*Positive Social Behavior
and Morality*

SOCIALIZATION
AND DEVELOPMENT

Positive Social Behavior and Morality

SOCIALIZATION AND DEVELOPMENT

ERVIN STAUB
DEPARTMENT OF PSYCHOLOGY
UNIVERSITY OF MASSACHUSETTS
AMHERST, MASSACHUSETTS

Volume 2

ACADEMIC PRESS   New York   San Francisco   London   1979
A Subsidiary of Harcourt Brace Jovanovich, Publishers

Figure 4.1 on page 105 is from Diana Baumrind, Child care practices anteceding three patterns of preschool behavior. *Genetic Psychology Monographs,* 1967, **75,** 43-88, Fig.2. Copyright 1967 by The Journal Press.

ACADEMIC PRESS, INC.
111 Fifth Avenue, New York, New York 10003

United Kingdom Edition published by
ACADEMIC PRESS, INC. (LONDON) LTD.
24/28 Oval Road, London NW1 7DX

Library of Congress Cataloging in Publication Data

Staub, Ervin.
    Positive social behavior and morality.
    Socialization and development.

    CONTENTS: v. 1. Social—personality determinants——
v. 2. The development of positive social behavior and
morality.
    1. Social psychology. 2. Altruism. 3. Helping
behavior. 4. Interpersonal relations. I. Title.
HM251.S755   301.1   77—92246
ISBN 0—12—663102—6 (v. 2)

PRINTED IN THE UNITED STATES OF AMERICA
79 80 81 82   9 8 7 6 5 4 3 2 1

To Adrian, Daniel, and All Our Children

Contents

Preface   xi
Acknowledgments   xv
Contents of Volume 1   xvii

chapter 1

Positive Social Behavior, Morality, and Development   1

The Nature of Positive Social Behavior   2
The Origins of Positive Social Behavior   4
Determinants versus Development   5
The Determinants of Positive Behavior: A Brief Review   8
    Personality, Consistency, and Specificity in Positive Behavior   13
The Origins of Personality and Positive Behavior   16

chapter 2

Major Approaches to Development   21

Identification—Internalization Approach   22
    Identification   23
    Internalization   29

vii

Social-Learning Approach   34
Cognitive Developmental Approach   38
   Research and Basic Issues   46

chapter 3

*Development with Age: Prosocial Behavior, Social
Cognition, and Related Characteristics*   59

Changes in Prosocial Behavior with Age   61
   Changes in Cooperation and Competition with Age   65
Changes in Consistency with Age   68
Changes in Different Types of Role Taking with Age   69
   The Beginning of Role Taking   69
   The Relationship between Different Kinds of Role Taking 73
Affective Role-Taking   77
Thinking about Others' Intentions and Motives   80
Moral Judgment, Role Taking, and Cognition   83
The Growth of Altruistic Motivation   86

chapter 4

Socialization: Basic Styles and Issues   89

Parental Control, Controlling Styles, and the Socialization
of Morality   91
   The Consequences of Forceful Control   92
   Differences in the Affective Bases and in the Socialization of
   Transgression and Prosocial Behavior   99
   Patterns of Parental Practices, Parental Control, and Child Behavior 103
The Relationship between Parents and Children   110
   Parental Affection, Nurturance   110
   Naturalistic Research on the Effects of Nurturance 113
   Experimental Research on the Effects of Nurturance 115
   Variations in the Nature of Nurturance   124
The Learning of Standards, Self-Reinforcement, and
Self-Regulation   127
   The Learning of Standards   128
   The Influence of Previously Learned Self-Reactions 130
   Cognitive Self-Control   133

chapter 5

Socialization: Practices That Promote Prosocial Development 137

What Is Learned, and Other Issues 137
The Conditioning of Prosocial Behavior 140
   Operant-Conditioning Procedures 141
   Classical Conditioning Procedures 145
Learning through Observation 150
   Learning through Self-Attribution 151
   The Effects of Television 153
   Role Playing and Enactive Learning of Positive Behavior 157
Reasoning by Parents: Induction 160
   Naturalistic Research on Reasoning and Induction 161
   Experimental Research on Reasoning and Induction 167
   Verbal Influences on Moral Judgment and Behavior 173
Values and Value Orientations of Parents and Children 178

chapter 6

Natural Socialization: Participation in Positive Behavior and Experiential Learning 189

Focusing Responsibility on Children and Learning by
Participation 189
Experimental Research on Learning by Participation and
Interactive Experience 198
   Direct Instruction for and Participation in Prosocial Action 198
   Participation, Teaching Others, and Induction 205
   How Does Experiential Learning Occur? 215
Interactive Experience, Role Taking, and Experiential
Learning 217

chapter 7

Peer Socialization: The Influence of Peers on Positive and Negative Behavior and Personality 221

The Role of Peers in the Development of the Affectional System 221
Reciprocity in Children's Interactions 223
Popularity, Peer Interaction, and Adjustment 228

Social Behavior and Popularity   228
Role Taking, Social Skills, Attitudes toward Others, and Popularity   232
The Long-Term Consequences of Popularity and of Negative
Interpersonal Relationships   237
Improving Peer Relations   240
Socialization and Peer Relations   243
The Influence of the Nature and Rules of the Peer Group
and of the Extended Environment   244

chapter 8

Summary and Conclusions: The Development of
Positive Social Behavior and Morality   *251*

Classes of Socializing Influences   251
Interrelationships and Changes of Influences   255
Divergence in Personality as a Source of Development   257
Antecedents of Different Kinds of Positive Social Behavior   259
Principles of Change   261
The Outcomes of Socialization for Prosocial Behavior   265
Deficiencies in Research   265
A Developmental Theory of (Pro)social Behavior   268
Education in Positive Behavior   272
Culture, History, and the Universal Applicability of Our
Understanding of Development   274

References   277
Author Index   299
Subject Index   305

Preface

This is the second of two related volumes on positive social behavior and morality. The first volume is concerned with the wide range of influences that lead people to behave in a positive fashion toward other people or inhibit them from behaving positively—that is, with how varied forms of positive behavior are determined (Staub, 1978a: It will be referred to in this book as Volume 1). The present volume (Volume 2) is concerned with how the tendency to behave positively, or the personal values, beliefs, and other characteristics that make positive behavior more (or less) likely, develop through socialization, through the influence of peers, and through the child's varied experiences. Although the two volumes are related and enlarge upon each other, the material in them is organized in such a way that each can be meaningfully read independently and that each constitutes an independent whole.

When I first conceived of writing a book on this topic—a long time ago—the amount of available material was limited. An explosion of research and writing on the many topics that I consider relevant to positive social behavior and morality has been taking place in the 1970s, and I have been determined to keep up with this explosion, to present and to integrate its products. Thus, in Volume 1 I examine research and theory on such varied topics as people helping others in emergencies, sharing, generosity, and positive exchange relationships and positive behavior among friends and intimates, in an attempt to understand and to elucidate the commonalities and diversities of the influences on such behaviors and of the motivations that affect them. I became increasingly convinced that in order to understand positive behavior we have to view it as an expression of varied aspects of people's personalities and of the circumstances that surround, and are sometimes created by, them. Consequently, in order to understand and elucidate the development of positive behavior and of positive aspects of personal morality, we have to concern ourselves with the development of varied aspects of personality and social behavior. A further consequence of this view is that in educating children in varied forms of prosocial behavior—in attempting to provide them with experiences that will lead to learning and to change—we cannot narrowly focus on positive *behavior* but have to concern ourselves with values, competencies, and other personal characteristics that will together enhance their responsiveness to others' needs and their desire to promote others' welfare.

In trying to understand the growth of children's positive behavior, I became interested in seemingly neglected influences on children's growth and development. These include children's learning by experience, defined here not only in the sense of opportunities for role taking, which Piaget and Kohlberg have emphasized, but also in terms of actual involvement in varied kinds of activities and in terms of the way they experience these activities—their "learning by doing." I also became concerned with the importance of the long-term influence of peers on each others' personalities and behaviors. Discussion of these topics, under the headings of *natural socialization* and *peer socialization,* follows an examination of more traditional theory and research.

In the course of writing this book and of conducting research, I have come to regard social, personality, and developmental psychology as strongly interrelated. I have come to feel, moreover, that we should move beyond recognizing this interrelationship as an ideal and should attempt to make it a reality. I hope that the two books will help, at least to a small extent, to serve this purpose. They deal extensively with material traditionally belonging to each of these domains of psychology. Moreover, in Volume 1 I describe a model or theory that elaborates on how personality and the nature of circumstances (social–situational influences) may join in affecting behavior. In Chapter 8 of this volume, I present rudimentary ideas for a developmental theory of social behavior, an attempt to provide a framework for considering how relevant personality characteristics and situational influences may develop, change, and join together in different ways with increasing age.

I hope that readers will be patient with references made in this book to Volume 1. Frequently, as material is presented in Volume 2, there are relevant issues discussed, theoretical ideas presented, or research reviewed in Volume 1. For those readers who want to consider specific topics in greater depth, such cross references may be useful.

He and She. A brief note about the use of "he" and "she" in this book. I laboriously included in my manuscript "he" and "she" in most sentences in which I used a third-person pronoun, as well as "him" and "her" and "herself" and "himself," whichever was appropriate. My copy editor—about whom I know only that she is a woman and that she lives in California—conscientiously erased all the feminine pronouns, leaving the masculine ones. At about this time I read a column by Tom Wicker, the *New York Times* columnist. He described various proposals to deal with the issue, providing examples of some of the most exquisitely convoluted language I have seen anywhere, examples that I certainly did not want to follow. Wicker suggested that when we first make a general reference to the race (of humanity) we use "whatever awkward formulation may be necessary to include both camps." Then writers can proceed to use pronouns referring to their own sex. I shall follow this suggestion.

I hope this book at least implicitly communicates my belief in his and her common humanity and equal rights, including the right to kindness and consideration and to equal well-being. Unfortunately, having stated this, I am still left with following tradition by using the masculine pronoun in the book. Here is *my* suggestion for the future: that we all write in Hungarian, which has a single third-person pronoun (ö) for he, she, and it.

Acknowledgments

I would like to thank various people whose positive influence on me gains expression, I hope, in these two volumes. Several people influenced me while I was a graduate student at Stanford, and they continued to do so later as colleagues and friends. Walter Mischel had an important influence on my thinking about psychology, and my association with him led me to want to do research and writing in psychology. Eleanor Maccoby also has strongly affected my way of thinking about psychology. Al Hastorf and Al Bandura were important sources of knowledge and inspiration. During his term as visiting professor at Stanford, Arnold Lazarus taught me, in clinical work, a greater appreciation of human complexity. Perhaps it is not surprising, in view of these varied intellectual influences, that I came to regard social, personality, and developmental psychology as strongly interrelated, at least as an ideal, if not as a reality. Furthermore, during my graduate school years, conversations with Perry London about his attempts to study characteristics of "rescuers," people who, during World War II, saved Jews and other minorities persecuted in Nazi Germany, made me wonder about the willingness of human beings to sacrifice themselves for others, as well as about their willingness to close their eyes to the suffering of others.

In beginning my independent research in my first job at Harvard and later, in beginning to write this book, my colleague and friend, Robert Rosenthal, was always a willing listener, a source of ideas, and a generous source of encouragement. Lane K. Conn, also a colleague and friend at Harvard, was an important source of both ideas and support. He contributed to my personal growth in ways that, I hope, have found some expression in this book. Many students collaborated with me in research that I discuss or refer to in this book. I am grateful to all of them. Dan Jaquette and Sumru Erkut at Harvard and Helene Feinberg at the University of Massachusetts made particularly important contributions. Lynne Feagans was a highly competent, reliable, and hardworking research assistant while we conducted at Harvard some of my early research on helping and sharing behavior.

I am grateful to the many people, both children and adults, who participated in my research. My early research with children was conducted primarily in Watertown, Massachusetts. After 1971, much of my research with children was conducted in Amherst, Massachusetts. I am grateful for the extensive cooperation given me by teachers, by principals (particularly Mr. John Dalton, Mr. Michael Greenebaum, and Ms. Nancy Morrison), and by the superintendent of the Amherst schools, Mr. Donald Frizzle.

Many people helped with these two books, typing, collecting references, and participating in other aspects of preparing them. I am particularly grateful to Vivian Goldman and Terry Shumann.

I was determined, until recently, not to follow the tradition of authors thanking their families, "without whose support the book could never have been written." I came to feel, however, that much more than tradition is involved and that such expressions of gratitude may actually give families less than their due. When one is really involved in writing a book, one is sometimes a marginal member of one's family. I am grateful to Sylvia and my children for their acceptance of my involvement and for their willingness to bear with me.

Finally, I am grateful to the National Institutes of Mental Health. Grant No. MH23886 supported the research that my students and I have been conducting since 1973 and enabled me to spend time and energy on research and writing.

Contents of Volume 1

Preface
Acknowledgments

chapter 1

Positive Behavior, Morality, and Human Nature

Prosocial Behavior: Definition, Significance,
and Relationship to Morality
Morality and Human Nature
Genetic Origins of Altruism

chapter 2

*Personality, the Situation, and the Determination
of Prosocial Behavior*

Why People Behave Prosocially
A Theoretical Model for Predicting Prosocial Behavior
Other Personality Influences on Goal Activation and Behavior
Supporting Research
Classes of Influences on Prosocial Behavior

chapter 3

Determinants of People Helping Other People in Physical Distress

The Early Research of Latané and Darley
The Influence of Others
Stimulus Characteristics That Affect Helping
Spontaneous (or Impulsive) Helping
Temporary States of the Actor, Stimulus Overload,
Urban–Rural Helping, and Personality
Summary of Situational Influences
Personality and Helping Others in Physical Need
The Influence of Combinations of Personal Characteristics
and of Situations

chapter 4

Observing and Causing Harm to Others: Affective, Cognitive, and Behavioral Consequences

Empathy and Prosocial Behavior
Just World, Devaluation, and Aggression
Harmdoing, Transgression, and Their Consequences
Conclusions, Issues, and Limitations of Research

chapter 5

Prosocial Behavior in Response to Varied Needs

Social Influence
Stimulus Influence
Decision Making, Personal Norms, and Helping Behavior
Individual Characteristics and Helping Behavior

chapter 6

Orientation to the Self and Others: The Effects of Positive and Negative Experiences, Thoughts, and Feelings

The Effects of Success and Failure, Moods, and Self-Concern
on Positive Behavior
The Psychological Consequences That Mediate the Effects
of Positive and Negative Experiences and States

chapter 7

*The Connection between Self and Others: Similarity,
Attraction, and Common Group Membership*

Conditions That Affect the Bond between the Self and Others

chapter 8

*Exchange and Reciprocity in Positive
and Negative Behavior*

The Nature of Social Exchange
Reciprocity and Equity in Social Exchange

chapter 9

*Cooperation and Intimate Relationships:
Further Explorations in Human Transactions*

Determinants of Cooperation
Inducing Cooperation and Its Consequences
The Development and Maintenance of Intimate Relationships
Relationships: Their Formation and Nature
Self-Disclosure
Principles of Interaction in Extended Relationships
A Model of Interpersonal Relationships

chapter 10

*Summary and Conclusions:
The Determinants of Positive Behavior*

Limitations of Our Knowledge: Future Goals
How Does Positive Behavior (or Its Absence) Come About?
The Influence of Cultures

References

Subject Index

*Positive Social Behavior
and Morality*

SOCIALIZATION
AND DEVELOPMENT

Positive Social Behavior, Morality, and Development[1]

Human beings can be kind, compassionate, and loving. They may help others in need, people who are hurt, distressed, or deprived. Sometimes they will suffer extreme hardship or risk their own lives, not only for the sake of family or friends, but even to protect and enhance the well-being of persons unknown to them, or that of their tribe or society. They frequently engage in cooperative activities that contribute to the welfare of others as well as their own. But human beings can also be extremely cruel, selfish, and inhuman in their treatment of others. Even the same people can be kind and generous under some circumstances and cruel under others, depending on circumstances in their lives, the

---

[1] Much of this chapter deals with basic issues, such as the definition of positive behavior, notions of consistency and predictability, and others that were extensively discussed in Volume 1 (Staub, 1978a). Some of the chapter expands on issues that were touched upon in the first volume (e.g., the relationship between the study of determinants and the study of the development of positive conduct), and some of the discussion is specific to introducing this volume. Thus, readers familiar with the first volume will find that Chapter 1 includes a summary and review of some material familiar to them. Other readers may want to turn to Volume 1 for an extensive discussion of the meaning of morality and of basic issues such as the significance of intentions in defining prosocial behavior and, of course, for a thorough review of the social, situational, and personal influences on varied forms of positive behavior in both children and adults.

1

specific conditions that exist, and their attitudes toward particular persons or groups.

I discussed in Volume 1 many of the influences that affect the likelihood of positive conduct. The existing evidence suggests to me that certain personality characteristics make it more likely that people will think and feel in ways that will lead to positive behavior or inhibit negative behavior. What are these characteristics, and how do they develop? Consider, for example, a man who had had two operations 10 days earlier. On his first day out he goes to the beach with his girlfriend. Suddenly he sees a woman drowning in deep water. Why is it this man, from all the people on the crowded beach, who jumps into the water and pulls out the drowning woman?—an act for which he received a Carnegie Hero Medal (Volume 1, Chapter 1).

The Nature of Positive Social Behavior

Positive social behavior is defined for the purpose of this book as behavior that benefits other people. In order to behave positively, a person has to understand another's needs, desires, or goals and act to fulfill them. Positive acts can take many and varied forms. A person may respond to verbal requests for food, clothing, or other material objects or may *initiate* help after having noticed the existence of need. People give to charities. They respond to friends or strangers who are in physical distress, who have been injured or are feeling sick. When someone appears upset, unhappy, depressed, in psychological distress or need, we may be able to respond sensitively, sympathetically, and to be truly helpful, or we may attempt to help but do more damage than good. We can respond to injustice that we directly observe, or we may respond to our knowledge of injustice or deprivation that people suffer and engage in protracted, purposeful behavior to correct the injustice. We can initiate friendly positive interactions with other people or engage in cooperative activities that provide mutual benefit. We may respond in a positive manner to the moods, desires, hopes, and needs of our friends and loved ones. We can contribute to other people's positive feelings and welfare in many ways.

There are many dimensions along which prosocial behavior can be classified: the degree of benefit it produces for another person; the degree and kind of sacrifices it requires from the actor; whether it is a single act or part of an ongoing relationship between individuals; and others.

Prosocial acts can also be classified on the basis of the presumed intention or motive of the actor, presumed since we can rarely definitely establish why a person acted to benefit another. Motives and intentions are only known to the actor—sometimes not even to him or her—and we can only make considered judgments about them. I would like to differentiate two levels of intentions. If a person voluntarily engages in behavior that, under ordinary circumstances, would benefit another person—that is, his or her behavior is not coerced—this person intends to benefit the other. However, *why* this person wants to help or to benefit another may vary. The reason may be the desire to enhance another person's well-being, a truly altruistic motivation. Even though the actor may both anticipate and experience satisfaction, the act is performed for the sake of another, and the satisfaction arises out of having benefited someone (see Volume 1, Chapter 1). Another reason may be the desire or intention to do what is one's duty or obligation. This contrasts with concern about the welfare of others, so that satisfaction (or dissatisfaction and guilt) arises out of having done one's duty (or having failed to do so) rather than out of having enhanced someone's welfare. The desire to gain benefits of varied kinds for oneself may also be a reason for positive conduct (see following section on determinants of positive behavior). Although all voluntary acts that would ordinarily benefit others will be regarded as positive behavior, the degree of altruistic intention of the actor, or, more generally, the actor's motivation for acting prosocially, can vary.

Behavior that has consequences for the welfare of other human beings or for the social group is thought to be guided by moral values and principles. Proscriptive values and standards prohibit action that would harm others (thou shalt not). Usually, people perform such acts because they satisfy a need or impulse or bring about material or social advantage. Prescriptive values and principles tell people what they ought to do (thou shalt). Much of prescriptive morality is prosocial in nature; it prescribes behavior that will benefit other people.

It is usually assumed that the interests of the self and of other people are in conflict. Frequently, in order to benefit others, one has to sacrifice time, effort, material possessions, physical welfare, and potentially even life itself. However, the relationship between the self and others can be perceived and experienced in varied ways, ranging from antagonism to conflict to identification with others. At the extreme, a person can experience others' goals, desires, and aspirations as his or her own. Parents are most likely to have such identification with their children, but it can occur among lovers and other intimates and, depending on the social structure, perhaps even among members of a whole social group. Facing a common danger or sharing important experiences may increase identification. In hunting or gathering societies (Cohen, 1972) cooperation was necessary for survival and probably advanced the development of the social organization. A substantial degree of interdependence must have existed among members of such societies.

However, social groups that live under similar circumstances, for example, scarcity of food, can develop quite different adaptations. The Siriano Indians of eastern Bolivia live in an almost continual state of semistarvation. If possible, they will avoid sharing food: They will lie about how much food they have and eat during the night to avoid detection by others. These people are selfish, unconcerned about others, unwilling to help others. In contrast, the Bushmen of the Kalahari Desert, who also experience scarcity in food, developed highly cooperative social arrangements for the distribution of food. Obviously, different cultures can create different social arrangements and moral orientations among members to deal with similar life conditions. The values and norms of a culture—the family organization, the institutions, the roles that exist—will exert strong influence on behavior and contribute to the development of individual characteristics, which, jointly with social rules and other influences exerted by the culture, affect prosocial and antisocial conduct.

The Origins of Positive Social Behavior

What are the bases of positive and negative conduct? Philosophers, geneticists, and psychologists made varied assumptions about "human nature." Both philosophers and psychologists entertained each of the following three conceptions: that human beings are basically "bad," meaning that they are selfish and only concerned about their own welfare, and that either a social organization has to be created that will force them to consider the interests of others or socialization has to produce an internal "structure" (for example, the superego) that will accomplish this; that human beings are basically good or have the potential to be good, a view usually accompanied by a specification of conditions that corrupt human beings, such as the nature of society or its institutions, and sometimes a specification of conditions that will enable them to fulfill their basic potential for goodness, such as therapy or self-knowledge gained in other ways; and, finally, that the conditions of man living in a social group can lead to enlightened self-interest, to an understanding that one's interests and the interests of others are interrelated, and that cooperation and mutual help are needed to live harmoniously with others. This last view implies that one's satisfaction of one's own needs and desires is dependent on one's willingness to contribute to other's welfare, as well as the assumption that human nature is neither basically good nor bad but that man has the potential for developing optimal social characteristics.

In recent years, controversies about the origin of both human aggression and human altruism took place among scientists concerned with the genetic basis of human behavior. Wilson's (1975) sociobiology, his attempt to suggest biological bases for human social behavior, Campbell's (1965, 1975) varied contributions, and Trivers' (1971) proposal of a genetic basis of "reciprocal altruism" led to much interest in genetic sources of altruism (see Volume 1).

One focus of theorizing has been to demonstrate the possibility of the transmission and spread of genes that would promote altruism, within the constraints of currently acceptable evolutionary theory. Some argued that kin selection or some other mechanism of gene transmission could serve and has served as the basis of the spread of altruistic genes and that, consequently, altruism has a genetic basis. Furthermore, various authors described and/or attempted experimental demonstration of "altruistic" behavior among animals, suggesting that such behavior is genetically determined rather than learned. Genetically based altruism among animals makes, for these authors, the genetic basis of human altruism seem likely.

Whatever the extent of a genetic base for human altruistic or positive conduct (see Volume 1, Chapter 1), it is clear that human beings are extremely variable in their manifestations of kindness toward each other. Although genetic potential must exist for kindness as well as for aggression, it is socialization and experience that must determine whether a particular individual will acquire characteristics that lead to a tendency to behave prosocially. That socialization and experience are important is not only suggested by the tremendous variability in positive behavior among individuals in a culture such as ours but also by the tremendous variation among cultures. How characteristic positive and negative behaviors of cultures are can vary dramatically. For example, on the same island, New Guinea, the Arapesh are kind, gentle, and cooperative people, and the Mundugamor are aggressive and uncooperative (Mead, 1935). As I noted, moreover, cultures can adjust to existing life conditions, such as scarcity, in profoundly different ways.

Determinants versus Development

How does the child's behavior toward other people come to be guided by moral rules, norms, or principles? How does it come to be guided by consideration for the welfare of others? A newborn child is, presumably, amoral; his actions are guided by self-interest, by the desire to gratify his needs and impulses, without consideration of the consequences to others.[2] Age and maturation alone are usually not assumed to change this "amorality."

Until recently, research and theory about the development of morality focused on how children learn or develop principles and values that prohibit socially undesirable behavior as well as the tendency to actually inhibit such behavior (Maccoby, 1968). The behaviors of interest included cheating and other forms of dishonesty, as well as behavior that harms others physically, verbally, or by doing damage to people's "extended self," for example, their property. As Maccoby (1968) puts it, developmental psychologists were concerned with how children learned the "thou shalt nots" but not with how they learned the "thou shalts." Adherence to, versus transgression of, rules laid down by adults and, thus, obedience, has been one of the important foci of this research, with the resulting implication that obedience is moral, disobedience is immoral. This, of course, is a questionable assumption.

In the last decade, together with the dramatic rise of interest in the *determinants* of prosocial behavior, there has been a dramatic rise of interest in the *development* of morally desirable tendencies, in how children come to behave in a manner that benefits others even when this demands self-sacrifice on their part.

The research about the determinants of positive conduct among children (and adults) that was reviewed in Volume 1 provides little direct information about how development takes place. Knowing that certain circumstances and personality characteristics affect the likelihood of positive behavior does not tell us how differences among persons in positive behavior develop. At the same time, it seems desirable to use information gained by personality and social psychologists about the determinants of some form of action in order to set the goals for developmental research. If we have reliable information and reasonable theories about what psychological processes (what kinds of thoughts and feelings) affect prosocial behavior and what personal characteristics affect the likelihood that these psychological processes will be active on varied occasions, we can pose questions for research on development. We

---

[2] However, at a very early age infants demonstrate an affective orientation toward others, in the form of distress reactions to the sounds of another child's crying (no such response was made to equally loud noise of a different kind). Such behavior is seen in the first 2–4 days of life (Levine & Hoffman, 1975; Simner, 1971). Thus, characteristics of the human organism that demonstrate involvement with others and perhaps provide an origin of a positive orientation toward others appear very early.

can then ask how personality characteristics and ways of relating to the social world that seem important influences on positive behavior—such as prosocial values and norms, empathic capacity, and varied competencies—are acquired by children.

Research about the determinants of prosocial behavior begins to take on a developmental character when it explores determinants at various ages and thus provides information about the extent to which the same or different influences operate as a function of a person's age. With regard to personality characteristics as potential determinants of behavior, even if the same ones operate throughout life (e.g., values, empathic capacity, and competencies), their influence will vary with age, since many of them gradually develop with increasing age.

A major approach to the study of development is to explore the type of socialization practices that parents and other socializers use and to evaluate what socializing practices are related to the development of personal characteristics relevant to prosocial behavior.

Another approach, which is usually called the developmental approach, is to consider how various characteristics of children change with age and combine or modify each other. For example, the capacity to take another person's point of view is sometimes, although not always, positively related to prosocial behavior (Volume 1, Chapter 5). Such role-taking capacity may contribute to empathy, which in turn affects helping. Role-taking capacity itself might be partly a function of other, perhaps more basic, cognitive capacities of the child. The manner in which these cognitive capacities develop and affect role taking might thus become of interest. A further example of this approach is Hoffman's (1975b) analysis of how very early forms of distress that is evoked in young children by others' distress is enhanced and elaborated with the development of object constancy and other cognitive skills.

In order to understand development we also need to ask how variations in different types of life experiences of children, including their experiences in interactions with other people that go beyond the discipline and teaching implied by the term "socialization," contribute to the development of characteristics that might enhance prosocial behavior. Cognitive developmental theory focuses on certain types of experiences as a source of development. For a meaningful exploration of the effects of life experiences, the distinction between *socialization,* which of course provides many of children's experiences, and other experiences will have to be considered. I shall discuss extensively the influence of participation in positive conduct and other *natural socialization experiences* on the tendency for positive behavior.

As I shall later elaborate, a focus on age alone, with reference to maturation and to unspecified or unexplored experiences that are associated with age, is insufficient for the understanding of children's learning and development. As a result of differences in socialization practices, in the content of what children are taught, in the characteristics of the environment, individual differences in children will emerge at an early age: in cognitive capacities, in affective and value orientations, in competencies. The capacities and characteristics of children at any one time will affect what children learn from seemingly the same experiences and from influences that are directed at them. Although this can be hardly questioned, the significance of current characteristics moderating the impact of new experiences has frequently been neglected in research or theorizing about children. An important contribution of life-span developmental approaches (Stein & Baltes, 1976) is the emphasis on the psychological processes that characterize children, rather than on age alone, and on how the child's characteristics and the environment join and interact in affecting development.

The major question for this book is: How do personality characteristics develop in children that enhance the likelihood (*a*) that under circumstances that make positive social behavior appropriate or desirable internal processes will be activated that enhance prosocial behavior, and/or (*b*) that children will seek out opportunities to help others. In other words, how does the tendency to behave prosocially develop?

The Determinants of Positive Behavior: A Brief Review

What influences affect prosocial behavior? What is the meaning of a tendency to behave prosocially? These questions will be discussed briefly before examining the sources of development.

A staggering amount of research (considering that almost all of it was conducted within the last decade) shows that varied aspects of situations affect positive behavior. However, situations must exert their influences as a function of how they are perceived by people, what meaning they have to them, what motivation they give rise to. Since persons vary, few situations will have uniform effects on their behavior. If on occasion people's behavior approaches uniformity, the meaning of the situation, the social norms that guide behavior in response to it, and relevant social values and motives must be dominant and/or uniformly adopted by people in the culture. The following summary of aspects of situations that affect positive behavior is derived from Volume 1.

1. The extent to which the nature of a stimulus for help (someone's physical or psychological need, its degree, nature, and manner of presentation), the surrounding conditions, and social influence exerted by other people provide an unambiguous indication that someone needs help. The less ambiguity, the more help will follow. Ambiguity frequently gives rise to concern that some action that would provide help may be inappropriate or may appear foolish.

2. The degree of need for help. Usually, the greater the need, the more help will follow. However, exceptions do exist, partly because when someone's distress, discomfort, or the danger to a person are great, which make the need for help great, frequently the costs associated with helping, the sacrifices demanded from a helper, or the potential danger for a helper are also great.

3. The extent to which responsibility for help is focused on a particular person rather than diffused among a number of people. The more clearly circumstances focus the responsibility on a particular person, the greater the likelihood that this person will provide help. Responsibility is focused on a person if he is the only witness to another's need; if he is the only person who is in a position to help, although not necessarily the only witness; if he has special skills that are required for helping; if he has a special relationship to the person in need; if a leadership position makes this person the natural one to take charge; and in other ways.

4. The degree of impact of the instigating stimuli. Closeness in space and the length of exposure to a distressed person, as well as the ease or difficulty of getting away from his or her presence (affecting length of exposure), would strongly affect impact. Greater impact leads to more helping.

5. The extent to which circumstances require self-initiated rather than responsive help. Sometimes the stimulus for help and/or the surrounding conditions clearly indicate not only that help is needed but also the kind of action that is required; a potential helper may even receive a specific request for a specific act. At other times, a person may have to decide both that help is needed and what needs to be done. When more decision making and greater initiative are required, the likelihood of help is smaller.

6. The costs of helping. How much effort, time, energy, material goods, and risk to oneself is demanded? The greater such direct costs, the less help can usually be expected. Indirect costs, a person's having to give up activities that would lead to the satisfaction of his own goals, also reduce helping.

7. The extent to which the circumstances suggest that the type of

action that is required to help is socially acceptable or that it may be undesirable, inappropriate, or socially unacceptable. For example, situational rules may exist—that a child is to continue working on a task, or that going into a strange room in a strange environment is inappropriate (Staub, 1970b, 1971b, 1974)—that inhibit responses to sounds of another person's distress.

8. The existence of a relationship to the person in need, its degree and kind. Clearly, our relationships to other people frequently place special obligations on us to respond to their needs and to promote their welfare. The existence of a close relationship, as well as certain other conditions (knowledge of shared group membership or of similarities in opinion, beliefs, and personality), can lead to identification with another person, and this makes the arousal of empathy and of other motives that promote help more likely. Other conditions, ones that give rise to antagonism, may make help less likely. An ongoing relationship also provides others' needs with greater impact, since it makes it difficult for a person to physically remove himself.

9. Positive or negative experiences concurrent with or just prior to the need for help. These create varied psychological states: positive or negative moods, different levels of temporary self-esteem, or differences in other internal states. Positive states usually enhance, negative states sometimes (depending on varied factors) diminish, help for others. Presumably, a person's own psychological state affects both his or her capacity to perceive or consider others' needs and the relationship between the self and others. I proposed a theory of "hedonic balancing" that specifies how people balance their own and other people's states of well-being at any particular time. A person considers his own current state of well-being relative to his usual state of well-being and compares and balances the discrepancy with his perception of another person's current well-being relative to his judgment of another's usual well-being (Volume 1, Chapter 6).

How do circumstances affect positive conduct? Why do people respond helpfully to another's needs or to the opportunity to benefit someone? Both the description of situational influences and the following discussion of motives are presented as if they applied equally to all forms of positive conduct. Within limits, that is true; however, special forms of positive conduct are also likely to have unique influences on them or the same influences active with different intensities. For example, psychological reactance, a resistance to limitations on freedom of action that is placed on people by others' need for help, is less likely to be aroused when someone unexpectedly suffers physical distress, particularly when helping places no extended demand on time or energy. Psychological reactance is more likely to be aroused when the need is relatively mild and/or when a person requests a favor that may be out of context for the relationship. Furthermore, in close relationships special principles that we, as yet, know little about are likely to affect positive conduct. Interpersonal relations and positive interactions are certainly transactional: Past actions by one person affect subsequent responses by another, which in turn influence the next behavior of the first actor, and so on. Reciprocity, which is an important principle of exchange and interaction in human relationships, applies less strictly in close relationships than among relative strangers, probably because in close relationships benefits that people provide for each other and sacrifices they make can be balanced over longer time intervals (Volume 1, Chapter 8).

Three classes of motives that promote positive behavior have been emphasized in the literature. First, people may be motivated by their desire for *self-gain.* They may help in order to gain social approval or to avoid disapproval or criticism for not helping someone. That is, positive behavior may be due to adherence to social values and norms or to existing conditions that specify the desirability of engaging in prosocial conduct. People may also hope to achieve material gain by helping others. Since reciprocity is a powerful principle in guiding human interactions, another person may be expected to reciprocate positive acts and to provide some needed service or to show gratitude in the form of material rewards. Positive conduct may also serve a desire to establish close contact, initiate friendly relationships, or promote intimacy, since people like those who are kind to them.

Second, the motivation for positive behavior may be adherence to values, beliefs, and norms that were internalized, adopted as one's own, and/or developed in the course of experience. Adherence to one's own beliefs, values, and norms can lead to self-reward, to positive affect, and to enhanced self-esteem, whereas deviation can lead to self-punishment, to anxiety and guilt, and to diminished self-esteem. Norms of social responsibility, reciprocity, equity, belief in the just world, and others were proposed as either social or personal norms that influence behavior: To varied extents, there is evidence of their influence. Beyond specific values, beliefs, and norms, people vary in broad value orientations. I suggested that people can be characterized by their prosocial orientation—the extent to which they tend to regard other human beings positively, are concerned about others' welfare, and experience a sense of personal responsibility for others' welfare. Prosocial orientation gives rise to a prosocial goal, a motive that is satisfied by helping others and by increasing others' welfare. Presumably, people can be meaningfully characterized by a number of different value orientations that have relevance to positive conduct. A person may be concerned with maintaining the social order, the stability of society. This may give rise to the motivation to help others under certain conditions but may inhibit positive action at other times when, for example, social action is required to benefit an oppressed group or to enhance equality and equity among members of the society.

Third, empathy, the vicarious experience of another person's emotion, appears to provide an important motivation to behave positively. The vicarious experience of another's distress and its anticipated reduction, or the anticipated satisfaction or joy that another person may experience, can motivate positive conduct. Traditionally, a firm distinction has been drawn between values and norms on the one hand and empathy on the other. However, the arousal of empathy by circumstances must depend on a person's orientation toward other people, on beliefs and values that lead to interpreting events in certain ways, and to feelings of identification with other people. Thus, prosocial orientation or, more specifically, valuing other people and their welfare is likely to be a precondition for the arousal of empathy.

As I noted, certain motivators of positive behavior can sometimes diminish positive conduct. The related beliefs that the world is or should be just and that equity should characterize human relationships —people getting what they deserve—can lead to the desire to create justice or equity by helping others. Under varied circumstances, however, belief in a just world can lead to justification of another's suffering rather than to help, to the assumption that a person who suffers must deserve it, and to a justification of the status quo, even if it appears to have substantial inequities, on the assumption that the people who have less must have deserved less.

Variation in how people perceive and evaluate other human beings and experience the connection between themselves and others affects the likelihood that prosocial values and norms appear relevant and that empathic affect is aroused by others' feelings and condition. Most people learn some degree of identification with others who are the members of the same "in-group." One influence on prosocial behavior must be how narrowly or broadly an in-group is defined. A child can learn either that only his or her family or that also his or her tribe or religious or racial group or people of the same nationality are also like him or are reasonable objects for identification. Potentially people may come to consider all human beings as like them or similar to them in some important, basic ways. Depending on what is learned, the applicability of a person's prosocial values and norms to varied groups of people, and the possibility of identification with them may vary greatly.

Personality, Consistency, and Specificity in Positive Behavior

Certain personal characteristics of individuals should make it more likely that psychological processes that motivate positive behavior, in contrast to those that inhibit such behavior, are aroused. Although many studies have found that certain personal characteristics are associated with positive behavior, only in limited domains have the relations between personality and positive behavior received sustained attention. For example, the relationship between role taking, moral judgments, and positive behavior in children has been explored in a number of studies (Volume 1, Chapter 5). The joint influence of personality and situational variations has been explored to a limited extent.

In Volume 1 (Chapter 2) I described a model that aimed to specify the manner in which situations and personality jointly affect behavior. According to this model we have to consider the varied motives, conceptualized as personal goals, that characterize individuals. These can be defined in terms of end states or outcomes that are desirable to persons. For most people their personal goals can be arranged in a hierarchy, according to their importance. Associated with each goal is a cognitive network that affects the manner in which situations are interpreted. We also need to consider the circumstances. Depending on the nature of particular circumstances one or more personal goals may be activated. Personal goals may combine, their satisfaction potentially satisfied through the same actions, or they may conflict with each other. In one situation the desire to do well in an achievement-related activity, the desire to benefit someone, the desire to gain the approval of other people, and other personal goals may all be activated. Which personal goals will be pursued in action is a function of the importance for a person of the goal relative to other goals, the activating potential of a situation for varied goals that the person possesses, and whether goal conflict is created (and how it is resolved). A person who has a strong achievement goal but a very weak prosocial goal would experience little conflict if in the course of pursuing some important achievement-related activity someone needed help. However, a person with both a strong achievement and a strong prosocial goal might experience intense conflict. According to this model, in addition to personal goals and activating potentials, other personal characteristics, particularly varied competencies (which include a sense of control over events, plans and strategies for action and the capacity to generate plans, and specific competencies to perform acts that would provide help) and perceptual tendencies (the speed of evaluating the meaning of events, as well as a tendency toward role taking) also enter into determining how a person will act. The variations in situations that were previously described as affecting positive conduct can be regarded as situational dimensions that either vary in their activating potential for prosocial goals or vary in the extent to which they demand competencies or role taking in order for helping to occur.

The motivation to help or benefit others, which may arise from a prosocial value orientation and specific prosocial values, is likely to enhance positive conduct. People's feelings about themselves—their self-esteem or ego strength—are also important. Differences in self-esteem and ego strength are likely to be related to differences in the belief that one can control or influence events and, thus, that one can affect others' fates. Furthermore, specific experiences may be more or less likely to create in people positive and negative psychological states such as happiness, joy, sadness and distress, and self-concern or freedom from it, depending on their self-esteem and their usual psychological states. Stable individual differences in self-esteem and moods are likely to further affect positive behavior by affecting people's willingness to initiate interpersonal interaction, which is often a precondition for help, by freeing persons of concern about themselves and enabling them to attend to others, as well as by affecting their relationship between the self and others. The latter may be expressed in the capacity to identify with others and in hedonic balancing. A substantial amount of research, on which these statements are based, was reviewed in Volume 1 (Chapter 6).

This brief review of research findings and theory about the determinants of prosocial behavior clearly suggests that such behavior is multidetermined. Varied personality characteristics and situations jointly increase the likelihood that psychological processes that affect positive conduct arise. What does this say about consistency in positive conduct, about whether people will consistently act or not act prosocially? According to the theoretical model that I have briefly described here (see also Volume 1, Chapter 2; Staub 1978b, 1979), whether a person behaves prosocially or not in a specific instance depends not only on what characteristics this person possesses that are directly relevant to prosocial conduct but also on his other personal goals and on surrounding conditions. All this implies, in my view, that with enough knowledge of a person's characteristics and of the surrounding circumstances positive behavior becomes understandable and predictable but not necessarily consistent from one time to another. A few studies have measured relevant personality characteristics and varied situations and have made relatively successful predictions of behavior (Feinberg, 1977; Grodman, 1978; Staub, Erkut, and Jaquette as described in Staub, 1974; see also Schwartz, 1977; Volume 1, Chapter 2; Staub, 1979).

Does this mean that no consistency in behavior can be expected? It does not. Individuals with strong prosocial motivation (who also possess a belief that they can influence events, as well as relevant specific competencies) are likely to behave more prosocially across varied situations than persons with a weak prosocial motivation (and/or without other relevant characteristics). When behavior is considered across many circumstances, other motives may dominate the behavior of such persons some of the time, but their prosocial motivation would gain expression at other times. That is, over a large number of instances sometimes circumstances would activate goals that conflict with a prosocial goal, but a strong prosocial goal would gain expression at other times. At least a moderate degree of consistency would, therefore, be apparent. By examining behavior across varied circumstances the tendency not to act prosocially would also become apparent.

Some consistency in prosocial behavior has, in fact, been found. When only two or three specific acts were measured, frequently no associations were found (Midlarsky & Bryan, 1972; Staub, 1971d). However, as the just mentioned theoretical considerations would suggest, consistency has been found when varied prosocial behaviors were summed and related to the sum of another set of prosocial behaviors, or when positive acts were correlated with teachers' ratings or peer ratings of children's positive behavior or consideration for others (for reviews, see Mussen & Eisenberg-Berg, 1977; Rushton, 1976; Volume 1; Staub, 1979). Sums of positive acts, teachers' ratings, and peer ratings all are indices of how a person behaves across varied occasions or situations. For evaluating consistency, examining relationships between sums or averages of large numbers of prosocial acts initiated by a person or enacted in response to stimuli that might elicit positive conduct seems most useful. Teacher and peer ratings may partly represent a perception or evaluation of generalized positivity–negativity or some other global perception or evaluation of children rather than provide an accurate index of behavior (Staub, 1971a).

Several studies (see Volume 1, Chapter 5) showed some consistency in behavior and coherence of positive behavior with how the child was perceived by peers and with the child's perception of events and people (see, for example, Dlugokinski & Firestone, 1973, 1974; Krebs & Stirrup, 1974). Consistency in aggression (Olweus, 1977) and honesty have also been found (see Staub, 1979). Two unpublished studies focusing on consistency in children's behavior over time (e.g., stability) were described by Mussen and Eisenberg-Berg (1977). In the first phase of a longitudinal study (Block & Block, 1973) nursery-school children were extensively observed. Nurturance toward other children, expressions of sympathy toward them, and understanding of others' perspectives were significantly related to each other. In elementary school, 5 or 6 years later, observationally based indices of socially responsible and altruistic behaviors were again significantly related. Of special interest is the fact that significant relationships were found between indices of social responsibility and altruism in nursery school and in elementary school, over 5–6-year intervals. These behaviors showed substantial stability ($r = .60$ for boys, $r = .37$ for girls).

In another longitudinal study (Baumrind, unpublished data), ratings by nursery–school teachers of generosity, helpfulness, empathy, and other prosocial characteristics were significantly associated with the amount of rewards children shared a year later. The children earned their rewards by their performance on a task and could share them with another child who did not have time to finish the task and consequently did not earn rewards. Children who were rated the year before as aggressive and as having trouble with delaying gratification shared less.

On the whole, not enough research has been devoted to assessing consistency and stability in behavior, and, specifically, in positive behavior. Moreover, differentiated predictions about consistency and stability are needed. Some beginnings have been made in this direction (e.g., Bem & Allen, 1974; Volume 1, Chapter 2). For example, as implied above, people can be expected to be consistent primarily in domains of activities that are important for them and in those that are related to important personal motives and/or to habitual ways of expressing these motives, and not in domains of activities that are unimportant for them. Thus, people with a strong prosocial motivation, but not those with weak prosocial motivation, can be expected to show consistency in prosocial behavior.

The Origins of Personality and Positive Behavior

According to the previous discussion, whether a person is kind, generous, helpful, and cooperative and whether he is inclined to interact with others in ways that benefit them is affected by many facets of his personality. These, in turn, are the result of the total complex of a person's socialization and experience. To understand the development of positive conduct or, more generally, moral conduct, it is necessary to take a broad perspective and consider how personality and social behavior develop. A tendency for prosocial behavior, and also positive morality, cannot be the result of highly specific, limited influences; they will come about as the result of varied, interrelated influences. For example, it is unlikely that morality can be advanced through discussion of moral issues and conflicts if a person lives in a hostile and threatening environment that leads to fear of other people and hostility toward them and to constant concern with physical or psychological survival. Varied influences jointly affect a number of personal characteristics that make positive behavior and a moral orientation toward the world likely.

What are influences on personality development? Mussen and Eisenberg-Berg (1977) list agents of socialization such as "parents, teachers, cultural and religious institutions, the mass media [p 7]." As I noted earlier, we need to consider both children's socialization and their varied experiences. Parents and teachers exert influence by the manner in which they interact with children, by how they discipline them, by what they try to teach them, by the kinds of examples they provide them, and in other ways. They also exert influence, together with the larger culture, by the structure of environment they provide. How is the family group organized? How democratic or autocratic is it? What are roles available to children (and to adolescents and adults) in the family and in the culture? What are the duties, the obligations, and the tasks assigned to children or adopted by them? What is the structure of the peer group, and how does it affect interactions among children? What are the behaviors children are led to engage in, and those directed at them? In the following chapters I shall examine the influence exerted on children by agents of socialization as well as by "natural" socialization, the influence of children's participation in activities and the experiences that result, and peer socialization, the long-term influence of interacting with peers. Before that, varied approaches to personality and social development will be considered: These approaches identify some of the principles by which learning and development take place as a result of socialization and experience.

Cultural influences will not be independently considered but will be examined in relation to the types of socializing influences they exert. The basic question for us is not whether in one culture people are more or less prosocial—about which we have little systematic information anyway—but, if such differences exist, what characteristics of the culture, what socialization practices and experiences undergone by members of the culture, bring about these differences. In some cultures there may be dominant forces that lead to either more or less positive conduct, and also to relative uniformity in behavior. In other cultures, such as ours, variability in the extent to which individuals behave prosocially or antisocially is great.

When cultural or subcultural differences in positive conduct exist, their origins are difficult to establish. Usually, cultures differ in a variety

of characteristics. Finding significant correlations between certain characteristics of the culture and characteristic behaviors of members rarely
convincingly establishes that the behavioral differences are the result of
the specific correlated cultural characteristics. For example, Madsen and
his associates (Madsen, 1971; Volume 1, Chapter 5) conducted many
studies in which children who were from a rural background showed
greater cooperation in playing games than did children from urban
backgrounds. Mexican American children cooperated more than did
Anglo American children (Kagan & Madsen, 1971; Knight & Kagen, 1977);
Israeli kibbutz children cooperated more than Israeli children from other
settings did (Shapira & Madsen, 1969). Possibly greater familiarity among
group members and interdependence in the functioning of people in
certain settings, such as villages or kibbutzim, lead them to learn to be
cooperative rather than individualistic or competitive. The family structure in which children grow up may also vary across some of these
groups: This can affect children's experiences and their cooperative or
competitive orientation. Variation in family structure may represent
variation in a specific form of interdependence, as well as variation in
other dimensions of experience. Graves and Graves (1978) found that on
Cook Island older children who came from nuclear families showed more
competitive and rivalrous reward choices than did children of the same
socioeconomic level who came from extended families.

However, the differences in behavior may also have other sources. In
much of this research the children could gain rewards for cooperation,
whereas they forfeited their rewards if they competed. (Hence, competition is regarded as "irrational" in this setting.) The rewards may
have been more valuable to rural than to urban children. Moreover, the
rural children may be accustomed to more supervision, more knowledge
of their behavior by adults; consequently, they may feel less free to act
uncooperatively. There may be different rules for "game playing" in
urban and rural areas and/or in different cultures; in some there may
be greater, in others lesser, emphasis placed on winning, specifically in
games. Thus, the findings may not generalize to other activities. To select
among various alternative explanations, experimental studies that systematically vary the extent of prior supervision, the value of rewards,
group norms, and other relevant variables may be useful and may
succeed in establishing which are more or less important influences on
cooperation.

The same considerations apply to research on socialization. Extensive
correlational studies are needed to determine the relationships between
parental child-rearing practices, other aspects of children's socialization,
and children's characteristics, as well as experimental studies that, in the

framework of (it is hoped) lifelike and meaningful experiences that children are exposed to, explore which are critical influences and which are correlated but are not, in themselves, important ones. One cannot, of course, be certain that the findings of experimental studies demonstrating the influence of particular conditions explain the meaning of correlations, but frequently the findings support each other and can progressively enlarge our understanding.

Culture, socioeconomic level, and urban versus rural environment are summary variables. Even some personal characteristics such as sex are best regarded as such. They do not directly identify or without further knowledge even imply differences in psychological processes. With regard to sex, it is clear that sex differences in prosocial behavior are highly complex (see Volume 1). Under some conditions women and girls act more positively than men and boys but, under others, less so, and frequently no differences were found. Some of the differences in behavior seem to be the result of differences in what behavior is regarded as sex-appropriate, as well as of differences in competence. Women help less a person, apparently stranded, who is standing next to a car with its hood up (West *et al.*, 1975). Women may feel less competent than men in helping when a car is involved, and they may feel that approaching a man who needs such help is inappropriate for them. However, men and women do not differ in providing help for a physically distressed man on the street (Staub & Baer, 1974). Females tend to divide rewards between themselves and another person, or between two other people, more equally; males divide rewards more equitably. Apparently, females are less concerned than are males with giving everybody what he or she deserves but, instead, value equality and are concerned with the feelings of the recipient (Volume 1, Chapters 4 and 5).

What differences in the characteristics of males and females may lead to differences in behavior? Females report more prosocial values and express more concern about other people's welfare. Recently, on the basis of a review of research, Hoffman (1977a,b) suggested that girls are more empathic than are boys. However, since in most studies empathy was measured by verbal statements of children, without evidence of real affective reactions, these studies may, again, have demonstrated females' greater concern about and sensitivity to others. What are the origins of such differences in the characteristics of males and females—which, presumably, on occasion affect their behavior? Are there, possibly, any genetic differences? What socialization practices and experiences are they exposed to that lead to different characteristics and behavior? Research findings about these and related questions, to the extent they exist, will be examined.

In summary, the following chapters will examine theory and varied types of research that may shed light on how socialization and experience lead to the development of characteristics that affect the tendency for behaving prosocially in interaction with other human beings. Understanding the origins of such characteristics can help parents and educators to foster their development.

Parents may have conflicts about the kinds of characteristics they value and want to promote in their children. They may wonder whether prosocial behavioral tendencies will interfere with their child's pursuit of self-interest. Seemingly, the contrary is true. First, positive behavior is always discriminative in nature (when not, one can regard it as maladjusted), its form and frequency affected by a person's other motives and by the existing circumstances. Second, the tendency to behave positively seems to promote self-interest in varied ways, by improving interpersonal relationships and the satisfaction a person might gain from them and by contributing to effective and satisfying personal adjustment (see Chapter 7). Since human relationships are reciprocal in substantial ways and degrees (Volume 1, Chapters 8 and 9), positive conduct is likely to lead to direct self-gain through reciprocation. Finally, the tendency by members of a social group to engage in positive behavior is likely to create a harmonious, cooperative, well-functioning society, which contributes to the welfare of all.

Major Approaches to Development

To provide a background for an examination of the development of prosocial tendencies, I shall first discuss three dominant theoretical approaches to children's development. These approaches are (a) the identification–internationalization approach,[1] (b) the social-learning approach, and (c) the cognitive developmental approach. It is important to note that it is difficult to find a contemporary researcher who relies solely on either of the first two approaches in their original forms. However, although important convergence has taken place, these approaches represent different theoretical origins for both current research and theory. The purpose of the following discussion is not to categorize but to identify concepts, clarify issues, and point to convergences as well as to differences.

With regard to each of these approaches, three questions ought to be asked. First, what antecedent conditions do investigators who are guided by the approach focus on—that is, what influences (independent variables) are of interest to them in exploring the sources of children's learning or development? Second, by what mechanisms does learning or

---

[1] This theoretical approach does not have a traditional designation. I named it identification–internalization approach from its two major constructs (see pages 22–34). The approach is a derivative of psychoanalytic thinking and has been used in some form by various developmental psychologists, starting at about the 1950s.

change come about? What principles are involved? Third, what is learned? What consequences (or dependent variables) are of primary interest?

Identification–Internalization Approach

The identification–internalization approach derives its basic concepts from both psychoanalytic theory and learning theory. The combination probably originated with Dollard and Miller's (1950) translation of psychoanalytic concepts into learning terms, which resulted in the application of psychoanalytic concepts to children's learning and development. Researchers who used this approach to moral development have been primarily concerned with the kind of socialization experiences that lead to the learning of moral values and beliefs by children. They have been concerned to a lesser degree with whether these socialization experiences or the resulting moral values affect behavior. They studied parental child-rearing practices as the source of learning or development. These practices can be subdivided into (a) discipline techniques—how the parents respond to transgression or wrongdoing by the child or how the parents attempt to bring about obedience—and (b) relationship variables—the quality of interaction between the parents and the child; the atmosphere of the home.

Discipline techniques have been categorized in different ways by different investigators, including love oriented versus object oriented, love withdrawal, reasoning, power assertion, and physical punishment. The relationship variables include parental warmth versus coldness, and permissiveness versus control, but other categorizations are, of course, possible. Another class of influence, parental values, which may guide a variety of parental behaviors toward the child, has been neglected by many investigators. Related to parental values or to be regarded as an independent class are the kinds of children's activities that the parents promote or attempt to inhibit, that is, the "content" of child rearing. Although it is important, from both theoretical and practical perspectives, to determine what it is that children are encouraged to do or are inhibited from doing, little attention has been paid to the content of parental child-rearing.

Hoffman (1963, 1970a) distinguished between three types of parental child-rearing (discipline) practices: power assertion, love withdrawal, and induction. Power assertion refers to the use of physical punishment, the deprivation of material objects or privileges, the direct application of force, or the threat of any of these. The parents capitalize on their physical power over material resources in controlling the child. In love withdrawal the parents give semidirect, nonphysical expression of anger or disapproval when the child has engaged in some undesirable behavior; for example, they ignore the child, refuse to speak or listen to him, or threaten to leave him. In induction, the parents give explanations or reasons why the child should not behave in certain ways, or why he should change his behavior. These explanations focus on the consequences the child's undesirable behavior has on others. Obviously, most parents are likely to use a combination of these child-rearing practices, but parents vary in their emphasis on, or frequency of use of, these techniques.

How do these relatively global techniques lead to learning? Often the manner in which they are expected to operate is *not* specified. Instead, the relationship between socializing practices and the child's values or behavior is treated as an empirical question. Psychologists guided by a social-learning approach imply or state that these techniques lead to change or learning through well-known principles, such as reinforcement and punishment. For example, the withdrawal of love or privileges might be regarded as punishment that decreases the probability of the punished behavior. However, the applicability of these principles to parent–child interactions and whether parents' behavior toward their children is best described in terms of rewards or punishments that have differential consequences have not yet been subjected to careful analysis.

In contrast to considering child-rearing practices as forms of direct tuition, other theorists and researchers assume that learning takes place through identification. Depending on parental practices, children identify with their parents to a greater or lesser degree, which determines the extent to which they will adopt parental values, standards, or behaviors. The important consequence of identification is usually thought to be a general tendency to learn from parental example and to internalize values, standards or beliefs. Once children internalize them and accept them as their own, positive emotional consequences result from adhering to these values, standards, and beliefs, and negative consequences (e.g., guilt) result from deviating from them. Identification and internalization are concepts of substantial importance; I shall examine their history and meaning next.

Identification

The notion that children learn through identification with their parents was proposed by Freud. Identification has become an overused, often poorly and variably defined concept, but properly conceptualized it might have value. After all, many research findings suggest that even temporary conditions of perceived similarity with others may lead to greater adoption of their goals or concern with their interests (Volume 1, Chapter 7). Adopting the interests and goals of others as one's own and wanting to be like others may be regarded as forms of identification.

Most contemporary psychologists define identification as imitation of a global, general kind (Bronfenbrenner, 1960; Kagan, 1958), that is, as a tendency to imitate a variety of characteristics and behaviors of another person. This is contrasted with the imitation of specific acts under specific circumstances. However, Bandura (1969a,b) regards the antecedents of specific and general imitation as the same, and thus he does not differentiate between the two kinds of imitation. Gewirtz and Stingle (1968) also believe that there is no distinction between identification and what they call *generalized imitation*.

According to Kohlberg (1963), the root meaning of identification is a tendency to model one's behavior after another's. Identification is distinguished from imitation in three ways: (*a*) It is a motivated disposition rather than an instrumental response; that is, it is maintained without obvious extrinsic or situational rewards when perceived similarity to the model is intrinsically rewarding for the child. (*b*) Similarity to the model is maintained in the absence of the model. (*c*) Modeling is relatively global, in that many aspects of the model's behavior are reproduced.

As a measure of identification, an index of global similarity is often used—for example, between the child's responses in projective test situations and his perceptions of the responses his parents would make in that situation. However, such perceived and/or imagined similarity, as well as actual similarity in the behavior of the parents and that of the child, may come about in a number of ways. Similarity may be due to parents' reinforcing the child's responses that are similar to their own, rather than to imitation for intrinsic reasons. Furthermore, children may imitate parents because—trusting the parents' competence or judging from the parents' success—they believe that imitation will lead to success in achieving some external outcome, in accomplishing a task or gaining a desired resource.

Kagan suggested (1958) that identification is an

> acquired cognitive response within a person(s). The content of this response is that some of the attributes, motives, characteristics, and affective states of a model (*M*) are part of *S*'s psychological organization. The major implication of this definition is that the *S* may react to events occurring to *M* as if they occurred to him. . . . the motivation to command or experience desired goal states of a model is salient in the development and maintenance of identification [p. 298].

According to Kagan, the reinforcement for the acquisition of "identifying responses" is the resulting perception of similarity between the person and the model.

A *motivated disposition* seems the crucial and defining aspect of identification. Some of the confusion associated with the concept of identification may be the result of many writers, starting with Freud, implying that the motivated disposition itself and one of its consequences —the tendency to imitate the parent—are one and the same thing, and calling both identification. It is useful to separate (*a*) the nature of this motivated disposition; (*b*) its antecedents, (what brings it about); and (*c*) its consequences. There actually may be several different types of antecedents, leading to somewhat different motivated dispositions, which have somewhat different consequences. However, I believe that it is desirable to define the motivated disposition alone as identification. The primary component of the motivated disposition is the desire of the child to be like the parent. Generalized imitation may be a consequence of this motivated disposition.

Why do children identify with their parents? What brings about a motivated disposition? Freud (1938) had a complex theory of identification (Brown, 1965) but proposed two major reasons for, or sources of, identification. One type of identification, referred to as *developmental* or *anaclitic* identification, is assumed to result from the desire of the child to reproduce the gratifications provided by a love object, the parent. According to both Sears, Maccoby, and Levin (1957) and Mowrer (1950) many attributes of the parent become secondarily reinforcing to the child, because they are associated with gratification of a variety of needs. When the parents are not around, or when there is a threat of loss of love because the parents punish the child by withholding love, or when the child fears that this will happen because of his potential or actual transgression, the child decreases his anxiety and gains reassurance and satisfaction by rehearsing parental roles and by adopting characteristics of the parents, thereby reactivating parental love. Discussions of developmental identification thus imply that in part it is based on the child's anxiety and thus on negative reinforcement, and in part it is motivated by the positively reinforcing capacity of being like the parents. Parental warmth, love, nurturance, or affection are regarded, however, as crucial components of developmental identification; without them loss or withdrawal of love would have little meaning, and the possibility of regaining affection would not exist. The *experiential* component of the motivated disposition in developmental identification is basically unknown; presumably it includes the feeling of affection and the desire to be like the parents.

Another kind of identification proposed by Freud (1938) is identification with the aggressor. This results from the desire to neutralize a threat from a feared individual. The conception of "defensive" identification grew out of the conception of the Oedipus complex. The child who has incestuous desires toward the parent of the opposite sex comes to fear retaliation from the same-sex parent; to minimize this threat he or she assumes the characteristics of the "aggressor." Evidence for this type of identification is primarily anecdotal and/or impressionistic. For example, the behavior of inmates of concentration camps, who came to act (e.g., dress, march) like their guards and torturers, has been interpreted as caused by identification with the aggressor (Bettelheim, 1943).

One contemporary theory of identification that apparently derives from the defensive-identification idea was proposed by Whiting (1959). In his view children identify with their parents, imitating their behavior or acting out their roles, because they envy the status of the parents. The child will experience status envy when another person has "more efficient control over resources than he has [Whiting, 1960]," the resources being anything that the child desires. Brown (1965) commented that Whiting's theory comes close to preserving Freud's explicit ideas about identification, "making them into a more sensible package." It recognizes that the parents' status and power extend beyond the sexual domain, and it also recognizes the significance of this for the child. Furthermore, according to status-envy theory the child would identify with the same-sex parent because he loves or desires the opposite-sex parent and the same-sex parent has control over the desired "resources." Another theory of identification, the social-power theory (Mussen & Distler, 1959), suggests that children identify with the controller of resources, the one who has the power to supply the resources that are needed for gratification. As Brown (1965) points out, it is unclear to what extent this theory is different from Whiting's. In the example Whiting gives for status envy the envied person enjoys the resources, and also has the power over the resources that makes it possible for him to enjoy them.

The different theories suggest somewhat different motivational states. Developmental identification conceptions emphasize an intrinsic desire to be like the parent; they propose that being like the parent is rewarding, that it enhances positive feelings or decreases negative ones. The status-envy notion implies that being like the parent may be perceived as instrumental in gaining access to external resources. However, as I noted, the subjective components of such motivational states are little known.

These conceptions of identification primarily focus on the conditions that produce identification. It seems reasonable for more than one of these conceptions to be correct. The motivational state that can be called identification might follow from different types of antecedent conditions; the joint existence of several conditions might increase the likelihood of identification. For example, the evidence that will be reviewed in Chapter 4 suggests that a combination of a reasonable degree of parental control (and thus control over the child's resources), warmth, and affection might be highly effective in promoting identification. If different types of conditions can give rise to identification, the nature of the motivated disposition, the parental characteristics that stand out in the child's perception, and the kinds of characteristics that the child will adopt might all differ. Imitating a dominant parent who is very much in control of the family's resources would have different consequences from imitating a loving, affectionate parent. The nature of the motivation and the kinds of intrinsic rewards that result from imitation might also be different.

Unfortunately, identification has received more attention from theorists than from researchers, possibly because the confusions surrounding the concept have made operational definitions and careful research difficult. Developmental identification has received the most attention as an explanatory concept. Sometimes love withdrawal and/or positive, loving characteristics of parents have been measured. These presumably give rise to a desire to be like the parent, and this motivation is expected to lead the child to imitate parental characteristics. Researchers have usually omitted the direct measurement of the motivated disposition; they have, instead, concentrated on the measurement of imitation, or similarity between parent and child.

Hetherington conducted several experiments on identification. In one study (Hetherington, 1965) the effects of parental dominance were examined. Dominance was measured by bringing the parents together, after each parent had independently decided how to handle a hypothetical problem with their child, and asking them to discuss the problem and arrive at a common solution. Percentage of talking, as well as yielding, provided the index of dominance. Hetherington reasoned that children would identify with the dominant parent and, consequently, would imitate his or her behavior. The 4- to 11-year-old subjects imitated the dominant parent's choice of pictures, an aesthetic preference measure, to a greater degree. Dominance of the mother was associated with somewhat less frequent sex-role behavior of boys and less similarity to the father. Dominance of the father was associated with greater similarity of girls to their fathers. Paternal dominance seemed to be a particularly important source of identification among boys; girls' imitation of the mothers was enhanced more by maternal warmth (Hetherington & Frankie, 1967).

Some evidence that an affectionate, positive relationship between parents and children does lead to identification comes from a study by Hoffman and Saltzstein (1967). The measure of identification in this study followed the lines I suggested earlier, in that motivated disposition rather than actual imitation was measured. This measure was provided by the sum of children's responses to questions about their orientation toward their parents, such as admiration ("Which person do you admire most or look up to most?"), desire to emulate ("Which person do you want to be like when you grow up?"), and perceived similarity ("Which person do you take after mostly?"). Power assertion by parents, evaluated independently from information provided by the parents themselves, was negatively correlated with identification, but induction oriented toward adults (explaining to the child the consequences of his behavior on adults) was positively related. In addition, highly significant positive correlations were obtained between reports of mothers' affection and the children's maternal identification scores.

In another publication, Hoffman (1971) described the relationship between this index of internalization and various measures of children's moral cognition and behavior. Hoffman suggested that such relationships might be limited because of the difficulty children might have in inferring the parents' values, moral evaluations of events and people, feelings of guilt, and the like, given their own limited cognitive skills and the scant information that parents often provide about such matters to their children. The findings showed that boys' identification with fathers, particularly among middle-class children, was related to indices of internalized moral values and to rule conformity. Given what he regarded as a relative paucity of significant relationships, Hoffman (1971) suggested that identification is not an "all pervasive process in moral development." As I shall progressively elaborate, learning and development must be the result of multiple influences, and identification is certainly only one of these.

Hoffman and Saltzstein found that the maternal use of induction and other practices relates to a greater degree to both boys' and girls' values and behavior than paternal use of specific practices. In contrast, identification with fathers had a stronger influence among boys than identification with mothers (Hoffman, 1971). Is it possible that the influence of mothers is more piecemeal, in that children learn from mothers as a function of relatively specific influences, whereas the influence of the father is more global, less differentiated, and demonstrates more generalized imitation? This might result from the usually less frequent contact with the father. Perhaps because of less frequent contact, fathers also attempt less to provide specific direction or guidance. Consistent with these findings and the reasoning are reports by Mullison (1969) and Katz and Rotter (1969). Mullison (1969) found that father identification of boys is associated with appropriate sex-role preferences but mother identification is not associated with sex-role preferences by either boys or girls. Katz and Rotter (1969) found a positive relationship between the interpersonal trust orientation of fathers and sons, although not of mothers and children. Other findings by Hoffman (1970b) and Rutherford and Mussen (1968), which are reviewed in conjunction with research on socializing influences, can also be interpreted in this manner.

As suggested earlier, evidence that directly demonstrates the origins and consequences of identification is minimal; this is also true of evidence about identification as it relates to the specific domain of prosocial orientation or behavior. Clearly, one would not expect socialization to take place only through the medium of identification. However, we do need to know to what extent the motivated disposition implied by identification, in contrast to specific influences working through a variety of other avenues, leads to the kind of learning and development that we are concerned with here. Some writers (Bossard & Boll, 1956) proposed that an *empathic complex,* a particular emotional linkage between a child and significant persons in his environment, is an important determinant of the kinds of characteristics that the child tries to adopt, the kind of person he wants to become, or the kind of person he tries not to become. The last notion is based on reports made by some individuals, that their intense dislike of a person led them to try to be different from that person. Self-report data from several groups of subjects showed that most people report that a few such positive and negative identifications (the subjects did not use this term, however) had substantial influence on them. Identification with the mother was most frequently reported.

Internalization

Many writers consider the internalization of societal values and standards as the essential step in moral development. Internalization can result from identification or come about in other ways. Early in the child's life, parents and other members of the social group begin to administer sanctions for deviation from moral values, norms, or standards of conduct, and rewards for adherence to them. Children usually learn at an early age what is expected of them, and they behave according to these expectations to gain reward and avoid punishment. The concept of internalization is used to explain how the individual becomes governor of his own moral actions, by accepting the moral values of his society as his own and guiding his actions by them.[2]

The notion that the moral standards of society are internalized by the individual was first elaborated by Freud (1938). Internalization takes place, according to Freud, when a part or portion of the external world is abandoned as an object and is taken into the ego so that it becomes an integral part of the internal world. This occurs by means of identification. The new physical agency that results carries out the functions that have previously been carried out by people in the external world. That is, outer regulation is replaced by inner regulation.

Hoffman (1970a), elaborating on the idea of internalization, wrote,

> the individual does not go through life viewing society's central norms as externally and coercively imposed pressures to which he must submit. Though the norms are initially alien, they are eventually adopted by the individual, largely through the efforts of his early socializers—the parents—and come to serve as internalized guides so that he behaves in accord with them even when external authority is not present to enforce them. That is, control by others is replaced by self control [p. 262].

Aronfreed (1968) wrote that "the concept of internalization is . . . often used to refer to the child's adoption of social norms or rules as its own, and the resulting evaluative control of its behavior by some of the most complex functions of cognitive and verbal processes [p. 16]."

According to the Freudian conception, internalization leads to the development of the superego, the Freudian equivalent of conscience. The superego is an internal governing agency that is a depository of standards of right and wrong. It guides behavior according to these standards and observes and judges conduct in relation to them, punishing deviation from them. This punishment takes place through affect or emotion —particularly guilt (or moral anxiety), which results from violation of moral standards. The superego is primarily noncognitive and nonrational; many of the internalized values and standards may be unconscious and consequently unavailable for rational examination. Often these standards are overly severe and punitive. In contrast to Freud, contemporary researchers on internalization tend to emphasize not the tyranny of such standards, but the conditions under which values and

---

[2] In general, no serious attempts have been made by the psychologists who studied internalization to define which societal values and norms are morally relevant. In the popular view and also in research efforts, values, norms, and related behavior that do not necessarily affect other people's welfare are assumed to have moral significance. They include orderliness, cleanliness, obedience, and sexual conduct, which is often regarded as morally undesirable.

standards do or do not get internalized, and the extent to which they guide behavior. Internalized standards are not all proscriptive; prescriptive standards refer to ideals and desirable values (thou shalts). The "agency" that contains these standards is referred to as the *ego ideal*.

What criteria can we use to evaluate the presence of internalization? Theoretically, "self-controlling acts would be evidence of internalization—those motivated by the wish to avoid self-condemnation or merit self-approval.' [Maccoby, 1968, p. 259]." In line with this Hoffman suggests that internalization is characterized at least by freedom from subjective concern about external sanctions. Relevant to this distinction between anticipated external consequences and freedom from subjective concern about external sanctions is the question of the role of absent reference groups and the possibility that behavior may be based on adherence to the norms of such reference groups (Hoffman, 1970a). Bandura (1969a) also noted this possibility. Several writers have gone further and have assigned a unique role to adherence to norms or standards of conduct motivated by a relationship to special agents—parents, reference groups, or even God. Kelman (1958) distinguished between behavior guided by compliance, by identification, and by internalization. In his scheme identification refers to adherence to a standard or value on account of a personal relationship, out of deference to, respect for, or the desire to please another person. Campbell (1964) also suggested that people may adhere to a standard out of respect for others but found that, among college students, over time conduct came to deviate from standards more when adherence was based on respect for parents than when it was due to internalized values. Hoffman (1970a) distinguished between the effect of fear of a punitive response from a reference figure and the effect of a positive attitude toward a reference figure. The latter is associated with a desire to please, based on love and admiration, and a concern about hurting or disappointing the reference figure. According to Hoffman, this second attitude may be considered internalization.

Four distinctions representing different forms and degrees of internalization seem useful. First, behavior may be directed by external consequences that have a high probability of occurrence, as suggested by discriminative stimuli that are present. The presence of an adult who usually punishes aggression would thus inhibit aggression. Second, behavior may be directed by the fear of anticipated negative consequences or by the expectation of positive consequences that are primarily in the actor's imagination or are unlikely to occur, such as punishment by supernatural beings. Third, behavior may be directed by the desire to please or not to disappoint others, even though they are not present and the behavior is private. Fourth, behavior may be directed by self-imposed consequences for deviation from or adherence to standards of conduct. The distinction between the last two kinds of influences is a worthwhile one. There seems to be subjective validity for the distinction; people facing moral dilemmas, preparing to make sacrifices, often think of what other people who are important to them would think of them and how they would evaluate their actions.

Can some of these distinctions actually be measured, or are they conceptual niceties? Is it ever possible to evaluate the subjective state of a person to the extent that one knows whether he is free of concern about external consequences, including concern about others' evaluation of him? Can one ever know that, as Hoffman (1970a, p. 264) stated, an "individual experiences the standards as an obligation to himself?" Certainly even people who are capable of viewing events in relation to highly internalized standards will, under many circumstances, be concerned about the external consequences of their actions.

Internalization tends to be evaluated in part by what people say about their thoughts and feelings, in part by how they act privately when they are not under surveillance. Internalized values presumably have a cognitive component: the knowledge of standards and the manner of thinking about right and wrong. This emphasis on the cognitive component is in contrast to the views of Freud, who believed that the content of the superego is mostly unconscious. Second, there is an affective component—expression of negative feelings, specifically guilt following transgression, which is usually contrasted with expressed fear of external consequences or absence of negative consequences. Presumably, positive emotions result from adherence to standards, although this aspect has been neglected both in theory and in the measurement employed in research. Positive emotions may be particularly likely to follow adherence to prescriptive standards—sharing, helping, considerate behavior. Perhaps as a consequence of the focus of past research and theory on proscriptive morality, the tyranny of moral values has been emphasized more than the pleasure of positive conduct or of restraint from negative conduct. Third, internalization is manifested in *behavior,* in adherence to moral standards despite personal gains associated with deviation or lack of external pressure for adherence. The desire to confess wrongdoing, the desire to "repent," and the desire to compensate for damage that one has done are also regarded as indices of internalization. They imply knowledge that what one has done is wrong, feelings of distress about it, and motivation to correct the wrong. There is, however, a problem with confession as an index of internalization. As Hill (1960) noted, the child may learn to confess because confession has instrumental value, that is, it results in reinforcement; parents often reward their child or forgive his transgression if he confesses voluntarily.

The cognitive and affective components of internalization are usually evaluated by measuring the child's reactions to transgression, such as guilt, self-criticism, reparation of damage caused, or confession of wrong-doing. These reactions may indicate that the child knows the standard by which the transgression would be judged wrong and that the child reacts emotionally to the transgression. Internalization has commonly been measured through projective story completions. The child is asked to complete a story that describes another child's transgression. It is assumed that the child identifies with the hero of the story and therefore his story completion shows his own beliefs and feelings. To what extent this assumption is justified is not known, but it must have some validity because relationships have been found between story completions and parental practices on the one hand and the child's behavior on the other hand (Hoffman, 1970a; Maccoby, 1968). The child's feelings are evaluated on the basis of what he *says* about *another* child's feelings, and the presence of real emotional experience by the child is not measured.

The types of moral concepts that the child employs and the nature of his judgments about situations that involve conflicting moral standards are also used to evaluate the degree of internalization. This technique was derived from the work of Piaget and Kohlberg, who used it to collect data in support of the cognitive-developmental position. Finally, the child's resistance to the temptation to act contrary to moral norms (or expectations of an authority) has been used as a measure of degree of internalization. This has been done through projective story completion or through evaluation of the child's behavior in response to a real temptation in the laboratory. In the latter case the child is usually alone and has been led to believe that no one is likely to find out about any transgression. Since no negative external consequences would follow from such deviation, resistance to temptation is assumed to indicate the presence of internalized standards. However, under such circumstances the child may still worry about detection and punishment; he may not be free of subjective concern about consequences.

Probably any one of the criteria that have been used to measure internalization can be criticized on some grounds. For example, behavioral attempts at reparation might result from the child's learning that such action leads to good social relationships. The expression of guilt in projective stories following wrongdoing by the hero might demonstrate a child's knowledge that such a feeling is socially valued. After all, most children must continually hear some variant of "you should feel bad for having done that." It is not surprising, therefore, that children with higher IQs, who are more able to learn about and adjust to their social world, express more internal moral judgments (Hoffman, 1971). It is unclear to what extent this relationship indicates a more developed conscience, more effective self-presentation, or both, by more intelligent children.

Internalization is perhaps best conceived of as a matter of degree. The more cognitive and affective statements a child makes that are characteristic of internalized values and form an interrelated set of cognitions, the greater one's confidence would be in the degree and, depending on the type of measurement, the range of his internalized values. Naturally, the greater the relationship between such measures of cognition and behavior under private circumstances—the greater one's ability to predict behavior from internalized values—the greater is one's confidence in the measures used and in the theory on which the predictions are based.

Social-Learning Approach

The social-learning approach focuses on how specific principles of learning—reinforcement, punishment, and modeling—determine what children learn and how they develop. The effects of various forms of verbal communications to children, particularly on their prosocial behavior, has also been studied. The term *social learning* gained attention through the social-learning theory of Rotter (1954); however, the approach acquired influence as a behavioristic orientation to child development. Social-learning theory both analyzed the development of social behavior in terms of principles of learning and considered the conditions under which learning is more or less likely to take place. Several conditions that have been studied as potential influences on learning have been derived from theory and research related to the notion of identification, for example, the degree to which a model's nurturance or power affects the extent to which the child imitates the model.

Because the approach was originally primarily behavioral, the consequences of learning have primarily been evaluated in terms of behavior. Moreover, researchers were not greatly concerned with cognitive mediators of learning, such as beliefs, values, or interpretations of events. However, emotional mediators, such as the anxiety that results from punishment through classical conditioning, have been considered important, certainly as inhibitors of undesirable conduct (Aronfreed, 1968, 1976). The lack of emphasis on cognitive mediators has been a relative one: For some time Rotter (1954), Mischel (1966, 1968, 1973), and Bandura (1969a,b) have all used the concept of expectancy of reward and punishment as a determinant of action. Thus reinforcement, punishment, and modeling were thought to have cognitive consequences, although relatively simple ones (e.g., expectation of outcomes), which in turn determined behavior. Bandura (Bandura, 1969a, 1971, 1977; Bandura & Walters, 1963) stressed the distinction between the learning of a behavior, which is dependent on the observation of a model alone, and the subsequent performance of the behavior, which is determined by the expectation of reward or punishment. This expectation was regarded as a function of several factors, including the observation of what happens to a model following his or her behavior, that is, vicarious reinforcement or punishment.

Rotter and Mischel have used another cognitive concept, that of the subjective value of the outcome of the behavior. In their system behavior is determined by the combined influence of the expectation of a positive outcome and the subjective value of that outcome for the person. Aronfreed (1968) emphasized cognition, but mainly as the conditioned stimulus for anxiety reactions that inhibit transgression of rules. Thoughts, verbalizations, and what people say to themselves can be highly effective conditioned stimuli in Aronfreed's view.

Later research and theory have placed increased importance on cognitive mediators of behavior. Some of the cognitive concepts focus on the manner in which people guide or regulate their conduct. Using plans and strategies for action (Mischel, 1973, 1976) or by the way they talk to themselves (Meichenbaum, 1974), people can regulate their progress toward a goal or a valued outcome. The way we talk to ourselves can also have motivational effects. Self-reactions, such as cognitive and affective self-reinforcement and self-punishment, are receiving increasing attention. Such self-reactions can motivate and guide action; they are important in maintaining adherence to standards of conduct (Bandura, 1971, 1976; Masters & Mokros, 1974). These conceptualizations are discussed in later chapters. The belief that people reinforce themselves for adherence to learned standards of conduct and punish themselves for deviation, not only materially but also internally by what they think and how they feel, represents an important rapprochement with the internalization approach. At the same time, because of the emphasis on the specificity of the influences considered, on operational definitions, and on the resulting ability to derive hypotheses and to explore them experimentally, the concepts that have been adopted and transformed by researchers guided by the social-learning approach are beginning to receive experimental verification and/or disconfirmation.

I suggested a further conception of how cognitions mediate behavior. In this conception, individuals possess networks of interrelated cognitions that have motivational potentials, that embody and define personal goals. When goals are activated by circumstances they give rise to the desire to reach certain outcomes as well as to tension that is maintained until the goal is either satisfied or deactivated (Volume 1, Chapter 2; Staub, 1979).

A convergence between identification theory and behavioral social-learning theory can be seen in the writings of Bandura (1969a, 1976, 1977). First he emphasized how behavior is controlled by its external reinforcing consequences and by discriminative stimuli that signal the kind of consequences that are likely to follow an act. In a well-known example, Bandura (1969a) described the motorist who arrives at an intersection late at night. Nobody is in sight. If he stops and waits patiently for the light to turn green he exhibits great control, but his behavior is clearly under the directing influence of an external (discriminative) stimulus. In many instances the controlling stimuli are unknown, and consequently behavior may be attributed to internal controlling agents even though it is under the control of discriminative stimuli. (We should note, however, that even when behavior is guided by discriminative stimuli, the motivation for action may be the result of expectations of self-reactions rather than external reactions.)

Bandura (1969a) proceeded to analyze how behavior can become, as a function of various learning conditions, "independent of specific situational contingencies and outcomes [p. 617]." He distinguished between several kinds of intrinsic reinforcement controls. One of these is intrinsic sensory consequences (for example, consequences of visual and auditory stimuli); the reinforcing effect of these is usually the result of a great deal of learning. Satisfaction gained from listening to music is an example of this. Another one is anticipatory consequences, when behavior is maintained by imagined rewards and punishments. A third mechanism "involves a process in which response patterns are largely controlled by their *self-evaluative consequences* [p. 618]." People may adopt standards of behavior that generate self-rewarding or self-punishing consequences, depending on how behavior compares to the self-prescribed standard. Positive and negative self-reinforcement may prevail over externally imposed or expected consequences. Bandura strongly suggests that maintaining standards for self-reinforcement probably does require some degree of social support, even if only from a few individuals who represent a valued reference group. This seems very likely to be the case. The handful of highly active abolitionists, for example, who traveled the United States in the early nineteenth century to stir up support for the abolition of slavery experienced much hardship and abuse (Tomkins, 1965). Apparently, however, they kept in touch with one another, urged one another on, and provided important mutual support.

The conception of self-reward and self-punishment that is a function of adherence to or deviation from (internalized) standards is extremely important for an internalization view. Guilt, obviously, is a form of self-punishment. However, past research on moral development includes few demonstrations of how self-reinforcement processes guide behavior. Usually it has been implied that if a person shows knowledge of a norm and ascribes negative feelings to a character in a projective story who transgressed a norm he also experiences these feelings himself, and they will guide his actions. Unfortunately, not even the correlation between such responses in projective stories and "moral" behavior is well established. When such a relationship is found to exist, that does not by itself establish that adherence to values or standards is maintained by self-punishment or self-reward.

Much of the research conducted in the behavioral social-learning framework must be regarded as research on the determinants of children's behavior, rather than research that demonstrates how learning or development take place. Usually only the immediate consequences of reinforcement, punishment, and modeling are evaluated, and thus their effects on behavior can be considered only as a demonstration of social influence, rather than of learning. Only rarely have researchers explored the long-term effects of experimental treatments or the generalization of treatment effects to behavior similar to but not identical with the behavior that was modeled. Moreover, much of the research has not been truly developmental because it has not considered the cognitive capacities, emotional development, and other personality characteristics of children that might modify the effects of particular learning procedures. (The same also tends to be true of research guided by other approaches.) The child's characteristics or the level of his development is likely to modify the meaning of particular experiences for him.

Much of the research conducted in this framework is "analogue" research. The experimental treatments provide children with varied kinds of modeling and reinforcing or punitive experiences, and the consequences of these experiences on relevant behavior are evaluated. It is implied or assumed that the treatment procedures create experiences that are analogous to those that children would have in interacting with adults and other socializers. This is an assumption that needs to be supported by independent research examining the manner in which reinforcement, punishment, and modeling experiences occur in the child's everyday life. A related issue that needs to be considered is whether events, or behaviors directed at the child, have the same effects when they occur in a parent–child interaction and when they occur in interaction with other adults in an unfamiliar setting. As I argued in Volume 1,

(Chapter 9), the behavior of an intimate is likely to have different effects than similar behavior on the part of a stranger.

In a sense, then, much of the research has an "as if" quality. It demonstrates influences that *might* be important in affecting children's behavior and their development. However, some indication of the validity of this research is provided by the correspondence and meaningful relatedness of a substantial variety of research findings from experiments guided by the social learning approach and by correlational studies that explored the relationship between indices of parental child-rearing practices and indices of children's behavior, or their values and standards (see Chapters 4 and 5). Further research that bridges the gap between the laboratory and real life is needed, and the ecological validity of laboratory findings has to be further established. Moreover, the ecological validity, the lifelike nature, of the conditions of laboratory research has to be increased.

The social-learning approach, with various modifications, has been highly influential in guiding research on children's positive social behavior. Other aspects of this approach are described in Chapters 4 and 5.

Cognitive Developmental Approach [3]

Social-learning theory and identification theory assume that children learn the moral standards, norms, and behaviors characteristic of their society by being directly taught, by learning from the examples of their parents and other socializing agents, or by identifying with and adopting characteristics of socializers. Cognitive developmental theory makes different basic assumptions (Kohlberg, 1958, 1969, 1976; Piaget, 1932; Turiel, 1969).

Piaget proposed that cognitive development proceeds through a series of stages, each stage representing a particular organization of the manner in which people perceive the world and think about it. Thinking at each stage, in other words, is characterized by certain principles. To move from one stage to another, a reorganization has to take place, one that results in new principles taking the place of the old ones. The stages are hierarchical, each succeeding stage representing a more ad-

---

[3] This theoretical approach will be examined in greater detail in this chapter than the other two approaches were, for two reasons. First, research related to this approach is less extensively examined in later chapters than is research related to the other two approaches, so that further discussion of this theory is less imbedded in later chapters. Second, cognitive developmental theory has had considerable popularity in recent years among researchers concerned with moral development.

vanced organization. The progression through stages is invariant in sequence; that is, the development of each person's thinking has to proceed through these stages in the same order.

Piaget (1932) applied this theory to moral development. He examined children's feelings about rules for a game of marbles, their reactions to stories of moral conflicts, and their evaluations of others' actions. On the basis of his data Piaget suggested that children move from *heteronomous* morality, characterized by evaluating right and wrong on the basis of the consequences of an action, to *autonomous morality,* in which the actor's intentions determine the evaluation of the act. Children in the heteronomous stage judge the child who breaks a larger number of cups accidentally as deserving greater punishment than the child who breaks fewer cups intentionally; a reversal takes place when the autonomous stage is reached. The two stages have other characteristics. In the heteronomous stage moral realism prevails—rules are regarded as absolute and as actually existing in nature. The autonomous stage is characterized by moral relativism. Rules are regarded as man-made and adjustable according to the circumstances.

Extensive research has been devoted to exploring Piaget's concerns and hypotheses and to verifying his conclusions (Lickona, 1976; Karniol, 1978). The research findings suggest that young children are able to consider intentions in evaluating conduct earlier than Piaget thought; when accident and intention cues are explicit, they tend to evaluate on the basis of intentions (Karniol, 1978). However, children and adults continue to be affected by consequences in evaluating conduct, particularly when these consequences are extreme, whether negative or positive (Volume 1, Chapter 4). Surber (1977) found, using Piaget type stories in which intentions varied from positive to negative and consequences from neutral to negative, that intentions and consequences both affected judgment among subjects who ranged in age from kindergarteners to adults. The major change appeared to be a decrease in the weight assigned to consequences with increasing age. Change, furthermore, appeared continuous rather than stagelike.

Kohlberg and his associates greatly expanded and modified moral stage concepts. Their theory of moral development has two basic aspects: the theory of stages and the interaction theory of development. Before discussing them, it is worthwhile to ask what determines the morality of a particular action or point of view in this approach. According to Kohlberg it is impossible to determine a person's morality on the basis of what this person does or what beliefs he states. As an example of this, Turiel (1969) relates an anecdote about Thoreau. Rather than pay his taxes, Thoreau went to jail, because he did not believe that he ought to be taxed. His friend Emerson, walking by, saw Thoreau through the window of his cell, and asked, "Henry, what are you doing in there?" Thoreau, who believed that Emerson ought also to have refused to pay his taxes, replied: "Waldo, what are you doing out there?" Which, then, is good or right: Being in jail, or not being in jail? To find out the morality of a person's beliefs or actions one has to know his *reasons* for them. Moral reasoning, the manner in which a person thinks about right and wrong, defines the level of a person's moral development, in Kohlberg's cognitive developmental approach. An important distinction is drawn between the content of a person's thinking—the kinds of rules, standards, and values a person advocates, whether he thinks an act is honest or dishonest—and why a person holds a standard, the reasoning a person employs in evaluating whether an act is right or wrong, which is referred to as his *cognitive structure*. Structures define principles or processes by which one interprets events and guides one's moral dealings with the social world.

One of the underlying assumptions of this theory is that people process information according to certain rules of logical operations, and some of these rules are epistemologically better than others. Morality is reasoned about in the same manner as is external reality. Development consists of the replacement of one logic system with a better one. Each logic system is a complete whole, qualitatively different, so that a change involves reorganization of the system rather than simple elaboration. Moral development is predicated on cognitive development. Cognitive structures have to be advanced enough to create the precondition for change in moral structure. The impetus for change, as we shall see, is the perceived inadequacy of a given set of rules, or system of reasoning, to account for new experience.

Moral reasoning develops, according to the theory, through six stages, which are invariant in sequence. Each person starts at Stage 1, and to reach a more advanced stage he has to go through each of the intermediate stages. The stages are regarded as universal in that they are rooted in the structure of the human mind. Every person, in every culture, has to go through the same sequence, although different individuals may progress up to different points and reach different final stages. The theory originally assumed (Kohlberg, 1964) that once a person has reached a particular stage there will be no downward movement, no regression, because the more advanced stages are more adequate in dealing with experience. However, regression has been found to occur (Kohlberg & Kramer, 1969).

Kohlberg derived the stages through the evaluation of moral judgments in conflict situations. He developed a series of stories that describe conflict situations. The main character in each story has to decide on a course of action when he is faced with two conflicting moral norms. As suggested earlier, it is not the decision about how to act, but the reasons given to justify this decision, that determine the level or stage or morality. The most often cited moral dilemma used by Kohlberg (1958, pp. 41–42) is the following:

> In Europe, a woman was near death from a rare form of cancer. There was one drug that the doctors thought might save her, a form of radium that a druggist in the same town had recently discovered. The druggist was charging $2,000, ten times what the drug cost him to make. The sick woman's husband, Heinz, went to everyone he knew to borrow the money, but he could only get together about half of what the drug cost. He told the druggist that his wife was dying and asked him to sell it cheaper or let him pay later. But the druggist said, "No." So Heinz got desperate and broke into the man's store to steal the drug for his wife.
> Should the husband have done that?

On the basis of the kind of judgments individuals make, Kohlberg concluded that there are three levels of development, each of which is divided into two stages (see Table 2.1).

Kohlberg (1976) gives a succinct description of the meaning of the three levels:

> One way of understanding the three levels is to think of them as three different types of relationships between the *self* and *society's rules and expectations*. From this point of view, *Level I* is a *preconventional* person, for whom rules and social expectations are something external to the self; *Level II* is a *conventional* person, in whom the self is identified with or has internalized the rules and expectations of others, especially those of authorities; and *Level III* is a *postconventional* person, who has differentiated his self from the rules and expectations of others and defines his values in terms of self-chosen principles [p. 33].

Kohlberg has also suggested that a different "socio-moral perspective" underlies each level of moral judgment. These are a "concrete individual" perspective at Level I, a "member of society" perspective at Level II, and a "prior to society perspective" at Level III. For example, at Level II there is a shared viewpoint that focuses on this individual's relationship to the group. "The conventional individual subordinates the needs of the single individual to the viewpoint and needs of the group or the shared relationship [Kohlberg, 1976, p. 36]." In contrast, at Level I a person would think only about his interests and those of others he cares about.

Table 2.1

Classification of Moral Judgment into Levels and Stages of Development [a]

Level	Basis of moral judgment	Stage of development
I	Moral value resides in external, quasi-physical happenings, in bad acts, or in quasi-physical needs rather than in persons and standards.	Stage 1: Obedience and punishment orientation. Egocentric deference to superior power or prestige, or a trouble-avoiding set. Objective responsibility. Stage 2: Naively egoistic orientation. Right action is that instrumentally satisfying the self's needs and occasionally others'. Awareness of relativism of value to each actor's needs and perspective. Naive egalitarianism and orientation toward exchange and reciprocity.
II	Moral value resides in performing good or right roles, in maintaining the conventional order and the expectancies of others.	Stage 3: Good-boy orientation. Orientation toward approval and toward pleasing and helping others. Conformity to stereotypical images of majority or natural role behavior, and judgment by intentions. Stage 4: Authority and social-order-maintaining orientation. Orientation toward "doing duty" and toward showing respect for authority and maintaining the given social order for its own sake. Regard for earned expectations of others.
III	Moral value resides in conformity by the self to shared or shareable standards, rights, or duties.	Stage 5: Contractual legalistic orientation. Recognition of an arbitrary element or starting point in rules or expectations for the sake of agreement. Duty defined in terms of contract, general avoidance of violation of the will or rights of others, and majority will and welfare. Stage 6: Conscience or principle orientation. Orientation not only toward actually ordained social rules but also toward principles of choice involving appeal to logical universality and consistency. Orientation toward conscience as a directing agent and toward mutual respect and trust.

[a] From Kohlberg, 1967, p. 171.

At Level III a person's commitment to moral principles precedes his taking or accepting society's perspective. Such a person "holds the standard on which a good or just society must be based [Kohlberg, 1976, p. 36]."

Whereas the content of a person's moral beliefs presumably depends on the society he lives in, the theory of stages implies that individual morality does not develop by internalization of societies' moral standards. These standards are relative to each society; if morality developed through direct tuition there could be no universal stages, and no invariant sequence, since individuals would learn different things in different societies. Kohlberg assumed, following Piaget, an interactionist theory of the development of moral stages. In the course of development, people interact with their environment; it is the variety of experiences they have, the nature of this interaction, that determines the extent to which structural changes take place and lead to movement toward higher stages of morality. Direct tuition has no special significance. The significance of parents, peers, and schools lies in shaping the child's opportunities for varied experiences and social interactions.

The type of experience that is especially significant is role-taking experience. Kohlberg (taking his views in part from Mead and symbolic interactionism) suggests that higher stages are characterized by an increasing ability to engage in reciprocal role-taking, to consider an action from an increasingly wider perspective. At the most advanced stage, which is characterized by justice and the sacredness of human life as the principles by which morality is to be determined, it is as if the person considers events from the perspective of all humanity in evaluating right and wrong. The environment can accelerate or retard moral development by enhancing or limiting opportunities for interaction that involves taking the roles of others.

What does variation in role-taking opportunities mean in terms of everyday experience? Kohlberg (1969) implies that it may mean some of the following:

1. Frequent interaction with others in varied situations and occupying different roles in these situations in relation to others.
2. Participation in varied social groups. A member of a group may consider the effects of a decision on himself, as well as on other members of the group.
3. Leadership in a group. Leadership provides additional and different opportunities for role taking. The leader has to consider the point of view of each member and the effect of a decision or action on them, in addition to viewing the event from his own perspective.

4. Membership in groups having potentially conflicting aims. Membership in such groups may make it necessary for the individual to examine the implications of the conflicting consequences of action on different people, or on different ideals or goals.

The specific mechanism by which change in cognitive structure is supposed to take place is *equilibration*, just as in Piaget's theory of structural change in cognition. Underlying the concepts of equilibrium and disequilibrium are Piaget's notions of *schemata*, the representation of experience in cognition; *assimilation*, the perception and interpretation of new experience in terms of existing cognitive representations; and *accommodation*, change in cognitive representations when they cannot, in their existing form, satisfactorily account for new experience. Turiel (1969) writes:

> According to Piaget (1947, 1967) movement from one cognitive structure to the next occurs when the system is in a state of disequilibrium. When a child who is in a state of disequilibrium is presented with operations that are developmentally close enough for him to consider, his assimilatory and accommodatory functions may act in complementary fashion to establish greater equilibrium (Langer, 1967). The child deals with the environmental event in accordance with structures available to him. Change may occur when the inability to completely assimilate events to the existing structure leads to disequilibrium that motivates attempts to achieve new equilibrium. This more highly equilibrated stage allows better assimilation of the new experience [p. 126].

In the course of their experience, children encounter situations that activate disequilibrium because of the conceptual contradictions in them. Change may be brought about by presenting children with such conceptual contradictions, but children will notice them and react to them with disequilibrium only if the contradiction is within their reach— close enough to their stage of development. According to the theory, disequilibrium has energizing properties, affective components that motivate change. It also has organizational components that lead to restructuring or accommodation. Stages are seldom "pure." Individuals are usually in the midst of developmental change; they are characterized by a dominant stage, but elements of the stage below and above this stage are also part of their reasoning. The highest stage should show the least "stage mixture." It should be the most stable and best equilibrated, since no further change follows. Fixation at low stage levels may also result in relatively little stage mixture, according to the theory (Turiel, 1969).

Kohlberg (1976) specified three aspects of "experience" that are likely to affect development in moral reasoning. Role-taking opportunity is one aspect. The moral atmosphere of the group or institution in which the child lives is another. By *moral atmosphere* Kohlberg means the "justice structure" of the environment. He quotes from Rawls (1971) to define this: "the way in which social institutions distribute fundamental rights and duties and determine the division of advantages from social cooperation [p. 7]." Kohlberg suggests that two institutions in which children were least and most advanced in their moral development, the American orphanage and the Israeli kibbutz, differed both in role-taking opportunities afforded to children and in moral atmosphere. The third aspect of experience that contributes to development in moral reasoning is cognitive–moral conflict, which can result from exposure to experiences arousing internal contradictions in a person's reasoning structure or from exposure to reasoning by significant others that is at variance with a person's own.

Other writers, quite varied in their theoretical perspectives (Aronfreed, 1976; Garbarino & Bronfenbrenner, 1976), also emphasize the importance of at least a moderate degree of conflict for moral development to take place. Garbarino and Bronfenbrenner differentiated between *monolithic, anomic,* and *pluralistic* settings. In a monolithic setting all "social agents and entities" are organized around the same set of goals; in an anomic setting there is almost no integration among goals; in a pluralistic setting,

> social agents and entities represent somewhat different expectations, sanctions and rewards for members of the society. These differences generate intergroup conflict which is largely regulated by a set of "ground rules" (such as a constitution) and a common commitment to integrative principles or goals (such as a religious ethic) [p. 75].

Under such conditions of moderate environmental contradictions, with a "delicate balance of diversity and consensus," moral development is likely to be enhanced.

Garbarino and Bronfenbrenner (1976) report data purportedly supporting their conception. They correlated a measure of pluralism derived from a factor analysis of sociopolitical indices (Vincent, 1971) and originally interpreted as an index of democracy but consistent with their view of pluralism, and scores on a measure of moral pluralism administered in 13 cultures. The latter was derived from 12-year-old children's performance on a Moral Dilemmas test (Bronfenbrenner, 1970a). This test measured the extent of children's willingness to engage in behavior that was urged by adults (which would result in a positive score on the test) or to go along with behavior urged or supported by peers (which would result in a negative score on the test). The test consisted of 30 hypothetical moral conflict situations (for example, going to a movie recommended by friends but disapproved of by parents, neglecting homework to join friends, or leaving a sick friend to go to a movie with other children). The greater the balance between the degree to which children reported that they would engage in adult-advocated or peer-advocated behavior (the closer the score to zero), the greater the child's moral pluralism, according to Garbarino and Bronfenbrenner. Actually, there was only one culture in which there was a negative score on the test, possibly because the children, who worked on the test in their school, were unwilling to admit too strong an inclination to act contrary to adult authority. A high negative correlation was found between societal pluralism and moral-dilemma scores, showing that with greater societal pluralism there is less authority orientation among children, less tendency to report behaving in ways advocated by authority. As Garbarino and Bronfenbrenner note, however, the differences among cultures can be completely accounted for by East–West differences, the West being represented by the democracies, the East by Communist countries; no correlations were apparent within each group. Consequently, it is unclear whether social pluralism or particular socialization emphases account for variation in the degree to which children report that they behave in the manner advocated by authority figures rather than by peers. In addition, the meaning of near-zero scores on the test is not clear, and the "moral" meaning of some of the conflict situations might also be questioned.

In another study that supports the notion that cognitive conflict is important in moral development, Maitland and Goldman (1974) reported that children who had to reach a concensus in the course of a group discussion of moral dilemmas—which demanded agreement on how to resolve moral conflicts—showed increase in moral judgment scores from a pretest to a posttest. Children who simply discussed the moral dilemmas but did not need to reach a consensus and those who spent time individually considering the dilemmas and justifying their choices showed no change.

Research and Basic Issues

I shall discuss here a limited amount of the evidence about the validity of the cognitive developmental theory. Some of the research is reviewed in later chapters in the course of examining influences that promote positive behavior and a prosocial value orientation. Briefly, the major claims of the theory, such as the stagelike organization of moral reasoning, the invariant sequence of stages, interaction and the opportunity for role-taking experiences as a source of development, and equilibration as the process by which development takes place, have not yet received substantial support. Kurtines and Grief (1974), in a thorough review, suggest not only that evidence is lacking for the invariance of stages but also that there is some evidence that the stages are *not* invariant. However, existing data primarily represent insufficient evidence, partly due to problems with the instrument to measure the stages (Kurtines & Grief, 1974; Rubin & Trotter, 1977) and to the lack of sufficient use of research strategies with which crucial aspects of the theory could be tested.

A very basic issue is the extent to which the evidence suggests that people are best characterized by the particular principles of morality that the six stages represent. As I noted in Volume 1, various philosophers and psychologists made assumptions about man's basic nature as either "good" or "bad." Kohlberg's theory clearly assumes that human beings are potentially good, since without inculcation of values and standards, simply through varied experiences, people will progressively evolve higher levels of morality. These higher levels of morality represent an unfolding of innate potentials. Given such a theoretical base, it is reasonable to ask to what extent the six stages are derived inductively (as Kohlberg [1958] claims), empirically derived from how subjects reasoned about moral dilemmas, and to what extent the system is deductive, representing basic assumptions or beliefs about different moral orientations. There is, of course, nothing wrong with a theory that represents basic assumptions that are then progressively verified. But are the principles that characterize the six stages of Kohlberg (see Table 2.1) accurate characterizations of people's moral thinking, their reasoning about issues of morality? Do they provide a more adequate characterization than would other systems, and are they better predictors of behavior? We do not yet have adequate answers to these questions.

Existing data clearly show age trends; moral reasoning appears to become more advanced with age in a variety of cultures (Kohlberg, 1969). However, the findings do not establish that development is stagelike rather than continuous. An instrument that is scored for stages has to provide stage scores. The findings show, however, extensive stage mixture as the rule, possibly because of the continuity of moral reasoning and not just because people are usually in transition between stages, as proponents of the theory claim. Nor do the findings provide evidence for invariant stages. The data are mostly cross-sectional, although a limited amount of longitudinal data examining change over limited time intervals is available (Kramer, 1968; Holstein, 1976). To establish invariance of sequence it would be necessary to examine changes in the moral reasoning of the same individuals over time—that is, to collect extensive longitudinal data.

Holstein (1976) examined changes in the moral reasoning of adolescents and of their parents over a 3-year interval. Both her data dealing with younger adolescents and Kramer's (1968) data dealing with older adolescents show that change in moral reasoning is sequential, at least from the preconventional to the conventional level. That is, the change is from the lower to the higher level of reasoning, as Kohlberg's theory would predict. However, when individual stages are examined, the progression is not stepwise; Stage 1 or 2 subjects can jump to Stage 4. Since there was a 3-year time interval between the first and second testing of subjects, it is possible that they passed through the intervening stages during this period. Holstein found that over the 3-year interval adults and adolescents who were originally at a higher stage were more likely to regress, to change in the "downward" direction, whereas lower-stage subjects were more likely to have advanced. The study included the college-educated parents as subjects and also showed that "moral justifications tend to stay at the conventional level over time [Holstein, 1976, p. 60]."

Holstein notes that with a strongly cognitive schema such as Kohlberg's and with the moral judgment stages originally defined and empirically tested with young white males (Kohlberg, 1963), the problem arises of what to do with such "irrational" moral sentiments as compassion, sympathy, and love. Women, who tend to show such sentiments to a greater degree (see Volume 1, Chapter 5) in response to moral conflict, are categorized at a low level of development in Kohlberg's schema. Moral sentiment is likely to be a strong influence in both conflict resolution and moral conduct; concepts like prosocial orientation, and value orientations in general, which clearly imply a strong affective component, tend to take them into consideration.

The "advance" (or change) in moral reasoning with age is a phenomenon one would expect; it would be predicted by a variety of theories. Increased cognitive maturity may enable children to handle certain moral concepts. The changing life circumstances of children and adolescents—changes that probably have some universality across cultures—may also account for moral advancement. Very young children are autocratically treated, by necessity, since they cannot exercise self-control or be reasoned with. Demands may be enforced by physical means, such as punishment, bodily separation from objects, and removal of the child from places. As the child becomes older the nature of control over the child is likely to become less direct, less physical, less authoritarian, and more verbal. It is not surprising, on this basis alone, that younger children evaluate right and wrong by the consequences of actions, in terms of rewards and punishments, and that this would change with age, given the changing reality of children's lives. The change in moral reasoning from Stage 1 to "conventional" morality would also be expected by theories of internalization, which assume that children move from concern with immediate rewards or punishments for their actions to concern with social consequences such as approval and disapproval and to internalization of values and standards.

In most of the cultures in which age trends were explored, moral reasoning did not advance above the level of conventional morality, Stages 3 and 4. It did so only in our own society, a modern, Western, industrialized culture. This has been interpreted by cognitive developmental theory as the result of differences in the opportunity for varied experiences that include role-taking opportunities. However, our culture includes the mode of thought that is characteristic of principled moral reasoning. Principles of justice, the sanctity of human life, and the concept of a social contract are important components of Western religious, philosophical, and political tradition. Exposure to them, combined with certain types of experiences that lead some people to use these components actively in their own thinking, is a likely origin of principled moral reasoning for most people who employ such reasoning. In addition, our society certainly incorporates varied value orientations and promotes varied goals, which would be likely to induce motivational and value conflicts that individuals have to resolve for themselves.[4]

As I already implied, the similar age trends in moral reasoning across cultures might in part result from similarities in socialization. Most cultures are likely to emphasize certain basic moral concerns that are important for the functioning of the social group and the survival of its members, even though different cultures allow different exceptions. Respect for the life and property of others may be dominant among these concerns. Gouldner (1960) suggested that the norm of reciprocity is universal across cultures. Other universal moral concerns, which arise because certain conditions promote human survival in groups, might exist.

One type of research attempted to show that children who are exposed to reasoning discrepant from their own and somewhat more advanced will prefer that reasoning to reasoning somewhat below their own stage (regression) or to reasoning far beyond their stage (a discrepancy too great to handle), and they will be influenced by this reasoning in their subsequent moral judgments (Rest, 1973; Rest, Turiel, & Kohlberg, 1969; Turiel, 1966; Turiel & Rothman, 1972). Turiel's (1966) data

---

[4] Incidentally, the frequency of Stage 6 reasoning appears to be extremely low. In two studies that my associates and I conducted, with over 100 female subjects in one study and over 100 male subjects in the other study, not a single person demonstrated Stage 6 reasoning (Staub, 1974).

show only a tendency for children to adopt reasoning that is one stage above rather than one stage below that of their own. Rest *et al.* (1969) and Rest (1973) found that preference is greater for reasoning above the subject's own stage, whether it is one or two stages above it, whereas comprehension is greater for reasoning below the subject's own stage. Thus, these data provide only slight support for the theory.

Nonetheless, the underlying conception seems sound. First, the findings of Turiel on change and of Rest and his associates on preference represent, in a specific domain, an important principle, probably fairly widely held, although infrequently applied by developmental psychologists: The child's level of development, whether cognitive, affective, or of another type, is likely to affect his capacity to learn from experience, as well as what he learns. Second, children may be more likely to learn ways of thinking about the world that challenge their desire for mastery, that are somewhat novel, that provide an opportunity for exercising their cognitive competence, that lead to a new level of adaptation. However, this may only be true of children who have not learned to be afraid of novelty and of demands on their intellect. That is, individual differences are likely to exist in the degree to which children will be stimulated by more advanced reasoning than their own.

An interesting point with regard to the study by Turiel (1966) and the one by Blatt (1969), in which an attempt was made to advance subjects' moral development through class discussion, is that these relatively direct interventions are considered to bring about changes by creating disequilibrium and leading to structural change. In contrast, experiments demonstrating that exposure to the example of models can affect children's subsequent moral reasoning (Bandura & MacDonald, 1963; Cowan, Pederson, Babigan, Izzo, & Trose, 1969) are regarded as of dubious significance, not having the capacity to create structural change. Presumably the latter process does not make children realize the greater adequacy of a more advanced mode of reasoning. It is unconvincing to assume, without further evidence, that these two types of procedures bring about change in moral reasoning by different means.

The issue of continuity versus discontinuity, in development in general and in moral reasoning in particular, has been a source of heated debate. If different stages represent different principles that guide thinking about morality, can change from one principle to the next be continuous? Seemingly, a person would be guided by one principle or by another, but it is difficult to imagine in-between principles. Maybe it is partly such reasoning that lead to the assumption of reorganization leading to change and, hence, "discontinuity." But now, with extensive evidence of stage mixture (Turiel, 1969), the argument about continuity versus discontinuity may be largely semantic. A person's reasoning about moral issues consists of many and varied elements. A particular element of thought probably either represents one principle or another or some form of unclarity or groping in a person's thinking as to how to see or interpret something—by what principle. Another element or aspect of thought may, at the same point in time, represent another mode of thinking, another principle by which morality is viewed. The change in a single aspect of thought is probably the result of a new insight or awareness, not of the addition of something that results in a little bit of change. However, in-between states consisting of unclarity, groping, or unstable change to a new principle may be common. A child who in the morning can only consider how a friend feels may in the afternoon be able to consider the perspective of a larger group; the next morning, it may be only the friend again. The elements in the conglomeration of thought that is evoked by tests of moral reasoning can be regarded as representing discrete stages, their combination as representing stage mixture. However, they certainly do not represent a sudden, dramatic reorganization but, instead, a different pace at which different elements change. Change may appear more discrete at the molecular, more continuous at the molar level.

Although in many respects lacking in supporting evidence, cognitive developmental theory contains concepts and emphases that are useful to consider and to include in a broader theoretical framework. First, the theory focuses on cognition. It attempts to elaborate on the manner in which children and adults think, to a substantially greater degree than the other two approaches have done so far. For example, the measurement of internalization focused to a large degree on the verbally stated affective consequences of internalized values and standards. A child's network of cognition about certain issues—with which Kohlberg's work concerns itself—is likely to have affective consequences, and the relationships between the cognitive and affective aspects, and between each of them and behavior, are important.

Second, the theory focuses on the child's interaction with his environment as a source of development. The usual focus on socialization resulted in insufficient emphasis on the role of peer interaction, and interpersonal experiences of all kinds, in the development and growth of the child. Although cognitive developmental theory emphasized the importance of experience with peers and of role-taking opportunities, very little research evidence has bearing on this point. Kohlberg (1969) interprets findings that urban children and those in higher socioeconomic groups develop faster, reaching higher stages of reasoning at earlier ages than rural children and those in lower socioeconomic groups, as the result of differences in role-taking opportunities. Urban children presumably have more complex and varied environments, and opportunities to assume a larger variety of roles. Lower classes do not feel as great a sense of participation in the economy and the government as do higher socioeconomic groups. Consequently lower-class children have less reason to look at the social order from a variety of perspectives, and they develop slower (and presumably reach a lower terminal point) in moral reasoning. However, socioeconomic groups differ in parental child-rearing practices (Bronfenbrenner, 1961) as well as parental values (Kohn, 1959, 1963). Differences in moral reasoning might be the result of direct, tuitional influences. There may also be important urban–rural differences in both moral values and child-rearing practices.

One task is to clarify what is direct tuition and what is experiential learning. Hamm (1976), in criticizing Kohlberg's oft-proclaimed view that teaching moral virtue does not work—partly because teaching different "contents" in contrast to structure does not contribute to development, partly because children can learn morality only from experience rather than from tuition—suggests that part of the problem is Kohlberg's "highly specialized use of 'teach' [p. 4]." Apparently children cannot be taught because in order to develop understanding the child himself has to grasp the principle or rule that is to be understood. But of course a teacher can lead the child to understanding in many ways, including the Socratic method of asking highly structured questions.

Another task is the identification of processes through which learning or development comes about. For example, Holstein (1968) found that the moral judgment of 13-year-olds was related to the extent that parents encouraged them to participate in the discussion and resolution of differences in moral opinions and hypothetical situations between mother, father, and child. Parents who encouraged children to participate and were rated as taking their children's opinions seriously tended to have more children with moral reasoning at the conventional level, Stages 3 and 4 (70%). Those who did not encourage children in this manner tended to have fewer children with mature, conventional moral judgment (40%). Kohlberg (1969) interprets these findings as evidence that providing children with role-taking opportunities leads to more advanced moral reasoning. Obviously, however, the parents who encouraged participation probably reinforced the child's tendency to think about moral issues. In the course of discussions they probably explained their own positions about moral issues, thereby modeling their own values and moral thinking. Moreover, parents who discuss such matters with their children might be more likely to interact with them and socialize them in ways that contribute to advanced moral thinking. Thus learning might have come about in a variety of ways other than equilibration resulting from greater role-taking opportunity.

It seems important to explore the extent to which those experiences in interaction with other people (particularly peers) that do not involve tuition but provide role-taking opportunities contribute to personality development, moral development, and the manner in which children behave toward others. It is also extremely important to find out how the effects of direct socialization and of interactive experiences combine, how they interact. Will selfishness by others toward oneself be interpreted differently as a function of values and beliefs learned from parents? Research on prejudice among children demonstrates that once children learn prejudicial attitudes toward blacks, interaction by itself does not eliminate these prejudices (Proshansky, 1966). It is likely that what children are taught by their parents and what they learn from interacting with them orient the children toward interpersonal experience with others and affect what they learn from it. Clearly, subjective experience is not a direct function of objective reality. Although cognitive developmentalists acknowledge that a child's level of cognitive and moral development affects the way he perceives and interprets reality, that child's emotional orientation toward other people, beliefs about other people's values and intentions, and many other factors are also likely to modify the meaning of his experience.

The theory is important also because it points to equilibration as an important principle of learning or development. There are many lines of thinking that converge to suggest the reasonableness of this. Adaptation-level theory (Helson, 1964) and a variety of motivational theories suggest our tendency to attend to, and move toward, stimulation that is somewhat different from what we are accustomed to. Theory and research about exploration, curiosity, competence, and the concept under which these have recently come to be summarized, *intrinsic motivation* (Deci, 1975, 1979), all emphasize the facts that, in our informational interaction with the world around us, we respond to discrepancies between what we know and what we perceive and that we attempt to deal with such discrepancies by developing new integrations.

However, how the principles of equilibration apply to learning in the social–moral domain remains to be demonstrated. Relevant in this regard is Cowan, Langer, Heavenrich, and Nathanson's (1969) replication–extension of the Bandura and MacDonald (1963) study. They were able to change, by modeling procedures, children's judgments of an act as more or less naughty to be either more according to the act's consequences or more according to the intentions of the actor, but the effect of modeling was somewhat greater when it was in the direction of more advanced reasoning. (The children were to judge a child in one story who attempted to steal a cookie and in the process broke a cup, and a child in another story who while opening a door knocked over a tray and broke 15 cups.) Is this difference due to an innate preference for more advanced (and more novel) reasoning? Or is it due to other factors, such as parental socialization being in the direction of more advanced reasoning, so that the modeling of judgment in terms of intentions is consistent with what children hear from their parents, whereas modeling of judgment in terms of consequences is inconsistent with it.

The theory implies that the different value orientations that are characteristic of the different stages of reasoning are not the end points of different types of development; rather, they are different points along a particular dimension that has only one "natural" end point. All others represent developmental stages in children and arrested development in adults. It is questionable whether this is so. For example, Kurtines and Grief (1974) suggest, on the basis of data presented by Hogan (1970), that Stages 5 and 6 might represent "alternative, but equally valid, forms of moral thought." Hogan developed a scale to discriminate utilitarian and instrumental attitudes toward the law from a disposition to invoke "intuitive" reasoning which he viewed to be the types of morality represented by Stage 5 and Stage 6 reasoning, respectively. The scale strongly discriminated between people who chose professions that uphold the law, such as policemen, and others who believed in civil disobedience for promoting social change. Moreover, people scoring at the two extremes on the scale tended to have different personality characteristics. The scale might tap different value orientations. The question of different value orientations, discussed briefly in Chapter 1, is a meaningful one and will be explored in later chapters.

A final point of interest is the relationship between moral judgment as measured by Kohlberg's test and behavior. Although the development of moral thought is of interest in its own right, and the elements of the theory might be useful in understanding the development of varied characteristics, the significance of this approach is substantially affected by the extent to which moral reasoning correlates with behavior. Kohlberg has usually implied that no such relationship is necessary, since at all stages reasoning can lead to different conclusions about the right conduct. This may be so in situations of moral conflict. When, however, one course of action has moral implications (e.g., helping a person in need), and a second course of action does not (continuing to read a good novel), more advanced moral reasoning would presumably promote help for others in need and inhibit acts that would harm others or the social group. Evidence reviewed in Volume 1 (Chapters 3 and 5) does demonstrate a positive relationship between moral reasoning and prosocial behavior, under certain conditions. In addition, several studies have showed some relationship between honesty and moral reasoning (Burton, 1976).

An issue of substantial significance enters here. Cognitive developmental theorists imply that the reasoning that a person demonstrates in dealing with moral dilemmas that researchers present to them is also characteristic of a person's reasoning in everyday life, in facing varied life situations, when the reasoning has implications for behavioral choices. However, reasoning about moral dilemmas may represent either a person's competence, his or her highest capacity (in terms of the stages), or the person's preferred mode of presenting his thinking to other people. Even if such reasoning represents a personally preferred mode of thinking, life circumstances can exert pressures that will lead a person to employ different and perhaps more self-serving principles (lower stage reasoning) in evaluating what is right and wrong. If this is so, then we have to concern ourselves not only with the kind of circumstances that lead people to behave consistently with the way they reason about moral issues, but also with how circumstances affect the manner in which people *think* about moral issues. There is recent evidence that the content of moral dilemmas, the nature of issues they deal with (Levine, 1976; Urbach & Rogolsky, 1976), the identity of the protagonists (Levine, 1976), and whether people think about hypothetical situations or an actual situation they experienced (Haan, 1975) all affect their stage of reasoning (see Volume 1, pp. 126–127).

Rarely have investigators concerned themselves with children's reasoning about self-sacrifice for the sake of others' welfare and about the conflict between their own interests and the interests of others. Eisenberg-Berg (in Mussen & Eisenberg-Berg, 1977) found that young children's reasoning about prosocial moral dilemmas is more advanced than their reasoning about Kohlberg type dilemmas. Presumably children have relatively frequent experience with the necessity or desirability of making sacrifices for others' sake, and are frequently exposed to adult influences in the domain of prosocial behavior.

Several investigators extended the domain of cognitive developmental theory and/or dealt with important issues (Damon, 1977; Selman, 1976; Turiel, 1975). Turiel (1975), for example, explored children's conception of social rules, distinguishing between conventional and moral rules. Damon (1977) used interviews to examine children thinking in four domains: positive justice—concepts of fairness and equitable distribution of valued resources; social rules that have moral force; authority and reasons for complying with its demands; and friendship. Damon found a developmental progression in children's thinking, a change to higher "level" reasoning with increasing age. He also found some correspondence between children's reasoning about hypothetical situations and when confronted with the same kinds of issues in structured situations in the laboratory that were similar to real life situations. In the authority-obedience domain the correspondence was good. In the positive justice domain, the children went through similar developmental progression in reasoning when they dealt with hypothetical situations and faced the structured situation, but their reasoning in the latter case (their "developmental level") was lower.

Damon also attempted to explore the relationship between reasoning and behavior. In some domains he found no behavioral measure that differentiated among children. In the domain of positive justice he found a weak relationship between children's reasoning about fair distribution of rewards and their actual distribution of rewards in a group situation. Damon suggests that when self-sacrifice is demanded, lower levels of reasoning may be used to rationalize action.

Can we ever make more accurate predictions about behavior? I believe so. First, we can examine situational influences on moral reasoning. If we explore reasoning and behavior in response to identical or similar circumstances, and the relationship between them, we may find the magnitude of the relationship greater. Second, moral reasoning, or children's conception of various issues, may not by itself provide an index of motivational orientation. Children's cognitions about various domains of morality may have to be more broadly sampled and/or their affective reactions also evaluated, in order to gain an index of their motivations for enhancing others' welfare, or for acting according to some principle (see Chapter 8). Third, and most importantly, even if moral reasoning was an acceptable index of motivation, as with other individual characteristics, the level of moral reasoning can be expected to exert influence on behavior in conjunction with other personality characteristics, and as a function of situational activation.

With regard to the influence of moral values, a specific consideration might be relevant. Kohlberg (1969) has long contended that specific values that people hold (honesty, helpfulness—the "bag of virtues"), which represent the content of what people think with regard to morality, are both unrelated to moral behavior and deficient in many ways as representatives of moral thought. At the same time, the principles that people employ in thinking about moral issues, the structure of their thought, can frequently lead to completely opposite decisions about right conduct. For example, social-contract (Stage 5) reasoning can be employed to justify either the belief that Heinz, who stole the drug, should be punished or that he should not be punished.[5] People might apply principles of reasoning, as represented by stages, in relation to specific values they hold, and it might be their personal values that determine what conduct they regard as morally correct. Thus, the accuracy of the prediction of moral behavior might increase if both level of moral reasoning and individual values are considered.

---

[5] People may frequently employ "moral" reasoning to justify behavior they prefer for self-serving, nonmoral reasons. Sometimes they may do this deliberately, to justify their conduct in front of others; at others times they may justify self-serving action to themselves, without even being aware of doing so. The use of justifications—thinking or reasoning that justifies negative behavior or inaction in response to others' need— has been extensively discussed in Volume 1 (Chapter 4). Often it would be difficult to separate justifications from moral reasoning, since there are no objective criteria for what is right or wrong conduct. Both societal rules and moral philosophy are imperfect guides as to what is right and wrong (Volume 1, Chapter 1).

Development with Age: Prosocial Behavior, Social Cognition, and Related Characteristics

The meaning of a *tendency to behave prosocially* has been repeatedly considered. To some degree it is a consistency in behaving prosocially under different circumstances, in different ways, in response to different needs. However, although such consistency has been found (Emmerich, 1977; Firestone, Kaplan, & Russell, 1973; Krebs & Staub, 1971; Rushton, 1976; Rushton & Wiener, 1975; Rutherford & Mussen, 1968), the model I proposed (Volume 1; Staub, 1979) suggests that consistency is likely to be limited because varied situations activate different combinations of goals and require behaviors that call for different kinds of competence. Therefore, the emphasis in the model has been on the predictability of behavior. When behavior in many situations is considered, consistency is likely to be found, its degree greater across situations in which a particular person's prosocial motivation will be dominant over other motives. The development of a tendency to behave prosocially refers to the development of both consistency in behavior and personality characteristics (e.g., values, role-taking capacity, empathy) that are likely to make prosocial behavior or its outcome valued and thereby lead to prosocial action under certain activating conditions.

The term *development,* as used in this chapter, refers to increased likelihood or presence with age, without implying influences that bring about change or principles by which change comes about. In conventional usage, development and learning are usually distinguished. *Development* is used to refer to change with age due to maturation of varied capacities of the organism and/or to the unfolding of innate potentials in the course of experience, such as cognitive capacities or moral reasoning. As used by cognitive developmental psychologists, the term development also suggests that change is qualitative, that it is not simply the result of something having been added to the knowledge, skill, or capacities that were present, but that it is the result of a reorganization within the organism and/or the appearance of a new skill or capacity. Learning theorists, in contrast, usually regard change as continuous, and what is learned is not considered as representing the unfolding of innate potential but the acquisition of something by the organism. Thus, development implies a certain sequence of change, whereas learning does not imply that change will be in a particular direction. Developmentalists assume, moreover, that change is the result of experience, particularly experience in interaction with peers, whereas learning is regarded by development-alists as the result of direct instruction, specific tuitional influences imposed on the child.

Some of the differences in assumptions may be due to the different content areas that were traditionally the focus of interest. In considering cognitive development, it is unlikely that a person, having acquired a certain capacity or skill, will unlearn it. Change in cognitive functioning seems to move from simple to complex, to be hierarchical in nature. As I discussed in the previous chapter, the nature of change in the realm of moral reasoning is less clearcut. Moreover, a distinction between the unfolding of potential and the acquisition of something new seems more justified in certain realms, primarily in relation to basic physical capacities and aspects of intellectual capacity. The potential of the organism, in general, fosters or limits what will be learned but does not determine the direction of change. Furthermore, a distinction between the "experiences" that an organism has and direct environmental influences is often not easy. Does verbal praise by other children represent a direct environmental influence, a reinforcer, or does it provide the recipient with an opportunity for role taking, or both? Depending on the characteristics of the inter-acting children and their environment, it can represent either or both.

With regard to most characteristics that this book deals with—such as values, beliefs, affective responsiveness, and positive behavior—change may come about in varied ways, represented by varied principles: rein-forcement, punishment, identification, modeling, and the resolution of disequilibrium, all discussed in the previous chapter. Self-perception—the perception of one's own behavior, its consequences, and attributions that one makes about the self and aspects of the environment that are affected by one's behavior—is a further principle by which change can come about (see the next chapter; also Bem, 1972; Volume 1, Chapter 5). A useful classification of experience may be in terms of its degree of force or impact on the child. In general, highly forceful behavior directed at children may be less likely to lead to change through the resolution of disequilibrium and through self-perception than less forceful behavior.

In the rest of this chapter, research on age-related changes in prosocial behavior and in individual characteristics that may contribute to prosocial behavior is examined. A limitation of most of this research is that it does not provide information about the reasons for changes in behavior, about the experiences or learning opportunities that foster or impede change. Beyond the examination of changes in behavior, the discussion will focus on changes in forms of social cognition, particularly the capacity to view events from others' perspectives. Unfortunately, information about other age-related changes, such as in personal values, empathy, and the like, is minimal or nonexistent. Role taking and social cognition are of substantial significance for prosocial behavior; however, they will seem of even greater significance in our discussion because of the lack of developmental information about the other characteristics. Beyond changes with age, the knowledge of the interrelationship among developing characteristics is important. For example, are role-taking skills affected by or dependent on the development of basic cognitive capacities? Do they, in turn, contribute to the development of other characteristics relevant to prosocial behavior, such as moral reasoning? [1]

Changes in Prosocial Behavior with Age

Some time ago researchers reported that 4-month-old infants cry in response to another infant's distress (Arlitt, 1930; Humphrey, 1923). Simner (1971) found that 2-day-old infants cried intensely when they heard another infant's cry. This did not seem to be the result of noise alone. The infants cried less intensely when they heard equally loud sounds of other kinds, including computer-simulated infant cries. Sagi and Hoffman (1976) replicated Simner's findings with infants whose average age was 34 hours (in contrast to Simner's 71), and with several stimuli instead of one. Exposure to another infant's cry again resulted in more crying than exposure to either a synthetic cry of the same inten-

---

[1] Information about the interrelationships between role taking, empathy, and moral reasoning on the one hand and positive behavior on the other hand helps to elucidate what psychological processes contribute to positive actions. The available information is reviewed in Volume 1, mainly in Chapter 5.

sity or silence. Moreover, female infants tended to respond to sounds of crying somewhat more than males ($p < .06$). However, although nonsignificant differences in the same direction were also found in the four previous studies of Simner (1971), cries by a female newborn were always used as the stimulus. Thus, either the nature of the stimulus or differential sensitivity, maybe of empathic kind, might be responsible.

The infants' reaction to sounds of crying, which may be regarded as a form of primitive empathy, is not prosocial behavior, but it may be a rudimentary basis of empathic responsiveness that leads to prosocial behavior. Such a reaction might be innate, or it might be a form of self-conditioning. Conditioning has been demonstrated in the early weeks of the infant's life (Kessen, Haith, & Salapatek, 1970). Possibly even soon after birth the natural association between the child's experiences of distress and his own crying results in conditioning and makes sounds of others' distress conditioned stimuli that evoke distress reactions. However, we cannot rule out the possibility that sounds of crying and distress are innate releasers of distress in infants (Leventhal, 1974).

Rheingold, Hay, and West (1976) reported that very young children engage in several behaviors that they called sharing: showing or giving objects to others and partner play. Partner play involves giving someone else an object and then proceeding to play with it while the other person has possession of it. They found such behavior among 15-month-old infants, and its frequency increased from 15 to 24 months of age. These behaviors were exhibited toward mothers and fathers, and also, though less frequently, toward unfamiliar persons. All children showed some "sharing," but individual differences in frequency did exist. According to anecdotal reports, such behavior begins between 9 and 10 months. Rheingold et al. (1976) did not speculate about the motives for these acts. These behaviors indicate some role taking and the desire to share one's perspective or interest. They also show some understanding that the perspective of another person is different. Consideration of the meaning of these behaviors enlarges, perhaps, our perspective on prosocial behavior. They appear to express the child's desire to have other people see or possess things that the child is interested in (or to have them know what the child knows or feels), to have them share the child's perspective; if so, these behaviors are expressions of self-interest. On the other hand, the sharing of one's perspective, interests, thoughts, or views of events with other people can also be regarded as a generous act. This duality may characterize many interpersonal social acts: the desire to give and thereby receive, a specific act representing a mixture of selfish and generous motives. Such mutual giving—sharing and accepting—can have positive consequences for both participants.

Several investigators found evidence of some increase in sympathetic and helpful reactions in the first few years of life (Berne, 1930; Murphy, 1937; Stern, 1924). Murphy extensively observed interactions among nursery-school children and also provided them with specific opportunities to be helpful. Although among the youngest children helpfulness was rare, it increased with age; sharing of materials, attempts to console a child in distress, warning others of danger, helping another child to become a part of a new group, even attempts to interpret another child's wishes to a stranger were found. Children who were more sociable, who interacted more with others, tended to be both more helpful and more aggressive. Children who were more competent motorically provided more active forms of assistance, and children who were more competent verbally offered more verbal forms of help. Other studies also found helping behavior of varied kinds in groups of nursery-school children (Baumrind, 1971, 1975; Friedrich & Stein, 1973; Hoffman, 1963). Hoffman found a relatively high incidence of direct, unsolicited aid to children in distress and expressions of concern for other children's needs.

Yarrow and Waxler (1976), in two 40-minute sessions, exposed children to opportunities for sharing (in response to requests from adults), for comforting adults, and for helping an adult pick up some spilled objects. The children ranged in age from 3 years to 7½ years; there was a successive 6-month age difference between groups of children. Except for a decrease with age in one form of comforting (responding solicitously to an adult who pinched her finger in a drawer), no relationships were found between age and prosocial actions. The adult's request and the nature of the needs seem to add a strong element of social desirability to most of these behaviors.

In the same study, the interactions among the younger children, who were in nursery school, were observed and coded. Murphy (1937), who found a positive relationship between helpfulness and aggression, assumed that in young children both kinds of behaviors were expressions of general sociability. In contrast, Yarrow and Waxler (1976) found no linear relationship between prosocial and aggressive behaviors. They reasoned, however, that frequent aggression by children may indicate hostility and difficulty in relating to other children, and that less frequent aggression may be situationally produced. If this were so, the two would have different meanings. They explored the relationship between aggression and prosocial behavior separately in children above and below the mean in aggressive behavior. Again, there was no relationship between aggression and helping. However, sharing and comforting, which were themselves related, were significantly positively related to aggression among boys who were less aggressive. In contrast, aggression was fairly highly, although not significantly, negatively related to sharing and comforting among the more aggressive boys. As separate analyses also showed, the relationship between aggression and these forms of prosocial behavior was curvilinear. Among girls, who were generally less aggressive, no relationships were found. These findings suggest that whether an association exists between aggression and prosocial behavior, and the nature of that association, may depend on the characteristics of the children who are studied, on how aggressive (or prosocial) they are. Differences in the characteristics of the children may be one reason for the discrepancy between these findings and those of Murphy. Another source of difference may be that socializers' beliefs about what behaviors are acceptable or permissible or desirable alter the frequency of aggressive and prosocial behavior of children and the relationship between their behaviors. That changes occurred in socializers' views and practices over the 40-year time span between these studies is probable.

Clearly, preschool children are aware of and sometimes respond to one another's needs. Unfortunately, helpfulness in freely interacting groups of older children, particularly the relationship between age and prosocial behavior, has rarely been studied. Among young children relatively little sacrifice of material possessions has been noted. In a variety of studies, changes with age in willingness to make such sacrifices, under highly structured circumstances, have been investigated.

Research findings are consistent in showing that as children get older they donate more of the material goods in their possession for charity; for other children who are absent but described to them as needy, poor, or in some ways deprived; or simply for classmates (Elliott & Vasta, 1970; Handlon & Gross, 1959; Midlarsky & Bryan, 1967; Rushton, 1975; Rushton & Wiener, 1975; Ugurel-Semin, 1952). The children in these studies ranged from kindergartners to sixth-graders. Green and Schneider (1974) used subjects varying in age from 5 to 14. They found an increase with age in the number of candy bars their subjects donated to other students in the school and the number of children who picked up pencils knocked over by an experimenter, although the latter behavior reached asymptote and did not differentiate among the oldest children. Green and Schneider found no differences in the amount of time children volunteered to make books for poor children. The subjects tended to profess good intentions at all ages. There is also evidence that fourth-graders share more with their peers than do third-graders in an interactive situation, where two children are together and only one child possesses candy or a drawing pencil (Staub, 1973; Staub & Noerenberg, 1978).

In contrast, one experiment that examined children's reactions to distress sounds from another child found that change with age was curvilinear (Staub, 1970b). Helping behavior increased from kindergarten through first to second grade, whether children heard the distress sounds alone or in pairs. Helping by children who were alone when they heard the sounds remained at the same level in fourth grade, but then declined substantially in sixth grade. When children heard the distress sounds in pairs, helping started to decline in fourth grade, and it declined to the same low level as with lone children in sixth grade. These findings and the apparent reasons for them as suggested by other research (Staub, 1971b)—that children were concerned with potential disapproval if they did not follow rules of proper social behavior, such as not going into a strange room—point to the limitation of considering behavior changes without establishing the reasons for them.

In an unfamiliar experimental situation, concern about behaving appropriately, in a socially desirable fashion, can be high even if a child who has an opportunity to donate some rewards for other children is alone in a room while donating. Donating to needy others is a socially highly desirable act, and as children grow older they certainly become increasingly knowledgeable about its social value. The uniformity of research findings showing that donations increase with age may be due to this growing awareness. Whether it was this awareness, greater concern about others' welfare, or belief in equity that impelled older children to donate more remains unexplored. Older children may even have placed less value on the material goods to be sacrificed; this also could have led them to greater generosity.

Changes in Cooperation and Competition with Age

Cooperation with other children also increases with age. Here I am referring to cooperation between children in naturalistic settings such as a nursery school; the term *cooperation* refers here to interactive activities in the course of which the children's behaviors are supplementary. Building a tower out of blocks with each child adding blocks to the tower is an example of cooperation. Parten (1932) found that through the preschool period children move from solitary play to "looking on," to parallel play, to associative group play, and finally to cooperative play. Similarly, Gottschaldt and Frauhauf-Ziegler (1958) report in a German study that, although 2- to 3-year-olds show no cooperation, 3- to 4-year-olds partially cooperate and 4- to 6-year-olds are able to cooperate completely in working toward a goal. Similar progression in cooperation with age was found by Zak (1968) and by Hirota (1951) in Japan. Meister (1965) observed the development of group cooperation and reported that groups of 7- to 11-year-olds cooperate within an authoritarian structure, but groups of children 12 years old and older have an egalitarian, leaderless quality. He related this to Piaget's notion of decentering and to change from heteronomous to autonomous morality.

Competition, the desire to do something better than others, also increases with age. Both Greenberg (1932), in observing block building by Viennese children, and Leuba (1933), examining children working on a pegboard, found that although no competitive behavior was seen among younger children, competition was dominant among children 5 and 6 years old and older. McClintock and Nuttin (1969) also reported an increase in competition from second through fourth to sixth grade among Belgian and American boys who played a game that provided an opportunity for the children to maximize the difference between their own outcomes and those of their partners.

No systematic evidence is available about age changes in different classes of cooperative and competitive behavior, or in the conditions that elicit cooperation or competition among young children. (For a review of influences on cooperative and competitive behavior, see Volume 1, Chapter 9). Cook and Stingle (1974) attempt to explain the development of cooperation with concepts provided by Mead and Piaget. Mead (1934) suggested that cooperation can only be established when one can distinguish between oneself and others, when one can take the role of the other. Piaget (1932) stressed that egocentrism makes cooperation impossible: "In order to cooperate one must be conscious of one's self and be able to situate it with respect to common thought [p. 96]." Although both statements may be correct, it is probably possible to train very young children in cooperative behavior through reinforcement and modeling (Azrin & Lindsley, 1956). The complexity of this behavior may be enlarged and its application extended as the children become older and their perspective-taking ability increases.

It might also be the case that one of the causes of *competition* in young children is the emerging ability of the self to distinguish and separate itself from others. In the course of this process of separation, the desire to establish and view the self as a distinct entity might contribute to competition. Competition may be a means by which this separateness is asserted and further developed.

In the kind of research that has been considered so far, cooperation centered on a common goal, such as building a tower, or playing a game in which each child had to do something to achieve a mutual goal. Competition referred primarily to attempts to do better than others in activities that children engaged in individually. In other research, cooperation and competition were pitted against each other in each specific act a child performed. These studies employed laboratory games in which a child had to make a series of moves to further another's goal if he was to cooperate. He could also attempt on each move to hinder the other and/or achieve his own goal. Cooperation in some of these games (Madsen, 1971) means that first one child, then another, makes moves that help the other person win. Competition deprives each of reaching his goal and winning rewards and is therefore regarded as irrational.

Kagan and Madsen (1971), in using one such game, the Circle Matrix Board, found that 4- to 5-year-old American children are more cooperative than 7- to 9-year-olds. Madsen (1971) found similar age difference in another game, a "marble pulling task," among American children, but found no increase with age in irrational competition among Mexican children. On another task Kagan and Madsen (1972) found that older children are more competitive, or "rivalrous," in the sense that they attempt to maximize the difference in their own favor by lowering the performance or the gain of a peer. Rivalry increased as age increased from 5–6 years to 8–10 years among both Mexican and American children, but it increased more in the latter group.

Not only the assertion of separateness and individuation is likely to be involved in the increase of competitiveness with age. At least in America, very young children begin to play games in which the object is to win; many children learn that winning is what games are all about. It is not surprising, therefore, that they become increasingly motivated to defeat their opponents in games. Clearly, we have to exercise caution in generalizing from these findings to other behavioral domains. We do not know the range of activities in which competition and rivalry come to dominate over cooperation. However, the emphasis on competition and winning in our culture certainly does extend into spheres beyond playing games.

Severy and Davis (1971) found in their observations of interactions among nursery school children varying in age from 3 to 5 years that normal children helped each other more than did retarded children. However, on varied indices helping increased with age among retarded children and decreased among normals. According to the authors, the social context encouraged among normals competitiveness and other behaviors that would satisfy self-interest, whereas teachers believed that cooperation was useful and appropriate among retardates and encouraged it.

The findings in a cross-cultural study conducted by Graves and Graves (1978) suggest that conditions that foster achievement orientation in a child may affect "rivalry." These authors gave children the opportunity to choose among varied ways of dividing money between themselves and another child. They compared 5–8-year-old children in New Zealand and on Cook Island—which has a relatively traditional culture. The children in New Zealand made substantially more rivalrous choices and fewer generous choices than did those in Cook Island. They usually maximized their own gain in both cultures, but, when they sacrificed their own interests, children in New Zealand did so to make other children receive less (rivalrous choice), whereas those in Cook Island did so to make other children receive more. When no sacrifice was involved, the former children were less likely to benefit another than were the latter.

Graves and Graves (1978) also examined the choices made by older Cook Island children. With increasing age, rivalry increased, generosity decreased, and a sex difference appeared, boys becoming more rivalrous than girls. These authors suggested that the children's experience in Western-type schools was the cause of these changes with age. They suggested that the teachers directly encouraged competitiveness, although they had no data on this point. Several findings indicated that the increase in rivalry occurs primarily among children involved in the school experience. Academic performance and indices of conformity to school (the state of the child's uniform, how well kept the child's hair was, etc.) were strongly positively related to rivalry. Possibly, among children who got involved in the school experience there was an increase in achievement motivation—in the desire to do well, of which a frequent (but not inevitable) aspect is to want to do better than others. However, due to the correlational nature of the data, assumptions about causal influences must be tentative.

Competition tends to increase with age, perhaps partly because children increasingly make self–other comparisons. Environments that deemphasize the pursuit of individualistic goals may minimize increase in competition and may contribute to cooperation—which also tends to increase with age, when cooperation in social interaction rather than in games is considered. Environments that emphasize individualistic goals and achievement orientation may increase competition and rivalry.

Changes in Consistency with Age

One study (Henshel, 1971) examined the relationship between children's values and corresponding behavior at different age levels. Henshel found, with female participants, increased consistency with increasing age between values about honesty and the degree to which children acted honestly. She used four items on a questionnaire to measure three components of a value placed on honesty: the affective ("what one finds desirable"), the cognitive (knowledge of right and wrong), and the intentional ("what one would do"). Cheating was measured by the number of errors that children did not report in correcting their own errors on a spelling test. There was no significant change with age, either in the value placed on honesty or in honest behavior. However, there was a progressive increase from fourth to seventh grade in the relationship between children's values and their "cheating" behavior (fourth, $r = -.02$; fifth, $r = -.35$, $p < .05$; sixth, $r = -.63$, $p < .001$; seventh, $r = -.78$, $p < .001$). An unfortunate procedural detail makes interpretation of these findings uncertain: Following the spelling test, the papers were corrected, kept by the experimenter for a week, and then returned to the children, who were asked to correct them. This procedure introduces the possibility that older children who expressed stronger values might have been more concerned that their scores were recorded during the intervening period, and they might be caught cheating.

However, in the early research of Hartshorne and May there was also a change in consistency with age; older children were more consistent in their moral conduct than younger ones, specifically in their performance on various measures of honesty. Moreover, those older children who were consistent tended to be honest, whereas those who were inconsistent tended to be dishonest (Hartshorne, May, & Shuttleworth, 1930). This finding might indicate that some of the children developed personal values that guided them to honest conduct. Others may have developed such values to a lesser degree and behaved honestly only when honesty served the satisfaction of some other personal value or goal, or when they were concerned about being caught and punished. Still others may have developed personal values about honesty that were applicable only to specific conditions. Another example of increasing consistency with age may be seen in Feshbach and Feshbach's (1969) finding of a positive relationship between a measure of empathy and aggression among younger boys (4–5 years old) and a negative relationship among older boys (6–7 years old). At a younger age, both aggression and helpfulness may be expressions of general sociability, as Murphy (1937) suggested. However, with increasing age empathy begins to be an inhibitor of aggression. I suggested in Volume 1 that varied motivators of positive behavior, including prosocial values and empathy, can function as inhibitors of harm-producing actions (see also Staub, 1971c).

Changes in Different Types of Role Taking with Age

The Beginning of Role Taking

The relationship between role taking and prosocial behavior, and the reasons for expecting role taking to contribute to prosocial behavior, were examined in Volume 1 (Chapter 5). Sometimes role taking was positively related to prosocial behavior, such as generous or cooperative acts; sometimes it was unrelated. Perhaps the influence of role taking is sometimes direct, so that individual differences in role taking directly affect prosocial behavior. However, I suggested that the capacity to view events from another's perspective does not mean that, on particular occasions, a person will do so. Moreover, when a person does consider and perceive how another views an event or is affected by an event, that does not guarantee that he will vicariously experience the other's emotions. Perceiving another's distress can lead to a feeling of satisfaction —if one is angry with someone or dislikes the other, or if one is the kind of person who gets satisfaction from others' distress. Role taking can indirectly contribute to positive behavior by contributing to the development of other characteristics, such as moral values and empathy, which in turn affect prosocial behavior. Furthermore, role taking in combination with other characteristics, such as prosocial values that may motivate both role taking and the desire to benefit another, can be expected to contribute to prosocial conduct.

It has been widely assumed that the young child is egocentric; this concept of Piaget's refers to the child's lack of differentiation between his own point of view and that of others, the child's inability to take another's point of view. The primary cause of egocentrism is the child's tendency to center his attention on one detail of an object or event (Piaget & Inhelder, 1956), a tendency called *centration*. A very important development in the child's cognitive capacities is the ability to *decenter,* to attend to more than one aspect of an object, event, or situation. Decentration, in turn, contributes to further cognitive development. By enabling the child to see more than one aspect of an object or event, it creates disequilibrium, which leads to cognitive growth. Role taking is the opposite of egocentrism. It is the capacity to take the position of another person, to see and understand events from his or her perspective or, in its most developed form, the "understanding of the nature of the relation between one's self and other's perspectives [Selman, 1973, p. 5]."

A variety of different kinds of role taking have been described and studied. They include perceptual role-taking, the ability to consider what is seen by a person who is looking at an object from a different physical perspective; communicative role-taking, the ability to describe an object to another person in a manner that enables the other to identify it and/or differentiate it from other objects; affective role-taking, a child's ability to identify another person's feelings; and cognitive role-taking, the ability to communicate to another or consider events from another's perspective, on the basis of information available to the other person, rather than acting as if information that is available to oneself was also available to the other. [The term *cognitive egocentrism* has also been employed (Rubin, 1973) to describe the degree to which children use speech to talk to themselves rather than to communicate; it refers to the use of private rather than public speech.]

Several issues are important with regard to the measurement and definition of these role-taking capacities. Measurement techniques vary. One important dimension of variation is the degree to which a response that indicates role taking demands advanced verbal capacity by children. For example, subjects in Borke's study (1971) could represent the feelings of a character in a comic strip by picking out a figure representing the proper feelings and pasting it into the last frame of the comic strip in which the main character was missing. Nearly 60% of subjects 3 to 3½ years old and 92% of subjects 3½ to 4 years old could do this correctly. In other studies subjects had to identify the feelings of an actor in a picture or comic strip verbally (Burns & Cavey, 1957; Gates, 1923; Walton, 1936), and correct responses were low for 3- to 4-year-old children. Burns and Cavey found an increase in accuracy from second to sixth grade on such a task. In Borke's study, in fact, when children had to name the character's feelings, only 44% of the 3- to 3½-year-olds and 69% of the 3½- to 4-year-olds could do so correctly.

Another dimension along which procedures vary is the degree of complexity of the materials used for testing (i.e., the difficulty of the task). The same type of role-taking ability has been tested with tasks that appear to demand greatly varying degrees of cognitive ability. Very young children are capable of role taking when the materials used in testing them are sufficiently simple. For example, Masangkay, McCluskey, McIntyre, Sim-Knight, Vaughn, and Flavell (1974) found that half their 2-year-old subjects and nearly all the 3-year-olds were able to perform a perceptual perspective-taking test correctly. Each child was shown a piece of cardboard with a different picture on each side. The child had to determine which picture would be seen by the experimenter, who sat opposite him and saw the opposite side of the cardboard. On this task the child and the experimenter had views of different whole objects. On another task, the child had to differentiate between his view of a part of an object and the view of the experimenter, who saw the same object from the opposite side. Although this task proved more difficult, and 3- to 4-year-olds performed at chance level, the 4- to 4½-year-olds performed nearly perfectly. This study and others (Huttenlocher & Presson, 1973; Shantz & Watson, 1971; Shatz & Gelman, 1973) suggest that children are capable of simple forms of role taking at a much earlier age than was originally assumed (Piaget & Inhelder, 1970) or has been found in other studies (Ambron & Irwin, 1975).

Such evidence of early role-taking makes more credible certain anecdotes in the literature about extremely early role-taking behavior by children and prosocial acts that grew out of this behavior (Borke, 1971; Hoffman, 1975b). Hoffman, for example, describes an incident between Michael, aged 15 months, and his friend Paul, who were fighting over a toy. Paul started to cry. "Michael appeared disturbed and let go, but Paul still cried. Michael paused, then brought his teddy bear to Paul but to no avail. Michael paused again, and then finally succeeded in stopping Paul's crying by fetching Paul's security blanket from an adjoining room. [p. 612]." Although there can be several explanations for this incident, Hoffman's major point is that this very young child could assess the "specific needs of another person which differed from his own [p. 612]." (Specific imitation as an explanation was ruled out by the parents' claim that Michael never saw Paul being comforted by a blanket.)[2]

The evidence continues to grow that young children have greater understanding of other people than has been implied by Piagetian theory, which assumed that children are originally highly egocentric and that the capacity to decenter evolves gradually. A derivative of this assumption was that young children cannot engage in prosocial and cooperative acts that are based on an understanding of others' needs (Piaget & Inhelder, 1969). Cooperation or prosocial behavior among young children would, presumably, be based on conformity to authority or to rules. However, both the experimental research discussed above and additional experimental research, as well as studies of children's behavior in natural free-play situations, show that very young children are capable of varying their communications to peers or to adults as a function of their goals in the interaction and of the characteristics of the other person, including age, cognitive limitations, or need for information (Gelman & Shatz, 1977; Lempers, Flavell, & Flavell, 1977; Mueller & Brenner, 1977; Spilton & Lee, 1977; Wellman & Lempers, 1977).

The existing evidence may mean that the cognitive prerequisites of role taking (and of effective and positive interpersonal behavior) develop earlier than was originally assumed. In contrast, some writers suggest that the state of infants and young children is not egocentrism but sociocentrism. Children are social from the beginning, as a result of man's evolution as a social species. Infants, in this view, are "genetically biased toward social behavior; they are preadapted to an ordinary expectable social environment [Stayton, Hogan, & Ainsworth, 1971, p. 1059]."

It is reasonable to assume that children will have social understanding of certain kinds at an extremely young age. They have to develop social understanding in order to know what to do to get their needs satisfied, to elicit responsiveness in other people. They seem to imitate

---

[2] As I noted earlier, understanding another's perspective need not lead, by itself, to attempts to help. The behavior also depends on the motivation of the role taker. An anecdote I heard from a friend demonstrates this: A 2-year-old, having been frustrated and angered by an age-mate, picked up the other child's teddy bear, a favorite toy and security blanket, and threw it out the window. An understanding of the other's probable emotional reaction was presumably present.

behavior directed at them at an extremely early age, perhaps partly because this appears to lead to a sequence of reciprocal exchanges, often to mutual imitation, with another person. The apparent reinforcing value to infants of their success in bringing about a change in their environment, to act as an agent, seemingly an aspect of what is now called intrinsic motivation, would lead them to try out varied behaviors and to learn from their outcomes. Understanding of the social environment is a prerequisite of successfully exerting influence, and children are likely to develop at least a rudimentary understanding, but probably much more than that at a very early age.

This "understanding" does not come about in an emotional or social vacuum. The reciprocal exchanges I noted—of smiles, of actions, of sounds—the social games, the behaviors by which the child requests the satisfaction of his needs, some of the needs themselves, which are fundamentally social, and the resulting and accompanying emotional ties between infants and others are expressions of the child's genetically based social bias, of the importance of a supportive social environment, and of the interrelationship of emotional and cognitive development. The latter involves the development of a sense of self, of the understanding of one's relationship to others, as well as role taking. Some of the preceding reasoning about the child's learning of effective interaction with his social world and of the exercising of control in relation to it suggests that role taking would develop faster in a social environment where interaction with infants is relative free, not highly restricted by rules (such as feeding on schedule, not picking up infants when they ask for it, etc.). Such relatively restrictive rules were frequently followed some time ago, such as 30–40 years ago, even more so in Europe than in the United States. Piaget's finding may have been affected by this.

The Relationship between Different Kinds of Role Taking

To what degree are the different types of role-taking skills alike? To what degree are they dependent on the same (or different) cognitive capacities and prior learning? How do different kinds of role taking relate to one another? How do role-taking skills change with age?

Simple measures of perceptual role-taking seem, essentially, to be measures of decentering. Other forms of role taking may demand, however, more advanced, different, or additional cognitive skills and/or information or knowledge about the world. This seems true of a frequently used measure (Flavell *et al.,* 1968) of what is sometimes referred to as *cognitive role-taking.* The child is asked to describe what happens in a series of seven pictures depicting a boy running away from a dog, climbing an apple tree to escape, and then eating an apple. Then three pictures of the chase by the dog are removed and the child is asked to tell what story another person would create from the remaining pictures. This task requires the suppression of information available to the subject, the breaking up of the coherent whole of the story he previously told, and reliance on the new stimulus array only. Moreover, the measure is sometimes scored for the frequency and nature of inferences the subject makes about the motives for the boy's actions. Clearly this is a more complex task than perceptual role–taking.

Of particular interest to us is affective role-taking, since that is likely to be involved in prosocial actions to the greatest degree. Affective role-taking, and its measures, can be quite simple, or highly complex. A child may simply be asked to identify a person's affect relying on facial cues. More commonly, a sequence of events is depicted in pictures or words, and the child is asked to indicate how the character feels at the end. The inferences that are required may be minimal, but with complex verbal stories they may be quite sophisticated. Moreover, role taking may be measured not only by the identification of affect, but also by the nature, degree, and elaboration of inferences about the internal states, feelings, and motives of a story character. Another complexity is introduced when particular situations or sequences of events imply particular feelings, but the person depicted in pictures (or in a story) actually reacts in an unusual, idiosyncratic way to those events. To what extent will children be able to disregard the cues provided by the preceding story sequence and attend to the facial expression of feelings? In a situation like this, whether a person is being tested by a psychologist or faces the situation in real life, that person may attend to the sequence of events and describe how another person would feel on the basis of how he himself would feel. This would be a projection of the observer's own reaction, an egocentric response. However, relying on the sequence of events rather than on indices of the emotional response can also represent not projection but the use of accumulated knowledge about the world: People in general tend to react to certain classes of events with certain feelings. They are frightened, rather than happy, when they are being chased by a tiger. When a particular person reacts with happiness to being chased by a tiger (Kurdock & Rodgon, 1975), an observer usually has to be able to suppress knowledge of how he himself and others in general would react, and to read expressive cues accurately in order to perceive the happiness.

Such judgments are demanded of us frequently in life, but they represent a complex demand. Accurate affective role-taking may require knowledge about how people react emotionally to different kinds of events; it may require an understanding of the psychological meaning of events and knowledge about the antecedents of different classes of human emotions. Then this knowledge may have to be disregarded, suppressed, in order to consider the idiosyncratic reaction of a particular person.

There is extensive evidence that the different kinds of role taking—as well as other types of social cognitions involving the child's understanding of his social world (Shantz, 1975)—all increase with age (Looft, 1972; Nahir & Yussen, 1977; Rubin, 1973; West, 1974; see also Shantz, 1975). Moreover, research findings indicate that there is some relationship among the various role taking skills. Generality has been expected on the basis of the conception advanced by Piaget that egocentrism is an inability to differentiate between one's view and that of others that is not tied to any particular "content" area. However, as the preceding discussion already suggests, there are substantial differences in cognitive and informational demands that various forms of role taking place on a person, apart from similarities that exist.

In a study that tested both age-related changes and generality Rubin (1973) found that scores on measures of several types of egocentrism all decreased from kindergarten to second, to fourth, and to sixth grade. Included were perceptual egocentrism, communicative egocentrism, "role-taking egocentrism"—a measure of the child's ability to infer others' thought (e.g., what a character thought about what other characters in the picture were thinking; an example of the most complex form of this was provided as "the boy is thinking that the girl is thinking of the other")—and "cognitive egocentrism," a measure of private speech, the degree to which children talked to themselves while working on a puzzle.

All scores except those for cognitive egocentrism measures were significantly related to one another and to scores on a measure of conservation; all loaded highly on the same factor in a factor analysis. That Rubin's cognitive egocentrism scores were unrelated to other measures is not surprising in the light of other findings, showing that private and social speech are very highly positively related ($r = .68$; Kohlberg, Yaeger, & Hjartholm, 1968). Consistent with Vygotsky's conception, private speech appears to have an important self-guiding function, in that children use it to provide directives to themselves. It seems to stand side by side with social speech, rather than being negatively related to it. Until private speech "goes underground," children are able to shift from one to the other, as required by circumstances.

Rubin's (1973) finding of a positive relationship among varied forms of role taking is consistent with only some research findings, not with all. In several studies in which performance on two or more different role-taking tasks was intercorrelated, no significant relationships were found (Finley, French, & Cowan, 1973; Rothbaum, 1973; Sullivan & Hunt, 1967).

In another study that found positive relationships, one conducted in Holland (Van Lieshout, Leckie, & Sauts-Van Sousbeek, 1973), 143 children, 3–5-year-olds, participated. Nine tasks (including affective and perceptual role-taking tasks) were used. The scores on eight tasks intercorrelated significantly. The correlations were moderate in size, ranging from .20 to .48.

In an extensive review Shantz (1975) suggests "that there is, at best, only a moderate relationship among the various role-taking skills [p. 300]." The reason for the differences in findings is not clear. Some types of role taking may be more highly related than others, and similarities (and differences) in the methods of measurement and the children's ages may also affect relationships. Shantz points out that investigators treated role taking as identical to decentration, although Piaget's theory specified decentration as necessary but not sufficient for role taking to emerge. Role-taking skills probably share a simple form of decentration as a common precondition for them; this may result in quite low but frequently still significant correlations. Apart from decentration, other cognitive capacities and knowledge about psychological processes might, to different degrees, be involved in different role-taking skills.

Shantz also notes that no studies included tests of cognitive abilities that are theoretically unrelated to role taking. She suggests that such an inclusion would allow the determination of the extent to which different forms of role taking are related to one another to a greater degree than to measures of theoretically independent cognitive capacities. It would be important to determine what cognitive capacities are involved to greater and lesser degrees in different types of role taking.

A study by Rushton and Wiener (1975) is relevant to the question of generality versus specificity of role-taking skills and of other aspects of cognitive functioning. These authors pointed to an apparently widespread assumption that different levels of cognitive development will lead to corresponding differences in intellectual and social behavior (Bruner, 1966; Flavell, 1963; Kohlberg, 1969). Rushton and Wiener suggested that the existence of generalized levels of cognitive functioning had not yet been determined. They administered seven cognitive tasks and three measures of altruism to 7- and 11-year-old subjects. The cognitive tasks included two measures of role taking (perceptual and communicative), and measures of cognitive complexity and conservation. On all cognitive tasks, performance substantially improved with age. However, with age and verbal IQ partialled out (their influence statistically eliminated), performance on these measures was uncorrelated; this was true also of the two measures of role taking. In contrast, there were some relationships among the behavioral measures, some generality across prosocial acts.

Affective Role-Taking

The perception, identification, or accurate inference about others' feelings must be one of the most important signals of others' needs for attention and help and a precondition therefore of attempts to help. Consequently, affective role-taking is particularly significant for prosocial behavior. As noted, the capacity to identify and understand others' feelings is present early in some forms, and it develops with age.

Preschool children can differentiate between pleasant and unpleasant emotions expressed in photographs and can select the photograph that shows a particular emotion. However, their verbal limitations are evident; they have difficulty *labeling* emotions on the basis of facial expressions (Izard, 1971). By 4 years of age, children tend to correctly identify situations that typically evoke various emotions, such as happiness, joy, sadness, fear, and anger, when nonverbal procedures are used (Borke, 1971; Mood, Johnson, & Shantz, 1974). However, there are differences in children's ability to do so as a function of the emotion and of cultural background and social class. Both American and Chinese children were able, at 3 years of age, to identify a situation that evoked happy feelings. Accuracy increased from age 4 to age 7 in identifying situations that evoked fear, sadness, and anger; the children had the greatest difficulty with situations that led to anger (Borke, 1973). Younger Chinese children were more accurate than American children in identifying sad situations, and social-class differences were found in both cultures. Again, this emphasizes the important but largely unexplored influence of socialization, at least in affective perspective-taking.

Several writers have suggested that a child's ability to identify another's feelings in a particular situation may represent not role taking but projection; the situation is familiar to the child who simply describes how he would react. Accurate identification when a person's expressed feelings are congruent with the situation can be the result of projection, of learning from experience and tuition that people in general tend to react to certain situations in certain ways, or of affective perspective-taking, the ability to identify how the particular person in question reacts. A number of studies show that similarity between a subject and the person whose emotions are to be judged increases accurate identification of affect. For example, the capacity of both boys and girls to make accurate judgments about another child's affect is greater with same-sex children (Deutsch, 1974; Feshbach & Roe, 1968). Racial similarity also increases the capacity to understand how another child feels (Klein, 1971). Finally, in a study in which children heard adults discussing situations that the children themselves probably did not encounter (e.g., not having enough time to prepare a dinner party before the guests arrive), although they probably observed their parents encountering them, 10½-year-olds were significantly better in identifying emotions of anger, happiness, anxiety, and sadness than 8½-year-olds. Other findings also show greater attention to and ability to identify feelings of adults on the part of older children (Flapan, 1968).

These data do not make it possible for us to differentiate among possible explanations of young children's capacity to identify what situations lead to what emotions. All the processes may be linked together, their relative importance as yet undifferentiated. Clearly, the data can mean that young children's ability to identify the feelings of story characters primarily represents self-descriptions, their indication of how they themselves would react. Or they may mean that children can make better judgments about such emotions when they have had more opportunity to learn from their own experience. However, the findings may also be interpreted as showing genuine affective perspective-taking, and they may indicate that in order to understand how a person is affected by an event, one has to know something about that person, the event, and his or her relationship to the event. With increasing age, children's knowledge of the meaning of events, for varied kinds of people, is likely to expand. Again, in addition to abstract cognitive capacities that underlie role taking, personal experience and socialization are implicated.

A further complexity in affective role-taking is introduced, as already discussed, by idiosyncratic reactions to events by people; to an observer, these reactions must often seem incongruous. Burns and Cavey (1957) used a series of picture frames with the main characters showing incongruous affect in the last frame. For instance, one sequence showed a boy upset at a birthday party; another showed a child smiling in the dentist chair. Preschoolers described the child's feelings on the basis of the situation, and children between 5 and 7 years of age were better at identifying the incongruous affect or noting the conflict. In a study by Deutsch (1974) preschoolers were again better at identifying affect from the situation than from facial expression, and their accuracy was greater in congruous than incongruous situations. The children in Deutsch's study were exposed to short filmed episodes, in which adult actors showed affect that was sometimes congruous and sometimes incongruous with the situation (e.g., one episode showed an adult giving another adult a cup of tea, at which the latter either smiled or frowned in response).

In a study with surprising findings, Kurdock and Rodgon (1975) measured perceptual role-taking, cognitive role-taking (using the Flavell measure described earlier), and affective role-taking of children from kindergarten through sixth grade. To measure affective perspective-taking they showed children black ink drawings depicting a child of the same sex as the subject in situations that evoked emotions of happiness, sadness, fear, or anger. A brief verbal narration was provided, and then the child was asked, "How does he/she feel?" "Half of the drawings . . . showed the characters expressing an emotion that was inappropriate to the situation described [Kurdock & Rodgon, 1975, p. 645]." For example, happiness followed either getting a new toy (appropriate), or dreaming of being chased by a tiger (inappropriate). Three scores were derived for affective perspective-taking: the number of correct responses in the four appropriate-affect stories, the number of correct responses in the four inappropriate-affect stories, and the number of "projections," that is, the child's description of the main character's feeling in the inappropriate affect stories according to preceding cues rather than to expressed feelings.

All except one index of role taking significantly increased with age, gradually increasing from kindergarten to sixth grade in a linear fashion. Only inappropriate affective perspective-taking decreased with age, also in a linear fashion; projections also increased. Males were significantly better than females at perceiving inappropriate affect. Intercorrelations among measures in the total sample and at different grade levels showed no clear-cut pattern of relatedness among different kinds of role taking.

The findings that older children rely more on situational cues than on facial expression when the two are incongruous is somewhat inconsistent with Burns and Cavey's findings, although not greatly, since the age range was substantially different. It also seems contrary to predictions that might be derived from past research findings in this area. One may speculate that increasing knowledge of how people usually react to certain situations can lead children, at certain ages, to exercise their competence in using such information. It is possible, furthermore, that in middle childhood, as children become more able to make inferences about feelings, intentions, and motives (Flapan, 1968), they are engrossed in focusing on other people's internal processes, which they try to predict from their understanding of preceding events or surrounding conditions, rather than by focusing their attention on facial expressions. Perhaps, however, the trend found by Kurdock and Rodgon continues into later childhood. In everyday life we are frequently called upon to understand others' feelings on the basis of something that has happened or is happening to them, as well as from their facial cues or other emotional expressions. Since people frequently hide their feelings from others, particularly the negative ones, we may come to rely more on situational cues than on facial cues. Research findings do show that adults use situational information in judging feelings of others. Furthermore, adults tend to adjust their perceptions of facial cues to fit the situation (Tagiuri, 1969). Clearly, the manner in which people deal with incongruity should be explored further, in light of the intriguing possibility that, as they get older, people tend to minimize incongruity, and therefore incorrectly perceive others' emotional expressions.

In everyday life, incongruity between the usual or normative emotional response to a situation and particular individuals' reactions is fairly common (consider, as an example, that children frequently feel upset at birthday parties—because they feel competitive with others in games, or because they feel they got less of something, or for other reasons). This lends further significance to a possible decline in people's perceiving incongruous reactions as they get older.

What information we rely on and how we deal with informational conflict probably depend not only on cognitive maturity and age, but also on the circumstances that focus attention on one or another kind of information, and on the set or orientation of the person making the judgment. All these influences are likely to operate in experimental studies, and they should be explored.

Thinking about Others' Intentions and Motives

With increasing age children think more about another person's intentions or motives; they consider internal psychological processes to a greater degree (Flapan, 1968; Piaget, 1932). This is important, since willingness to help another person, reciprocating others' kindness or aggression, and evaluation of other people as good or bad (and the behavior that resulted from the evaluation) all seemed, in research described in Volume 1 of this work, to be affected by attributions of motives and intentions.

In a study conducted by Flapan (1968), girls 6, 9, and 12 years of age were shown episodes of a movie and were asked to report on what happened in the movie. With increasing age simple descpritions of what happened declined. They gave way first to attempts at explaining what was happening in social interactions, and then to inferences about thoughts, feelings, and intentions of the actors. Moreover, the younger children's major explanation of the actors' behavior was situational, but older children came to use first the actors' feelings and motives in explaining their actions, and then the manner in which the actors perceived the behavior or personality of other actors—that is, their interpersonal attributions. The major shift toward consideration of internal states occurred between 6 and 9 years of age. For example, 9- to 12-year-olds were increasingly likely to say that an actor was happy or sad because of how someone else felt toward him, perhaps because a parent did not love him. Six-year-olds tended to explain the cause of someone's feelings by reiterating the situation.

As in research with role taking, in which simpler methods or methods requiring less verbalization were successful in demonstrating role taking in very young children, so, with a simple task and a procedure that required simple responses, Green (1977) was able to demonstrate that kindergarteners understand the causal influence of certain events on people's emotions. Moreover, there was a significant positive relationship between causal attribution scores of girls and teachers' judgments of their role-taking skills. This makes sense, since attributing an emotion to another person usually involves role taking, or, alternatively, the capacity to make inferences about others' internal states is necessary for certain types of role taking. However, alternative explanations, such as both scores' being an expression of general intelligence, are possible.

A great deal of research attempted to show, following Piaget's (1932) original studies, that children's judgments of other people as good or bad, or their judgments of whether the behavior of others is praiseworthy or blameworthy, are increasingly determined by their perceptions of the intentions of the other persons rather than by the consequences of their actions. In Piaget's procedure, and in many replications, two stories are presented to the child:

> In one, a child acts from bad intentions (such as malice or greed) causing a small amount of damage, while in the second story another child with good intentions (such as obedience, helpfulness, generosity) causes a large amount of damage. The general finding has been that the seriousness of the outcome is the major determiner of blame judgments up to the age of 8 or 9, whereas the intention of the actor is the basis for assigning blame in older children [Shantz, 1975, p. 290].

There are a variety of problems with these procedures (Shantz, 1975). For example, the amount of damage and the type of intention are covaried. Bad intentions and small damage and good intention and large damage usually go together, so that the independent influence of each cannot be determined. Second, in some stories the actors' intention (e.g., to steal a cookie), and the responsibility for the outcome or consequences, such as breaking the jar (whether it was intended or accidental), are confounded. Although an actor with good intentions who tried to be helpful but caused some damage is never presented as someone who intended the damage, actors whose behavior was the result of selfish or other negative motives sometimes cause the damage accidentally, sometimes intentionally; most often, however, the responsibility for the damage is not specified and has to be determined by the reader. For example, a child who is angry at another may engage in some behavior that is negative in nature. It ends up hurting the other child, but whether the harm was intended or not may be unspecified. Finally, only recently have investigators started to examine what judgments follow when actors appear to have positive (in contrast to the conventionally used neutral) intentions.

Clearly, the use of intentions in making judgments of another's character, personality, or praise- or blameworthiness increases with age. When the consequences of a child's behavior are positive, children come to evaluate the behavior as a function of the actor's intentions at an earlier age (about 6); negative consequences seem to focus the children's judgment on the outcome more forcefully, and they come to judge the behavior in terms of the actor's motives at a somewhat later age (Costanzo, Coie, Grument, & Farnill, 1973). This is consistent with the finding that when the negative consequences of some behavior are severe, children tend to judge the behavior by its consequences, although at the same age (6) when the consequences are milder they tend to judge the behavior by the actor's intentions (Armsby, 1971).

In this realm again, recent research findings suggest that children are able at an early age to consider and evaluate acts on the basis of intentions. Karniol (1978), based on her review of such research, using Piaget's paradigm, in which intentions and consequences were not so intertwined that the independent influence of intention cues could not be evaluated, concludes that "children do evaluate on the basis of intentions and ignore consequence information when accidental and intentional acts are explicitly specified [p. 76]." On the whole, the research findings suggest, however, that young children may have difficulty in making inferences about intentions versus consequences in everyday life, when they have to derive information from and base their judgments on the varied cues imbedded in the events that occur.

As the social-psychology literature that was noted in Volume 1 suggests, the tendency to judge individuals whose behavior has severe negative consequences as responsible persists into adulthood. Such judgments may partly reflect people's personal experience that both other people and the law take them to account when they cause accidents of serious consequence.

It is likely that attributions of intentions to others and inferences about their internal states as the basis of judgments about their behavior and character continue to develop through childhood, and even in adulthood, since often many complex factors are involved in making such judgments. In this domain also, research needs to be done on the development of individual differences and on the child-rearing and experiential factors that contribute to them.

Moral Judgment, Role Taking, and Cognition

As noted earlier, moral judgment increases with age (Kohlberg, 1969). Both Piaget (1932) and Kohlberg (1969) saw cognitive growth and role taking as intimately involved in the development of moral reasoning. A number of experiments attempted to demonstrate that role taking and moral judgment, or certain cognitive capacities and moral judgment, are linked in some fashion.

Two issues need to be considered. First, both role taking and moral judgment—particularly of the Piagetian type—are what Gerwitz (1968) called *summary variables*. They are multidimensional constructs that are often treated as single dimensions. The relative independence of different kinds of role taking clearly suggests this. With regard to moral judgment, Kohlberg (1969) argued that Piaget's stages are not true stages, that the different elements that characterize each of the two stages do not represent a whole. For example, judgments of intentionality of wrong-doing and of proper restitution of damages that resulted from some action might be relatively independent. With regard to Kohlberg's stages, the degree to which the different elements that are used to define each stage are intercorrelated has not been reported.

The second issue involves the theoretically expected relationship between role taking and moral judgment and the measurement of these constructs. On the one hand both Piaget and Kohlberg assume that role taking is a prerequisite for moral judgment. On the other hand, the ability to consider events from an increasingly broad perspective is a central aspect of increasing moral maturity in Kohlberg's view; a person who is at the most advanced, principled level of reasoning will consider the perspective of all of humanity in reasoning about moral conflicts. Thus, role taking is an inherent aspect of moral judgment. As currently measured, simple forms of role taking are different from moral judgment. However, increasingly complex forms of role taking that involve inferences about social reality come to be increasingly similar to moral judgment (Selman & Byrne, 1974). For example, considering the difference between a person smashing a cup in anger and accidentally knocking it over involves differentiation between motives, which is related to role taking. Judging the "wrongness" of the act on the basis of intentionality intimately involves such role taking. If the relationship between role taking and moral judgment is to be explored meaningfully, it seems important to measure role taking in its basic, cognitive forms, or at least without the social-informational elements that some complex role-taking tasks include and may share with moral judgment.

In one study of the relationship between role taking and moral judgment, Selman (1971) used a cognitive role-taking task—a hiding-and-guessing game. In this game different amounts of money are hidden under different boxes and the child is supposed to guess how another person would reason about the hidden money. Using Kohlberg's stories to measure moral judgment Selman found that 8- to 10-year-olds who reasoned at a more mature (conventional) level possessed better role-taking skills than those who reasoned at less mature (preconventional) levels. However, the reverse did not hold: An advanced role-taking ability was not similarly associated with advanced reasoning. On this basis Selman proposed that role taking is a necessary skill for advanced moral judgment but is not sufficient for it. Kuhn (1972) also found a significant relationship between role-taking skills measured by a hide-and-guess game and moral judgment in 5- to 7-year-olds. Rubin and Schneider (1973) found an $r = .59$ correlation between role-taking scores based on the number of distinctive features a child used in describing a picture to an experimenter who could not see it, and level of moral judgment. Ambron and Irwin (1975) used perceptual, cognitive (hide-and-guess games), and affective measures of role taking, with 5- and 7-year-olds. There was a significant relationship between cognitive role-taking and the tendency to judge a child's naughtiness as a function of the intentionality of some harm this child caused. The latter was evaluated in a classic Piagetian story, in which one child caused harm intentionally and another caused harm accidentally. The character who had positive intent did more damage. Affective role-taking was marginally related to children's basing their judgment on intentionality, whereas perceptual role-taking was unrelated. (However, the perceptual role-taking task used in this study might have been overly difficult. Children at both age levels performed poorly on this task; there was no improvement with age, as was seen on the other two role-taking measures.) Judgment of the proper restitution for damage was unrelated to role taking.

The relationship between cognitive capacities and moral judgment has also been studied. Keasey (1975) suggests not only that cognitive development facilitates moral development, but also, on the basis of his research, that major cognitive transformations, the shift to concrete and to formal operations, have quite specific effects on moral development and facilitate the emergence of Kohlberg's second and fifth stages of moral reasoning.

The existence of a relationship between role taking and moral judgment makes sense. The ability to consider events from the point of view of specific others should contribute to the ability to consider what is right and wrong from the standpoint of all people. Role taking may exert its influence on behavior through its contribution to moral judgment and values. It may also exert its influence in other ways, as noted, such as enhancing feelings of empathy with other people. Feshbach and Roe (1968) found that for children to report that they had feelings similar to those of a child character in a picture-series story, they first had to identify that child's feelings. In simple physical-distress situations another's feelings may be obvious, but in many other situations they are not. Obviously, accurate identification of another's feelings is necessary—and this often demands good affective perspective-taking skills—before feelings of empathy can arise.

In conclusion, it seems that role taking advances with age. The findings by Kurdock and Rodgon (1975) of increased difficulty in perceiving other people's incongruous affective responses to events present an interesting puzzle in the otherwise apparently straightforward growth of role taking with age. Other social–cognitive skills, such as attributing intentions to others and making inferences about others' internal states, advance with age. Unfortunately, the specific cognitive capacities that contribute to role taking have not been identified. Most research to date has ignored the highly important questions of what conditions facilitate and what conditions inhibit the development of role-taking skills, as well as the related question of how individual differences in role taking develop. I shall review the research that has dealt with these questions in subsequent chapters.

There has been insufficient study of the continued development of role taking into adulthood. One study demonstrated a continued increase of role taking with age in the realm of considering others' moral judgments and further showed that moral judgments are not fixed but can vary as a result of influences acting on a person (see Chapter 2). Yussen (1977) found that people can place themselves in the role of other people who vary in the social role they occupy. He found that, with increasing age, subjects at grade levels 9, 10, and 12 and in college who were asked to respond to a moral reasoning questionnaire from the standpoint of themselves, an average policeman, and an average philosopher were increasingly able to respond differentially. College students were most affected in their responses by the social role they were asked to assume. To some extent, the increasing differentiation may correspond to cultural stereotypes. However, Yussen notes that the instructions to assume the role of philosopher resulted in more advanced responses than did instructions to subjects to *fake* "good responses" (McGeorge, 1975) and that

responses to the policeman role differed from responses to the self role
in ways other than level only. With increasing age, people can increasingly think about moral issues from varied perspectives.

Various aspects of role taking may continue to develop beyond childhood. There can be substantial variation in the "depth" of role taking.
Role taking can range from simple identification or awareness of what
another person thinks or feels to entering into another's inner world and
elaborately considering another person's thoughts, feelings, intentions, or
motives. As we more extensively enter into another's thoughts and feelings,
we may experience empathy or identification with the other person to a
greater degree. Consequently, the impact of role taking on our behavior
is likely to be greater. We need to explore in what realms the capacity
for increasingly elaborate role taking develops with age, the influences
that foster or inhibit its development, and the extent to which people
who have the capacity tend to engage in such role taking and how it
affects their behavior.

The Growth of Altruistic Motivation

Briefly, a model proposed by Hoffman (1975a) of the development
of "altruistic motivation" is worth considering here. This is an optimistic
model, probably more so than justified by our current knowledge. The
model implies that altruistic motivation will develop out of the natural
growth and experiences of the child, although Hoffman (1976) also recognizes the importance of child-rearing influences. However, he assigns a
major role to role taking and to other cognitive capacities. The assumptions in the model about how various developing capacities of the child
intertwine represent an excellent use of a developmental approach.

Empathic distress, according to this model, is present very early in
life. It is part of the organism's potential, and can result from very early
conditioning experiences. It may even be released by particular stimuli
to which reactivity is innate. As I have noted, self-conditioning might be
an important part of early empathic distress in infants.

As a next step, children develop *person permanence,* an awareness
of the existence of others as separate physical entities. At this time the
child knows, when someone is in distress, that it is the other, not he,
who is in distress. The earlier, "parallel" affective reactions are gradually
transformed into "reciprocal, sympathetic concern for the victim," or
sympathetic distress. The child cannot distinguish between the quality
of his own and others' internal states, and assumes that they are identical.
Role-taking ability, which is present very early in some form, gradually

develops. The child also develops and more firmly possesses a sense of personal identity, of continuity of the self and therefore of others. These developing capacities lead to the further evolution of sympathetic distress. The child becomes able to perceive another's independent emotional state in a particular situation and to understand that it might be different from what he does or would feel. As he becomes aware of others' continuous existence, he becomes able to respond not only to their feelings in a particular situation but also to their general life circumstances and how they relate to the current circumstances. With further cognitive development he may be able to comprehend the plight of entire groups of people. The motivational core, the push for action, is provided by empathic distress, but this emotional state is enlarged, refined, and shaped; action is guided by the altered ability to process information about others.

We know that person permanence, role taking, and a sense of personal identity all develop in children, that a cognitive sense of both the self and others develops. It is questionable, however, that the development of such cognitive capacities, even in combination with primitive empathic responsiveness, is sufficient to produce altruistic motivation. The quality or content of the sense of others and self is likely to be highly important—for example, whether others are seen as malevolent or benevolent and whether the self is perceived positively or negatively. The child's experiences can accelerate or retard the cognitive aspects of development—how clearly the child perceives himself and others as separate entities, how firm the boundaries of self are, and how well he can take the role of others. They will certainly affect the qualitative aspects of development. The life conditions that the child experiences and the nature of his socialization are likely to be highly important, therefore, for the development of altruistic motivation. The kinds of socialization and experiences that are likely to contribute to prosocial behavior are considered in subsequent chapters.

view verbal communications by parents have to be associated with punishment if they are to guide later behavior. The verbal representations or cognitions that the child learns function as conditioned stimuli that control the child's behavior by eliciting anxiety. The anxiety-eliciting capacity is the result of the punishment the child receives in conjunction with the parental verbalizations. In a series of experiments Aronfreed showed that when punishment (for example, aversive noise or a loud *no*) for some activity is accompanied by verbalizations that provide the child with a "cognitive structure" children later resist temptation more. The children are also more likely to use the verbalizations following transgressions, perhaps as means of self-punishment, than children not exposed to verbalization. In Aronfreed's studies, however, extremely minimal verbalizations were used by experimenters, which could not possibly have extensively affected the manner in which the child thought about or evaluated the activity. For example, the word *blue* accompanied the prohibited or punished activity in one verbalization condition, but not in the punishment-alone condition.

In an extensive review of the literature on moral development (dealing mainly with the antecedents of proscriptive morality, since research on prosocial behavior was just starting at that time) Hoffman (1970a) argued that the evidence for the importance of love withdrawal, which until then was considered the most effective child-rearing technique in the development of conscience, was questionable. Instead, he proposed that a certain type of reasoning by the parent was the most important antecedent of internalized values and corresponding behavior. He suggested the importance of induction, of the parent pointing out the harmful consequences of the child's undesirable behavior on others (how certain actions hurt other people, cause feelings of disappointment, and so on) for the development of internalized moral values and moral behavior. He also differentiated among types of induction as a function of whether the consequences of the child's behavior for parents, or other people, particularly peers, were pointed out. Induction is a specific form of reasoning. Although reasoning refers to a mode of discipline, induction refers both to the use of that mode and to a particular content area. Parents who reason with their children in this manner, particularly those who employ other-oriented induction, communicate values to them that emphasize the importance of the welfare of human beings.

Naturalistic Research on Reasoning and Induction

Hoffman and his associates conducted a series of naturalistic studies to evaluate the consequences of induction and to compare them to the consequences of other socializing techniques. In the first study (Hoffman,

1963), children's interactions in nursery school were observed. A relationship was found between induction and socially responsible behavior—positive, constructive behavior in interactions—but only among children whose parents were low in their use of power assertion. The relationship was not found among those whose parents were high in power assertion, or in the total sample.

In another study parental use of power assertion, love withdrawal, and induction was related to several measures of moral development (Hoffman & Saltzstein, 1967). Parental discipline techniques were determined separately on the basis of parents' and children's responses. Both parents and children received the description of four concrete situations (child talked back to parents, child had not done well in school, and so on) and were asked to indicate the absolute frequency of use of each of 10–14 practices (representing the discipline categories) that were listed following each situation. They were asked to indicate the first, second, and third practice most frequently used. From the responses, weighted and summed scores were derived. A fourth technique, parental induction with regard to peers, was assessed from parents' responses as to how they would have dealt with two situations in which a child's transgression had harmful consequences for another child.

Parental discipline techniques were correlated with indices of the subjects' internalized morality. Two "cognitive" indices were used. One, the intensity of guilt the child experienced following transgression, was evaluated by the completion of projective stories about children who committed transgressions. Guilt scores were based on "evidence of conscious self-initiated and self-critical reactions [Hoffman & Saltzstein, 1967]." Their intensity was rated on a 6-point scale. Extreme actions by the hero, such as personality change or suicide, received the highest ratings. Another measure of internalization was the moral reasoning children used in judging severe (hypothetical) transgressions in Piaget-type stories, about persons committing crimes. They were to decide, for example, which of two crimes was worse and to judge crimes with extenuating circumstances. Responses were coded as external ("you can get put in jail for that"), internal ("that's not right, the man trusted you"), or indeterminate. The sum of internal responses constituted the child's moral judgment score.

In addition to these cognitive measures, the child's overt reactions to transgression were evaluated by asking teachers how the child reacted when "caught doing something wrong" (denied it, blamed someone else, looked sad or cried, accepted responsibility, tried to rectify it on his own initiative) and by asking mothers whether the child confessed (reported on his own) when he did something that he knew his parent would not approve of. Consideration for others was also measured in this study, by using sociometric ratings by other children. They nominated the first, second, and third child most likely "to care about the other children's feelings" and "to defend a child being made fun of by the group." The two scores were weighed and summed.

The subjects were seventh-grade middle- and lower-class children. In the middle-class sample power assertion by the mother was associated with "weak moral development" (e.g., many significant negative correlations). The use of parent-oriented induction by the mother was associated with advanced moral development and was significantly positively related to most cognitive and behavioral measures. Many of the significant relationships were found only between the child's perception of parental practices and measures of the child's moral cognition or behavior. This was particularly the case with the negative relationship of power assertion and the positive relationship of induction with teachers' ratings of the child's acceptance of responsibility. In light of such findings, it is important to gather more knowledge about what parental behaviors affect how children perceive their parents.

The number of relationships between the father's practices and indices of moral development was relatively small. Induction by both mothers (with regard to the consequences of the child's behavior on parents as well as peers) and fathers (with regard to parents) was associated with peer ratings of consideration for other children. Interestingly, power assertion by both mothers and fathers was also associated with ratings by peers of boys' consideration for others. The association was based on parental reports of power assertion. Most of the relatively few correlates of the father's practices were behavioral: confession, the teacher's report of accepting responsibility, and consideration for others. Perhaps the mother, who has more everyday contact, provides the cognitive base, which is reflected in cognitive indices of moral development, but the father's influence is necessary if this is to be translated into action.

In the lower-class sample the correlations between parental practices and measures of moral development were generally low; only a few scattered correlations reached significance. Given this paucity of relationships it seems important that parental practices were related to children's consideration for others. There was a positive correlation between induction (toward parents) by mothers and girls' consideration for other children, and between power assertion by mothers and boys' consideration for other children. Both of these correlations were based on children's reports of parental practices. Power assertion by parents was involved, in both middle- and lower-class samples, in boys learning to show consideration for others.

It is unfortunate that in this study, which is one of the few to explore parental practices and cognitive and behavioral indices of development together (including an index of prosocial behavior), the interrelationships among the indices of moral development were not reported. Neither were the relationships among parental practices, so that the existence of patterns of practices and their influence could not become evident. Clearly, parents who use power assertion also use induction to some degree; different patterns or combinations would be expected to have different consequences. Affection by parents, which, as reported in Chapter 4, has also been found to relate in this study to children's consideration for others, might be correlated with other practices. The degree of independent and combined influence of various practices, and the degree to which behavior might have been mediated by cognition cannot be estimated from the data.

In a later study Hoffman (1975a) measured the relationship of the importance of altruistic values to parents, their use of victim-centered discipline, and parental affection, to peer ratings of fifth-grade children's consideration for others. Parental values were evaluated by a questionnaire. Victim-centered discipline—the parents' encouraging reparation, apology, or the expression of concern about the feelings of a victim—were measured by parents' reports of how they would have responded, when the child was 5 or 6 years old, to the child causing harm to someone. The data relating to affection were reported in Chapter 4. The fathers' altruistic values were positively related to consideration for others among both boys and girls; the mothers', only among girls. The mothers' reports of victim-centered discipline were highly significantly related to boys' consideration for others, whereas fathers' reports of victim-centered discipline were highly related to girls' consideration for others. Again, unfortunately, relationships among parental measures, and the degree to which the correlations with the children's consideration for others were independent, were not reported. It might be expected that parental values get expressed in various ways, one of which is victim-centered discipline, so that altruistic values and victim-centered discipline would be related. Parental affection may be somewhat related to both.

What Do Children Learn from Induction? Hoffman's findings and theory suggest that induction might be an important antecedent of the tendency to behave prosocially. How might induction affect children? According to Hoffman (1970a), it has two major consequences. First, induction directs the child's attention to others' distress and explains the nature of it if it is not obvious (when the distress is psychological, for example). This may often elicit empathic responses. Second, induction communicates to the child that he is responsible for the distress. The first of these functions implies that the child learns to recognize others' feelings, to anticipate how certain events, particularly his own behavior, might affect other people. Consequently induction might affect role taking, the ability to consider events from others' points of view. To the extent that role taking enhances the likelihood of empathic reactions, directly or by contributing to the development of empathic reactivity, children who frequently experience induction would be more likely to respond empathically to others. The second function of induction suggests that children exposed to it would acquire a sense of responsibility for others' welfare, or at least for their own behavior toward others.

Consistent induction is likely to have varied consequences. Minimally, unless it is ignored, it increases children's ability to infer others' emotions and thus will increase their perceptual sensitivity. Second, to the extent that it implies or directly communicates behavioral alternatives in response to stimulus conditions involving others' welfare, induction teaches children strategies or plans for action. Third, induction must frequently be associated with direct or indirect punishment (or reinforcement) of the child, including the expression of displeasure (or pleasure—see the discussion of positive induction later in this chapter) so that the cognitions that the child acquires become conditioned stimuli, eliciting affect, as Aronfreed suggested. This emotion can be empathic in nature, since the child is likely to be made to experience negative affect when the induction points to harm, and positive affect when it points to positive consequences of the behavior.

Although a conditioning view of the effectiveness of induction and other types of reasoning is probably correct, as far as it goes, it assigns a relatively subsidiary role to cognition. The manner in which the child learns to interpret his environment, and his own relationship to it and role in it, would be strongly affected by parental reasoning and induction. What parents tell children about the world, about other people, and about ways of interacting with people will shape the kinds of attributions children make about the motives or intentions that guide others' behavior, will influence how they evaluate people, events, and behaviors, and will affect the kinds of strategies and plans that they develop for relating to other people. These in turn are likely to affect behavior, partly through the emotional reactions that evaluations and attributions create.

Verbal communications, together with the parents' behavior, may also shape children's conception of their own similarity to or difference from others. If children come to conceive of others as similar to themselves on important dimensions defining "humanness"—basic needs, feelings, and the like—a close self–other connection may result, the capacity for empathy and identification with others may be enhanced, and a wide range of applicability of prosocial values may develop. As research reviewed in Volume 1 (Chapters 6 and 7) suggested, the manner in which the connection between the self and others is defined is an important determinant of responsiveness to others. Furthermore socializing experiences, experiences in interacting with parents and other people, and the content of verbal information children receive may jointly determine their specific beliefs and values (such as a belief in justice), what standards they employ in determining equity, the nature of hedonic balancing they engage in, and so on. As the discussion on self-regulation suggested, what children think about and imagine, the way they evaluate events and their own behavior, can guide their actions. If children adopt some of the thinking and values to which induction exposes them, thoughts and images that evolve from them and then accompany their behavior might lead to greater prosocial conduct, and to self-reward and self-punishment as a function of adherence to these values.

Through induction and verbal interaction with others and by other means, children may learn systems of cognitions by which they interpret and evaluate events. Only one type of event is their own behavior. In addition, children may come to value the importance of the welfare of other people, to consider others' distress as bad and others' well-being as desirable. Given such interpretations, the observations of others' distress or others' well-being is likely to lead to varied emotions in the observer–interpreter, including emotions corresponding to those of the other person—that is, to the experience of empathy.

The assumption I make is that a network of cognitions that guides the interpretation of certain kinds of events (with different networks for other kinds of events) also affects emotional reactions. This assumption is in line with contemporary theories of emotion (Arnold, 1960; Lazarus, 1966; Leventhal, 1974; Schachter & Singer, 1962), which assume that emotions are a function of both physiological arousal and the interpretation of events. Several writers (Arnold, 1960; Lazarus, Averill, & Opton, 1969; Leventhal, 1974) assume that how events are assessed determines both whether physiological arousal (or central nervous system activation) will result and the nature of the emotion experienced. If so, the manner in which one interprets one's own behavior or other people's experiences is likely to determine to what extent (and what kinds of) emotions are aroused.

A variety of experiments show that verbal communications can affect emotional reactions (Lazarus & Alfert, 1964; Leventhal, Singer, & Jones, 1965; Nisbett & Schachter, 1966; Staub, 1968, 1972b; Staub & Kellett, 1972). Emotional reactions to others' distress, to viewing a film of an operation that is part of an initiation ceremony in a primitive tribe (Lazarus & Alfert, 1964), and to feared and aversive stimuli (Staub, 1968; Staub & Kellett, 1972) can all be affected by prior verbal communications, presumably because the verbal communications affect how these stimuli or events are interpreted (for an extended discussion, see Volume 1, Chapter 4).

In the preceding discussion, heavy emphasis was placed on the importance of cognition in guiding behavior. Several functions, although not necessarily independent ones, have been attributed to cognition. Even this does not adequately represent, probably, the important and complex ways in which thinking and imagining guide behavior. Although it is fashionable, in recent psychological theorizing, to acknowledge that human beings are cognitive organisms and that cognition must be a powerful influence on behavior, all too often we pay lip service to this relationship and invoke cognition as an easy explanatory principle (in place of reinforcement, for example). Unfortunately, frequently that is all we can do. The nature of the relationship between cognition and behavior, which has to be tremendously complex given the extreme complexity of human cognitive processes and the unconscious nature of some of the determinants of our behavior, is only beginning to be elucidated.

Experimental Research on Reasoning and Induction

Although the naturalistic studies do suggest the importance of verbal communications by parents and particularly of induction as contributors to children's tendency to behave prosocially, early laboratory studies have been less successful. I reviewed the experimental research on verbal influences on children's positive behavior in Volume 1 (Chapter 5). There, I distinguished among three types of verbal influence. Some verbal communications expressed the desirability of sharing, of donating to others, and communicated to children that this was a good thing to do. Such normative statements, referred to as "preaching" (Bryan & Walbeck, 1970a,b; Eisenberg-Berg & Geisheker, 1978; Rushton, 1975), were usually ineffective in inducing children to donate material possessions to others. This is consistent with the findings of Hartshorne, May, and Shuttleworth (1930) that experiences such as being a member of the boy scouts —where children seem to be exposed to normative ideals—are not associated with willingness for greater self-sacrifice. However, verbal communications of this kind *can* affect positive behavior, depending on surrounding conditions and, presumably, on children's personalities.

Eisenberg-Berg and Geisheker (1978) found that, when normative statements of donations were delivered by a person who had power over the children, the school principal, they enhanced subsequent donations, but they did not when they were delivered by a low-power person, the principal of another school. In a second group of experiments, children were directly told what to do; these verbal communications prescribed a standard of conduct and a strategy for executing the standard. Such verbal communications usually enhanced donations; this research will be further examined in the next chapter. A third group of experiments employed inductive statements.

In an early laboratory study (Staub, 1971d) induction did not increase prosocial behavior. In this study "positive induction" was used. Hoffman and his associates used the term *induction* to refer to parents' pointing out the negative consequences of the child's undesirable behavior on other people. However, pointing out the positive consequences of desirable behavior, the increased welfare of other people, the positive emotions that such behavior induces, and the like, is also likely to be important in the development of a tendency to behave prosocially. Presumably the incentive value of acting prosocially will be greater, because of the anticipated self-reward or anticipated positive empathic experience, when people can foresee and consider the benefits that their behavior will produce. The satisfaction from having acted prosocially would also be greater. Positive induction is also likely to contribute to an awareness of one's power in benefiting other people, presumably contributing to a sense of responsibility for helping others.

In my study, kindergarten children were told in one experimental group about several situations in which a child needed help and ways of providing help (Staub, 1971d). In another condition, in addition, the children were told about positive consequences of help, the manner in which help benefits the child in need, and its positive consequences on the victim's physical and emotional welfare. These induction statements were also employed in conjunction with role playing, where the children enacted the roles of the helper and of the helped child, exchanging roles so each child could take both roles. Although role playing affected later prosocial behavior (see the discussion of role playing presented earlier in this chapter), induction did not increase help for a distressed child in an adjoining room or sharing with a child whose parents could not buy a birthday present for him. However, induction decreased the children's helping an adult pick up paper clips she accidentally dropped. In another study Midlarsky and Bryan (1972) found that verbal communications of an inductive type affected children's donations and had a delayed and generalized effect. However, they had no control group, and thus it is not clear whether communications in one treatment group about positive consequences increased donating, or communications in another group about the undesirability of donating for the recipient and subject decreased donating. The latter might have happened, as it did in the study conducted by Rushton (1975). That pointing out the beneficial consequences of donating for others has no effect on later sharing behavior was also found by Sims (1974) in a study with 9- and 10-year-old black children. However, Sims also included in her study a racial-identification induction condition, in which the shared group membership of subjects and of the recipients of the donations was stressed. This condition enhanced donations in comparison to modeling, induction, and control treatments. Moreover, the greater the number of candies that children possessed, the greater was the effect of this type of induction. This finding is consistent with the research reviewed in Volume 1 (Chapter 7) that showed that conditions that lead to identification with others —such as presumed similarity in personality or opinions, or shared group membership—enhance positive behavior. Either past experiences that lead to identifying with other people (that is, personality characteristics of children) or existing conditions or verbal communications that lead to identification may provide a basis for considering and being affected by others' needs. Once identification exists, induction may more easily increase responsiveness.

In a further study Sims (1978) again found that induction had no effect on fourth-grade girls' donations, but self-induction—the use of questions to elicit an expression by children themselves of the consequences of various positive and negative behavior on other children's feelings—enhanced subsequent donations by girls, in comparison to children in both the induction and a control group. Answering such questions may involve the child to a greater degree than hearing others describe the consequences of positive behavior, and it may therefore activate the motivation to behave generously. In all of the aforementioned studies, induction did not increase positive behavior. However, Dlugokinski and Firestone (1973) found that induction increased the generosity of children who reported that their parents practiced induction with them at home. Past induction may have led to concern by children about others' welfare, which was activated by the induction statements. In a study with findings somewhat discrepant from those I have just reviewed, Eisenberg-Berg and Geisheker (1978) found that an inductive statement enhanced generosity by both third- and fourth-grade girls and boys, consistent with findings that will be reported later in this section. However, the pattern of average donations suggests that the effect was primarily due to the girls' behavior.

Varied conditions associated with induction, which I shall discuss below, are likely to determine how induction affects children. An examination of possible reasons for the differences in the findings of naturalistic studies—in which parental use of induction was associated with moral cognition and positive behavior—and the predominant findings of the experimental studies that were reviewed may indicate some of the conditions that contribute to the effectiveness of induction.

First, stimulus differences might exist; that is, the kinds of verbalizations might differ. Verbalizations employed in the different laboratory studies varied, and most of them were probably different from those employed by parents. Depending on the content of verbal communications, different motives might be attributed to the communicator, as stressed earlier, and different values might be transmitted. Moreover, the verbalizations that parents were asked to report in the Hoffman studies were primarily negative in nature. Most of the experimental studies attempted to induce prosocial behavior by positive statements. The former, then, measured parents' use of verbalizations following an act, whereas the latter employed verbal inducements preceding an act. Thus, a difference in timing is involved.

Another reason for the difference in findings may be that parental induction produces effects in conjunction with correlated variables. Certainly, parental induction can take place in the context of ongoing control by the parent over the child. Baumrind (1967, 1971), for example, found that extensive reasoning by parents was part of a pattern of practices she called *authoritative*. Because parental induction is used in conjunction with the child's behavior (as suggested, often immediately following it) and because parents can influence the child to act in a manner consistent with the verbal message, the verbalizations are associated with the child's behavior and over time may become employed by the child to guide his own behavior. The verbal statements that Hoffman and Saltzstein (1967) described as inductive included statements of disappointment by parents for the child's action; those described by Hoffman (1975a) as victim-centered included demands for reparation and apology, which clearly had direct implications for the child and his behavior. In laboratory experiments the experimenter or model is a stranger and therefore has had no past opportunity to establish authority, to indicate his expectations about children acting according to values communicated to them. This person usually says things that lay down no specific rules but communicate values, the desirability of outcomes or actions. In addition, the child has no reason to expect future interaction with or control by this person. The verbal communications by this person usually precede the opportunity for action. Under these circumstances it may be relatively easy for children to ignore what they are told. Without continuing interaction, induction may evoke psychological reactance, resentment because of the implied limitation on children's freedom by demands that they be "good."

A third difference is that in naturalistic studies a global measure of prosocial behavior was usually employed. For example, some studies used sociometric ratings by the child's peers of his consideration for others, which is a summation of the behavior of the child as perceived by others across many situations. Such an index allows for much variation in behavior. As research on consistency in personality shows, consistency is usually found when such summary measures of behavior are employed. Prediction of behavior in a specific setting at a specific time is extremely difficult because of the varied determinants of action that operate under particular circumstances (Block, 1977; Mischel, 1968; Staub, 1978b; Staub & Feinberg, 1978; see also Volume 1, Chapter 2 of this work). Laboratory studies measure such specific behavioral responses. Thus, there is a difference in response classes that are measured in the two kinds of research.

An implication of the foregoing discussion, and of the repeatedly suggested importance of the performance of prosocial behavior in learning later prosocial behavior, is that when induction statements accompany children's actual participation in prosocial action, it becomes more likely that the consideration of positive consequences will become associated with prosocial behavior in the child's thinking and that it will later guide his or her behavior. Other circumstances, such as induction statements by people who have exercised control over the child and/or will exercise continuing control, can be expected to have similar effects.

In several studies we attempted to integrate induction with relevant concurrent experiences (e.g., participation in a prosocial activity). In one study (Staub, 1975b; Staub & Fotta, 1978) the children participated on several occasions. Induction statements were administered each time, in conjunction with the children's activity. The procedures created some continuing control over the child, and they provided the opportunity for an association between words and action to develop. Induction first depicted the positive consequences that were to follow from prosocial acts and then depicted the positive consequences already produced by them. Fifth- and sixth-grade children spent four 40-minute sessions either making puzzles for hospitalized children or making drawings for an irrelevant purpose. Half of the subjects, whatever their activity, had some of the expected positive consequences of making puzzles for hospitalized children pointed out to them in the first two sessions and some of the actual positive consequences described in later sessions. The other half simply engaged in their own activity and were given a brief description of its purpose in the first session.

The children who made drawings and also experienced induction were told that other children were making puzzles for hospitalized children and that they themselves might have a chance to make puzzles. In this context, the positive consequences of the puzzle-making activity were described. This condition gave us the opportunity to evaluate the effects of positive induction experienced without actual participation in prosocial action. In the first two sessions, the induction statements pointed out, among other things, that the hospitalized children who were to receive the puzzles would be less bored, that the puzzles would keep them occupied so they would think less about their illness. Some actual positive consequences of their prosocial activity were pointed out to children in the third and fourth sessions. They were told that the puzzles they had completed had been delivered to hospitalized children, and the good feelings of the recipients, their pleasure in and enjoyment of the puzzles, were described.

The children received, about a week after the last training session, lists of the first names of hospitalized children of the same sex. A brief description of the reason for hospitalization was included for each child. They were asked to write letters to these children within 3–4 days and drop the letters into a collection box. They also received a large envelope containing stationery for two letters, but they were told that they could write more. Just before they received the stationery, they were asked to indicate on a sheet of paper whether they would be willing to make more puzzles for hospitalized children and, if so, how many they would make. The treatments affected the number of letters that children wrote to hospitalized children; both a significant two-way and a significant three-way interaction (with sex) were found. Participation in prosocial activity combined with induction increased the number of letters that participants wrote in comparison to the other three treatment groups (neutral activity, neutral activity with induction, prosocial activity without induction). This was primarily due to the large number of letters that girls wrote in this condition. Boys wrote relatively few letters in all experimental groups; there was a significant sex difference across all conditions. Writing letters may be a more congenial activity for girls of this age. In addition, as we will later see from the findings of other experiments, boys may be less affected by verbal communications or may even react negatively to them.

Treatments and sex also interacted in their effects on children's expression of intention, producing a significant three-way interaction. As before, the combined treatments substantially increased girls' expressed willingness to make puzzles for the hospitalized children. However, participation in the prosocial activity or induction, but not their combination, increased boys' expressed willingness to help. Unfortunately, our later research (Staub & Jancaterino, in Staub, 1975b) found that there is relatively little relationship between the intentions children express and what they actually do. In sum, the combination of participation in a prosocial activity and having the positive consequences of this activity emphasized to them increased the subsequent prosocial behavior and the expressed prosocial intent of girls, as expected, but not that of boys.

The two measures that were described were both delayed tests, administered 1–2 weeks after the children participated in the training sessions. One of them was a generalized measure, of a different prosocial behavior, the other a measure of intention to do more of the same activity that children were trained on. A third measure was administered immediately after the last training session: Children received gift certificates for their participation and had the opportunity to donate some of them so that toys could be bought for hospitalized children. Behavior on this measure was unaffected by treatments. Possibly the children felt that they earned and deserved their gift certificates. Such a feeling would have reduced, in all conditions, their willingness to share them immediately after the treatment (Long & Lerner, 1974; Staub, 1973; Volume 1, Chapter 6). This possibility was tested in a subsequent experiment in which half the children received gift certificates immediately after their participation in experimental procedures that involved prosocial activities; the other half received the certificates a week later. The passage of a week was expected to decrease a sense of deserving the rewards and the resulting unwillingness to part with them (Staub & Jancaterino, in Staub, 1975b). In this study children who taught other children to make puzzles donated more of their puzzles than children who participated in the same activities but did not teach. Strong positive relationships appeared in two of three teaching groups between the length of time that elapsed between training and testing and the number of puzzles that children donated. This experiment will be discussed in the next chapter, together with additional experiments that we conducted to examine the joint effects of positive induction and participation in positive behavior on later prosocial behavior.

Verbal Influences on Moral Judgment and Behavior

Verbal influences on values and moral reasoning, which themselves are mediators of prosocial behavior, have been explored in a variety of experiments. In Chapter 2 I briefly mentioned two assumptions of such research when it is inspired by cognitive developmental theory. First, exposure of children to such reasoning is regarded not as direct tuition but as the stimulation of disequilibrium. Second, exposure to a higher stage of reasoning will have greater influence than exposure to a lower stage, because only the former is expected to stimulate disequilibrium. Several experiments showed preference by children for advanced levels of reasoning (Rest *et al.*, 1969) in comparison to reasoning below their own stage. Turiel (1966) also found that exposing children to thinking one stage above their own increased their subsequent usage of such thinking. However, this change was only slightly greater than the increase in children's usage of reasoning one stage below their own following exposure to such reasoning. The treatments consisted of exposure to advice by an adult experimenter about the resolution of two hypothetical moral dilemmas.

Blatt (1969) had sixth-grade children participate in a program of classroom discussions of moral dilemmas, three times a week for 3 months. "Blatt's procedure was to elucidate the arguments of the Stage 3 children as against the Stage 2 children on hypothetical moral conflicts, then to pit the Stage 3's against the Stage 4's, and finally to himself present Stage 5 arguments [Kohlberg, 1969, p. 403]." The reasoning of 45% of the children moved up one stage, in contrast to 8% in the control group. A majority of Stage 2 children moved up to Stage 3, and a majority of Stage 3 children moved up to Stage 4. There was little change from Stage 4 to Stage 5. Obviously, extensive and intensive influence was directed at the children in this study. Kohlberg (1969) suggested that one reason for the greater effect of this procedure than of those in other studies was lengthy exposure and that another reason was that it induced greater conflict through disagreement. "Presumably a sense of contradiction and discrepancy at one's own stage is necessary for reorganization at the next stage [Kohlberg, 1969, p. 403]."

One might suppose, however, that the children clearly perceived that the adult regarded certain types of reasoning as more desirable, more valuable than others, and that they experienced the social influence exerted on them; it was either explicitly stated or implicitly implied that higher stage reasoning was better. One cannot determine how much children's reasoning was affected by cognitive conflict that was induced and the resulting acceptance of more "adequate" ways of thinking, or to what extent the training could be construed as instruction in reasoning that was valued by the adult, which children adopted according to the limit of their cognitive abilities. Moreover, neither do we know whether the primary change involved the children's competence in reasoning (see Chapter 2) or their preferences and habitual modes of thought.

Two experiments demonstrated that, in fact, exposure to reasoning by adults can induce children to think either at more advanced levels or at less advanced levels. Bandura and MacDonald (1963) tested children's judgment of others on Piaget-type (1932) items in terms of intentions underlying an act and the consequences of the act—for example, whether an act is worse if a person has good intentions but accidentally breaks a larger number of cups (if so judged, a heteronomous stage is indicated) or worse if the person's intentions are bad but consequences are less serious (here an autonomous stage is indicated). Children reasoning in one of these ways were exposed to adults who made the opposite-type judgment and were reinforced for these judgments. The resulting change in the children's subsequent judgments was substantial. It generalized to new items and was about equal whether it was in a more advanced or less advanced direction. Cowan *et al.* (1969), questioning Bandura and MacDonald's findings and conclusions, conducted a similar study but modified the procedure somewhat. They had highly similar findings, with children's judgments changing in either direction following exposure to models. Kohlberg (1969) suggested that the changes resulting from the exposure to models in Bandura and MacDonald's study were not structural. There is no general moral stage factor in Piaget's dimensions of morality, he reasoned. Rather, there are several independent factors, one of which is judgment of intentionality. The findings of Bandura and MacDonald (and hence of Cowan) "do not represent actual learning or 'unlearning' of basic concepts of intentions, but a learning to weight them more or less heavily as opposed to consequence [Kohlberg, 1969, p. 408]."

In these studies, verbal communications by models and verbal discussions affected children's judgments, evaluations, or reasoning about situations of moral relevance. Although there is evidence that the children preferred more advanced reasoning, they remembered less advanced reasoning better than their own. There is little evidence that change in a particular direction is more likely. It is also difficult to conclude with confidence from the research that certain changes are qualitatively different from other ones. Finally, it is difficult to know to what degree in different studies the children's thinking changed through conflict and reorganization and to what degree they accepted and used, in particular contexts, ways of thinking or judging that they were exposed to, without structural change. The differential consequences of the two kinds of changes have not been extensively explored.

It is reasonable to assume that children have to be exposed to sufficiently elaborate experiences to come to understand more advanced levels of reasoning than their own and to acquire sufficient competence in such reasoning to show generalization in applying it to novel, unfamiliar moral dilemmas. What is "sufficient" experience has been, to some extent, indicated but not delimited by these studies; presumably, it also depends on the exact level of the child's reasoning capacity at the start and perhaps on other characteristics, such as cognitive capacities and openness to experience. In a further, relevant study Brody and Henderson (1977) exposed first-grade children to both peer and adult models who were either consistent, inconsistent, or conflicting in their moral judgments and who either did or did not provide rationales for their judgments. Several conditions resulted in more mature moral judgments by experimental than by control subjects; but only when children were exposed to consistently mature moral judgments by models, combined with rationales for the judgments, did children show greater numbers of both mature judgments and mature moral explanations than did control subjects. Thus, explanation by models of why they made particular judgments was important.

A study by Turiel and Rothman (1972) explored the effects on children's behavior of exposure to reasoning about such behavior one stage above and one stage below their own. Seventh- and eighth-grade middle- and upper-class boys were the subjects. Their task was to administer punishment to a person for mistakes that this person made on a learning task. The punishment consisted of taking away chips representing money, which the "learner" previously won. Two adults, who were participating before the child, began to argue as to whether they should continue with the procedure or not, in response to protests by the learner ("Please don't take my chips"). The experimenter asked them to discuss their disagreement privately. Then they presented their views to the subject; one of them argued, at a level one stage above the subject's reasoning (which had been evaluated on a pretest), that he should continue. The other one argued, at a level one stage below the subject's, that he should stop. Other subjects received the argument to continue one stage below their level of reasoning, and the arguments for stopping one stage above. Children who reasoned at the Stage 2 and Stage 3 levels were unaffected by the arguments; they tended to continue with the procedure. Children who reasoned at a Stage 4 level were influenced by reasoning one stage above their own; they tended to stop or to continue depending on which type of reasons were presented to them at the more advanced level of thinking. Possibly children whose reasoning was at a more advanced stage were more capable of considering their own thinking, the adult's reasoning, and their behavior in relation to each other, and were more likely to integrate all factors. All subjects tended to prefer reasoning by the adult that was one stage above their own, even if their behavior was unaffected by it.

In a replication with excellent controls and a significant extension of the study just mentioned Rothman (1976) again found that Stage 4 subjects were strongly affected by arguments to stop that were presented one stage above their own level of reasoning. Such arguments had similar effects whether subjects were exposed to two adults, one who wanted to stop and another who wanted to continue, or to a single adult who wanted to stop and presented arguments for doing so one stage above the subject's own. In a hypothetical choice situation, the effect of reasoning presented by adults within a story had the same effect on hypothetical behavioral choices, "one plus" arguments leading Stage 4 subjects to stop. Stage 3 subjects tended to continue with the task regardless of the reasoning they were exposed to, both in their real and hypothetical choices. Stage 4 subjects who were exposed to one plus reasoning to continue tended to do so. Exposure to a single adult who wanted to stop and provided arguments to children at a stage below their own slightly increased the frequency of stopping, particularly by Stage 4 children. If these children have some desire of their own to stop punishment, varied influences will move them in this direction, the more "adequate" from the standpoint of their level of development the greater the effect.

That subjects were similarly affected by adult reasoning in hypothetical and real choice situations is important. The extent to which Kohlberg's and other investigators' tests of moral reasoning only measure competence in reasoning or reflect the kind of thinking that people engage in facing real-life situations is an important, continuing question. In this study, reasoning externally supplied to subjects in hypothetical and in real situations affected them similarly; perhaps people's own reasonings in hypothetical and real situations also have similar effects on their actions. However, in real-life situations, when nobody suggests appropriate reasoning, some situational cues may activate the most advanced moral reasoning a person is capable of; other cues may activate reasoning at less advanced levels. The latter may occur when self-concern is aroused by circumstances.

Under what circumstances will reasoning directed at children affect their later capacity to reason, and their later behavior? In the Turiel and Rothman study and in the Rothman study children whose behavior was affected by the reasoning they heard also showed temporary shifts in their own reasoning to a more advanced stage, in their answers to postexperimental questions. However, in the Turiel and Rothman study, which measured long-term effects, the changes did not persist or generalize to dilemmas on the posttest. Rothman also reported that Stage 3 subjects who were exposed to advanced reasoning to stop vacillated while they continued, and showed some advanced reasoning in their answers to postexperimental questions. Continued exposure to reasoning by adults that stimulates children's thinking and indicates the value of certain types of thinking might have cumulative effects over time. However, to the extent that such reasoning implies the desirability of certain kinds of conduct, as it usually does in real life, the change in children's thinking will be more likely if they are also led to engage in behavior consistent with the reasoning.

Values and Value Orientations of Parents and Children

I have suggested, in the preceding review of the literature, that a variety of parental practices contribute to children's prosocial values and sense of responsibility for others—to their prosocial orientation—and to other personal characteristics that are in turn important determinants of positive behavior.

The parents' varied values, together with their conception of children's nature, are likely to be extremely important in determining the manner in which they interact with their children. Presumably the use of practices that contribute to the development of prosocial orientation, in contrast to other practices, is in part an expression of a value orientation by the parents. Consider, for example, that with the changing age of children different disciplinary and/or socialization practices are required. If there is to be reasonable consistency in the spirit or meaning of the parent's approach to the child, parental practices and behaviors have to be derived from stable values. Loevinger's (1959) analysis of parental control and guidance applies here. Children, in her view, always try to evade parental control in their attempt to satisfy their desires and express their impulses, and continually devise new strategies to do so. Parents, consequently, have to change their own strategies in exerting control over the children. Some basic theory or philosophy is required to successfully socialize the child; this unites and/or gives rise to specific strategies for control and also communicates to the child that reason—rather than impulse—is at work.

I am implying that parental values or value orientations might be the basis of parental controlling practices, of the content of verbal communications to the child, and, of course, of parental behaviors that serve as examples for the child. They probably shape even other aspects of the child's life. Naturally, they cannot account for the entirety of the parents' behavior toward the child: Unconscious forces, affective dispositions unrelated to the child (but still expressed toward him), the parents' capacity for impulse control and self-regulation, and their skill, knowledge, and competence in dealing with and educating the child are all important. All these combine and create a structure in the child's life, shape his environment and the nature of interactions among people in the child's environment and their ways of relating to the child. This structure has profound effects, since it is incorporated by children and provides them an overlearned but mostly implicit blueprint of what people are like and what human interactions are feasible.

When parents have clear ideas that guide their interactions with children and serve as a basis for the guidance they provide them, there may be less unintended and less haphazard influences exerted on children. Baumrind (1971) reported that authoritative parents had clear ideas about how they wanted their children to behave. A parental value orientation can be the basis of such ideas: It is likely to be a persistent influence that gains expression in varied ways.

Parents have values about and value orientations with regard to different aspects of life. At least three types of values or value orientations seem relevant to parents' influence on children: personal values that guide a person's life in relation to other people, society, and work; values about child rearing, how parents think about children and what they regard as the right way of treating, disciplining, educating, and relating to children; and finally parental values as goals with regard to the kind of person they want their child to become. Obviously, some relationship is likely to exist among values in these three realms, but the degree of the relationship and the degree of consistency and inconsistency may vary greatly. Furthermore, different people may express their values in behavior to a greater or lesser degree, and in a more or less consistent manner. Unfortunately, we know little about these matters so far.

Parental values and value orientations are not only likely to gain expression in child rearing and in the parents' relationship to the child, but are also likely to affect the degree to which children model their parents, or respond to reinforcement and other parental behaviors. Earlier the discussion strongly suggested that imitation of prosocial behavior by a model is affected by the kinds of motives that appear to guide the model's behavior, the reasons for the model's actions. Children who begin to perceive their parents as unkind, unconcerned about other people, and hypocritical in their prosocial actions might learn to discount prosocial acts by their parents and remain unaffected by their example.

Furthermore, parents who verbally express values but do not follow them in their own behavior might have children who experience conflict, uncertainty about their conduct, themselves unable to translate values into action, or at least unable to engage in prosocial conduct of sufficient magnitude to provide them with a sense of satisfaction for acting as they feel they ought to be acting.

Differences in socialization certainly lead to children learning different specific values, but they may also contribute to differences in broad value orientations. Prosocial orientation is one such value orientation. The principles of reasoning that characterize the different stages of development in the cognitive developmental view can also be thought of as different value orientations. Many writers proposed schemas to represent different value orientations or different principles of individual morality. As I noted (Volume 1, Chapter 1), Durkheim proposed (1961) that some people are characterized by a responsible orientation toward societal rules, a concern with the maintenance of the rules and regulations of the social order. Others are less reliable in this regard but they are concerned with the "good" and are able and willing to make sacrifices to help others. The latter seem to be concerned with the welfare of individual human beings rather than rules and the more abstract social good. Presumably a combination of these orientations and a reasonable integration of them within a person are also possible.

Some research has explored individual differences in moral orientations. One dimension of value orientation in both parents and children was examined by McKinney (1971). He differentiated between proscriptive and prescriptive value orientations in college students and proposed that these are the result of different emphases by parents in rearing children. Some parents reward the child for doing what is good and punish the child for not engaging in desirable or good behavior (prescriptive child-rearing), whereas others punish children for doing something bad and reward them for not engaging in bad behavior (proscriptive child-rearing). Clearly such parental practices represent different value orientations with regard to what is expected of children. McKinney (1971) found that there were individual differences in college students' value orientations on the prescriptive–proscriptive dimension, and that students with a prescriptive value orientation perceived their parents as more rewarding than those with a proscriptive orientation. As the results of the study to be discussed next also suggest, it seems reasonable that the differences in perception would be accurate expressions of differences in parental rewards and punishment that follow from prescriptive–proscriptive orientations. Parents who want to promote desirable conduct (the "thou shalts") would find it easier to do so by rewarding it when it happens rather than by punishing its absence. Parents who would want to inhibit undesirable behavior (the "thou shalt nots") would find it easier to do so by punishing undesirable behavior when it occurs rather than by rewarding its absence.

In a subsequent investigation Olejnik and McKinney (1973) measured 4-year-old children's value orientations, their generosity, and their parents' value orientations. The children's value orientations were measured by asking them the questions, "What makes a good boy?" (or girl) and "What makes a bad boy?" (or girl), and scoring the number of good behaviors or avoidance of good behaviors, respectively, they gave as responses (prescriptive), in contrast to avoidance of bad behaviors and bad behaviors they gave as responses (proscriptive), and computing the difference between the two. Children's generosity was measured by the number of candies they donated for poor children (of 18 pieces they received). Parental value orientation was measured by a questionnaire in which parents were asked to indicate how much they would reward or punish 24 behaviors. The behaviors included doing bad, avoiding bad, doing good, and avoiding good. Scores for prescriptive and proscriptive orientations and for the frequency of use of rewards and punishments by parents were computed.

Parents whose value orientations were prescriptive had children who tended to give candy, whereas parents whose value orientations were proscriptive had children who tended not to give. Not only were these differences significant, but the association between parental value orientation and children's generosity was also significant when considered separately with regard to parents' use of rewards for doing good things (prescriptive) or for not doing bad things (proscriptive) and punishment for not doing good things (prescriptive) or for doing bad things (proscriptive). When differences in value orientation were controlled (statistically partialled out), the parents' use of reward and punishment did not, by itself, affect generosity. However, parents with a prescriptive orientation tended to use more rewards and fewer punishments than parents with a proscriptive orientation.

Finally, there was a significantly larger number of givers among children who themselves had a prescriptive orientation than among children who had a proscriptive orientation. The relationship between the parents' value orientations and the children's value orientations was, unfortunately, not reported.

Another study that concerned itself with differences in children's value orientations and their origins was conducted by Hoffman (1970b). In this study, as in previous research (Hoffman & Saltzstein, 1967), children were divided into two groups, one with external moral orientation and one with internalized moral values. The latter group was subdivided; subgroups that could be classified as humanistic or conventional in their internalized moral orientation were selected. Children who were both humanistic, in that they showed in projective story completions and moral judgments concern about the welfare of human beings, and flexible in applying standards, in that they considered extenuating circumstances for a person's behavior and justified deviation from social rules on the basis of such extenuating circumstances, were called humanistic. The children who justified moral judgment in terms of violation of institutional standards and tended to rigidly apply these standards regardless of the circumstances were called conventional. The two internal groups differed from the external group, but not from each other, on several independent measures of internalization: story-completion guilt intensity, teachers' rating of acceptance or denial of responsibility for misdeeds, and parental reports of confession after wrongdoing.

Hoffman (1970a) summed up the differences between the two internal groups in the following manner:

> The humanistic–flexible and conventional–rigid groups appear to be two variants of an internalized conscience which differ not only in the manifest content but also the hierarchical arrangement and motivational basis of their moral standards. Thus, in making moral judgments about other people's violations, the humanistic–flexible subjects tend to stress the consequences for others and are more likely to take extenuating circumstances into account. Their story completions suggest they are more tolerant and accepting of their own impulses. . . . They also appear to experience guilt primarily as a direct result of harmful consequences of their behavior for others, rather than unacceptable impulses in themselves. The conventional–rigid subjects, on the other hand, are more likely to give a religious or legal basis for their moral judgments and to ignore extenuating circumstances. . . . guilt stems less from the amount of harm actually done to others than from awareness of unacceptable impulses; and they tend to avoid expressing these impulses even in fantasy [p. 339].

These conclusions were based on varied data beyond those used to assign children to membership in the two groups. A major source of data was children's responses to projective stories. In one story the hero and a friend are on their way to a ball game, as they pass a small child who seems lost. The hero wants to stop but the friend convinces him that the child will be found anyway, but they will miss part of the game if they stop. The next day the hero discovers that the child was fatally struck by a car. Humanistic boys (although not girls) showed significantly more guilt on this story than conventional boys, but they did not differ in guilt on another story where the consequences of a transgression, cheating on an athletic contest, were not apparently harmful to anyone.

The humanistic value orientation appears to be similar to the prosocial orientation I have emphasized. The degree to which children who feel guilt about not having done something good or desirable will also have a desire to do good, or anticipate guilt for not responding to a human need, would be important to explore. The desire to do good and a feeling of guilt for not doing good or for causing harm should frequently coexist. To what extent is this so? To what extent are there individual differences, so that some people's motivations to help others are based on positive affect, on the experiencing or expectations of positive emotion from benefiting others, whereas others' motivations are based on negative affect? As I implied earlier, the likelihood that people with different value orientations will engage in prosocial behavior can be expected to vary. Humanistic children may be expected, for example, to respond more than conventional children to another person's distress or need, and to be less inhibited by rules of appropriate social behavior (Staub, 1974). They may have learned to consider and order the importance of various societal rules as a function of how they relate to human needs that exist at any one time. However, the actual relationship between humanistic (or prosocial) value orientations and behavior is largely unexplored. DePalma (1974) found second- and third-grade humanistic boys to be more generous in donating candy for a needy child in one experimental condition (when children received mild punishment before, in another phase of the study) but not in another condition (when they received greater punishment) than boys who had a "rigid" orientation. Rigidity was one aspect of the conventional moral orientation described by Hoffman. In several studies my students and I found that a prosocial orientation—measured in a relatively primitive way, by using a combination of tests relevant to prosocial values and to feelings of responsibility for others' welfare [1]—was positively related to helping someone in either physical or psychological distress (Staub, Erkut, & Jaquette, in Staub, 1974; see also Feinberg, 1977; Grodman, 1978; Volume 1, Chapter 2). Prosocial orientation and circumstances sometimes jointly affected helping. For example, Grodman found that more prosocial subjects were generally responsive to a person in psychological distress and generally more helpful, but a high cost of help reduced some forms of help to the level shown by low prosocial subjects.

---

[1] My associates and I have been developing a measure to specifically test a prosocial orientation or goal—as well as measures of achievement and approval goals, so that the joint (conflicting or additive) influence of varied motivational orientations on behavior can be evaluated (Staub, 1979).

Hoffman reported differences in the child-rearing practices of conventional and humanistic children, based on both parents' and children's reports. Parents of both groups of internal children showed more affection, used more induction, and used less power assertion than did parents of external children. In addition, parents of the conventional children more often reported love withdrawal as a discipline technique. They used love withdrawal particularly in response to the child's expression of anger but also in response to accidental damage caused by the child, and in other situations. Hoffman (1970a) concluded, on the basis of his review of the research on moral development, that love withdrawal does not "contribute to an internalized moral orientation but only to the inhibition of hostile impulses [p. 339]." He further speculated that love withdrawal in combination with low power assertion and frequent use of induction may lead to the inhibition of impulses in general. This may account for impulse inhibition as the characteristic basis of moral orientation that he found in conventional children. Mussen *et al.* (1970) reported that mothers' negative reactions to their children expressing anger and other impulses, although such reactions contributed to certain forms of honesty, were negatively associated with prosocial conduct.

In contrast to the tendency of parents of conventional children to use love withdrawal, regardless of the exact circumstances, parents of humanistic children appeared discriminative in their discipline practices. They used little love withdrawal. They tended to attend to reasons behind the child's actions. They dealt with anger firmly, but rather than using threat they tended to focus on the instigating disagreement, asking the child also to do so. Although they disapproved of destruction of other children's property even in response to instigation, and focused on the other's hurt feelings, just like conventional parents, they also demanded that their child attempt to repair the damage or help the other child repair the damage. Although the two groups of parents did not differ in the frequency of induction, parents of conventional children tended to use induction to point to or highlight the harm that the child's action caused the *parent*. Somewhat surprisingly, humanistic parents used more power assertion than conventional ones. Hoffman reasonably speculated that this may be necessary for the child to heed induction. To accidental damage, these parents responded in a permissive manner; apparently they inferred no negative intent and thus did not see the damage as within the child's control. The major differences seem to be the flexibility of the discipline used by parents of humanistic children—its dependence on context—and the difference in the use of love withdrawal.

Hoffman also discussed parental characteristics and identification with parents. Children in both internalized groups reported more identi-

fication with parents—emulation, liking, the desire to be like them—
than children who were externally oriented.

Parents of the two internal groups differed somewhat. One piece of
information came from responses to a story in which a boy told a lie to
protect a friend who was being teased by his peers. Fathers of boys and
mothers of girls of humanistic children were more likely to approve of
the lie than were parents of conventional children, and their responses
paralleled those of their children. These same-sex parents of humanistic
children were more likely than were parents of conventional children to
report that their own child would react as they did. Fathers of humanistic
boys tended to say significantly more often that the lying was right because it saved the other boy's feelings. On sentence-completion items
humanistic boys, completing the sentence, "The main thing about my
father is . . . ," tended to give more personal responses, such as "good
sense of humor" and "enjoys driving," and fewer power-structure responses, such as "too strict" or "not strict enough." This corresponds with
Hoffman's expectation of more "positional" identification by conventional children (identification of a defensive character, related to power
structure) and more personal identification by humanistic children (related to the child's desire to emulate personal characteristics of the
parent). According to Hoffman (1970a), when humanistic boys experience
conflict between conventional and humanistic norms,

> The father's unambiguously empathic response [as in the lying situa-
> tion just described] may then have an especially powerful effect
> because he is not just expressing his values didactically, but re-
> inforcing the empathy experienced by the child at the time and
> helping him resolve his own ambivalence [p. 342].

These findings and the related discussion are suggestive. However, the
judgment that fathers of humanistic children have an empathic quality
is based on only a few specific responses to moral judgment stories and
to subsequent probes, and not on any knowledge of the fathers' behavior.

This research on value orientations (rather than specific values) represents a beginning only. There is some, but not substantial, additional
evidence of the relationship of parental values to children's behavior
(Hoffman, 1975a). The existence of particular value orientations and
the origin of these orientations and of important specific values of children need to be explored. For example, how do individual differences
come about in the valuing of deserving, or equity, or justice in the world,
and in valuing mercy as well? For a start, different types of value orientations and their frequencies might be empirically tested. We need descriptive knowledge. Are there people who have value orientations that

center on reciprocity in human interactions, or on trust and brotherhood? I do not mean to provide these words as names of value orientations. I simply wish to ask whether there are certain constellations of values that frequently arise, in our culture and in others; what they are, and what behavioral consequences follow or are associated with them. What are their origins? We know very little about the answers to such questions.

There is some evidence of differences among children coming from bureaucratic families and those coming from entrepreneurial families. The former appear to be guided to a greater degree by a sense of responsibility toward other people. The latter's helpfulness is more reciprocal in character; their help is more contingent on receiving help from others (Berkowitz, 1972). Is the nature of their family's interaction with the outside world and consequently the nature of the child's experience of the world the origin of these differences, or do the differences stem more directly from differences in parental guidance?

There is also evidence that individual differences exist in trust in other human beings, in belief in the truthfulness or the reliability of what other people say (Rotter, 1971). There is, moreover, a relationship between college students' memories of their parents being trustworthy, keeping their words, not only about good things but also with regard to threat or punishment, and the students' scores on a measure of trust (Into, 1969). Whether such personal reports are reliable has to be checked. But it makes sense that such direct personal experience would affect the development of a personal belief in trust.

The different stages in Kohlberg's system may be regarded as value orientations that embody different primary principles as well as a hierarchy or organization of component values. As the examples of value orientations that I have discussed suggest, I believe that other value orientations are also likely to exist. Some of these a cognitive developmentalist may regard as content based, not structurally different—the structure of reasoning that underlies them may not differ. For example, one person may come to develop a prescriptive value orientation based on the general principle "Do good," whereas another may develop a proscriptive value orientation and come to be guided by the principle "Don't cause harm." We do not have enough empirical knowledge to specify what value orientations exist and what systems of classification or organization of them may be useful. Various writers suggested different value orientations. This brief review suggested some; Kohlberg's stages specify some. Garbarino and Bronfenbrenner (1976) suggested five moral judgment and behavior types: self-oriented, authority-oriented, peer-oriented, collective-oriented, and objectively oriented. Other writers proposed further systems of classifications. What empirically prevalent constellation of values are frequent still needs to be explored.

Value orientations, in my view, are general principles that organize constellations of specific standards and values. As Hogan (1973) suggested, human beings are rule-formulating and rule-following organisms. Value orientations imply specific standards and are likely to be the source of specific rules that people generate in response to specific situations. For example, humanistic orientation, with its emphasis on concern about other human beings' welfare, implies a variety of more specific standards prohibiting harm to others and promoting positive conduct. Value orientations must also have important emotional concomitants: They give rise to or embody affect that motivates and reinforces conduct. Values, value orientations, and behavioral tendencies develop not only through direct socialization but also through learning that results from the child's participation in varied activities and through interactive experience with peers. These sources of development are reviewed in the next two chapters.

Natural Socialization: Participation in Positive Behavior and Experiential Learning

Focusing Responsibility on Children and Learning by Participation

At several points in Chapter 4 I suggested that enacting or rehearsing prosocial behavior is important if children are to learn to behave prosocially. I also suggested that certain types of influences on children, such as verbal communications, will acquire meaning and gain acceptance when they are experienced in conjunction with ongoing prosocial action.

I have previously suggested (Staub, 1975a, 1975b, 1978c; Staub & Feinberg, 1978) that an important influence on children learning to behave prosocially is the focusing of responsibility on them by parents and other socializing agents to engage in behavior that enhances others' welfare. Focusing responsibility refers to the demand by the parent that the child engage in prosocial behavior. It does not refer to a method of discipline, such as love withdrawal or power assertion, which does not specify what values and behavior the parents wish to promote. Like induction, focusing responsibility on children to behave prosocially refers to a particular content area, to a particular type of behavior the parents wish to promote. Although responsibility assignment is likely to lead to knowledge of desirable behavior, knowledge of "family norms" or social norms, it can only be expected to lead to internalization and

189

self-guidance if socializers employ effective controls so that the child will actually behave prosocially. Thus, effective focusing of responsibility on children might result from a combination of parental values and parental actions that induce behavior consistent with these values in the child. However, focusing responsibility on children for activities that are in some sense prosocial might also be motivated by other values and by self-interest. At the extreme parents may insist that the child work around the house to the point of exploitation and an inequitable distribution of labor. Obviously the motives for responsibility assignment, equity, and many other conditions may determine its effect on the child.

A distinction may be made between two types of responsibility assignment, according to the degree to which they are structured. The need to act prosocially may emerge in the course of ongoing events; and may result in sharing toys with others, helping someone who had an accident or hurt himself in other ways, or consoling someone who is upset. Rewarding children for doing these things, punishing them for not doing them, and generally communicating to them that they are expected to behave prosocially under conditions like these would be one form of responsibility assignment. Such *less-structured* responsibilities may lead to the development of initiative on the part of children, since they often have to use their own judgment to determine what prosocial action is appropriate. Responsibility assignment may also be *more structured;* a child may be expected to take care of a younger sibling whenever the mother is not home or when she is otherwise occupied, or may have obligations for the maintenance and welfare of the family or some of its members. The more clearly specified the task—what it is, how it is done, and when it is done—the more structured the responsibility assignment.

An early study found that children who had pets acted more sympathetically toward their peers (Bathurst, 1933). Although the responsibility of taking care of pets might have increased these children's sensitivity to others, it is also possible that more sensitive children are more interested in having pets. Baumrind (1971, 1975) reported that part of the pattern of child rearing by parents of friendly and sociable children was the assignment of household duties to children. Mussen *et al.* (1970) reported that encouragement of responsibility by mothers was associated with peers' perceptions of a child's helpfulness, particularly in boys. Other relevant data came from several sources.

Evidence that provides tentative support for the influence of "structured" responsibility assignment on prosocial behavior comes from the cross-cultural research of John and Beatrice Whiting (1969; 1975). These investigators examined the behavior of children in six cultures and the relationship between the characteristics of the culture, child rearing, and children's behavior. They found that in some cultures children were more altruistic (they made more responsible suggestions to others, were more helpful, and so on), whereas in other cultures children were more egoistic (they sought help and attention for themselves). These cultures differed in a number of characteristics, including social organization and level of technological development. However, what was most strongly related to and in the researchers' view responsible for the differences among cultures in children's altruistic-egoistic tendencies was the degree to which children were assigned responsibilities that contributed to the maintenance of the family. The more the children had to tend animals, take care of younger siblings, and assume other "responsible" duties, the more altruistic their behavior. The children were found to be most egoistic in the "Yankee" town in the United States, in "Orchardtown." There, children's obligations in the family consisted primarily of keeping order in their own rooms, which was unlikely to give them much of a sense of importance for contributing to the welfare of the family.

Whiting and Whiting noted that parents did not use induction or gentle persuasion in the cultures that assigned extensive responsibility to children; rather, they exerted influence in a straightforward manner, to make sure that children actually did their (prosocial) tasks. What children learn from actually engaging in prosocial behavior will depend on a variety of surrounding conditions: the manner in which they are induced to do it, whether they are reinforced for it, the degree of satisfaction that they experience from the activity itself, the degree to which they learn to gain satisfaction from the positive consequences of their action, how demands on them compare to demands placed on other children in their culture, and so on.

If strong force is exerted on children to behave prosocially, a variety of negative consequences might follow. First, psychological reactance might be created, resulting in resistance or in children's trying to outsmart the authority exerting force. They may either not behave prosocially, or, if they do, they will make external rather than internal attributions about reasons for their prosocial behavior. However, several conditions might alter such consequences. First, in some cultures responsibility for others' welfare and efforts to contribute to the welfare of the group might be basic, universally enforced elements of the culture, so that the need to behave that way and the value underlying it will not be questioned. Moreover, a child's contribution to the welfare of his family or group can be so necessary, and important, that participation in prosocial behavior confers importance on the child.

When children's participation in prosocial activity is enforced over a period of time—even if this is done in a manner that on a single occasion might lead to resentment, reactance, and external attribution for acting prosocially—they might accept the values and norms inherent in such conduct and come to guide their behavior according to them. A person who consistently behaves in a particular way would find it difficult to maintain that he does so for purely external reasons.

One culture that seems to use responsibility assignment extensively, according to Bronfenbrenner (1970b), is the Soviet Union. The whole social milieu of children is shaped to make them learn that their conduct affects other children and others' conduct affects them, and that they are responsible to follow the rules of the collective and to make others follow the rules. A variety of methods are set up to make children assume responsibility for their collectives—which are defined at various levels: a small group the child is a member of, the child's whole class, his school, and his society. These methods include shaming, depriving a group of privileges when any one member's behavior is objectionable, and making children responsible for supervising and monitoring one another's activities. Thus children are both objects of others' supervision and agents in monitoring and guiding others' behavior. One specific example is that elementary-school children are assigned younger classmates, for whom they are responsible. They walk the child to school and are expected to help the child with any problems, particularly schoolwork. Their responsibility for the younger child is part of the curriculum; they receive a grade. Another example is that classwork is done in groups of about five peers, with each member responsible for all others. Still another example: When a child has been late in coming to school, one or two other children get the task (from their teacher, or from their small collective) to stop by his house and escort him to school in the morning. Bronfenbrenner (1970b) reported relatively low occurrence of disruptive and inconsiderate behavior among children in the Soviet schools.

In addition to such practices in schools, parents are educated in practices that will maximize rule obedience and cooperative behavior. Manuals in child rearing, which include specific examples of how to deal with particular problems, are prepared for both teachers and parents. Structured assignment of responsibility, and the opportunity to participate in prosocial behavior, often in a manner that might be intrinsically satisfying because it puts the child into a position of importance, seem fundamental aspects of these child-rearing practices, together with group supervision and enforcement of responsible activity.

What might be the effect of children's experiences in Russian schools on their prosocial behavior toward individuals in everyday settings—

for example, on their willingness to respond to someone in an emergency? Although Bronfenbrenner describes instances in which teachers encouraged prosocial behavior in interaction among individual children and discouraged negative behavior, it seems that the primary aim of the social education children receive is to instill a sense of responsibility toward the group and the collective society (Tschudnowski, 1974). An important aspect of this is rule-following behavior and a subjugation of one's interest to the group. It would be important to know to what extent this sense of responsibility is evoked when there is no accountability to an authority and when individual initiative is required. Would intensive socialization in following rules interfere with individual initiative?

In many societies, including our own, the older children in a family, particularly if the family is large, are especially likely to have responsibility focused on them to care for their younger siblings and protect them from mishaps and to assume various responsibilities in maintaining the family. Bossard and Boll (1956) provided detailed descriptions of the characteristics of large families, on the basis of an interview–questionnaire study of 100 such families. In these families responsibility was frequently focused on older children to care for the younger ones, to administer discipline while doing so, and often to run the house. These authors noted that several personality types developed among the children. One was the "responsible" type, which was seen most often in children, particularly older girls or the oldest one, who had responsibilities in the rearing of the younger children. Since the family circumstances often made it necessary for older children to assume responsibility, such a child could consider her role an important and meaningful one. Such responsibilities might therefore be accepted as legitimate and a sense of responsibility for others might become internalized. However, because such responsibilities are not a way of life for children in our culture, so that in comparison to others the child may feel heavily burdened, sometimes rebellion ensues. This might be particularly likely if the child or adolescent feels exploited because the parents and other children do not sufficiently share in the care of the family. Both issues are exemplified in the report of a girl, the oldest of eight children:

> By the time I was in the third grade, I was always helping mother while the others played with the neighboring children. This made me old beyond my years, serious, and quite responsible for all that went on in the household. . . . Each Saturday, my mother went into the city six miles away for the groceries and stayed for the day. In the evening she and dad visited friends and came home about midnight. From age fifteen to nineteen, I found myself responsible for seeing that the housework was finished, cooking lunch and dinner for the children, and caring for the newest baby. At night, I bathed

six children, washed their heads, and tucked them into bed. Saturday
nights continued like this until I rebelled. I wanted to have time
for dates like other girls had [Bossard & Boll, 1956, pp. 159–160].

I am proposing that involvement with responsible activities will
lead to a sense of personal responsibility toward others, which, as the
research showed (Volume 1, Chapters 2, 3, 5), is an important influence
on prosocial behavior. However, the nature, magnitude, and other
aspects of such responsible activities would modify what is learned from
them. Actually, the girl in the foregoing example, even though she ultimately rebelled against her exploitation, might still have acquired a
prosocial tendency that she expressed in her interaction with others.

The proposed relationship between birth order and prosocial behavior has been found in experimental studies of children's reactions to
sounds of distress from another child in an adjoining room. Oldest siblings tend to be most helpful (Staub, 1970b, 1971a,d), whereas youngest
ones tend to be least helpful (Staub, 1970b). In pairs of children who
together heard sounds of distress and did not actively help by going into
the adjoining room, upon the return of the experimenter about a minute
and a half after the distress sounds were over, the children in the pairs
who were oldest siblings were more likely to report that something
happened, or to be the first to respond to the experimenter's questions,
than children in other birth positions (Staub, 1970b). These findings are
somewhat surprising, because oldest siblings appear less certain of themselves in social situations and are less popular with their peers (Hartup,
1970). That they initiate more helping acts may be the result of greater
demands placed on them to be responsible for others' welfare. An alternative hypothesis should also be considered, however: Oldest siblings
have a more intense relationship with their parents and, to the degree
that the parents hold prosocial values, they are more likely to adopt
them.

Like older siblings, older children who are part of a social group
may have responsibility focused on them to respond to the needs of
younger children, or awareness of their greater competence may lead
them to assume responsibility and to respond helpfully to the needs of
younger children.

Children who spend substantial amounts of time in a social group
in which the ages of peers vary may learn to be helpful by observing
helpful acts done by older children, by experiencing such acts when they
are directed at them, and by acting in a "responsible" prosocial manner
when they themselves are older. Bizman, Yinon, Mitzvari, and Shavit
(1978) found, in fact, that children 5 years of age and older in age-

heterogeneous kindergartens in Israeli cities and kibbutzim were more helpful than same-age children who came from age-homogeneous kindergartens. The former children were more likely to choose helpful alternatives in deciding what was the best response to two situations that were described to them, and they shared more pretzels that they won in a game with children who would not have a chance to play. The authors note that the 5-year-olds in the heterogeneous kindergarten "already learned with older children when [they] were only four years old [Bizman *et al.*, 1978, p. 156]." Since apparently they did so in the same kindergarten, whereas children attended the homogeneous kindergarten for a shorter time, the findings may have been affected by the greater familiarity of children in the heterogeneous kindergarten both with the setting and with the other children, the recipients of their generosity. There were no differences between city and kibbutz children in this study.

In several foregoing examples, responsibility was focused on children with some degree of pressure, although in some cases, as with older siblings, responsibility may be "naturally theirs." Because of their greater competence, older siblings may naturally assume the roles of protector of younger siblings from harm and of caretaker for them. Sometimes these and other responsibilities will be regarded by children, or can be presented to them, as a privilege rather than a duty. The role they are cast into, the demands placed on them, indicate trust in their competence or ability, have prestige attached to them, and might have varied intrinsically rewarding aspects. Given these surrounding conditions participation in prosocial activity would not produce reactance or resistance. On the contrary, it would be a rewarding experience to the actor. In earlier writings (Staub, 1975a,b; Staub & Feinberg, 1978) I distinguished between children being the targets of instruction, instruction being aimed at them, and children learning through participation in activities that are meaningful and rewarding to them (indirect instruction).

What experiences might be regarded as indirect instruction? At an early age a child might be asked to "help Mommy." The implication that the child's help is needed makes the child a valued collaborator. In the cultures that Whiting and Whiting studied the children's responsible duties were important for the maintenance of the family. The children may have gained a sense of importance from being collaborators in an important enterprise.

An incidental finding of one of our experiments (Staub & Buswell, unpublished research) also suggested the positive results of children acting as collaborators of adults, and of indirect instruction. We used several procedures in this study in our attempt to enhance prosocial behavior. In one treatment group one child, the subject, was working on a task, while another child, a confederate, was doing other things in the same room. Sometimes these were play activities, but in the course of other "activities" the confederate needed help (for example, once she fell off a chair, and another time she could not reach an object high up on a shelf). Using a buzzer as a signal, we tried to teach our subjects that under some circumstances, when another person needs help, it is "appropriate" (Staub, 1971b) to interrupt whatever they are doing in order to provide help. The confederates, children from the same population as the subjects, were taken to the experimental room by the experimenter before the subjects entered and trained to engage in a variety of activities in response to cue cards. They performed these activities after the subject joined them in the room. Either 1 day or 1 week after the training, both the subjects' and the confederates' helping and sharing behavior was evaluated. The confederates attempted to help significantly more in response to sounds of distress by another child than subjects in any of four experimental groups. A number of these children spontaneously verbalized the principle that we tried to teach the subjects in the experimental session, that one ought to help others when they need help.

Children who are provided with the opportunity to teach other children benefit the child they teach, but being given the responsibility to teach can be viewed by them as a privilege, and might be intrinsically rewarding. There has been, since the 1960s, an apparently nationwide movement in the schools to use older children as tutors for younger ones (Allen, 1976; P. Lippitt, 1969; R. Lippitt, 1968; Thelen, 1969). This has been called *cross-age tutoring.*

In such programs, both well-functioning children and children with behavioral problems are used as tutors. Informal reports provided by the writers cited suggest that participation may improve the academic performance of both the child being taught and the tutor (who is usually the focus of interest). It may reduce the behavioral problems of both participants and may result in greater self-confidence as well as other positive personality changes in the tutor. Based on her observations, Lippitt (1968) wrote that "dramatic" changes result from participation as tutors and explained this as a result of the students' being in a collaborative effort with the teachers. In a few primarily unpublished studies, when low achieving or poorly motivated children tutored younger children for an extended period, the tutors showed positive gains in self-attitudes or self-concepts (see Feldman, Devin-Sheehan, & Allen, 1976).

What kind of learning results from doing? Focusing responsibility on children will, minimally, make them aware of parental and/or societal values. When they are successfully induced to engage in prosocial behavior, in a consistent fashion, they might learn, at the least, that people are expected to do things for others; that other people regard such behavior as an obligation, and that one can expect rewards for doing so and punishment for not doing so. Under certain conditions children are likely to internalize values and norms of prosocial conduct. First, they might come to believe that people ought to assume responsibility in relation to other people. Second, they may come to regard it as their own obligation to assume responsibility for others. If they evaluate their own behavior as internally guided, they might come to regard themselves as people who do and will assume responsibility when others' welfare is involved. Their concern about others' welfare and their empathic capacity may also increase. Some of the conditions that may make these consequences more or less probable have already been mentioned. They include (probably in our culture, where values of individuality and self-interest often conflict with prosocial values, and where children's contributions, in many segments of society, are not essential for survival) not overly coercive ways of inducing children to behave responsibly or prosocially and an association between prosocial behavior and cognitions that amplifies reasons for and positive consequences of behaving prosocially. Participation in responsible prosocial action can be induced so it will be perceived as an important, privileged activity, or as a collaborative activity with an adult socializer, or as an activity that is intrinsically satisfying. The association of the rewarding nature of such responsibilities with others' welfare and with the sense of power or competence that results from being able to enhance others' welfare might lead the child to view his own interests as identical with those of others—or at least as associated rather than conflicting. Helping others might then be experienced not as a sacrifice, but as a contribution to the self, the increase in others' welfare resulting in empathic reinforcement—in a parallel change in the actors' own emotions. (Such a change in personal orientation will not, of course, always gain expression in behavior, which is determined in a complex fashion—see Chapter 1; Volume 1.)

Learning by doing and by participating may be regarded as examples of experiential learning. Teaching others, or participating in helping other people, can also provide opportunities for role-taking experiences in interaction with others, which, according to cognitive developmental theory, is crucial for the moral development of children. The notion of interactive experience as a source of learning and development and the exploration of experiential learning is extremely important not only from the cognitive developmental perspective, but from any perspective that seriously concerns itself with the child's growth and development. The dimensions of experiences that contribute to the development of prosocial behavior and morality in general will have to be progressively elaborated and defined, and the processes by which they induce learning and the kind of learning or change that results from them will have to be specified. Moreover, children's personalities—what they have learned from parents, the kinds of persons they have already become—will determine the effect of particular experiences on them. Depending on prior learning and experience they will perceive objectively identical experiences differently and they will learn different things from them.

Experimental Research on Learning by Participation and Interactive Experience

Direct Instruction for and Participation in Prosocial Action

A variety of experiments suggest that telling children what to do will affect their behavior, at least in the short run, as much as or more than exposure to a model. This has been found in studies in which verbalizations to children clearly specified that they were expected to donate (Grusec, 1972; Grusec & Skubicki, 1970; Rice & Grusec, 1975; see Volume 1, Chapter 5). Experiments in setting standards for self-reinforcement showed that verbally imposing standards on children resulted in greater adherence to the standards than did exposure to models (Masters and Mokros, 1974, Chapter 4). Other studies also show that focusing responsibility on people for others' welfare, in a specific manner, affects their behavior. In one study (Staub, 1970a), first-graders' attempts to help a child apparently in distress in an adjoining room were greater when they were left "in charge" by the experimenter, to "take care of things," and subsequently heard the distress sounds. Moreover, kindergarten children, whose helping behavior did not increase as a result of responsibility being focused on them, perhaps because they were too young to know what to do upon the experimenter's return, tended to deny that they heard distress sounds more often than those who did not have responsibility focused on them, presumably because they feared disapproval for not helping. In another study Tilker (1970) found that subjects who were asked to observe another person administering shocks to a learner, in a Milgram-type situation, were more likely to interfere with the further administration of shocks when they were made responsible for the learner's welfare, and when there was more feedback about the consequences of the shocks, that is, more signs of distress of the person receiving the shocks.

These studies show the immediate consequences of imposing standards of conduct on people or making them responsible for others' welfare. By frequently or regularly assigning responsibility to children (and adults?) in this manner, the consequences described earlier may occur. However, one cannot assume from the immediate consequences of responsibility assignment on behavior in the same setting that more extensive responsibility assignment will produce generalized and enduring consequences. Other experimental studies, however, have provided further information about delayed or generalized effects of responsibility assignment and participation in prosocial action.

Groups of experiments that were reviewed in Volume 1 showed that the experience of positive behavior affects subsequent performance of similar behavior and/or related feelings. Being part of a group of cooperating individuals enhanced liking for both others in the group and persons outside the group (for example, class members) by children (Chapter 9). When people were induced to engage in a single positive act of some sort they were more likely to engage in a second positive act, in comparison to persons in control groups (Chapter 5).

Rosenhan and White (1967) found that children who donated more of the rewards that they earned when they privately played a bowling game were those who donated in the model's presence during a training period, when the model and the child took turns playing the bowling game. These researchers proposed that the rehearsal of modeled behavior was an important contributor to later prosocial behavior. Possibly, however, the individual characteristics of certain children led them to donate both in the model's presence and in her absence.

In an experiment with fourth- and fifth-grade subjects, White (1972) explored the contribution of rehearsal to later donating behavior. In one of the treatment groups, guided rehearsal (GR), the children played the bowling game in the experimenter's presence and won two gift certificates on two out of five trials. The experimenter told the child beforehand that "what we would like you to do is to give one certificate to the orphans each time you win two." When they won, the children were reminded to donate. This might be considered a condition in which responsibility was directly focused on children. In the observation plus unguided rehearsal condition (UR) the subject and experimenter took turns, each winning twice. The experimenter each time put one of his gift certificates into a "charity box," but gave no cues to the child as to what he or she should do. In the observation condition the experimenter alone played five games, won on two, and donated half her winnings. In a control group the experimenter simply pointed out the charity box and then left the child to play the game alone. In all conditions except the control group half of the children were left alone to play the game immediately after the training period (Session 1) and they again played the bowling game alone 5 days later (Session 2). This was called the *played-immediately condition.* The other half of the children only played the bowling game 5 days later (*played-later condition*). In the control group all children played only immediately after training.

An analysis of the data of the played-immediately condition showed that, across the two sessions, children in the GR condition donated most, followed by those in the UR, observation, and control conditions. For males, the GR condition resulted in significantly more donations in Session 1 than any other treatment. For females the same was true numerically but the difference with the UR condition was not significant. For females, UR enhanced donating over the control condition. In Session 2 differences were generally not significant although children, particularly females, tended to donate more in the two rehearsal conditions than those in the other two conditions.

An analysis compared donations by children in the played-immediately condition during the first session, and donations by children in the played-later condition—that is, the amount children donated at the first opportunity, which was either immediately after training or 5 days later. The average donation in the GR played-immediately group was 4.8 for males and 4.5 for females; their combined average in the delayed group was 1.97. In the UR played-immediately group, the average donation was 1.6 for males and 2.9 for females, and 1.40 in the delayed group. In the observation-alone group the average donation was .5 for males and 1.3 for females, and 1.37 in the delayed condition. The analysis showed significantly fewer donations in both rehearsal conditions on delayed than on immediate testing, the difference particularly large in the GR condition, somewhat smaller in the UR condition. Somewhat more donations were found in the observation-alone condition when testing was delayed. A further important finding emerged from a comparison of Session 2 sharing by children in the played-immediately condition and in the delayed condition. In this analysis a comparison was made of the donations of children 5 days after training. The children either did or did not have a prior opportunity to donate. No significant difference was found between children as a function of this prior experience to donate. Overall, guided rehearsal subjects donated significantly more than observation plus unguided rehearsal subjects, and subjects in the latter group donated more than those in the observation group. Girls donated more than boys.

The findings showed that telling children to donate and then observing them while they had the opportunity to donate result in substantial donations immediately after training and somewhat more donations at a later time, than resulted from other procedures. Children who were more subtly induced to "rehearse" also tended to donate more than children who simply observed a model. On the basis of the greater decline in donations from Session 1 to Session 2 among children in the guided-rehearsal than in the unguided-rehearsal condition, White stressed the superiority of the latter over the former as a means of inducing pro-social behavior. However, children in the guided-rehearsal condition donated at least numerically more at every point in time, and substantially more immediately after their training experience, which accounts for the greater decline from Session 1 to Session 2. Despite the greater decline in their donations from the immediate test, children who experienced guided rehearsal tended to donate more than other children 5 days after the experimental session, suggesting some persistence of the influence of prior rehearsal. A covariance analysis to evaluate how the amount children donated earlier affected later donations would have been useful. Children in the guided-rehearsal condition who donated a great deal during the first private testing might have felt that they had done their share and therefore donated less later. As the result of prior giving the total amount that they had for themselves was apparently less than what the other children had. What a person has already done for others is likely to influence later actions. Most people must feel, under many circumstances when they have shared or helped, particularly when the recipients are not in immediate and observable need, that they have done their share for the time being. Given the same recipients for the children's donations and otherwise the same circumstances, this might have been true in White's study.

A suggestive finding is that children in the guided-rehearsal condition "stole" more (took more) unearned rewards for themselves than did children in the unguided rehearsal. This suggests resentment in response to the pressure to make sacrifices. However, it was the children who did not respond to this pressure by donating, who resisted it from the beginning, who later stole candy. None of the children in the guided-rehearsal condition stole in Session 1. Of the 13 guided-rehearsal subjects who did not donate at all in Session 1, 6 stole in Session 2; only two additional children stole in Session 2 in this condition. The number of children who stole in the observation and control conditions was not different from those in the unguided-rehearsal condition, and fewer children in the unguided-rehearsal condition stole than in the guided-rehearsal condition. These findings suggest a personality difference. Some children reacted to the demand for donations in the guided-rehearsal condition resentfully, not sharing and later taking "unearned" gift certificates.

In summary, both focusing responsibility and then having children donate, and inducing children to donate without verbally focusing responsibility on them, increased later donations. However, some children did appear to respond negatively to the verbal demand to donate, presumably as a result of characteristics that they developed in the course of their prior experience. White did not present information about how many children donated during the training, actually "rehearsed" in the presence of the experimenter, and how this and variations in amounts they donated related to later donations. Such information is important, given the intention to evaluate the effects of rehearsal.

In another study White and Burnam (1975) had fourth- and fifth-grade girls play a game. The girls had to push buttons, and they won five pennies when the "right" combination of two buttons was pushed. They had the opportunity to donate this money to needy orphans. Some children were told they could donate, but that they did not have to (permissive instructions). Others were told that the experimenter would like them to donate some of the pennies each time they won (constraining instructions). Some children took turns with the experimenter in playing the game (public donation condition) and others watched the experimenter play (private donation condition). The experimenter donated different amouts: either 80% or 60% or 40% or 20% or none of her winnings. In a no-modeling control group the experimenter put pennies that she had won into a dispenser. Then the experimenter left, telling the child that she would not return, and that after the child finished playing, when the buzzer rang, she could take what she won and return to her classroom. The children then played alone, winning on six trials. An analysis of children's private donations across all conditions showed that constraining instructions resulted in substantially more donations. There was also a complex interaction in the effects of different instructions, the amount donated by the model and grade level. The amount that children donated while taking turns with the experimenter (public donation) was affected both by modeling (children donated more in the 80, 60, and 40% modeling conditions than in the 20% and no-modeling conditions) and by instructions (children again donated more in the constraining instruction conditions). A covariance analysis of the public donation conditions, eliminating the influence of differences in public donations on subsequent private donations, showed only a grade effect; fifth-graders donated more.

The constraining instructions forcefully stated a situational rule, which children then followed shortly afterward while playing the game by themselves. The children who had the opportunity to donate both publicly and privately acted in a similar way in the presence of the experimenter as they acted in her absence. Eliminating variations in public donations also eliminated differences in the effects of treatments on private donations.

In another study Dressel and Midlarsky (1976) examined verbal and modeling effects on children's donations. They exposed children either to a generous model, who sometimes donated all, other times half of what she won (four pennies) on each winning trial of a bowling game, or to a greedy model, who donated nothing. Before playing the game the model either stated a variety of reasons for donating to needy children in a local orphanage, using both inductive and normative statements, and later added further "exhortations," or made verbal statements about her desire to win and keep the rewards, exhorting greed. The model played the game for 10 trials and then, while the child played for 10 trials, the model stood behind the child, telling him or her on some trials either to donate or to keep the rewards. Thus, the model's example, her exhortations, and her demands to donate varied. Different types of inconsistencies among the three influences resulted from the procedures. After the children played the game in the model's presence, the model was called away, and they continued to play privately for 20 trials, with continued opportunity to donate. Both the model's behavior and the demands that the child be charitable or selfish significantly affected donating in the model's presence, but, of the two, what the model told the child to do accounted for a substantially greater proportion of the variance. When children donated privately the influence of the model's behavior disappeared but the demands on the child continued to have a substantial influence, and exhortation also had a significant effect, both in the expected direction. There was also a marginally significant interaction between demands and exhortations, and a significant three-way interaction between these variables and sex. When the model both demanded and exhorted charity, children donated a high percentage of their money when they played privately. Girls' donations were high only in this condition; they were relatively low in the other three combinations of demands and exhortations. The treatments had more of a combinatorial influence on boys, with inconsistent demands and exhortations leading to intermediate levels of donations.

Focusing responsibility on the child to donate (making demands) and/or verbally giving reasons to donate had substantially greater effect on private donations than did behavioral modeling. The authors suggest that this might have had something to do with the age of the children, who were seventh- to ninth-graders. They might have been more capable of perceiving and integrating verbal communications than younger children. The "best" predictor of the subjects' private donations was their public donation; there was a highly significant relationship between the two. Thus, again, a rehearsal effect was found, prior prosocial behavior influencing later prosocial behavior. Demands substantially affected the children's prosocial behavior in the presence of the model. Exhortations to donate, verbal reasons, might have acquired an influence that affected private behavior by their association with the children's earlier, publicly performed prosocial behavior.

Inconsistency between the model's practices and her demands on the child, in either direction, resulted in more negative evaluation of the model than did the model's consistency. Previous research with younger children showed that what the model does and what the model says affect the evaluation of the model, but inconsistency itself between the model's practices and exhortations has no effect (Bryan & Walbek, 1970a,b). In contrast, inconsistency between a standard for self-reward that an adult imposed on the child (a stringent rule) and a standard imposed on himself (a lenient rule) resulted in stealing by children (Rosenhan et al., 1968). Thus inconsistency between an adult's actions and rules that he imposes on the child, which deprive the child of rewards, might lead to negative reactions by children and affect the adults' later capacity to exert influence over the child (Midlarsky et al., 1973).

Finally, in a study that was described in Chapter 4, Grusec et al. (1978) also found that direct instruction to children to donate enhanced later prosocial behavior, particularly when their donations following the direct instruction were attributed to the kind of person they were. Both White's (1972) interpretation of guided rehearsal as ineffective even though its influence was stronger on an immediate test and remained at least as strong or stronger on a delayed test than of other treatments and Grusec et al.'s (1978) expression of surprise over the influence of direct instruction ("This failure to find less donation in direct instruction than in modeling conditions is puzzling; it attests, if nothing else, to the desire to comply that apparently exists in the experimental paradigm we have used here [p. 56].") are indications that the reasoning developed and the conclusions suggested in this chapter are contrary to current theories. According to current views, direct influence, such as telling children how to behave, is unlikely to be effective in socializing them for desirable conduct. It is assumed that direct influence will not lead children to make self-attributions or to internalize values or reasons that would later again promote such behavior. The theory that has been presented in this chapter suggests, however, that participation in positive behavior can be an important source of later behavior. When children are induced, without undue force, to participate in positive behavior, the likelihood that their later behavior will be affected may be greater than it is following exposure to varied other influences, frequently even modeling and induction, particularly when these do not succeed in inducing positive behavior. However, what represents undue force needs to be further explored and defined. Sometimes the joining of two influences has less effect on children than one or both of the separate influences (Staub, 1971d, 1972b), perhaps because the combination is too forceful. Setting a behavioral rule for children does not seem to be a forceful procedure. Direct instruction for positive behavior, under circumstances when children are likely to see no alternative to following the instructions, may not arouse psychological processes that would interfere with learning or arouse them to a lesser degree than some other procedures. They may arouse less resistance than other verbal communications that do not set a rule but exert pressure to voluntarily behave prosocially, to make voluntary sacrifices for others.

Participation, Teaching Others, and Induction

My students and I conducted a series of experiments to explore the influence of participation in various types of prosocial activities—sometimes by itself, sometimes in combination with induction—on various types of subsequent prosocial behavior.

As I already reported, in one of these experiments (Staub, 1975b; Staub & Fotta, 1978) the combination of repeated participation in a prosocial activity (making puzzles for hospitalized children) and induction increased girls' but not boys' subsequent prosocial behavior and expressed prosocial intentions; boys were somewhat affected by the separate procedures.

In another study (Staub, Leavy, & Shortsleeves, 1975) we explored the effects of teaching others on children's later prosocial behavior. Some fifth- and sixth-grade girls learned a prosocial activity, first-aid techniques; others learned a neutral activity, making puzzles. In one condition the girls were individually trained in these activities and then practiced them for a period of time (no teaching). In another condition the girls were told, before the training period, that they would teach these activities to younger children; following the training each subject did indeed teach a younger child. Teaching another child resulted in participants writing significantly more letters to hospitalized children, about a week after the training session, clearly a generalized and delayed effect of the training. Interestingly, there was an interaction in the effects of teaching and its content: The experience of teaching had a greater effect on children who taught a younger child to make a puzzle. At least two interpretations of this seem reasonable. First, the children who taught first-aid skills did not directly benefit the learner, but potentially benefited other people whom the learner could in turn help. In contrast, the children who taught puzzle making were told that the purpose of this was to enable children to make their own toys, which might be satisfying to them. These children might have felt that they were directly benefiting the child they taught, which may have resulted in a stronger association between the satisfaction experienced in teaching and the awareness of benefiting another person. Second, learning and teaching first-aid skills was more complicated, and perhaps the participants experienced less mastery and consequently less satisfaction from their role.

A potentially important finding of this study was that ratings by the experimenter (who observed the children through a one-way mirror) of the teacher's responsiveness to the child she taught—the teacher considering the younger child's ability in setting the pace, listening and responding to the learner, and so on—were significantly positively related to the number of letters that the teacher wrote. Responsiveness by the teacher was also significantly related to the learner's responsiveness to the teacher. First, existing characteristics of some children might have enabled them to be more responsive as teachers, perhaps experiencing more satisfaction as a result, and being more affected by the experience. Second, the characteristics of the learner may have affected the teacher's and the learner's responsiveness to each other, with a similarly positive effect on the teacher. Both could be true. However, responsiveness by teachers was also a function of the children's experience in training. Children who participated in the training with one of the experimenters later wrote more letters than those who participated with the other experimenter, regardless of treatment conditions. Similar differences were found in the influence of the two experimenters on the children's responsiveness to each other. It should not be surprising at this point that the characteristics of a "socializer," no matter how temporary a socializer that person is, modify her influence.

As in our earlier study (Staub & Fotta), the experimental treatments did not affect the number of gift certificates that children donated for needy children immediately after the training, probably for similar reasons. They received these gift certificates for their participation, and could put their donations into a box outside the room on their way back to the classroom. Having just earned them, and believing that they deserved them, they might have been unwilling to part with them, in all treatment conditions.

In a further experiment we attempted to explore the effects of three experimental procedures—participating in a prosocial activity, teaching others, and induction—on subsequent prosocial behavior (Staub & Jancaterino as presented in Staub, 1975b). I will communicate some of the complex findings and experiences with this project that highlight important issues about the methodology of such research.

In exploring the effects of teaching, we intended to make several improvements. In the previous experiment, the content of instruction varied in different experimental groups. In this experiment the content was the same, puzzle making, but the reason for making the puzzles was varied. In one of the direct instruction (no teaching) groups children learned to make puzzles so they could make some for hospitalized children, then continued to work on the puzzles for a while (prosocial group). In another group children learned to make puzzles for hospitalized children but were also given a list of induction statements to read and rehearse that pointed out the benefits that making puzzles for hospitalized children were likely to produce (prosocial–induction group). They were told that knowing the consequences of their behavior was likely to make helping others enjoyable. Then they spent some time working on the puzzles.[1] In a third group (not prosocial) children learned to make puzzles and then spent time working on them; they were asked to do this because it might be enjoyable for them to learn to make their own toys. In three parallel conditions children taught another child puzzle making. In the prosocial teaching group children learned to make puzzles so they could teach younger children to make puzzles for hospitalized children. Then they taught a younger child how to make the puzzle. In a second teaching group children also received and rehearsed the list of induction statements, to be used while teaching the younger child. They were told that the younger children would find helping more enjoyable if they knew the consequences of their behavior, and that they would be more likely to help. In a third group the children taught the younger child how to make puzzles because "it might be enjoyable for children to learn how to make their own toys." With subjects varying in sex, we had a $2 \times 3 \times 2$ design (teaching–not teaching; prosocial activity–prosocial activity with induction–no prosocial activity; and sex).

Following the treatment sessions, subjects' willingness to donate gift certificates was tested. They received the gift certificates either 1 or 2 days

---

[1] This group served primarily as a control for the teaching–prosocial–induction group described later. In that group, teachers read and rehearsed induction statements so that they could use them in teaching other children. Although reading and rehearsing induction statements to make the task more enjoyable might have appeared contrived to the children in the no-teaching condition, we wanted both to expose children who did not teach to induction and to equate their degree of familiarity with the induction statements, because that might be an important determinant of whether children are affected by them.

after the treatment or several days, mostly 5–6, afterward, and then they were asked to donate some of the gift certificates to a group of needy children.

Eleven days after the gift-certificate test, the next posttest, the envelopes test, was administered. Each subject received two large manila envelopes and was told that he or she might want to fill the envelopes with pictures, stories, or poems, cut out of magazines or copied from magazines and books, and other items. The children were told that these envelopes would be given to children who did not have families and had few attractive objects or toys of their own. Finally, 2 weeks after the envelopes test, the subjects were administered the puzzles test. They received three large envelopes containing unmade puzzles of the same kind that they had previously worked on. When they received the puzzles, they were asked how many of these puzzles they thought they would make for hospitalized children (intentions measure). The puzzles that they actually made were collected in 3 days.

Scores for both the envelopes test and the puzzles test were derived by two independent raters on the basis of how much work the material that the children handed in represented and, in the case of the envelopes test, how much material sacrifice it involved. Agreement between the raters was over 90% in both cases.

Analyses of variance showed a significant effect of teaching on donating gift certificates. Children who taught other children donated more gift certificates. There was a highly significant sex effect; girls donated more. The timing of the test of donation was varied, to explore the possibility that children who receive gift certificates later, when the feeling of deserving might be less acute, would share more. Correlations computed within each treatment group between the number of days that the donation test followed the treatment and the number of gift certificates that children donated showed that in the three nonteaching groups and in one of the teaching groups (prosocial–no induction) the relationship was negligible. However, in the other two teaching groups, the longer the delay after the treatment session, the more gift certificates children donated. This might be interpreted as support for the hypothesis that teaching would enhance children's donations when their feeling that the gift certificates were earned and deserved was less acute.

The other measures of helping were affected by treatments only in interaction with sex or children's "quad" or classroom membership. All subjects came from one of two open classrooms, with about 100 children in each. Girls helped more than boys, marginally significantly more on the envelope test ($p < .10$) and substantially more on the puzzles test ($p < .002$); girls also intended to make more puzzles ($p < .001$). In addition, on both the envelopes test ($p < .01$) and the puzzles test ($p < .01$) children who came from Quad 1 helped significantly more than children who came from Quad 2.

The treatments did not affect children's envelopes test scores. On the intention to make puzzles, there was a significant teaching by sex interaction ($p < .05$) and a significant prosocial treatment by sex interaction ($p < 05$). Girls were unaffected by either treatment, whereas boys who taught intended to make more puzzles than boys who did not teach ($\overline{X} = 3.42$ versus 2.07) and boys who were in the not-prosocial group intended to make fewer puzzles than boys in the prosocial–induction and prosocial groups. Finally, the analysis of variance of the puzzles scores showed a significant prosocial treatment by quad membership interaction ($p < .05$). The pattern of means showed that in Quad 1 the prosocial treatment enhanced most strongly the amount that children worked on the puzzles for hospitalized children, but in Quad 2 the prosocial–induction treatment did so. One of the two treatment groups did elevate helping behavior in each quad in comparison to the nonprosocial group.

The extent to which the children's sex and the classroom that they came from affected prosocial behavior on all the measures was impressive. The sex effect was stronger than in most of our prior research. In this experiment we deviated from our previous practice of using experimenters of one sex, usually females, with all subjects. Instead, female experimenters conducted the treatment sessions with girls, and male experimenters conducted them with boys. Therefore the sex differences might, in part, be caused by the sex of the experimenter, which covaried with the sex of the subject. Are females more influential with girls, or more influential in general, than males are with boys or with either boys or girls?

As reported earlier, there were significant experimenter effects in the first study. Additional analyses in this later experiment showed that helping behavior varied not only according to sex (of the experimenters and subjects) but, to some extent, also as a function of which of the two male or two female experimenters conducted the session (although there were no experimenter by treatment interaction effects). Combined with other researchers' findings about experimenter effects, these findings strongly suggest the need for research in this area. More must be learned about the differences in the effects of male and female experimenters (and socializing agents) with boys and girls, as well as differences in the influence of experimenters as a function of their manner of interaction with children.

The difference in behavior related to quad membership points to another important issue. The atmosphere established in a classroom, whether it is primarily cooperative or competitive, whether it is more or less friendly, and so on, can have important effects on the behavior of children independently of the socioeconomic and cultural composition of classrooms. In addition, the attitude of teachers toward the children's participation in a project can have important effects. I believe that at least part of the reason for the quad differences was a difference in the teachers' attitudes. As the experiment progressed, we encountered difficulties in Quad 2 in securing the continued cooperation of the teachers. The results might well reflect the attitude that these teachers communicated to the children. It was also interesting that on our first measure, the donations of gift certificates, there was no significant quad effect. On the other measures, which took place later, after conflicts became apparent, there were significant quad effects.

A related issue to that of the influence of teachers is how our subjects perceive what we do, what they tell each other about it, and what meaning a project acquires and what attitudes develop toward it. The shared evaluation of a project that probably inevitably develops may be as powerful a determinant of the children's behavior in it as anything specific that we do. It is important to learn about such shared evaluation among children, but it is difficult to do so. Perhaps asking half the subjects in our experimental groups to describe their thoughts, feelings, and opinions about the experiment, and evaluating the behavior of the other half, might provide such information.

We conducted another elaborate experiment, with fourth-, fifth-, and sixth-grade children, to explore further the effects of induction, of participating in a prosocial activity, and of teaching on children's varied prosocial behaviors (Staub & Feinberg, 1977a). We again made several changes, what we regard as improvements, in our procedures. A deficiency in the last study was the lack of a control group in which children would have a truly neutral experience. As my conception of the influence of participation in prosocial activity evolved, it led to the belief that both kinds of participation, making puzzles for hospitalized children, and teaching others—either to do some good in turn or to do something beneficial to or enjoyable for the learner—would increase later prosocial behavior. Thus, all the treatment conditions in the previous experiment might be expected to increase, to some extent, later prosocial behavior. Therefore, in this experiment, we included a control group in which children were simply asked to make toys during the training. They were not given a specific reason for doing so. We also thought that induction might be more effective if children could participate in thinking up the benefits that would result from their activity. Therefore, in the treatment group where children experienced induction they were asked to suggest what benefits might follow from making toys for hospitalized children. The experimenter wrote down their ideas, suggesting others so that the same basic set of positive consequences was always included. It is important to note that we sacrificed somewhat the ability to draw theoretical conclusions, for meaningfulness. In all relevant experimental groups children were briefly told about some beneficial consequences of making toys for poor hospitalized children, since to ask children to do that without some explanation seemed artificial and unreasonable. Thus we contrasted minimal with elaborate induction. We also thought that puzzle making might be too restrictive an activity, that some children might not like it. Therefore, we had materials prepared for a variety of different toys that children could make (puzzles; pogo horses; fish with a magnet and a fishing line with a magnet; beanbags) about equal in difficulty, and the children could select which toy they wanted to make.

Treatments varied the reason for the children's being asked to make toys. In one group they were asked (participating individually, one child at a time) to make them for poor hospitalized children whose parents could not provide them with toys. In another group the reason was the same but children also experienced induction. In a third group the subjects were asked to make toys to help art teachers find out what kinds of toys children like to make and are good at making, thereby helping the art·teachers to prepare the best materials for art classes. In all these conditions the children participated in some prosocial activity (participation conditions). In a fourth condition, the children were simply asked to make the toys, without a particular reason. In all groups, after the treatments were administered and the children were trained to make a toy, they proceeded for 15 minutes to make toys, and then continued to make toys (a different one, if they so desired) in another session 2 days later. In another set of three experimental conditions (teaching) the children experienced the same training as in the three participation conditions, but in preparation for teaching a younger child to make toys, for the reasons described (for example, so that the younger child could make toys for hospitalized children). After the training experience, each child proceeded to teach a younger child for 15 minutes. Two days later they taught again; the learner was another younger child of the same sex. Half of the subjects from each group received and had the opportunity to share gift certificates 1–2 days after the second experimental session (already a delayed posttest), and were administered the toy-making posttest about 2 weeks after that. The other half were administered these tests in the reverse order. In the toy-making posttest, after children selected the kind of toy they wanted to make they received materials for four toys, and were told to make as many toys as they wished.

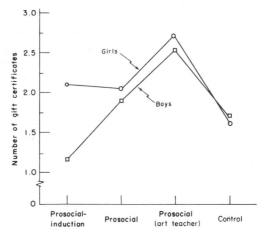

Figure 6.1

The average number of gift certificates that children donated in each experimental group.

About 2 weeks following the second, delayed posttest, children were asked to write letters for hospitalized children, in a manner similar to that described earlier.

The teaching and participation conditions had comparable effects on all dependent measures; therefore, the parallel teaching and no-teaching (participation) conditions were combined for further analyses. The effects of various forms of participation were compared to one another and to the effects of the control treatment.

The number of gift certificates that children shared was significantly affected by treatments ($p < .04$). The children in the prosocial–art teacher condition shared significantly more than those in the control group or those in the prosocial–induction group. As Figure 6.1 indicates the latter difference is due to the low level of sharing by boys in the prosocial–induction group. The analysis of toy scores showed a significant treatment by sex interaction ($p < .03$). As with gift certificates, boys in the prosocial–art teacher condition had substantially and significantly higher scores than those in the other treatment groups. Girls, on the other hand, made more toys in the prosocial–induction group than in the other groups (Figure 6.2). Analyses of the number of letters that children wrote to hospitalized children, and the amount of effort expended in letter writing, showed only a significant sex difference; girls did more than boys. The findings clearly show that in comparison to a control group, participation in a prosocial activity of a certain kind, helping an art teacher (and thereby, indirectly, the art teacher's pupils) enhanced

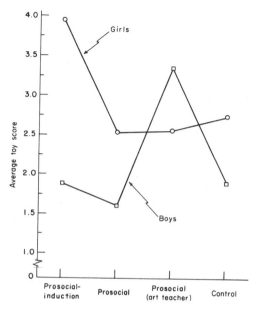

Figure 6.2
Average toy scores in each experimental group.

boys' later prosocial behavior. The same activity also enhanced girls' prosocial behavior on one measure, sharing gift certificates; helping hospitalized children and experiencing induction enhanced girls' prosocial behavior of another kind.

It is important to emphasize that the nature of the activities of children in the prosocial and prosocial–art teacher conditions was identical; only the stated reasons for their activities were different. The substantial effect of the prosocial–art teacher treatment on boys' and on girls' sharing of gift certificates may be due to one or more of several factors: that helping in this condition was not a behavior that would be regarded as "good" (or even goody-goody), thus creating reactance; that their involvement in or help with the selection of materials or activities for art classes made the children feel important; and that this was a kind of goal they could understand and empathize with. The helping behavior of boys in this condition was as great as that of girls in any treatment group. Thus, although in these studies there was a tendency for girls to behave more prosocially, some conditions appear to induce boys to prosocial behavior.

It seems clear from these findings, and earlier ones, that elaborate verbal communications that point out the consequences of positive behavior on other children, combined with actual participation in such prosocial behavior, frequently enhance girls' later prosocial behavior but either have no effect on boys or decrease boys' later prosocial behavior. Bernstein (1975) also found that a verbal communication of an inductive nature decreased the number of puzzles that seventh-grade boys later made for hospitalized children; it slightly (not significantly) increased the number of puzzles that girls made. When this verbal communication was accompanied by another kind that provided personal information about the would-be recipients of the puzzle, the decrease in boys' helping behavior did not occur.

What may be the explanation of the sex difference in reactions to verbal communications? A variety of other experiments also showed that girls are more responsive to verbal communications than boys (Grusec & Skubicki, 1970; Hovland & Janis, 1959; Staub, 1972b) in that their attitudes or behaviors are more likely to be affected by them. For one thing, in everyday life there may be less control exercised over boys than girls, in that verbal communications that give guidance or direction to them are less frequently enforced and translated into behavior. If so, then boys may learn to disregard verbal influence attempts to a greater degree. Second, if boys are taught to be independent and self-directing to a greater degree than girls, they may resent verbal communications or other influence procedures that would diminish their freedom more than girls; these would be more likely to evoke reactance and opposition. This may be particularly true of communications that promote other people's welfare, because such communications invoke social norms that have an obligatory character. If greater reactance is created, the boys' prosocial behavior would be reduced more.

One finding may be viewed as providing support for the latter proposition. Analyses were performed in which the effects of the order of administering the tests of sharing gift certificates and making toys were evaluated. Order had no effect on sharing gift certificates. However, with toy scores as the dependent variable, a highly significant treatment by sex by order interaction was found ($p < .01$). This appeared mainly due to boys making significantly and substantially fewer toys in the prosocial–induction group than in other groups when toy making was their first posttest ($\overline{X} = .29$). However, they made more toys in this than in other conditions when toy making was their second posttest ($\overline{X} = 2.91$), even though the tendency in the other experimental groups was for children to make fewer toys on the delayed than on the immediate posttest. If induction statements evoked reactance and this diminished toy making by boys on the immediate posttest, it is reasonable to assume that in a period of over 2 weeks this reactance would have declined.

How Does Experiential Learning Occur?

Teaching others and participating in prosocial behavior can be regarded as examples of what may be called *natural socialization*. Socialization mostly refers to the influence of socializers on children through the child-rearing techniques they employ and through direct tuition. Natural socialization refers to participation in activities and interpersonal experiences that result in some kind of learning. Socialization is involved here in an indirect manner, in that socializing agents can lead the child to participate in these activities and can create surrounding conditions that will maximize learning from such participation, but they do not directly teach the child to behave prosocially. Learning is primarily the result of the experience of, or participation in, an activity. Parents, teachers, and socializers in general are heavily involved in such indirect socialization in the child's everyday life. The circumstances that exist in the child's life are also important in determining whether the child will get involved in such activities. The various examples of natural socialization that have been explored seem to lend themselves to application, to being used in schools and other settings to promote children's prosocial behavior, and, more generally, to promote the development of positive characteristics such as self-esteem and positive orientation toward others.

A related type of learning occurs through role playing, which may be regarded as "as if" participation (Staub, 1976). Although in the course of role playing children do not aim to reach the same goals at which the real behavior (like helping someone) would aim, they do perform the behavior and may have some of the experiences that are usually associated with it. Role playing is at least partly an enactive form of learning, as are other types of participation. Moreover, since in role playing the behavior has an "as if" quality, variations in and experimentation with behavior are possible, and learning may take place that would not occur in the course of the real performance of the behavior. The shifting or exchange of roles can contribute to the development of awareness of others' perspectives, to role taking.

What are the significant elements of such experiences, which determine whether children's later prosocial behavior is affected or not? To briefly summarize earlier discussion, several (interrelated) conditions seem important:

1. A sense of benefiting others, of doing something that increases others' welfare.

2. A sense of responsibility for others' welfare. Certain conditions may focus responsibility on children to a greater degree, make

them feel that they are personally responsible for another person's welfare; other conditions may do so to a lesser extent or not at all. However, too much responsibility or too great a need by another person or lack of identification with beneficiaries of one's behavior may not activate or may interfere with processes that would lead to learning through participation.

3. A sense of the significance of one's activities, a belief that they are important and worthwhile.

4. A sense of agency or personal effectiveness. I would not expect participation in positive behavior that creates a sense of incompetence in the actor to enhance later positive behavior.

5. Other conditions that make the experience a satisfying one, in contrast to an unpleasant one: for example, the nature of the activity, whether it is liked or disliked.

6. Verbal communications to children can affect the degree to which self-attribution takes place (see section on "Learning through Self-Attribution," Chapter 5) and can contribute to the development of a cognitive network about the self, the welfare of others, and the behaviors for benefiting others that would enhance later positive behavior.

7. The opportunity for role taking, which may enable a child to appreciate others' needs and their related feelings.

Presumably, not all of these conditions have to be present at the same time.

To summarize again, in addition to those mentioned, several kinds of changes may result from experiences that include the just mentioned components. The association between benefiting others and the experience of self-enhancement or self-gratification may contribute to the expectations of gratification from benefiting others. It may also contribute to experiencing empathy with others. Over time a person may come to respond with an experience of empathic reinforcement to others' increased welfare that results from his actions. Having responsibility focused on the self may contribute to a sense of responsibility or obligation toward others. Having engaged in positive behavior may lead to setting higher standards for future positive conduct. Having benefited others, awareness of one's capacity to benefit others may increase. Clearly, some of these changes are interrelated.

An important task of future research in this and in other domains is to explore the cognitive and affective consequences of learning opportunities and the relationship between these consequences and behavioral ones. Do the presumed consequences really follow? Are they the mediators of the increased positive behavior that follows participatory learning? As I have repeatedly suggested, how existing personal characteristics modify experiential learning is also important. There is some indication that personality modifies how having engaged in some behavior affects people (Volume 1, Chapter 5).

Interactive Experience, Role Taking, and Experiential Learning

What is the relationship between role taking in interaction with peers as a form of experiential learning, which was assigned the central role, in both Piaget's (1932) and Kohlberg's (1969; 1976) theory, as a source of development, and the kind of experiential learning that I have emphasized? The two types of learning are related, complement each other, but are also different from each other. Piaget regarded the adjustments required in interaction with others, the demand for coordination between individuals to resolve conflict and engage in cooperation, as sources of cognitive and moral growth. Thus, the more opportunity for peer interaction (and the more varied roles available to children in the course of interaction), the greater the expected rate of change in role taking and in moral reasoning. Although the research on the influence of exposure of children to reasoning more advanced than their own and on the influence of guiding children's moral discussions (Chapters 2 and 5) suggests that socializers have an important role, the theory stresses that children learn from their own experience.

My reasoning about experiential learning is similar on the last point: Socializers exert influence, but their effect is indirect. The actual learning or change results from the child's own experience. Extensive opportunities for interaction may lead to the development of role taking and sensitivity to others. They may also promote children's tendencies to consciously process their experiences, to make attributions (to the self or to external agents), and to evaluate aspects of their environment. Thus, the opportunity for varied interactive experiences may make it more likely that children learn from participation. However, for children to engage in positive (in contrast to negative) behavior, adults and the rules or structure of an environment have to provide guidance. Progressively, such behavior can become self-maintaining. Thus, more directive influence is required by adults than that posed by Piaget and Kohlberg, for experiential learning of a behavior tendency and of related values and norms to occur.

Does the opportunity for interactive experience contribute to the development of role taking and moral reasoning? Based on Piagetian theory, several investigators assumed that environments that allow or lead to more early peer interaction would lead to the development of greater role-taking skills. None of the studies explored affective role-taking: They focused on perceptual, communicative, or cognitive role-taking. Hollos and Cowan (1973) found no differences in the role-taking capacity of children in farming communities in Norway and those in nonfarming communities (which provided presumably greater opportunities for social interaction). West (1974) found no differences between children from Israeli kibbutzim, moshavs (which are cooperative agricultural settlements, but not as communal as kibbutzim), and cities. Hollos and Cowan suggested that, beyond minimal threshold level, the sheer amount of social interaction does not affect the development of role-taking skills. In West's view, a basic level of varied social experience is necessary for the development of decentered thought, and other factors must be looked to as sources of individual differences in role-taking skills.

Beyond the amount and even the variety of social experience it allows, the rules and structure of a social environment can be expected to affect the nature of peer interaction. For example, how restrictive environments are would affect the extent to which children consider the consequences of their behavior on others and why others behave toward them as they do, in contrast to children's primarily following existing rules and interpreting behavior as normative.

In contrast to the preceding studies, Nahir and Yussen (1977) found that first- and fifth-grade kibbutz children were better able to modify their descriptions of objects as a function of the age of the children who were the recipients of their communications than were city children. First grade kibbutz children were also significantly better than city children at describing pictures to other children, without including information that was available to them but not represented in the pictures. These tasks seem to involve communicative skills that experience with peer interaction should contribute to: The findings have face validity. The differences in the findings of the varied studies may be partly due to different role-taking tasks that were employed.

Differences in opportunities for interactive experience, in socialization practices, and in rules laid down for children in groups must combine and jointly affect development. With regard to city and kibbutz, socialization practices appear to differ, at least as judged by reports of children about their experiences with their mothers, fathers, peers, and teachers (Avgar, Bronfenbrenner, & Henderson, 1977). Children in the kizzutz received more support and less discipline at home than did children in the city. Kibbutz parents were more concerned with encouraging autonomous behavior than were city parents. In reporting about their experiences outside the family, kibbutz children received more support than city children but also experienced more discipline from teachers and peers. Moshav children fell in between city and kibbutz children on all these dimensions but were closer to kibbutz than to city children.

It seems that older kibbutz children (the subjects were fifth, sixth, and seventh graders) receive a substantial amount of support and encouragement for autonomy by their parents, but discipline and responsibility in interacting with others is promoted by teachers and peers. The combination of emphasis on autonomy—which presumably included stressing the child's own responsibility—and the emphasis by teachers and by the peer group on responsibility in social interaction, as well as joint possession of play material with peers from an early age, can enhance cooperation and diminish competition among kibbutz children (in games, this has been found in comparison to children in the United States, in West Germany, and in Israeli cities; Madsen & Shapira, 1977) and probably contribute to other types of positive social behavior.

One of the profound issues facing research and theory on personality and social development and on the development of positive behavioral orientations is exploration and specification of the manner in which varied parental practices or socializing influences directed at specific children by parents and others, natural socialization and learning by participation, and the nature of the environment and the peer interaction it promotes jointly affect what children learn, how they develop, and even the principles by which their learning and development occur. Not only are these influences intertwined in shaping children, but the personal characteristics that children develop also enter into the transactions between them and their environments and affect further development. How these varied influences join in contributing to development will be discussed in the concluding chapter. Before that, the socializing influences of peer interaction will be examined.

Peer Socialization: The Influence of Peers on Positive and Negative Behavior and Personality

Adults are not the only important socializers of children. After the first few years of life children spend just about as much time in the company of peers as they spend in the company of parents, if not more. With the current trends toward play groups, day care centers, and compensatory education, many children begin to spend substantial amounts of time in the company of their peers in their first or second year. Peers exert great influence on one another in a variety of ways, and they are certain to be important socializers of each other.

Unfortunately, research about the long-term effects of the many ways in which peers influence one another is barely existent. Therefore, most of the generalizations about long-term effects, which are of primary concern here, will have to be based on demonstrations of immediate influences; they suggest what might be, not what is.

The Role of Peers in the Development of the Affectional System

In Volume 1 (Chapters 6, 7; 2, 4) the probable influence of positive or negative affective orientations toward others on behavior was considered. Liking and affection for other people is probably a precondition for feelings of empathy and also affects feelings of responsibility for others' welfare. Liking and affection may be necessary for a prosocial goal, for the motivation to benefit others. Hostility, in contrast, tends to give rise to aggression (Staub, 1971c).

The importance of parents in the development of an affectional system has already been briefly discussed (Chapter 4, section on "Relationship between Parents and Children"). Research findings with monkeys show that interaction with peers also contributes to a positive affectional system and to the formation of appropriate social relations. Harlow and Harlow (1962) found that monkeys who were reared with their natural mothers but were deprived of contact with peers during early life (for either 4 or 8 months) showed more wariness in their play and hyperaggressiveness than those who had peer contact. The Harlows concluded that monkeys deprived of the opportunity to form affectional ties to peers during the first year fail to learn the modulating and controlling systems needed for effective social relations.

There is further evidence that when other relationships are lacking (a parent–infant relationship) the opportunity to interact with peers helps to develop an early affectional system and normal social relationships. In the Harlow studies, whether an infant monkey was reared with its natural mother, with a "surrogate" mother (an inanimate figure made of terry cloth or wire), or no mother, those animals who were also reared with peers appeared to be similar to ferally reared animals in their later social and sexual behavior. The relevance of these findings to humans, that peer relations among humans also have positive and sometimes compensatory effects, was suggested by Freud and Dann's (1951) account of six German Jewish children whose parents were killed in concentration camps. These children were in the same camp and in close contact with one another for several years, from a few months of age until age 3–4. At that time, when taken to England, their behavior toward adults was bizarre in many ways. They acted wild, restless, and demonstrated no positive feelings for persons outside their group. But they appeared to care greatly for one another and acted as a cohesive, closely knit unit with almost no jealousy, rivalry, or competitiveness. Sharing and mutual support was usual. Over time, they began to develop relationships with their caretakers. The authors suggest that these children were saved from a "deficient" development, psychosis, delinquency, or the like, by the close relationship they had with one another.

Beyond this case history there is, unfortunately, little research evidence about the consequences for human beings of variations in early peer relations. Early peer relations of a positive kind may contribute to the development of interpersonal skills and positive inclination toward other people. The nature of a child's relationship to his peers in later years further affects his feelings about other people. Whether he will feel positively or negatively toward people may in turn affect the nature of his initial interactions, the likelihood that he will "move toward people" and engage in positive acts, and the kinds of relationships he develops.

Reciprocity in Children's Interactions

Extensive research evidence shows that people believe in reciprocity in interactions with others—for example, that one should help those whose help one received and should not harm such people (Gouldner, 1960)—that they usually prefer reciprocal to nonreciprocal relationships, even if the latter results in personal gain that they do not have to repay, and that people tend to reciprocate benefits (as well as harm). This research, together with conditions that affect reciprocity, was reviewed in Volume 1 (Chapter 8).

In their everyday interactions, children tend to behave reciprocally from an early age on. Even infants show reciprocity in the amount of interest they show in each other (Lewis & Rosenblum, 1975; Lewis, Young, Brooks, & Michalson, 1975). There is a positive relationship between the frequency with which children initiate verbal and motor acts toward others, and the frequency of such acts initiated toward them (Bott, 1934; Kohn, 1966). There is also a positive relationship between children initiating positive or negative behavior toward other children and others initiating positive or negative behavior toward them. In one study children who initiated acts to dominate others had dominating acts directed toward them, whereas those who initiated "integrative" acts had such acts directed toward them (Anderson, 1939). Observing children at a median age of 5 years and 11 months, Kohn (1966) found that friendly behavior constituted 86% of children's responses. A high positive correlation existed between the frequency of positive acts initiated by and directed toward a child ($r = .68$, $p < .05$). More active children had fewer positive acts initiated toward them ($r = -.45$, $p < .10$), apparently because children with high levels of activity tended to initiate negative acts. Charlesworth and Hartup (1967) found that the more a child reinforced others the more reinforcement he received. The most reinforcing children tended to scatter their reinforcements toward many other children, and received many reinforcements in return. Leitner (1977) found that preschool children who initiated interactions more frequently were more frequent recipients of others' initiations of interactions. Children who more frequently responded agreeably to others' initiations (complied, went along with, accepted, allowed another child to join in, and so on) received more agreement when they initiated interaction than did children who gave fewer agree responses. Friendly initiations resulted in agreement more frequently, whereas initiating interaction in a demanding manner (commanding, shoving, taking something away, screaming, demanding, fighting) resulted in coercive responses (threaten, hit, yell, and so on) more frequently than did friendly or "whiny" initiations.

In addition to widespread reciprocity, there is complementarity in peer interactions. Evidence for both reciprocity and complementarity was provided by the findings of one of our studies. We observed and coded second- and third-grade children's interaction on many dimensions in three open classrooms for half a year (Staub & Feinberg, 1977b). What is the relationship between children's behavior and behavior directed at them? A great deal of reciprocity was found, as well as some complementarity or accommodation. Consider the following as an example of both: A factor analysis of girls' positive behaviors provided one factor that may be called *responsive*. Girls who had high scores on this factor expressed positive emotion toward others, had positive physical contacts with others, and shared in response to requests by other children. Scores on this factor were positively related to scores on a factor that was derived from the factor analysis of positive behavior directed at the children, with expressions of positive emotions, helpfulness, and sharing in response to requests having high loading on this factor. Scores on the responsive factor were significantly negatively related to factor scores derived from the factor analysis of negative behavior directed at children. Responsive behavior by girls was significantly positively related to several specific categories of behavior directed at them: physical affection, verbal interaction, positive emotion, cooperation, and humorous verbal and nonverbal acts. Presumably due to the high level of interaction represented by a high score on the responsive factor, these scores were also associated with conflict with other children. The responsive pattern was negatively related to minimal interaction with others, interaction that involved nothing more than sitting at a table and exchanging materials in working on tasks. Interestingly, it was also negatively related to requests of help by others. There is reciprocity, as well as accommodation, evidenced in the pattern. The responsive pattern does not include offers of and the tendency to provide help, and other children tend not to request help.

Substantial reciprocity was also found in boys' interactions. Aggressive behavior by boys and aggressively defensive behavior—boys defending themselves aggressively when someone attacked them—were strongly associated with aggressive and aggressively defensive behavior directed at them. Specifically, aggressive defense by a boy is associated with aggressive defense directed at the child, aggression directed at the child, instrumental aggression directed at the child, and submission toward the child. The same behavior is negatively related to various positive behaviors, particularly sharing. Positive behaviors by boys are correlated with positive behaviors directed at them, and are mostly negatively related to aggressive behavior directed at them. In some cases, highly specific reciprocity exists. Sometimes this is a function of the nature of the activity; a child cannot have conflict with others, cannot cooperate with others, without a partner who participates in such interactions. At other times, however, specific reciprocity does not stem from the nature of the activity, as in the case of the substantial relationship $(r = .52)$ between humorous behavior by boys—verbal or physical (enactive) humor—and humorous behavior directed at them. Humor seems to have a positive function in boys' interactions,, since it is related to various positive behaviors.

Kohn (1966) interpreted his findings as suggesting that children create their own environment; they get what they give. However, it is possible that they give what they get, that because of certain characteristics they possess other children will initiate positive or negative acts toward them and they will reciprocate. Thus the positive acts of some children may not be reinforced by others, depending on the recipient's attitude toward or evaluation of the child. The studies reported earlier did not deal with differences in the degree of reciprocation of positive acts as a function of the characteristics of individual children. Interaction among group members was usually studied after the group existed for a period of time. Over time, relationships in a group may stabilize and nonreinforced positive acts may decline in frequency and be less in evidence.

There is evidence that children who are anxious in their social interactions are less popular, less accepted by their peers, as shown by sociometric choices (Hartup, 1970). Children who are perceived as anxious and in some sense "needy" might initiate positive behaviors toward other children, but because of the manner in which they perform such behaviors or because they are negatively evaluated for other behaviors, their positive initiative might not be reciprocated. The evidence soon to be reviewed, that children who have better capacity for role taking are more popular with their peers, suggests a related possibility: When children's "positive" acts are not appropriate—they do not fit group norms and the individual needs of other children and consequently are not positive from the standpoint of the recipient—they will not be reciprocated.

Exceptions to strict reciprocity in children's behavior are certain to exist. One type of exception has been suggested by the findings of Campbell and Yarrow (1961). In a study of boys in a summer camp they found that children who were liked by others and were perceived to fill socially appropriate roles—"socially effective" children—initiated and received a high frequency of "friendly-sociable" acts. Children who were less socially effective initiated and received fewer such acts. However, the highly socially effective children also initiated a high frequency of "aggressive–disruptive" acts, but had a much lower frequency of such acts directed at them. Campbell and Yarrow (1961) suggest that acceptance by peers provides "greater freedom of action, less feeling of constraint by the accepted child, and perhaps, too, a greater likelihood that aggressive–disruptive acts by favored children are reinterpreted by peers in acceptable frameworks [p. 12]."

Reciprocity within the social group (as well as accommodation and other modes of adjustment that a child develops) may lead to and/or strengthen the habitual patterns of interaction between a child and his peers. Some children may learn to act more positively toward others and receive positive reactions in return; others may act more negatively and receive negative acts initiated toward them. Still others may engage in successful (reinforced) aggression. Patterson, Littman, and Bricker (1967) found that aggressive behavior by preschool children is maintained by "reinforcement," which takes various forms: success in taking away a toy from another child, submission and crying by the victim, and the like. Although aggressive children may experience such reinforcement, the behavior that others initiate toward them may be negative. Children who habitually act in a hostile and aggressive way toward others may receive hostility or avoidance in return. If so, such children may begin to dislike, distrust, and perhaps fear other people. Their relationships with peers are not likely to be a source of pleasure or satisfaction. As yet, evidence of the stability of such interactive patterns over time is minimal.

Actually, what behaviors are perceived by peers as positive and negative, that in turn evoke positive and negative reactions, is a complex issue. As Campbell and Yarrow (1961) found, aggressive behavior is not always associated with reciprocal aggression, and, as research reviewed in the next section will show, it is not necessarily associated with unpopularity. What perceptions, behavioral reactions, and peer evaluations result from aggressive behavior probably depend on its form or nature and on the total pattern of behaviors and characteristics of the aggressively behaving child. Problems in personality development may arise even more when a child is the frequent victim of aggression. A recipient of aggression may engage in reciprocal aggression and experience an aggressive interactive pattern. But some children may evoke aggression directed at them and/or deal with the aggression in ineffective, possibly negative ways—including submission and avoidance—that reinforce and perpetuate aggressive behavior toward them. Support for some of this reasoning comes from Olweus (1977). He conducted two longitudinal studies—extending over 1- and 3-year intervals—of the stability of boys' acting aggressively, of their being recipients of aggression, and of their popularity with (being liked by) peers. The information about children was based on ratings by three raters from each class of children, with one-third of these raters the same at the beginning and at the end of the study, the other two-thirds different. The ratings had a reasonable degree of reliability. Both behaving aggressively and receiving aggression were stable over time. The average correlation of ratings over time was $r = .72$ for the 1-year interval and $r = .66$ for the 3-year interval. There was little relationship between children's aggression and their popularity. However, the children who were targets of aggression tended to be unpopular.

Reciprocity does not necessarily lock children into a negative pattern. Negative reactions by others may reduce negative behavior, particularly if children come to understand the relationship between their own behavior and others' reactions. It is not known, however, how easy or difficult it is, once an interactive pattern has been established, for children to change behavior directed at them by changing their own behavior. What enables children to be successful agents in changing existing interactive patterns, and others' perception of themselves? That behavior is affected by others' reactions, by differential reinforcement from peers, was shown by Hartup, Glazer, and Charlesworth's findings (1967): Positive behavior by children in a nursery-school setting was stable from fall to spring, highly positively related, whereas negative behavior was not. The interactive behavior patterns of very young children, as those in the Hartup *et al.* study, may be less stable and more easily modified by other children's reactions than the interactive behavior of older children. Campbell and Yarrow (1961), who attempted to evaluate the stability of children's reputations (others' sociometric evaluations of them) and of their interactive behavior found that reputation tends to be stable, possibly to a greater degree than behavior. If so, change in behavior that is inconsistent with how others perceive a child might not be reinforced or has to show some persistence before it gets reinforced.

Several investigations found that reinforcement by a child who is not a friend, or by an unpopular or disliked child, has greater effect on children's behavior than reinforcement by a liked or popular peer, or by a friend (Hartup, 1964; Patterson & Anderson, 1964; Titkin & Hartup, 1965). Unpopular children reinforce others infrequently, which is one of the probable sources of their unpopularity. When they do, perhaps, the unexpected and unfamiliar nature of their behavior enhances its impact. It may therefore be that changes in the behavior of such children would be successful in changing behavior directed at them. However, whether reinforcing behavior on their part will have a cumulative and long-term effect, resulting in a change in the behavior directed at them and in their reputation, needs to be explored.

In addition to negative interaction patterns, an important source of negative orientation toward people may be isolation by peers. Some children may be the objects of neither positive nor active negative behavior; although sometimes rejected, they may be mostly ignored. The consequences of such isolation may be different from those of a negative reciprocal pattern of interaction with peers, but they are probably highly negative. Of course, the personality characteristics of the child, the home environment and the support the child receives at home, and other factors would modify the meaning and influence of experiences with peers.

In sum, the existence of stable patterns in peers' interactions is important because children who develop a persistent negative pattern of interaction with other children might develop personality characteristics that substantially decrease the likelihood of their later positive behavior. Being persistently the object of negative behavior may affect a child's self-concept and self-esteem, leading to a negative orientation toward the self. In addition, it may also lead to a negative orientation toward other people, to fear of others and hostility toward them. It may also lead to firmly established negative, hostile strategies (or submissive, or other kinds) of interaction and behavioral competencies, and habitual modes of relating to others in a negative manner. A lasting positive reciprocal pattern of interaction might have the opposite effects.

Popularity, Peer Interaction, and Adjustment

Social Behavior and Popularity

A large group of studies examined the relationship of both children's behavior toward their peers and a variety of their personality characteristics to acceptance, liking, and other forms of evaluation by peers. In most of these studies sociometric measures were used to determine popularity or acceptance (the two terms will be used synonymously). Sociometry uses the strategy of asking children (or adults) to nominate others as best friends, seating companions, playmates, or partners for other activities. The index of the child's popularity or liking by his peers is usually the total number of nominations received, or that number weighted by whether the child was nominated first, second, or third as a companion or friend, or some variant of such procedures. If other types of questions are asked, peers' perceptions and evaluations of a child's leadership, consideration for others' welfare, or other behaviors and characteristics can be assessed. Sociometric measures are reasonably reliable and stable, even over rather lengthy time periods such as a year or two (Oden & Asher, 1977; Sells & Roff, 1967). Unfortunately, information about an important index of the validity of the measure—the manner in which other children *behave* toward their more or less popular peers—is not extensive, and not entirely consistent. There is, however, an extensive network of other correlates of sociometric measures, providing construct validity.

A very large number of correlates of popularity have been identified. For our purposes, they may be differentiated into behavioral correlates, which indicate what kinds of interactive, social behaviors by children are associated with popularity and acceptance, and nonbehavioral correlates. This division is not straightforward, since the latter include IQ, school grades, physical attractiveness, and athletic capacity, some of which are likely to be associated with different interactive behaviors.

Sociable, friendly children, who take initiative in interacting with others, appear to be popular with their peers. In an early study Marshall and McCandless (1957) found that friendly social interaction, consisting of associative play, friendly approach, and conversation of a friendly nature, was significantly and fairly substantially ($r = .57$) related to a sociometric measure of preference among preschool children, as well as to teachers' judgment of children's sociometric status. This is one of the few studies in which the relationship between how each child was judged by others on the sociometric measures and behavior toward the child was reported. There was a moderate but significant relationship between the popularity of the child and friendly behavior directed at the child. Hostility by children in interaction with other children was unrelated to how popular they were. In a study by Moore and Updegraff (1964) there were three small groups of preschool subjects, somewhat differing in age. The authors measured popularity by having children select four classmates they especially liked and four whom they did not like. As in most studies with young children, the subjects were presented with pictures of their classmates when asked to make their sociometric choices. With the three groups combined, nurturance and giving—offering affection, attention, reassurance, and protection in interaction with other children—was marginally significantly related to popularity scores derived from the combination of positive and negative judgments. Dependence on other children, as measured by children seeking physical contact, reassurance, attention, and help, was also marginally positively related to popularity. Considering the rather positive nature of the behaviors subsumed under dependence, the relationship to popularity, at least among preschool children, is not surprising. Dependence on adults was significantly negatively related to popularity in the youngest group of preschoolers (ranging from 3 years 2 months to 3 years 10 months in age) but unrelated in the other two groups. Possibly dependence on adults in young children interferes with their interaction with peers.

An extension and clarification of the earlier findings was provided by Hartup *et al.* (1967). They measured acceptance and rejection of nursery-school children by their peers, and related them and the difference between them (which they called "status") to children's behavior in interaction with one another. They summed a variety of primarily positive behaviors (such as attention and approval; affection and personal acceptance; and submission) under the label of *positive reinforcement* and a variety of negative behaviors under the label of *negative reinforcement*. In one nursery-school class they collected behavioral and sociometric measures twice, both in the fall and in the spring, in another class only once. Positive reinforcement and acceptance scores were stable, but negative reinforcement, rejection, and status scores were not. Perhaps children learned from their interactions with peers and modified their negative behavior over time. The relationship between providing positive reinforcement for others and being accepted by them was substantial and significant each time it was measured. The relationship between negative reinforcement of peers and rejection by them was also significant, two of the three times measured. However, positive reinforcement was unrelated to rejection (children who positively reinforced others were not rejected less often) and negative reinforcement was unrelated to acceptance (children behaving negatively were not less accepted). Status scores seemed less useful, providing fewer and less clear-cut relationships, than acceptance and rejection separately. Rejection was not simply lack of preference. A child who is not a preferred friend or companion of his peers need not be one who is disliked by them.

In another study, Gottman (1978) found that peer acceptance and frequency of peer interaction were unrelated to each other among 3–5-

year-old preschoolers. Children who were not accepted by others were not social isolates; they were part of ongoing interactions among peers. Also, children who had low frequency of peer interaction were not usually withdrawn, shy, and fearful. Gottman described one group of children who were not accepted as "tuned out" and "hovering"—a combination that seemed to identify children who had interpersonal problems. We need to specify further the pattern of child behaviors and interactions that represents problems in adjustment.

Research with older children confirms that friendly, sociable behavior is associated with popularity and acceptance, and that the lack of friendly, sociable behavior is not associated with rejection. To quote from Hartup (1970, p. 388), "Peer acceptance [among elementary-school children] has been found to be positively related to friendliness, outgoing behavior, and amount of participation (Bonney, 1944; Bonney & Powell, 1953); lack of withdrawal as perceived by peers (Winder & Rau, 1962); the frequency with which kindness is expressed to peers (Klaus, 1959)." Among adolescents, the findings are similar. Perhaps they suggest a slight shift in emphasis, in that among younger children positive social behavior seems of substantial importance for popularity, but among adolescents sociability and being "good company" acquire a somewhat greater weight (Elkins, 1958; Keislar, 1953; Marks, 1954). Some of the studies again showed that low sociability is not associated with rejection (Feinberg, Smith, & Schmidt, 1958).

As already indicated, aggressive or negative behavior is often unrelated to acceptance but several investigators found that it is related to rejection by peers (Hartup *et al.*, 1967; Moore, 1967). That is, the selection of liked peers is unaffected by how aggressive they are, but the designation of disliked peers is affected by aggression. The aggressive behavior of children who are liked by others may take more appropriate, acceptable forms, may be more justified by the circumstances, may be more "reality oriented" (Hartup, 1970) and less immature. For example, Lesser (1959) found strong negative relationships between both verbal and indirect aggression and popularity in fifth- and sixth-grade boys, but a moderate positive relationship between popularity and provoked physical aggression. Still, as suggested earlier, an additional factor may be that aggression by children who are more popular on account of their other behavior and characteristics is more acceptable to their peers, perhaps even when it takes somewhat immature forms. In contrast, children who are not well liked may not be able to affort the luxury of aggression or other disagreeable behavior and are rejected for it.

An additional aspect of the child's behavior that contributes to his popularity among his peers is the degree to which it is socialized: follows group norms and shows a flexibility in adjusting to the group. Peer acceptance has been associated with compliance to the routines of the group and acceptance by the child of his situation (Koch, 1933); to quote Hartup (1970, p. 389) again, it is associated with "adjustment to, and cooperation with, group rules (Lippitt, 1941); and peer perceptions of conformity (Moore, 1967)."

Role Taking, Social Skills, Attitudes toward Others, and Popularity

A variety of skills and capacities of children are likely to contribute to popularity because they contribute to the effectiveness and sensitivity of the children's interpersonal interactions. Rubin (1973) found, for example, that less egocentric children, as measured by a test of communicative egocentrism, were more popular in kindergarten and first grade, although not among older children. Deutsch (1976) also used a measure of communicative egocentrism, with preschool children, and found that children who had greater communicative skills were more popular on a behavioral measure of popularity (the frequency of friendly interactions with other children). However, a sociometric measure of popularity was unrelated to communication skills and to the behavioral measure of popularity.

In another study Gottman, Gonso, and Rasmussen (1975) used six measures of "social skills" quite varied in nature, two of which were significantly related to friendship choices. Children who were more often nominated as friends performed better on a measure of referential communications skills, where they had to send to another child clue words that would enable the other child to guess one of two words in a word pair (e.g., house–car). Friendship choice was also related to the child's performance in role playing, in which he showed how he would attempt to make friends with a new child in school. Performance on several other tasks, however, was unrelated to popularity. The other tasks included labeling emotions in facial expressions, and communicative and perceptual role-taking tests. Consistent with previous findings, children with more friends gave and received more positive reinforcement in their classroom interactions. However, significant grade (third or fourth) and social class (middle-income or lower-income classrooms) interactions were found in the distribution of positive reinforcement. An interesting difference in social class was that in the middle-income group friendship was associated with verbal reinforcement, but in the lower-income group it was associated with nonverbal reinforcement.

That role-playing skills are related to popularity has also been shown in a study by Mouton, Bell, and Blake (1956) with a small number of sixth-grade children. The participants played three roles: a child who is sad because he was not invited to his best friend's party; a child who is extremely angry at a playmate (for some self-selected reason); and a mischievous student who is called into the principal's office. Each subject's performance of each role was rated by three different observers (nine observers altogether), on 10· dimensions. Ratings on 8 of the dimensions were highly reliable but also strongly interrelated; apparently all provided an index of "effectiveness in role." The subject's behavior in the three roles was consistent. The ratings correlated from $r = 70$ to $r = .97$. Subjects were divided into high, medium, and low popularity groups and into high, medium, and low role-playing groups. The relationship between popularity and role playing was significant for all 8 dimensions, for all three roles.

Communicative abilities and role-playing skills might be involved in interpersonal relationships in several ways. First, children who are better at communication tasks should be more effective in expressing themselves and easier to listen to and interact with. Similarly, children who are better at enacting different roles are, presumably, clearer in expressing themselves and better in letting others know about their feelings, desires, and intentions. This would make it easier, less demanding, and more satisfying to interact with them. It is also possible that both communicative skills and role-playing skills are indicative of better role-taking. Children who communicate better might also be able to perceive more accurately what others communicate to them. Children who can enact varied roles might also be able to recognize how others feel, to identify the meaning of others' behavior, and to react appropriately and sensitively. Naturally, skills in perceiving and thinking about others' behavior and feelings, skills in communicating with others, and the ability to respond to others behaviorally in an effective fashion would contribute to positive interpersonal relationships. Among younger children the ability to communicate effectively and to perceive communications accurately would be a relatively advanced interpersonal skill, contributing to effective interaction. Among somewhat older children the capacity to adopt varied roles and perceive others' intentions accurately might be the advanced skill.[1]

---

[1] In our study of reciprocity in children's interactions (Staub & Feinberg, 1977b) we explored varied personality and behavioral correlates of children's behavior and of behavior directed at them. One finding about the relationship between "empathy" and behavior directed at children seems to be of substantial significance in light of currently popular methods of research on empathy. We measured children's descriptions of the feelings of characters in varied pictures we showed them, as well as their reports of how they felt looking at these pictures. Currently, when children report that they experience a feeling similar to the feeling of a character in a series of pictures

Although the reasoning given suggests that children with better *role-taking capacity* would behave more sensitively toward others and would be better liked, there are both conceptual and empirical complications. In Chapter 3 as well as in Volume 1 (Chapter 5) I suggested that role taking may enable children to perceive others' feelings and needs better but that their behavior toward others will also depend on their motivation. Some may be motivated to respond positively to others' feelings and needs, whereas other children may use their understanding of others' internal states in self-serving ways. Thus, both behavior in interaction with others and popularity may depend on a constellation of characteristics of which role playing is one component and prosocial orientation and self-esteem may be others. A consequence of this may be the instability of relationships between varied forms of role taking and specific prosocial acts (reviewed in Volume 1, Chapter 5); sometimes positive relationships were found, but not always.

Varied findings show complexities in relationships between role taking, the capacity to make inferences about others, and social-interactive behavior. Krebs and Stirrup (1974) found no relationship between

---

or in a story, this is taken as an indication of the child's empathic reaction, and a tendency to report parallel feelings to those of picture or story characters is taken as an indication of empathic capacity or tendency. We distinguished between parallel empathy—a child reporting feelings similar to those of characters in pictures—and reactive empathy—a child reporting emotions indicating that he feels with the characters in the picture, responds to their condition, and reacts to it with some emotion of his own. Looking at a poorly clothed black child standing next to a grungy and nearly empty refrigerator, with a somewhat forlorn expression on his face, leads some children to report feeling poor or deprived. These we code as parallel empathic responses. Reports of feeling sorry for the boy or angry at his deprivation were taken as indices of reactive empathy.

Among girls, parallel empathy scores had few behavioral correlates. However, girls who had high reactive empathy scores were the recipients of varied positive behaviors from other children, including cooperation and the expression of positive affect. Considering everyday experience, it seems that our empathic response to others rarely takes the form of experiencing the same emotion. Empathy may not usually take the form of feeling sad when someone else feels sad or of feeling insulted when someone else feels insulted. Rather, we may react to others' affect with feelings of our own that are other-centered (rather than self-centered) and responsive to their affective state. Their sadness may evoke sorrow or sympathy. Children or people who primarily report parallel feelings may not, in fact, respond sensitively to others and/or may be attempting to gain social approval. (It is possible, however, that, in the course of developing empathic orientation toward others, children go through a period in which they experience parallel feelings.) Among boys in our study, reactive empathy was almost never reported. Both parallel empathy and accurate inferences by boys about the feelings of characters in the pictures were somewhat related to *negative* behaviors directed at boys.

two measures of cognitive role-taking and specific forms of positive behavior by 7- and 8-year-old children in interaction with each other, but
there were significant positive relationships of role taking with a composite prosocial score and with teachers' ratings of prosocial and cooperative behaviors. However, since *IQ* on formal tests and teachers'
ratings of IQ correlated with all measures, IQ may have affected the relationships to an unspecifiable degree. Barrett and Yarrow (1977)
measured the inferential ability of children by having them interpret
videotaped social episodes in which an emotional experience abruptly
changed the behavior of the central character. The 5–8-year-old subjects
attended a summer camp. Among the children who showed high inferential ability, self-assertive behaviors and prosocial behaviors in their
interactions with others were significantly positively related to each
other, whereas no significant relationships were found among children
with a low inferential ability. Social inferential ability by itself was unrelated to children's prosocial behavior. In this study and in most
others, the extent to which general intelligence enters into relationships
between role-taking capacities and behavior was unexplored. The findings
of Krebs and Stirrup (1974) suggest that IQ may at least contribute to
such relationships.

Children with better role-taking and inferential abilities may not
engage in more positive acts than other children, but their overall pattern of relating to peers may be more effective. Perhaps their behavior
is more responsive to the behavior of others. They may be better at
managing interpersonal relationships, both appropriately defending
themselves and discriminately responding to others' needs.

Findings of Campbell and Yarrow (1961) point to the involvement
in popularity of the manner in which children perceive others and think
about others. In a summer camp, 8- to 12-year-old boys were asked to
select those cabin mates who were their friends. In addition, children
who filled socially appropriate positive roles were selected on the basis
of "guess who" items. Such an item consists of a description or a profile
of a child (e.g., a leader), and children are to supply names of children
to whom the description applies. Children were assigned social-effectiveness scores on the basis of both selections. There were no relationships
between social-effectiveness scores and the content categories children
used in describing others (among the categories included were "mild
dependence," "fearfulness," "submission," "nurturance," and "indirect
aggression") except for a marginal positive relationship with the category
"affiliative." However, there were strong relationships between social
effectiveness and both the degree of organization children used in describing others and their inferences about other children. Children who

showed a high degree of organization rather than giving unrelated details or global statements, such as "she is nice," and children who made interpretive statements about personality, motivation, or behavior ("sometimes he's good so he won't be beat up" in contrast to "she is always willing to help you") were judged as more socially effective.

Obviously, considering others' motives and personalities would increase the child's ability to behave toward others in a sensitive or at least relevant manner. That the ability to perceive oneself and others accurately is important was further shown by Goslin (1962), who found that less popular children, in contrast to more popular children, perceived themselves differently from the way other children perceived them. They also perceived other children differently from the way the rest of the group perceived them and predicted poorly how they would be perceived by the rest of the group.

In several studies, children's attitudes toward others and themselves have been found related to children's acceptance by their peers. In one study (Loban, 1953) with subjects in the ninth to twelfth grades, accepted peers were designated as having behavioral characteristics that showed sensitivity rather than insensitivity toward others. Children who had sensitive behavioral characteristics ascribed to them reported more concern about interpersonal relationships, more worry about their own behavior, and more awareness of personal inadequacies and failures. Less sensitive children ascribed to the ideal of being free of control. In another study, Reese (1961) found that children who scored in the middle range on a measure of self-esteem were significantly more popular than children low in self-esteem. The high-self-esteem group was between the other two in popularity and not significantly different from either. The pattern of acceptance by children of same-sex others was similar but more pronounced, in that all three self-esteem groups were significantly different. An important finding was that acceptance by others was positively related to accepting others, to rating other children as friends and indicating liking for them. Klaus (1959) also found that children who were popular ascribed more positive characteristics to other children than those who were unpopular. In other studies Horowitz (1962) reported that unpopular children had derogatory self-concepts, and Coleman (1961) reported the same finding for adolescents.

The only slightly surprising finding is that children with moderate rather than high self-esteem are best liked. Some of the findings of the Loban study suggest an explanation. Children with very high self-esteem may be so satisfied with themselves that they are unquestioning of their relationships to others and as a result are somewhat insensitive to them. Children whose self-esteem is positive but moderate may monitor their interactions with others more carefully, with the hope of improving them. This reasoning is supported by research findings of Reykowski and Jarymowicz (1976). These Polish investigators found that children with a medium level of self-esteem were more prosocial than children whose self-esteem was either very high or very low. In one study, children with a medium level of self-esteem demonstrated greater accuracy in perceiving the problems and emotions of a child portrayed in a film about 10- to 11-year-old school children. Reykowski and Jarymowicz also found that an elaborate procedure that aimed at increasing children's self-esteem enhanced low-self-esteem children's sensitivity in perceiving the feelings and problems of the child in this film, as well as their expressed intention for positive conduct (see Volume 1, pp. 309–310). This finding is relevant to intervention, which is discussed in the next section. My reasoning here is also consistent with the report by Coopersmith (1967) concerning the characteristics of boys having high, low, and medium self-esteem. Those with medium and high self-esteem were similar in many ways, and different from those with low self-esteem. They showed more initiative and greater persistence in their activities, and they were better able to handle criticism. However, those whose self-esteem was in the middle range were more concerned about their relationships to others than those whose self-esteem was high; they were more concerned with self-worth and with the manner in which they might be evaluated by others.

A variety of additional characteristics of children have been found to correlate with popularity. Some of these are behavioral and/or are likely to be expressed in behavior. For example, scores on paper-and-pencil tests of anxiety correlate negatively with popularity, to a relatively low but significant degree, in the majority of studies (Hartup, 1970). The tendency to feel anxious is likely to gain expression in the children's behavior. Physical attractiveness, athletic ability, and other characteristics, the social–behavioral correlates of which might vary, have also been found to relate significantly positively to popularity. Academic achievement and IQ have been found related to both peer acceptance and peer rejection (Sells & Roff, 1967).

The Long-Term Consequences of Popularity and of Negative Interpersonal Relationships

Popularity, rejection, and isolation are likely to differentially shape a child's personality, affecting his attitudes toward others, interpersonal skills, adjustment, and future interactions. Their influence on development may be substantial. In discussing the relationship between friendly, sociable behavior and popularity Moore (1967) wrote,

> To know that popular children perform a preponderance of friendly
> behaviors is not to say that their friendliness is the "cause" of their
> popularity. It is just as reasonable to hypothesize that being well-
> liked inspires a child to perform friendly behavior as it is to hy-
> pothesize that performing these behaviors causes the child to be
> well-liked [p. 236].

The research findings suggest that popularity can have different
initial bases. Some children might be liked, initially, because of their
interactive style, the manner in which they relate to others. The origins
of their positive relating to others might be both in the children's positive
attitudes toward others and themselves, and in the social skills through
which these attitudes gain expression. Other children may be popular
because they are physically attractive, or athletic, or have some other
valued or idealized characteristic. In a sense, these children do not have to
work for their popularity. Although it is reasonable to think that positive
behavior that is directed at them would induce friendly, positive behavior in such children, perhaps it does not always do so. It would be
worthwhile to investigate reciprocity in behavior separately among children with these two (and other) different bases for popularity.

Unfortunately, there is little information about how combinations of
characteristics are related to popularity. Since relationships between
single characteristics and sociometric measures of popularity, although
significant, are generally fairly low, it may be that, of the children who
are physically attractive or athletic, it is mainly those who also possess
certain behavioral characteristics who are popular among their peers. It
is also possible that various characteristics contribute to popularity in
an additive fashion.

Particularly when popularity involves a child's interactive style,
we are likely to deal with an evolving system. Positive interactions are
likely to be reciprocal, positive behaviors are likely to be reinforced, and
popular children may acquire further behavioral skills and learn from
their interactive experience in the cognitive domain. Perhaps they learn,
as Piaget suggested (1932), that reciprocity is the logic of interpersonal
relations, and also extend their belief in the benevolence of their environment, their positive orientation to or acceptance of others, and
continue to develop their self-esteem. Children who have difficulties in
interaction with others, who are rejected or isolated, might develop mis-
trust and dislike for others and perhaps a negative evaluation of themselves. It is a further possibility that popularity that is based not on
social behavior and attitude toward others but on such "impersonal"
characteristics as physical attractiveness or athletic prowess will not lead
to the same kind of positive development. Children with such character-

istics are likely to be the recipients of positive behavior, which might of course lead to reciprocity on their part and to development along the lines described. However, children with certain valued characteristics might be the recipients of positive behavior without having to reciprocate or demonstrate sensitivity to others. As a result they may not develop sensitivity and interpersonal skills, or cognitive capacities such as role taking. Again, direct evidence on this point is lacking. Tangentially one may note that boys with highly masculine interests in adolescence, who tended to be self-confident and valued by others (popular) at the time, were found to lack confidence and leadership in their thirties in comparison to boys who were more "feminine" in their values during adolescence (Mussen, 1961, 1962).

The evidence that children's position of being accepted or rejected by others transfers to other groups is also nearly nonexistent. Among preschoolers Gellert (1961) found that the dominant members of dyads tended to be the same children during three different testing sessions. That is, over time (but not over different members of dyads) power relations did not fluctuate. Information is needed, however, about the degree to which peer status transfers from group to group. There is evidence that leadership in groups is influenced by circumstances, including the group tasks and differences in members' expertise on those tasks (Hartup, 1970). It is possible, however, that leadership fluctuates primarily among the more popular children. It would also be important to collect evidence about how feelings toward others and self-esteem are affected by having high or low status in a group over a long period of time. Children who are members of a stable school-class may often face such a situation, since peer preferences remain relatively stable over time (Oden & Asher, 1977; Sells & Roff, 1967).

There are indications that lack of popularity or isolation in childhood can be associated with varied problems in adulthood. In one study a group of servicemen who received bad-conduct discharges and had been patients in a child-guidance center were rated by their childhood counselors as having significantly poorer peer adjustment than other former patients who had satisfactory service records (Roff, 1961). However, those in the group in question may have been generally more disturbed, and therefore received worse ratings of peer adjustment and had greater difficulty in adjusting to the service.

Other research shows that unpopular children have a high frequency of representation in a community-wide psychiatric register later in life (Cowen *et al.,* 1973). Moreover, nearly one-third of adult manic depressives and schizophrenics were social isolates in childhood, although the proportion of social isolates in a normal control group was close to zero (Kohn & Clausen, 1955). Roff, Sells, and Golden (1972) found, in a sample of 40,000 children in 21 cities, that with the exception of the lowest socioeconomic class, low-peer-acceptance scores were highly positively related to delinquency 4 years later. Social isolation was even found to be related to various factors that in turn are highly correlated with suicide rates (Stengel, 1971).

We do not know, of course, the direction of causation in these relationships. As Hartup (1970) wrote, "there is clear consensus that a child's general adjustment is related to his popularity with peers . . . it is possible to conclude that neurotic disturbance is likely to be associated with low peer evaluation [p. 391]." Children who have psychological difficulties in childhood might be negatively evaluated or isolated; the early difficulties may continue and develop into later ones independently of peer relations, although it is reasonable to think that they would be exacerbated by poor peer relations, which can result from the child's psychological problems. The starting point could also be rejection or isolation by peers, this giving rise to adjustment problems in childhood.

Most likely we are dealing with an evolving system, so that early personality and behavioral problems result in negative reactions by peers and negative peer reactions lead to behavioral and personality problems. Whatever the starting point, unless reversed, the evolution of this pattern may lead to later difficulties in adjustment and to individual characteristics that would decrease the likelihood of positive social behavior. Changes in life circumstances and new learning opportunities may slow down, halt, and even reverse this process.

The information that is available about peer relations and evaluations does suggest that positive interactions with others and characteristics that enhance positive interactions contribute to satisfactory adjustment. Intervention in the form of enhancing a child's capacity to direct appropriate positive behavior at other people and be responsive to others might improve the child's adjustment. Even in instances in which basic adjustment is satisfactory and thus is not an issue, such enhanced capacity for positive relationships is likely to contribute to satisfaction in life. With children who have problems in peer relations, intervention may be of dramatic importance.

Improving Peer Relations

Assuming the persistence of a negative pattern of reciprocal peer interactions or of negative evaluation by peers and unpopularity or isolation, or any aspect of this, what procedures may help children to improve their peer relations? On the basis of research findings and my reasoning about them, role playing, varied forms of participatory learning, and verbal communications that help children understand the consequences of their behavior on others as well as others' motives and needs all seem potentially effective procedures. Many children who tend to engage in negative behavior may do so because they have no skills or plans and strategies for positive social behavior that would enable them to satisfy their goals—including involvement with peers, play, recognition, and possession of play materials. They may also lack strategies for asserting or defending themselves in relatively socially acceptable ways. Furthermore, if they attribute negative motives to others, they would frequently respond to others' behavior with retaliation.

A number of studies attempted to improve children's peer relations, using some variants of the procedures listed above. Oden and Asher (1977) "coached" children in social skills. Third- and fourth-grade children, low on peer acceptance, played with another child on six occasions. They were either coached on five of these occasions or simply played with the other child (peer pairing). In a control group, children played by themselves, with another child in the room. The experimenter discussed with children who were coached three concepts: participation in play, communication during play, and "validation support" (being friendly, nice, and "fun"). The stated purpose of this discussion was to make the game more fun and to make playing with another person more fun. The coach probed the child's understanding of these concepts, asked for examples, and asked for examples of opposite types of behavior. The coach also suggested to the child to try out some of the ideas during the immediately following play session and told the child that she will check back with him to see if it worked. That children could immediately try out or rehearse behaviors that were discussed is important for the acquisition of new behaviors, as I argued at length.

The coaching significantly increased the acceptance of coached children by peers, in comparison to the other two treatment conditions, by both partners in the play sessions and by nonpartners. A one-year follow-up showed that children who were coached continued to improve (their acceptance by others for play activities was just below the class average). Participants in the peer-pairing group made slight gains, whereas the sociometric ratings of control subjects remained unchanged. In the course of the play sessions, children's interactions were also assessed. There were no gains in positive behavior in the play setting parallel to gains in peer acceptance. However, in the play setting popular and unpopular children behaved in a similar fashion, and interactive behavior in the classroom was not evaluated.

In another study (Rosen, 1974), disadvantaged black children showed less sociodramatic play in their free-play activities than did advantaged children. Instruction and guided participation in sociodramatic play over an extended period—40 1-hour sessions—increased children's productivity in working on tasks, increased their cooperative behavior in a game developed by Madsen to test cooperation–competition (the cooperation board), and increased both perceptual role-taking and children's capacity to choose appropriate birthday presents for various people—mother, brother, sister, teacher. The intervention consisted of the experimenter's being with and entering into play with children during their free-play period in their kindergarten. The intervention was specifically tailored to children; twice a week, current behavior profiles were constructed for each child to guide intervention so that the child could learn the sociodramatic play he lacked. The experimenter brought toys that would evoke role taking. She worked with children individually, but, once they seemed capable of sociodramatic play, she worked with them in groups, introducing new ideas, themes, and incidents.

Clearly, the complex treatment procedure was guided by a primary conception, but many elements are intertwined in it, so that the contribution of specific elements is undeterminable. Moreover, the experimenter spent less time with children in control groups (10 hours) in leading them in activities and in communicating to them adults' interest in children's play activities.

In another study, by Zahavi and Asher (1978), aggressive preschool children were verbally instructed by their teacher in three "concepts": "the harm that results from aggression, its lack of effect as an interpersonal strategy, and the benefits that result from prosocial alternatives [p. 146]." Choosing 8 of the most aggressive children out of a total population of 19, each child was individually instructed in the three concepts, and the teacher asked questions, encouraged desired responses, and, if necessary, stated the "desired response." The teacher made a summary statement about each concept before discussing the next one. The training lasted for 10 minutes, on a single occasion. Somewhat surprisingly, given the limited instruction, it affected children's interactive behavior. A time-lagged design was employed; following baseline observation, 4 aggressive children were instructed, another observation period followed, then the second group of 4 aggressive children were instructed, with a third observation period at the end. Aggression significantly decreased for the instructed children, and changes in behavior followed the instruction sequence, appearing for the children who were instructed first during the second observation period and remaining at the lower level at the third period, and appearing for the children who were instructed second during the last observation period. There was a slight numerical increase in the positive interactive behavior of the instructed children. The behavior of the nonaggressive children did not change.

The just cited studies provide further evidence that role playing, verbal communications (that provide information about the consequences of certain acts and set standards), and learning through participation—in all of the studies children could immediately apply any cognitive learning that took place to interpersonal interaction—can contribute to positive behavior of varied kinds.

These studies may be considered as preliminary attempts. Peer socialization may be a powerful influence on the development of children's personalities, and the modification of a persistent negative pattern of peer interaction and of unpopularity and isolation may be one of the most important ways that we can help children. Since such interventions can take place in schools or in any organized settings where peer interaction takes place, they may be easier to affect than intervention in parent–child relations. Moreover, such interventions can be presented and conducted in a straightforward manner as learning of social–interpersonal skills, without implications for therapy.

In my view, presenting children with descriptions of situations that can occur in everyday interactions, having them role play such situations with exchange of roles, providing them with feedback (for example, in the form of presenting to them video films of their performance), and leading them in a discussion that is tied in with the role playing—of the consequences of their behavior on others, the motivation and intentions that underlie varied behaviors of other people, and of how their desires and goals can be satisfied by prosocial means—is likely to be highly effective in bringing about substantial and lasting changes in peer relations.

Socialization and Peer Relations

Presumably some of the child-rearing practices that were discussed earlier lead to the desire to behave positively toward others, to interpersonal competence, role-taking ability, initiative in social interactions, and other characteristics that enable the child to interact in a positive, responsive manner with peers and gain their liking and acceptance. As a consequence the child starts off in a good position to learn by, benefit from, and further develop his prosocial tendencies in interaction with peers.

A number of the research projects that were previously reviewed in examining the relationship between parental practices and children's characteristics used positive behavior in interaction with peers (Baum-rind, 1967, 1971; Hoffman, 1963) or peers' perception of children's consideration or helpfulness (Hoffman, 1975a; Hoffman & Saltzstein, 1967; Mussen *et al.*, 1970) as measures of children's prosocial behavior. They showed that induction, parental affection, and patterns of practices that were discussed in Chapter 4 contribute to positive behavior toward or perception of helpfulness by peers.

Other research examined child-rearing practices similar to some that were earlier suggested as antecedents of a prosocial behavior tendency and found them positively related to popularity. A consistent finding across the relatively few relevant studies is that children whose parents are pleased with them tend to receive more favorable evaluations from their peers than children whose parents are dissatisfied with them. Winder and Rau (1962) reported, for example, that fathers of high-status boys gave positive evaluations of their sons' competence. The parents of high-status boys also provided them with more supportive reinforcement. They discouraged aggressive behavior but used relatively little aggressive punishment or deprivation of privileges. Elkins (1958) also reported a positive relationship between satisfaction of parents with their children and sociometric status. Parental affection too was positively related to peer status. It also works in the other direction; accepted children report greater satisfaction with their home lives and describe their families as more cohesive (Elkins, 1958; Warnath, 1955).

Several experiments suggest that good relationships with the father contribute to good peer adjustment (Hoffman, 1961; Lynn & Sawrey, 1959; Wyer, 1965). Hoffman found that boys whose mothers were dominant were less successful in exerting influence on their peers, and were likely to be aggressive and unfriendly. When the father was dominant in disciplining the child, the child was likely to be forceful in initiating friendships and to have higher power in the peer group. Moreover, affection from both the mother and the father was significantly related both to boys' liking of other children and to others' liking for them. Affection from the father was also related to effective skills in peer interaction. Absence of fathers (Lynn & Sawrey, 1959) and lack of communication between children and fathers was associated with poor peer relations.

The Influence of the Nature and Rules of the Peer Group and of the Extended Environment

So far the importance of positive peer relations has been stressed. The nature of a peer group and the rules by which it functions are likely to affect the patterns of interaction among children in the group, the relationship of the children to the outside world, and generally the kind of learning and development that may result from the child's experience with his peers. Certainly, if every child in a group of young children has his own toys and each is encouraged to respect property rights—based on the rationale that conflicts will be minimized—interactions are likely to be different from those in a group where all toys are community property that is to be shared. Or, if in a group of children every behavior is directed by rules laid down by adults, the opportunities for growth and development through interactive experience will be restricted in comparison to groups in which children are allowed greater freedom and self-determination. Leitner's (1977) finding of more social initiation by children, particularly of a friendly kind, in a less structured than in a more structured school supports this point (although one cannot be certain that the schools differed only in degree of structure). On the other hand, for the optimal functioning of the group and optimal development of its members, it is probably necessary to set certain basic rules, which are enforced, that protect the welfare and interests of members of the group but do allow considerable freedom.

To some extent all children's groups, whether they are as formal as nursery schools and classrooms, or as informal as gangs or groups that develop at street-corner meeting places, develop some of their own rules. There is evidence that even aggression in street-corner groups, both among members and toward the outside world, is guided by quite specific, although mainly unverbalized, rules (Miller, Geretz, & Culter, 1961).

The rules of the adult world and of children are surprisingly often consistent: Children adopt their parents' values in some fashion in most societies and derive rules and standards from them to guide their conduct in interaction with their peers (Hartup, 1970). The degree to which this is so is certain to vary, however, across cultures, subcultures, and families in a culture. Mead (1970) speculated that cultures vary, both in comparison to each other and over time, in the extent to which individuals' behavior in them is guided by the influence of peers *(cofigurative cultures)* in contrast to social values and norms that members internalized *(postfigurative cultures)*. In cofigurative cultures parents presumably educate their children to be concerned about evaluation by peers and to derive standards of conduct from peers in contrast to internalizing values and standards that parents promote and guiding behavior according to them. Hollander and Marcia (1970), in studying white middle-class fifth-graders, found reliable differences in children's peer orientation; that is, they found variation in the extent that children used peers in contrast to parents or their own beliefs as standards. The authors found a significant relationship between the extent that parents tended to use peers as a standard for the child and the child's own peer orientation. The latter was measured by the children's interview reports, questionnaire responses, and sociometric ratings by other children. Unfortunately, information about parental peer orientation was available only from the children's reports, not from an independent source.

Bronfenbrenner and his associates conducted investigations in a variety of countries on the influence of peers and adults on children's behavior. In these studies, in addition to cultural variations, the influence of the particular context of the children's lives, the social setting, was also explored. The researchers used Bronfenbrenner's (1970a) moral dilemma test, which measures the extent to which children report that they would engage in behavior that was urged by peers but conflicted with adult standards. Some of the items have little to do with prosocial or moral behavior (e.g., going to a movie recommended by friends but disapproved of by parents), whereas others do relate to prosocial behavior (leaving a sick friend to go to a movie with a friend). The items were developed through interviews with parents, teachers, and children, to make sure that children and adults disagreed about their desirability.

Fifth-graders in the United States reported much greater willingness to engage in peer-advocated but parent-disapproved behavior than Soviet children of the same age. Moreover, when children were asked to report how they would act if they were supervised, Soviet children reported that they would misbehave less, whether their behavior was supervised by peers or parents. These findings are not surprising. In the Soviet Union extensive supervision is exercised over children, and peers are also used as agents in supervising children's adherence to adult rules. Not only does this make it understandable why supervision by adults and peers would both reduce "misconduct," but the continuous, rigorous supervision makes it less likely than in the case of American children that subjects truthfully reported what they thought they would do. American children reported that they would deviate less from adult standards if they were supervised by parents but would deviate more if they were supervised by peers, in comparison to reports by children of how they would act when they are unsupervised.

Related to the issue of truthful reporting as well as to cultural differences in reports of conformity are comparisons of German and American children's reports, done by Devereux (1972). He assumed—and found—that because socialization in Germany is more authoritarian, German preadolescents would report more conformity to adult standards than would American preadolescents. Moreover, the German subjects showed a significant increase in their reports of conformity to adults and of "guilt–anxiety" over misconduct when the measure was administered with a teacher present, whereas the American children did not.

Bixenstine, DeCorte, and Bixenstine (1976) replicated the findings about the effects of supervision by peers and parents on American children's reports of how they would act. In their study children's reports of their willingness to engage in peer-promoted behavior that deviated from adult standards increased with age, from third to eighth grade, then leveled off at eleventh grade. With increasing age children also judged the conduct described by the items on the test as less wrong and reported less favorable attitudes toward adults in general and their fathers in particular. Bixenstine *et al.* explain the age differences as the result of less favorable feelings about adults.

A study by Turiel (1976) also reported a decrease in "moral knowledge" with age (perhaps similar in meaning to the decrease in judgments of wrongness found by Bixenstine *et al.*), but an increase in levels of moral reasoning. Unfortunately Turiel did not report the items of his moral knowledge test, and Bixenstine *et al.* did not differentiate among items in their analysis. It is reasonable to expect that children in our culture would ascribe less, with increasing age, to items about obedience to authority, acting according to rules, or unconditional statements about honesty or other standards. Since our culture appears to emphasize individualism, such values and behaviors expressing them would come to be less valued with age; other values and behaviors might not be.

Evaluation of the wrongness of the items, children's self-report of how they would behave, and Turiel's findings of decrease in moral knowledge might all be the result of children's increasing critical evaluation of standards and rules that are set by adults for young children. Many standards may come to be regarded in less absolute terms by older children and held important only if they serve some moral principle or basic value. In fact, although probably more slowly than children would want, adults' values about and expectations of children's behavior at different ages must also change. These reasons, and increasing identification with peers, may primarily account for reports of increased willingness by older children to engage in peer-promoted deviation from adult standards. However, Bixenstine *et al.*'s (1976) findings of children's increasingly less favorable evaluation of adults in general and of their fathers in particular is of interest in itself. If they are reliable findings, are they only characteristic of our culture? Or are they characteristic of others too? Do they represent the increasing capacity of children to evaluate others' behavior critically and their desire to separate themselves from others, including their parents? If cultural differences exist, what are their causes and consequences?

The apparently contrasting influence in our culture of peers and adults on certain behaviors of children might have positive consequences. As Garbarino and Bronfenbrenner (1976) suggest, contrasting influences on children might create diversity and complexity, which children have to come to terms with. If the complexity and diversity are not too great, the conflicts they produce not too severe, in the course of dealing with and resolving the conflicts children are likely to develop and grow in the realm of morality.

It is unfortunate that we know so little about the kinds of group structures that best contribute to children's personal and moral development. We know that certain conditions lead to cooperation and induce positive behaviors; cooperative tasks or group atmospheres lead to more prosocial behavior (Bryant & Crockenberg, 1974) and greater feelings of benevolence toward others in the group and even toward outsiders (Volume 1, Chapter 9). In democratically organized groups, children work on tasks and interact more constructively than in groups with authoritarian adult leadership (Lippitt & White, 1943). But the consequences of variations in environmental structure and rules that are applied to groups—as well as to individual children—need to be extensively explored.

The importance of group structures, standards, and atmosphere might be similar to the importance of nurturance, parental control, and natural socialization in relation to individual children; they may provide preconditions for optimal development and may lead to certain kinds of interactive experiences. From another perspective, Kohlberg (1976) reasons that the moral atmosphere of the group is one of the basic conditions for moral development. The American orphanage and the Israeli kibbutz are found, in Kohlberg's casual analysis, at the opposing extremes of moral atmospheres; children in the orphanage show very low levels of moral reasoning, children in the kibbutz show very high levels. However, the two groups differ in a tremendous number of ways. Here again, more research is needed.

Increasingly, I am moving in this discussion from the rules guiding interaction in the peer group to the nature of the larger environment. The structure, organization, and rules of an environment can influence behavior directly and shape personality and, thereby, affect behavior indirectly. Only recently have psychologists begun to realize the necessity to systematically explore the influence of environments. As an initial step, various psychologists suggested that we begin to classify environments and suggested or explored dimensions along which environments may be classified (Mischel, 1976; Moos, 1974). Trickett (1978) examined the perceived environment—what he called the social ecology—of varied schools. He found differences among rural, urban, suburban, vocational, and alternative schools in the three dimensions that he explored: involvement, affiliation, and support among students and between students and teachers; orientation toward learning, expressed in task orientation and competition; and order and organization, rule clarity, teacher control, and innovation. Differences in these aspects of the school environment must have impact on children's personalities and social development.

The nature of the family, the school, a neighborhood, an ethnic or religious group in which one holds membership, and one's society can influence parental socialization and natural socialization and can provide rules for peer interaction, as well as set ideals to live by. Consider, as just one example, the tremendous variations in opportunities that different societies offer for children to assume meaningful responsibilities for the welfare of members of their family and of those outside the family. Or consider the extent to which they stress competitiveness or cooperation, achievement or other values and behavioral orientations, or are democratically or autocratically organized. We shall have to explore how the larger environment affects the type of influences that we have considered and how it joins with and modifies these influences in shaping children's personalities and social development, as well as prosocial orientation and behavior.

Summary and Conclusions: The Development of Positive Social Behavior and Morality

chapter 8

Classes of Socializing Influences

Varied influences on children appear to promote personal characteristics that increase the likelihood of positive behavior (see Table 8.1).

Certain parental socializing practices—including modes of interaction with the child and tuitional influences and their patterning—appear to contribute to positive orientation toward others. Affection and nurturance, effective but reasonable modes of control, reasoning with the child, and, specifically, the use of induction and the modeling of positive conduct by parents were important elements that I specified.

Another class of influences on children that I proposed as highly important is natural socializing experience. Parents can induce the child to engage in positive behavior in the home, both in the course of the flow of their everyday experience and as part of specific responsibilities that the child has to assume. Without this, the child is not likely to acquire or retain the cognitions and affects that induction, modeling, and other influences may initially induce. Inductive statements and the observations of others' behavior may become disconnected from behavior irrelevant to the child's own conduct. In contrast, having such responsibilities in the home, as well as parents inducing the child to engage in positive behaviors outside the home and people in other settings inducing

251

Table 8.1

The Development of Personality, with Emphasis on Prosocial Orientation

Classes of influences on children	Principles of learning and development	Consequences or outcomes
1. Parental (adult) socialization	1. Conditioning–punishment	I. Personal characteristics
a. Quality and style of interaction	2. Identification	1. Value (and affective) orientations
warmth and affection		
effective control	3. Resolution of cognitive disequilibrium or discrepancy	2. Specific values, standards
reasoning		
b. Content of influence	4. Observational learning	3. Beliefs about and evaluations of people, events, situations
what is modeled		
induction	5. Inferring qualities of self (self-perception) and of environment	⎱ Personal goals (1–3)
2. Natural socialization participation in prosocial behaviors (e.g., caring for others, teaching others)		4. Perceptual tendencies role taking speed of defining events
3. Peer socialization		5. Self-esteem
4. Nature of environment degree of structure, nature of rules, distribution of authority, and other aspects		6. Competencies locus of control plans and strategies specific competencies
		II. Behavior The function of varied personal characteristics and current environmental influences

the child to assume responsibilities for others' welfare and to engage in positive behavior, may all be important sources of learning and development, both in themselves (given supporting circumstances) and in conjunction with other influences.

Peer socialization is a third class of important influences. Few would question the fact that peers exert important socializing influence on each other. Although directly relevant data are limited, I suggested what I believe are reasonable hypotheses about the development of patterns of interactions among children and their long-term consequences. Children who experience different patterns of interaction would learn different behavioral skills and would develop different beliefs about and feelings toward their peers as well as toward themselves in relation to their peers. The characteristics and behavioral skills with which children enter the peer group, as well as the rules and structure of the peer group—largely set by adults among younger children, but even then partly a function of the characteristics of the individual children, of the adults supervising them, and of other factors, including amount of space and availability of toys—may all affect the patterns of interactions that are permissible and possible within the peer group and the patterns that individual children will enter into.

This brings us to the fourth class of influences, the nature of the child's environment. There are varied environments that the child lives in and experiences, and environments have varied levels. For example, parents may set rules that siblings must follow in their interactions. They may specify and enforce the level of aggression that is permissible among the children and the kinds of positive behaviors they must engage in. They may specify how much authority older children may exercise over younger ones. The nature of the rules that parents set for interactions among their children and the modes of interactions they expect between themselves and their children may be similar or quite different. Conceivably, some parents allow or encourage relatively democratic modes of interaction among their children—the use of reason and joint decision making—but act in an autocratic fashion in their own interactions with them.

Three basic environments of children in our society are the home, the school, and peer groups outside the school; their structures and natures may be similar or different. The rules imposed by adults, the tasks of interactions, the physical nature of the environment and what activities it permits, the characteristics of other children and adults, and the material objects available (their abundance and variety) make up the structure and nature of the environment. From a different perspective, we may consider rights or privileges, their distribution among children and between children and adults, or how fair and just the environment is. Other aspects and levels of the environment can also be considered: its ethnic or religious character, the nature of society as a whole. Such aspects of the environment can exert their influence relatively directly through rules that guide behavior or can affect parental treatment of the child. One study showed that the existence of a kinship network and church attendance, as well as other conditions, affected the parents' treatment of children in low income families (Giovannoni & Billingsley, 1970). On the whole, we know woefully little about the long-term effects of different kinds of environments on children.

I would expect an environment in which there is reasonable structure (and effective control) that limits harmful interactions among children and encourages positive interactions, interdependence among members of the group so that cooperation and positive behavior in response to need occur naturally, a fair amount of autonomy that children are allowed so that they can learn and develop effective modes of interaction and conflict resolution, and basically democratic and just relationships between children and adults to contribute to prosocial orientation, high self-esteem, a sense of competence, role taking, and positive social behavior.

I implied in the preceding chapters that the adult socialization practices that contribute to the development of prosocial behavior tendencies and to related value and affective orientations are *optimal,* in the sense that they contribute to a tendency not only for prosocial behavior but also for desirable personal characteristics. These include high self-esteem, the capacity for self-assertion, and the ability to take one's own interests into account. The personal characteristics and behavioral tendencies that result may contribute to effective adjustment, good relationships to other people, a sense of satisfaction with oneself, and personal well-being. However, if children have to deal with peers or school environments or a society that exposes them to insensitivity and cruelty, the tendency to approach others positively, as well as related personal characteristics such as sensitivity and responsiveness, may be dysfunctional. Thus, whether certain characteristics are optimal or not depends on what environment a person lives in and needs to adapt to.[1] Moreover, if children are exposed to such "negative" environments, the parental practices that were described as contributing to prosocial behavior may not do so. Parents

---

[1] I recognize that what are optimal characteristics can be argued endlessly. What I regard as optimal is based on values and ideals I hold about human life and about ways for human beings to live together. Others, who start from different values, may not regard these characteristics as optimal.

need to adjust their practices and help the child adapt his developing prosocial orientation and behavior to aggressive, cruel, or unjust environments. Otherwise, not having the cognitive, affective, and behavioral skills to cope with such environments, the child may experience the impact of these negative environments as even greater than he would with parental practices that lead to more aggressive behavior and less concern for others.

Interrelationships and Changes of Influences

I have noted in the chapters dealing with parental socialization (4 and 5) the need to consider patterns of practices and to explore correlates of varied patterns while also trying to identify the influence of specific practices that are part of the pattern. The preceding discussion points to the need to go beyond patterns of parental practices to patterns of influences of different kinds.

The interrelationship among different kinds of socializing influences is an issue of substantial importance. Varied kinds of influences certainly modify each other's effects. Graves and Graves (1978) reported that, when Cook Island children are presented with alternative ways to distribute rewards between themselves and another child, with increasing age their rivalry increases (the extent to which they maximize the difference between themselves and the other child, even when this does not lead to greater benefits for the self but only diminishes the gains of the other) and their generosity decreases (the extent to which children make choices that benefit the other child at no cost to themselves). These researchers attribute the change to the Western-type schooling that children are exposed to on Cook Island. They present some evidence that children who are more involved in the school—judged from their neatness in school and their grades, for example—show more rivalry. There was very little increase in rivalry with age among children who lived in extended families; this occurred primarily among children who lived in nuclear families. The findings do not indicate whether children who come from extended families get less involved with school and develop less of a competitive orientation or whether these children do get involved with school but the interdependence among family members and the responsibilities that children may have to assume in extended families counteract the competitive orientation that involvement with school fosters. In either case, this seems to be an instance of different types of influences combining and joining in affecting how children develop.

Another example of varied constellations may come from a comparison of what I suggested as important in our society, a combination of inducing children to assume responsibility for others' welfare and to participate in positive behavior with positive induction, and what Whiting and Whiting (1975) reported as correlates of positive behavior in some other societies. In less technologically advanced societies than ours, where participation in activities that contribute to the maintenance and welfare of families was a regular part of children's lives, parents apparently engaged in little induction. Children nonetheless showed helpful behavior, made helpful suggestions to others, and sought relatively little help and attention for themselves in comparison to children in other societies. The structure of the environment and the children's natural socializing experiences may have led children to experience certain existing rules and modes of behavior as "givens," as integral parts of reality.

I briefly noted (for example, in Chapter 4 in the discussion of control and autonomy) an important issue: That, over time, parental practices inevitably change. They (and probably other influences) must change to promote the child's further development of positive characteristics. Parent–child interactions may change as a result of parents themselves changing or gaining experience, changing family dynamics sometimes due to the birth of other children, or changes in cultural values. However, a primary reason for change must be the change in the growing child. The manner in which practices change would partly depend on the characteristics of the child. If the child develops the capacity for delay of gratification, self-control, and the ability to guide his behavior according to rules set by parents and societal dictates, presumably parents can treat the child in a less instructional, more democratic fashion—if they are inclined to do so. We need more research and theory in this domain. How do parental practices change with the increasing age of children? How do they change as a function of the characteristics of the child?

Baumrind (1975) wrote that, in interviews in her studies, authoritative and harmonious parents (the latter term referring to a small group of parents who established harmony, equanimity, and rationality in the family and had control—in the sense that children tried to intuit what the parents wanted—but did not directly exercise control) made frequent references to the child's stage of development. They saw the duties and obligations of parents and children as a changing function of the child's development. These parents' ideology focussed on believing in the norm of reciprocity, in reciprocal duties and obligations of parents and children. Their practical application of the concept of reciprocity depended on what the child was able to do. Thus, part of the reason for the effectiveness of authoritative parents may have been their awareness of the changing needs and competencies of the child, this presumably leading to changing demands placed on the child as well as to changes in what the parents offered the child in forms of care, ways of spending time together, and their manner of guidance. However, in Baumrind's studies the children were preschoolers. The continued effects of varied patterns of childrearing and the actual changes in parent–child interactions need to be explored.

What kinds of changes in parental practices may be necessary to continue to promote prosocial behavioral tendencies? One may be a greater reliance on self-control by children, accompanied by an increase in the autonomy that is granted to them. Another may be an increase in the extent to which parents guide the child toward natural socializing experiences—participation in varied activities that would promote the child's further development—and a decrease in attempts to directly teach the child. The nature of induction that is employed with the child, or of reasoning in general, has to change. In their first few years it may be useful to tell children what is good or bad to do. Already at an early age "preaching" may become counterproductive, but pointing out beneficial or harmful consequences of varied acts on people's psychological and physical welfare becomes useful. At a still later age—probably by preadolescence—communications have to be more sophisticated and less direct, building on what the child presumably already knows. On the one hand, adult communications may at that time put behavior and their consequences into a larger context and may focus on human beings living together in social groups and on the conditions that are necessary to promote mutual welfare. On the other hand, they may elaborate and differentiate to a greater extent among internal psychological experiences of people, thus enabling the child to perceive and respond to subtle emotions, psychological states, and motives of other people in a sensitive and differentiated manner. It would be worthwhile to develop and test hypotheses about "optimal" changes with the child's age in all four classes of socializing influences (Table 8.1).

Divergence in Personality as a Source of Development

A basic but neglected issue is how the developing personality of children affects both the kind of influences that are later directed at them and what they learn when they are exposed to identical experiences and influences. Children appear different at birth, in varied characteristics including the amount and intensity of crying, their ease or difficulty of being soothed, their cuddliness (to what extent they mold their bodies to adults who hold them or try to minimize contact), and their activity level (Escalona, 1968; Freedman, 1965; Korner & Grobstein, 1976). We know little about the extent to which, or the manner in which, these differences give rise to divergent development. It is certainly the case, however, that interactions among human beings are transactional and that from birth on children and adults exert mutual influence on each other. Although the transactional nature of interactions means that relationships to which both the child and his parents contribute evolve and continuously develop, one might think that the influence of adults when the child is very young is greatly dominant. However, recent research findings show substantial mutuality in infants' and adults' contributions to the developing interactive system (see Bronfenbrenner, 1977).

The developing personality of the child will shape the reactions of other people to the child, will guide the child's perceptions of events and the meaning the child derives from experiences, and will enter into all facets of the child's cognitive, affective, and behavioral experiences. Thus, as children's personalities begin to diverge, the personalities themselves become a highly important influence on their further development. This continues into adulthood, since people's personalities and interactive behavior continue to shape their experiences. For example, in varied cultures children were found to differ in how competitive or cooperative they were in playing a game with a peer, their behavior affecting their partner's responses. Competition, in particular, evoked competitive responses (Toda, Shinotsuka, McClintock, & Stech, 1978). This was also found among adults (Kelley & Stahlesky, 1970).

How existing personality characteristics affect further development is of profound significance. Research and theory have, nonetheless, largely ignored the issue. We need to assess children's personal characteristics and interactive behavior at varied points in time and to consider their influence in conjunction with socializing influences. One focus of our assessment may be the personal characteristics presented in Table 8.1. These characteristics, which I regard as important influences on positive behavior, may also shape the further development of personality. Other characteristics, such as the degree of identification and cooperation with adults or the degree of an oppositional tendency that developed toward them, would directly affect the socializing process. They can be expected to have profound effects on further development.

I have described many potential influences on the child and have implied many possible combinations. A reader may throw up his or her hand in desperation. Specifying too many determinants may seem like specifying none; they lose their utility. Although focussing on a limited set of influences is certainly easier, doing so denies the true natures of the phenomena. One of the burdens that psychology has had to deal with in the course of its history is the lure of grand ideas that often take the place of attention to the genuine complexity of human functioning and to the efforts that are necessary to begin to unravel this complexity. But how can one deal with this complexity? First, we may want to describe and clarify phenomena as they exist in nature. Whereas many different combinations of influences on children are possible, there are probably only a few dominant patterns that are frequent in a culture. One reason for this is that dominant cultural and subcultural values that guide the treatment of children are likely to exist. Another is a seemingly natural and probably frequently occurring relatedness among certain practices (e.g., reasoning with children, granting them autonomy, and nurturance), which may partly derive from an inherent consistency among them. Second, the existence of a variety of influences and their proposed inter-relationships does not mean that specific hypotheses about subsets of these influences are not meaningful to explore. However, a concern about how influences join should lead to better-informed hypotheses.

Antecedents of Different Kinds of Positive Social Behavior

The research and theory that I have examined in this book did not focus on differences among the antecedents of varied kinds of prosocial behavior. Unfortunately, we do not yet have research that would identify differences in antecedents. Moreover, the motivational bases of varied positive acts can be—although need not always be—similar.

I want to distinguish at least among a few types of positive conduct: Sensitivity and responsiveness to others' psychological states; cooperation and helpfulness in everyday interactions; the willingness for material sacrifice, to share with and give to others; responsiveness in suddenly oc-curring emergencies; and the willingness to take great risks and to engage in substantial potential or actual sacrifices. Finally, the desire to engage in social and/or political action in order to improve the welfare of other people in one's society (or in the world) is an important form of positive conduct. These different types of positive behaviors place different de-mands on a person, embody different degrees and kinds of costs, and often result in benefits of different magnitudes and kinds. Some of these posi-tive behaviors depend on a person's value orientation and specific values that modify or extend the basic value orientation. Others also demand specific skills—such as the capacity to take others' roles and to make in-ferences about others' psychological states, varied competencies (including the knowledge of how one might exert influence on the political system), courage, and other characteristics.

Although different types of positive conduct can be based on similar motives, they require different combinations of personal characteristics. For example, Christians who participated in underground activities to save Jews and other persecuted individuals in Nazi Germany were characterized by having been exposed to at least one parent highly concerned with morality and right conduct. They were marginal members of their social group—and thus may have felt less need to conform or to accept their society's dehumanizing views of Jews and of other minorities. These individuals were also adventurous. They participated in varied dangerous activities before they joined in the attempt to save lives (London, 1970). They apparently possessed courage and enjoyed danger and adventure.

Most of the research has dealt with the origins of positive behavior toward other individuals. However, attempting to influence how one's society or some part of it functions, in the hope of improving the welfare of its members, is an important type of positive behavior. Most research and theory on personality and social development has dealt with the development of how an individual relates to himself (for example, his self-esteem), the personal motives he develops (achievement, affiliation, and others), and his interpersonal behavior. Even in the realm of moral development, the primary concern has been with the individual's relationship to other individuals.

Inevitably, people also develop a relationship to the system they live in and toward systems in general. At one extreme, they may have little concern with the system, pursuing their individual goals, whereas, at another extreme, they may have an intense desire to change the system— by political activity, by social action, or by revolutionary means. Such activities can be based on a desire for improving human welfare or for extending justice, but they can also be based on the desire to improve one's own fate or on other self-related motivation, such as a desire for power.

The origins of social action and political action and a differentiated analysis of the origins of different kinds of prosocial behavior are important. Involvement with social and political action may vary in likelihood and in form, depending on socialization and on the interrelationship of varied socializing influences (Block, Haan, & Smith, 1969; Rosenhan, 1970). In Russia, the government attempts to create uniform socializing influences by coordinating what children are taught, how they are treated, and how their environment is organized in the school, in youth groups, and even in the home (by "educating" parents). In a country where this happens, assuming that parents do actually conform to governmental influence, children do not have to deal with and create their own resolutions of divergent influences. Since the educational practices rely on children's assuming responsibilities for others' welfare, such socialization may promote cooperation and a sense of duty and obligation toward authority and the system but may retard individuality and autonomy. In our society, there is at least moderate divergence among different types of socializing influences; this may contribute to a sense of individuality, of independence, and, to some degree, of moral autonomy. Although the socialization we expose children to may frequently not include important antecedents of a prosocial behavioral tendency, it *can* lead to greater willingness to attempt to influence how society functions. (Beyond differences in socialization, the existence of repression would, of course, inhibit political and social action.)

Ideologies and apparently high ideals that serve as the ideological basis of social action, political action, and revolution have frequently led to inhuman conduct. Human beings seem able to engage even in mass murder for high-minded reasons. A milder equivalent of the cognitive processes that probably enable people to do this can occur in response to any type of human need—justifications that make the need appear small, that make the person in need seem not deserving of help, or that in other ways eliminate the need for action or justify inaction. Justifications are cognitive activities that enable people to pursue their own desires and to act in self-serving ways. Sometimes justifications can appear highly moral. There is extensive evidence that justifications can affect positive behavior (see Volume 1, particularly Chapter 4).

We ought to explore their origins. Individuals may greatly differ in the extent to which they employ an advanced capacity to reason morally for self-serving rather than for truly moral purposes. The belief that the world is just and the accompanying desire that justice be maintained is frequently associated with devaluation of sufferers and the denial of the rights of those who are deprived or underprivileged, apparently on the basis that they must be undeserving (Volume 1, Chapter 4). How does this kind of functioning come about? It may be the result of parents's stressing mutual obligations among persons and concern about fairness and justice to the exclusion of mercy and concern about the welfare of individual human beings. If parents guide the child to perceive others' fate and their own primarily in terms of whether or not it is just, such consequences may follow. "Deserved" suffering would, then, not evoke sympathy, and no need to mitigate it would be seen. The origins of the tendency to use justifications seem highly important to understand.

Principles of Change

One of the deficiencies of past theories has been that they focussed on one or another principle or mechanism as the source of change or development, often implying or insisting that only that single principle was involved. I believe that children change, learn, and develop through varied principles (Table 8.1, Column 2). Although all these principles and perhaps others are probably always involved, specific socializing influences and the child's developing personality can lead to change occuring more through some principles than through others. What determines their relative influence? Do the principles by which learning takes place affect *what* is learned? These are basic questions to explore.

Varied theories attempted to specify conditions that are conducive for change to occur through specific principles (see Chapters 2 and 4). For example, warmth and affection, parental power, and power over the distribution of resources were among the conditions proposed as important for learning to occur through identification. Large bodies of research have attempted to identify the conditions that maximize learning through conditioning and punishment. The time intervals between stimulus, response, and reinforcing sequences have been examined in order to identify optimal intervals. The consequences of patterns of reinforcement—whether reinforcement is continuous (always follows some behavior) or variable in frequency or has other properties—have been identified. The opportunity for extensive interaction with peers and for role taking has been proposed as an important source of change through the (creation and) resolution of cognitive disequilibrium. It has been proposed that the application of limited force in exerting influence on children is crucial if change is to occur through dissonance reduction. I suggested that the same is true for change to occur through self-attribution and changed self-perception. Whereas research on cognitive dissonance focussed on what children learn from not engaging in certain activities—such as not playing with prohibited toys—I focussed on how change occurs through participation in positive activities. The conditions that are involved in another type of learning—people making inferences about their environments—have not been specified. Simply the observation of other people's behavior and of events in the environment is probably sufficient, but how these observations are categorized may depend on the structure of the environment and on the existing personality of the person, such as personal constructs and perceptual and cognitive sets.

Other levels of analyses are also possible. If the child is under consistent, regular, highly specific external control, learning is likely to take place primarily by conditioning and punishment. The child is likely to be characterized by an external orientation, the desirability of conduct evaluated in terms of its external consequences. When the child is under such direct reinforcement (and punishment) control, and particularly when the force that is employed by agents of socialization is relatively great, there is a reasonable likelihood in a society like ours, in which children experience divergent inputs, that an oppositional tendency may develop. Children then may begin to devise strategies to subvert the authority of adults.

It is possible, however, for an environment to offer clear rules and fairly extensive structure without resulting in the development of an oppositional tendency. In some of the societies that Whiting and Whiting (1975) described, children appear positively socialized even though extensive structure exists. However, the children become responsible, participating members of the society relatively early, and they may define their own interests and those of the adults as identical rather than opposing. Consequently, identification is likely to occur. When adults and children are set in opposition due to inconsistency by adults, to lack of control or overly forceful control, to arbitrariness and hostility, or to conflicting rules, I would expect identification as a basis of learning to be limited. Negative identification and the desire to be different may be more likely.

An environment that provides reasonable structure—which is necessary for normal development—but also a fair amount of autonomy may lead children to learn through the resolution of cognitive disequilibrium and through making inferences about the self and the resulting continuous development of morally relevant self-perceptions. Making inferences about the self and about the environment is inevitable. However, the extent to which children see themselves as agents that control events or as pawns of a powerful environment will vary. Attributing prosocial qualities to the self and explaining positive behavior by the qualities of oneself, as well as making the kinds of inferences about the world that enhance the chance of positive behavior, are likely to result from an absence of overbearing external guidance. Moreover, in an oppressive and threatening environment children are less likely to experiment with varied roles, varied perspectives, and varied ways of relating to others. Unfortunately, much of this is speculation. We have not learned to assess by what principles children learn and develop outside the laboratory, partly because we have not concerned ourselves with the extent to which environmental conditions affect the principles or mechanism by which children change.

To continue with speculation, I would expect a combination of reasonable structure that gives children security, influences that are slight or moderate in "force" that lead them to behave prosocially, a generally benevolent environment, and freedom in interacting with peers and in assuming varied roles to be conducive for experiencing cognitive disequilibrium and for learning through the resolution of disequilibrium and through feedback from varied experiences. These conditions will certainly affect, however, *what* the child learns; several of them were described as origins of a prosocial behavioral tendency.[2]

When change in children comes about through different primary principles, some basic differences in what they learn or in how they develop should be evident. I suggested that conditioning and punishment as dominant principles are likely to lead to an external orientation. Learning through identification involves an orientation toward other people that may continue throughout life. In itself, the child's identifying with others has important meaning and implies connectedness and the fact that other people can be an important source of reference for the child. However, the conditions that lead to identification are likely to affect what the nature of this orientation to others will be, what kinds of people will be important to the child and why. Whether the child identifies with people in authority, with people who are nurturant, or with people demonstrating other characteristics is presumably affected by the source of the child's identification with parents and other early socializers. Change through the resolution of cognitive disequilibrium has a seemingly impersonal quality in cognitive developmental theorists' presentation. Moreover, the nature of the principled stages of moral reasoning implies an impersonal orientation toward others as an outcome of change, an orientation to principles, not to individuals. In contrast, I suggested that this mechanism of change is likely to be dominant in an environment that is affectively not threatening, inhibiting, or restricting. The outcomes are probably not abstract cognitive orientations but instead represent affective involvement with people. Relatively strong external guidance, both the use of and emphasis on authority may induce strong beliefs in principles, without empathic involvement with human beings. Obviously, these are, again, speculative hypotheses.

---

[2] Giving children responsibilities, having them engage in prosocial acts that benefit others, can appear to them as a privilege, a sign of their own importance and appreciation by others. However, for practical purposes it is. important to note that to induce children to assume regular responsibilities can also be difficult. This is particularly true when such responsibilities are not basic, customary aspects of childrens's socialization. Initially, it may require a fair amount of pressure, direct control, power assertion— what I referred to as *force*—to have children assume responsibilities. If the responsibilies and obligations do not unreasonably tax the child's capacities and are not unreasonably onerous, as they become habitual the necessity to employ force may diminish or disappear. The child may come to experience these behaviors as self-directed and as a source of satisfaction, with the attendant change in the evaluation of the activities and their outcomes (see Chapter 6).

The Outcomes of Socialization
for Prosocial Behavior

Deficiencies in Research

All along in this volume I suggested personal characteristics that may result from different socializing experiences. On specific occasions these personality characteristics, in combination with situational influences, are assumed to give rise to psychological processes—thoughts and feelings—that presumably mediate positive behaviors (see Volume 1). Specific psychological processes were frequently inferred from the relationship between independent variables and behavioral outcomes. Occasionally, researchers attempted to gain more direct information about these psychological processes. They examined physiological reactions to stimuli and considered how subsequent behavior was related to the magnitude of the physiological reactions, or they collected verbal information about what people thought or how they felt in response to influences directed at them. The latter was usually done in postexperimental questionnaires, following the behavioral response, so that the extent to which people responded to their own behavior rather than to the stimuli that impinged on them could not be ascertained. The influence of personality in interaction with situations was rarely explored, even though such research could provide information about psychological processes (see later in this section).

We have come to appreciate the significance of cognitive and affective processes and have, ideologically, given up the psychology of the empty organism, which focussed on stimulus–response connections alone. However, when we make inferences about internal processes, the information that we collect usually remains so far removed along an inferential chain from what a person thinks and feels that our inferences remain quite tentative. Usually, varied assumptions about what perceptions of events, what meanings attributed to events, and what motivations come about and affect behavior in response to experimental treatments remain tenable.

When experimental procedures (or socializing practices) bring about lasting increase (or decrease) in positive behavior, we are often left to speculate as to what changes occurred in the actors' personalities. Even less information is collected about changes in perceptual, cognitive, or affective tendencies, in the internal processes that seemingly stable personal characteristics give rise to. Thus, similar lacunae of knowledge exist when we consider current influences on behavior (the determinants of behavior) and when we consider the outcomes of socialization and the development of positive behavior. In socialization research there is usually some evaluation of children's thinking, their verbally reported affects, or their behavior, but the interrelationships among thoughts, affects, and behaviors are rarely assessed.

Could these deficiencies be remedied? Inevitably, we shall always have to make inferences about internal psychological processes. We are unlikely to ever know for certain how a person thinks and feels. But can we gather data that would provide better bases for inferences, more information about internal states than stimulus–response connections do by themselves? Two strategies seem useful. I suggested in Volume 1 that we should conduct experiments in which two groups of subjects are exposed to each experimental treatment. In one group, the treatment experiences would be followed by an attempt to evaluate cognitive and affective reactions by using questionnaires, interviews, projective stories, and observations of facial and bodily reactions. In another group, we would evaluate behavioral responses. If parallel changes occur, the inference that the cognitive and affective reactions mediated behavioral effects will become more reasonable.

We may also find that, using certain strategies, good indices of psychological processes can be derived without interfering with behavioral reactions, so that the relationship between psychological processes and behavior in the same persons can be explored. For example, Leiman (1978) extended a body of research that showed that ratings of facial expressions are reliable and valid measures of emotional reactions (see Volume 1, Chapter 4), in order to study the relationships between empathy and sharing. Leiman had children watch a videotaped story in which a child discovers that his favorite marble collection was stolen. The film ends with a close-up of the sad face of this child. The observers were unobtrusively filmed, and their reactions were rated as showing negative (empathic), neutral, or positive affect. In another group, the children did not watch the video story. Afterwards, the children could either play with a game that, when its crank was turned, produced a marble for the child who was the television actor or with another game. Children who did not watch the film produced an average of 37 marbles; those who watched but responded nonempathically produced an average of 73 marbles; and children who responded empathically produced an average of 104 marbles, all three groups significantly different from each other. Empathic reactions were seemingly involved in motivating children's prosocial behavior.

Another strategy, one that could be used concurrently with the first one, is the inclusion of relevant personality measures in experimental studies. Such designs, which have been called semiexperimental, can serve several important functions. Differences in relevant characteristics should give rise to different reactions to events. A person who demonstrated a greater empathic orientation on personality measures would be expected to respond with greater concern for a distressed person's welfare and with more affective involvement than would a person who demonstrated less empathic orientation. If, for example, differences in empathic orientation combine with induction procedures in affecting prosocial behavior, so that more empathic persons provide more help following induction than do less empathic persons, we have reason to believe that induction activated empathy. We can then make more informed and justified inferences about how behavior is mediated. (Similarly, when we expose children to experiences that are expected to promote some characteristic, knowledge of the interactive effects of these experiences and of already existing differences in personality will enable us to make more reasonable and more justified inferences about the kinds of learning and change that occurred.)

Experimental research is not the only culprit. In socialization research, frequently only the relationship between parental practices and aspects of children's cognitive functioning—their internalized values, as represented by projective stories, or their moral reasoning—is explored. Sometimes, teacher ratings and sociometric ratings by peers are used as indices of children's behavior. We have little information about how discriminative these ratings of, for example, consideration for others or aggression are. Ratings may often represent popularity, liking, and other global positive or negative reactions to the child (Staub, 1971a). Rarely is the child's interactive behavior observed and its relationship to parental practices explored, and, when that is done, usually children's personalities, their perceptual cognitive and affective functioning, are not assessed.

We need to do research in which the whole chain is explored: the influences that are directed at children (including personal characteristics that may modify their impact), changes in personality and in psychological functioning that they produce, and behavioral effects.[3]

---

[3] I believe that extending the effort that is necessary to get information about every component in this chain would greatly expand our knowledge of human development, but the need to do so has not been much stressed. For example, Bronfenbrenner (1977) discussed the need to do research on human development that considers the varied levels of influences on children, the need to consider the influence of each of these levels (ranging from parents to schools to the nature of society), and their interactions. He stressed the transactional, reciprocal character of human interactions and the need to study dyads, triads, and interactive systems with even more members. These suggestions are clearly consistent with the views I expressed in this chapter, and he made other pertinent suggestions as well. However, Bronfenbrenner focussed on sys-

A Developmental Theory of (Pro)social Behavior

The rudiments of a theory of social behavior were described in Volume 1, Chapter 2, and are briefly summarized in Chapter 1 of this volume. At various points in Volume 1 I suggested that the theory can summarize and explain research findings on how positive social behavior is determined and can point to future research. Can this theory be extended to include developmental components?

The theory was based on the assumption that we need to specify how personal characteristics and the characteristics of the environment join together to affect social behavior. It specified personal characteristics that are important to consider if we are to understand how positive behavior is determined, the manner in which these characteristics may combine, and how the motivation to behave in certain ways is activated by characteristics of the person and of the environment. The characteristics of the person and of the environment also determine whether this motivation, once activated, will gain expression in behavior. I believe that a theory of social behavior needs to be descriptive of persons and of their environments and that it also needs to be dynamic so that we can predict how the personal characteristics and environmental conditions will be organized in relation to each other. I proposed that personal goals, the motivational construct in the theory, are the primary organizers.

The descriptive terms of this theory can be considered as the relevant outcomes of socialization. Column 3 in Table 8.1 presents some of the personal characteristics that are important for predicting positive social behavior. Volume 1 (particularly Chapter 2) elaborates on how these characteristics join in affecting behavior. Using a descriptive system of this kind, we can begin to assess the specified characteristics of children from an early age on. We can test the relationship between influences directed at children, the principles by which they learn, and the outcomes. We can also evaluate how well our theory predicts at different ages how personal characteristics and situations combine in affecting behavior.

Some personal characteristics listed in Table 8.1 give rise to the motivation for prosocial behavior. I specified value orientations and the specific values, standards, and beliefs that a person holds as giving rise to varied personal goals. Past theories of how positive behavior is motivated, although useful, are limited in scope. Moral reasoning, empathic ca-

---

tems, roles, and interactions without emphasis on how the consequences of development must be evaluated at the individual level in terms of personality and of psychological processes, as well as of behavior. The psychological mechanisms of the individual filter experience and shape new experiences both through perception and through actions that affect the interactive system.

pacity, and other personal characteristics can give rise to motivation for positive behavior: They can be usefully subsumed, I believe, under the concept of personal goals. If we consider any one of these potential motivators alone, our capacity to understand and to predict behavior may remain poor. For example, an advanced capacity for moral reasoning may not by itself give rise to a desire to benefit a person in need. Even if it does, as a potential motivator of behavior it has to compete with other potential motivators, such as the need for achievement, the desire to gain approval, or hostility toward people in authority and a strong motivation to put them in their place. To be able to compare the influence of different and sometimes conflicting motives, it is worthwhile to think of them in identical conceptual terms and to measure them in similar ways. The concept of a personal goal, as I defined it, refers to the value or desirability for a person of a related set of outcomes, to the cognitive network that a person possesses in relation to these outcomes and to related events or phenomena, and to tension systems that move a person toward the goal. Personal goals also imply a potential that certain situations possess for activating certain goals (activating potential).

How can an empathic orientation toward others be conceptualized in terms of a personal goal? Empathy does not arise out of nowhere in response to another person's emotional state. The tendency to respond empathically must be coded and expressed in individual characteristics. Empathic responsiveness may be coded primarily in the form of a value orientation (e.g., prosocial orientation) that under certain conditions gives rise to empathic affect. Norms or standards for specific actions can also be derived from this value orientation. Other value orientations, such as an orientation toward duty and obligations toward other people, may give rise to standards (of a different sort) that guide conduct and to affects associated with adherence to or deviation from the standards but may not give rise to empathic reactions. These two value orientations, associated with (or based on) different cognitive networks and specifying somewhat different preferred outcomes, can be regarded as the bases of two different prosocial goals.

Other goals, for example, the desire to affiliate with others or the need for approval, can also lead, under certain circumstances, to a tendency to behave prosocially. Some people may learn to satisfy such goals by habitually engaging in prosocial behaviors that are sources of approval and provide opportunities for affiliation. Thus, habitual ways of expressing personal goals are important to assess. Specific values and standards that persons hold may indicate what the ranges of applicability for people of general value orientations and affective tendencies that give rise to prosocial goals are. The antecedents of different types of prosocial goals, which may arise from different value orientations, and of different specific values and standards that persons hold need to be explored (see Staub, 1979).

According to the theory, a strong prosocial orientation that gives rise to a prosocial goal that is characterized by the desire to improve others' welfare and by a positive evaluation of other people, concern about others' welfare, and a feeling of responsibility for others' welfare (embodied in cognitive networks that can give rise to affective reactions) will make it likely that a person will show moderate consistency in positive behavior across varied settings. Such a prosocial orientation is likely to have the capacity for role taking associated with it. It is not impossible, however, to imagine a set of socializing influences that leads to a strong prosocial orientation with relatively limited role-taking capacity. For example, when parents and other adults do not express their own feelings, do not point out how the child himself feels, and do not discuss differentiated internal states of other people and when the culture encourages children to be relatively inexpressive of internal states, children may develop a limited capacity for role taking. Other influences, which include the modeling of positive behavior by adults and verbal communications that stress the desirability of positive behavior (see Table 8.1), could lead to a strong prosocial orientation. Given a strong prosocial orientation and limited role-taking capacity, we may predict positive behavior when others' need is relatively obvious but not in response to slight cues of psychological distress or of need by others. Similarly, the knowledge of a child's level of self-esteem may lead to differential predictions about the child's initiating positive behavior under different circumstances. Under conditions of ambiguity, I would expect primarily children whose self-esteem is high and/or who perceive themselves as capable of influencing events to initiate helpful responses. Low self-esteem children may respond to others' need mainly when the need is unambiguous and/or the actions by which others can be helped are relatively unequivocal. Self-esteem may also modify the extent to which prosocial behavior is affected by experiences that modify temporary mood and other temporary psychological states. I am briefly giving examples and am thereby summarizing discussion, from both Volume 1 and Volume 2, that indicates how varied personal characteristics enter into affecting behavior.

Personal characteristics can be classified according to the extent to which they are directly relevant to positive behavior (direct) or are not directly relevant but are still likely to exert influence (indirect). Prosocial orientation and specific values and norms that make helping other people desirable are direct characteristics. Self-esteem is indirect when its influence on a person's willingness to initiate public behavior is considered. Self-esteem is also a somewhat direct characteristic in that it can affect a person's experience of the connection between the self and others, the extent of a bond (see Volume 1, Chapter 6). Specific competencies, such as the capacity to swim, are highly indirect, but when there is a necessity to save someone from drowning they can strongly affect helping. Role-taking capacity seems relatively direct in that it is important for sensitivity to others' psychological states. In this book I have focussed on the development of directly relevant personal characteristics. I have also suggested that certain indirect characteristics may be the by-products of the "optimal" socialization practices that lead to the development of directly relevant characteristics.

Table 8.1 and the preceding discussion present a system that can, it is hoped, be used to generate further research. Both global and specific hypotheses can be developed. As an example, our goal can be to specify influences on children that we believe promote both a strong prosocial goal and a goal that potentially leads to motivational conflict. Achievement may be such a goal. We can assess socializing influences on children, and their personal characteristics, in varied ways. Having tested the relationship between socializing influences and personal goals and having identified children with this combined motivational orientation, we can make differential predictions about circumstances in which the prosocial goal would be dominant and about others in which the achievement goal would exert the dominant influence. In still other circumstances the two goals may join and strengthen each other or may mutually inhibit each others' expression. Both observational research, with the activation potential of varied situations for prosocial and achievement goals specified, and experimental research, in which the activating potential of situations can be systematically varied, could be used to test predictions. I realize that this example points to years of research, but it suggests one potential use of the approach that I am presenting.

Another example of generating hypotheses may be to identify socializing practices (and analogues) that would, while leading to a strong prosocial goal, maximize or minimize competencies for prosocial behavior. Can we specify such socializing influences and identify the children exposed to them? Can we then differentially predict positive behavior as a function of demands placed on the child's competencies?

Naturally, characteristics that promote positive behavior will progressively develop with age. However, the determinants of positive behavior may also change with age. In younger children, prosocial behavior may be more the result of norms and standards imposed by the culture and may be less autonomous, less guided by their own values, than in older children. Aspects of this difference are almost certainly relative. Some children from an early age on appear to demonstrate a positive affective orientation toward other people and concern for others' welfare. Nonetheless, different motivations may be primary at different ages. One of our goals may be to specify how the determinants of positive behavior change and what characteristics may be primarily influential in affecting positive behavior at different ages.

Past theories have been limited by a focus on only one or another principle or mechanism of change, by a focus on primarily one kind of outcome—such as moral reasoning or behavior—and by giving rise to the application of only certain kinds of research methodologies. In my view, many and varied methodologies and kinds of information are important. We need to evaluate the structure of children's environments. We need to evaluate behaviors directed at children (and the *principles* that guide socializers, which may inform us of aspects of their behavior that otherwise we would consider unimportant or would not even notice). We need to evaluate children's perceptions of their environment and of behaviors directed at them, what meaning they assign to them, their affective reactions to them, and how their cognitive networks and affective orientations change as a result of their experience. These evaluations ought to take place both in naturalistic and in experimental settings. We ought to explore what systematic differences exist between children's behavior in everyday life settings and in the laboratory. There is evidence that young children, for example, show systematic differences in their interaction with parents in the home and in the laboratory. Bronfenbrenner (1977), who reviews some of the research, notes that such differences do not make our research invalid as long as we are aware of their nature and meaning.

Education in Positive Behavior

The material presented in this book is so clearly relevant and applicable to educating children to behave prosocially in varied settings including homes, schools, peer groups, or summer camps that only a few issues need to be considered here.

Many of the procedures that were employed in the experimental research can be transferred to other settings and applied to children's ongoing experience: role playing, inducing children to participate in positive activities, their exposure to television and live models, and others. That many of these procedures do not represent direct tuition, that the child is not preached to or somehow directly taught to be "good," makes them more acceptable, I believe, in applied settings. But, beyond these specific procedures, the practices that, when employed by parents, appeared useful in promoting characteristics that lead to positive behavior are likely to have similar effects when employed by teachers. Affection and nurturance, effective but reasonable control, and the other practices that were discussed can be expected to have positive consequences when employed in the classroom. A cooperative atmosphere in the classroom is likely to lead to positive feelings toward others and to increased cooperation, as the research findings (reviewed primarily in Volume 1, Chapter 9) suggest.

What if there is conflict between the environment and practices employed at home and in the school, the home providing a negative environment, the school a relatively optimal one? Will the school be effective in counteracting the home? Presumably, it can be if the child is engaged and becomes a truly participating member of this environment. The child has to acquire the capacity to effectively discriminate between the two environments, to understand the different possibilities for prosocial interactions in them. The characteristics of the child as he enters the school, the extent to which adults have the time and the capacity to educate or socialize the child for how to interact with others in a positive manner, may be crucial in enabling the child to become a genuine participant. However, adults with whom the child may come to identify in such an environment frequently disappear from the child's life. Given the continued impact of the home, the benevolent and prosocial socialization provided by teachers and by peer relations would have to be relatively enduring if it is to help the child develop characteristics that enable him to develop prosocial peer relations in other settings and prosocial interactions with other adults.

If positive social behavior is an expression of a child's personality and social development, which I have stressed all along, then education and intervention have to involve and influence varied aspects of personality. Role playing, for example, may be a useful procedure because it actively involves cognition, affect, and behavior and can lead to corresponding changes in each. In the course of role playing, the child can be guided to consider the consequences on others of varied forms of behavior and the reactions that varied acts may evoke. He probably will have components of the emotional experience that is present when the same behaviors are performed in real interactions. He learns behavioral skills and strategies for interaction. If intervention and education are to have substantial influence on positive behavior, we need to consider the environment in which the child lives, the circumstances he has to deal with. If children live in an aggressive environment, intervention or education that promotes their capacity to defend their own interests and to assert themselves may be a precondition for learning positive interactive behavior that is motivated by prosocial rather than by other (defensive) goals. Experiencing cruelty as an everyday event may make it impossible for children to consider higher principles of morality in resolving moral dilemmas as anything but an intellectual exercise. Considering their own life circumstances in terms of moral principles and understanding injustices they suffer may be a precondition for a genuine change in moral reasoning.

An important aspect of education in positive behavior is the opportunity it provides for testing and confirming hypotheses. If we find that exposing children to certain experiences will have a lasting effect on their cognitions, affects, and behavior, we can verify the findings of laboratory analogue research. Thus, intervention that is properly designed, with its effects tested, can be an important domain for collecting data and testing theories.

Culture, History, and the Universal Applicability of Our Understanding of Development

Recently, a controversy has been raging among social psychologists about the extent to which our understanding of human social behavior is necessarily limited to a particular culture and, even within a culture, to a particular time period. Some argue that the psychological functioning of human beings is a function of the cultural context, so that our theory and data have limited applicability.

How universal can our understanding be of how human beings function and of how they develop? Triandis (1978) argued that, if we made our theoretical terms sufficiently abstract, they will have universal applicability across cultures and among human beings. I suggested (Volume 1, Chapter 10) that the terms in the theoretical model I presented are sufficiently abstract but also concrete enough so that we can develop operational measures and test predictions. I noted that the goals that people possess may vary tremendously across cultures and historical periods, but it seems impossible to imagine human beings without motives, here conceptualized as personal goals.

Consider, for example, cooperative and competitive behavior. Children may engage in either kind of behavior in order to maximize their own gains. However, coordinating effort with another person to achieve mutual (shared) gains and the desire to maximize one's gains relative to other persons (even if that means that one sacrifices some absolute gain) can become valued goals in themselves. Mead (1937) classified 13 "primitive" societies according to the extent to which they were characterized by cooperative, competitive, and individualistic goals. The dominant goal orientation varied across these societies, but each could be characterized as demonstrating and propagating these goals to different extents. I suggested (Volume 1, Chapter 10) that in different cultures different aspects of the environment that are relevant to positive behavior may be dominant and that we can speak of a "dominance classification" of the environment. When an aspect of the culture is dominant, relatively uniform motives, values, or behavior may characterize members of the culture in relevant domains. The dehumanization of Jews in Nazi Germany and slavery in America prior to the Civil War can be regarded as dominant aspects of the environment. Cultures may vary in the extent to which they emphasize the common humanity of all persons or devalue outsiders, even members of subcultures. One or another pole of this dimension can be dominant in a culture. Aspects of the environment that lead to cooperative versus competitive behavior and to the inculcation of cooperative and competitive values can be dominant. If this occurs, individuals are likely to shape their own environment, since their behavior determines other people's responses to them and the kind of interactions they will engage in (Kelley & Stahlesky, 1970; Toda *et al.*, 1978).

Are personal characteristics that affect positive behavior in one culture the same as those that affect it in another culture? Do they combine and interact with each other and with situations in the same manner? Some elements of a theory that describes how positive behavior is determined can be universally valid.

Consider the possibility that, in some cultures, role taking may be minimally relevant because members of the culture learn to express or demonstrate their need for help in highly visible, even ritualized fashion. This would be consistent with the theory, since role taking should not make much difference when the need is clearly and strongly expressed. However, it is difficult to imagine that all human needs, including psychological ones, would have such explicit manifestations. In some domains, role taking must still enter into determining behavior. But role taking will join with other characteristics, perhaps in the manner my rudimentary theory suggests, in affecting behavior.

With regard to development, I suggested that a limited number of principles or mechanisms of change operate. As I noted in discussing principles of change, different environmental conditions may lead to change occurring more by one or by another mechanism. Thus, different principles may be differently involved across cultures. Are the same influences necessary for the development of positive behavior in different cultures? First, positive behavior can result from varied motives. According to Cohen (1972), in many cultures the Western concepts of empathy and of altruistic motivation are alien concepts, but the interdependence of persons and the expectations of benefits to the self that will result from positive conduct are recognized and accepted. Thus, positive behavior may be part of a clear although probably often implicit understanding of social exchange, reciprocity, and mutual gain. In some social groups, mutual surveillance may ensure continued positive behavior.

Different motives may give rise to somewhat different forms of positive behavior. In our society, too, much positive behavior may represent social exchange motivated by expectations of gains that will result from reciprocity (see Volume 1, Chapter 8). This kind of prosocial behavior is important, since it results in benefits for others and for the self and contributes to the harmonious functioning of society. (Since motives are usually mixed, when people habitually engage in positive social exchange both values and beliefs about the interrelatedness of one's own and of others' welfare and values that emphasize others' welfare are likely to be components of their motivation.) Different influences would promote the development of different motives for positive behavior (see section on value orientations, Chapter 5); that, however, presents no problem for a theory of the development of social behavior.

Are the same environmental conditions necessary in different cultures for the development of concern about and the desire to benefit others? Probably, some basic components are crucial. Nurturance, in the form of expression of love and affection, may not be as basic as the child's perception of benevolence by adults, a concern with the child's welfare, and/or a desire to promote the child's interests (Baumrind, 1975; Coopersmith, 1967; Whiting & Whiting, 1975). The necessary conditions may also vary as a function of the combination of different influences that the culture embodies. Verbal induction may be more necessary in our culture than in some others because we do not induce children to participate to any significant degree in positive behavior and we encourage individuality, with some focus on the self inherent in it.

I have clearly implied, in this concluding chapter, my belief that we need to consider and study the varied aspects of the phenomena related to positive behavior and morality—developmental, social psychological, and personality aspects—in conjunction. The system or model I described is based on this belief. In addition to expanding research and theory, an important task is intervention, education, or application—ideally in a form that also tests hypotheses. Can we reduce the willingness of human beings to inflict harm and to tolerate harm inflicted on others, and can we increase their willingness to make sacrifices for others' sake? I waver between optimism and pessimism about our capacity to affect the nature of interrelatedness among human beings—but what a fantastic adventure it would be to really try.

References

Allen, M. K., & Liebert, R. M. Children's adoption of self-reward patterns: Model's prior experience and incentive for nonimitation. *Child Development*, 1969, *40*, 921–926.

Allen, V. L. *Children as teachers: Theory and research on tutoring.* New York: Academic Press, 1976.

Ambron, S. R., & Irwin, D. M. Role taking and moral judgment in five- and seven-year-olds. *Developmental Psychology*, 1975, *11*, 102.

Andersen, H. H. Domination and integration in the social behavior of young children in an experimental play situation. *Genetic Psychology Monographs*, 1939, *21*, 287–385.

Arlitt, A. H. *Psychology of infancy and early childhood.* New York: McGraw-Hill, 1930.

Armsby, R. E. A reexamination of the development of moral judgments in children. *Child Development*, 1971, *42*, 1241–1248.

Arnold, M. *Emotion and personality.* New York: Columbia University Press, 1960.

Aronfreed, J. The origins of self-criticism. *Psychological Review*, 1964, *71*, 193–218.

Aronfreed, J. *Conduct and conscience.* New York: Academic Press, 1968.

Aronfreed, J. Moral development from the standpoint of a general psychological theory. In T. Lickona (Ed.), *Moral development and behavior.* New York: Holt, 1976.

Aronfreed, J., & Paskal, V. Altruism, empathy and the conditioning of positive affect. Unpublished manuscript, University of Pennsylvania, 1965.

Aronfreed, J., & Paskal, V. The development of sympathetic behavior in children: An experimental test of a two-phase hypothesis. Unpublished manuscript, University of Pennsylvania, 1966.

Avgar, A., Bronfenbrenner, U., & Henderson, C. R. Jr. Socialization practices of parents, teachers, and peers in Israel: Kibbutz, moshav and city. *Child Development*, 1977, *48*, 1219–1227.

Azrin, N., & Lindsley, O. The reinforcement of cooperation between children. *Journal of Abnormal Social Psychology*, 1956, *52*, 100–102.

Bandura, A. *Principles of behavior modification*. New York: Holt, 1969. (a)

Bandura, A. Social-learning theory of identificatory processes. In D. A. Goslin (Ed.), *Handbook of socialization theory and research*. Chicago: Rand-McNally, 1969. (b)

Bandura, A. *Social learning theory*. New York: General Learning Press, 1971.

Bandura, A. Self-reinforcement: Theoretical and methodological considerations. *Behaviorism*, 1976, *4*, 135–155.

Bandura, A. *Social learning theory*. New Jersey: Prentice Hall, 1977.

Bandura, A., Grusec, J. E., & Menlove, F. L. Some social determinants of self-monitoring reinforcement systems. *Journal of Personality & Social Psychology*, 1967, *5*, 449–455.

Bandura, A., & Kupers, C. Transmission of patterns of self-reinforcement through modeling. *Journal of Abnormal & Social Psychology*, 1964, *69*, 1–9.

Bandura, A., & MacDonald, F. The influence of social reinforcement and the behavior of models in shaping children's moral judgment. *Journal of Abnormal & Social Psychology*, 1963, *67*, 274–281.

Bandura, A., & Mischel, W. Modification of self-imposed delay of reward through exposure to live and symbolic models. *Journal of Personality & Social Psychology*, 1965 *2*, 198–705.

Bandura, A., & Perloff, B. Relative efficacy of self-monitored and externally imposed reinforcement systems. *Journal of Personality & Social Psychology*, 1967, *7*, 111–116.

Bandura, A., & Walters, R. H. *Adolescent aggression: A study of the influence of child training practices and family interrelationship*. New York: Ronald Press, 1959.

Bandura, A., & Walters, R. H. *Social learning and personality development*. New York: Holt, 1963.

Barrett, D. E., & Yarrow, M. R. Prosocial behavior, social inferential ability, and assertiveness in children. *Child Development*, 1977, *48*, 475–481.

Bathurst, J. E. A study of sympathy and resistance among children. *Psychological Bulletin*, 1933, *30*, 625.

Baumrind, D. Child care practices anteceding three patterns of preschool behavior. *Genetic Psychological Monographs*, 1967, *75*, 43–88.

Baumrind, D. Current patterns of parental authority. *Developmental Psychology*, 1971, *4*, 1–101.

Baumrind, D. *Early socialization and the discipline controversy*. Morristown, New Jersey: General Learning Press, 1975.

Baumrind, D., & Black, A. E. Socialization practices associated with dimensions of competence in pre-school boys and girls. *Child Development*, 1967, *38*, 291–327.

Bell, R. Q. A reinterpretation of the direction of effects in studies of socialization. *Psychological Review*, 1968, *75*, 81–95.

Bem, D. J. Self-perception theory. In L. Berkowitz (Ed.), *Advances in experimental social psychology*, Vol. 6. New York: Academic Press, 1972.

Bem, D. J., & Allen, A. On predicting some of the people some of the time: The search for cross-situational consistencies in behavior. *Psychological Review*, 1974, *81*, 506–520.

Berkowitz, L. Social norms, feelings and other factors affecting helping behavior and altruism. In L. Berkowitz (Ed.), *Advances in experimental social psychology*, Vol. 6. New York: Academic Press, 1972.

Berne, E. V. C. An experimental investigation of social behavior patterns in young children. *University of Iowa Studies in Child Welfare*, 1930, *4*, No. 3.

Bernstein, M. R. Helping in children: The effects of recipient-centered verbalizations, the role of empathy. Unpublished masters thesis, University of Massachusetts, 1975.

Bettleheim, B. Individual and mass behavior in extreme situations. *Journal of Abnormal & Social Psychology*, 1943, *38*, 417–452.

Bixenstine, V. E., DeCorte, M. S., & Bixenstine, B. A. Conformity to peer-sponsored misconduct at four grade levels. *Developmental Psychology*, 1976, *12*, 226–236.

Bizman, A., Yinon, Y., Mivtzari, E., & Shavit, R. Effects of the age structure of the kindergarten on altruistic behavior. *Journal of School Psychology*, 1978, *16*, 154–160.

Blatt, M. The effects of classroom discussion programs upon children's level of moral judgment. Unpublished doctoral dissertation, University of Chicago, 1969.

Block, J. Advancing the psychology of personality: Paradigmatic shift or improving the quality of research. In D. Magnusson & N. S. Endler (Eds.), *Personality at the crossroads: Current issues in interactional psychology*. Hillsdale, New Jersey: Lawrence Erlbaum, 1977.

Block, J., & Block, J. H. Ego development and the provenance of thought: A longitudinal study of ego and cognitive development in young children (Progress report for National Institute of Mental Health Grant No. MH 16080, January, 1973).

Block, J. H., Haan, N., & Smith, M. B. Socialization correlates of student activism. *Journal of Social Issues*, 1969, *25*, 143–177.

Bonney, M. E. Relationships between social success, family size, socioeconomic home background, and intelligence among school children in grades III to V. *Sociometry*, 1944, *1*, 26–39.

Bonney, M. E., & Powell, J. Differences in social behavior between sociometrically high and sociometrically low children. *Journal of Educational Research*, 1953, *46*, 481–495.

Borke, H. Interpersonal perception of young children: Egocentrism or empathy? *Developmental Psychology*, 1971, *5*, 263–269.

Borke, H. The development of empathy in Chinese and American children between three and six years of age: A cross-cultural study. *Developmental Psychology*, 1973, *9*, 102–108.

Bossard, J. H. S., & Boll, E. S. *The large family system*. Philadelphia: University of Pennsylvania Press, 1956.

Bossard, J. H. S., Boll, E. S., & Boll, H. S. Child behavior and the empathic complex. *Child Development*, 1957, *28*, 37–43.

Bott, M. Personality development in young children. *University of Toronto Studies, Child Development Series #2*. Toronto: University of Toronto Press, 1934.

Brehm, J. W. *A theory of psychological reactance*. New York: Academic Press, 1966.

Breland, K., & Breland, M. *Animal behavior*. New York: Macmillan, 1966.

Brody, G. H., & Henderson, R. W. Effects of multiple model variations and rationale provision on the moral judgments and explanation of young children. *Child Development*, 1977, *48*, 1117–1120.

Bronfenbrenner, U. Freudian theories of identification and their derivatives. *Child Development*, 1960, *31*, 15–40.

Bronfenbrenner, U. Some familial antecedents of responsibility and leadership in adolescents. In L. Petrulo & B. L. Bass (Eds.), *Leadership and interpersonal behavior*. New York: Holt, 1961.

Bronfenbrenner, U. Reaction to social pressure from adults versus peers among Soviet day-school and boarding-school pupils in the perspective of an American sample. *Journal of Personality & Social Psychology*, 1970, *15*, 179–189. (a)

Bronfenbrenner, U. *Two worlds of childhood*. New York: Russell Sage Foundation, 1970. (b)

Bronfenbrenner, U. Toward an experimental ecology of human development. *American Psychologist*, 1977, *32*, 514–532.

Brown, R. W. *Social psychology*. New York: Free Press, 1965.

Bruner, A. Facilitation of classical conditioning in rabbits by reinforcing brain stimulation. *Psychonomic Science*, 1966, *6*, 211–212.

Bryan, J. H. Children's cooperation and helping behaviors. In E. M. Hetherington (Ed.), *Review of child development research*, Vol. 5. Chicago: University of Chicago Press, 1975.

Bryan, J. H., & Walbeck, N. Preaching and practicing generosity: Children's actions and reaction. *Child Development*, 1970, *41*, 329–354. (a)

Bryan, J. H., & Walbeck, N. The impact of words and deeds concerning altruism upon children. *Child Development*, 1970, *41*, 747–757. (b)

Bryant, B., & Crockenberg, S. Cooperative and competitive classroom environments. *JSAS Catalog of Selected Documents in Psychology*, 1974, *4*, 53.

Burns, N., & Cavey, L. Age differences in empathic ability among children. *Canadian Journal of Psychology*, 1957, *11*, 227–230.

Burton, R. V. Honesty and dishonesty. In T. Lickona (Ed.), *Moral development and behavior*. New York: Holt, 1976.

Campbell, D. T. Ethnocentric and other altruistic motives. In D. Levine (Ed.), *Nebraska symposium on motivation*, 1965, *13*, 283–311.

Campbell, D. T. On the conflicts between biological and social evolution and between psychology and moral tradition. *American Psychologist*, 1975, *30*, 1103–1126.

Campbell, E. Q. The internalization of moral norms. *Sociometry*, 1964, *27*, 319–412.

Campbell, J. D., & Yarrow, M. R. Perceptual and behavioral correlates of social effectiveness. *Sociometry*, 1961, *24*, 1–20.

Cantor, N. L., & Gelfand, D. M. Effects of responsiveness and sex of children on adults' behavior. *Child Development*, 1977, *48*, 232–238.

Cautela, J. R. Covert sensitization. *Psychological Reports*, 1967, *20*, 459–468.

Chandler, M. J. Egocentrism and antisocial behavior. The assessment and training of social perspective—talking skills. *Developmental Psychology*, 1973, *9*, 326–332.

Charlesworth, R., & Hartup, W. W. Positive social reinforcement in the nursery school peer group. *Child Development*, 1967, *38*, 993–1002.

Coates, B., Pusser, H. E., & Goodman, I. The influence of "Sesame Street" and "Mister Rogers' Neighborhood" on children's social behavior in the preschool. *Child Development*, 1976, *47*, 138–144.

Cohen, R. Altruism: Human, cultural or what? *Journal of Social Issues*, 1972, *28*, 39–57.

Coleman, J. S. *The adolescent society*. Glencoe, Illinois: Free Press, 1961.

Cook, H., & Stingle, S. Cooperative behavior in children. *Psychological Bulletin*, 1974, *81*, 918–933.

Coopersmith, S. *Antecedents of self-esteem*. San Francisco: Fremont, 1967.

Costanzo, P. R., Coie, J. D., Grument, J. F., & Farnill, D. A reexamination of the effects of intent and consequences on children's moral judgment. *Child Development*, 1973, *44*, 154–161.

Cowan, P., Langer, J., Heavenrich, J., & Nathanson, M. Social learning and Piaget's cognitive theory of moral development. *Journal of Personality & Social Psychology*, 1969, *11*, 261–274.

Cowdry R. W., Keniston, K., & Cabin, S. The war and military obligations; Private attitudes and public actions. *Journal of Personality,* 1970, *38,* 525–549.

Cowen, E. L., Pederson, A., Babigan, H., Izzo, L. D., & Frost, M. A. Long-term follow-up of early detected vulnerable children. *Journal of Consulting & Clinical Psychology,* 1973, *41,* 438–446.

Damon, W. *The social world of the child.* San Francisco: Jossey-Bass, 1977.

Davidson, G. C. Appraisal of behavior modification techniques with adults in institutional settings. In C. M. Franks (Ed.), *Behavior therapy: Appraisal and status.* New York: McGraw-Hill, 1969.

Deci, E. *Intrinsic motivation.* New York: Plenum, 1975.

Deci, E. Intrinsic motivation and personality. In E. Staub (Ed.), *Personality: Basic issues and current research.* Englewood Cliffs, New Jersey: Prentice-Hall, 1979 (in press).

DePalma, D. J. Effects of social class, moral orientation, and severity of punishment on boys' moral responses to transgression and generosity. *Developmental Psychology,* 1974, *10,* 890–900.

Deutsch, F. Female preschoolers perceptions of affective responses and interpersonal behavior in video-taped episodes. *Developmental Psychology,* 1974, *10,* 733–740.

Deutsch, F. Observational and sociometric measures of peer popularity and their relationships to egocentric communication in female preschoolers. *Developmental Psychology,* 1976, *10,* 745–747.

Devereux, E. D. Authority and moral development among German and American children: A cross-national pilot experiment. *Journal of Comparative Family Studies,* 1972, *3,* 99–124.

Dienstbier, R. A., Hillman, D., Lehnhoff, J., Hillman, J., & Valkenaar, M. C. An emotion-attribution approach to moral behavior: Interfacing cognitive and avoidance theories of moral development. *Psychological Review,* 1975, *82,* 299–315.

Dlugokinski, E. L., & Firestone, I. J. Congruence among four methods of measuring other-centeredness. *Child Development,* 1973, *44,* 304–308.

Dlugokinski, E. L., & Firestone, I. J. Other-centeredness and susceptibility to charitable appeals: Effects of perceived discipline. *Developmental Psychology,* 1974, *10,* 21–28.

Dollard, J., & Miller, N. E. *Personality and psychotherapy.* New York: McGraw-Hill, 1950.

Dressel, S., & Midlarsky, E. Preaching, practicing and demanding charity: Effects on donation behavior and evaluations of the model. Unpublished manuscript, 1976.

Durkheim, E. *Moral education.* New York: Free Press, 1961.

Eaton, J. W., & Weil, R. J. *Culture and mental disorders.* New York: Free Press, 1955.

Eisenberg-Berg, N., & Geisheker, E. The "who" and "what" of it: The effects of content preachings and power of the preacher on children's sharing. Unpublished manuscript, Arizona State University, 1978.

Elkins, D. Some factors related to the choice status of ninety eighth-grade children in a school society. *Genetic Psychology Monographs,* 1958, *58,* 207–272.

Elliot, R., & Vasta, R. The modeling of sharing: Effects associated with vicarious reinforcement, symbolization, age, and generalization. *Journal of Experimental Child Psychology,* 1970, *10,* 8–15.

Emmerich, W. Evaluating alternative models of development: An illustrative study of preschool personal–social behaviors. *Child Development,* 1977, *48,* 1401–1410.

Eron, L., Walder, L. O., & Lefkowitz, M. M. *Learning of aggression in children.* Boston: Little, Brown, 1971.

Escalona, S. K. *The roots of individuality.* Chicago: Aldine, 1968.

Farber, I. E. The things people say to themselves. *American Psychologist*, 1963, *18*, 185–197.

Feinberg, H. K. *Anatomy of a helping situation: Some personality and situational determinants of helping in a conflict situation involving another's psychological distress.* Unpublished doctoral dissertation, University of Massachusetts, Amherst, 1977.

Feinberg, M. R., Smith, M., & Schmidt, R. An analysis of expressions used by adolescents of varying economic levels to describe accepted and rejected peers. *Journal of Genetic Psychology*, 1958, *93*, 133–148.

Feldman, R. S., Devin-Sheehan, L., & Allen, V. L. Children tutoring children: A critical review of research. In V. L. Allen (Ed.), *Children as teachers.* New York: Academic Press, 1976.

Ferguson, L. R. *Personality development.* Belmont, California: Brooks/Cole, 1970.

Feshbach, N. D., & Feshbach, S. The relationship between empathy and aggression in two age groups. *Developmental Psychology*, 1969, *1*, 102–107.

Feshbach, N. D., & Roe, K. Empathy in six and seven year olds. *Child Development*, 1968, *39*, 135–147.

Festinger, L., Freedman, J. L. Dissonance reduction and moral values. In P. Worchel & D. Byrne (Eds.), *Personality Change.* New York: Wiley, 1964.

Finley, G. E., French, D., & Cowan, P. Egocentrism and popularity. Paper presented at the 14th Inter-American Congress of Psychology, São Paulo, 1973.

Firestone, I. J., Kaplan, K. J., & Russell, J. C. Anxiety, fear, and affiliation with similar-state *vs.* dissimilar-state others: Misery sometimes loves nonmiserable company. *Journal of Personality & Social Psychology*, 1973, *26*, 409–414.

Fischer, W. F. Sharing in preschool children as a function of amount and type of reinforcement. *Genetic Psychology Monographs*, 1963, *68*, 215–245.

Flapan, D. *Children's understanding of social interaction.* New York: Teachers College Press, 1968.

Flavell, J. H. *The developmental psychology of Jean Piaget.* Princeton, New York: Van Nostrand-Reinhold, 1963.

Flavell, J. H., Botkin, P., Fry, C., Wright, J., & Jarvis, P. *The development of role-taking and communication skills in children.* New York: Wiley, 1968.

Freedman, D. G. Hereditary control of early social behavior. In B. M. Foss (Ed.), *Determinants of Infant Behavior, III.* New York: Wiley, 1965.

Freud, A., & Dann, S. An experiment in group upbringing. In R. Eissler *et al.* (Eds.), *The Psychoanalytic Study of the Child*, Vol. 6. New York: International Universities Press, 1951.

Freud, S. *The basic writings of Sigmund Freud.* New York: Modern Library, 1938.

Friedrich, L. K., & Stein, A. H. Aggressive and prosocial television programs and the natural behavior of preschool children. *Monographs of the Society for Research in Child Development*, 1973, *38* (4, Serial No. 151).

Friedrich, L. K., & Stein, A. H. Prosocial television and young children: The effects of verbal labeling and role playing on learning and behavior. *Child Development*, 1975, *46*, 27–38.

Garbarino, J., & Bronfenbrenner, U. The socialization of moral judgment and behavior in cross-cultural perspective. In T. Lickona (Ed.), *Moral development and behavior.* New York: Holt, 1976.

Gates, G. S. An experimental study of the growth of social perception. *Journal of Educational Psychology*, 1923, *14*, 449–461.

Gelfand, D., Hartmann, D. P., Cromer, C. C., Smith, C. L., & Page, B. C. The effects of institutional prompts and praise on children's donation rates. *Child Development,* 1975, *46,* 980–983.

Gellert, E. Stability and fluctuation in the power relationships of young children. *Journal of Abnormal & Social Psychology,* 1961, *62,* 8–15.

Gelman, R., & Shatz, M. Appropriate speech adjustments: The operation of conversational constraints on talk to two-year-olds. In M. Lewis & L. A. Rosenblum (Eds.), *Interaction, conversation, and the development of language.* New York: Wiley, 1977.

Gewirtz, J. L. On designing the functional environment of the child to facilitate behavioral development. In L. L. Dittmann (Ed.), *Early childcare: The new perpectives.* New York: Atherton, 1968.

Gewirtz, J. L., & Stingle, K. G. Learning of generalized imitation as the basis for identification. *Psychological Review,* 1968, *75,* 374–397.

Ginott, H. G. *Between parent and child.* New York: Avon Books, 1965.

Giovannoni, J., & Billingsley, A. Child neglect among the poor: A study of parental adequacy in families of three ethnic groups. *Child Welfare,* 1970, *49,* 196–204.

Goslin, D. A. Accuracy of self perception and social acceptance. *Sociometry,* 1962, *25,* 283–296.

Gottman, J. M. Toward a definition of social isolation in children. *Child Development,* 1978, *48,* 513–517.

Gottman, J. M., Gonso, J., & Rasmussen, B. Social interaction, social competence, and friendship in children. *Child Development,* 1975, *46,* 709–718.

Gottschaldt, D., & Frauhauf-Ziegler, C. Über die Entwicklung der Zusammenarbeit im Kleinkindalter (On the development of cooperative behavior in young children). *Zeitchrift für Psychologie,* 1958, *162,* 254–278.

Gouldner, A. W. The norm of reciprocity: A preliminary statement. *American Sociological Review,* 1960, *25,* 161–179.

Graves, N. B., & Graves, T. D. The cultural context of altruism: Development of rivalry in a cooperative society. Unpublished manuscript, 1978.

Green, F. P., & Schneider, F. W. Age differences in the behavior of boys on 3 measures of altruism. *Child Development,* 1974, *45,* 248–251.

Green, S. K. Causal attribution of emotion in kindergarten children. *Developmental Psychology,* 1977, *13,* 533–534.

Greenberg, P. J. Competition in children: An experimental study. *American Journal of Psychology,* 1932, *44,* 221–248.

Grings, W. W., & Lockhart, R. A. Effects of "anxiety-lessening" instructions and differential set development on the extinction of GSR. *Journal of Experimental Psychology,* 1963, *66,* 292–299.

Grodman, S. M. The role of personality and situational variables in responding to and helping an individual in psychological distress. Unpublished dissertation, University of Massachusetts, 1978 (in preparation).

Grusec, J. E. Power and the internalization of self-denial. *Child Development,* 1971, *42,* 93–105.

Grusec, J. E. Demand characteristics of the modeling experiment: Altruism as a function of age and aggression. *Journal of Personality & Social Psychology,* 1972, *22,* 139–148.

Grusec, J. E., Kuczynski, J., Rushton, P., & Simutis, Z. M. Modeling, direct instruction, and attributions: Effects on altruism. *Developmental Psychology,* 1978, *14,* 51–57.

Grusec, J. E., & Skubicki, L. Model nurturance demand characteristics of the modeling experiment and altruism. *Journal of Personality & Social Psychology*, 1970, *14*, 352–359.

Haan, N. Hypothetical and actual moral reasoning in a situation of civil disobedience. *Journal of Personality & Social Psychology*, 1975, *32*, 255–270.

Hamm, C. Dialog: Cornel Hamm talks with Don B. Cochrane. *Moral Education Forum*, 1976, *1*, 3–6.

Handlon, B. J., & Gross, P. The development of sharing behavior. *Journal of Abnormal & Social Psychology*, 1959, *59*, 425–428.

Hapkiewicz, W. G., & Roden, A. H. The effects of aggressive cartoons on children's interpersonal play. *Child Development*, 1971, *42*, 1583–1585.

Harlow, H., & Harlow, M. Social deprivation in monkeys. *Scientific American*, 1962, *207*, 136–146.

Harris, M. B. The effects of performing one altruistic act on the likelihood of performing another. *Journal of Social Psychology*, 1972, *88*, 65–73.

Hartman, D. P., Gelfand, D. M., Smith, C. L., Paul, S. C., Cromer, C. C., Page, B. C., & Lebenta, D. V. Factors affecting the acquisition and elimination of children's altruistic behavior. *Journal of Experimental Child Psychology*, 1976, *21*, 328–338.

Hartshorne, H., May, M. A., & Shuttleworth, F. K. *Studies in the nature of character*, Vol. III: *Studies in the organization of character*. New York: Macmillan, 1930.

Hartup, W. W. Friendship status and the effectiveness of peers as reinforcing agents. *Journal of Experimental Child Psychology*, 1964, *1*, 154–162.

Hartup, W. W. Peer interaction and social organization. In P. H. Mussen (Ed.), *Carmichael's manual of child psychology*. New York: Wiley, 1970.

Hartup, W. W., Glazer, J. A., & Charlesworth, R. Peer reinforcement and sociometric status. *Child Development*, 1967, *38*, 1017–1024.

Helson, H. *Adaptation-level theory*. New York: Harper, 1964.

Henshel, A. The relationship between values and behavior: A developmental hypothesis. *Child Development*, 1971, *42*, 1997–2007.

Hetherington, E. M. A developmental study of the effects of sex of the dominant parent on sex-role preference, identification and imitation in children. *Journal of Personality & Social Psychology*, 1965, *2*, 143–153.

Hetherington, E. M., & Frankie, G. Effects of parental dominance, warmth and conflict on imitation in children. *Journal of Personality & Social Psychology*, 1967, *6*, 119–125.

Hicks, D. J. Imitation and retention of film-mediated aggressive peer and adult models. *Journal of Personality & Social Psychology*, 1965, *2*, 97–100.

Hildebrandt, D. E., Feldman, S. E., & Ditrichs, R. A. Rules, models and self-reinforcement in children. *Journal of Personality & Social Psychology*, 1973, *25*, 1–5.

Hill, W. E. Learning theory and the acquisition of values. *Psychological Review*, 1960, *67*, 317–331.

Hirota, K. Experimental studies of competition. *Japanese Journal of Psychology*, 1951, *21*, 70–81.

Hoffman, L. W. The father's role in the family and the child's peer-group adjustment. *Merrill-Palmer Quarterly*, 1961, *7*, 97–105.

Hoffman, M. L. Parent discipline and the child's consideration for others. *Child Development*, 1963, *34*, 573–588.

Hoffman, M. L. Moral development. In P. H. Mussen (Ed.), *Carmichael's manual of child development*. New York: Wiley, 1970. (a)

Hoffman, M. L. Conscience, personality, and socialization technique. *Human Development*, 1970, *13*, 90–126. (b)

Hoffman, M. L. Identification and conscience development. *Child Development,* 1971, *42,* 1071–1082.

Hoffman, M. L. Altruistic behavior and the parent-child relationship. *Journal of Personality & Social Psychology,* 1975, *31,* 937–943. (a)

Hoffman, M. L. Developmental synthesis of affect and cognition and its implications for altruistic motivation. *Developmental Psychology,* 1975, *11,* 607–622. (b)

Hoffman, M. L. Empathy, role-taking, guilt, and development of altruistic motives. In T. Lickona (Ed.), *Moral development and behavior: Theory, research and social issues.* New York: Holt, Rinehart and Winston, 1976.

Hoffman, M. L. Personality and Social Development. In M. R. Rosenzweig & L. W. Porter (Eds.), *Annual Review of Psychology,* 1977, *28,* 295–321. (a)

Hoffman, M. L. Sex differences in empathy and related behaviors. *Psychological Bulletin,* 1977, *84,* 712–720. (b)

Hoffman, M. L., & Saltzstein, H. D. Parent discipline and the child's moral development. *Journal of Personality & Social Psychology,* 1967, *5,* 45–57.

Hogan, R. A dimension of moral judgment. *Journal of Consulting & Clinical Psychology,* 1970, *35,* 205–212.

Hogan, R. Moral conduct and moral character: A psychological perspective. *Psychological Bulletin,* 1973, *79,* 217–232.

Hollander, E. P., & Marcia, J. E. Parental determinants of peer-orientation and self-orientation among preadolescents. *Developmental Psychology,* 1970, *2,* 292–302.

Hollos, M., and Cowan, P. A. Social isolation and cognitive development: Logical operations and role-taking abilities in three Norwegian social settings. *Child Development,* 1973, *44,* 630–641.

Holstein, C. B. Parental determinants of the development of moral judgment. Unpublished doctoral dissertation, University of California, Berkeley, 1968.

Holstein, C. B. Irreversible stepwise sequence in the development of moral judgment: A longitudinal study of males and females. *Child Development,* 1976, *47,* 51–62.

Horowitz, F. D. The relationship of anxiety, self-concept, and sociometric status among fourth, fifth, and sixth grade children. *Journal of Abnormal & Social Psychology,* 1962, *65,* 212–214.

Hovland, C. L., & Janis, I. J. *Personality and persuasibility.* New Haven: Yale University Press, 1959.

Hughes, C. C., Tremblay, M. A., Rapoport, R. N., & Leighton, A. H. *People of Cove and Woodlot: Communities from the viewpoint of social psychiatry.* New York: Basic Books, 1960.

Humphrey, G. The conditioned reflex and elementary social reaction. *Journal of Abnormal & Social Psychology,* 1923, *17,* 113–119.

Huttenlocher, J., & Presson, C. C. Mental rotation and the perspective problem. *Cognitive Psychology,* 1973, *4,* 277–299.

Iannotti, R. J. Effect of role-taking experiences on role taking, empathy, altruism and aggression. *Developmental Psychology,* 1978, *14,* 119–124.

Inoff, G. E., & Halverson, C. F. Jr. Behavioral disposition of child and caretaker-child interaction. *Developmental Psychology,* 1977, *13,* 274–281.

Into, E. C. Some possible childrearing antecedents of interpersonal trust. Unpublished master's thesis, University of Connecticut, 1969.

Izard, C. E. *The face of emotion.* New York: Appleton, 1971.

Jensen, R. E., & Moore, S. G. The effect of attribute statements on cooperativeness and competitiveness in school-age boys. *Child Development,* 1977, *48,* 305–307.

Kagan, J. The concept of identification. *Psychological Review*, 1958, *65*, 296–305.

Kagan, S., & Madsen, M. C. Cooperation and competition of Mexican, Mexican-American and Anglo-American children of two ages under four instructional sets. *Developmental Psychology*, 1971, *5*, 32–39.

Kagan, S., & Madsen, M. C. Rivalry in Anglo-American and Mexican children of two ages. *Journal of Personality & Social Psychology*, 1972, *24*, 214–220.

Karniol, R. Children's use of intention cues in evaluating behavior. *Psychological Bulletin*, 1978, *85*, 76–86.

Katz, H. A., & Rotter, J. B. Interpersonal trust scores of college students and their parents. *Child Development*, 1969, *40*, 657–661.

Keasey, C. B. Implications of cognitive development for moral reasoning. In D. J. DePalma & J. M. Foley (Eds.), *Moral development: Current theory and research.* Hillsdale, New Jersey: Lawrence Erlbaum, 1975.

Keislar, E. R. A distinction between social acceptance and prestige among adolescents. *Child Development*, 1953, *24*, 275–284.

Kelley, H. H., & Stahleski, A. J. Social interaction basis of cooperators' and competitors' beliefs about others. *Journal of Personality & Social Psychology*, 1970, *16*, 66–91.

Kelman, H. C. Compliance, identification, and internalization: Three processes of opinion change. *Journal of Conflict & Resolution*, 1958, *2*, 51–60.

Kessen, W., Haith, M. M., & Salapatek, P. H. Infancy. In P. Mussen (Ed.), *Carmichael's manual of child psychology.* New York: Wiley, 1970.

Klaus, R. A. Interrelationships of attributes that accepted and rejected children ascribe to their peers. Unpublished doctoral dissertation, George Peabody College for Teachers, 1959.

Klein, R. Some factors influencing empathy in six and seven year old children varying in ethnic background. Unpublished doctoral dissertation, University of California, Los Angeles, 1971.

Knight, G. P., & Kagan, S. Development of prosocial and competitive behaviors in Anglo-American and Mexican-American children. *Child Development*, 1977, *48*, 1385–1394.

Koch, H. L. Popularity in preschool children: Some related factors and a technique for its measurement. *Child Development*, 1933, *4*, 164–175.

Kohlberg, L. The development of modes of moral thinking in the years ten to sixteen. Unpublished doctoral dissertation, University of Chicago, 1958.

Kohlberg, L. Moral development and identification. In H. W. Stevenson (Ed.), *Child psychology.* Chicago: University of Chicago Press, 1963.

Kohlberg, L. Development of moral character and moral ideology. In Hoffman & Hoffman (Eds.), *Review of child development research,* Vol. I. New York: Russell Sage Foundation, 1964.

Kohlberg, L. Moral and religious education and the public schools: A developmental view. In T. Sizer (Ed.), *Religion and public education.* Boston: Houghton Mifflin, 1967.

Kohlberg, L. Stage and sequence: The cognitive-developmental approach to socialization. In D. Goslin (Ed.), *Handbook of socialization theory and research.* Chicago: Rand McNally, 1969.

Kohlberg, L. Moral stages and moralization: The cognitive-developmental approach. In T. Lickona (Ed.), *Moral development and behavior.* New York: Holt, 1976.

Kohlberg, L., & Kramer, R. B. Continuities and discontinuities in childhood and adult moral development. *Human Development*, 1969, *12*, 93–120.

Kohlberg, L., Yaeger, J., & Hjortholm, E. The development of private speech: Four studies and a review of theory. *Child Development,* 1968, *39,* 692–736.

Kohn, M. L. Social class and parental values. *American Journal of Sociology,* 1959, *4,* 337–351.

Kohn, M. L. Social class and parent–child relationships: An interpretation. *American Journal of Sociology,* 1963, *4,* 471–480.

Kohn, M. The child as a determinant of his peers' approach to him. *Journal of Genetic Psychology,* 1966, *109,* 91–100.

Kohn, M., & Clausen, J. Social isolation and schizophrenia. *American Sociological Review,* 1955, *20,* 265–273.

Korner, A. F., & Grobstein, R. Individual differences at birth: Implications for mother–infant relationship and later development. In E. Rexford, L. Sander, & T. Shapiro (Eds.), *Infant psychiatry.* New Haven, Connecticut: Yale University Press, 1976.

Kramer, R. B. Changes in moral judgment response pattern during late adolescence and young adulthood: Retrogression in a developmental sequence. Unpublished doctoral dissertation, University of Chicago, 1968.

Krebs, D. L., & Staub, E. Personality and varied forms of helping. Unpublished research, Harvard University, 1971.

Krebs, D. L., & Stirrup, B. Role taking ability and altruistic behavior in elementary school children. Paper presented at the annual meeting of the American Psychological Association, New Orleans, August, 1974.

Kuhn, D. The development of role-taking ability. Unpublished manuscript, Columbia University, 1972.

Kurdock, L. A., & Rodgon, M. M. Perceptual, cognitive, and affective perspective taking in kindergarten through sixth grade children. *Developmental Psychology,* 1975, *11,* 643–650.

Kurtines, W., & Greif, E. B. The development of moral thought: Review and evaluation of Kohlberg's approach. *Psychological Bulletin,* 1974, *81,* 453–470.

Langer, J. Disequilibrium as a source of development. Paper read at the Society for Research in Child Development, New York City, April, 1967.

Lazarus, A. A., & Abramovitz, A. The use of "emotive imagery" in the treatment of children's phobias. *Journal of Mental Science,* 1962, *108,* 191–195.

Lazarus, R. S. *Psychological stress and the coping process.* New York: McGraw-Hill, 1966.

Lazarus, R. S., & Alfert, E. The short circuiting of threat by experimentally altering cognitive appraisal. *Journal of Abnormal & Social Psychology,* 1964, *69,* 195–205.

Lazarus, R. S., Averill, J. R., & Opton, E. M. Towards a cognitive theory of emotion. In M. Arnold (Ed.), *Feelings and emotions.* New York: Academic Press, 1969.

Lefkowitz, M. M., Eron, L. D., Walder, L. O., & Huesmann, L. R. *Growing up to be violent: A longitudinal study of the development of aggression.* New York: Pergamon Press, 1977.

Leiman, B. Affective empathy and subsequent altruism in kindergarteners and first graders. Paper presented at the annual meeting of the American Psychological Association, Toronto, Canada, August, 1978.

Leitner, M. P. A study of reciprocity in preschool play groups. *Child Psychology,* 1977, *48,* 1288–1295.

Lempers, J. P., Flavell, E. R., and Flavell, J. H. The development in very young children of tacit knowledge concerning visual perception. *Genetic Psychology Monographs,* 1977, *95,* 3–54.

Lepper, M. R. Dissonance, self-perception, and honesty in children. *Journal of Personality & Social Psychology*, 1973, *25*, 65–74.

Lepper, M. R., Sagotsky, G., & Mailer, J. Generalization and persistence of effects of exposure to self-reinforcement models. *Child Development*, 1975, *46*, 618–630.

Lesser, G. S. The relationships between various forms of aggression and popularity among lower-class children. *Journal of Educational Psychology*, 1959, *50*, 20–25.

Leuba, C. An experimental study of rivalry in young children. *Journal of Comparative Psychology*, 1933, *16*, 367–378.

Leventhal, H. Emotions: A basic problem for social psychology. In C. Nemeth (Ed.), *Social psychology: Classic and contemporary integrations*. Chicago: Rand McNally, 1974.

Leventhal, M., Singer, R., & Jones, S. Effects of fear and specificity of recommendation upon attitudes and behavior. *Journal of Personality & Social Psychology*, 1965, *2*, 20–29.

Levine, G. Role-taking standpoint and adolescent usage of Kohlberg's conventional stage of moral reasoning. *Journal of Personality & Social Psychology*, 1976, *34*, 41.

Levine, L. E., & Hoffman, M. L. Empathy and cooperation in 4-year olds. *Developmental Psychology*, 1975, *11*, 533–534.

Lewis, M., & Rosenblum, L. A. *Friendship and peer relations*. New York: Wiley, 1975.

Lewis, M., Young, G., Brooks, J., & Michalson, L. The beginning of friendship. In M. Lewis and L. A. Rosenblum (Eds.), *Friendship and peer relations*. New York: Wiley. 1975.

Lickona, T. Research on Piaget's theory of moral development. In T. Lickona (Ed.), *Moral development and behavior: Theory, research, and social issues*. New York: Holt, 1976.

Liebert, R. M., & Allen, M. K. Effects of rule structure and reward magnitude on the acquisition and adoption of self-reward criteria. *Psychological Reports*, 1967, *21*, 445–452.

Liebert, R. M., & Poulos, R. W. Television as a moral teacher. In T. Lickona (Ed.), *Moral development and behavior: Theory, research, and social issues*. New York: Holt, 1976.

Lippitt, P. Children teach other children. *Instructor*, 1969, *78*, 41–42.

Lippitt, R. Popularity among preschool children. *Child Development*, 1941, *12*, 305–322.

Lippitt, R. Improving the socialization process. In Clausen (Ed.), *Socialization and society*. Boston: Little, Brown, 1968.

Lippitt, R., & White, R. K. The "social climate" of children's groups. In R. G. Barker, J. S. Kounin, & H. F. Wright (Eds.), *Child behavior and development*. New York: McGraw-Hill, 1943.

Loban, W. A study of social sensitivity (sympathy) among adolescents. *Journal of Educational Psychology*, 1953, *44*, 102–112.

Loevinger, J. Patterns of parenthood as theories of learning. *Journal of Abnormal & Social Psychology*, 1959, *59*, 148–150.

London, P. The rescuers: Motivational hypothesis about Christians who saved Jews from the Nazis. In J. Macauley & L. Berkowitz (Eds.), *Altruism and Helping Behavior*. New York: Academic Press, 1970.

Long, G. T., & Lerner, M. J. Deserving, the "personal contract," and altruistic behavior by children. *Journal of Personality & Social Psychology*, 1974, *29*, 551–556.

Looft, W. R. Egocentrism and social interaction across the life span. *Psychological Bulletin*, 1972, *78*, 73–92.

Lynn, D. B., & Sawrey, W. L. The effects of father-absence on Norwegian boys and girls. *Journal of Abnormal & Social Psychology,* 1959, *59,* 258–262.

Maccoby, E. E. The development of moral values and behavior in childhood. In Clausen (Ed.), *Socialization and Society.* Boston: Little, Brown, 1968.

Madsen, M. C. Developmental and cross-cultural differences in the cooperative and competitive behavior of young children. *Journal of Cross-Cultural Psychology,* 1971, *2,* 365–371.

Madsen, M. C., & Shapira, A. Cooperation and challenge in four cultures. *Journal of Social Psychology,* 1977, *102,* 189–196.

Maitland, K., & Goldman, J. Moral judgment as a function of peer group interaction. *Journal of Personality & Social Psychology,* 1974, *30,* 699–704.

Marks, J. B. Interests, leadership, and sociometric status among adolescents. *Sociometry,* 1954, *17,* 340–349.

Marshall, H. R., & McCandless, B. R. A study in prediction of social behavior of preschool children. *Child Development,* 1957, *28,* 149–159.

Marston, A. P. Imitation, self-reinforcement, and reinforcement of another person. *Journal of Personality & Social Psychology,* 1965, *2,* 255–261.

Masangkay, Z. S., McCluskey, K. A., McIntyre, C. W., Sims-Knight, J., Vaughn, B. E., & Flavell, J. H. The early development of interferences about the visual perception of others. *Child Development,* 1974, *45,* 357–366.

Masters, J. C., & Christy, M. D. Achievement standards for contingent self-reinforcement: Effects of task length and task difficulty. *Child Development,* 1974, *45,* 6–13.

Masters, J. C., & Mokros, J. R. Self-reinforcement processes in children. In *Advances in child development and behavior,* Vol. 9. New York: Academic Press, 1974.

Masters, J. C., & Santrock, J. W. Studies in the self-regulation of behavior: Effects of verbal and cognitive self-reinforcement. *Developmental Psychology,* 1976, *12,* 334–348.

McClintock, C. G., & Nuttin, J. Development of competitive game behavior in children across two cultures. *Journal of Experimental Social Psychology,* 1969, *5,* 203–218.

McGeorge, C. The fakability of the defining issues test of moral development. *Developmental Psychology,* 1975, *11,* 108.

McKinney, J. P. The development of values; Prescriptive or proscriptive? *Human Development,* 1971, *14,* 71–80.

McMains, M. J., & Liebert, R. M. Influence of discrepancies between successively modeled self-reward criteria on the adoption of a self-imposed standard. *Journal of Personality & Social Psychology,* 1968, *8,* 166–171.

Mead, G. H. *Mind, self, and society.* Chicago: University of Chicago Press, 1934.

Mead, M. *Sex and temperament in three primitive societies.* New York: Morrow, 1935.

Mead, M. *Cooperation and competition among primitive peoples.* New York: McGraw-Hill, 1937.

Mead, M. *Culture and commitment: A study of the generation gap.* Garden City, New York: Natural History Press/Doubleday, 1970.

Meichenbaum, D. Examination of model characteristics in reducing avoidance behavior. *Journal of Personality & Social Psychology,* 1971, *17,* 298–307.

Meichenbaum, D. *Cognitive behavior modification.* Morristown, New Jersey: General Learning Press, 1974.

Meichenbaum, D., & Goodman, J. Reflection-impulsivity and verbal control of motor behavior. *Child Development,* 1969, *40,* 785–797.

Meichenbaum, D., & Goodman, J. Training impulsive children to talk to themselves: A means for developing self-control. *Journal of Abnormal Psychology*, 1971, *77*, 115–126.

Meister, A. Perception and acceptance of power relations in children. *Group Psychotherapy*, 1956, *9*, 153–163.

Midlarsky, E., & Bryan, J. H. Training charity in children. *Journal of Personality & Social Psychology*, 1967, *5*, 408–415.

Midlarsky, E., & Bryan, J. H. Affect expressions and children's imitative altruism. *Journal of Experimental Research in Personality*, 1972, *6*, 195–203.

Midlarsky, E., Bryan, J. H., & Brickman, P. Aversive approval: Interactive effects of modeling and reinforcement on altruistic behavior. *Child Development*, 1973, *44*, 321–328.

Miller, R. L., Brickman, P., & Bolen, D. Attribution versus persuasion as a means of modifying behavior. *Journal of Personality & Social Psychology*, 1975, *31*, 430–441.

Miller, W. B., Geretz, H., & Culter, H. S. Aggression in a boys' street corner group. *Psychiatry*, 1961, *24*, 283–298.

Mischel, W. Theory and research on the antecedents of self-imposed delay of reward. In B. A. Maher (Ed.), *Progress in experimental personality research*, Vol. 3. New York: Academic Press, 1966.

Mischel, W. *Personality and assessment*. New York: Wiley, 1968.

Mischel, W. Towards a cognitive social learning reconceptualization of personality. *Psychological Review*, 1973, *80*, 252–283.

Mischel, W. *Introduction to personality* (2nd ed.). New York: Holt, 1976.

Mischel, W., & Ebbesen, E. B. Attention in delay of gratification. *Journal of Personality & Social Psychology*, 1970, *16*, 329–337.

Mischel, W., Ebbesen, E. B., & Zeiss, A. Cognitive and attentional mechanism in delay of gratification. *Journal of Personality & Social Psychology*, 1972, *21*, 204–218.

Mischel, W., & Grusec, J. Determinants of the rehearsal and transmission of neutral and aversive behaviors. *Journal of Personality & Social Psychology*, 1966, *3*, 197–205.

Mischel, W., & Liebert, R. M. Effects of discrepancies between observed and imposed reward criteria on their acquisition and transmission. *Journal of Personality & Social Psychology*, 1966, *3*, 45–53.

Mood, D., Johnson, J., & Shantz, C. U. Affective and cognitive components of empathy in young children. Paper presented at the Southeast Regional Meeting of the Society for Research in Child Development. Chapel Hill, North Carolina, 1974.

Moore, S. G. Correlates of peer acceptance in nursery school children. In W. W. Hartup & N. L. Smothergill (Eds.), *The young child*. Washington, D.C.: National Association for the Education of Young Children, 1967.

Moore, S. G., & Updegraff, R. Sociometric status of preschool children related to age, nurturance-giving, and dependency. *Child Development*, 1964, *35*, 519–524.

Moos, R. H. Systems for the assessment and classification of human environments. In R. H. Moos & P. M. Insel (Eds.), *Issues in social ecology*. Palo Alto, California: National Press Books, 1974.

Morris, W. N., Marshall, H. M., & Miller, R. S. The effect of vicarious punishment on prosocial behavior in children. *Journal of Experimental Child Psychology*, 1973, *15*, 222–236.

Mouton, J. S., Bell, R. L., & Blake, R. Role playing skill and sociometric peer status. *Group Psychotherapy*, 1956, *9*, 7–17.

Mowrer, O. H. *Learning theory and personality dynamics*. New York: Ronald Press, 1950.

Mowrer, O. H. (Ed.) *Morality and mental health*. Chicago: Rand-McNally, 1967.

Mueller, E., & Brenner, J. The origins of social skills and interaction among play-group toddlers. *Child Development,* 1977, *48,* 854–861.

Mullison, D. C. Identification and sex-role preference. Senior honors thesis, University of Michigan, 1969.

Murphy, L. B. *Social behavior and child personality: An exploratory study of some roots of sympathy.* New York: Columbia University Press, 1937.

Mussen, P. H. Some antecedents and consequents of masculine sex-typing in adolescent boys. *Psychological Monographs,* 1961, *75,* (2, whole No. 506).

Mussen, P. H. Long-term consequents of masculinity of interests in adolescence. *Journal of Consulting Psychology,* 1962, *26,* 435–440.

Mussen, P. H., & Distler, L. Masculinity, identication, and father-son relationships. *Journal of Abnormal Social Psychology,* 1959, *59,* 350–356.

Mussen, P. H., & Distler, L. Child rearing antecedents of masculine identification in kindergarten boys. *Child Development,* 1960, *31,* 89–100.

Mussen, P. H., & Eisenberg-Berg, N. *Roots of caring, sharing and helping.* San Francisco: W. H. Freeman, 1977.

Mussen, P. H., & Rutherford, E. Parent–child relations and parental personality in relation to young children's sex-role preferences. *Child Development,* 1963, *34,* 589–607.

Mussen, P. H., Rutherford, E., Harris, S., & Keasey, C. B. Honesty and altruism among pre-adolescents. *Developmental Psychology,* 1970, *3,* 169–194.

Nahir, H. T., & Yussen, S. R. The performance of kibbutz and city reared Israeli children on two role-taking tests. *Developmental Psychology,* 1977, *13,* 450–455.

Nisbett, R. E., & Schachter, S. The cognitive manipulation of pain. *Journal of Experimental Social Psychology,* 1966, *2,* 227–236.

Oden, S., & Asher, S. Coaching children in social skills for friendship making. *Child Development,* 1977, *48,* 495–506.

Olejnik, A. B., & McKinney, J. P. Parental value orientation and generosity in children. *Developmental Psychology,* 1973, *8,* 311.

Olweus, D. Aggression and peer acceptance in adolescent boys: Two short-term longitudinal studies of ratings. *Child Development,* 1977, *48,* 1301–1313.

Parke, R. D. Nurturance, nurturance withdrawal, and resistance to deviation. *Child Development,* 1967, *35,* 1101–1110.

Parten, M. B. Social participation among pre-school children. *Journal of Abnormal & Social Psychology,* 1932, *27,* 243–269.

Patterson, G. R., & Anderson, D. Peers as social reinforcers. *Child Development,* 1964, *35,* 951–960.

Patterson, G. R., Littman, R. A., & Bricker, W. Assertive behavior in children: A step toward a theory of aggression. *Monographs of the Society for Research in Child Development,* 1967, *32* (113).

Piaget, J. *The moral judgment of the child.* London: Kegan Paul, 1932.

Piaget, J. *La psychologie de l'intelligence* (The psychology of intelligence). Paris: Armand Colin, 1947.

Piaget, J., *Six psychological studies.* New York: Random House, 1967.

Piaget, J., & Inhelder, B. *The child's conception of space.* London: Routledge, 1956.

Piaget, J., & Inhelder, B. *The psychology of the child.* New York: Basic Books, 1969.

Piaget, J., & Inhelder, B. *Mental imagery in the child.* New York: Basic Books, 1970.

Proshansky, H. M. The development of intergroup attitudes. In L. W. Hoffman & M. L. Hoffman (Eds.), *Review of child development research,* Vol. 2. New York: Russell Sage Foundation, 1966.

Provence, S., & Lipton, R. C. *Infants in institutions*. New York: International Universities Press, 1962.

Rawls, J. *A theory of justice*. Cambridge, Massachusetts: Harvard University Press, 1971.

Reese, H. Relationships between self-acceptance and sociometric choices. *Journal of Abnormal & Social Psychology*, 1961, *62*, 472–474.

Rest, J. Patterns of preference and comprehension in moral judgment. *Journal of Personality*, 1973, *41*, 86–109.

Rest, J., Turiel, E., & Kohlberg, L. Level of moral development as a determinant of preference and comprehension of moral judgments made by others. *Journal of Personality*, 1969, *37*, 225–252.

Reykowski, J., & Jarymowicz, M. Elicitation of the prosocial orientation. Unpublished manuscript, University of Warsaw, 1976.

Rheingold, H. L., Hay, D. F., & West, M. J. Sharing in the second year of life. *Child Development*, 1976, *47*, 1148–1158.

Rice, M. E., & Grusec, J. E. Saying and doing: Effects on observer performance. *Journal of Personality & Social Psychology*, 1975, *32*, 584–593.

Roff, M. Childhood social interactions and young adult bad conduct. *Journal of Abnormal & Social Psychology*, 1961, *63*, 333–337.

Roff, M., Sells, S. B., & Golden, M. M. *Social adjustment and personality development in children*. Minneapolis: University of Minnesota Press, 1972.

Rosen, C. E. The effects of sociodramatic play on problem-solving behavior among culturally disadvantaged preschool children. *Child Development*, 1974, *45*, 920–927.

Rosenhan, D. The natural socialization of altruistic autonomy. In J. Macauley & L. Berkowitz (Eds.), *Altruism and helping*. New York: Academic Press, 1970.

Rosenhan, D., Frederick, F., & Burrows, A. Preaching and practicing: Effects of channel discrepancy on norm internalization. *Child Development*, 1968, *39*, 291–301.

Rosenhan, D., & White, G. Observation and rehearsal as determinants of prosocial behavior. *Journal of Personality & Social Psychology*, 1967, *5*, 424–431.

Rothbaum, F. Taking the perspective of another: A study of 11 and 13 year old children. Unpublished manuscript, Yale University, 1973.

Rothman, G. R. The influence of moral reasoning on behavioral choices. *Child Development*, 1976, *47*, 399–406.

Rotter, J. B. *Social learning and clinical psychology*. Englewood Cliffs, New Jersey: Prentice-Hall, 1954.

Rotter, J. B. A new scale for measurement of interpersonal trust. *Journal of Personality*, 1967, *35*, 651–665.

Rotter, J. B. Generalized expectancies for interpersonal trust. *American Psychologist*, 1971, *26*, 443–452.

Rubin, K. H. Egocentrism in childhood: A unitary construct? *Child Development*, 1973, *44*, 102–110.

Rubin, K. H., & Schneider, F. W. The relationship between moral judgement, egocentrism, and altruistic behavior. *Child Development*, 1973, *44*, 661–665.

Rubin, K. H., & Trotter, K. T. Kohlberg's moral judgment scale: Some methodological considerations. *Developmental Psychology*, 1977, *13*, 535–536.

Rushton, J. P. Generosity in children: Immediate and long-term effects of modeling, preaching, and moral judgment. *Journal of Personality & Social Psychology*, 1975, *31*, 459–466.

Rushton, J. P. Socialization and the altruistic behavior of children. *Psychological Bulletin*, 1976, *83*, 898–913.

Rushton, J. P., & Wiener, J. Altruism and cognitive development in children. *British Journal of Social & Clinical Psychology*, 1975, *14*, 341–349.

Rutherford, E., & Mussen, P. Generosity in nursery school boys. *Child Development,* 1968, *39,* 755–765.

Sagi, A., & Hoffman, M. L. Empathic distress in the newborn. *Developmental Psychology,* 1976, *12,* 175–176.

Schachter. S. *The psychology of affiliation: Experimental studies of the sources of gregariousness.* Stanford, California: Stanford University Press, 1959.

Schachter, S., & Singer, J. E. Cognitive, social, and psychological determinants of emotional state. *Psychological Review,* 1962, *69,* 379–399.

Schaefer, E. S. A circumplex model for maternal behavior. *Journal of Abnormal & Social Psychology,* 1959, *59,* 226–235.

Schaefer, E. S. Children's reports of parental behavior: An inventory. *Child Development,* 1965, *36,* 413–424.

Schwartz, S. H. Normative influences on altruism. In L. Berkowitz (Ed.), *Advances in experimental social psychology,* Vol. 10. New York: Academic Press, 1977.

Sears, R. R., Maccoby, E. E., & Levin, H. *Patterns of child rearing.* New York: Harper, 1957.

Sears, R. R., Rau, L., & Alpert, R. *Identification and child-rearing.* Stanford, California: Stanford University Press, 1965.

Sells, S. B., & Roff, M. Peer acceptance–rejection and personality development. Final Report, Project No. OE 5–0417, United States Department of Health, Education, and Welfare, 1967.

Selman, R. L. The relation of role-taking to the development of moral judgment in children. *Child Development,* 1971, *42,* 79–91.

Selman, R. L. A structural analysis of the ability to take another's social perspective: Stages in the development of role-taking ability. Paper presented at the meeting of the Society for Research in Child Development, Philadelphia, 1973.

Selman, R. L. Social–cognitive understanding: A guide to educational and clinical practice. In T. Lickona (Ed.), *Moral development and behavior.* New York: Holt, 1976.

Selman, R. L., & Byrne, D. F. A structural–developmental analysis of levels of role-taking in middle childhood. *Child Development,* 1974, *45,* 803–806.

Serbin, L. A., Tonnick, I. J., & Sternglanz, S. H. Shaping cooperative cross-sex play. *Child Development,* 1977, *48,* 924–929.

Severy, L., & Davis, K. Helping behavior among normal and retarded children. *Child Development,* 1971, *42,* 1017–1031.

Shantz, C. U. The development of social cognition. In E. M. Hetherington (Ed.), *Review of child development research,* Vol. 5. Chicago: University of Chicago Press, 1975.

Shantz, C. U., & Watson, J. S. Spatial abilities and spatial egocentrism in the young child. *Child Development,* 1971, *42,* 171–181.

Shapira, A., & Madsen, M. C. Cooperative and competitive behavior of Kibbutz and urban children in Israel. *Child Development,* 1969, *40,* 609–617.

Shatz, M., & Gelman, R. The development of communication skills: Modifications in the speech of young children as a function of the listener. *Monographs of the Society for Research in Child Development,* 1973, *38* (5, Serial No. 152).

Simner, M. L. Newborn's response to the cry of another infant. *Developmental Psychology,* 1971, *5,* 136–150.

Sims, S. Socialization and situational determinants of sharing in black children. Unpublished doctoral dissertation, University of Michigan, 1974.

Sims, S. A. Induction, self-induction and children's donation behavior. Paper presented at the 49th Annual Meeting of the Eastern Psychological Association, Washington, D.C., March, 1978.

Spilton, D., & Lee, L. C. Some determinants of effective communication in four-year-olds. *Child Development*, 1977, *48*, 968–977.

Staub, E. The reduction of a specific fear by information combined with exposure to the feared stimulus. *Proceedings, 76th Annual Convention of the American Psychological Association*, 1968, *3*, 525–527.

Staub, E. A child in distress: The effects of focusing responsibility on children on their attempts to help. *Developmental Psychology*, 1970, *2*, 152–154. (a)

Staub, E. A child in distress: The influence of age and number of witnesses on children's attempts to help. *Journal of Personality & Social Psychology*, 1970, *14*, 130–140. (b)

Staub, E. A child in distress: The influence of modeling and nurturance on children's attempts to help. *Developmental Psychology*, 1971, *5*, 124–133. (a)

Staub, E. Helping a person in distress: The influence of implicit and explicit "rules" of conduct on children and adults. *Journal of Personality & Social Psychology*, 1971, *17*, 137–145. (b)

Staub, E. The learning and unlearning of aggression: The role of anxiety, empathy, efficacy and pro-social values. In J. Singer (Ed.), *The control of aggression, violence: Cognitive and physiological factors*. New York: Academic Press, 1971. (c)

Staub, E. The use of role playing and induction in children's learning of helping and sharing behavior. *Child Development*, 1971, *42*, 805–817. (d)

Staub, E. Instigation to goodness: The role of social norms and interpersonal influence. *Journal of Social Issues*, 1972, *28*, 131–151. (a)

Staub, E. The effects of persuasion and modeling on delay of gratification. *Developmental Psychology*, 1972, *6*, 168–177. (b)

Staub, E. Children's sharing behavior: Success and failure, the "norm of deserving," and reciprocity in sharing. Paper presented at the symposium "Helping and sharing: Concepts of altruism and cooperation" at the meeting of the Society of Research in Child Development, Philadelphia, March, 1973.

Staub, E. Helping a distressed person: Social, personality, and stimulus determinants. In L. Berkowitz (Ed.), *Advances in experimental social psychology*, Vol. 7. New York: Academic Press, 1974.

Staub, E. *The development of prosocial behavior in children*. Morristown, New Jersey: General Learning Press, 1975. (a)

Staub, E. To rear a prosocial child: Reasoning, learning by doing, and learning by teaching others. In D. DePalma & J. Folley (Eds.), *Moral development: Current theory and research*. Hillsdale, New Jersey: Lawrence Erlbaum. 1975. (b)

Staub, E. The development of prosocial behavior: Directions for future research and applications to education. Paper presented at Moral Citizenship/Education Conference, Philadelphia, June, 1976.

Staub, E. *Positive social behavior and morality, Vol. 1: Social and Personal influences*. New York: Academic Press, 1978. (a)

Staub, E. Predicting prosocial behavior: A model for specifying the nature of personality–situation interaction. In L. Pervin & M. Lewis (Eds.), *Internal and external determinants of behavior*. New York: Plenum Press, 1978 (b).

Staub, E. Socialization by parents and peers and the experiential learning of prosocial behavior. In J. H. Stevens & M. Mathews (Eds.), *Mother/child, father/child relationships*. National Association for the Education of Young Children, 1978. (c)

Staub, E. Understanding and predicting social behavior with special emphasis on prosocial behavior. In E. Staub (Ed.), *Personality: Basic issues and current research*. Englewood Cliffs, New Jersey: Prentice-Hall, 1979 (in press).

Staub, E., & Baer, R. S. Jr. Stimulus characteristics of a sufferer and difficulty of escape as determinants of helping. *Journal of Personality & Social Psychology,* 1974, *30,* 279–285.

Staub, E., & Buswell, S. Incidental effects of helping an adult teach other children prosocial behaviors. Unpublished research, University of Massachusetts.

Staub, E., Erkut, S., & Jaquette, D. Personality, variation in the permissibility of action and response to another's need for help. Unpublished research, Harvard University.

Staub, E., & Feinberg, H. Experiential learning and induction as means of developing prosocial conduct. Unpublished research, University of Massachusetts. Amherst, 1977. (a)

Staub, E., & Feinberg, H. Positive and negative peer interaction and some of their personality correlates. Unpublished research, University of Massachusetts, Amherst, 1977. (b)

Staub, E., & Feinberg, H. Personality, socialization, and the development of prosocial behavior in children. In D. H. Smith & J. Macauley (Eds.), *Informal social participation: The determinants of socio-political action, leisure activity, and altruistic behavior.* Jossey-Bass, 1978, in press.

Staub, E., & Fotta, M. Participation in prosocial behavior and positive induction as means of children learning to be helpful. Unpublished manuscript, University of Massachusetts, Amherst, 1978.

Staub, E., & Jancaterino, W. Learning to be helpful by participation in a positive behavior: The effects of teaching others. Unpublished research, University of Massachusetts.

Staub, E., & Kellett, D. S. Increasing pain tolerance by information about aversive stimuli. *Journal of Personality & Social Psychology,* 1972, *21,* 198–203.

Staub, E., Leavy, R., & Shortsleeves, J. Teaching others as a means of learning to be helpful. Unpublished research, University of Massachusetts, Amherst, 1975.

Staub, E., & Noerenberg, H. Deserving, reciprocity and transactions in children's sharing behavior. Unpublished manuscript, University of Massachusetts, Amherst, 1978.

Stayton, D. J., Hogan, R., & Ainsworth, M. D. S. Infant obedience and maternal behavior: The origins of stabilization reconsidered. *Child Development,* 1971, *42,* 1057–1069.

Stein, A. H., and Baltes, P. B. Theory and method in life-span developmental psychology: Implications for child development. In Reese, H. W. (Ed.), *Advances in child development and behavior,* 1976, Vol. 11, New York: Academic Press.

Stein, A. H., & Friedrich, L. K. Television content and young children's behavior. In J. P. Murray, E. A. Rubinstein, & G. A. Comstock (Eds.), *Television and social behavior,* Vol. II: *Television and social learning.* Washington, D.C.: U.S. Government Printing Office ,1972.

Stengel, E. *Suicide and attempted suicide.* Middlesex: Penguin, 1971.

Stern, W. *Psychology of early childhood: Up to the sixth year of age.* New York: Holt, 1924.

Sullivan, E. V., & Hunt, D. E. Interpersonal and objective decentering as a function of age and social class. *Journal of Genetic Psychology,* 1967, *110,* 199–210.

Surber, C. F. Developmental processes in social inference: Averaging of intentions and consequences in moral judgment. *Developmental Psychology,* 1977, *13,* 654–665.

Taguiri, R. Person perception. In G. Lindzey & E. Aronson (Eds.), *The handbook of Social Psychology,* Vol. 3. Reading, Massachusetts: Addison-Wesley, 1969.

Tchudnowski, P. Paper delivered at the Conference on Mechanisms of Prosocial Behavior. Sponsored by the Committee of Psychological Sciences of the Polish Academy of Sciences, Poland, October, 1974.

Thelen, H. A. Tutoring by students. *School Review,* 1969, *77,* 229–244.

Theroux, S. S. The effects of modeling on cooperation in young children. Unpublished dissertation, University of Massachusetts, 1975.

Thomas, A., Chess, S., Birch, H. G., Hertzig, M. E., & Korn, S. *Behavioral individuality in early childhood*. New York: New York University Press, 1963.

Thomas, K., Chess, S., & Birch, H. G. *Temperament and behavior disorders in children*. New York: New York University Press, 1968.

Thompson, W. R., & Grusec, J. Studies of early experience. In P. H. Mussen (Ed.), *Carmichael's manual of child psychology* (3rd ed.), Vol. 2. New York: Wiley, 1970.

Tilker, H. A. Socially responsive behavior as a function of observer responsibility and victim feedback. *Journal of Personality & Social Psychology*, 1970, *14*, 95–100.

Titkin, S., & Hartup, W. W. Sociometric status and the reinforcing effectiveness of children's peers. *Journal of Experimental Child Psychology*, 1965, *2*, 306–315.

Toda, M., Shinotsuka, H., McClintock, C. G., & Stech, F. J. Development of competitive behavior as a function of culture, age, and social comparison. *Journal of Personality and Social Psychology*, 1978, *36*, 825–839.

Tomkins, S. S. The constructive role of violence and suffering for the individual and for his society. In S. S. Tomkins & C. E. Izard (Eds.), *Affect, cognition, and personality*. New York: Springer, 1965.

Triandis, H. C. Some universals of social behavior. *Personality and Social Psychology Bulletin*, 1978, *4*, 1–16.

Trickett, E. J. Toward a social-ecological conception of adolescent socialization: Normative data on contrasting types of public school classrooms. *Child Development*, 1978, *49*, 408–414.

Trivers, R. L. The evolution of reciprocal altruism. *Quarterly Review of Biology*, 1971, *46*, 35–37.

Turiel, E. An experimental test of the sequentiality of developmental stages in the child's moral judgments. *Journal of Personality & Social Psychology*, 1966, *3*, 611–618.

Turiel, E. Developmental processes in the child's moral thinking. In P. Mussen, E. J. Langer, & M. Covington (Eds.), *Trends and issues in developmental psychology*. New York: Holt, 1969.

Turiel, E. The development of social concepts: Mores, customs, and conventions. In D. DePalma & J. M. Foley (Eds.), *Moral development: Current theory and research*. Hillsdale, New Jersey: Lawrence Erlbaum Associates, 1975.

Turiel, E. A comparative analysis of moral knowledge and moral judgment in males and females. *Journal of Personality*, 1976, *44*, 195–208.

Turiel, E., & Rothman, R. The influence of reasoning on behavioral choices at different stages of moral development. *Child Development*, 1972, *43*, 741–756.

Turner, D. & Balow, B. Social learning theory and group behavioral change. Paper presented at the annual meeting of the American Educational Research Association, 1972.

Ugurel-Semin, R. Moral behavior and moral judgment of children. *Journal of Abnormal & Social Psychology*, 1952, *47*, 463–474.

Urbach, N. M., & Rogolsky, S. Moral judgment in altruism and honesty situations. Unpublished manuscript, Institute for Child Study, University of Maryland, 1976.

Van Lieshout, C. F., Leckie, G., & Smits-Van Sonsbeek, B. The effect of a social perspective-taking training on empathy and role-taking ability of preschool children. Paper presented at the meeting of the International Society for the Study of Behavioral Development, Ann Arbor, Michigan, 1973.

Vincent, J. Scaling the universe of states on certain useful multivariate dimensions. *Journal of Social Psychology*, 1971, *85*, 261–283.

Walton, W. E. Empathic responses in children. *Psychological Monographs*, 1936, *48*, 40–67.

Warnath, C. F. The relation of family cohesiveness and adolescent independence to social effectiveness. *Marriage & Family Living*, 1955, *17*, 346–348.

Weissbrod, C. Noncontingent warmth induction, cognitive style, and children's initiative donation and rescue effort behaviors. *Journal of Personality & Social Psychology*, 1976, *34*, 274–281.

Wellman, H. M., & Lempers, J. P. The naturalistic communicative abilities of two-year-olds. *Child Development*, 1977, *48*, 1052–1057.

West, H. Early peer-group interaction and role-taking skills: An investigation of Israeli children. *Child Development*, 1974, *45*, 1118–1122.

West, S. G., Whitney, G., & Schnedler, R. Helping a motorist in distress: The effects of sex, race, and neighborhood. *Journal of Personality & Social Psychology*, 1975, *31*, 691–698.

White, G. M. Immediate and deferred effects of model observation and guided and unguided rehearsal on donating and stealing. *Journal of Personality & Social Psychology*, 1972, *21*, 139–148.

White, G. M., & Burnam, M. A. Socially cued altruism: Effects of modeling, instructions, and age on public and private donations. *Child Development*, 1975, *46*, 559–563.

Whiting, B., & Whiting, J. W. M. *Children of six cultures*. Cambridge, Massachusetts: Harvard University Press, 1975.

Whiting, J. W. M. Sorcery, sin, and the superego: A cross-cultural study of some mechanisms of social control. In M. R. Jones (Ed.), *Nebraska symposium on motivation*, 1959.

Whiting, J. W. M. Resource mediation and learning by identification. In I. Iscoe & H. W. Stevenson (Eds.), *Personality development in children*. Austin: University of Texas Press, 1960.

Whiting, J. W. M., & Whiting, B. The behavior of children in six cultures. Unpublished manuscript. Cambridge, Massachusetts: Harvard University Press, 1969.

Wilson, E. O. Sociobiology: The new synthesis. Cambridge, Massachusetts: Belknap Press of Harvard University Press, 1975.

Winder, C. L., & Rau, L. Parental attitudes associated with social deviance in preadolescent boys. *Journal of Abnormal & Social Psychology*, 1962, *64*, 418–424.

Wyer, R. S. Effect of child-rearing attitudes and behavior on children's responses to hypothetical social situations. *Journal of Personality & Social Psychology*, 1965, *2*, 480–486.

Yarrow, L. J., & Pedersen, F. A. Attachment: Its origins and course. In W. W. Hartup (Ed.), *The young child*. National Association for the Education of Young Children, 1972.

Yarrow, M. R., & Scott, P. M. Imitation of nurturant and nonnurturant models. *Journal of Personality & Social Psychology*, 1972, *23*, 259–270.

Yarrow, M. R., Scott, P. M., & Waxler, C. Z. Learning concern for others. *Developmental Psychology*, 1973, *8*, 240–261.

Yarrow, M. R., & Waxler C. Z. Dimensions and correlates of prosocial behavior in young children. *Child Development*, 1976, *47*, 118–125.

Yussen, S. R. Moral reasoning from the perspective of others. *Child Development*, 1976, *47*, 551–555.

Zahavi, S., & Asher, S. R. The effect of verbal instructions on preschool children's aggressive behavior. *Journal of School Psychology*, 1978, *16*, 146–153.

Zak, J. Studies of the development of interaction among preschool children. *Psychologie Wychowa Woza*, 1968, *11*, 75–85.

Author Index

A

Ainsworth, M. D. S., 72, 126
Alfert, E., 166, 167
Allen, A., 16
Allen, M. K., 129, 133
Allen, V. L., 196
Alpert, R., 122
Ambron, S. R., 71, 84
Anderson, D., 228
Anderson, H. H., 223
Arlitt, A. H., 61
Armsby, R. E. A., 82
Arnold, M., 166
Aronfreed, J., 30, 34, 35, 45, 93, 95, 97, 99, 132, 145, 146, 148, 153, 160, 161, 165
Asher, S., 229, 239, 241, 242
Averill, J. R., 166
Avgar, A., 218
Azrin, N., 66, 141

B

Babigan, H., 50
Baer, R. S., 19
Balow, B., 154
Baltes, P. B., 8
Bandura, A., 24, 31, 34, 35, 36, 50, 53, 112, 116, 128, 129, 130, 131, 132, 133, 138, 141, 175
Barrett, D. E., 235
Bathurst, J. E., 190
Baumrind, D., 16, 63, 91, 92, 93, 103, 105, 106, 108, 109, 110, 114, 160, 170, 179, 190, 244, 256, 276
Bell, R. Q., 93, 94, 232
Bem, D. J., 16, 61, 95
Berkowitz, L., 186
Berne, E. V. C., 63
Bernstein, M. R., 214
Bettelheim, B., 26
Billingsley, A., 254
Birch, H. G., 93
Bixenstine, B. A., 247
Bixenstine, V. E., 247
Bizman, A., 194, 195
Black, A. E., 106
Blake, R., 232
Blatt, M., 50, 174
Block, J., 15, 171
Block, J. H., 15, 260
Bolen, D., 152
Boll, E. S., 29, 193, 194
Bonney, M. E., 231
Borke, H., 71, 77

299

Bossard, J. H. S., 29, 193, 194
Botkin, P., 158
Bott, M., 223
Brehm, J. W., 98
Breland, K., 139
Breland, M., 139
Brenner, J., 72
Bricker, W., 226
Brickman, P., 124, 152
Brody, G. H., 176
Bronfenbrenner, U., 24, 45, 46, 52, 112,
    186, 192, 193, 218, 246, 248, 258,
    267, 272
Brooks, J., 223
Brown, R. W., 25, 26
Bruner, A., 76
Bryan, J. H., 15, 64, 116, 119, 124, 138,
    146, 147, 150, 167, 168, 204
Bryant, B., 248
Burnham, M. A., 148, 202
Burns, N., 71, 78, 79
Burrows, A., 129
Burton, R. V., 55
Buswell, S., 195
Byrne, D. F., 83

C

Cabin, S., 123
Campbell, D. T., 5
Campbell, E. Q., 31
Campbell, J. D., 226, 227, 235
Canton, N. L., 94
Cavey, L., 71, 78, 79
Chandler, M. J., 158, 159
Charlesworth, R., 223, 227
Chess, S., 93
Christy, M. O., 131
Clausen, J., 240
Coates, B., 155
Cohen, R., 4, 275
Coie, J. D., 82
Coleman, J. S., 236
Cook, H., 66, 154
Coopersmith, S., 92, 111, 237, 276
Costanzo, P. R., 82
Cowan, P., 53, 75, 175, 218
Cowdry, R. W., 123
Cowen, E. L., 50, 239
Crockenberg, S., 248
Crower, C. C., 143
Cutler, H. S., 245

D

Damon, W., 55, 56
Dann, S., 222

Davidson, G. C., 143
Davis, K., 67
Deci, E., 53, 97
DeCorte, M. S., 247
DePalma, D. J., 183
Deutsch, F., 77, 78, 232
Devereaux, E. D., 246
Devin-Sheehan, L., 196
Dienstbier, R. A., 94, 97
Distler, L., 26, 113
Ditrichs, R. A., 130
Dlugokinski, E. L., 15, 138, 169
Dollard, J., 22
Dressel, S., 148, 203
Durkheim, E., 180

E

Eaton, J. W., 130
Ebbeson, E. B., 134, 135
Eisenberg-Berg, N., 15, 17, 55, 167,
    168, 169
Elkins, D., 231, 244
Elliot, R., 64
Emmerich, W., 59
Erkut, S., 14
Eron, L. O., 93, 160
Escalona, S. K., 257

F

Farber, I. E., 139
Farnill, D. A., 82
Feinberg, H. K., 14, 171, 183, 189, 195,
    210, 224, 233
Feinberg, M. R., 231
Feldman, R. S., 196
Feldman, S. E., 130
Ferguson, L. R., 126
Feshbach, N. D., 68, 77, 85
Feshbach, S., 68
Festinger, L., 95
Finley, G. E., 75
Firestone, I. J., 15, 59, 138, 169
Fischer, W. F., 142
Flapan, D., 78, 79, 80
Flavell, E. R., 72
Flavell, J. H., 71, 72, 73, 76, 158
Fotta, M., 171, 205, 206
Frankie, G., 28
Frauhauf-Ziegler, C., 65
Frederick, F., 129
Freedman, D. G., 257
Freedman, J. L., 95
French, D., 75
Freud, A., 222
Freud, S., 23, 25, 26, 30, 32, 132
Friedrich, L. K., 63, 153, 154, 155, 156, 157

Frost, M. A., 50
Fry, C., 158

G

Garbarino, J., 45, 46, 112, 186, 248
Gates, G. S., 71
Geisheker, E., 167, 168, 169
Gelfand, D. M., 94, 142, 143, 144
Gellert, E., 239
Gelman, R., 71, 72
Geretz, H., 245
Gerwitz, J. L., 24, 83
Ginott, H. G., 125
Giovannoni, J., 254
Glazer, J. A., 227
Golden, M. M., 240
Goldman, J., 46
Gonson, J., 232
Goodman, I., 155
Goodman, J., 135
Goslin, D. A., 236
Gottman, J. M., 230, 231, 232
Gottschaldt, D., 65
Gouldner, A. W., 49, 223
Graves, N. B., 67, 68, 255
Green, F. P., 64
Green, S. K., 81
Greenberg, P. J., 66
Greif, E. B., 47, 54
Grings, W. W., 141
Grobstein, R., 257
Grodman, S. M., 14, 183
Gross, P., 64
Grument, J. F., 82
Grusec, J. E., 116, 117, 122, 126, 138, 151, 198, 204, 214

H

Haan, N., 55, 260
Haith, M. M., 62
Halverson, C. F., 94
Hamm, C., 52
Handlon, B. J., 64
Hapkiewitz, W. G., 160
Harlow, H., 222
Harlow, M., 222
Harris, M. B., 148
Harris, S., 100
Hartmann, D. P., 94, 142, 143, 144
Hartshorne, H., 69, 167
Hartup, W. W., 108, 194, 223, 225, 227, 228, 230, 231, 232, 237, 239, 240, 245
Hay, D. F., 62
Heavenrich, J., 53

Helson, H., 53
Henderson, C. R., 218
Henderson, R. W., 176
Henshel, A., 68
Hetherington, E. M., 27, 28
Hicks, D. J., 138
Hildenbrandt, D. E., 130
Hill, W. E., 32
Hillman, D., 94
Hillman, J., 94
Hirota, K., 65
Hjartholm, E., 75
Hoffman, L. W., 244
Hoffman, M. L., 6, 7, 19, 22, 28, 29, 30, 31, 32, 33, 61, 63, 71, 86, 93, 111, 113, 114, 115, 126, 161, 162, 164, 170, 181, 182, 183, 184, 185, 244
Hogan, R., 54, 72, 126, 187
Hollander, E. P., 245
Hollos, M., 218
Holstein, C. B., 47, 48, 52
Horowitz, F. O., 236
Hovland, C. L., 214
Huesmann, L. R., 160
Hughes, C. C., 130
Humphrey, G., 61
Hunt, D. E., 75
Huttenlocher, J., 71

I

Iannotti, R. J., 159
Inhelder, B., 70, 71, 72
Inoff, G. E., 94
Into, E. C., 186
Irwin, D. M., 71, 84
Izard, C. E., 77
Izzo, L. D., 50

J

Jancaterino, W., 173, 206
Janis, I. J., 214
Jaquette, D., 14, 183
Jarvis, P., 158
Jarymowicz, M., 237
Jensen, R. E., 152
Johnson, J., 77
Jones, S., 166

K

Kagan, J., 24, 25
Kagan, S., 18, 67
Kaplan, K. J., 59
Karniol, R., 39, 82
Katz, H. A., 29
Keasey, C. B., 84, 100

Keislar, E. R., 231
Kellett, D. S., 166, 167
Kelley, H. H., 112, 258, 275
Kelman, H. C., 31
Kenniston, K., 123
Kessen, W., 62
Klaus, R. A., 231, 236
Klein, R., 77
Knight, G. P., 18
Koch, H. L., 232
Kohlberg, L., 24, 33, 38, 39, 40, 41, 42, 43,
    44, 45, 47, 48, 49, 51, 52, 54, 55, 56,
    75, 76, 83, 84, 174, 175, 186, 217, 248
Kohn, M. L., 52, 223, 225, 240
Korner, A. F., 257
Kramer, R. B., 40, 47, 48
Krebs, D. L., 15, 59, 234, 235
Kuhn, D., 84
Kupers, C., 128, 131, 133
Kurdock, L. A., 74, 78, 79, 85
Kurtines, W. 47, 54

L

Langer, J., 44, 53
Lazarus, R. S., 166, 167
Leavey, R., 205
Leckie, G., 76
Lee, L. C., 72
Lefkowitz, M. M., 93, 160
Lehnhoff, J., 94
Leighton, A. H., 130
Leiman, B., 266
Leitner, M. P., 245
Lempers, J. P., 72
Lepper, M. R., 128, 153
Lerner, M. J., 173
Lesser, G. S., 231
Lcuba, C., 66
Levanthal, H., 62, 166
Levin, H., 25
Levine, G., 55
Levine, L. E., 6
Lewis, M., 223
Lickona, T., 39
Liebert, R. M., 129, 130, 133, 160
Lindsley, O., 66, 141
Lippitt, P., 196
Lippitt, R., 196, 232, 248
Lipton, R. C., 126
Littman, R. A., 226
Loban, W., 236
Lockhart, R. A., 141
Loevinger, J., 178
Long, G. T., 173
Looft, W. R., 75
Lynn. D. B., 244

M

Maccoby, E. E., 6, 31, 33, 116
MacDonald, F., 50, 53, 175
Madsen, M. C., 18, 67, 219, 242
Mailer, J., 128
Maitland, K., 46
Marcia, J. E., 245
Marks, J. B., 231
Marshall, H. M., 145
Marshall, H. R., 229
Marston, A. P., 130
Masangkay, Z. S., 71
Masters, J. C., 35, 128, 131, 133, 134, 198
May, M. A., 68, 167
McCandless, B. R., 229
McClintock, C. G., 66, 258
McClusky, K. A., 71
McGeorge, C., 85
McIntyre, C. W., 71
McKinney, J. P., 96, 180, 181
McMains, M. J., 129
Mead, G. H., 66
Mead, M., 5, 43, 245, 274
Meichenbaum, D., 35, 133, 135
Meister, A., 65
Menlove, F. L., 116
Michalson, L., 223
Midlarsky, E., 15, 64, 124, 138, 139, 146,
    147, 148, 150, 168, 203, 204
Miller, N. E., 22
Miller, R. L., 152
Miller, R. S., 145
Miller, W. B., 245
Mischel, W., 34, 35, 122, 129, 130, 134,
    135, 138, 171, 248
Mitzvari, E., 193
Mokros, J. R., 35, 128, 198
Mood, D., 77
Moore, S. G., 152, 229, 231, 232, 237
Moos, R. H., 248
Morris, W. N., 145
Mouton, J. S., 232
Mowrer, O. H., 25, 132
Mueller, E., 72
Mullison, D. C., 29
Murphy, L. B., 63, 64, 68
Mussen, P. H., 15, 17, 26, 29, 55, 59, 100,
    102, 113, 114, 115, 122, 184, 190, 239, 244

N

Nahir, H. T., 75, 218
Nathanson, M., 53
Nisbett, R. E., 166
Noerenberg, H., 64
Nuttin, J., 66

O

Oden, S., 229, 239, 241
Olejnik, A. B., 96, 181
Olweus, D., 15, 227
Opton, E. M., 166

P

Page, B. C., 143
Parker, R. D., 116
Parten, M. B., 65
Paskal, V., 145, 146, 148
Patterson, G. R., 226, 228
Pederson, A., 50
Pederson, F. A., 126
Perloff, B., 130, 131
Piaget, J., 33, 38, 39, 43, 44, 66, 70, 71, 72, 73, 75, 76, 80, 81, 83, 84, 175, 217, 238
Poulos, R. W., 160
Powell, J., 231
Presson, C. C., 71
Proshansky, H. M., 53
Provence, S., 126
Pusser, H. E., 155

R

Rapaport, R. N., 130
Rasmussen, B., 232
Rau, L., 122, 231, 244
Rawls, J., 45
Reese, H., 236
Rest, J., 49, 50, 174
Reykowski, J., 237
Rheingold, H. L., 62
Rice, M. E., 198
Roden, A., 160
Rodgon, M. M., 74, 78, 79, 85
Roe, K., 77, 85
Roff, M., 229, 237, 239
Rogolsky, S., 55
Rosen, C. E., 241
Rosenblum, L. A., 223
Rosenhan, D., 116, 123, 129, 150, 199, 204, 260
Rothbaum, F., 75
Rothman, R., 49, 176, 177, 178
Rotter, J. B., 29, 34, 35, 112, 186
Rubin, K. H., 47, 70, 75, 84, 232
Rushton, J. P., 15, 59, 64, 76, 124, 138, 150, 167, 169
Russell, J. C., 59
Rutherford, E., 29, 59, 100, 113, 114, 115

S

Sagotsky, G., 128
Salapatek, P. H., 62
Saltzein, H. D., 28, 113, 114, 162, 170, 181, 244
Santrock, J. W., 133, 134
Sauts-Van Sousbeek, B., 76
Sawrey, W. L., 244
Schachter, S., 111, 166
Schaefer, E. S., 91, 92
Schmidt, R., 231
Schneider, F. W., 64, 84
Schwartz, S. H., 14
Scott, P. M., 94, 116, 117, 121, 122, 125, 140
Sears, R. R., 25, 111, 122, 160
Sells, S. B., 229, 237, 239
Selman, R. L., 55, 70, 83, 84
Serbin, L. A., 142
Severy, L., 67
Shantz, C. U., 71, 75, 76, 77, 81
Shapira, A., 219
Shatz, M., 71, 72
Shavit, R., 193
Shinotsuka, H., 258
Shortsleeves, J., 205
Shuttleworth, F. K., 69, 167
Sim-Knight, J., 71
Simner, M. L., 61, 62
Sims, S., 169
Singer, J. E., 166
Singer, R., 166
Skubicki, L., 116, 198, 214
Smith, C. L., 143
Smith, M., 231
Smith, M. B., 260
Spilton, D., 72
Stahleski, A. J., 112, 258, 275
Staub, E., 10, 14, 15, 19, 36, 49, 59, 64, 65, 68, 90, 98, 109, 111, 112, 115, 116, 119, 121, 133, 138, 157, 158, 166, 167, 168, 171, 173, 183, 189, 194, 195, 196, 198, 205, 206, 210, 214, 215, 222, 224, 233, 267, 270
Staub, E. (Volume 1),* 1, 2, 3, 5, 6, 7, 8, 10, 11, 13, 14, 15, 16, 18, 19, 20, 24, 36, 37, 39, 48, 54, 55, 57, 59, 61, 69, 90, 95, 97, 98, 102, 111, 124, 132, 133, 137, 144, 148, 150, 160, 166, 167, 169, 171, 173, 180, 183, 194, 197, 198, 199, 217, 221, 223, 234, 237, 248, 261, 265, 266, 268, 270, 271, 273, 274, 275, 276
Stayton, D. J., 72, 126

* The following page numbers refer to *Positive Social Behavior and Morality, Vol. 1: Social and Personal Influences.*

Stech, F. J., 258
Stein, A. H., 8, 63, 153, 154, 155, 156, 157
Stengel, E., 240
Stern, W., 63
Sternglanz, S. H., 142
Stingle, K. G., 24
Stingle, S., 66, 154
Stirrup, B., 15, 234, 235
Sullivan, E. V.,
Surber, C. F., 39

T

Tagiuri, R., 79
Tchudnowski, P., 193
Thelen, H. A., 196
Theroux, S. S., 154
Thomas, A., 93, 94
Thompson, W. R., 126
Tilker, H. A., 198
Titkin, S., 228
Toda, M., 258, 275
Tomkins, S. S., 36
Tonnick, I. J., 142
Tremblay, M. A., 130
Triandis, H. C., 274
Trickett, E. J., 248
Trivers, R. L., 5
Trotter, K. T., 47
Turiel, E., 38, 39, 44, 49, 50, 55, 174,
   176, 177, 247
Turner, D., 154

U

Ugurrel-Semin, R., 64
Updegraff, R., 229
Urbach, N. M., 55

V

Valkenaar, M. C., 94
Van Lieshout, C. F., 76
Vasta, R., 64
Vaughn, B. E., 71
Vincent, J., 45

W

Walbeck, N., 124, 167, 204
Walder, L. O., 93, 160
Walters, R. H., 35, 112
Walton, W. E., 71
Warnath, C. F., 244
Watson, J. S., 71
Waxler, C. Z., 63, 117
Weil, R. J., 130
Weiner, J., 59, 64, 76
Weissbrod, C., 115, 116
Wellman, H. M., 72
West, H., 75, 218
West, M. J., 62
West, S. G., 19
White, G. M., 116, 148, 150, 199, 201,
   202, 204
White, R. K., 248
Whiting, B., 190, 191, 195, 256, 263, 276
Whiting, J. W. M., 26, 190, 191, 195,
   256, 263, 276
Wilson, E. O., 5
Winder, C. L., 231, 244
Wright, J., 158
Wyer, R. S., 244

Y

Yaeger, J., 75
Yarrow, L. J., 126
Yarrow, M. R., 63, 94, 116, 117, 119, 121,
   122, 125, 140, 157, 158, 159, 226,
   227, 235
Yinon, Y., 194
Young, G., 223
Yussen, S. R., 75, 85, 218

Z

Zahavi, S., 242
Zak, J., 65
Zeiss, A., 135

Subject Index

A

Acceptance
  attitudes toward others affecting
      peer, 236
  by peers and self-esteem, 236–237
  and rejection by peers, 230–232
Affect
  cognitions and, 127–128, 165–167
  differences in transgression versus
      prosocial behavior, 99–100
  and internalization, 32
  interpretations of events and, 165–167
Affection, parental, 110–112, *see also*
      Nurturance
Affectional system
  in monkeys, 222
  peer influences on development of,
      221–223
  prosocial motivation and, 221–222
Affective role-taking, 74–75, 77–80
  age changes in, 78–80
  incongruity affecting, 78–80
  personal experience and, 78
  projection versus, 77–78
  similarity to others and, 77–78
  situational versus facial cues, 78–80

Age and age changes
  in behavior, 68–69
  in competition, 65–68
  in cooperation, 65–68
  in donating, 64–65
  egocentrism and, 75–76
  methodologies needed to study, 272
  and moral reasoning, 47–50
  in prosocial behavior, 60–65, 271–272
  in role taking, 69–80
  sacrifice and, 64
  in sharing, 62
  in value–behavior relationships, 68–69
Aggression and aggressive
  and acceptance or rejection by peers,
      231–232
  behavior and television programs,
      154–155
    effects of, 160
  behavior in peer interactions, 224–225
  popularity and, 231–232, 225–227
  prosocial behavior and, 63–64
  versus prosocial television programs,
      153–157
  punishment and, 92–93
  reciprocal, 226–227
  social skills, improvement of, 242–243

Aggressive-defensive behavior, 224–225
Altruism and altruistic
    childrearing practices and, 100–103
    cognitive skills contributing to, 86–87
    genetic sources of, 5
    intentions, 3–4
    motivation, 86–87
    values and victim-centered discipline,
        164
Analogue research, 120–121
Anxiety
    popularity and, 237
    social interactions and, 225–226
Attitudes
    peer acceptance and, 236–237
    toward others affecting popularity,
        232–237
Attributions, *see also* Self-attributions
    self and internal and external, 150–153
Authority or authoritative parents, 93,
        104–106, 108–110
    practices of, 256–257
Autonomy, 256
    and responsibility, 219
Awareness of others, altruistic moti-
        vation and, 86–87

B

Behavior
    cognitive mediators of, 35–36
    imitation of, 24
    influence of expected outcomes on, 35
    internal versus external stimuli
        affecting, 36
    peer-advocated and parent-
        disapproved, 246–247
    reinforcement controls affecting, 36–37
    self-reactions affecting, 35
    television programs affecting, 153–157
    verbal influences affecting, 173–178
Behavioral skills learned through role-
        playing, 157–160
    by delinquent boys, 158–159
Birth order, prosocial behavior and, 194

C

Centration and decentration, 69–70
Change
    conditions conducive to, 262
    principles of, 261–264
Childhood adjustment, peer evaluation
        affecting, 240
Children
    development of person permanence,
        86–87
    perceptual ability of, 80–83
    social understanding by, 72–73
    sociocentric state of, 72
Children's interactions
    complementarity in, 224–225
    frequency of, 223–224
    positive versus negative, 223–224
    reciprocity and, 223–228
Civil rights activities
    and parental hypocrisy, 123–124
    and parental practices, 123–124
Classical conditioning
    age differences in effects of, 146–147
    conditioned versus unconditioned
        stimuli, 145–147
    empathic responsiveness and, 145–147
        behavioral effects, 146–147
    sharing and, 146–148
Coaching to improve peer relations, 241
Cofigurative cultures, 245–246
Cognitions
    and affect, 127–128, 165–167
    conditioning and, 139–140
    development through induction, 166
    relation to action, 159–160
    and self-regulation, 133–136
Cognitive development, generality in, 76
Cognitive developmental theory, 7, 38–57
    concepts of development, 51–52
    equilibration/disequilibrium, 44
    experiences affecting development,
        44–45
    interactionist theory, 43
    role-taking, 43–44
    validity and issues, 46–57
Cognitive self-control, 133–136
Cognitive skills
    contributing to altruistic motivation,
        86–87
    and role-taking, 7–8, 73–76
    and self-control, 133–136
Communicative egocentrism, 232
Communicative skills
    peer interaction and, 218
    role-playing skills affecting inter-
        personal interaction, 233–235
Competency affecting positive behavior, 19
Competition
    achievement orientation and, 67–68
    causes of, 66–67
    cooperation versus, 66–68
    definition of, 66
    development of influences on, 18
    development of with age, 65–68
    environmental effects on, 68
    individuation and, 66–68
    sex differences affecting, 68

Complementarity in peer interaction, 224–225
Conditioned behavior, externally caused versus self-caused, 140–141
Conditioned versus unconditioned stimuli, 145–147
Conditioning procedures
  age differences in effects of, 146–147
  aversive versus reinforcing, 141
  behavior resulting from aversive, 143–145
  classical, 145–150
    producing empathy, 145–146
  cognitive reactions to, 141
  instrumental, 148–150
  modeling and direct instruction, 151–153
  operant (instrumental), 141–145
  punishment, 143–145
  reinforcement in, 141–142
  self-attribution through, 151–153
  sharing and, 146–148
  sympathetic reactions by, 148–150
  verbal versus material reinforcement, 142–143
  enhancing moral development, 45–46
Consistency
  of behavior, and values and nurturance, 123–124
  change in value behavior relations, 68–69
  and coherence, 15–16
  of behavior and hypocrisy, 123–124
  of induction, consequences of, 165
  and predictability, 14
  in prosocial behavior, 14–16, 59
  and stability, 15–16
Control by parents, 256–257, *see also* Parental control
  effects on identification, 262–263
  effects on learning, 262–263
Conventional moral orientation, 181–187
  child identification with parent and, 184–187
  childrearing and, 184–185
  parental characteristics and, 184–187
Cognitive disequilibrium, 263–264
Cognitive distraction as self-guidance, 134–135
Cognitive network and empathic responsiveness, 269
Cooperation
  age changes and, 65–68
  competition versus, 65–68
  definition of, 65

environmental effects and, 68
influences on children, 18–19
modeling and, 154
sex differences in, 68
Cross-age tutoring, 196
Cultures and cultural
  adaptations to environment, 4
  cofigurative and postfigurative, 245–246
  context of development, 274–276
  differences in behavior, 4–5
  differences in focusing responsibility, 190–192
  effects on standards, 130
  environmental influence of, 274–276
  influences of peers and adults on behavior, 245–247
  influences on positive behavior, 275–276
  socialization, 17–18, 260–261
  values and norms, 4

D

Decentration, 69–70
Delay of gratification, and self-guidance, 134–135
Delinquent children, role-taking skills and effects on, 158–159
Dependence, popularity and, 229–232
Determinants of positive behavior
  ambiguity, 9
  appropriateness, 9–10
  degree of need, 9
  direct and indirect costs, 9
  instigating stimuli, 9
  positive or negative moods, 10
  relation to person in need, 10
  responsibility, 9
  self-initiation versus responsive help, 9
Development and developmental
  and age, 8
  approaches to the study of, 7
  cognitive-developmental approach, 38–57
  of competition with age, 65–68
  of cooperation with age, 65–68
  culture, history, and universal applicability, 274–276
  by equilibration, 53–54
  identification–internalization approach, 21–34
  versus learning, 59–60
  and the life span, 8
  of personality, 17
  personality effects on, 257–259
  principles or mechanisms, 60–61
  social learning approach, 34–38
Developmental approach, 7–8, 34–35, 59–61

Developmental change
  current personality and, 50
  principles or mechanisms, 60–61
Developmental identification and pro-
    social behavior, 114–115
Developmental theory of (pro)social
    behavior, 268–272
Direct influence, 204–205
Direct instruction
  modeling and induction versus, 204–205
  and participation in prosocial action,
    198–205
Dissapproval, children's fear of, 64–65
Discipline techniques, 22
  by fathers, 163
  moral development and, 161–164
  and parental values, 164
Disequilibrium by verbal reasoning,
    173–174
Dissonance theory, 95–96
Distress, responsiveness to, 64–65
Donating and donations
  age changes in, 64–65
  effects of teaching others on, 207–209
  sex differences in, 207–209
  induction effects on, 173
  permissive versus constraining
    instruction for, 202
  rehearsal versus modeling affecting,
    199–202
  verbal and modeling effects on, 327–329

E

Education
  influencing social development, 273–274
  in positive behavior, 272–274
  in homes and schools, 272–274
Egocentric and egocentrism, 72
  age-related changes in, 75–76
  in children, 69–70
  and decentration, 69–70
  popularity and, 232
  and role-taking, 69–71
  types of, 75–76
Emotion and emotional reactions due to
    interpretations, 166, *see also* Affect
Empathic responsiveness, cognitive
    networks and, 269
Empathy and empathic
  by classical conditioning, 145–148
    behavioral effects, 146–147
  distress in infants, 19, 61–62, 86
  as motivation to help, 12
  primitive, 61–62
Enactive learning, 157–160

Environmental influences
  education in positive behavior
    through, 272–274
  on peer groups, 244–249
  and role-taking skills, 217–218
  school versus home, 272–274
  structure and nature of, 254
  types of, 253–254
  in various cultures, 274–275
  extensive versus reasonable control,
    263–264
  principles of learning and, 263–264
  and socialization, 262–264
Equilibration and disequilibrium, 53–54
Experience and experiential learning
    and development, 52–53
Experiential learning, 189–198
  interactive experience, role-taking, and,
    197–198, 217–219
  kinds of learning from, 196–198
  as natural socialization, 215
  occurrence of, 215–217
Experimental research
  desirable strategies of, 266–268
  development of hypotheses, 271–272
  effects of subject's evaluation, 210
  experimenter effects in, 209–210
  lasting effects of analogue procedures,
    265–266
  methodologies to study age change,
    272
  personality measures in, 266–267
External attribution, self or internal
    versus, 151–152
External orientation, 264

F

Family and families, responsibility and,
    193–194
Fathers, effects of childrearing by, 163,
    see also Parental childrearing
    practices
Force, its effects in childrearing, 92–99

G

Generosity
  infants and, 62
  nurturance and, 114–115
Guilt
  humanistic versus conventional values
    and, 181–183
  versus positive emotion in moral
    behavior, 99–100
  self-punishment and, 131–132

H

Harmonious parents, practices of,
256–257
Hedonic balancing, 14
Helping and helpfulness
aggression and, 63–64
effects of participation and induction,
205–215
fear of disapproval and, 64–65
heterogeneous versus homogenous
groups and, 194–195
by older versus younger peers, 194–195
psychological reactance to, 10–11
reactions by children, 63
responsibility and, 190
situational influences on, 9–12
History and historical understanding of
development, 274–276
Honesty
childrearing practices and, 100–103
consistency with age, 69
Human beings, characteristics of, 1–2
Humanistic moral orientation, 181–187
child identification with parent
and, 184–187
childrearing and, 184–185
parental characteristics and, 184–187
Human nature, assumption about
origins, 4–5
Hypocrisy
by models, 124
by parents, 123–124

I

Identification
with aggressor, 26
of children with humanistic or
conventional parents, 184–187
as cognitive response, 24–25
conditions producing, 26–27
developmental type, 25
with dominant parent, 27–28
empathic complex as, 29
environmental structure and, 263–264
imitation versus, 24
measures of, 24
as motivated disposition, 25
experiential component of, 25
with parents, 23–29
and positive behavior, 14
sex-role preferences, 28–29
social power theory, 26
status envy theory, 26
Identification–internalization approach,
22–34

Imitation, *see also* Modeling and Models;
Observational learning
for intrinsic reasons, 24
need for attention increasing, 121–122
and nurturance, 116
perception of models and, 124
Indirect instruction, 195–196
Individual differences affecting change,
8, *see also* Personality
Induction, 22–23, 160–178, 355–356,
see also Reasoning
affecting emotional reactions, 166–167
and conception of self and others,
165–166
consequences of, 164–167
decreasing positive behavior, 168–169
development of cognitions through, 166
effects on donating, 173
experimental research on, 167–173
increasing responsiveness by identification, 168–169
integrated with relevant experiences,
171–173
sex difference in effects of, 172–173
naturalistic research on, 161–164
versus experimental research, 170–171
parental versus experimental, 170–171
participation and, 205–215
sex differences in, 208–209, 211–212
personality and effects of, 170–171
plans and strategies, 165
positive versus negative, 168–173
responsibility and, 164–165
role-taking and, 164–165
Inferences and inferential ability
age changes in, 80–82
inferences about others, 80–83
of others' intentions and motives, 80–83
Instruction
collaboration and indirect, 195–196
cross-age, 196
effects of inconsistency in, 204
improving peer relations by, 241–243
participation in prosocial action versus
direct, 198–205
Instructional learning
effects of, 151–153
versus modeling, 151–153
Instrumental (operant) conditioning, 148–
150
Intelligence as affecting role-taking and
inferential abilities, 234–235
Intentions
altruistic, 2–3
inferences about others', 80–83

Interactive behavior
  affecting development, 247–258
  reciprocity in and stability of, 227
Interactive experience, 198–219
  experiential learning as, 197–198, 217–219
  with peers and communicative skills, 218–219
Internalization
  affective components of, 32
  and behavior, 32
  cognitive components of, 32
  conflicting moral standards and, 33
  effects of punishment and reinforcement, 96–97
  and ego ideal, 30–31
  evaluated by reactions to transgressions, 33
  forms of, 31–32
  origins of, 29–30
  and reference groups, 31
  and the superego, 30–31
  of values, 23, 29–34
  verbal discipline and, 160–161
  verbal reasoning and, 97–98
Internalized values versus peer group evaluations, 245–246
Internal states and role taking, 74–75
Interpersonal interactions
  communicative and role-playing abilities affecting, 233–234
  egocentrism and popularity, 232
  improvement of, 240–243
Interpersonal relationships, long-term consequences of, 237–240
Interpretation of events and emotional reactions, 166
Intervention
  to improve peer relations, 241–242
  influencing social development, 273–274
Intrinsic motivation, 72–73
Intrinsic reinforcement, 36–37
Isolation by peers, 228
  consequences of, 228
  interactive behavior patterns and, 228
Israeli socialization practices, 218–219

J

Judgments about others' goodness and badness, 81–83
  based on consequences of behavior, 82–83
  measurement of, 81–83
Justifications, 261
Just World phenomenon, 12

L

Leadership, popularity and, 239
Learning
  conditions affecting principles of, 262–264
  versus development, 59–60
  direct instruction versus modeling, 151–153
  by doing, 189–197
  effects of, 151–153
  enactive, 157–160
  environmental–structural influences on, 263–264
  experiential, 189–198
  influences on, 59–60
  kinds of, from participation, 196–198
  nurturance enhancing, 112
  through observation, 150–160
    and television, 153–157
  principles or mechanisms of, 60–61
  selectivity in, 121–123
  through self-attribution, 151–153
  of standards, 128–130
Love withdrawal, 22–23

M

Material reinforcement, verbal reinforcement versus, 142–143
Modeling and models
  acquisition of standards by, 128–130
  affecting social interaction, 154
  cooperative, 154
  direct instruction and focusing responsibility versus, 151–153, 198–202
  embedded, 121
  lasting effects of, 138–140
  learning by and effects of, 150–151
    on prosocial behavior, 150–151
    on values, 150–151
  loss of value of, 139
  nurturance, 115–116
  parental values affecting, 179–180
  role playing and, 157–158
  selectivity of, 121
  and self-reinforcement, 131
  standard-setting by, 133–134
Moral conduct, development of, 16–20
Moral development
  by arousal of dissonance, 95–96
  conflicts enhancing, 45–46
  cultural effects on, 45–46, 49
  and discipline techniques, 161–164
  interactionist theory, 43
  logic systems of, 40–41

moral pluralism and, 45–46
moral reasoning and, 39–40
reasoning and, 160–161
role taking and, 43–44, 52–53
socialization leading to, 22
socioeconomic status and, 51–52
stages of, 38–39
Morality
    autonomous, 39
    determining a person's, 39–40
    heteronomous, 39
Moral judgment
    age-related changes in, 84
    cognitive capacities and, 84
    modeling of, 175
    role taking and, 83–86
    verbal influences on, 173–178
Moral reasoning, 39–40
    age trends in, 47–50
    behavior and, 54–55
    cognitive structure of, 44
    competence versus performance in, 54
    continuity versus discontinuity, 50–51
    cultural effects on, 49
    evaluation of, 40–41
    in everyday life, 54
    experiences affecting development, 44–45
    moral sentiments and, 48
    regression of, 40
    role taking and, 52–53
    stages of, 40–43
    tuition versus experiential learning, 52–53
    and value orientations, 54
    values and, 56–57
Moral (value) orientations
    and child's identification with parent, 184–187
    conventional versus humanistic, 181–187
    childrearing and, 184–185
    parental characteristics and, 184–187
Moral values, influence of mothers versus fathers on, 115, *see also* Values
Mothers versus fathers
    differences in mode of influence, 28–29
    influences on moral values, 115
Motivation
    altruistic, 86–87
    diminishing positive behavior, 12
    empathy, 12
    and personal goals, 13–14
    promoting positive behavior, 11–12, 14–15, 268–269
    prosocial orientation, 11–12
    and self-esteem, 14

self-gain, 11
Motives, perception of others', 80–83

N

Naturally occurring responsibility, 195
Natural socialization, 7, 251, *see also* participation
    definition of, 215
    participation and experiential learning as, 189–219
Needs, parents' responsiveness to, 124–127
Nurturance
    and consideration for others, 113–115
    and consistency in children's values and behavior, 123–124
    effects on transgression and positive tendencies, 122–123
    experimental research on, 115–124
    and generosity, 114–115
    and imitation, 116
    and learning, 112
    modeling and, 115–119
    and moral development, 112, 115
    naturalistic research on, 113–115
    versus nonnurturance, 116–117
    parental, 110–112
    popularity and, 229–232
    and selectivity in learning, 121–123
    a source of identification, 112
    variations in, 124–127
    with and without control, 116–117

O

Obedience–disobedience, 6
Observational learning, 150–160, *see also* Imitation; Modeling and models
    by television, 153–157
        aggressive versus prosocial programs, 153–157
Operant (instrumental) conditioning, 141–145
    aversive procedures, 143–145
    behavior resulting from, 144–145
    verbal versus material reinforcement, 142–143
Oppositional tendency and psychological reactance, 98–99

P

Parental childrearing practices, 106–110
    changes with child's age, 256
    and children's characteristics, 100–103
    control versus autonomy, 256
    discipline techniques, 22

Parental childrearing practices (*cont.*)
  education in school environment and,
    272–274
  effects of fathers', 163
  honesty and altruism through, 100–103
  induction, 22–23
  love withdrawal, 22–23
  material versus social reinforcement, 96–
    97
  moral development and, 161–164
  parent relationship to child, 100–103
  and parents' values and value orienta-
    tions, 178–179
  patterns of, 103–110
  popularity and, 244
  power assertion, 22–23
  prescriptive versus proscriptive, 180–181
  to promote positive behavior, 257
  reasoning, 97–98, 160–161
  relationship variables, 22
  social behavior and, 103–110
  threat versus punishment, 95–96
  victim-centered discipline, 164
Parental control
  consequences of forceful, 92–99
  consistency of, 93
  importance of, 92
  and nurturance versus nonnurturance,
    116–117
  patterns of, 103–110
  by physical punishment, 92–93
  range of standards, 91–92
  socialization by, 91–92
  studies showing effects of, 103–110
Parental socialization, 7–8
Parental values
  affecting modeling of parents, 179–180
  discipline techniques and, 164
  influencing childrearing practices, 178–
    187
  types of, 179
Parent–child relationship
  affecting peer status, 244
  children identifying with parents, 184–
    187
  and selectivity in imitation, 121
  values and value orientations in, 178–187
Participation, 355–356
  affecting later behavior, 204–205
  direct instruction and, 198–205
  effects of in prosocial activities, 205
  effects of teaching others, 205–215
  induction and, 205–215
    sex differences in, 208–209, 211–212
  learning and, 198–219

  in positive behavior and experiential
    learning, 189–198
Participation in prosocial activities
  induction integrated with and en-
    hancing, 171–173
  sex differences in effects of, 172–173
Peer acceptance
  attitudes toward others affecting, 236
  versus rejection due to aggressive be-
    havior, 231–232
  self-esteem affecting, 236–237
  social behavior and, 231–232
Peer and teacher ratings, 15–16
Peer evaluation affecting childhood adjust-
    ment, 240
Peer group
  evaluations versus internalized values,
    245–246
  influences of rules and nature of, 244–
    249
Peer influences
  and age effects on values, 247–248
  and development of positive behavior,
    221–249
Peer interaction
  and acceptance and rejection by peers,
    230–232
  affecting role-taking skills, 217–218
  aggressive behavior and, 224–225
  boys versus girls, 224–225
  communicative skills and, 218
  complementarity in, 224
  effects of stability of, 228
  personality development and stable, 228
  popularity and, 228–249
  reciprocity in, 224–225
  responsiveness in, 224–225
  and status, 374–375
Peer isolation, 228
Peer perception, popularity and, 235–236
Peer-promoted behavior, adult standards
    versus, 247–248
Peer relations
  cultural influences on, 246–247
  development of affectional system and,
    221–223
  father and son relationship affecting, 244
  improvement of, 240–243
    procedures for, 240–243
  positive orientation and, 243–244
  socialization and, 243–244
Peers, responsibility for, 219
Peer socialization, 221, 240–244, 253
Peer status, 388–389
  affecting self-esteem, 239–240
  parent–child relationship and, 244

Permissive or permissiveness, parents',
    105–106, 108–110
Persistence and self-reactions, 134–135
Personal goals
    affecting positive behavior, 13–14
    conflicting, 13–14
    as motivators of prosocial behavior, 268–
        270
    situations activating, 13–14
Personality
    characteristics, 259–260
        motivation for prosocial behavior and,
            268–269
        relevant to positive behavior, 270–271
        popularity and children's, 237
    development and stable peer interaction,
        228
    influences on development of, 17, 257–
        259
    measures in experimental studies, 266–
        267
    origins of, 16–20
    prosocial behavior and, 89–90
    relevant characteristics of, 13–14
        competencies, 13–14
        perceptual tendencies, 13–14
Plans and strategies, 139–140
Popularity
    aggression and, 225–226, 231–232
    anxiety and, 237
    from childhood to adulthood, 239–240
    childrearing practices and, 244
    children's characteristics and, 237
    dependence and, 229–230
    egocentrism and, 232
    as an evolving system, 238–239
    initial bases of, 238
    long-term consequences of, 237–240
    measurements of, 228–229
    nurturance and, 229–230
    peer interaction and, 228–249
    peer status and, 239–240
    personal characteristics affecting, 238
    reciprocity and, 226–228
    role-taking, social skills, and attitudes
        affecting, 232–237
    self-esteem and, 236–237
    social behavior and, 228–232
    social-effectiveness and, 235–236
Positive induction, 168–173
Positive orientation toward people
    affection versus hostility and, 111–112
    moral development and, 112
    nurturance versus nonnurturance and,
        110–111
Positive social (prosocial) behavior

age-related changes, 61–65
aggression and, 63–64
anticipated emotions and, 99–100
by aversive conditioning, 143–145
birth order and, 194
classical conditioning and, 145–150
classifications of, 2–3
competency and, 19
conditioning of, 140–150
consistency and stability of, 14–16, 59
cultural differences affecting, 274–276
definition and nature of, 1–4
determinants versus development, 5–13
education in, 272–274
    in homes and schools, 272–274
effects of participation and induction,
    205–215
expectation of punishment and, 145
identification with person in need, 12
instrumental conditioning, 148–150
intentions and, 2–3
kinds of, 259
    antecedents of, 259–261
long-term effects of treatments,
    215–216
modeling effects on, 150–151
motivations diminishing, 12
motivations for, 2–3, 11
by older versus younger peers, 194–195
origins of, 4–5, 260–261
parental childrearing patterns and, 103–
    110
parental responsiveness affecting, 126–
    127
peer influence and, 221–249
personality characteristics and, 259–260
personality development and, 90
predictability of, 14–15
primitive empathy and, 61–62
reciprocity guiding, 10–11
and role taking, 69–70
self-attribution and, 95–96
self-guidance and, 135–136
self-interest and, 20
sex differences and, 19
situational influences and, 13–14
socialization of affective bases, 99–103
socialization versus genetic origins, 5
Postfigurative cultures, 245–246
Power assertion, 22–23
Power inducing charity and helpfulness,
    117
Praise as reinforcement, 143
    versus instructional prompts, 143
Prescriptive childrearing, 180–181
    affecting generosity, 181

Prohibitions, severe versus mild, and self-attributions, 153
Proscriptive childrearing, 180–181
 affecting generosity, 181
Prosocial action, direct instruction and participation in, 198–205
Prosocial conditioning, 145–150
Prosocial development, socialization practices for, 137–187
Prosocial orientation, 110–111
 age changes in characteristics promoting, 271–272
 characteristics of, 270
 external orientation versus, 264
  changes in, 264
 and humanistic value orientation, 181–187
 role taking and, 270
 self-esteem and, 236–237, 270–271
 socialization influences on, 270
 deficiencies in research in, 265–268
 outcomes of, 265–272
Prosocial television
 aggressive programs versus, 153–157
 programs, differential effects, 155–157
 sex differences in effects of, 156–157
Prosocial values, development through induction, 165–167
Psychological processes, 14
 experimental strategy for testing, 266–267
 facial expressions and, 266
 in positive behavior, 13–14
 reactance to helping, 12
Psychological reactance
 to helping, 10–11
 and oppositional tendency, 98–99
 in response to forceful influence, 98–99
 in response to reinforcement and modeling, 139
Punishment
 aggression and, 92–93
 behavior guided by verbal, 160–161
 in childrearing, 23
 consequences of physical, 94–95
 expectation of, 145
  behavior resulting from, 145

R

Race or racial identification and prosocial behavior, 168–169
Reasoning, 160–178, *see also* Induction
 advanced versus lower stages of, 173–178
 experimental research on, 167–173
 naturalistic research on, 161–164

 power assertion versus, 161–162
 self-serving versus moral, 261
 stimulating disequilibrium, 173–174
Reciprocity
 affecting positive behavior, 10–11
 aggression and, 226
 anxiety and, 225–226
 boys versus girls, 224–225
 in children's interactions, 223–228
 complementarity and, 224–225
 nonreciprocal patterns and, 226
 popularity and, 226–227
 positive and negative patterns of, 226–227
 and self-gain, 20
 socially effective children and, 226
 stability of behavior and, 227
Reinforcement
 in conditioning, 141–142
 effects of, by various peers, 228
 lasting effects of, 138–140
 loss of value of, 139
 verbal versus material, 142–143
Rejection and acceptance by peers, 230–232
Relationships between parent and child, 110–127
Reputation, stability of, 227
Research techniques
 adequacy of, 137–138
 to evaluate cognitive–affective reactions, 148
 lasting effects of treatments, 138–140
Responsibility
 autonomy and, 219
 birth order and, 194
 cultural differences in structured, 190–191
 focusing on children, 189–198
 forceful assignment of, 191–192
 helpfulness and, 190
 imposed standards of, 198–199
 in large families, 193–194
 natural, 195
 for others' welfare and induction, 164–165
 and participation in positive behavior, 189–198
 peer interaction and, 219
 rehearsal versus modeling of, 199–202
 structured, 190–191
 sympathy and, 190
 types of, 190–191
Responsibility assignment in the Soviet Union, 192–193
Responsive behavior
 peer interaction and, 224–225

reciprocity and, 224–225
Responsiveness by parents
  affecting prosocial orientation, 126–127
  to child's needs, 124–127
  effects on development, 125–127
Rivalry
  children and, 67–68
  schools' influence on, 68
  sex differences, 68
  socializing influences and, 255
Role taking, 7, 43–44, 69–80
  advances with age, 85–86
  affected by peer interaction, 217–218
  affecting popularity, 232–237
  affective, 74–75, 77–80
  age-related changes in, 84
  children's capacity for, 71–72
  cognitive, 73–74
  communicative abilities affecting inter-
    personal interaction and, 233–235
  and enactive learning, 157–160
  as experiential learning, 217–219
  induction and, 164–165
  measurement techniques of, 70–71
    children's verbal capacity affecting, 70–
    71
  modeling and, 157–158
  moral judgment and, 83–86
  and moral reasoning, 52–53
  and peer interaction, 217–218
  and prosocial behavior, 69–70
  sensitivity and, 233–234
  sex differences, 157
  skills learned through, 157–158
    by delinquent boys, 158–159
  social environment and, 72–73
  specificity versus generality of skills, 76
  types of, 43–44, 70
    relationship between, 73–76

S

Sacrifice, age changes and, 64
Self and others
  conflict of interest, 3–4
Self-attributions
  affecting behavior, 152–153
  affecting consistency of behavior, 152–
    153
  effects of, 151–153
  external attributions and, 151–153
  modeling and, 152–153
  promoting change, 95–96
  prosocial behavior and, 95–96
  treatments producing, 151–153
Self-caused behavior, 141

Self-concept, popularity and, 236–237
Self-control, cognitive, 133–136
Self-criticism, 131–132
  anxiety and, 132
Self-esteem
  boys' personality characteristics and,
    236–237
  popularity and, 236–237
  prosocial orientation and, 236–237, 270–
    271
Self-evaluations, 127
Self-gain, 20
Self-guidance
  cognitive and verbal, 134–135
  and delay of gratification, 134–135
  expectancy of rewards and, 135–136
  and prosocial behavior, 135–136
Self-induction, 169
Self-interest, expressions of, 62
Self-punishment, 34–37
  criticism and, 132
  guilt and, 131–132
  reasons for, 132
  self-reinforcement versus, 131–132
Self-reactions, 127–128
  influence on behavior, 130–133
  persistence and, 134–135
Self-regulation
  learned through television, 155
  by self-reward and self-punishment, 127–
    128
Self-reinforcement, 130–133
  and guilt, 131–132
  influences on, 131
  learning techniques of, 132–133
  modeling and, 131
  self-concept and, 131–132
  or self-punishment, 131–133
  standards of, 130–131
  verbal, 133–135
Self-reward, 34–37
Self-verbalization, standard setting and,
  133–134
Sensitivity
  to psychological needs by parents, 124–
    125
  role-taking skills and, 233–234
Sex differences
  in effects of induction and participa-
    tion, 172–173, 208–209, 214
  in mothers' and fathers' influence, 28–29
  in positive behavior, 19
Sharing
  aggression and, 63–64
  classical conditioning and, 146–148
  by infants, 62

June, 1972 but no agreement was reached (see Chapter Eight). An agreement could be modelled after the General Agreement on Tariffs and Trade (GATT), which has set basic principles of fair trading practices and has led to the reduction of tariffs and other trade barriers.

A problem might arise with countries like Japan which believe that government subsidies should be given to industry for pollution control. Such subsidies produce distortions of costs as compared to countries where manufacturers are required to pay their own pollution control costs. Also, differing production techniques present an obstacle to any standards agreement. For example, the American steel industry still relies basically on the open-hearth production method, while many other countries use the oxygen method, which produces two to three times more pollutant per ton of steel.

Any agreement on standards would initially include only the industrialized countries; economically and morally, the less developed countries could not be forced to meet the same initial standards. However, negotiating a date when such standards would have to be met, and the sanctions to be imposed if they were not met, might prove to be a messy political problem.

DEFINITIONS AND CLASSIFICATIONS

Pollution, therefore, is a worldwide problem, and so are its costs. Before discussing specific kinds of pollution in the following chapters, however, we need to define some of the concepts that will be used, for example, what is a pollutant? what is waste? what are the components of the "cost" of environmental protection? In part these definitions are necessary for clarity, in part because the way we define things strongly influences the way we think about them. The remaining sections of this chapter define a number of terms, then classify pollutants according to their physical, chemical, or behavioral characteristics, and finally discuss the important distinction between normative pollution levels and optimal pollution levels.

110. Some Definitions

Pollutant. A pollutant, in a very general sense, is anything animate or inanimate that by its excess reduces the quality of living. Thus, sulphur dioxide is a pollutant, so is excessive noise, and so is an epidemic of rats.

One idea that is important in understanding pollutants and pollution is that, while man is unquestionably a polluter, man is not (in a pollution context), a consumer. "Consumer" is a word invented by schools of business and by Madison Avenue, and has no real application to a discussion of pollution. Man consumes nothing, whether it be the food he eats, the automobiles he drives, or the clothes he wears. He merely "uses" things, and, according to the law of Conservation of Matter, discards exactly the same mass of material after use. Sometimes, as in the case of a building or a dam, disposal is postponed for a very long time. Much of the weight of each year's production is transformed into gas and released into the atmosphere without any special treatment. But the concept of nonconsumption still holds, and becomes especially important when we begin to think in terms of reconversion.

Directly related to the concept of nonconsumption is the fact that there is not really an air pollution problem or a water pollution problem, but rather a materials disposal problem. To eliminate air and water pollution may simply mean transforming them into the problem of disposing of solid waste, another pollution problem.

Waste. Waste, the component of most pollution, is defined as some substance that our society does not as yet have the intelligence to use, or that our present economic system prevents us from using or reusing. Waste disposal—which is what people do with waste—is not capable of economic definition because it is really a misnomer. Disposal is usually used to denote the process of burning, diluting, grinding up, or spreading things around so that they won't be offensive or be noticed. It is a little like the lazy housewife who, when asked what she did with her garbage, said "I just kick it around until it gets lost."

Disposal. Disposal is really just a conversion process. When we convert iron ore to iron, we call it smelting or refining; when we convert the iron into a car, we call it manufacturing. When we stop using the car and abandon it, we call it waste disposal. In the latter case we have converted the automobile into a large chunk of iron oxide. We could as well, if not as easily, have melted the car and converted it back into iron.

If our present technology does not allow us to reuse iron oxide,[18] an alternative method of disposal might be to take these chunks of metal from compressed automobiles to the mid-Western plains, to Kansas or Saskatchewan, and use them as building blocks for the construction of mountains which could then be used for skiing and other recreation. These would be mountains of fairly pure iron, which could be mined when our economics changed or iron ore became scarce.

In the same sense the use of water is merely a conversion from clean water to dirty water. The reconversion of water would be the cleaning of it. In economic terms there is no producer and no consumer of water, only consecutive steps in the conversion process.

All this suggests a shift in emphasis from the temporary expedient of waste disposal to the more permanent solution of waste recycling and reconversion. However, if producers manufacture synthetic materials that are not degradable (reconvertable) by nature, the conversion cycle is broken; after use, someone must unmake these things using the same technology. This implies that before designing things and converting resources to new forms, producers should have in mind a plan for reconversion and recycling. Some nerve gases, for example, can be broken down into nonpoisonous components; some equally potent gases cannot be safely converted, and must be disposed of in the ocean or similar places.

Some kinds of reconversion are hard to envision; for example, collecting old newspapers, cleaning the print off them, and reusing them for something else. Experiments are taking place; for example, in Beltsville, Maryland, where cattle are being fed pure newsprint cellulose with amino acids and other additives, which the ruminants change into protein. One may visualize a factory where old newspapers go in one end and steaks come out the other. That is the sort of objective to which recycling is striving!

Landfill is another form of reconversion or recycling, in this case again using wastes as a construction material. Untreated waste (garbage, sewage sludge, building rubble) is buried in layers, each covered by several inches of compacted earth. This technique has transformed thousands of acres of low-value land into parks, playgrounds, golf courses, and other useful facilities.

Reconversion and recycling would be helped by a tax on waste (for example on throw-away containers) imposed on the basis of the difficulty of recycling. There always seems to be some perverse component that gets in the way of economic recycling; the aluminum ring that a twist-off cap leaves around the neck of a soft drink bottle makes it uneconomic to grind such bottles into cullet for glassmaking, and the cost of removing the metal, either before or after grinding, is prohibitive. Similarly, the tin coating and lead solder on the otherwise steel "tin can" largely exclude it from being economically recycleable. The government could also help through discriminatory purchasing policies, as federal government purchases account for about 6 percent of all packaging expenditures. If government were to insist upon tin-free steel cans or aluminum-ring free soft drink packages, industry would have a powerful economic incentive to alter its technology.

Cost of Environmental Protection. To continue with definitions, the *cost* of environmental protection, to society, is the sum of expenses incurred to prevent environmental damage, plus expenses incurred through not preventing environmental damage. Thus:

Cost of environmental protection = expense of preventing environmental damage + expense of environmental damage not prevented.

The expense of preventing environmental damage is easily measured; it is the total expense incurred by public and private parties to prevent damage caused by waste products. Expenditures by public bodies for sewage treatment, and by private corporations to remove soot from smoke are good examples.

The expense incurred from environmental damage *not* prevented is much more difficult to identify and to measure. Conceptually, it is the expense of pollution; the money value of the damages caused by waste products after they are released into the environment.

The following are three components of such expenses:[19]

Expense of environmental damage not prevented = public expenditures to avoid pollution damage + private expenditures to avoid pollution damage + the money equivalent of the welfare cost of protection.

The first component of this equation is public expenditures to avoid pollution damages—not to prevent pollution, but to prevent the damage that pollution causes. For example, the cost of treating drinking water to prevent typhoid epidemics is such a public expenditure, while the expense of sewage treatment is an expenditure to prevent pollution.

The second component of the equation is expenditures made by private parties to avoid pollution damage. Examples are the expenditures that individuals who live in areas of air pollution make compared with those who live in cleaner-air areas for dry cleaning of clothes, painting of houses, home air-purification systems, and so on.

The third component of the equation is the money equivalent of the welfare cost of pollution—the dollar value of the reduction of public welfare from pollution damage that is not prevented. This includes, for example cost of foregone or lower earnings or of increased commuting expenses where families move away from city centers to escape air pollution. A manufacturer that moves to a new location to secure clean water, but that must then pay higher transportation costs for raw materials or finished goods, incurs such costs. Similarly, the value of pleasures foregone or diminished —the lack of local swimming because of polluted water, or the decreased aesthetic value of a littered landscape—are real losses in welfare that at least some people are willing to pay to have reduced.[20]

Given these components of cost, the problem facing the economist is to minimize the total cost of environmental protection; the cost of preventing environmental damage, plus the cost of environmental damage not prevented.

A final area of definition concerns the boundaries of a polluted area which are relevant for the study or control of the pollution problem at hand. Unfortunately, such boundaries are seldom if ever well defined. No area is completely isolated from other areas, since many pollutants are fairly mobile, and different pollutants affect areas of vastly different sizes. Airborne soot of a given size range may affect an area of from 20 to 400 square miles, while radioactive gases may contaminate the entire atmosphere. Different wastes discharged into a water system can affect either large or small areas before they are diluted or degraded below noxious concentrations. Areas of population concentration such as metropolitan areas would seem natural areas for the study of pollution, but this is not feasible where pollutants and pollution victims are mobile over greater distances, as is true with automobiles without emission control systems.

If an arbitrary choice of area must be made, most often it consists of choosing a political area, because pollution control is closely tied to political unit decisions. A political unit such as the State of Maine is clearly too large for some kinds of pollution control and too small for others; some pollution from the Canadian Maritime provinces affects people in Maine, while some pollution from Portland, Maine does not even extend to North Portland. But the residents of Maine do have some political clout in controlling those pollutants which arise within their state, and less clout (but perhaps some influence) in abating pollution which arises outside Maine's borders.

111. Classification of Pollutants

Now that we have defined the most common concepts to be used in the following analysis, it might be helpful to classify kinds of pollutants according to their physical, chemical, or biological characteristics, or according to their behavior when released into the environment. Various pollutants may be usefully classified in terms of their toxicity, the productivity of their source, their durability, avoidability, and the costs of abatement.[21]

Toxicity. Probably the most critical criterion for classifying pollutants is the toxicity of the pollutant to plant and animal life. However, there are wide differences of opinion on the short-term and cumulative effects of various dosages of toxic pollutants, for example, the extent to which toxic materials are concentrated by successive organisms in the food chain and by long-lived organisms such as man.

Productivity. A second basis for classifying pollutants is by the economic benefit which arises from the activity which causes the pollution. It is often said that a paper mill smells like money to those who live nearby. If most of those living near the mill depend on it for their livelihood and have no reasonable alternative sources of income; if temperature inversions occur only occasionally and dangers to health are minimal; then residents of the area may prefer the odor to the alternative of shutting down the source of pollution.

Durability. The durability criterion requires that the highest priority in pollution prevention be given to conditions requiring many years or decades to clean up, and that lower priority be given to pollution the effects of which can be remedied fairly quickly when efforts are made to do so. Thus, in the case of water pollution the highest priority would be assigned to controlling the pollution of large lakes in which the water is retained for decades, and a lower priority to the prevention of population of fast-flowing rivers the beds of which are flushed yearly by spring floods.

Avoidability. The economic damage caused by pollution varies with the ease with which people may avoid using the polluted resource. Thus, in an area with substantial ground water, numerous unpolluted streams and ample precipitation, the pollution of one particular stream does not impose large opportunity costs on prospective users. The same quantity of stream pollution would impose much higher costs if there were no readily available alternatives to the use of the water, either because other streams were already polluted, or because alternative streams did not exist.

Adoption of an avoidability criterion means that air pollution would be given greater priority than water pollution, since people are under no physiological or other compulsion to come into contact with water in any particular place (except for drinking and washing water, which is normally treated), while there is no way for people to avoid breathing polluted air if they live or work in an area where air pollution exists. By the criterion of avoidability, air pollution is to people what water pollution is to fish.

Cost of Pollution Abatement. Some industries have wastes that are much more expensive to treat than are those of other industries. Given a similar set of physical conditions, waste-water treatment plants for industrial use may be quite expensive compared with treatment plants for sewage. If the self-cleansing capacity of a waterway is considered as a productive natural resource to be used for the public benefit, that benefit is maximized if the resource is used to substitute for the most costly industrial and municipal waste treatment. A cost-of-pollution-abatement criterion implies that the public interest is better served by diverse water-treatment standards than by uniform ones that require a predetermined level of waste treatment by all industries and municipalities.

112. Normative and Optimal Pollution

A final concept of importance for following chapters is the distinction between normative and optimal pollution levels.

The chapters which follow are not concerned with any concept of a normative (or "ideal") environment, or with normative levels of pollution, since no idealized standards do or can exist. There are no definitions of normative environmental conditions that have any moral superiority over others, except by reference to the selfish needs of one portion of society over another. For example, is it good or bad for plants to alter the atmospheric composition in favor of oxygen, or for animals to do so in favor of carbon dioxide by breathing oxygen and by eating plants? Is it worse to kill stands of cedar by industrial fumes, than to cut cedar trees in order to build housing for the poor?

A number of pollutants are natural constituents of the air. Even without man's technology, plants, animals, and natural activities would cause some pollution—volcanic action would release sulphur dioxides, and surface winds would stir up particulate matter. There is no way to remove all pollution from the air. The "right" composition of the atmosphere is that which contains some oxygen, some carbon dioxide, and some hydrogen sulfide, in combinations which permit organized society to pursue the greatest possible satisfaction for its human members.[22]

The "correct" solution to our current environmental problems will not produce pure air, or pure water, but rather some optimal state of pollution. The cost of this optimal state is best expressed in terms of the other goods—such as more housing, more ballet, more medical care—that must be foregone in return for somewhat cleaner air and water. Society will be willing to forego one ballet company, or one housing development, only if the resources that would go into it yield less human satisfaction than would the same resources if they were devoted to the elimination of air or water pollution. Trade-off by trade-off, an economist would divert our productive resources from current goods and services to the production of a cleaner, more pastoral nation up to the point where society values the next ballet or house more highly than it values the next unit of environmental improvement that the diverted resources would create.[23]

REFERENCES

[1] Alvin Toffler, *Future Shock* (New York: Random House, 1970).

[2] There are economic incentives that might encourage a voluntary reduction in population growth. We might subsidize or pay in full the cost

of abortions and voluntary sterilizations, and seek ways to give women more equality in educational and job opportunities so as to aid them in developing professional interests to compete with family interests. Using the tax system, we might stop taxing single persons more heavily than married ones. We could grant a standard exemption for the first two children in a family, and thereafter levy a tax on an increasing scale. For those who do not pay a tax, we could give women between the ages of 17 and 45 who already have two children a cash bonus each year they do not get pregnant. Each man or woman who volunteers for sterilization could be given a similar cash bonus or tax credit.

[3]Barry Commoner, *Is There An Optimal Level of Population?*, a paper presented to the Annual Meeting of the American Association for the Advancement of Science, Boston, Mass. (December 29, 1969).

[4]Paul Ehrlich, *The Population Bomb* (New York: Ballantine Books, Inc., 1968), in particular pp. 15-67.

[5]Paul R. Ehrlich and Anne H. Ehrlich, *Population/Resources/Environment: Issues in Human Ecology* (San Francisco: W. H. Freeman, 1970), p. 300.

[6]The Olin Corporation, producer of 20 percent of the U.S. supply of DDT, announced on June 30, 1970 that it was going out of the DDT business. Olin's announcement came after a suit to halt the discharge of DDT from Olin's Redstone Arsenal plant into the Wheeler National Wildlife Reserve had been filed in U.S. District Court for the District of Columbia by the Environmental Defense Fund, National Audubon Society, and National Wildlife Federation. The suit alleged that the concentrations of DDT in the Olin discharge ditch at the point of discharge from the plant ran as high as 460 parts per billion, when 1 to 3 parts per trillion of DDT caused such accumulation in the fatty tissues of fresh water fish as to render them unfit for human consumption, and 2 to 3 parts per trillion caused reproductive failure among many species of carnivorous birds and fish in other ecologically comparable areas.

[7]F. Bator has suggested that there are three possible, but not mutually exclusive types of externalities that may lead to market failure: ownership externalities, technical externalities, and public goods externalities.
     In the case of ownership externalities, the basic cause of market failure is the inability of the owner of a factor of production (because of legal or other reasons) to charge for the value of his services. Ownership externalities play an important part in the failure of the private market to provide a sufficient quality of water for outdoor recreation.
     Technical externalities are due either to indivisibilities or to increasing returns to scale. Production may occur when price equals marginal cost and exceeds average cost, with the position representing a local

profit maximum rather than a global profit maximizing point. Thus, there is failure by signal.

Public goods externalities occur when an individual's consumption of a good leads to no subtractions from any other individual's consumption of that good. Thus, there is no set of market prices for public goods which is useful for individual production and/or consumption decisions. In the absence of a set of market prices to ration any fixed supply of public goods, a private market for public goods will fail by existence.

Source: F. Bator, "The Anatomy of Market Failure," *Quarterly Journal of Economics*, No. 72 (August, 1958). An illustration of how a blend of the three types of externality conditions leads to market failure in the provision of water recreational facilities in an estuary is given in Paul Davidson, F. Gerard Adams, and Joseph Seneca, "The Social Value of Water Recreational Facilities Resulting from an Improvement in Water Quality: The Delaware Estuary," in Kneese and Bower, *Water Research* (Baltimore: Johns Hopkins Press, 1966), pp. 179-187.

[8]See Otto A. Davis and Andrew Whinston, "Externalities, Welfare, and The Theory of Games," *Journal of Political Economy*, No. 70 (June, 1962), pp. 241-262, for an excellent discussion of the measurement of externalities.

[9]The best overview of the topic known to the writer is A. R. Prest and R. Turvey, "Cost-Benefit Analysis: A Survey," *The Economic Journal* (December, 1965), pp. 683-731.

[10]Estimate in the Second Annual Report on the State of America's Environment by the Council on Environmental Quality (1971). The figure of $105 billion represents a doubling of the 1971 rate of spending on environmental protection from all sources by 1975. Of the total funds it is projected that 23 percent would go to air pollution control, 36 percent to water pollution control, and the rest to solid waste management.

[11]To polluting industries that plead poverty it might be pointed out that identical defenses were once raised on behalf of slavery, child labor, and the working conditions and housing associated with the early Industrial Revolution in England. The same defenses are offered for migrant farm workers camps in California and the southwest.

[12]U.S. Bureau of the Census, *Census of Manufacturers, 1967* (Washington, D.C.: U.S. Government Printing Office, 1968).

[13]For an overview on the fallacies of GNP see Kenneth E. Boulding, "Fun and Games With The Gross National Product—The Role of Misleading Indicators in Social Policy," in Harold W. Helfrich, ed., *The*

Environmental Crisis (New Haven, Conn.: Yale University Press, 1970), pp. 157-170.

[14]See John Cornwell, "Is The Mediterranean Dying?", *The New York Times Magazine* (February 21, 1971), pp. 24-25, 47-57.

[15]For a succession of U.S. type environmental horror stories in a Soviet setting, see Marshall I. Goldman, "The Convergence of Environmental Disruption," *Science*, No. 170 (October 2, 1970), pp. 37-41. The discussion which follows is based on this article, and on Marshall I. Goldman, "The Pollution of Lake Baikal," *The New Yorker* (June 19, 1971), pp. 58-66.

[16]Goldman, "Convergence," pp. 38-39.

[17]Goldman, "Convergence," pp. 41-42.

[18]In the remelting of automobile bodies, it is the small amount of copper in the wiring and the motors which pollutes the steel. If we were concerned about being able to convert car bodies back into iron we would design automobiles with aluminum harnesses and ferrite magnets which would oxidize and come off as slag so that we could get a better grade of steel.

[19]The classification and much of the analysis comes from J. H. Dale's *Pollution, Property and Prices* (Toronto: University of Toronto Press, 1968), pp. 12-26.

[20]The amount of information available on the third component is scant; our knowledge of how to collect such information is extremely limited. The average citizen has only the vaguest idea of what air pollution costs him in terms of lower earnings or increased commuting fees, to say nothing of the cost of excess cleaning, painting, or health bills. A statistician might try to collect such data by comparing per capita expenditures on these items in locations with different amounts of air pollution, but the data collection problems and costs are staggering. How would a statistician go about measuring the value of damage done to such intangibles as aesthetic enjoyment of natural environments located several hundred miles away, and which our citizen visits only at intervals of several years? How would he calculate the value of a day's sickness because of bronchial irritation caused by sulphur dioxide particles in the air? The respondent will want to know whether we are talking about a work day or a vacation day of illness; whether the malady is sufficient to require a day in bed, bed plus drugs, or a hospital visit plus curtailment of smoking for a month. And those are simple questions compared with the proper one of asking the respondent how much he would be willing to pay to prevent the sulphur dioxide content of the air in his city from exceeding, say, five parts per million more than ten days a year—especially when one is also unable to tell him speci-

fically what the effects of such a concentration on his personal health might be.

[21]The classification criteria are elaborated in R. Stepp and S. Macaulay, "The Pollution Problem," *Legislation and Special Analyses of the American Enterprise Institute for Public Policy Research*, 90th Congress, 2nd Sess. (No. 16, 1968), pp. 26-30.

[22]A thoughtful expansion of these ideas is contained in Lectures One, Eight, and Nine of the Harvard Alumni Summer College Lecture Series (1970), given by Leonard M. Ross.

[23]There is an economically optimal level of purity for a portion of the environment, say a river. Writers have argued that this level of purity will be obtained if the parties involved can bargain over the level of pollution to be tolerated. A willingness to pay for what one desires indicates the relative value of pollution or nonpollution to each of the parties; the one with the highest value will have his way. However, where *many* parties are affected by the actions of one or more persons, it may prove impossible to organize for bargaining purposes. This problem is discussed in more detail in Chapter Five. See also Ronald H. Coase, "The Problem of Social Cost," *Journal of Law and Economics* (October, 1960), pp. 6-15.

2

Air

Pollution

Baa, baa, black sheep,
What's dirtied up your wool?
Soot, smoke, sulphur
Of which the air's so full.
Soot from the foundries
Sulphur from the stacks,
And that's why we sheep now wear
Black coats on our backs.

200. The Extent of Air Pollution

Air pollution is not a recent world phenomenon. As early as the beginning of the Industrial Revolution many communities endured levels of smoke pollution that would be considered intolerable by present standards. In the last half of the 19th century, a number of citizen groups picketed the British Parliament to protest the smoke-laden air of London; their protests were lost in the desire of the government for industrial development at any price. In the U.S., the cities of Chicago and Cincinnati passed smoke control laws in 1881; by 1912, 23 American cities with populations over 200,000 had passed similar laws, although they were seldom enforced. By the 1930's and 1940's, smoke pollution had become sufficiently bad in eastern and midwestern industrial cities to cause improved smoke pollution legislation to be passed and enforced, with control efforts primarily focused on cutting down smoke from fossil fuels, particularly coal.

Although the number of recorded fatal air pollution incidents has not been large, the precedent does exist. In 1930 in the Meuse Valley in Belgium, 63 people died and more than 100 became seriously ill from a combination of particulate and sulphide pollution. In 1948, in the Monongahela River Valley in Pennsylvania, almost half the population of the town of Donora became ill and 17 died from air pollution which built up under a low-level temperature inversion. In London, in December of 1952, an estimated 4,000 excess deaths occurred during a two week period, followed by another incident in December of 1962 producing an estimated 300 excess deaths.

In the United States the present dimension of air pollution is severe. According to the United States Public Health Service, a total of 43 million persons in over 300 U.S. cities live under an air pollution hazard rated as major. An additional 30 million people live in 850 other cities with air pollution that is less than severe, but too serious to be classified as minor.[1] Testimony before a Senate committee in 1963 indicated that about 7,300 U.S. cities and towns, housing 60 percent of the population of the United States, had at that time a discernable air pollution problem of one kind or another.[2]

201. The Sources of Air Pollution

In terms of total national air pollution, the automobile is the greatest single contributor by weight. Nonautomotive sources of air pollution include emissions from the consumption of fossil fuel by industries such as pulp and paper, iron and steel, petroleum, refining and smelting, and chemicals; power plants which use fossil fuels to produce electricity; disposal of solid wastes by combustion; and the heating of homes, offices, and plants by fossil fuels.

Automotive emissions include carbon monoxide, hydrocarbons, oxides of nitrogen, lead compounds, sulfur dioxide, and particulate matter. It is estimated that 90 million automobiles and trucks annually discharge into the air 66 million tons of carbon monoxide; 6 million tons of nitrogen oxides; 12 million tons of hydrocarbons; a million tons of sulfur oxides; a million tons of particulate matter; and 190 thousand tons of lead compounds. The total from nonautomotive sources is 25 million tons of sulfur oxides, 11 million tons of hydrocarbons, and 5 million tons of carbon monoxide.

Industrial air pollution is not restricted to industrial centers of the United States. A twenty-four member combine called Western Energy Supply Transmission Associates (WEST) are in the process of building six of the largest fossil fuel power plants in the world in and around the Colorado Plateau, with the potential of turning the Four Corners area of Utah, New Mexico, Arizona and Colorado into a major pollution zone.

Already the single 2.1 million kilowatt plant at Farmington, New Mexico emits as much particulate matter per day—250 tons—as New York and Los Angeles combined. The plume of smoke and ash, which was the only man-made landmark that the Apollo 8 astronauts could consistently photograph from lunar orbit, drifts across more than 200 miles of Indian reservation. New Mexico ordered the company to make the stacks at Farmington 99.2 percent pure by the end of 1972, or shut down. The plant is installing wet scrubbers that will reduce the ash to 15 tons a day, but when all six plants are operating in the desert by the late 1970's, even if equipped with wet scrubbers, they will still emit 350 tons of fly ash a day. If not forced to clean up, they will also emit 2,160 tons of sulfur oxides a day—more than Chicago or New York City, and 850 tons (yes, tons) of nitrogen oxides per day. The nitrogen oxide figure rivals that of Los Angeles, which produces in the area of 900 tons a day from its millions of automobile exhausts.

Estimates of the total quantity of air pollutants released daily in the U.S. range up to 400,000 tons. While probably accurate, such figures are only relevant when compared with the total volume of air involved—a figure which to my knowledge has never been estimated. In the absence of such a comparison, the impact of simply stating quantities of pollutants in tons is likely to be several times greater than it might be in the true relationship.

202. The Primary Components of Air Pollution

The earth's atmosphere has only a limited capacity to assimilate wastes or to carry them away. Most particulate matter which is released to the atmosphere probably settles out fairly quickly; it may be that an equilibrium dust concentration in our atmosphere has already been achieved. But carbon monoxide, oxides and lead compounds do not settle out; they remain (or are transformed to other compounds by sunlight), to permanently alter the composition of the atmosphere.

Although a large number of substances pollute the air, the health hazard actually arises from the direct or indirect effect of from five to ten substances. The principal candidates for inclusion in this group are discussed below—some experts might add one or two others, some might delete one or two. Most sources of these substances can be identified, and their quantities metered on a sample basis, in ways that are not extremely expensive. For most pollutants there are a large number of control methods offering a combination of cost and effectiveness possibilities. For example, sulfur dioxide is created in the burning of fossil fuels. It can be removed from smokestack gases after burning, or removed from the fuel in the refining process, before burning. Fuels with low sulfur content can be substituted for fuels with high sulfur content. The time pattern of burning can be changed so that little high-sulfur fuel is burned when pollutant concentrations are high. Or, the location or degree of the activity for which the fuel is consumed can be altered. The health significance of a number of common air pollutants is indicated as follows:

Carbon Monoxide. The toxic effects of carbon monoxide on the body are well known. By combining with hemoglobin more rapidly than does oxygen, inhaled carbon monoxide interferes with the capacity of blood to transport oxygen to the tissues. A concentration of 30 parts per million (ppm)[3] of carbon monoxide for more than four hours will produce measurable impairment of physiologic functions such as vision and psychomotor performance. These effects are enhanced by any additional illness which decreases oxygen intake in the lungs, or the ability of the circulatory system to distribute oxygen to the body. Cigarette smokers, for example, may have carboxyhemoglobin levels as high as 8 percent. Concentrations higher than 30 ppm carbon monoxide are frequently observed in urban traffic. If this exposure is maintained for 6 hours, or for less time if exercise is carried out, significant effect on cognitive performance is also noted. Researchers Alfred C. Hexter and John R. Goldsmith have reported a significant association between death rates and the levels of carbon monoxide existing in urban communities. They found that, all other things being equal, there were 11 more deaths a day in Los Angeles when the carbon monoxide concentration averaged 20.2 ppm (the highest concentration observed during their four-year study period) as when the concentration averaged 7.3 ppm (the lowest concentration observed).

About 98 percent of the carbon monoxide that is released into the atmosphere each year comes from automobiles, which means that people may be exposed to high concentrations of the gas when they walk the sidewalks or pursue outdoor activities. Of the United States' largest cities, the highest eight-hour average concentrations of carbon monoxide have been found in downtown Chicago, with readings of 40 ppm. In New York, the eight-hour averages in midtown traffic have been in the range of 20 to 30 ppm. New standards announced by the federal government will require those figures to be reduced to no more than 9 ppm.

Hydrocarbons. Some hydrocarbons interact with oxides of nitrogen in sunlight, producing smog, ozone, eye irritation, and damage to vegetation. Hydrocarbons may have a carcinogenic (cancer-producing) effect in some compounds, but this has not been conclusively proven. The primary concern with hydrocarbon emissions is their participation in the photochemical reaction producing smog.

Nitrogen Oxides. Nitrogen dioxide is directly toxic to man and animals; other oxides contribute to photochemical reactions. The gas is relatively insoluble and can be directly inhaled, producing damage at the alveolar and lower bronchial level. Chronic respiratory disease and death have resulted from accidental exposure to high concentrations of nitrogen dioxide in mines and in farm silos. Animal studies have shown pulmonary damage with several species exposed to concentrations at 5 ppm or less; with continuous exposure, some effects have been found at 0.5 ppm. Continuous exposure also appears to increase susceptibility to bacterial infection in animals.

Most nitrogen oxides emitted from automobile exhausts are in the form of nitric oxide. A chain reaction involving hydrocarbons and activated oxygen converts the nitric oxide to nitrogen dioxide, which dissociates in sunshine to nitric oxide and atomic oxygen. Some of this atomic oxygen combines with molecular oxygen to form ozone. Ozone and related oxidents are irritating to mucous membrane, and produce eye and respiratory irritation in concentrations prevalent in Los Angeles, and occasionally in other urban areas. Evidence indicates that in the range of 0.1 to 0.15 ppm oxident (which occurs in Los Angeles), there is impairment of athletic performance of school children and more rapid impairment of lung function in persons with moderately advanced emphysema.

Lead. Lead has been known to be toxic for more than two thousand years. The symptoms of chronic lead poisoning—

weakness, apathy, lowered fertility, and miscarriage—have been recognized for several centuries. Overexposure to lead was probably a factor in the decline of the Roman Empire, because lead pipe was often used in Roman cities to carry water. Romans also lined their bronze cooking, eating, and wine storage vessels with lead to avoid the unpleasant taste of copper, thus trading the taste and symptoms of copper poisoning for the pleasant taste and more subtle poisoning of lead. Examination of the bones of upper-class Romans of the classical period shows high concentrations of lead; the lower classes lived more simply, drank less wine from lead-lined containers, and picked up far less lead poisoning.

Today in most industries and occupations which have a known hazard, lead exposure has been controlled. Most accidental exposures are by ingestion, usually through children eating lead-based paint, and through industrial exposure to fumes and particles of lead in the atmosphere. The latter may be more dangerous; only 10 percent of the lead ingested by mouth is absorbed from the gastro-intestinal tract, while about 50 percent of the inhaled lead of submicronic particle size is absorbed from the lungs.

Atmospheric lead became a major problem with the introduction of tetraethyl lead as a gasoline additive in 1924. Each gallon of gasoline contains about 2.5 cubic centimeters of tetraethyl lead, most of which is exhausted in the form of particles which remain suspended in the atmosphere. The range of blood lead is from 0.015 to 0.045 mg/100 ml of blood, with blood lead in occupationally-exposed groups such as traffic policemen ranging up to 0.06 mg. It has not been established whether this concentration is enough below the level in the blood where toxicity occurs to be safe. Persons with higher "normal" values may suffer subtle impairments of health, and perhaps impairment of enzyme systems in the body, although there may be no overt signs of disease. While it is recognized that infants are more sensitive to lead than adults, maximum permissible blood lead ranges for infants have not been established. The importance of atmospheric lead as a contributing factor to body lead and the narrow margin between normal and toxic levels in the body suggests the need for strong controls over any increased atmospheric levels in populated areas, with steps taken to reduce current levels of lead.

Carbon Dioxide. The problems associated with the production of large quantities of carbon dioxide are little understood, but have potentially vast implications. In just over a century, man has oxidized through burning a substantial portion of the earth's fossil fuels which have accumulated through millions of years. Assuming that the use of fossil fuels will continue to grow with increased economic activity, the amount of carbon dioxide in the atmosphere could rise to 150 percent of its 1970 level before the end of this century. The significance of this is not understood; it is known, however, that atmospheric carbon dioxide is one of the substances which help to retain radiated energy in the atmosphere. If measurable changes in temperature were to occur as a consequence of the carbon dioxide buildup, the effects on the world's climate and on the level of the oceans could be dramatic.

Particulate Matter. Most liquid and solid particles are submicroscopic; such particles are of 0.1 microns or less in diameter and serve as condensation nuclei which may absorb pollutants. Particles of this size acquire monomolecular layers of organic or inorganic chemicals while in the atmosphere or during passage through the upper respiratory tract. Such particles act as carriers for other pollutants and produce more serious health effects than larger particles which are intercepted in the nose or throat. Nuclei consisting of very small lead residues react with atmospheric iodine to form lead iodide, and concentrations of such nuclei may be significant in ice crystal formation. The effects of these concentrations on weather systems, notably on cloud formation and precipitation, have not yet been established but may be considerable.

Included with particulate matter are a number of substances which are potential health hazards at very low concentrations and which require stringent controls. Beryllium, for example, is emitted from industrial sources and from rocket fuel, causing lesions in the lungs, and producing serious respiratory damage and sometimes death if inhaled. Asbestos, which has long been recognized as an occupational hazard, is increasingly present in ambient air because of its use in construction materials, brake linings, and other products. Long exposure in industry produces the lung-scarring disease, asbestosis. Mercury, which has gained attention as a contaminant in tuna and swordfish, is causing concern also as an air pollutant. Mercury is often closely bound with sulphur compounds in the earth, and is freed when coal or oil is burned in power plant boilers to create steam. A high mercury content also occurs in fumes from stacks of municipal incinerators since paper is a major part of municipal refuse, and mercury also is used in the production of paper.

203. The Geographic Extent of Air Pollution

Two geographic types of air pollution—localized and generalized—are relevant both in public policy formulation, and in the consideration of specific abatement measures. A localized problem exists in a limited area—usually immediately downwind from a specific source of pollution, although factors of topography, meteorology, and the height of the stacks emitting pollutants may produce a localized problem at a considerable distance from the source. Because localized air pollution problems affect persons and property in limited segments of a community, they may be a matter of indifference to those areas of the city which escape pollution.[4]

Generalized pollution by definition affects a large area, although not necessarily large or small relative to localized pollution. The significant characteristic of generalized pollution is the complex mixing of pollutants which occurs in the atmosphere to the point where it is often impossible to distinguish one pollutant from another, or to identify their sources. Also, interactions in the atmosphere may produce secondary pollutants such as photochemical smog which differ from any of the original agents emitted.

Prevailing wind patterns and terrain in a given area determine the boundaries of an air shed, which can be thought of as analogous to the boundaries of a watershed or river valley. In California, for example, the prevailing westerly winds and inland mountains create several well defined urban air sheds, one in the San Francisco Bay area, another over and south of Los Angeles. The concept of an air shed is useful for some analytical and control purposes, although there are some problems with its use. It is much more difficult to predict air flows than water flows, and much more difficult to apply mathematical prediction tools in arriving at alternative means of air pollution abatement than water pollution abatement.

Control is made difficult also because air sheds do not generally correspond to existing political jurisdictions, and special commissions usually have to be set up and given appropriate supra-local or state powers before air-shed wide abatement can even be considered.

The upper boundary of an air shed is a ceiling resulting from lack of vertical air mixing due usually to a zone of stable temperature. Air temperature normally decreases with altitude. When temperature increases with higher altitude we have a condition known as a temperature inversion. Temperature inversions are common in all areas of the United States, occurring between 10 percent and 50 percent of the time at elevations of 500 feet or less. The intensity and duration of an inversion depend on how rapidly the earth cools at night and warms in the morning. Inversion conditions which develop over a city during the night frequently last until 3 or 4 hours after sunrise. Thus, pollution from the morning traffic peak may be held down in a city until late morning. Similarly, ground cooling may produce the beginning of an inversion at the time of the peak of evening traffic, often holding this pollution down, sometimes until morning.

204. Biological and Medical Effects of Air Pollution

A number of uncertainties in predicting the biological and medical effects of pollutants affect our ability to set long-term standards for air sheds, or to select long-term pollution control strategies. In particular, we know little of the effects of long-term exposure to relatively low concentrations of air-borne pollutants. Many of the constituents of air pollution—carbon monoxide, nitrogen oxides, and lead compounds—are well-known hazards, and toxicity standards for industrial exposure have been established for many of them. However, knowledge of the effects of moderate to low concentrations of air pollution which are continued year after year is generally not available because the necessary longitudinal studies have not been completed. If chronic or cumulative effects from prolonged exposure to relatively low concentrations of pollutants are important for certain segments of the population, such as children or the elderly, then pollution standards may have to be extremely stringent. Assessing the health effects in a human population requires continual reevaluation to better define air quality criteria. Air quality standards for pollutants in ambient air[5] have been set by state and federal regulatory agencies. However, due to the lack of health information on the effects of pollutants there should be no complacency where such standards are being met.

ECONOMIC APPROACHES TO AIR POLLUTION ABATEMENT

205. The Economic Cost of Air Pollution

Relatively unpolluted air is no longer a free good in our society. It costs money to trap pollutants before they escape into the air, and it costs money to escape to places where the air is relatively clean. Most people probably would be willing to pay for the benefits of increased longevity, decreased morbidity, and decreased nuisance that come with relatively cleaner air.

The singular characteristic of air pollution is its pervasiveness. Unlike water pollution, the extent of air pollution is limited only by the course of prevailing winds. We know that pollution of the atmosphere affects the health of human beings, of animals, and of plants;[6] it causes deterioration in property values and increased costs in a number of production processes;[7] it raises the rate of automobile and airline accidents;[8] it may substantially reduce agricultural productivity in affected areas.[9] A slow rise in the temperature of the earth has been attributed to air pollution. It is suspected of altering human genes so that mutations may occur resulting in the transmission of different characteristics to future generations.[10] Almost certainly, the major benefit from air pollution abatement is found in a general improvement in the quality of life rather than in one of the more measurable categories. It is therefore not surprising that there are fundamental problems in measuring the economic costs of air pollution.

For example, not only are current estimates of the total cost of air pollution highly speculative, but many economists in the field are pessimistic that any more accurate estimates will be forthcoming in the near future. It is possible that adequately funded studies of the costs of air pollution would be more productive than current writers seem to believe. However, the question is academic since no such studies are underway, and no funding for them appears likely in the near future.[11]

The lack of hard figures to measure air pollution costs would not be critical if there were a linear relationship between the level of air pollution and the cost of controlling it. Economists could simply make point estimates, and extrapolate to estimate intermediate values. Although some writers have assumed that the shape of air pollution cost and abatement functions are linear, it is unlikely even on *a priori* grounds that this is intended as any more than a convenient simplification. If such relationships are nonlinear, then effective policy determination requires comprehensive studies to estimate the true costs of air pollution and the benefits of abatement over a wide range of possible levels of pollution.

Harold Wolozin has proposed an S-shaped functional relationship between the level of pollution and the cost of abatement as is shown in Figure 2-1.

This is an *a priori* reasonable approximation of the likely shape of such a function.[12]

FIGURE 2-1

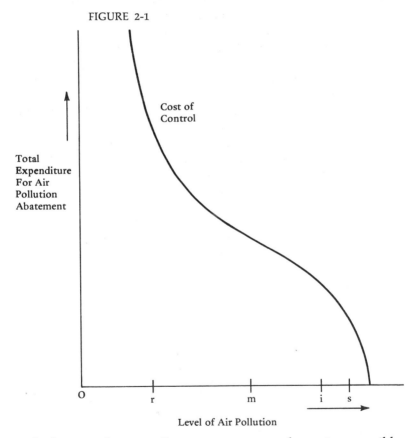

Level of Air Pollution

The horizontal axis on Figure 2-1 measures the various possible levels of pollution on some composite index. The vertical axis measures the total cost of abatement required to achieve each level of air quality measured on the horizontal axis. This static analysis assumes that technology is constant in the short run. The point at which air pollution is just detectable is indicated by "r;" the saturation point at which pollution is at dangerously high levels, by "s." As we move from "s" towards "r," outlays for air pollution abatement increase as we reach *successive levels* of purer air. The function indicates intitial low returns to scale as abatement is initiated at point "i," a long span over which returns to scale increase to point "m," and entry to an area of rapidly diminishing returns to scale as the air becomes cleaner.

As indicated previously, economists are concerned with an optimal level of air pollution—not perfectly pure air but some level of pollution which is acceptable in terms of the other goods that must be foregone by society to achieve the resulting cleaner air. Society accepts lower abatement expenditures—a smaller diversion of resources—at the cost of a disproportionate acceleration in the cost of air pollution.

In traditional microeconomic analysis, an optimal level of pollution would occur at that point where the total costs of pollution and of pollution control are minimized. In Figure 2-2 the Cost of Control curve is similar to that in Figure 2-1. The Cost of Pollution curve represents the cost of individual and social benefits foregone (health benefits, etc.) in the absence of air pollution control. This curve is also an S-function, with an initial range of minimal damage followed by a range of rapid rise in health and property damage costs relative to pollution levels, followed by a leveling off, although the latter might come only at a point where health costs due to morbidity and mortality were already unbearably high.[13]

The total cost of pollution and of control are at a minimum at

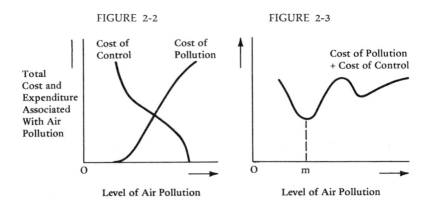

FIGURE 2-2   FIGURE 2-3

Cost of   Cost of
Control   Pollution

Total
Cost and
Expenditure
Associated
With Air
Pollution

Cost of Pollution
+ Cost of Control

O   O   m

Level of Air Pollution   Level of Air Pollution

point "m" on Figure 2-3. To reduce pollution to point "m" is the same as saying that we will spend money on air pollution controls until the incremental abatement dollar reduces the cost of pollution as much as the cost of control, but that we will not spend beyond that point. The S-shape of the individual cost curves in Figure 2-2 results in a total cost curve in Figure 2-3 with several minimum points, making very difficult the estimation of a true minimum point in the absence of realistic dollar values for costs and benefits of control at different levels of pollution.

It should be emphasized that simply knowing that the total benefits from any single level of pollution abatement are greater than the total cost of pollution at that level is not a sufficient basis for deciding that abatement should be increased. It is sometimes argued in noneconomic literature that increased pollution control is necessary in a certain case because the total cost of pollution exceeds the existing industry and government expenditures for research and control devices, but this fact alone does not tell us whether pollution abatement should be increased. For example, consider the following simplified example in Table 2-1.

TABLE 2-1

Cost and Benefit of Air Pollution Abatement

Percent Level of Air Pollution Abatement	Total Benefit to Society of Abatement	Total Cost to Society of Abatement	Net Value to Society of Abatement (Total Benefit minus Total Cost)
0	$ 0	$ 0	$ 0
20	100	25	75
40	180	75	110
60	250	175	75
80	305	300	5
99	320	450	−130

The total benefits to society from 80 percent abatement of $305 exceed the total cost to society of $300 at that level. However, the net value to society of abatement is less at 80 percent than it would be at 60 percent, 40 percent, or 20 percent. If our total cost and total benefit schedules are correct, then a 40 percent level of air pollution abatement is economically optimal. The conclusion that abatement should be increased from that point because benefits would exceed costs would be economically incorrect.[14]

The two sections which follow are indicative of some of the

better economic research which has been carried out on determining the costs associated with air pollution. The first considers health costs; the second considers costs from deterioration in residential property values.

206. Health Costs of Air Pollution

Much scientific effort has been expended to investigate short-term episodes of air pollution, while the more relevant question is probably the long-term health effects of growing up in and living in a polluted atmosphere. While a number of scientists have established that air pollution is associated with respiratory diseases of many types, including lung cancer and emphysema, the qualitative link is for our purposes of limited usefulness. To estimate the benefit of pollution abatement, we must know how the incidence of a disease varies with the level of air pollution.

A 1970 article by Lester B. Lave and Eugene P. Seskin which appeared in *Science,* reported an investigation of the effect of air pollution on human health and derived quantitative estimates of the effect of air pollution on various diseases. It also discussed the economic costs of ill health, and estimated the cost of effects attributed to air pollution.[15] For example, Lave and Seskin collected data for 114 Standard Metropolitan Statistical Areas (SMSAs) in the U.S. and attempted to relate total death rates and infant mortality rates to air pollution and other factors such as socioeconomic data. These data, death rates, and air pollution data were taken from various sources, and a series of statistical regressions were run. Their data showed that a 10 percent decrease in the minimum concentration of measured particulates in the United States would decrease the total death rate by 0.5 percent, the infant death rate by 0.7 percent, the neonatal death rate by 0.6 percent, and the fetal death rate by 0.9 percent. A 10 percent decrease in the minimum concentration of sulfates would decrease the total death rate by 0.4 percent, the infant mortality rate by 0.3 percent, and the fetal death rate by 0.5 percent.

By way of illustrating the difficulty in generating these figures, consider the sources of data available to the researcher. Epidemiological data are the kind of health statistics best adapted to estimating air pollution effects. These data are in the form of mortality and morbidity rates for a particular group of people, generally segmented geographically. Thus, an analyst could in theory try to account for variations in the mortality rate among the various census tracts in a city. However, while these statistics are tabulated by the government and are easily available, there are problems both from the varying accuracy in classifying the cause of death (since not all physicians take equal care in determining causation), and from the lack of information on unmeasured variables, such as smoking habits, occupational exposure to air pollution, and genetic health factors.

A second source of data available to the researcher is from episodic relationships. These data attempt to relate daily or weekly mortality or morbidity rates to indices of air pollution during the interval in question. These studies are of limited interest because they concentrate on the immediate determinant of death rather than on the initial cause of illness. A 30-year-old who is killed by an increase in sulfur dioxide concentrations is likely to be gravely ill in the first place. Thus, morbidity data are probably more useful than mortality data.

Lave and Seskin also reviewed a number of studies which quantified the relationship between air pollution and morbidity and mortality rates, and concluded that the evidence shows a substantial association between the two. Their conclusions could be challenged on the grounds that the relationships found by investigators are spurious because the level of air pollution is correlated with a third factor, which is the "real" cause of ill health. For example, many studies do not consider smoking habits, occupational exposure, or the general pace of life. Thus, it may be argued that city dwellers smoke more, get less exercise, and tend to be more overweight, thus having higher morbidity and mortality rates than rural dwellers. Were this true, air pollution as a causative variable might be irrelevant.

Apparently there is little systemic relationship between such third factors and the level of air pollution. An English study in which smoking habits were examined revealed little evidence of differences by residence. In several United States studies, the correlations between air pollution and mortality were greater when areas within a city (where more factors are held constant) were compared than when rural and urban areas were compared. Also, significant effects were found in studies comparing individuals within strictly defined occupational groups, such as postmen and bus drivers, where incomes and working conditions were comparable and unmeasured habits were likely to be similar.

Lave and Seskin attempted to translate their data on increased sickness and death from air pollution into dollar units to answer the question of how much society should be willing to spend to improve health. The normal procedure for estimating what society is willing to pay for better health is to total the amount that is spent on medical care, plus the value of foregone earnings resulting from disability and death. However, this total would seem to underestimate the amount that society is willing to spend to prolong life or relieve pain. For example, a patient with kidney failure can be kept alive by renal dialysis at a cost of up to $25,000 per year— a cost which is substantially in excess of foregone earnings, although today many kidney patients are receiving this treatment. Lave and Seskin defined direct disease costs as including expenditures for hospital and nursing-home care, and for services of physicians, dentists, and members of other health professions, plus the earnings foregone by those who are sick, disabled, or who died prematurely.

This method of calculation can be illustrated further using the case of bronchitis. The studies cited in the Lave and Seskin article indicated that mortality from bronchitis would be reduced by about 50 percent if air pollution is lowered to levels currently prevailing in urban areas with relatively clean air. The assumption was made that there would be a 25 to 50 percent reduction in morbidity and mortality due to bronchitis if air pollution in major urban areas were abated by about 50 percent. Since the medical expenses and foregone income related to bronchitis total about $930 million per year, Lave and Seskin concluded that from $250 million to $500 million per year would be saved by a 50 percent abatement of air pollution in the major urban centers.

Similar calculations were applied to lung cancer ($33 million annual saving based on a 50 percent reduction in air pollution), all other cancers ($390 million), respiratory disease ($1222 million), and cardiovascular morbidity and mortality ($468 million). These cost estimates are not all equally certain. For example, the connection between bronchitis or lung cancer and air pollution is well documented while the connection between all cancers or all cardiovascular disease and air pollution is more tentative.

Lave and Seskin's conclusion that the total annual cost saving from a 50 percent reduction in air pollution levels in major urban areas is $2080 million or more provides a first approximation to what the health cost savings from reduction of various forms of pollution might equal.

The Lave and Seskin article and similar articles also indicate

that researchers are not looking for one substance in air pollution to account for observed health effects, but rather are searching for an understanding of the complex chemistry of the atmosphere and the effects of that chemistry on human bodies. There are numerous diseases—caused in combination by infection, by hereditary predisposition, by allergy, by emotional factors, and by cigarette smoking—to which air pollution acts as a catalyst. The effect of pollutants on man is complicated by atmospheric factors of temperature and humidity, which have their own effects on health aside from their effect on pollutants in the atmosphere. Thus, in London in 1952, a number of deaths from respiratory tract ailments followed a concentration of 1.34 ppm of sulfur dioxide together with a high concentration of particulate matter and soot. In 1962 a higher concentration of 1.98 ppm of sulfur dioxide with a much lower level of particulate matter coincided with far fewer deaths. In Amsterdam in 1962, similar high levels of sulfur dioxide and much lower levels of particulate matter to that found in London coincided with virtually no increase in mortality or illness. High levels of particulate matter with low concentrations of sulfur dioxide have produced mixed results in both countries.

207. Residential Property Values and Air Pollution

There is evidence that air pollution affects residential property values, and that it may figure in people's calculations when they move. Some pollutants are undoubtedly reflected in property values; others may not be because of imperfect information. In a study by Ronald G. Ridker and John A. Henning, published in *The Review of Economics and Statistics* in 1967,[16] the authors attempted to provide evidence on the effect of air pollution on property values for single family dwellings in the St. Louis metropolitan area in 1960. The evidence consisted of estimates obtained through applying least-squares regression methods to cross-sectional data. The air pollution variable was treated by developing alternative estimates of the effects of air pollution, given other possible explanatory variables that might have been involved.

As indicators of characteristics of the property itself, Ridker and Henning included variables for median number of rooms in the house, percentage of houses recently built (as an index of housing quality), and number of houses per mile (as a measure of average lot size). As indicators of locational advantages and disadvantages, they included express bus travel time to the central business district, accessibility to highways and major thoroughfares, accessibility to shopping areas, and accessibility to major industrial areas. As indicators of neighborhood characteristics they obtained and quantified data on school quality, crime rates, persons per unit (as a measure of crowding), and occupation ratio (as a measure of the homogeneity of a neighborhood—the assumption being that people prefer to live in neighborhoods that are homogeneous with respect to occupational and social classes).

A further variable was included to indicate the effect of differences in property taxes, which are likely to be capitalized in the market value of the property. Another variable represented the percentage of non-white residents in a census tract (although no *a priori* judgments were made about what relation this might have to property values). A final variable of median family income was introduced as a proxy for the housing and neighborhood characteristics that had not been picked up by the other variables used in the study.[17]

On the whole (and considering that fifteen separate variables were involved), the hypotheses in the Ridker and Henning study tested out very well. The results were both statistically significant and fairly reasonable within the context of the St. Louis metropolitan area.

The researchers concluded that if the sulfation levels to which any single family dwelling unit is exposed were to drop by .25 mg. per 100 cubic centimeters per day (compared with a mean of 0.85, a range of approximately 0.35 to 2.75, and a standard deviation of .45), the value of that property could be expected to rise by about $245.[18] This would have produced a total increase in property values for the St. Louis SMSA of about $82 million. Invested at 10 percent, this amounts to a return of about $8 million annually. Ridker and Henning assumed it would cost about $8 million per year to shift to low-sulfur fuels that would cut sulfation levels enough to achieve the .25 mg. per 100 cubic centimeters per day level. However, other considerations are also relevant. First, property values other than those for single family dwellings would also rise, adding substantially to the benefit estimate. Second, benefits besides the increase in property values (health benefits, for example) would also be derived from a reduction in sulfation levels. Third, to bring about these property value and related benefits it would probably be necessary to reduce the levels of other pollutants that are correlated with sulfation levels, especially particulates, and this would substantially raise the cost estimates. Although the Ridker and Henning work is probably the best material to date on the relationship of residential property values and air pollution, it is clear that further work remains to be done before an adequate comparison between the benefits and costs of air pollution abatement—even when related only to changes in residential property values—can be made.

208. Control of Air Pollution

The debate among economists over air pollution control centers on whether polluters in the private sector (consumers or business) can be induced to voluntarily lessen or eliminate their pollution in response to market incentives or coercion, or whether the government must enforce control by legislative means. Under incentive systems, there is, of course, an option not to be persuaded. Wolozin quotes one businessman as follows:

> . . . if you would base pollution control on a system of incentives, you might be disappointed. The marginal dollar gained for pollution control is hardly as exciting as the marginal dollar gained in expanding sales, creating new products or improving technology . . . many if not most businesses have a shortage of key personnel and they would rather use this resource to develop the mainspring of their profits than to maximize their pollution subsidies.[19]

Market pressure could be exerted by imposing effluent fees or other charges that would reflect the marginal external costs of the air pollution. Other suggested economic incentives include tax credits for air cleaning equipment or alternative processes, outright payment by government for control devices, or government relocation cost payments.

The movement at present seems to be towards government assumption of direct responsibility rather than operation through market incentives. Except for the control of automobile emissions and the setting of overall national air quality standards, which are federal responsibilities, the establishment of enforcement regulations or incentives is a state and local responsibility. As we shall examine later in this book, both the *Clean Air Act of 1963* and its subsequent amendments, and the *Air Quality Act of 1967*, which replaced it, require states to undertake this responsibility. Prior to the Clean Air Act, only sixteen states had air pollution control legislation; today, all do.

Although the Air Quality Act gives state and local governments a primary role in protecting air quality, it gives the federal government authority to act in emergencies, responsibility to review and approve state and regional control programs, and authority to establish federal controls in states or regions which fail to establish their own controls. The Act requires the Department of Health, Education, and Welfare (HEW) to designate specific air quality control regions, which treat groups of communities as a unit for the purpose of setting and implementing air quality standards. HEW is required to develop and publish air quality criteria for pollutants or groups of pollutants, information on control techniques that identify the best methods available for reducing each pollutant emission at its source, and the cost of doing so.

After a criterion and information on control techniques for a pollutant are published, the Act sets a timetable which each state must follow in developing its own air quality standards (not lower than federal standards), and implementing them for each of the designated regions. Implementation plans can offer financial incentives as well as enforce controls. If any state fails to establish standards, or if the Secretary of HEW finds that standards are not consistent with the federal criteria, he can initiate action to insure that appropriate standards are met.

In May of 1971, the Environmental Protection Agency (see Chapter Seven) announced its first national air quality standards for six principal pollutants, to go into effect by July 1, 1975. The standards are for sulphur oxides, particulates, carbon monoxide, hydrocarbons, nitrogen oxides, and photochemical oxidants. The first two are of particular interest. The standard set for sulphur oxides is 1.03 ppm of air as an annual mean; for particulates, 75 micrograms per cubic meter. Most regions of the country can meet these standards by switching to low-sulphur fuels and by requiring plants to install electrostatic precipitators to capture soot. Seven cities—New York, Chicago, St. Louis, Baltimore, Hartford, Buffalo, and Philadelphia—are expected to have a hard time meeting the standards by 1975 because of currently high pollution rates. To meet the standards through an increased use of natural gas (replacing high sulphur coal), the seven cities combined would cause an increase in the national use of natural gas by almost 15 percent with half that increase going to New York City alone. However, as the National Academy of Engineering has pointed out, the difficulty with this solution is that the supply of natural gas will decline markedly in less than 10 years unless large new reserves are discovered.

In order that the legal deadline for carbon monoxide be met, not only would automobile manufacturers have to meet the Act's 1975 deadline of producing "clean" engines, but many cities would have to make drastic changes in their transportation systems by developing rapid transit lines from the suburbs and limiting private cars in their inner cities in peak hours.

The problem with hydrocarbons is equally severe. In many cities it is now common to find 2 to 3 parts of hydrocarbons to a million parts of air. The primary standard set by the Agency calls for a limit of 0.24 ppm as a maximum three-hour average concentration not to be exceeded more than once a year.

209. Approaches to Air Quality Standard Setting

In general, two approaches are available in the setting of air quality standards—constant pollution abatement, and selective pollution abatement.[20] Under the constant abatement solution, air quality standards are set well below the pollutant concentrations known to result in morbidity or mortality. All sources of a particular pollutant are expected to reduce their emissions in the same proportion as the desired reduction in air pollutant concentration. In one sense this is an equitable procedure, as a source that accounts for "x" percent of particulate emissions is thus responsible for "x" percent of the reduction in particulate concentration. In another sense it is inequitable, as it assumes different sources of pollution have similar costs of proportionately reducing that pollution. If the assumption is incorrect, it results in a solution which is far more costly for some polluters than others.

The best example of constant abatement is citywide or areawide standards requiring that each source of pollution reduce its emissions by a predetermined proportion. In its most naive form, this requires that a source located on the downwind side of an air shed must reduce emissions proportionately with a source located upwind thus removing any incentive that a firm has to relocate to reduce its effect on the level of air shed pollutant concentration.

Under the selective abatement solution, air quality standards are set at pollutant concentrations which, if exceeded, are known to result in morbidity or mortality. This approach recognizes that acute air pollution episodes can be predicted, and that varying degrees and methods of abatement are appropriate for different degrees of pollution. Thus, in the New York City-New Jersey Air Pollution Commission area, an initial alert is called if air pollutant concentrations exceed predetermined levels, or if stable weather conditions are forecast. A second alert is called if concentrations of air pollutants reach still higher levels, or if the first alert has not produced improved conditions. A third alert, which indicates a danger to public health, is called if the concentrations of pollutants reach even higher levels or if the second alert has been ineffective.

Successive levels of alert require that pollution control equipment be brought into use, that some polluting activities such as open burning be limited or terminated, that motor vehicle operation in affected areas be restricted, that the consumption of polluting fuels such as sulphur-heavy oil be restricted, and so on. A third-level alert might require measures as stringent as a curfew on lighting and heating (so that coal or oil fired generators can be cut back), restrictions on the use of fuel oil and diesel oil, and curtailment of all motor vehicle traffic in the metropolitan area except for emergency vehicles. This staged-approach implies among other things that companies do not have to utilize expensive pollution control equipment 100 percent of the time to satisfy air quality standards, but only when problem conditions are forecast. Further, all polluters do not have to abate to the same degree. The value of the staged-approach depends largely on how well weather conditions can be predicted. To date, meteorologists have had only limited success in forecasting air-pollution potentials accurately.[21]

Constant abatement both incurs the greatest abatement cost to society and also provides the best guarantee that there will not be an air pollution problem. Each variation in shifting from the constant abatement model to the selective abatement model is a refinement. As we move towards selective abatement there is a tradeoff; the probability of satisfying any given air-quality standard declines, while the probability of finding the least expensive solution to air pollution increases. Selective abatement carries the expected cost that air quality standards will not be met, while constant abatement carries the expected cost from not using the least-expensive approach to air pollution control. The optimal least-expected cost solution to the air pollution problem depends specifically on our knowledge of the environment and on our ability to forecast weather conditions.

Independently of the ability to forecast, general abatement will be more economic than selective abatement where the cost of implementing and supervising selective abatement is very high— where sources of pollution are small and numerous as with residential units, small incinerators, and automobiles.

The most efficient solution will also differ between cities or air sheds, each of which has its own unique characteristics and problems; each must determine for itself whether constant abatement or some variation of selective abatement is most efficient in meeting specific air quality standards. This means it is probably uneconomic for the federal government to establish national air quality standards or emissions standards, except perhaps at very minimal levels, or as guidelines.

AUTOMOTIVE AIR POLLUTION: A CASE STUDY

210. A Systemic Approach to Automotive Air Pollution

We have already noted that the automobile is the biggest single contributor by weight to air pollution. Some conclusions from a study commissioned in 1966 by the United States Department of Commerce provide further perspective on this major pollutant. The study, led by Dr. Richard Morse of MIT, was originally to consider the feasibility of electrically powered vehicles. The resulting Panel on Electrically Powered Vehicles subsequently broadened the scope of their inquiry to include other modes of transportation, and to consider the total complex of urban problems related to automotive air pollution.

The Morse study used a systemic approach to point out where new solutions might be fruitful. The systemic approach is illustrated by the observation that pollution control changes may affect more than just vehicles. In evaluating the effect of changing permissible pollutant levels, one must also examine possible impacts on transportation system design. For example, emission reduction would facilitate the design and construction of tunnels, and partially or totally underground highways. Ventilation requirements limit the extent of both tunnels and underground roads, and increase the cost of building and operating them. The reduction of ventilation requirements that would result from reductions in pollution emissions would free designers from many current constraints.

Also, emission reduction accompanied by noise reduction would permit extensive use of the air space over highways. In many cities, roads and access ramps use large amounts of land and destroy neighborhood integrity. Development of highway air space might offset these effects, but such development is likely to take place only if automobile emissions and noise are substantially reduced.

The concluding chapter of the Morse report conceives of vehicular air pollution as only one element in a complex of urban problems that begin with the existing spatial relationship of homes to jobs. There has been considerable debate as to whether this systemic approach is a feasible short-term one to the problem of vehicular air pollution, or whether the scope of the problem requires a more pragmatic short-term consideration only of the cost-benefit aspects of surface vehicle propulsion systems. For example, does the ultimate solution to automotive air pollution problems lie only with the design of vehicles powered by steam or electricity, which are attractive to the consumer and inherently free of toxic emissions? More basic, is surface transportation in urban centers a determining force, or can it be treated as a dependent variable which responds to external criteria? The conclusions of the Morse report are stated in the following excerpt.

THE AUTOMOBILE AND AIR POLLUTION*

One might reduce the level of polluting activity by
(a) Reducing the total amount of urban transportation.
(b) Reducing the total amount of motor vehicle travel throughout a metropolitan area
(c) Shifting some of the demand for motor vehicle travel to less polluting modes of transportation.
(d) Reducing total motor vehicle travel in severely affected areas

*Reprinted from Richard Morse, et al., The Automobile and Air Pollution; A Program for Progress (The Morse Panel), Report of the Panel on Electrically Powered Vehicles, Part II, Washington, D.C.: U.S. Department of Commerce (October, 1967). Reprinted by permission of Richard S. Morse, Chairman of the Panel. Portions of the original sections have been omitted.

(e) Reducing all motor vehicle travel in affected areas at affected times.

(f) Reducing the extent of motor vehicle travel in especially polluting aspects of driving (with possible further qualification to specific areas and/or times).

(g) Reducing travel by more highly polluting vehicles.

Reducing The Total Amount of Urban Transportation

There are basically two ways to reduce the total amount of urban transportation: to reduce the demand and/or to restrict the supply. To reduce the demand, two main approaches have been proposed. The first is to redesign sections of metropolitan areas to reduce need and demand for transportation, and to so design new areas. The second is to substitute communications services for direct transportation.

·   ·   ·

The lengths and frequencies of trips in a metropolitan area are functions of its structure as well as of its transport system and socio-economic characteristics. The relationships of homes to jobs, and to shopping, cultural, educational, and recreational facilities strongly influence the over-all amount of metropolitan travel. It has thus been suggested that the total demand for transportation might be reduced if one could

(i) Provide better spatial integration of residences and offices in communities, to reduce the home-work place separation. At one extreme, this could involve recreating villages or village-like environments that would be relatively self-contained. . . . A more moderate version of the same proposal might involve revising zoning practices to permit greater intermixing of residences and offices throughout metropolitan areas.

(ii) Substitute elevator for ground transport by judicious use of tall buildings. Tall buildings abet urban concentration, which has been both strongly supported and strongly attacked in the last few decades. . . .

(iii) Redesign Federal regulations and financial procedures to encourage developments containing homes, apartments, and jobs, to minimize the number of new "bedroom" communities miles away from places of employment.

The substitution of communications services for direct transportation has been a popular theme in projections for the future. It has been forecast that phonovision, closed-circuit television, facsimile transmission, remote computer operation, and devices yet unforeseen will make travelling all but obsolete. Yet evidence thus far suggests that transportation and communications reinforce each other: the better the communication the more transportation, and vice versa.

•   •   •

Reducing The Total Amount Of Metropolitan Motor Vehicle Travel

Basically, there are three ways to reduce the total amount of metropolitan motor vehicle travel: regulation, pricing, and shifting demand to other transport modes.

Regulation might involve (a) fuel rationing, using any of a graded spectrum of schemes, (b) limited registration of second and third cars (based on "evidence of need") in the metropolitan area, (c) extremely tight enforcement of traffic laws, (d) motor vehicle travel permits (i.e., rationed travel), etc.

Pricing might involve (a) substantially increasing fuel taxes throughout the metropolitan area and its environs and (b) substantially increasing vehicle registration and operator's license fees throughout the area, to reflect the cost of air pollution in the expense of automobile operation. In conjunction with (c) above, it might also include increasing fines for traffic violations.

The pricing schemes tamper less with normal economic and social functions but may lead to misallocation and maldistribution of resources without successfully reducing pollution. The schemes, for example, are all economically regressive. They thus affect most those with lower incomes, who own fewer vehicles and drive those they do own less than the overall average.

•   •   •

Shifting Demand To Less-Polluting Modes Of Transportation

Electric Vehicles. ...Electric cars need be considered for pollution-reduction only over the long-term. They are not expected to have any significant impact until at least 1980.

. . . If the new cars are truly as different and new as their most enthusiastic advocates claim, they will radically change the relationship between existing transportation modes and tend to create their own specialized markets.

Mass Transportation.   Mass transportation must be effective at the margin if it is to be effective at all in reducing pollution. It might be effective, for example, if it were to discourage additional one-car families from becoming two-or-more-car families. It might be effective if it were to remain sufficiently attractive and convenient to keep the passengers it now has. And it might be effective if its diversion of demand were to be sufficient to reduce peak-hour congestion in some areas and thus reduce the pollution caused by vehicles operating in highly inefficient driving modes.

Mass transportation as now conceived is not likely to be able to do much more. No matter how successful mass transportation is, it will not handle goods, which will continue to be carried mostly by truck. And, perhaps more important, mass transportation, even where it is expanding, is not the only form of transportation being built. New highways and highway improvements are underway or planned in many areas, and no cessation of road construction or improvement appears likely.

In many urban areas, mass transportation now carries an important fraction of people commuting to downtown. The question of interest for air pollution, however, is how many of those not now using mass transportation can be induced or persuaded to shift. For most urban areas, this number appears to be small, relative to the total number of people driving motor vehicles in the area for one reason or another.

With regard to the new San Francisco Bay Area Rapid Transit system, for example, the AAAS Commission on Air Conservation found: "Roughly 100,000 automobile trips per day are to be diverted to rapid transit. From the viewpoint of coping with traffic and congestion at the hours of most intensive demand, rapid transportation could make an important contribution. From the viewpoint of air pollution control, however, the transit solution, even if it meets the expectations of the Transit District, is only a minor portion of the whole. There are now [1965] about 4 million daily trips in the three-county area, 7 million in the entire Bay Region. These figures [are expected to] rise to 5.2 million and to 11 million, respectively, by 1975. The Transit District estimate that it would carry 258,600 trips per day means that it would absorb only about 5 percent of the passenger travel (in trips, not miles) in the three-county area, and 2.5 percent in the entire Bay Region."

Reducing Motor Vehicle Travel In Affected Areas

There are three basic ways of reducing motor vehicle travel in affected areas: regulation, pricing, and shifting demand to other modes.

Regulations that have been proposed include:

(a) Banning or regulating the use of internal combustion engine vehicles in affected areas (possibly only at certain times).

(b) Restricting traffic access to major arteries, bridges, tunnels, etc. leading into affected areas (possibly only at certain times).

(c) Reducing the number of parking spaces available for all-day or long-term parking in affected areas.

Pricing policies that have been proposed include:

(d) Instituting graduated, variable tolls on major arteries, bridges, tunnels, etc. leading into affected areas. Such tolls could be adjusted to help control traffic patterns and reduce traffic into affected areas at selected times.

(e) Substantially increasing long-term parking charges in areas used by commuters, while keeping charges relatively low for short-term (less than 4 hours) parking to encourage shopping, social, cultural, and recreational activities.

(f) Indirectly achieving (e) through selective taxation and legislation.

(g) Instituting vehicle use taxes (similar to wage taxes), to be collected from those who use vehicles regularly in affected areas.

Policies for shifting demand to other modes include:

(h) Improving public transportation in affected areas.

(i) Making non-polluting vehicles available for inexpensive rental, in conjunction with one or more of (a) through (g).

(j) Making parking spaces more available for all-day parking near collection points for non-polluting modes of transportation ("Park-and-ride").

(k) Improving taxi availability and service, in conjunction with (h) and (j).

The regulations restrict mobility and may reduce pollution at the expense of reducing the activities that attract people into affected areas. Good analysis and study would be needed to assess the regulations' impact.

The pricing policies have attractive aspects, but have the major disadvantages of being somewhat regressive and of working only indirectly to reduce pollution.

Reducing The Extent of Driving In Inefficient Modes

There are basically two ways of reducing the amount of driving in inefficient, highly polluting modes: introducing new vehicle configurations and concepts and improving traffic flow.

The former reduces inefficient driving by substituting non- or low-polluting power sources for the internal combustion engine. The main new vehicle configurations and concepts proposed are:

(a) Combination of car or truck powered by internal combustion engine with auxiliary transport system to reduce mileage driven— e.g., piggyback, moving pallet, road-rail system.

(b) Combination of short-range electric vehicle with long-range transport system—e.g., piggyback, "third-rail," electronic highways, "Urbmobile."

Improving traffic flow helps reduce pollution because vehicular pollution is created at a rate approximately inversely proportional to speed. An increase in speed from 20 to 30 miles per hour yields about a one-third reduction in pollutants, while a change from 20 to 40 miles per hour brings about a two-fold reduction. There is considerable room for improvement: Traffic on Manhattan streets during rush hour moves at an average speed of 8½ miles per hour, and on the approach expressways to Manhattan, speeds are as low as 13 miles per hour.

The two basic approaches to improving traffic flow are

(a) reducing traffic levels. Some ways are staggering working hours and encouraging a greater number of persons per individual vehicle.

(b) improving traffic flow at given levels of traffic. Some ways include better traffic control, new expressways, redesigned intersections and traffic bottlenecks, automatic control devices to govern individual vehicles (automated highway), better system labelling.

Reducing Travel By More Highly Polluting Vehicles

Some vehicles emit more pollutants than others. One might thus reduce average emissions per vehicle by reducing the proportion of travel done by more highly polluting vehicles.

Policies proposed for accomplishing this include:

(a) Imposing taxes or "polluting fees" related to emissions. . . .

(b) Causing polluting vehicles to be operated more efficiently. This might involve checking all cars and trucks for combustion efficiency, training mechanics better to service and maintain pollution-related systems. . . .

(c) Having motor vehicle taxes increase with increasing vehicle age.

Although some old cars burn fuel more completely than some new ones, statistically age is highly correlated with poor carburetion. Approximate, preliminary analysis indicates that this tax scheme would affect mainly the disadvantaged and poor, who tend to own older cars, and middle-income families owning two or more cars. In the first case, the taxes would be regressive and would seem unlikely to achieve much of the desired effect. In the second case, the increased tax might stimulate earlier "trading in" of old second cars but would drive off the road primarily cars being used far less than average.

● ● ●

Alternatives to Reduce The Impact Of Emitted Pollutants

There are basically two approaches to reducing the impact of emitted pollutants: reducing atmospheric pollutant concentrations in areas where they may affect people, property, or plants and reducing the impact of the pollutants on the sensitive receptors.

Policies proposed to reduce atmospheric concentrations include:

(a) Reducing local concentrations by :

(i) Enhancing local atmospheric transport, to disperse pollutants —e.g., enhancing natural micro-meteorological forces by shaping wind patterns (building location and design, major topographical changes, such as building or levelling hills), making best use of the winds available (highway location and design), and reducing the extent of construction (and forest denudation, etc.) favorable to stagnant conditions .

(ii) Providing artificial convection.

(iii) Preventing pollutants from accumulating in local atmospheres, by "sweeping" with adsorbents, molecular sieves, or reactive catalysts to remove pollutants as they are formed.

The forces involved in (i) are not well understood, but the possibilities appear attractive. Achieving (ii) is likely to be inordinately expensive; the atmosphere ordinarily tends to resist or overcome small-scale disturbances, and even assuming atmospheric cooperation the power and equipment costs involved are enormous. Alternative (iii) involves treating large volumes of air, but may be very attractive and effective in places where air is already collected and pumped as, for example, at tunnel ventilators or garage exhaust vents.

(b) Removing undesirable products from the general atmosphere:

(i) Chemically—react pollutants to form carbon dioxide and water or other less desirable compounds.

(ii) Physically—sweep, scrub, or scavenge pollutants from atmosphere. Enhance precipitation of particulates.

(iii) Biologically—introduce pollution predators, such as microbes or insects.

(i) and (ii) require contacting large volumes of air with other substances. The power needed simply to move the air effectively is likely to be so expensive that these alternatives will be most unattractive except where the air is moved anyway, as in tunnel ventilation.

The problem with (iii) is uncertain ecology. It is difficult to predict what else pollution predators might find appetizing, or what effects they might have on their surrounding biological system. (The "cure" may be worse than the problem.) It also may be difficult to "train" predators to feed only on undesirable substances.

(c) Reducing megalopolitan sprawl.

Through "downwind" and cumulative effects, filling in metropolitan areas is believed to exacerbate pollution. Areas that once received relatively clean air receive pollutants from new sources in filled-in areas upwind; these new pollutants compound the older area's existing problems. And pollutants that once were blown quickly out of the megalopolitan convection cells are believed to stay much longer when the megalopolis expands.

Policies proposed to reduce pollutant impacts include:

(a) Locating major highways such that pollution effects on surrounding neighborhoods are kept to a minimum.

(b) Reducing the biological effects of atmospheric pollutants on man by:

(i) Relocating pollutant sources relative to man so that the effective exposure is less.

(ii) Designing and distributing protective systems—e.g., gas masks, oxygen, anti-pollutant inoculations.

(iii) Making effective diagnosis and treatment of pollution effects readily available.

(iv) Developing a means for inducing tolerances and immunities to pollution effects.

(i) is likely to become quite important, although the design bases for it are ill-understood. (ii) may become necessary for especially susceptible people (i.e., heart patients, elderly people with respiratory ailments) in high-pollution areas. The need for (iii) and (iv), and the scientific bases on which to develop them, are still unclear.

Impacts Of Pollution Control Policies

Recommendations . . . that would result in significant reduction of air pollution are likely to change the pricing cost, performance characteristics, and accessibility of the transportation system. These changes could result in significant net costs or benefits to society.

Pollution control affects not only the transportation system but also products—automobiles, trucks and motor fuel—that account changes resulting from pollution control measures, therefore, could for a large part of the American gross national product Major have large impacts on the national economy.

If, to choose an extreme example, electric vehicles were to predominate some decades hence, vast amounts of petroleum now used to make gasoline would have to be converted into other products or be left unrefined or underground. Service stations would have to be converted to handle the new vehicles and their particular requirements. Electrical distribution networks would have to be extended and expanded in heavily populated areas to permit the distribution and use of recharging outlets. Batteries or fuel cells (or other energy conversion devices) would have to be designed to minimize the use and/or facilitate the recovery of scarce or precious materials.

211. Market Structure and Low-Pollutant Propulsion Systems

The possibility of electric or steam-powered automobiles representing a viable alternative to the internal combustion engine must be considered against the background of the market structure of the automobile industry. For several decades, three to five companies have dominated the domestic production of automobiles. The barriers to entry in the automobile industry are formidable. For example, economies of scale are such that to produce at near minimum cost, a company must turn out 250,000 or more units of the same model per year. The capital investment required for production of this magnitude is from $75 to $125 million. Also, a strong and expensive dealer system is required to market and service automobiles. Investment per dealership runs upward of $125,000 with $350,000 a minimum figure for a large dealership. Perhaps 200 such dealerships are required for minimum national coverage; the automobile manufacturer has the options of making this investment directly, or inducing dealers with franchises to make the investment against possible returns from sale of an untried product. Exclusive dealing arrangements prohibit most existing automobile dealerships from taking on competing product lines without permission from their parent franchisor. In addition, yearly model changes have been an important part of marketing strategy for American automobile manufacturers. New and smaller firms are at a distinct cost disadvantage in this area since the substantial retooling costs involved in such changes must be spread over the number of units produced during the model run.

Any substantial innovation in the automobile industry would require a serious reorientation in industry production, materials usage, and relationships with subcontractors and supporting industries. A steam-powered vehicle would use the same production and service facilities as do internal combustion vehicles, but would make obsolete existing transmission, ignition, and cooling systems and would require a completely new oil refining process to meet the fuel requirements of steam engines. However, an electric-powered vehicle would also make obsolete engine, power train, cooling system, and existing gasoline fuel supply facilities. It is doubtful that the automobile industry, as presently structured, would pursue either of these innovations in the absence of a strong competitive threat.[22]

Steam propulsion systems do not appear to have the potential for reducing the barriers to entry into the automobile industry. In all relevant aspects of production and marketing, a steam propulsion system would be close enough to existing internal combustion systems to utilize current facilities. A steam-propulsion innovator external to the existing automobile industry would require a fairly high rate of production for minimum cost. The possibilities of subcontracting for components is limited. If the innovator overcame the capital and production barriers and marketed an attractive product, he would likely face short-run competition from the existing industry which could adapt its production and service facilities to steampower if forced to by competition. It is doubtful that the capital investment required would be forthcoming when the potential payoff is so doubtful.[23]

On the other hand, the electric automobile does seem to have the potential for reducing barriers to entry into the automobile industry. Small economies of scale, and the ability to subcontract for major components such as motors, batteries, and control systems would greatly reduce the required amount of capital to produce electric cars. Low maintenance requirements and the estimated 100 mile range of electric vehicles would permit a simpler dealer network which could initially be limited to a few major urban centers.

The likelihood of a new product image for the electric automobile suggests that the importance of dynamic obsolescence as a marketing concept will be greatly reduced, at least initially. Since the barriers to entry are sharply reduced, a small innovator has an opportunity to survive all but the most predatory behavior on the part of existing manufacturers. Thus, while steam-propelled vehicles probably constitute less of a threat to existing market structure than do electric vehicles, entry barrier considerations suggest that an electric automobile innovation is the more likely of the two in the short-run.[24]

A third low-pollutant propulsion system, the gas turbine, should also be mentioned. The gas turbine has been a favorite experimental toy of various manufacturers, notably the Chrysler Corporation. While a gas turbine does not burn externally in the sense that a steam engine does, it does burn continuously, and therefore is cleaner than an internal combustion engine. Until recently, it was felt that heat and nitrous oxide emission problems with small turbines would make them ultimately impractical for passenger car adaptation. General Motors and Ford have concentrated on larger engines for use in buses and trucks, some of which are currently operating and are close to being competitive with diesel engines on a dollar-per-horsepower basis. The passenger car turbine is a logical next step. While the turbine shares or exceeds the high barriers to entry of the steam car in the automobile industry, it is the most likely of the low-pollutant propulsion systems to be introduced by existing automobile manufacturers. However, a great deal of work to reduce costs and operating problems will be necessary.

There is some chance that the internal combustion engine will become virtually pollution-free. Edward N. Cole, President of General Motors Corporation, has predicted that by 1974 GM would have available devices capable of reducing present air pollutants such as unburned hydrocarbons, carbon monoxide, and oxides of nitrogen to near zero. He said that this would be done with catalytic converters to convert nearly all hydrocarbons and carbon monoxide to water and carbon dioxide, and cutting sharply the oxides of nitrogen emissions. He emphasized that this would only be possible with unleaded and moderately high octane gasoline which the petroleum industry is beginning to develop.

212. Federal Standard Setting for Automotive Emissions

The federal emission standards which we have noted were initially set for motor vehicles in terms of ppm concentrations of the various pollutants found in the exhaust of vehicles. Such a measurement does not take into account the total volume of pollutants and might equate small engines with larger ones which consume far more fuel and expel more total pollution. The most recent federal standards are stated in terms of grams per mile, which accounts for differences in vehicle size and fuel consumption.

Testing is done on prototype cars provided by manufacturers, and the cars are averaged so that some may exceed the standards but be offset by others which are within them. This procedure has been criticized as has the use of production prototypes; critics maintain that the cars provided for testing are highly-tuned and do not approximate production-line models in their emissions characteristics. Also, once the new car has been driven for a short time its emissions tend to increase as the car goes "out of tune."

The federal government concerned itself first with crankcase hydrocarbon emissions—the PCV valve reduced these by 100 percent.

The next stage was to reduce the permissible emission of hydro-carbons and carbon monoxide from the exhaust. 1971 models were the first to control evaporative emissions of hydrocarbons from the carburetor and gas tank. In 1973, controls will be extended to nitrous oxides; in 1975, to particulate emissions.

The new standard for particulates is designed expressly to exclude leaded gasoline, which is the principal source of particulates in the exhaust. It is considered impossible to reduce particulate content of exhaust sufficiently to meet the 1975 standard, using leaded fuels. However, some petroleum companies have produced reduced-lead content fuels which might make the 1975 standard. The publicly stated reason for the exclusion of lead is to permit use of catalytic devices which may be effective in reducing gaseous emissions, but would be fouled by leaded fuels. The standard for particulate emission was set at 0.1 gram per mile, and the automobile industry was given five years to develop the hardware to meet this theoretical standard.

Table 2-2 shows the evolution in emissions standards through 1975. It is predicted that standards for 1980 will approximately halve the 1975 permitted emissions.

TABLE 2-2

| | | (grams per vehicle mile) | | | | |
	Uncontrolled	1968	1970	1971	1973	1975
Exhaust:						
Hydrocarbons	12.2	2.4	2.2	2.2	2.2	.5
Carbon Monoxide	79.0	35.1	23.0	23.0	23.0	11.0
Nitrous Oxides	6.0	6.0	6.0	6.0	3.0	.9
Particulates	.3	.3	.3	.3	.3	.1
Crankcase Hydrocarbons	3.7	0	0	0	0	0
Evaporative Hydrocarbons	2.8	2.8	2.8	.5	.5	.5
Totals:						
Hydrocarbons	18.7	6.2	5.0	2.7	2.7	1.0
Carbon Monoxide	79.0	35.1	23.0	23.0	23.0	11.0
Nitrous Oxides	6.0	6.0	6.0	6.0	3.0	.9
Particulates	.3	.3	.3	.3	.3	.1

The 1971 standards reverse the steady upward trend in total emissions, but only for a short period as the number of vehicles and their use are increasing rapidly. By 1980 increased total mileage will raise total emissions above present levels, assuming that the 1980 standards are half those of 1975.

The federal emission standards are also a point of friction between the United States and Europe and Japan, with Europeans and Japanese fearing that the legislation will be used as a nontariff barrier to reduce their share in the American automobile market. The stakes are high; Volkswagen sells half of its output in the United States, while companies like Volvo, British Leyland, Fiat, and Renault have smaller but significant shares of the export market. In part the problem arises because the 1975 standards are thought by the Europeans and Japanese to be way below anything that could possibly be injurious to health—with an official of British Leyland going so far as characterizing the American anti-pollution drive as "hysteria." [25]

European manufacturers have done little work in gas turbines, with the bulk of their research efforts going into electric or battery-operated cars. This technology is better suited for Europe, where distances covered by a car are much shorter than in the United States. With Europeans concentrating on electricity, and the possibility existing that U.S. manufacturers will proceed with gas turbines or some variation of the steam engine, there is a chance that European and American cars might have completely different types of propulsion systems in the future.

REFERENCES

[1] A simple counting of pollutees is misleading; there is some evidence that a relative absence of air pollution is a superior economic good—one which varies directly with real income. A study by the U.S. Public Health Service in Clarkston, Washington, a city with a pollution-producing kraft pulp mill, found that 44 percent of the local managers, proprietors, and professional people (who one would expect to have higher incomes and wealth) were "aware" of an air pollution problem and "concerned" about its effect on their health and property values. Only 32 percent of the clerical and skilled laborers, and 19 percent of the semi-skilled and unskilled workers expressed a similar awareness and concern. U.S. Public Health Service, *Community Perception of Air Quality: An Opinion Survey in Clarkston, Washington* (Washington, D.C.: U.S. Public Health Service, Publication 999-AP 10, 1965), pp. 45-55.

[2] Senate Committee on Public Works, *A Study of Pollution—Air*, 88th Congress, 1st Session (1963), vii. at 2.

[3]In talking about pollutant concentrations of parts per million (ppm), the reader should appreciate that serious health effects arise from extremely small quantities of pollutant. One part per million is roughly equivalent to an ounce of vermouth in 7,550 gallons of gin.

[4]Treatment of localized problems is discussed in Lester Goldner, "Air Pollution Control in the Metropolitan Boston Area: A Case Study in Public-Policy Formation," in Harold Wolozin, ed., *The Economics of Air Pollution* (New York: W. W. Norton & Company, Inc., 1966), pp. 127-161.

[5]The assumption of ambient air is itself part of an uncertainty. Knowledge of small-scale atmospheric convection and diffusion, and of the governing processes, is essential in relating air purity standards to the biological and physical effects of pollutants. Where pollutants are rapidly dispersed, higher emissions are acceptable. Where air is stagnant or atmospheric inversions are common so that pollutants accumulate, the most stringent standards are necessary.

[6]In general see J. R. Goldsmith, "Air Pollution," in A. Stern, ed., *Air Pollution and Its Effects* (New York: Academic Press, 1968), p. 547.

[7]There is great uncertainty on the quantitative effects of pollution on animals, plants, and materials, with many of the estimates only quasi-informed guesses. Thus, the most quoted figure for annual air pollution damage in the U.S. is $11 billion, which is derived from an estimate of costs in Pittsburgh in 1913. Economists calculated that smoke damage in Pittsburgh in that year, for cleaning, maintaining and lighting homes, businesses, and public buildings, amounted to $20 per capita per year. This figure was adjusted to 1959 prices and the updated estimate multiplied by the 1958 U.S. population to arrive at the figure of $11 billion. The President's Council on Environmental Quality estimated in 1971 that air pollution costs the United States $16 billion a year, made up of $6 billion in human mortality and morbidity, $4.9 billion in damage to crops, plants, trees and material, and $5.1 billion in lowered property values.

[8]*Public Health* (Johannesburg) No. 63 (1963), pp. 30.

[9]H. Wolozin and E. Landau, "Crop Damage from Sulphur Dioxide," *Journal of Farm Economics,*No. 48 (1966), pp. 394.

[10]Remarks of Dr. Haagen-Smit before the American Meteorological Society, Washington, D.C., January, 1968.

[11]Ronald G. Ridker completed in 1966 a detailed study of the economic costs of air pollution under the sponsorship of the Division of Air Pollution of the U.S. Public Health Service. Ridker considered the economic costs of diseases associated with air pollution; the cost of soiling

and materials damage; the cost of declining property values in polluted areas; and psychic costs and attitudes associated with a particular pollution episode in Syracuse, New York. His work is worthy of attention both as a first estimate of the value of benefits to be gained from expenditures on abatement, and for his discussion of strategies for measuring the costs of pollution. Reference: Ronald G. Ridker, *Economic Costs of Air Pollution: Studies in Measurement* (New York: Praeger Publishers, Inc., 1967).

[12]Harold Wolozin, "The Economics of Air Pollution: Central Problems," *Law and Contemporary Problems,* No. 33, pp. 229-233. An interesting illustration of curvilinear total damage and total cost of control functions with figures to illustrate their derivation is given in Azriel Teller, "Air Pollution Abatement: Economic Rationality and Reality," *Daedalus* (Fall, 1967), pp. 1085-1088.

[13]Cost and abatement curves may both be kinked, which means that the derived marginal curves would be discontinuous, introducing more uncertainty into the calculation of optimal levels of expenditure on air pollution. Each of these possibilities justifies increased research on determining the actual position and shape of cost and damage functions. Collection of data would be done separately for each specific air shed, and for specific pollutants (or groups of pollutants if they can be acted on together). Each community has its own characteristics and faces different meteorological, topological, and economic conditions. The appropriate tradeoffs will thus vary with each geographic area and pollutant being studied, which suggests that national estimates of pollution and control costs would not be useful for standard setting except as a first approximation, even if they could be made in marginal terms.

[14]The argument is developed in Azriel Teller, "Air Pollution Abatement: Economic Rationality and Reality," *op cit.,* pp. 1087-1088.

[15]Lester B. Lave and Eugene P. Seskin, "Air Pollution and Human Health," *Science,* Vol. 169 (August 21, 1970), pp. 723-733.

[16]"The Determinants of Residential Property Values With Special Reference to Air Pollution," *The Review of Economics and Statistics,* Vol. 49 (1967), pp. 246-257.

[17]The statistical problems faced were also important. In brief, if a model has been properly specified, then least square estimates will be unbiased. If, however, a variable that *a priori* judgment suggests should be included in the analysis is omitted, the regression coefficients for the remaining variables with which it is correlated will be biased. Biased estimates will also occur if a variable that *a priori* judgment suggests should be excluded is for some reason included in the regression analysis. The extent of such biases due to incorrect specification of the

model depends upon the degree of correlation between the variable in-correctly excluded or included, and the variables whose coefficients are critical to the analysis. There are no set methods for detecting and treating this problem; the Ridker and Henning analysis involved stepwise regressions to observe the effect on regression coefficients when new variables were included, and correlations of each independent variable against all others to observe the magnitudes of their multiple and partial correlation coefficients.

[18]An earlier study carried out by Professor Crocker and Anderson in St. Louis, Washington, and Kansas City, found that a 5 to 15 percent decrease in air quality correlated with a $300 to $700 decrease in property values.

[19]Quoted in Wolozin, "The Economics of Air Pollution: Central Problems," op. cit., p. 236.

[20]The categories can be broken down further. See Azriel Teller, *Air Pollution Abatement: An Economic Study Into The Cost of Control* (Ann Arbor, Michigan: University Microfilms, 1968); and Teller, "Air Pollution Abatement: Economic Rationality and Reality," op. cit.

[21]Teller reports that using one set of criteria over a one-year period, twelve stagnation cases occurred of which ten were forecast. Another eight were forecast but not verified. Source: Teller, "Air Pollution Abatement," op. cit., pp. 1092-1095.

[22]Ford Motor Company is engaged in a joint venture with Thermo Electron Corporation of Waltham, Massachusetts in designing an organic working fluid Rankine-cycle steam engine for automotive application. The target date for a go, no-go decision is 1975. See *Report by Thermo Electron to Division of Motor Vehicle Research and Development of the National Air Pollution Control Administration* (June, 1970).

[23]William P. Lear, who has spent about $12.5 million on steam-powered experiments, admits the steam engine is five times as complicated, burns 50 percent more fuel, is twice as heavy and twice as expensive as a gasoline engine of similar power output. The automotive steam engine has five different systems: boiler, feedwater pump, expander, condenser, and controls. There are still technological problems in each system; the prime problem exists with the lack of an efficient and compact condenser.

The steam engine does promise cleaner air and fewer automotive emissions. According to General Motors Corporation and based on results from its two experimental steam cars in May, 1969, the steam car emits 0.62 grams per mile of hydrocarbons while the standard 1970 V-8 powered car emits 2.2 grams per mile. Carbon monoxide emissions from a steam engine are 2.8 grams per mile against 23 grams for the gasoline-powered V-8. Oxides of nitrogen emitted from the steam engine are about 1 gram per mile, versus about 4 grams per mile for the gasoline engine. While distinctly lower, these steam car emissions would not meet proposed 1975 emission standards for oxides of nitrogen, and would not meet proposed 1980 standards for emissions of hydrocarbons.

[24]Robert Ayres of Resources for the Future, notes that if electricity were generated totally by fossil fuels, emission of oxides of nitrogen from an all-electric car stock would exceed those from a steam-powered fleet, but would be only one-quarter those from an internal combustion engine fleet. Sulphur dioxide would present a greater emission problem also. If nuclear fuels were used, the problems of radioactivity and thermal pollution would be aggravated but not proportionately because of the use of off-peak power for recharging.

[25]An exception is Volvo, which has agreed to adopt the American standards timetable to its own cars in Sweden.

3

Water

Pollution

Rub a dub-dub
Three men in a tub
And who do you think they be?
The skipper, the shipper
The nautical dripper,
Who spill oil on Flipper,
And foul up the sea.

300. The Nature of Water Pollution

Water pollution is generally more localized than air pollution, and sources of water pollution are generally easier to identify and control than sources of air pollution. The problem is still critical, however, since humans require water as well as air for survival.

A complete description of the physical, chemical, and biological aspects of water pollution would require an entire volume. One common classification system of water pollution differentiates between physical wastes, which may be inorganic, organic, radioactive, etc., and biological substances, such as bacteria and viruses. Another classification which is more useful for our purposes, distinguishes between nondegradable and degradable wastes based on their behavior in receiving waters. Nondegradable wastes are those which are diluted but are not appreciably reduced in weight in the receiving waters. Degradable wastes are reduced in weight by the biological, physical and chemical processes which occur in the receiving waters.[1]

Nondegradable Wastes. The combination of industrial waste, agricultural irrigation, and mine discharges presents the major nonnatural source of chlorides and metallic salts of local and regional waters. Nondegradable wastes are composed mainly of inorganic chemicals such as chlorides, synthetic organic chemicals, and inorganic suspended solids. A principal source of these wastes is industrial discharges which frequently contain inorganic or metallic salts, synthetic organic chemicals, and similar materials. Mining discharges may contain residues of copper, zinc, uranium, and other compounds. Acid drainage from mines is an acute problem in a number of coal producing areas. Agricultural irrigation also contributes nondegradable wastes, as the return flow from agricultural irrigation is generally much higher in dissolved salts (and chemicals from fertilizers) than was the original irrigation water.

There are several natural sources of chlorides and dissolved solids. Natural formations such as salt deposits result in high chloride concentrations in nearby groundwater and rivers. An increasingly important source of natural chlorides is seawater intrusion into groundwater near coastal areas following excess pumping from wells which results in a lowering of groundwater levels.

Nondegradable suspended solids consist primarily of sediment from natural and accelerated erosion of land surfaces and stream channels, and of colloidal clay particles from domestic and industrial wastes. In particular, storm runoff from agricultural land carries silt, clay, and fertilizers into water courses. Most of the suspended sediment settles out, but colloidal-size material does not. Both suspended sediment and colloidal matter cause turbidity in surface water, making the water less attractive, inhibiting the growth of oxygen-producing algae, and possibly damaging marine life.

There are a number of problems involved in identifying the significance of nondegradable wastes. Each type of receiving water has different characteristics with the result that the same waste has different impacts on water quality. The concentrations of pollutant involved, especially concerning chemical substances, are often on the order of a few parts per billion; the extent to which continued low-level exposures to such concentrations are harmful to plant and animal life, and the extent to which there are synergistic reactions still is not well understood.

Degradable Wastes. The most damaging source of degradable waste is industrial discharges; the most common source is probably domestic sewage. Organic waste, which is highly unstable, can be converted to stable inorganic material such as bicarbonates, nitrates, sulphates, and phosphates by bacteria and other organisms in bodies of water. If the receiving waters are not overloaded with wastes, the process (usually referred to as self-purification) proceeds aerobically through the action of bacteria using free oxygen. If the receiving waters become overloaded with degradable wastes the process proceeds anaerobically through the action of bacteria not requiring free oxygen. The anaerobic process produces hydrogen sulfide and other unpleasant gases. Both processes are duplicated in conventional waste treatment plants, which merely accelerate the reactions that take place in natural waters.

Bacteria are always present in natural waters, and most types are harmless to man. Some bacteria arise from waste discharges of warm-blooded animals. The measure of such waste content, called the coliform count, is used as a proxy for the real bacterial concern —those bacteria capable of causing typhoid, dysentery, hepatitis, and cholera. Most bacteria are considered degradable, since they usually die quite quickly after leaving the body.

Thermal waste is usually classified as degradable because heat is readily dissipated in receiving waters, either by evaporation through surface water or conduction in groundwater. The principal sources of thermal pollution are the generation of electrical energy (including nuclear energy), and cooling operations in the petroleum refining, iron and steel industries, and other industries. The thermal barrier caused by a rise in temperature of more than 4°F. in receiving waters may have the effect of sterilizing or killing fish and other marine life.

The quality of a waste discharge can be measured through biological oxygen demand (BOD), chemical oxygen demand (COD), alkalinity or acidity, electrical conductivity, or turbidity. The most common measure of organic waste load is BOD, which indicates the quantity of oxygen used in the decomposition of the waste. While the level of dissolved oxygen (DO) is certainly not the only parameter of water quality,[2] it is common in empirical studies to use DO levels as indices of threshold conditions necessary for various water activities. For example, we may postulate that at least 3 milligrams per liter (mg/l) of oxygen are necessary to eliminate offensive odors and therefore to allow boating, 4 mg/l for sport fishing, and 5 mg/l for swimming. Thus, for pragmatic reasons, DO levels are often used as a first estimate of the level of water quality.

The amount of oxygen and its rate of use are functions of the type and quantity of waste, and the chemical characteristics of the receiving waters. For example, toxic materials may reduce the rate of decomposition by inhibiting bacterial action. At higher water temperatures the oxygen saturation of water is relatively low, bacterial action is increased, and biochemical oxygen demand increases as wastes are degraded more rapidly. If the imbalance between available oxygen and oxygen demand becomes too great, decomposition may become anaerobic. On the other hand, certain factors restore dissolved oxygen to the water. This reaeration process depends on such factors as velocity of stream flow, area of air-water interface, and photosynthesis.

The effects of discharged wastes are interrelated in many complicated ways. For example, water turbidity affects the photosynthetic production of algae, which requires sunlight. Thus, waterways with high turbidity usually do not have the odor and water taste problems that accompany prolific algae growth. When efforts are made to reduce turbidity, and increase the clarity of the water, algae production and resulting odor and taste problems may increase dramatically.

301. The Problem of the Oceans

While most of this chapter is devoted to the economics of the comparatively simple problem of fresh water pollution, the more difficult and potentially much more serious problem of pollution of the oceans must be mentioned at least in passing. The famed oceanographer and undersea explorer, Captain Jacques Cousteau, has estimated that the damage done to the oceans in the past 20 years is somewhere between 30 percent and 50 percent of that which would be required for most life in the oceans of the world to die under the stresses of pollution, just as Lake Erie has died. He claims that the amount of life in the oceans is decreasing rapidly, with the decrease first noticeable in 1968. In 1970 the world catch of fish dropped for the first time in two decades.[3]

We have given so little thought and care to the oceans because people have assumed that their immensity protected them; man could do nothing to disturb so gigantic a force. While scientists still feel that the oceans can absorb a good deal of waste without irreparable damage to ecosystems or to humans, it is now recognized that we don't have to pollute all 140 million square miles of ocean before we suffer unacceptable consequences—we only have to pollute a good part of the 14 million square miles closest to shore.

The sea as we know, is shaped like a deep bowl. However, waste that we throw into the sea does not spread out evenly to be diluted, nor does it necessarily come to rest in the ocean's deepest parts. Rather, most pollution remains on the continental shelf, which occupies only about 10 percent of the surface of the sea, but where 90 percent of the fish which are consumed are spawned, raised, and caught. The shelf extends out from land for anywhere from two miles to hundreds of miles, and in general follows the contours of the continents themselves.

It is from rivers that most pollutants reach the continental shelf, although harborside industries add their share of effluents, heated water comes from power plants, ships at sea contribute sewage and garbage and trash, and both ships and tankers contribute oil and sludge. It is estimated that a million tons of oil are spilled accidentally into the world's oceans each year, and more is added from offshore drilling and pumping rigs, from onshore accidents, and from the deliberate dumping of oil residues at sea by oil transports.

Most pollution that reaches the deepest parts of the ocean probably comes via wind and rain rather than from polluted rivers. The atmosphere deposits in the oceans an estimated 200,000 tons of lead and a million tons of oil from engine exhausts each year, and as much as 5,000 tons of mercury, which comes primarily from fuel consumption but is also used in the papermaking process and released into the atmosphere when the paper is burned. Probably half the pesticides in the sea have come from the air where they are carried long distances by high altitude winds. Cousteau estimates that 25 percent of all the DDT compounds so far produced have already been absorbed by the sea.

When people impose sudden loads of chemical compounds on an ecosystem, the system may be drastically altered. For example, human sewage will decompose in the ocean if given enough time, because salt is lethal to the bacteria in these wastes. But when receiving waters become overloaded with sewage, some of the bacteria survive long enough to be taken up by shellfish, which feed by straining water through their systems. Once the bacteria are inside the shellfish they can thrive, protected from the salt. Infectious hepatitis germs collect there in numbers sufficient to make the shellfish a hazard for man to eat. Shellfish have been found to concentrate viruses such as polio up to 60 times the proportion of viruses in the surrounding water.

Even where the amount of pollutant in the ocean is minimal in terms of the volume of water, three things tend to increase the level of pollutants reaching the food chain. The first is the capacity of marine organisms to store pollutants, which are passed along the food chain. The second is the location of so much pollution on the continental shelf. The third is the longevity of many pollutants, for example DDT, which has a half-life of about 15 years.

There may also be dramatic synergistic (or multiplicative) effects of these wastes on the environment. Nickel is a relatively nontoxic metal, but put into water with copper effluent it multiplies the toxicity of the copper by a factor of 10. If you add iron and zinc and sewage and heated water from thermal plants there is a synergistic mix which reacts to itself as well as to the chemistry of the sea, with ultimate effects that can only be guessed at.

302. Fresh Water Uses

The aesthetic enjoyment of bodies of fresh water (and of that portion of the oceans immediately adjacent to land) is primarily a matter of visual perception. At a minimum this means that the water must be free from obnoxious floating or suspended substances, particularly domestic sewage and industrial waste such as oil.

For recreational activities which require water contact, the water must not only be aesthetically pleasing but must contain no substances which are toxic upon ingestion or irritating to the skin or eyes. Also, the water must be relatively free of pathogenic organisms. Most efforts to measure water quality for recreation purposes have centered on this last condition, and a wide range of standards have been invoked, ranging from 50 to 3000 bacteria per 100 ml. Such standards do not appear to be based on epidemiological evidence of a direct relationship between contact with contaminated water and bacterial infections. In one study, McKee and Wolf concluded that the risk to health from bathing in sewage-polluted sea water was negligible. If any risk exists, it is probably associated with chance contact with solid lumps of infected fecal matter.[4] A greater possibility of infection exists in fresh water than in saline water, but the level of probability involved is almost certainly less than has been commonly assumed. For the most part, nondegradable wastes have little impact on the aesthetic enjoyment or recreational use of water unless the substances are toxic, or suspended sediment exists in concentrations high enough to impart an unattractive color to the water.

On the other hand, the value of water as a habitat for aquatic life is reduced or destroyed by some waste discharges which do not necessarily render the water aesthetically displeasing to human beings. The effects of these discharges on fish and other aquatic life are difficult to predict because they vary with the physical and chemical composition of the water. Higher temperatures, excessive acidity or alkalinity, and a low concentration of dissolved oxygen can increase the sensitivity of fish to toxic substances or can themselves result in fish kills. Conversely, certain combinations of salts can neutralize each other whereas acting independently they would be harmful.

Perhaps the most important factor in determining the tolerance of aquatic life to a pollutant is the time-concentration relationship. While a single short-term exposure to a high concentration of pollutant may show no damaging effects, repeated exposures to the same concentration or continuous exposure to a much lower concentration may result in death. On the other hand, with gradual exposure many organisms can develop tolerance to concentrations that would otherwise be toxic.[5]

The amount and character of treatment which is necessary before water can be used for domestic purposes is related to the quality of the water intake. Water which contains organic substances from domestic sewage must be treated with large amounts of chlorine or other disinfectants to kill the bacteria. If the water is corrosive, saline, hard, or contains quantities of substances like iron or manganese, further special treatment may be needed. There is little empirical evidence on which to base a limiting standard for drinking water with respect to total dissolved solids. The standard of 500 milligrams per litre (500 parts per million) is often used, but with no apparent epidemiological basis.

The effect of water quality on irrigation use cannot be defined in terms of a single water quality variable.[6] The extent to which crop yields are reduced by water quality deterioration is a function of the type of crop, type of soil, extent of drainage, the type of salts already in the soil, and other factors. Even changes in the temperature of applied water may improve or reduce crop yields.

The range of water quality used in industrial operations is very wide, depending in part on whether the water is used for processing, as boiler feedwater, for cooling, or for sanitary purposes. Feedwater for high temperature boilers requires the highest quality standards of any industrial use. Next to boiler feedwater, the quality standards for process water which comes into contact with foodstuff is the most demanding. At the other extreme, cooling water can be almost any level of quality with respect to total dissolved solids and even dissolved oxygen levels. With proper treatment it is quite possible to use sea water for cooling purposes.

303. Prediction of Dissolved Oxygen Levels

The rate of biochemical oxygen demand combined with the rate at which oxygen is restored determines the level of dissolved oxygen in a waterway. In flowing water the combined effect of a degradable waste discharge and reaeration in the stream produces a decrease and then an increase in DO as the waste moves downstream. Factors that reduce the rate of BOD lengthen and decrease this "oxygen sag" of DO in the water, while factors that accelerate BOD have the opposite effect. The oxygen sag is also affected by the rate of reaeration, which itself depends on water characteristics, photosynthetic oxygen production, and many other factors.

Despite these complexities, engineers have been able to develop models which interrelate the many variables involved and predict (given the nature and spacing of waste loads), the levels of dissolved oxygen, the temperature, and other water quality characteristics for different zones of a body of water. Such models provide a basis for economic optimization studies of water quality management systems, and determine, for example, the proper capacity and design for a waste treatment plant. Basic equations describing DO behavior can be elaborated to handle complex situations, including multiple points of waste discharge, different kinds of waste, and differing oxygen saturation along the length of the stream.[7]

There are a number of complexities which can complicate the calculation of DO levels. Tracing the decomposition of organic waste in an estuary is made difficult by tidal actions, the large air-water interfaces, and the complex hydraulic characteristics of the body of water. Lakes present problems because their more stationary water is more susceptible to nutrient buildup (eutrophication), a process which is accelerated by organic wastes.

Nutrient enrichment tends to be accompanied by low DO levels, but the complex circulation patterns and temperature inversions combine to make the exact effect of organic waste discharges on water quality difficult to predict.

A final complication is that BOD proceeds in two stages. When an organic waste is discharged into a stream where DO levels are high, there is an immediate decrease in DO level as organic wastes are degraded by bacterial action. Thereafter, DO levels tend to recover. After five to seven days, a second stage BOD occurs as the nitrogen in the organic wastes is converted first to nitrite and then to nitrate by aeorbic nitrifying bacteria. The second stage is more diffuse and easier to predict than the first.

Lakes, reservoirs, and estuaries, like flowing streams, are subject to deposits of sludge banks, which if suddenly dispersed (for example through dredging) produce a "shock load" of oxygen demand. Stratification, the formation in essentially stationary bodies of water of thermal layers which prevent vertical mixing of water, complicates the analysis of DO levels in lakes and reservoirs. Plant nutrients take on special significance here because they tend to accumulate over time in relatively stationary bodies of water and contribute to the depletion of oxygen in the lower levels. In a tidal estuary, areas of water with low DO levels may be moved back and forth within the estuary for long periods of time rather than being dispersed into the ocean or undergoing vertical mixing with higher DO areas of water.

ECONOMIC APPROACHES TO WATER POLLUTION ABATEMENT

Given the complexities involved in calculating water quality standards and water pollution effects, it is helpful when taking an economic approach to water pollution optimization to attack the complex issue by first assuming away some of the complexities, and then solving the simplified problem that remains. The value of this exercise is not in the resulting answer, which is at best a first approximation, but in isolating the assumptions (and thus the knowledge required) to formulate a more realistic problem. Water pollution is more amenable than most other environmental problems to such an approach because so many of the variables involved are—at least potentially—capable of being quantified.

304. Economic Approaches to Water Pollution Assuming Complete Knowledge

Consider the problem faced by the citizens of the town of North Lake Tahoe, located on Lake Tahoe in Nevada.[8] The waters of Lake Tahoe were until a few years ago remarkably pure, but they have been increasingly polluted because the inflow of sewage effluent from the town slightly exceeds the capacity of the lake to cleanse itself. So far only the one pollutant (sewage) is involved, and it exists in approximately equal proportions from each citizen of the town.

The citizens of the town have several options or alternatives open to them in preserving the lake's water for drinking purposes. Each family can add chlorine pills to its drinking water at a cost of $6 per person per year (or $3 per half year, or $4.50 for 9 months). Or, engineering studies indicate that a water treatment plant can be built to remove all noxious wastes from the drinking water at a cost of $5 per citizen per year. One that will remove 75 percent of the wastes can be built for $3.50 per citizen per year, or one that will remove half the wastes for $2 per citizen per year. A further study indicates that within ten years Lake Tahoe will be unfit even for swimming unless a sewage treatment plant is also built, and this will cost each citizen $3.00 per year. The sewage treatment plant will solve only the swimming problem; the drinking water problem is solved only through the construction of the water treatment plant, or by the addition of chlorine pills to drinking water.

A final medical study indicates that if nothing is done, water pollution will result in one day's mild sickness per citizen per year. If 50 percent of the wastes are removed, sickness falls to three days per ten years (because the illness caused by sewage goes up faster than does concentration of pollutant). Similarly a plant that is 75 percent effective cuts sickness rates from water pollution to one day per citizen in ten years.

A quick survey of a sample of Lake Tahoe citizens indicates that each citizen is prepared to pay $2.50 per year for the privilege of swimming in the lake. A second survey shows that the average citizen will pay $10 to avoid a day's sickness. Thus, a treatment plant that is 100 percent effective is worth $10 a year to each citizen.

It is now possible to put together a simple matrix (see Table 3-1), in which we specify the alternatives open to the citizens of the

TABLE 3-1

Cost-Benefit Matrix For Water Pollution Abatement of Lake Tahoe

	Add Chlorine to Drinking Water				Build Water-Treatment Plant				Build Sewage Plant	Build Water-Treatment Plant and Sewage Plant				Do Nothing At All
1. Policy	(% of water treated)				(% of water treated)					(% of water treated)				
	100	75	50	0	100	75	50	0		100	75	50	0	m
	a	b	c	d	e	f	g	h		i	j	k	l	
2. Damage Avoided (per citizen)	$10.00	$9.00 (health)	$7.00	$0	$10.00	$9.00 (health)	$7.00	$0	$2.50 (swimming)	$12.50	$11.50	$9.50 (health and swimming)	$2.50	$0
3. Cost of Avoiding Damage (per citizen)	6.00	4.50	3.00	0	5.00	3.50	2.00	0	3.00	8.00	6.50	5.00	3.00	0
4. Net Benefit (#2 - #3)	4.00	4.50	4.00	0	5.00	5.50	5.00	0	-$.50	4.50	5.00	4.50	-$.50	0
5. Cost of Damage Not Avoided (per citizen)	2.50 (health)	3.50	5.50 (health and swimming)	12.50	2.50 (health)	3.50	5.50 (health and swimming)	12.50	$10.00 (health)	0	1.00	3.00 (health)	10.00	12.50
6. Total Costs Incurred (#3 + #5)	8.50	8.00	8.50	12.50	7.50	7.00	7.50	12.50	13.00	8.00	7.50	8.00	13.00	12.50

town. The alternatives are indicated horizontally at the top of the matrix, and calculations are made vertically. Citizens can make a decision based either on maximizing net benefit per citizen (No. 4), which is damage avoided less the cost of avoiding it, or by minimizing the sum of damage-avoidance costs plus value of damage not avoided (No. 6). The two solutions will always prove to be equivalent. The citizens decide to build a water-treatment plant to remove 75 percent of the sewage for $3.50 per year per citizen. They decide also not to build a sewage plant, and not to undertake any addition of chlorine tablets to drinking water.

On checking the calculations it is obvious that the answer obtained depends completely on the numbers assumed, and on their accuracy. If the cost of removing all the sewage from drinking water were actually $4.40 per citizen per year instead of $5.00, the net benefit from this strategy would be $5.60 instead of $5.00, the total cost incurred would be $6.90 instead of $7.50, and 100 percent abatement rather than 75 percent would be adopted. A mis-estimate from $5.00 to $4.40 could arise through engineering error, or the cost of building a plant might decline by the requisite 12 percent as water treatment technology improved. Thus, the choice of preferred strategy is highly sensitive to the estimation of the costs of water treatment. Similarly, a small increase (from $2.50 to $3.00 or more) in the amount that a citizen is prepared to pay for the privilege of swimming in the lake would mean that a sewage treatment plant would become part of the optimal solution.

Reaching a solution in the matrix was possible only because some very simplistic assumptions were made. It was assumed that the characteristics of the "average" citizen of North Lake Tahoe were known, i.e., the quantity of pollutant he contributed, the value he placed on a day's illness, and the value he placed on recreational swimming. We also assumed that the damages avoided by alternative solutions were known, and were measurable in dollars. We ignored the technical problem of interrelationships among pollutants by assuming that sewage was the only pollutant. Finally, we considered only the citizens of North Lake Tahoe, and ignored how sewage pollution affected residents on the south shore of the lake, and how the quantity of pollution originating on the south shore might vary depending on what was done by the citizens of North Lake Tahoe. Each of these assumptions is important; to assume away any one distorts the entire analysis.[9]

Some of this information is lacking because it is not available (although obtainable), and some because it is not obtainable given present measurement techniques. The technical problem of interrelationships among pollutants is certainly solvable, although complicated; ecologists claim that accurate estimates of the interrelationships among pollutants, and good predictions of the damage avoided by removing any combination of pollutants, can be made. As indicated earlier, the technical problem of measuring the value of avoiding a day's sickness is complex; people simply do not *know* what they might be willing to pay to avoid the imprecisely stated effects of pollution. If they did know, they might overstate their answer in the hope that someone else, "the government," would be more willing to correct the situation. If a respondent felt he would be required to contribute funds for pollution abatement equal to the damage he had suffered he might avoid the expense by understating his own damage in the hope that others would contribute enough to implement abatement anyway.

Nor would a simple voting system invariably work to insure an economic amount of pollution abatement. Thirty of the residents of North Lake Tahoe might incur health and swimming damage of $12.50 each, and twenty others damages of $17.50 each. A vote on an abatement proposal costing $13.50 per citizen per year then would fail, even though total community damages of $725 could have been avoided at a community cost of $675.

The most difficult factor to measure may be recreation values such as swimming rights. However, aesthetic enjoyment and freedom from health hazards are one of the largest components of water pollution problems and cannot be ignored.

305. Economic Approaches to Water Pollution Assuming Imperfect Knowledge

The opportunities for economic analysis to be used in choosing an optimal pollution-abatement policy from among all possible alternatives in a world where people differ and information is incomplete are somewhat limited. Once we discard the assumption of complete information, it is difficult and misleading to draw up a matrix showing an accurate dollar value of benefits and costs of all possible abatement strategies.

But difficult or not, something usually has to be attempted. Like most problems, the pollution of Lake Tahoe refuses to go away

TABLE 3-2

Town Commission Decision Matrix for Water Pollution Abatement of Lake Tahoe

1. Government Policy	Add Chlorine to All Drinking Water At Source	Build Water-Treatment Plant With Tax Funds (% of water treated) 100 75 50 0	Build Sewage Plant With Tax Funds	Build Water Treatment Plant and Sewage Plant With Tax Funds (% of water treated) 100 75 50 0	Do Nothing At All
2. Damage Avoided (per citizen)	Marked improvement in drinking water quality but deterioration in taste. Health benefits at least $10.00 per annum, probably much more.	Marked improvement in drinking water quality and some improvement in taste. Health benefits up to $10.00 per annum, perhaps more, and some aesthetic benefits which are difficult to measure.	Marked improvement in swimming, value is hard to measure.	Marked improvement in drinking water quality and in swimming, health benefits of up to $10.00 per annum or more plus aesthetic benefits plus value of swimming improvement which is hard to measure.	None
3. Cost of Avoiding Damage (per citizen)	$4.00	$5.00 $3.50 $2.00 $0	$3.00	$8.00 $6.50 $5.00 $3.00	$0
4. Net Benefit (#2−#3)	uncertain	uncertain	uncertain	uncertain	$0
5. Cost of Damage Not Avoided (per citizen)	Present danger to swimming and health hazard from swimming remain, value hard to measure.	Present danger to swimming and health hazard from swimming remain, value hard to measure. Some health hazard if water treatment less than 100 percent.	Health hazard from drinking water at least $10.00 per annum, probably more.	All damage avoided if 100 percent of water is treated, some health hazard from drinking water if treatment less than 100 percent.	All health hazards from drinking water and damage to swimming remain, value of $10.00 per annum or more.
6. Total Costs Incurred (#3+#5)	$4.00 per citizen plus damages to health and swimming.	Up to $5.00 per citizen plus damages to health and swimming.	$3.00 per citizen plus health hazard from drinking water.	$8.00 per citizen, or $3.00 to $6.50 per citizen plus damages to health and swimming.	Health hazards from drinking water and damages to swimming.

by itself. There is increasing citizen pressure for government to do something, so the North Lake Tahoe Town Council appoints a Commission to look into the facts, and they prepare their own revised matrix. It is apparent that some people are getting sick from drinking untreated water; that swimming in the lake is not as pleasant as it used to be, and is getting worse; that some residents have already installed individual water-treatment systems at considerable expense and that other people have sold their lakeside cottages but have been unable to realize enough from their sale to buy equivalent properties elsewhere. Only a small number of people are spending any money to abate water pollution damage on their own, and the damage suffered by those who do nothing is very difficult to quantify except in the most general terms.

Town engineers are able to tell the Commission what the per capita costs of avoiding damage are under the varying alternatives available. The cost of adding chlorine at the source is somewhat lower than it is when added individually. The cost of building a water-treatment plant and/or a sewage plant are the same as in the earlier example. The net benefit per capita (No. 4 in the matrix of Table 3-2) becomes uncertain or unknown for four of the five alternatives under a situation of incomplete knowledge. The total costs incurred are still the per capita costs of avoiding damage from No. 3, plus the residual damage as indicated in No. 5. Even in this example, the Commission has not considered water use problems other than fitness for swimming and drinking—for example quality of fishing, the growth of algae in the lake, or the buildup of sludge on the lake bottom. The citizens of North Lake Tahoe have also ignored (quite properly from their point of view) the impact of lake pollution costs on others, although it is obvious that some cost is imposed on everyone who lives on the circumference of the lake, and on all those who use it periodically for recreational purposes.

Nevertheless, the Commission puts together a Town Decision Matrix for Water Pollution Abatement, which, if less precise than the original cost-benefit matrix, is at least a systematic way of looking at the problem, particularly of weighing what is achieved (in No. 2) and what is not achieved (in No. 5), under each alternative. Such a decision matrix might help if the issue were put to voters for a decision (for example on raising taxes for water pollution abatement), but the voting scheme would likely prove unfeasible. As a minimum it would be necessary to have several elimination votes. Otherwise the policy of "Do Nothing At All" might win with a plurality but not a majority, while a majority of people would have preferred to compromise on a policy such as a moderate degree of water treatment which, although not their favorite, would have been preferred to the option of "Do Nothing."

Even solving the method of voting does not answer the question of who should vote—permanent residents of North Lake Tahoe certainly, and probably temporary residents of the town who are also land owners or property owners. But should people on the south shore who also have a stake in the quality of the water (and who incidentally are located in California rather than in Nevada) also be allowed to vote? It could be argued that everyone in northern Nevada and many people in northern California have some interest in the outcome, and should be allowed some voice in it. These problems, and that of citizen indifference, mean that voting is at best impractical, and at worst useless as a solution to this real-world pollution problem.

Given continued citizen pressure to do something about the problem, the Commission will choose some solution, based not on economics but on some sort of political reality. If the Commission chooses one of the policies with the lowest cost of avoiding damage (doing nothing, building only a sewage plant, or building a water treatment plant for only a small portion of the water taken from the lake), citizens who are concerned about pollution will see the lake and their drinking water continue to deteriorate, and will be unhappy. If the Commission chooses the most expensive policy (that of building a treatment plant for all the water plus a sewage plant), taxes will rise considerably and citizens who object less to pollution than to high taxes will be unhappy. The Commission will almost certainly choose some intermediate solution such as 50 percent water treatment, arguing that it is wiser to start with intermediate treatment and see how citizens react to the new pollution levels and tax load, and add on further water treatment and/or a sewage plant in the future if this seems appropriate. Such a political decision can be objected to as inferior, but only in comparison with an economic decision based on perfect information which of course we do not have. Lacking perfect information, the Commission's decision cannot be proven economically superior or inferior to the other available alternatives.

One outcome of a local-Commission type of decision is the tendency to a pollution-zoning of different areas. Different cities and towns will differ significantly in their pollution levels and in their tax assessments for pollution control, and people will be induced to move until they find the combination of water quality and tax level that they can tolerate. After people have sorted themselves out in relation to geographic pollution levels, the amount of political complaint about environmental pollution can be expected to decline.

For a much more complex economic analysis of a water pollution problem, consider the example which follows of the Delaware River Estuary.

THE DELAWARE RIVER ESTUARY STUDY: A CASE STUDY

306. General Background to the Delaware River Study

During the late 1950's, several state and interstate water pollution control agencies and the City of Philadelphia became concerned with the severe pollution of the Delaware Estuary. They requested the Public Health Service's Division of Water Supply and Pollution Control, now the Federal Water Pollution Control Administration, to develop a program for water pollution control in the Delaware Estuary. The Delaware Estuary Comprehensive Study (DECS) was undertaken in late 1961 in cooperation with the State regulatory agencies of New Jersey, Pennsylvania, and Delaware, the Delaware River Basin Commission, the City of Philadelphia, and a number of other interested parties. The study area encompassed the Delaware Estuary from Trenton, New Jersey to Liston Point, Delaware, including the estuarine reaches of its tributaries.

The decision-making body which resulted, the Delaware River Basin Commission, was at that time the only interstate-federal compact agency in the United States. The objective of the Commission was to devise, based on the study, a multipurpose water resources plan to upgrade the river and preserve it for a variety of uses; to bring the greatest benefits and produce the most efficient service in the public welfare.

The Commission in its study was thus faced with a magnified version of our simplified water quality problem, with some of the political jurisdiction issues stripped away but complicated by the necessity of dropping many of the simplifying assumptions, and of quantifying some of the values ignored in the example. The sections that follow discuss only a small portion of the total study, but indicate how the problems involved can be approached, given sufficient time and resources.

Using computers, the study devised a mathematical formulation of the entire Delaware estuary, and the researchers were able in a short time period to collect and analyze technical data on water quality that earlier would have required years.[10] The river mathematical model, an untested approach until the DECS application, has now become a proven mechanism for application to previously unsolvable water pollution problems.

During 1966 about 28,000 people were employed by the firms designated as substantial waste dischargers in the Delaware River Estuary area. For the 20 major industrial waste sources, the estimated dollar value of output was about $4 million. The total carbonaceous oxygen demanding waste load discharged into the estuary during 1966 was 1,400,000 pounds per day. About 65 percent of this discharge was from municipal discharges and 35 percent from direct industrial discharges. There was an oxygen demand of about 200,000 pounds per day exerted by bottom deposits of sludge and mud, which were the result of material discharged from storm-water overflows, from municipal and industrial waste effluents, and from dredging operations.

The vast majority of municipal waste effluent flows were discharged without disinfection and consequently contained large concentrations of coliform bacteria. During 1966 all municipal sources along the estuary gave at least primary waste treatment (about 30 percent removal of oxygen demanding load), and some waste treatment was as high as a 90 percent removal level. The amount of industrial waste reduction along the estuary ranged from none to a 95 percent removal of "raw" load. During 1966 the average removal of waste discharges along the estuary was about 50 percent of the raw load.

Population projections in the study area indicate increases of 30 percent between 1960 and 1975, and of 135 percent between 1960 and 2010. It was estimated that 1966 raw waste loads would increase by 2.3 times by 1975, and by 5 times by 2010. Industrial raw waste loads were expected to double from 1966 to 1975, and to increase by more than six times by 2010. Overall the total municipal and industrial waste load prior to treatment was expected to double between 1966 and 1975, and to increase by about 5½ times by 2010.

307. Water Quality Goals[11]

The procedure used in establishing water use and water quality objectives for the Delaware River Estuary was to investigate all feasible water uses, to determine water quality criteria sufficient to guarantee those uses, and to assign water quality goals to the various sections of the estuary according to the uses designated. Meetings of the Water Use Advisory Committee (WUAC) were held to elicit community feelings on possible swimming areas, on desirable fishing locations, on withdrawal of water from the estuary, and on intentions of potential industrial water-users. Based on the work of WUAC, the thousands of possible combinations of uses versus location were reduced to five sets of possible water use and associated water quality objectives. The five objective sets ranged from maximum feasible enhancement of the river under present technology to maintenance of existing levels of water use and water quality. For each set of objectives the costs were estimated and the benefits, where possible, were quantitatively evaluated. It was not required that the final objective be any one of the individual sets but could be composed of various features from each of the objective sets.[12] The five water use/water quality sets were as follows:

Objective Set I (OS I) represented the greatest increase in water quality levels among all the objective sets. Water contact recreation was anticipated in the upper and lower reaches of the estuary, with sport and commercial fishing envisioned in other areas. A minimum daily average DO level of 6.0 mg/liter was included for anadromous fish passage during appropriate periods. Fresh water inflow controls were proposed to overcome high chloride concentrations in several specific locations. OS I required 92–98 percent removal of all carbonaceous waste sources, plus instream aeration. An estuary-wide residual of 100,000 pounds per day of oxygen demanding wastes was permitted. There was considerable uncertainty as to the ability to achieve these reductions over the entire estuary. OS I required large-scale utilization of advanced waste treatment and reduction processes which had doubtful technical feasibility in 1966.

Objective Set II (OS II) anticipated a reduction in the area set aside for water contact recreation in OS I, a reduction in minimum DO levels with a concomitant reduction in sport and commercial fishing, and reduced chloride control as compared with OS I. OS II required removal of approximately 90 percent of the existing waste load with an estuary-wide residual of 200,000 pounds per day of oxygen demanding wastes permitted.

Objective Set III (OS III) was identical in all respects to OS II except that no DO criteria for anadromous fish passage were imposed, thus a further decrease in sport and commercial fishing potential was anticipated. Also, water quality standards at points of municipal water supply were reduced from those anticipated in OS I and OS II. OS III required removal of about 75 percent of the existing waste load with a residual load of about 500,000 pounds per day allowed.

Objective Set IV (OS IV) represented a slight increase over then-existing levels in water contact recreation and fishing in the lower reaches of the estuary. Generally, quality requirements were increased slightly over 1964 conditions in OS V, representing a minimally enhanced environment. OS IV called for about a 25 percent removal of existing waste loads with a residual load of 650,000 pounds per day allowed.

Objective Set V (OS V) represented a maintenance of 1964 water quality conditions, and was intended to prevent any further deterioration of water quality levels from those then in existence. OS V permitted a dumping of about 950,000 pounds per day of oxygen-demanding wastes along the reaches of the estuary.

308. Alternative Approaches To Water Quality Objectives

The methods considered for improvement of water quality in the river included limiting effluent discharge to the estuary by requiring reduction of wastes before discharge; piping of wastes to other places, where the discharges would have a reduced economic effect; regulation of stream flow; removal of benthic sludge deposits; instream aeration; and control of storm water discharges. It was concluded that a comprehensive program might incorporate several of these possibilities, but would have the greatest assurance of success if it depended primarily on reduction of waste at the source.

There are many ways of controlling the discharge of waste to achieve a specified water quality objective. The problem is to choose a system which balances the apparent equity of the solution to the individual waste discharger, the economic cost to the region, and the means of administering the water quality control program. The DECS used an economic model of dissolved oxygen conditions to investigate four alternate control programs for achieving desired DO levels in the estuary. The DO model is a good example of the sort of analytical technique available, and is discussed briefly below.[13]

The DECS computer model segmented the watercourse into 30 sections of 10,000 to 21,000 feet in length each; the segmentation permitted the prediction of effects of a change in waste loads in one section upon all other affected sections. Superimposed on this physical model of the estuary is a cost optimizing economic model (a linear programming formulation) which considers imputs such as: (1) location of a waste source with respect to the DO profile of the waterway; (2) the relative cost of removing waste at each source; (3) the maximum quantity of waste that can be removed at each source; and (4) the proximity of one waste discharge point to existing points. With cost data collected by sampling and survey methods, the study analyzed four programs for achieving alternative DO objectives in the estuary. The control programs considered were:

Cost Minimization (CM), which uses a mathematical programming solution to obtain the minimum total cost of waste treatment yielding the desired DO level for all individual polluters in the region.

The CM solution results in differing levels of treatment at different pollution points because treatment is concentrated at those points where the critical oxygen sag can be reduced most inexpensively.

Uniform Treatment (UT), which requires all waste dischargers to reduce their waste loads by the same percentage, with the percentage chosen being the minimum needed to accomplish desired DO levels.

Single Effluent Charge (SEC), which requires each waste discharger in the estuary to pay a uniform price per unit of oxygen demanding material discharged. The solution estimates the minimum single charge which will induce sufficient reduction in waste discharge to achieve desired DO standards.

Zoned Effluent Charge (ZEC), which uses a uniform effluent charge in each of a number of zones, instead of a uniform charge over all reaches of the estuary.[14]

The economic costs associated with the four programs are shown in Table 3-3 for two levels of water quality. The 3-4 ppm standard is the one that estuary authorities considered the maximum practically attainable in the estuary.

TABLE 3-3
Costs Associated with Various Control Programs

D.O. Objective	Cost Minimization (CM)	Uniform Treatment (UT)	Single Effluent Charge (SEC)	Zoned Effluent Charge (ZEC)
	(all figures in millions of dollars per year)			
2 ppm	1.6	5.0	2.4	2.4
3-4 ppm	7.0	20.0	12.0	8.6

While the CM solution is the most efficient in each case since it programs waste discharges at each point specifically in relation to the cost of improving quality, this comes at the cost of highly detailed information on treatment costs at each point, and an extremely inequitable distribution of costs.[15] The CM solution is closely approximated by the ZEC solution at the higher DO objective level. In effect ZEC "credits" upstream dischargers with the waste degradation that takes place in the stream, a necessary condition for full efficiency when effluent charges are used to achieve a minimum standard at a critical point in a waterway. The ZEC solution does not achieve the full efficiency of the CM solution because the basis for the "credit" is too broad.

An effluent charge of about 10 cents per pound of BOD would be needed for the ZEC solution; using this charge the administrative agency would collect $7 million per year in rent on the assimilative capacity of the watercourse.[16] For industry and municipalities, this is about the same as the cost of treatment only under a uniform treatment program. The study concluded that a charge at that level would not cause major regional economic readjustments such as the closing of industrial plants in the study area. Perhaps the great advantage of the ZEC or SEC approaches is that they require much less in the way of information and analytical refinement than does the CM solution.

309. Costs of Alternate Programs

The nature and amount of the current waste load in the estuary was determined by technical studies of rates of decay, reaeration, and other stream characteristics. Data on abatement costs and future waste load estimates was collected from existing municipal and industrial dischargers. Table 3-4 shows the estimated cost of achieving each objective set under three different cost-allocation formulas.

TABLE 3-4
Summary of Total Costs of Achieving Objective Sets 1, 2, 3, and 4 (Costs include cost of maintaining present (1964) conditions and reflect waste-load conditions projected for 1975-80). Flow at Trenton = 3,000 cfs

(million 1968 dollars)

	Uniform treatment			Zoned treatment			Cost minimization		
Objective set	Capital costs	O & M costs[1]	Total costs	Capital costs	O & M costs[1]	Total costs	Capital costs	O & M costs[1]	Total costs
1	180	280 (19.0)	460[2]	180	280 (19.0)	460[2]	180	280 (19.0)	460[2]
2	135	180 (12.0)	315[3]	105	145 (10.0)	250[3]	115	100 (7.0)	215[3]
3	75	80 (5.5)	155[3]	50	70 (4.5)	120[3]	50	35 (2.5)	85[3]
4	55	75 (5.0)	130	40	40 (2.5)	80	40	25 (1.5)	65

[1]*Operation and maintenance costs, discounted at 3 percent, twenty-year-time horizon; figures in parentheses are equivalent annual operation and maintenance costs in millions of dollars/year.*
[2]*High-rate secondary to tertiary (92-98 percent removal) for all waste sources of all programs. Includes in-stream aeration cost of $20 million.*
[3]*Includes $1–$2 million for either sludge removal or aeration to meet goals in river sections #3 and #4.*
Source: DECS p. 58.

An alternative to on-site waste reduction would be to pipe wastes out of the area of the estuary, presumably into the Atlantic Ocean. The obvious disadvantage of piping is that it merely moves the pollution problem from one location to another, perhaps externalizing pollution costs from one area to another. Table 3-5 shows the estimated cost of waste reduction versus piping for Objective Sets I through IV.[17]

TABLE 3-5

Capital Costs for Attainment of Objectives (millions of dollars) 1) By Piping of Wastes out of the Estuary; 2) By Reduction of Wastes at the Source

Obj. Set	Estimated [1] Diverted Flow (cfs)	1) Piping of Wastes Out of the Estuary			2) Waste Removal
		Piping	Chloride[2] Control	Total	
1	1200	125	40	165	180
2	1150	120	35	155	115
3	800	90	25	115	50
4	650	65	20	85	40

[1]It is assumed that industrial waste streams will be separated to allow cooling water to return to the stream.
[2]Estimated Capital Cost of additional storage necessary to counteract effects of diverted flow.
Source: DECS p. 68.

Rough estimates of the total cost of reaching the various DO objectives by mechanical aeration, including capital and operation and maintenance, are shown in Table 3-6. It should be noted that mechanical aeration meets DO objectives only, and additional expense would be necessary to meet other parameter objectives. Since large-scale in-stream aeration such as would be required for the Delaware has never been attempted except on a pilot-plant scale, considerable study would have to be devoted to the feasibility of the size of the system required. The cost estimates given thus are highly tentative. Also, it was anticipated that some problems might develop in interferences with navigation and recreation as well as in the creation of nuisance conditions, such as foaming.

TABLE 3-6
Estimated Total Cost to Reach DO Objective by
Mechanical Aeration

Objective Set	Cost (Millions of Dollars)
I	$70
II	40
III	12
IV	10

Economic projections showed that a substantial increase in waste production could be expected in the estuary area. To maintain any given objective set under increased waste loadings would increase program cost by an additional 5.0 to 7.5 millions of dollars per year from 1975 through 1985. No estimate of treatment costs after 1985 was attempted; it was felt that this would be misleading as other alternative methods of effluent treatment became feasible, as more efficient production processes became available, and as entirely new objective functions were undertaken.

310. Quantification of Benefits from Improved Water Quality

The next step undertaken by the DECS was to define and quantify the benefits of enhanced water quality in the Delaware Estuary. Quantification of benefits is a standard part of any engineering feasibility study. In this situation, a number of existing intangibles required that subjective value-judgments based on the estimated social satisfactions from improved water quality be made.[18]

Initially, data was collected from the major water-using industries along the estuary. DO and chloride levels were found to be the most important quality parameters to industrial water users. It was found that increased DO levels resulted in negative benefits (or increased costs) to water-using industries, primarily due to increased corrosion rates at the higher oxygen levels. The increase in cost ranged from $7 million for OS IV to $15 million for OS I. (This means that while humans seek higher DO levels, industry seeks lower levels). Chloride goals in OS II and OS III resulted in a benefit to industrial water users of almost $4 million per year,

with the chloride goal in OS I producing an additional benefit of
$2 million per year.

A study was then made to define and quantify the benefits that
would accrue to the commercial fishing industry. Although the
estuary itself does not support a commercial fish harvest of any
size, its water quality does influence commercial fish production in
adjacent areas.[19] In calculating benefits, a given species was considered to be beneficially influenced by improved water quality if
it must depend on water within the study area for survival at some
period in its life cycle. The estimated net commercial fishing benefits range from $3 million minimum to $5 million maximum for OS
IV to $9 million minimum to $12 million maximum for OS I.

The next step of the DECS was to quantify the recreational
benefits included in swimming, boating, and sport fishing. The
benefits associated with other activities, such as picnicking and
sightseeing, were seen as resulting from the improved aesthetic surrounding, but were considered to be non-quantifiable. The net
dollar benefits that might accrue in the 1975-1980 period from increased recreational possibilities for each objective set were produced by: (1) estimating the total recreational demand in the
Delaware Estuary region by applying national average participation
rates to the region's projected population; (2) estimating the
maximum capacity of the estuary under each of the objective sets;
(3) estimating the part of the total demand expected to be filled
by the estuary; and (4) applying monetary values to the estimated
total participation demand in the estuary to arrive at total estimated
benefits from recreation. The analyses indicated a tremendous latent
recreational demand in the estuary region that to some extent could
be satisfied by improved water quality. It was estimated that during
the period 1975-1980 the increase in total demand for the whole
region over the present demand would be about 43 million activity
days per year, and by the year 2010 would increase by almost 100
million activity days per year.

The problems associated with estimating a figure for benefits
from recreation are substantial. For example, suppose the report
claims $110,000 in swimming recreational benefits for a community
under OS III, but fails to recognize that the same swimming recreational benefits could be accomplished through an expenditure
of $80,000 for a community pool. Which alternative measure of
benefits should be accepted?

Some people would maintain that a public program which provides $1 million of benefits to one small segment of the population (recreational boaters), is inferior to a program that distributes $1 million of benefits to a broader sector of the population (swimming pools to poor inner city residents who cannot afford to travel to more distant parts of the estuary to swim). It is not clear whether cost-benefit analysis can be adapted to take into account the income distributive and benefit distributive effects of a recreation program, or for that matter of a sewage program. If such distributive effects cannot be quantified into the dollar units that are standard in cost-benefit analysis, how can such considerations be integrated into the planning process?

The estimated range of recreational benefits for each objective set is indicated in Table 3-7.[20] In this calculation, the benefits accruing to industry and the municipalities were seen as being small and as cancelling out because of the negative features of industrial water use. The ranges of recreational benefits were thus taken to be estimates of the total benefits from improved water quality in the estuary.

TABLE 3-7

Costs and Benefits of Water Quality Improvement in the Delaware Estuary Area[1]

(million dollars)

Objective set	Estimated total costs	Estimated recreation benefits	Estimated incremental cost minimum[2]	maximum[3]	Estimated incremental benefits minimum[2]	maximum[3]
1	460	160-350				
			245	145	20	30
2	215-315	140-320				
			130	160	10	10
3	85-155	130-310				
			20	25	10	30
4	65-130	120-280				

[1] All costs and benefits are present values calculated with 3 percent discount rate and twenty-year time horizon.
[2] Difference between adjacent minima.
[3] Difference between adjacent maxima.
Source: DECS data summarized in Kneese and Bower, Managing Water Quality: Economics, Technology and Instructions (Baltimore: Johns Hopkins Press, 1968), p. 233.

Table 3-7 indicates that OS IV appears to be justified, even when the lowest estimate of benefit is compared to the highest estimate of cost. The incremental costs suggest that going to OS III is marginal, but perhaps justifiable on the assumption that some of the more widely distributed benefits of water quality improvement may not have been taken into account. Clearly the incremental economic benefits of going to OS II or to OS I are outweighed by the incremental costs of doing so.

Note, however, that in addition to the benefits measured in the study there are numerous other uses that will be improved as a results of improved water quality. The water quality levels in any of the first four objective sets would reduce the rate of corrosion, delignification, and cavitation of piers, wharfs, bridge abutments, and boat engines and hulls. The quantity of debris, silt, oils, and grease that settle and block channels and cooling systems in boat engines would be reduced substantially. The dollar benefits attributable to these effects remain undefined.

Another important benefit of improved water quality is the improved aesthetic value of the river. Some of this benefit is included in the estimate of increased recreational value, but this estimate does not include the increase in value of property adjacent to the estuary, nor the enhanced value of parks and picnic areas adjacent to the watercourse.[21]

What is less apparent is that once the water quality reaches a threshold level at which several important recreational activities may occur, an additional increase in water quality may produce few if any new benefits. For example, once the bacterial standard for water contact recreation is such that swimming and water skiing can be authorized, no further benefit (except perhaps an unrecognized health benefit or some benefit from the existence of a "safety margin") results if bacterial levels are reduced further. In fact, improving DO levels above standard may produce negative benefits as well as increased costs because of the increase in oxygen-aided corrosion and similar effects.

The quantitative analyses also do not include the influence of secondary effects on the regional economy. For example, a unit of monetary benefit associated with commercial fishing use might be expected to generate at least an extra 15 percent in other benefits due to the interrelationship between the commercial fishing industry and the rest of the economy. This may occur in the form of increased wages, additional capital investment, or increased use of trades and services.

The use of a static analysis in the DECS conceals a number of additional factors: (a) the raw sewage load is growing at 8 percent a year; (6) undercapacity of abatement facilities can be corrected within 6 years if no preliminary planning has been done, or within 3 years if the necessary design work has been done on a contingency basis beforehand; and (c) the technology of waste treatment is evolving at a very rapid rate. How would these factors, incorporated into a dynamic rather than a static analysis, affect the conclusions arrived at by the DECS?

If a safety factor is felt necessary, should it be built into the objective set, or into the calculation of permissible waste loading in the objective set which we would like to achieve? Does the "location" of such a safety factor make any difference in terms of the ease of having the objective set adopted, the ease in resisting pressures from dischargers, or the avoidance of public disillusionment with pollution control and consequent loss of interest or overreaction? A safety factor was built into the objective set rather than in the permissible waste loadings in the DECS study to placate the large industrial and commercial representation on the advisory committees to the study.

311. What's Best for Philadelphia

The preceeding analysis has discussed the costs and benefits of water quality improvement for the whole of the Delaware Estuary area. However, voting on the various alternatives is done by the individual entities, primarily cities, which make up the Delaware Estuary compact, and it is enlightening to look at the political considerations facing these entities. The economic and political alternatives facing the City of Philadelphia were typical.

Under OS II, Philadelphia would be required to institute BOD removal of about 88 percent of its current raw sewage load at each of its three plants. OS III would require about 75 percent abatement at the current raw loading. The required percentage of BOD removal would rise as the raw load grew. The Philadelphia Water Department estimated that to build plants to allow the city to meet its requirements for the first 5 years would cost $60 million for OS III and $100 million for OS II. This would require a 20 percent increase in water-user charges—an increase in average annual family water cost from $25 to $30. When augmented secondary treatment became inadequate and tertiary treatment became necessary to meet OS II standards, average family water cost would go up to $37.50, probably within five years. Even such small increases in cost were considered politically unfeasible in Philadelphia. Also, the authorization to issue bonds for construction costs had to be sought separately, one plant at a time, and this magnified the political impact of the expenditures on the city's elected officials.

There is also some question as to what benefits Philadelphia would have received from a higher level of water treatment. A cleaner river would not make it any cheaper to produce palatable and safe drinking water for Philadelphians. There would be a small improvement in aesthetic values and some improvement in recreation possibilities in and near the city. But it is unlikely that an estimate of benefits could have been made which would come anywhere near equalling the cost of $60 to $100 million to Philadelphians.

There was also the problem of the alternative goods (more schools, lower taxes) which would have been foregone by citizens of Philadelphia if the higher cost standards of OS II had been chosen. Voters in the city had turned down three school bond issues between 1960 and 1965, and the school system generally was in need of extensive renovation and upgrading. To judge the true opportunity costs of any of the alternatives would have required information on methods of authorizing and financing alternative programs, on the requirements of the bond market, and on political considerations of the acceptability of various city objectives. Given such data, it is not clear that the resulting calculations would have been accurate enough to be worth doing. But making any judgment (or doing nothing) *assumes* such a calculation. A complicating factor is that the cost of construction of sewage treatment plants had been going up steadily at 5-6 percent per year, so that delay was not costless.

A strictly political question arises as to whether federal assistance would have been more likely if there had been an open fight between the city and DECS over standards, or if there was no fight. Given an uncertain timetable for federal appropriations, the city had to decide which timing of its decision would produce the best chance of being considered for a large share of federal aid. All these decision factors are repeated, of course, for every political unit in the compact, each of which had to vote on the various alternatives open.

312. Outcome

Essentially the same data as shown here were submitted to the three DECS advisory committees and to all subcommittee members. Through a long process involving numerous meetings and communications the chairmen extracted the view-points and expressions from their members and arrived at a consensus for their committees. At their eleventh meeting on March 28th, 1966, the advisory committees arrived at OS III as their compromise recommendation for the development of a water pollution control plan for the estuary.

Of the four control programs discussed (cost minimization, uniform treatment, etc.) a modification of the zoned system was adopted which did *not* contain an effluent fee but rather a waste-allocation formula. The effluent fee provision was dropped apparently on the philosophical basis that it sanctioned contamination of the environment and put the government in the business of licensing polluters and then cleaning up after them.

On deciding that the present oxygen consumption by pollutants (COD) in the waterway must be reduced, the Delaware River Basin Commission decided in 1967 to divide the estuary into four zones, each having a share of the waste-accepting capacity. Each zone's capacity was divided among its dischargers. Within each zone, all wastes were to receive a minimum of secondary treatment (removal of practically all suspended solids and reduction of oxygen-consuming pollutants by at least 85 percent). Except for storm water bypass, discharges containing human wastes or disease producing organisms must first be disinfected, thus protecting river recreation users and shellfish.

In June, 1968, 81 public and industrial dischargers with 92 plants were assigned a maximum permissible oxygen-consuming waste discharge allocation by the basin commission. The allocation was made by the Executive Director after a notice and hearing. A reserve for new dischargers was maintained, and the capacity can be reallocated whenever the reserve approaches depletion or the circumstances render the existing allocation inequitable. Provision was made for progress reports, inspection, surveillance, and non-compliance hearings and citations.

Given that a waste discharge permit system was adopted, it is curious that no consideration was given to making waste discharge permits negotiable. One might consider how such a system might work, what kind of governmental regulation of the discharge permit market might be required, and what existing problems not faced by the plan as adopted might be solved by it.

The commission also adopted the provisions that stream standards could vary within each zone, with higher oxygen requirements

[18]The Commission's position was sustained by the U.S. Court of Appeals for the District of Columbia Circuit in *Banzhaf* v. *Federal Communications Commission*, 405 F. 2d 1082 (1968).

[19]Public Law 91-222, signed into law on April 1, 1970.

[20]Cited in *Cigarette Labeling and Advertising, op. cit.*, pp. 190-191.

[21]The whole fairness doctrine question is considerably more involved than a short discussion would indicate. An excellent discussion of the doctrine and its application to an ecology case, that of misleading advertising for Standard Oil of California's F-310 gasoline additive, is found in Alan F. Neckritz and Lawrence B. Ordower. "Ecological Pornography and the Mass Media," *Ecology Law Quarterly* 1 (1971), pp. 374-399.

[22]*Red Lion Broadcasting Co.* v. *FCC*, 395 U.S. 367 (1969).

5

Economic Approaches

To Cost

Internalization

As I looked into the future
Far as human eye could see,
Saw a vision of the world
And all the wonder that would be.

Saw the landscape filled with chimneys
Oceans brown with floating scars,
200 million belching Chevys
The urban planners drunk in bars.

500. Economic Externalities Revisited

We have continued to point out that the discharge of pollutants imposes on some members of society costs which are inadequately imputed to the sources of the pollution by free markets. The result is more pollution than is desirable from society's point of view. Some sectors of society benefit from the existence of externalities. Those who buy the goods produced, and those who own land, labor, or capital inputs that are used in producing these goods, all benefit by not having to include the external costs involved in their selling price. The presence of externalities also leads to a misallocation of productive resources. For example, a newsprint manufacturer may pollute a river and thereby increase the cost of water treatment for a glass producer further downstream. From society's point of view the newsprint firm has understated its costs and is producing and selling too much, while not enough glass is being produced, because glass prices are overstated by the water-purification costs imposed by the newsprint effluent. Such a mis-allocation of productive resources—producing too much newsprint, not enough glass—constitutes economic inefficiency.

Economists have generally adopted the position that complete efficiency could be attained only if all external costs were somehow internalized to the firms that produced them. This approach was discussed and attacked in a 1960 article by R. H. Coase,[1] who argued that, given costless bargaining, efficient resource allocation could be achieved regardless of which party was required to bear the cost of the externality. According to the Coase argument, the absence of bargaining costs means that optimal resource allocation is independent of society's laws, or "starting rules"—whether in-cinerators have a right to pollute or nearby residents have the right to breathe clean air, or whether SSTs have the right to produce sonic booms or persons along the flight path the right to peace and quiet is irrelevant. Bargaining and side payments would produce the same end solution, independent of which position or assump-tion one started from, and there would be no increase in human satisfaction stemming from judicially-imposed liability.[2]

The important assumption here is that bargaining is costless, that there are no mediators, arbitrators, researchers, or others to reduce the amount of money transferred among the parties to the bargain-ing process.[3] Because the actual cost of bargaining is not zero and can be very high, actual bargaining to arrange pollution rights will be undertaken only when the increased value of production upon the rearrangement is greater than the costs of bringing it about.

501. Potential Solutions to Externality Problems

Again and again, the imperfect working of the free market is cited to justify almost any kind of governmental interven-tion in the free market. In the case of air and water pollution, the existence of external costs often leads people to think entirely in terms of direct regulation in the form of permits, registration, licenses, or administrative standards. These approaches have not proven very effective means of controlling environmental pollution. Control by means of regulation offers the polluter only the crudest form of economic incentive not to pollute—the only exception being where fines imposed for violations exceed the cost of com-pliance. Regulation may also turn out to be economically dysfunctional; for example, a strict application of a rule that "all wastes amenable to treatment must be treated" might result in large increases in production costs without producing any corresponding benefit to the environment. Also, any impetus for research and development of better effluent controls is missing so long as minimum legal pollution standards are being satisfied. Even where the marginal costs of additional control efforts are less than the marginal gains which would accrue to society, a polluter has no economic incentive to take these efforts under a regulatory scheme.

Given these defects in direct regulation schemes, it makes much more sense to investigate how externalities may be reduced or eliminated through restructuring of badly-functioning market mechanisms. Only when such restructuring appears totally impossible should the advantages of free decision-making be given up in favor of direct regulation.

The "Do Nothing" Alternative. A first approach to dealing with externalities is simply to ignore them. This is economically sound if the bargaining or transaction costs of any internalization scheme exceed the resultant gains in efficiency. A failure of private bargaining to arise may indicate that there are such high transaction costs as to preclude any increase in efficiency through cost internalization. It has been observed that: "The absence of a price [or a market] does not imply that either market transactions or substitute government services are desirable."[4] If private bargaining costs are too large to bring the externality into the price-bargaining system, then judicially or administratively imposed pricing or regulation might also be too costly to justify in terms of any possible efficiency gain. Thus, for example, emission control standards or control devices on outboard motors might be neither economic nor desirable no matter how imposed.

Zoning. The costs of administrative ordering may be so small relative to private bargaining costs that the private market should be displaced entirely, as is the case with emission-standard zoning. One problem is that while the expense of internalizing pollution costs can be estimated from existing agency expenditures, costs of taxation systems, or costs of litigation, the potential gains from controlling any one form of pollution are more difficult to measure. Thus, justification for either regulation or for administrative ordering must rest on either intuitive cost estimates, or on an *a priori* criterion of equity that does not require a cost-benefit justification.

Bargaining. If bargaining is economically feasible, it is the simplest way by which economic allocative efficiency can be achieved in a simple world of one polluter and one victim. Prior rights are assigned by a legislature or by the courts, to the interests which are considered most important—the creation of a market by rights-creation.[5] If the right to use scarce air and water resources belongs to the polluter, the victim can seek a contractual arrangement whereby he will pay the polluter to abate his pollution, assuming, of course, that the value of the reduction is worth more to him than the payment, and that it is cheaper to control pollution at its source. If the cost of pollution reduction becomes too high, the victim would probably choose to endure the pollution. From the standpoint of economic efficiency this would be acceptable as the value stemming from pollution control would then be less than the cost of resources required for control. If it were less expensive to correct the results of pollution where they are felt rather than at the source, as may be true with some forms of water pollution, the victim would prefer to clean up his own environment. This would also be economically efficient.

The same economic result is reached if assignment of prior rights dictates that the use of the environment belongs to the victim, and that the polluter must pay the costs of his pollution. Polluters would pay for the right to pollute up to the point where additional payments are greater than initial control costs. The victims would accept these payments up to such point as the payment failed to compensate for the additional costs incurred. Either way, cost internalization would result, with its burden being dependent on the assignment of prior rights.

However, this and most other bargaining models postulate a simple framework of one polluter, one victim, and are thus limited in value. Even where the one polluter-one victim conditions hold, it is unlikely that most single victims would have the resources to adequately bribe a large polluter to cease pollution. If several victims are involved, the freeloader effect will provide disincentives to a bargaining solution. Since air or water are common resources, one victim's payment will produce pollution reduction advantages which also accrue to his fellow victims. Each victim is motivated to do nothing and let others do the bribing. The resultant lack of incentive among all victims prevents any action at all. If it is the victim who has rights to pollution-free water or air, bargaining enforcement may be equally difficult because the victim rarely has the resources to bring a suit to enforce his rights—and knowing this, the polluter has little incentive to negotiate a settlement with any individual victim.

Extending the Firm. A perfectly valid approach to the internalization of social costs is to enlarge the size and scope of the firm so that all the costs and benefits of externalities accrue to the same entity. This might result in such a vast expansion that the costs of underspecialization might be greater than the gain from internalization. Probably the only meaningful way to internalize the costs of air pollution, which normally are spread over a wide area, would be to invoke public ownership. As both economic sophistication and the degree of pollution increase, it is probably inevitable that externalities will become the subject of increasing state-controlled allocation.

Consider the earlier case study of the Delaware River Estuary. Extending the firm in this case would imply putting the entire estuary under a single management so as to internalize all benefits and costs. But although extending the firm would eliminate some external costs, technical externalities would remain in the production of water recreational facilities and the proper allocation of resources into recreational facilities by a free market would fail.[6]

Private Actions. Another approach to internalization of costs is the private civil action to enjoin or to collect damages from offending polluters. This approach enables the victim to obtain fairly rapid satisfaction rather than waiting for the implementation of legislation, or for appeals to regulatory bodies to be resolved. It is also flexible since the victim can direct his action against new and complex pollutants, or base his claim on new forms of pollution damage. However, problems of proof, excessive costs, and lack of judicial precedent are barriers facing the private litigant. The topic of internalization of costs by private actions is an involved one, and is treated in more detail in Chapter Six.

Direct Taxation. It is sometimes argued that a direct

tax on pollutants can serve as a surrogate for costless bargaining. A direct tax does allow firms to maintain some degree of flexibility in finding the most efficient way to minimize their pollution, and hence minimize their tax load.

However, cost-incorporating taxes are subject to a number of criticisms. It is generally desirable to minimize the degree to which taxation is used to control behavior rather than raise revenue. It is also argued that a tax on one person, based on the cost or damage to another, will always produce an unstable equilibrium.[7] It is not clear how one would design a tax system which, if based on pollutants emitted, would not be subject to locational bias and arbitrariness. Finally, once an estimate of the total cost of pollution is made, the cost must be apportioned among polluters. However, the actual contribution of any one firm will depend on interactions among pollutants, on the direction of prevailing winds, on smokestack height, on timing of emissions during the day and by season, and so forth. Any equitable tax would thus have to encompass so many variables as to be unworkable, or would itself produce locational and other diseconomies through its application.

The desirability of a direct tax on pollutants is also relative to the extent to which the initial distribution of income in society is inequitable. If everyone had the same income, it would be equitable to tax persons who used goods that lead to pollution of the environment, either to pay the costs of restoring environmental quality or to compensate others for the damage caused them. But in a world where incomes are not equally distributed, such a tax leads to material goods (which comprise a relatively larger part of the budgets of the poor) becoming more expensive relative to services (which comprise a larger part in the budgets of the rich). This means the taxation of staple goods used by the poor to pay for protection of the recreational amenities of the rich.

Equitable or not, such taxes are being proposed. The Council on Environmental Quality has suggested a penalty tax on the sulphur content of coal, oil, and natural gas to go into effect in 1974.[8] Under the proposal, the tax would be imposed initially at a level of one cent per pound of sulphur content of coal burned in the first year, rising to 10 cents per pound by 1976. The objective would be to provide time and the incentive for conversion to the use of low-sulphur fuel and for adoption of methods for burning high-sulphur fuels without discharging sulphur dioxide into the atmosphere. The tax would be imposed on the producers of fossil fuels; a user of high-sulphur fuel who burned it without discharging sulphur dioxide into the air would receive a rebate of the tax that had been paid on the high-sulphur fuel.

One problem is that more than half of the sulphur-bearing fossil fuels used in the United States are consumed by public utilities, whose prices and profit levels are set by regulatory bodies that permit utilities to pass on to the customer all their costs of doing business. The utilities thus have no incentive to do research to find more economical ways of eliminating sulphur dioxide emissions. However, there is not enough low-sulphur fuel in the United States, regardless of costs, to meet the needs of utilities and other fossil-fuel users. Thus, the one real hope of eliminating sulphur dioxide emissions is improved technology in the use of these fuels.

E. S. Mills has recently proposed a scheme for direct taxation of pollutants that recognizes the interrelations of air pollution, water pollution, solid waste disposal, sewage, plastic containers, and the other paraphernalia of modern technological life.[9] His proposal is that the government collect a materials-use fee on specified materials at the time they are removed from the environment by the original producer, or are imported. The fee for each material would be set to equal the social cost to the environment if the material were eventually used in the most harmful possible way. The fee would be refunded to anyone who would certify that he had disposed of the material, with the size of the refund depending on the method of disposal. A full refund would be given for re-cycled materials; and ecologically harmless disposal would earn a large refund; disposal in the most harmful way would earn no refund at all.

The economic advantage of such a scheme is that whenever two or more materials could serve the same purpose, for example biodegradable and nonbiodegradable materials for containers, the fees would make their prices reflect social costs, including disposal, rather than merely private costs, and the original choices of materials would come nearer to being socially optimal. The combination of the schedule of refunds and direct costs would provide an accurate guide to individuals in choosing a method of disposal. Administratively, such a scheme avoids the problem of monitoring the disposal of goods by measuring the amount removed from the earth by the first producer, a much simpler problem. The burden of proof is placed on the individual and not on the pollution control agency. It is probable that specialized firms would arise to perform disposal services and provide certification of the method of disposal in order to earn the available refund for themselves and their clients.

There are some difficulties with Mills' scheme. It would have to apply over a wide geographic area, otherwise one location would be making refunds to those who disposed of materials that had paid the fee elsewhere. There would have to be some sort of refund for materials incorporated in very durable objects like buildings or dams (which might be considered as forms of harmless disposal rather than use).

Most importantly, there would be huge administrative costs involved in setting fees and certifying refunds. But Mills' scheme does provide a first approach to the correct problem, that of global materials usage, and it does so by utilizing the price system rather than administrative fiat to correct the divergence between private and social costs.

Subsidies, Tax Credits, and Effluent Fees. The need to internalize costs does not necessarily require that producers bear the total burden. Since the public benefits both from clean air and a productive industrial sector, it is sometimes argued that the public should pay some part of the cost of controlling pollution. A simple form of economic incentive to abate pollution would take the form of subsidy payments to stimulate reduction of emissions over the long run. Subsidies might be geared to a percentage reduction from total potential emissions, to an absolute reduction, or to the attainment of an emission standard set by a government regulation. A subsidy system can be thought of as equivalent to a tax, to be utilized with external benefits in the same way that a direct tax is utilized with external costs. A second economic alternative is one which provides tax credits for capital investment in pollution abatement facilities and accelerated depreciation for such equipment.

A third alternative often used in conjunction with subsidy or tax credit arrangements is the imposition of an effluent fee system, under which the polluter is made to bear the costs of his disposal directly. A schedule of emission fees predicated on the amount of damage done to the environment is applied to wastes discharged into the atmosphere or the water. Charges can also be imposed as a purely punitive measure without any relation to the damages actually done, or to the costs of treatment.

The three alternatives of subsidies, tax credits, and effluent fees are by far the most advocated and most widely practiced economic approaches to cost internalization. Since each is complex in design and impact, each is discussed separately below.

SUBSIDY PAYMENTS

502. Introduction

One argument frequently advanced in support of subsidies to industry for pollution control equipment is that the assets employed by industry in their abatement programs are economically unproductive; they neither add to revenues, nor decrease costs. A firm has little incentive to buy a device that does not help to produce salable products, or reduce production costs—even when the government offers to pay part of the cost. However, it sometimes happens that control devices enable the polluter to recover wastes with some economic value. To the extent that economic waste recovery is possible, firms may be induced to install pollution control devices by payment of only part of the cost by government.

It is also sometimes argued that cash payments for pollution abatement measures are to be preferred to tax credits because of ease of administration, because grants allow the government to avoid superimposing new loopholes in existing tax codes, and because grants enable preference to be given to smaller, financially weaker enterprises that are most in need of assistance in implementing pollution control.[10]

Subsidies, in the form of performance payments for pollution abatement rather than partial payments of capital expenditures, provide a continuing incentive to reduce emissions to the most economic level consistent with the level of subsidy payments. In practice, however, payments for reduction in discharge levels require an estimate of what the magnitude of pollutants might have been without any control devices, or any subsidy. The polluter has an obvious incentive to exaggerate the quantity of pollutants he would have discharged. As Edwin S. Mills notes:

> The trouble is precisely that which agricultural policy meets when it tries to pay farmers to reduce their crops. Jokes about farmers

deciding to double the amount of corn not produced this year capture the essence of the problem.[11]

Under a system of rewarding actual waste reduction, polluters would have an incentive to adopt, or at least to threaten to adopt, processes which produce a maximum amount of waste, in order to be able to collect a maximum of payments for restricting waste discharges. In equity, payments would probably have to be made on a continuing basis to firms which moved geographically as a means of reducing waste discharges in one local area. At one extreme, a case might be made for payments to potential dischargers who refrained from going into business—e.g., from locating anywhere—because of the payment for nonpollution. Moreover, subsidies could lead to higher net profits in pollution intensive industries, and perhaps produce a socially undesirable expansion of those industries.

It is questionable also whether accurate measurement of most emissions, and thus of emission reductions, is possible given our existing technology. It is certainly doubtful whether engineering estimates of emission volumes would satisfy the legal requirements of proof which an emission reduction subsidy system would impose.

An appropriate criticism of capital grant subsidies is that they are often incentives to undertake inefficient means of waste disposal. Changes in production techniques or in the fuel burned frequently are more efficient in reducing waste emissions than are end-of-the-line facilities. Most of the subsidy programs which have been enacted to date are limited to incentives for capital investment and have the result of making capital expenditures artificially cheap in relation to process or fuel changes, or to curtailment operations until an episodic danger had passed. Because of this, the most effective means of pollution abatement may in actuality be discouraged by subsidy payments.

Another frequent criticism of subsidy schemes is that it is inequitable to pay someone to refrain from an act which he has no right to commit in the first place, and that to pay a polluter to cease imposing a cost on the remainder of society is a form of blackmail. There are two possible replies to such a criticism: when the entire community is a beneficiary, it is not necessarily unsound economics (or unsound social policy) to have the community pay a portion of the cost of the improvement. More significantly, society is now asking the polluter to abate a nuisance which in all likelihood he had no way of knowing would ever be considered as a nuisance at the time his plant or facility was built. Most industrial polluters are simply doing on a larger scale what industrialists have always done; it is society that has changed the rules, not the polluter who has changed his behavior.

Whatever the pros and cons of subsidy payments, direct federal grants for capital equipment related to pollution abatement have been growing rapidly. Capital grants made through the Environmental Protection Agency and relating to water quality, air pollution, solid waste disposal, pesticide regulation, and radiation standards, almost doubled from $670 million in 1971 to $1.3 billion in 1972. By far the largest slice of the pie goes to local waste treatment plant grants. The federal government makes grants to cities for sewage treatment plants and to some industrial operations, and covers from 30 to 55 percent of the total cost depending on whether the state involved also bears part of the cost.

TAX CREDITS

503. Introduction

The term "tax credit," or "tax subsidy," or "tax expenditure" is used to describe special provisions of federal or state income tax systems which grant tax exemptions to achieve various social or economic objectives. Special provisions may take the form of deductions, credits, exclusions, preferred rates, or deferrals. In most cases the government has the option of using direct grants, direct loans, interest subsidies, federal insurance, or a guarantee of private loans to achieve the same ends as do the tax subsidies. The tax subsidy concept views a deduction as an imputed collection of the tax that would have been due had the deduction not been available, with a simultaneous grant of funds by the government to the taxpayer in the amount of the tax saving.

Although tax credits to aid in pollution control are a relatively new development, credits to induce similar activity or behavior in the national interest have a long history. The investment tax credit was introduced to encourage the purchase of equipment and machinery; preferential tax treatment of qualified pension plans was introduced to foster broader pension plan coverage; the corporate surtax exemption was aimed at encouraging small business; the deduction of home mortgage interest from taxable income was an inducement to home ownership; and so on.[12]

Federal tax credits aimed at cleaning up the environment had their beginning in 1966 with the suspension of the 7 percent investment tax credit. At that time an exception was made so that the credit could continue for pollution control equipment. In 1968, the tax-exempt status of industrial development bonds was revoked, but an exception was made for bonds the proceeds of which went into pollution control facilities. The federal law containing the major specific tax incentive for pollution control was passed in 1969, when the Tax Reform Act added Section 169 to the Internal Revenue Code. That section permits rapid, sixty-month depreciation allowances for newly-installed pollution control equipment.

The exemptions and tax incentive were motivated by industry arguments similar to those advanced in support of federal subsidy payments: that many industries would find it difficult to meet the cost of federal, state, and local pollution regulations without an exemption or incentive; that pollution control facilities do not add to earnings, cut costs, or improve competitive position; and that investment in pollution control produces a social benefit and the public should bear some of the cost of producing this benefit.[13] In each instance the Treasury, the Department of Health, Education and Welfare, and other government bodies opposed this special treatment for reasons ranging from erosion of the effectiveness of federal fiscal policy to the allegation that tax credits simply are not an effective stimulus to pollution abatement.

Secretary Finch of HEW pointed out that the cost to industry of effective pollution control under the then-existing regulations would average less than one-third of one percent of value added by all manufacturing and electric power industries, and that this relatively small cost did not appear to warrant federal cost-sharing.[14] The Secretary also argued that the proposed tax incentives were only available for investment in end-of-the-line hardware, producing an incentive for businesses to use hardware as a solution to every pollution problem to the exclusion of methods such as changes in fuel, in processing techniques, or in raw materials utilization.

Despite all opposition the investment tax credit was passed. Under the five-year rapid-amortization provision a taxpayer could deduct the total cost of pollution abatement equipment in five years, even though normal tax rules would establish a longer useful life for the property.

Viewed as a tax measure, the Treasury estimated that equipment with a 50 year useful life would have received a tax benefit from the new rapid write-off provision equal to a 20 percent investment credit. Viewed as an expenditure provision, the House, in effect, proposed to appropriate $400 million annually to share costs for an effort that, from the evidence available, needed no subsidy, and for an approach which, in the view of the experts, would in the long run be ineffective and inefficient.[15]

Not all pollution abatement equipment is covered by Section 169. The five-year tax write-off is limited to only a "certified pollution control facility," that is, a separate identifiable treatment facility used to abate air or water pollution. A building does not qualify as a pollution control facility under the provision unless it is exclusively for treatment; it must not include any equipment which serves a function other than pollution control. Facilities which only diffuse pollution, such as a smokestack on a plant, are not eligible for rapid write-off. Most importantly, Section 169 does not provide for writing off the cost of fuel desulphurization facilities, or of other facilities to remove pollutants from fuel, because such expenditures cannot be separated from other income-producing activities of the enterprise.

Individual states have been far ahead of the federal government in offering tax credits for antipollution investments. Starting in the early 1960's, state tax incentives took the form of property tax abatements (currently available in 21 states), sales and use tax exemptions (in 13 states), and accelerated write-offs or special tax credit (in 8 and 5 states, respectively).

Some of the state plans have been highly unsuccessful. New York State has since 1966 provided an investment tax credit of one percent of the cost of constructing or improving facilities to control air pollution or treat waste. However only 34 tax returns filed over the first 5 years of the plan claimed the special deduction. Apparently most companies found it more profitable to continue the state's already liberal rules governing the write-off rate for industrial assets, rather than switch to the new tax-credit scheme.

504. Virtues and Defects

A large number of claimed virtues and defects have been imputed to tax subsidies. In light of the extensive use of these tax devices, some consideration of the more common arguments is warranted.[16] Many of the virtues claimed for tax subsidies are subtle ones, which relate more to the common usage of the tool than to its economic impact.

For example, tax subsidies are often promoted with the observation that they involve less government bureaucracy and less red tape than do other alternatives. While it is possible (although doubtful) that tax incentives have in the past been less complex than, say, direct grants, this is not an advantage inherent to the technique. It is not the tax device that makes a program simple, but the substantive decision to produce a simple program. Much of the promotion of tax incentive programs may be a reaction to badly-designed direct expenditure programs; a more creative solution would be to design better direct expenditure programs.

A variant of the bureaucracy argument is that social problems are best solved by private rather than public decision-making, and that tax subsidies promote private decision-making and thus should be preferred. The rebuttal is parallel to the previous one; just as a direct grant program could be designed to involve a minimum of bureaucracy, so could a program be designed to provide a minimum of government control and a maximum of private decision-making. A tax credit allowed for pollution control expenditure is often cited as a method of government assistance that would promote private decision-making flexibility, as the taxpayer and not the government would select the control method and the amount of money to be invested in it. However, an expenditure program under which the government matched on a no-questions-asked grant basis some portion of all expenditures on pollution control would equally preserve private decision-making.

A much more substantial criticism of tax subsidies focuses on their lack of equity. They are worth more to high income taxpayers than to low income taxpayers, and they do not benefit those who are outside the tax system because of low incomes or tax-exempt status. This criticism is valid for virtually all pollution tax subsidies, which in general were never carefully structured to be equitable. By way of example, under the present tax structure every corporation pays a tax of 22 percent of its taxable income and a surtax of 26 percent of its income over $25,000. Thus, an expenditure for pollution abatement facilities for a corporation in the higher bracket, under Section 169, is subsidized by the government at 48 percent of the cost, while a corporation in the lower bracket is subsidized at 22 percent, and a firm with no profits at all in a tax year gets no assistance, although its obligations in installing facilities may be the same.

The real financial problem in private sector pollution is the inability of small businesses to pay for control devices. Not only do tax subsidies provide higher grants to larger firms, but they benefit only those with capital to invest and income to be sheltered—by definition almost excluding the smaller firms in the economy. For example, a $1 million investment in an electrostatic precipitator, when depreciated in sixty months under Section 169, benefits fully only businesses with $200,000 in yearly profits to shelter from taxation. Businesses with less than this in profit either get little or no benefit, or cannot use Section 169. Even larger firms in need of assistance might not get it under existing tax subsidy provisions. The unprofitable Penn Central Railroad could not benefit from Section 169, although it certainly has substantial need for assistance to meet its antipollution responsibilities.

Such inequitable and irrational side effects are not restricted to tax subsidies for pollution control, but are common to tax subsidies as a class of incentives.

> Many tax incentives look, and are, highly irrational when phrased as direct expenditure programs structured the same way. It is doubtful that most of our tax incentives would ever have been introduced, let alone accepted, if so structured, and many would be laughed out of Congress. What HEW Secretary would propose a medical assistance program for the aged that cost $200 million, and under which $90 million would go to persons with incomes over $50,000, and only $8 million to persons with incomes under $5,000? The tax proposal to remove the 3 percent floor under the medical expense deductions of persons over 65 would have had just that effect . . . What HUD Secretary would suggest a housing rehabilitation subsidized loan program under which a wealthy person could borrow the funds at 3 percent interest but a poor person would have to pay 7 percent or 8 percent? That is the effect of the five-year amortization of rehabilitation expenditures contained in the recent Tax Reform Act.[17]

Aside from equity considerations, it is unlikely that most large polluters need public financial assistance to meet pollution control requirements. It is even more debatable whether we want to promote the downgrading and elimination of small business which is inevitable as the cost of required pollution controls rise, and government gives disproportionate aid to the largest and most profitable companies.

Tax subsidies are also inequitable because some of the tax benefits go to taxpayers for activities which they would have performed without the benefits, thus the subsidy stimulates no additional activity. This is the case where tax subsidies are given to assist in meeting pollution standards required by law. However,the criticism applies equally to a similarly-structured direct grant program. For example, direct grants for industrial sewage treatment may be given to firms that for legal or other reasons would have treated their effluent anyway.

Another problem is the burden which tax subsidies place on the federal budget. While overall limits may be placed on federal spending by Congress, it is almost impossible to apply such limits to tax subsidies, which once passed become noncontrollable federal outlays. If tax subsidies were structured as direct expenditures there would be no logical basis for such immunity; the sheltering takes place solely because of the device through which they were granted. The existence of tax incentives greatly decreases the ability of the government to maintain control over its expenditures and priorities, both as to the programs to be funded and as to amounts to be spent on particular programs and areas.

The design of a subsidy or the regulations governing it may produce results which are counterproductive to the intended goal. It has been pointed out that a tax credit for pollution control equipment focuses on expenditures for machinery as a control method, perhaps to the exclusion of more efficient control techniques. If the tax credit applied only to equipment and not to its operation, preference would be given to facilities with low operating costs, even if they required very large capital outlays. For example, a firm seeking to remove cigarette butts from cooling water prior to pumping it back into a waterway might have them removed by an unskilled worker with a tea strainer at a cost of $5,000 per year. Or, the company might purchase an elaborate machine for $60,000 and with annual maintenance costs of $2,500 to do the same job. With a 100 percent tax credit, which is sometimes recommended in Congress, the machine would cost the firm less.

A more subtle problem arises in that state and federal agencies are burdened by tax subsidies with the need to process thousands of applications for exemptions to the variety of state and federal taxes; by law, they must provide businessmen with detailed certification to meet exemption requirements of Section 169. This burden (which is obviously not unique to tax subsidies, but could arise under direct grants) produces either a reduction in the agency's other enforcement and monitoring activities, or a very cursory examination of exemption applications which makes abuses of the tax subsidy quite predictable.

Finally, tax incentives are unlikely to lead to minimizing the total amount of pollution because they are generally applied uniformly within the jurisdiction of the government unit imposing the tax. However, to grant tax incentives on the basis of political boundaries is to ignore that a dollar spent to prevent the discharge of waste into a body of air or water already polluted to the limit of its ability to cleanse itself yields much greater social returns than the same dollar spent to prevent discharges into more assimilative bodies.

505. Comparison of Rapid-Amortization to Other Incentives

In analyzing the economic impact of a rapid-amortization provision such as that found in Section 169, it is useful to restructure the provision to conform to competing tax and non-tax types of pollution control assistance. Paul R. McDaniel and Alan S. Kaplinsky have worked out comparisons of rapid-amortization to direct grants, interest-free loans, government guarantee of conventional financing, and investment credits; the material presented here is based on their calculations.[18]

Direct Grants. If Section 169 were reformulated as a direct federal grant program, a summary of the grant provisions would read as follows:

Every corporation that purchases a $150,000 certified pollution control facility shall be eligible to receive a direct grant from the federal government on the following basis:

—a corporation with profits exceeding $25,000 for the year is eligible for a grant of $11,952;

—a corporation with profits under $25,000 for the year is eligible for a grant of $5,479;

—a corporation with no profits, or with a loss for the year, or which is nonprofit by nature, will receive no federal assistance;

—a corporation which follows pollution control policies not involving the purchase of pollution abatement hardware need not even apply.[19]

No elected legislature would vote a grant with such inequitable and irrational side effects, yet the United States Congress passed exactly such a measure in Section 169 of the Tax Reform Act of 1969.

An Interest-Free Loan. Section 169 can be viewed as providing an interest-free federal government loan in the amount of the difference between the taxes which would have been paid using regular depreciation on the pollution control facility, and the taxes actually paid under accelerated depreciation during the fiveyear write-off period. The loan is repaid after five years, when the corporation must forego depreciation deductions to which it would have been entitled had regular depreciation been taken. On a $150,000 pollution control facility, a corporation in the 48 percent tax bracket receives a loan that saves a total of $24,038 in interest, while the 22 percent tax bracket corporation saves only $11,029 in interest. An unprofitable corporation faced with purchasing a $150,000 facility receives no interest saving at all because it has no earnings. Such a firm must go to the regular commercial money market for funds with which to purchase the equipment.

Government-Guaranteed Financing. Section 169 can be formulated as a federal program which guarantees repayment of conventional corporate borrowing for pollution control purposes, thus securing a preferred interest rate for the borrower. On a full mortgage for the $150,000 expenditure in a market which normally charges 10 percent per annum, a corporation with more than $25,000 in profits receives the equivalent of a guaranteed loan at an interest rate of 7.98 percent. A corporation showing less than $25,000 in annual profits must pay the equivalent of an interest rate of 9.38 percent, while one with no profits or a loss must pay the full 10 percent rate of interest.

An Investment Credit. Section 169 can be reconstructed as an investment credit by determining the present value of the net tax saving resulting from using rapid amortization rather than conventional straight line depreciation. The rapid amortization provision is the equivalent of a 7.97 percent tax credit for investment in pollution control equipment for a corporation in the 48 percent tax bracket, a 3.65 percent tax credit for investment in the same facilities by a firm in the 22 percent bracket, and no tax credit for a firm which shows no profits. In each example a 10 percent imputed rate of interest is used, although results are comparable irrespective of the interest rate chosen.

Given the problems and the inequitable effects discussed above, it seems as a general rule that the burden of proof should fall on anyone proposing the use of a tax subsidy system for pollution control in any given situation. Proof must include a detailing of what advantages, if any, might be obtained by using the tax subsidy as compared to spending an equivalent amount of money on direct pollution grants, or comparable alternatives. It appears that the advantages of a tax system would have to be overwhelming to overcome the problems and loss of control that accompany even a well-designed tax subsidy system.

EFFLUENT FEES

506. Introduction

As we have already noted, much of our environmental degradation arises because the price system is not applied to many of our natural resources. Fresh air and clean water are resources that are converted in the productive process in the same way that coal and steel are converted. But while a price related to the cost of production is charged for fuel and raw materials, our air and water resources can in most cases be used without payment for the privilege.

The problem exists because people use costly materials with a high degree of efficiency, but apply very little care or diligence to the use of resources which are free. In New York City, where water is supplied by the city at no charge, taps are left running, water lines develop huge leaks and are not repaired, and a periodic water crisis is the usual result. For the same reason, the cleansing power of air and water is overused when no charge is made for these resources. Consider, for example, how inefficiently electricity or long distance telephone service would be used if they were available at no charge.

The economist responds to this problem by claiming that there is no excuse for supplying scarce resources free; that these resources should be available only at an appropriate price. Specifically, the economist calls for an extension of a tax or fee system, one that does not necessarily increase the overall burden of taxes but rather gives industry the opportunity to minimize its tax load by behaving in a way consistent with social goals.

For example, the accumulation of litter could be reduced by imposing a significant tax or fee on no-deposit, no-return containers, perhaps matched by a reduction in the excise tax on items in returnable containers. Such an approach has the virtue of being self-enforcing, and therefore not very costly. Its instrument is the production line meter rather than the regulatory agency inspector. Calculation of the total tax payable on disposable containers requires no more than a record of how many cases of such containers have been manufactured or used. There are no crimes to be discovered, no courtroom battles, and no disputes over appropriate levels of fines to be imposed. Such a tax/fee approach has the additional advantage of longevity. Because it is self-enforcing it will be equally effective five or ten years from now when public interest in the subject has diminished. Unlike a program dependent on the enthusiasm of a regulatory agency, a tax or fee does not require continued enthusiasm for the original cause.

An effluent fee system is analogous to this tax on containers in that it attempts to minimize the costs of pollution damage and pollution abatement by requiring a polluter to pay a periodic fee, based on the amount of his effluent. One approach is to set the fee to produce that amount of effluent yielding the minimum total cost of pollution plus cost of pollution control. This point is illustrated in Figure 5-1, which is the total cost of pollution and pollution control curve that appeared in Chapter Two. Operation at point 'a' motivates polluters as a group to use an optimal mix of abatement and fee payments to maximize their profits.

Alternatively, fees could be based on the cost of treating the discharged waste and returning it to its natural state. This is practical with liquid wastes, but impractical with air pollutants because of the difficulty of treating gaseous wastes centrally. The approach has proven promising for water pollutants, and has been used in the Ruhr basin Genossenschaften, and by some municipalities in the United States for determining sewage charges for industrial waste. Effluent fees might also be imposed at a purely punitive level without relation to either the cost of pollution or the cost of

FIGURE 5-1

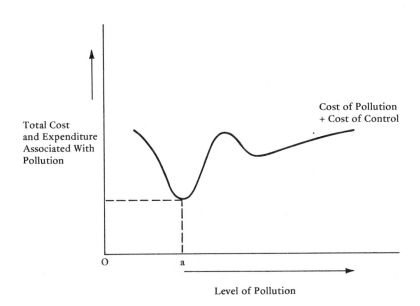

Level of Pollution

pollution control. However, this would induce individual polluters to undertake abatement to the left of the minimum total cost point on Figure 5-1.

Most commonly, however, effluent fees are based on some rough estimate of the average damage done to the environment and its members by a specific pollutant. For example, California state officials might conduct an investigation with respect to the Sacramento River basin, and conclude that 20,000 pounds of phosphates per month were being discharged into the river system by processing plants, and that the phosphates caused damage estimated at $50,000 per month to water supplies, navigation, individual firms, and public recreation along the 90 miles of waterway before the river flowed into the Pacific Ocean. The state government would then levy an excise tax of $2.50 per pound on the discharge of phosphates into the river. It would make similar calculations with respect to each of the other important pollutants in the waterway. Each polluter would be required to monitor his own discharges, and to calculate and pay a monthly fee reflecting its total polluting activity. Spot checks would be made on the operations of different polluters, much the same as government auditors make spot checks on the self-reporting activities of companies for income tax purposes.

Some polluting firms, aware of the technologies currently available, would purchase abatement equipment to reduce their tax burden to near zero. Other firms would find such equipment unavailable, and would respond by maintaining their existing production techniques but carrying a heavy emission fee burden. Some firms would choose to undertake some abatement and to pay some fees. In total, society would approach what was described in Chapter One as an optimal level of pollution; that level at which, to produce a dollar's worth of satisfactions in a less-polluted environment, it would be necessary to spend resources that were currently yielding more than a dollar's worth of social satisfactions in their current usage.

It should be noted that while the effluent fee system makes it unnecessary for an outside body to dictate to a polluter what abatement technology (if any) he should use, it does not remove the necessity of estimating the cost of the harm caused by specific effluents. The difficulties in such estimation have been discussed earlier. Theoretically, the effluent fee should be set equal to the cost of the marginal amount of harm done by the final unit of pollutant introduced into the environment. In practice, effluent fees would probably be set at the average level of harm done by a unit of effluent; marginal rates would be both difficult to calculate, and difficult to explain to the public. In most cases fees based on marginal harm would be higher than fees based on average harm, but the difference should not be so great as to invalidate the approach.[20] It should be recognized that the same average vs. marginal problem applies to the legislative approach to pollution control, although that approach is much more crude, and the differences involved much more significant than the average vs. marginal distinction associated with effluent fees.

It might also be possible to adapt the principles of two-level iterative planning as developed in Hungary and elsewhere to the specific problem of water pollution control. One such procedure requires the central authority to propose a scale of effluent fees to each polluter. Each polluter then makes his own cost calculations and reports back to the central authority the amount of effluent he will discharge and his total spending on abatement at each level of fees. Using this information, the central authority calculates a new schedule of fees, and the procedure continues until it converges to an optimal amount of pollution, and a least-cost combination of abatement to reach this optimal quantity.

507. Effluent Fees and Auto Emissions

A self-monitored effluent fee arrangement is best suited for stationary pollution sources producing significant amounts of effluent. Automobile emission fees would not be feasible if introduced at the owner level, because the monitoring of a large number of small-emission sources would introduce prohibitively high administration costs. A simple proposal is to sample the discharge of effluents from automobiles as they are manufactured, and to include in the sales tax on each car a fee based on the sampled effluent discharge. Sampling once at time of manufacture is inexpensive, but has the defect that it has no effect on cars once they leave the factory. Existing antipollution devices (blow-by devices, afterburners, and engine modifications) are not effective for more than one or two years without maintenance.

Thus, an effective application of effluent fees to automotive pollution would probably require both sampling of emissions at the time of annual inspection, and having the annual registration fee dependent on the result of the inspection. Ideally, one would charge a fee based on the average effluent per mile multiplied by the number of miles the car had been driven since its last inspection, and modified by whether the car was registered and driven within a metropolitan air shed.

A technological problem arises in that there is not currently available any inexpensive and reliable metering device for automobile effluents for use in an annual inspection. Federal automobile legislation has recognized these difficulties by avoiding any kind of fee system and opting for direct regulation at the manufacturer level.

508. Current Applications of Effluent Fees[21]

While effluent fee arrangements are only now coming into use in the United States, they have been in use in the Ruhr River basin in Germany for almost 60 years. The Ruhr and Emscher rivers flow approximately parallel to each other for about 75 miles in northwestern Germany until they both join the Rhine River near Duisburg. About 1904, users of the river basin area joined together and agreed to use the Emscher for the bulk of their effluent discharge, so that the Ruhr River would remain pure enough for recreational use. By 1930 seven Genossenschaften had been established in the Ruhr district, the Emscher River had been rerouted, diked, shortened, and about 90 percent of the liquid wastes from the area were being discharged into the Emscher rather than into the Ruhr. At four different points prior to where the Emscher empties into the Rhine, the Emschergenossenschaft operates treatment facilities to remove the wastes from its waters. The concentration of effluent into this single stream results in significant economies of scale in the eventual treatment of the waste.

Individual polluters discharging into the Emscher are charged effluent fees based on the quantity of their effluent, and on the average cost of treating each type of waste. The discharger thus is given an incentive to reduce his emissions to the extent that the cost of his own treatment is less than the charges levied by the Genossenschaft.[22] The possibility of saving on effluent fee costs has induced Ruhr industries to reduce the quantity of their emissions by instituting process changes and by recycling wastes.[23] Assessments on individual members of the Ruhr system are public obligations and can be enforced by law as taxes. Because of good relations between the associations and their members, there has never been a need for such enforcement. The Ruhr system is limited, as are the systems in use in the United States, to the abatement of water pollution. However, the method of determining discharge fees, if not the joint treatment concept, is applicable to the treatment of air pollutant discharges.

In the State of Vermont, the Water Resource Board has classified the waters of the state according to their intended uses and the minimum standards of effluents which may be discharged into each. A permit is required for each waste discharge. If the polluter is unable to meet normal standards required for issuance of a permit because his waste is not sufficiently treated, the Water Resources Board will issue a temporary permit but the discharger must pay an effluent charge based on the amount of damage to the waterway caused by his pollution. The charge per unit of pollutant varies to reflect the initial state of the waters involved, and the predicted economic damage done to other private and public users of the waterway. The Vermont charge system is not very close to the pure economic model of effluent fees discussed earlier, in that it merely superimposes an effluent charge on a more traditional permit system. However, the Assistant Attorney General of Vermont for Environmental Control has characterized the system as a necessary intermediate step in moving toward a system which relies exclusively on emission charges. An interesting interpretation of the Vermont statute is that the issuance of a temporary permit for discharge and the payment of effluent fees does not immunize the polluter from damages or injunctive relief from private suits, but the polluter is allowed to deduct any damages paid by him due to private suits from the effluent charge due the state.

The Regional Water Quality Act of 1970 introduced by Senator Proxmire comes closer to the pure economic model of emission charges. The proposed bill establishes a schedule of national effluent charges for all pollutants other than domestic sewage, with fees reflecting the quantity and quality of the waste discharged and the resulting damage to the quality of the waterway. The Water Quality Act would not preclude criminal or civil actions against the polluter, and would not allow him to deduct the cost of private damage actions from his effluent charges. An average effluent charge of 10 cents per pound of oxygen demanding material discharged (the figure recommended in the Delaware River Estuary study) would produce approximately $2 billion in revenue each year.[24] The revenue could be channelled to states or cities for the construction of waste treatment plants, or given to water management associations in the regions where the fees originated to further their abatement work.

509. Virtues and Defects of Effluent Fees

The biggest advantage of the effluent fee approach is that it is the least expensive method of producing a socially optimal level of pollution abatement.[25] The fee provides an inducement to the polluter to develop more efficient abatement techniques, or to install pollution control equipment. Pollution costs are completely internalized within the firm whether the polluter abates or pays the emissions fee if that is the least costly alternative. Pollution abatement equipment manufacturers are motivated to research new technology, knowing that markets for their devices are available if their costs can be kept below the known costs of emission fee payments. Further, determination of the most efficient method of abating a given firm's effluent is placed on corporate management, where it belongs, rather than in the hands of a regulatory agency. The corporation is not biased in choosing among abatement, process change, and fuel changes as is the case with tax incentive systems. The polluter is allowed to pay the effluent fee during a period of transition to new manufacturing processes, rather than being forced by sudden changes in the law to abate immediately.

A further advantage of cost internalization by effluent fees is the adjustment of consumer purchases in favor of lower cost (and lower fee-paying) producers. Depending on the ability of the polluter to pass on cost increases to his consumers, the demand for goods produced with minimal pollution should increase at the expense of high-pollution substitute goods. The reallocation of purchases results in a lower total pollution load for society as a whole.

There is great selectivity possible in the way in which effluent fees are applied. They are adjustable to the time of day, the season of the year, or the existence of special weather phenomena, such as atmospheric inversions. The entire fee schedule may be altered as our knowledge of the synergistic effects of certain combinations of pollutants grows. Polluters may be induced to locate in areas where their damage to the atmosphere or waterways is least, through altering the fees imposed for waste discharge in different geographic areas.

As compared with the least-cost program for the Delaware River Estuary, discussed in Chapter Three, the effluent fee program has the important efficiency advantage that it requires much less in the way of information and analytical refinement. The initial DECS report was sufficient to provide an estimate of the required fee, and changes could be made if responses to the charge indicated a need for adjustment. Since the DECS report did not consider the possibility of process change, the charge they recommended was probably too high. Under an effluent fee system the charge could be quickly adjusted downward when the problem was recognized.

As new technology developed, the effluent charge could be gradually reduced while the waterway standard was maintained, or the standard could be raised if this were considered desirable. The direct control measures implicit in the Delaware Estuary least-cost program (and of the effluent standard of the uniform treatment program) provide only a limited incentive to introduce new technology.

The argument most frequently cited by environmental enthusiasts opposed to effluent fees, and the one cited in the DECS report, is that the proposal creates a license to pollute. This suggests that the critic has in mind some alternative system of control that would both flatly prohibit pollution and would be economic in terms of alternative uses of available resources. Actually, the regulatory approach confers a much greater license to pollute. A regulatory order asks that pollution levels be reduced to some point which a government official finds practicable and feasible. When confronted with such an order, a firm has no incentive to improve its level of performance from that stated in the order. Until the order is issued, the firm has no incentive to do anything at all to reduce its effluent.

It is important to note that an insistence on the use of a regulatory approach instead of effluent fees does not imply the lack of a cost-benefit analysis (if only an implicit one). The assumption behind a regulation which bans all production or all pollution is that the costs involved are either infinite, or at least so much greater than potential benefits that the calculation is not worth making. This is certainly the case with the banning of dumping of mercury into lakes and streams, which was mentioned in the Preface.

There are two significant technical problems which must be overcome if effluent fee systems are to function efficiently. One is that current monitoring technology has not yet produced efficient, low-cost devices to measure all types of pollutants. Instruments capable of measuring several pollutants simultaneously are available, but their high cost makes it unlikely that they would be applied to the measurement of small-scale pollution sources. The problem is alleviated but not solved by the introduction of a self-monitoring scheme carried out by individual polluters, because this simply passes the high cost of available control devices on to industry, and says nothing about the simple unavailability of devices to measure a number of important pollutants.

The second technical problem is that of determining and quantifying the damage done by particular pollutants—a problem which has been discussed at length earlier. This problem is important because substantive due process requirements in law require that the cost-benefit relationship which forms the basis for the effluent fee schedule be reasonably accurate. There is some possibility that a polluter could challenge the validity of an effluent fee levy on the grounds that its fee calculations lacked scientific substantiation. The issue of legal acceptability of a cost-benefit analysis would not arise in an effluent fee scheme employing either the effluent standard-fee or the ambient air quality standard-fee approaches, which are discussed below. Under each of these two methods the fee schedule is prepared in relation to predetermined national standards rather than being based on estimates of pollution damages for a given area.

A further alleged weakness of effluent fee arrangements concerns the fact that some firms can pass the fee on to customers, thus eliminating their incentive to abate. It is not clear whether the entire burden of an effluent fee would or could be shifted to the consumer. The fact that effluent fees would be lower for rural polluters than for urban polluters, and lower for some competitors than for others, lessens the likelihood of prices simply being increased to cover the entire cost increase. The argument has greatest relevance when applied to public utilities, but even there the existence of a lag in obtaining regulatory rate-increases creates at least a short-term incentive for abatement.

The high degree of selectivity and flexibility inherent in waste discharge fees is sometimes viewed as a disadvantage as well as an advantage. Since the fee schedule is subject to continuous and rapid revision by pollution control agencies, industry may be frustrated in attempts to plan comprehensive abatement programs over the long term, and may be subjected to a rule of politically motivated men rather than one of equity. However, administrative controls could be introduced to guarantee against unjustified modifications, perhaps by guaranteeing existing fee rates which would not exceed stated limits within a given planning period.

In summary, the overriding advantages of emission charges are that when fees are imposed, all costs of pollution are internalized to the polluter, pollution abatement expenditures take on an economic rather than a social function, and flaws in the incentive-to-abate system which are common to other alternatives are corrected. Also, decision-making is decentralized, and individual polluters have very real incentives to adopt the most efficient means of abatement available. If fees are set at the proper level, a socially-optimal degree of abatement will take place. Six decades of German experience attest to the effectiveness of the effluent charge system; the several American experiments seem to point to a successful implementation of such systems, at least as applied to water pollution problems.

510. Administration of the Fee

The effective administration of an effluent fee plan requires an administrative agency to determine the cost-benefit relationship for all pollutants within its jurisdiction, to regulate and inspect self-monitoring reporting arrangements, and to calculate and enforce the resulting fee assessments. A question arises as to whether state, local, or airshed/watershed entities are best able to set up and administer such an effluent fee program.

The Air Quality Act of 1969 delegated all air pollution control responsibilities to state agencies. If an effluent fee plan could be implemented under this Act,[26] state legislatures would be responsible both for the enabling legislation and for supervision of control efforts.

Past experience with control efforts at various governmental levels indicates that local governments are probably better able than state governments to calculate the necessary cost-benefit relationships, to provide continuous monitoring and inspection, and to enforce fee payment. However, both local and state political entities are faced with a significant conflict of interest between their desire to protect the public welfare, and the economic reality that stringent pollution standards and high fee levels may induce new and existing industries to locate in more favorable jurisdictions.

A better approach might be to set up special pollution districts, conforming to airshed or watershed characteristics, to administer effluent fee control arrangements. These districts would almost certainly overlap existing city or county boundaries, and in many cases would encompass parts of several states. The pollution district would be identical with the area defined as appropriate for cost-benefit studies. The independent nature of the special district would make it less subject to pressure from large industrial polluters or local special interest groups. If such an arrangement produced overwhelming inter-jurisdictional disputes, it could be modified to one whereby the rule-making and fee-setting power of the pollution district authority was subject to challenge by city or state authorities in the courts on either procedural or substantive grounds. The authority would have primary responsibility for performing the initial cost-benefit studies and the setting of fees, for arranging for self-monitoring reporting systems, and for conducting economic studies of the business reaction to and economic impact of the various fees imposed.

The principal technical problem facing a control agency would be that of implementing a self-reporting monitoring program for the volume and nature of pollutants from individual sources. Ideally the agency would either provide each emitter with a standardized monitoring device to insure uniformity and accuracy, or it would certify available devices meeting agency standards. Until the necessary automatic monitoring devices were available at reasonable cost, the agency could require periodic samples to be taken and analyzed in lieu of continuous monitoring.

An administrative decision would have to be made as to whether the existence of an operating effluent fee plan should preclude private actions against polluters, or whether damages from such private actions should be deductable from effluent fee payments. Considerations of equity suggest that neither should be the case. A citizen subjected to pollution damage to his property or person would find little solace and no compensation in the increased fee that the polluter would pay to some autonomous agency. Further, if a quasi-monopolistic polluter such as an electric utility were actually able to pass much of its emission fee payments on to the consumer by way of higher prices, the individual citizen might find himself paying twice—for the emission fee, as well as suffering damage from the pollution. The retention of private as well as effluent-fee remedies would provide additional economic incentive for a quasi-monopolistic polluter to internalize his costs of pollution. For a polluter in a competitive industry (and if the cost-benefit calculations of the effluent-fee setter were correct), the existence of double liability would induce the polluter to abate his level of pollution below that level which was economically optimal from the standpoint of the whole society.

No such efficiency problem arises with alternate public remedies such as injunctive relief, which should not be displaced by the implementation of an effluent fee arrangement. For example, periodic pollution incidents arising from short-term fuel substitution may result in extraordinarily high pollution levels over a short period of time which would not significantly increase an effluent fee charge that is based on an average emission level over a period of time. Such a situation would warrant injunctive or similar relief.

511. A Pollution Standard—Effluent Fee Approach

An effluent fee administered by a special pollution control district may be combined with air or water quality standards for the district, providing an abatement standard upon which the effluent fee schedule is based. Such an approach has several names: here it will be called a pollution standard-effluent fee approach.

The air or water quality standard could be considered as a maximum standard above which the emitter could not pollute. Such a maximum standard could be set at the highest level of pollution acceptable without serious health effects. The effluent fee schedule below this maximum standard would provide a continuing incentive for the polluter to abate to a lower level of emission.

Alternately, the effluent fee schedule could be sharply increased at levels above the air or water quality standard applied to the district, and lowered below that standard. This would create an important incentive to abate to the standard level, and a less powerful incentive to abate below that level. Such a plan abandons the basic "cost-internalization to produce efficiency" approach, since the polluter pays a fee unrelated to the actual damage caused. However, this combined approach retains most of the other advantages of the effluent fee. The pollution standard effluent fee approach may also be more politically acceptable than an effluent fee approach which relies completely on a profit maximization incentive.

512. Conclusion

It is obvious that solutions must be found that are more likely to prevent the continuing deterioration of the environment than those which have been tried to date. Given the nature of our capitalistic society, economic incentives seem to have the greatest chance of successfully internalizing the social costs of pollution to the polluting firm.

Under existing regulatory plans, no incentive is offered for a polluter to abate beyond the minimum requirements of the law; in fact there is an economic incentive to continue to pollute at the same level as one's competitors. The various tax incentive and subsidy schemes which we have discussed recognize the nonproductivity of pollution abatement equipment, but it is doubtful whether such programs actually provide any incentive to either pollution control or to the internalization of pollution costs. A more serious problem is the unintended impact and side effects of incentives delivered through the tax system.

The most promising approach we have discussed is the effluent fee system, which overcomes the basic flaw in tax incentive and subsidy systems in that pollution abatement expenditures for end-of-line treatment or for production changes take on an economic function. An equally important advantage to an effluent fee system is the decentralization of the abatement decision-making process so that individual decision-makers have real economic incentives to adopt the most efficient available means of emissions abatement.

Another significant method of forcing industry to internalize the social costs of their production processes is private environmental litigation—an approach which is discussed in detail in the next chapter.

REFERENCES

[1]R. H. Coase, "The Problem of Social Cost," *The Journal of Law and Economics*, Vol. III (October, 1960), pp. 1-44.

[2]By way of illustration, assume that an optimal mix between soldiers and civilians is to be determined in a free market, with bargaining and side-payments permitted. There are two alternatives: taxpayers can bargain inductees into the military with higher payments, or everyone is drafted with the possibility of the highest bidders buying their way out. Coase argues that efficiency is served in either case because the tax cost of recruiting soldiers with dollars is equivalent to the cost of foregone national income of refusing to let soldiers buy their way out. Coase also argues that an identical soldier-civilian mix will result under either rule, with the last person to volunteer under a bid-in system also being the last person to buy his way out under a property-rights system.

[3]There are other assumptions inherent in a discussion of a bargaining solution; a small number of parties, equal in economic power, and in full possession of information concerning their own and their adversaries' positions, which confront an externality situation in an economy

in which resource allocation is in every other respect optimal. In most environmental pollution cases the parties involved are far from equal insofar as organization, power, and information are concerned. The typical situation is one in which one or more sources of pollution, associated with a large economic interest, affect a large and diffuse group of victims whose individual interests are harmed relatively little. Moreover, there is often no signal to the victims that important values are being destroyed. Consider a hundred fishermen who are faced not with dead, floating fish, but with a decline in their catch. No one fisherman finds it worth his while to bargain (or knows with whom to bargain), or even to generate information. The fisherman also finds that the costs of organizing a group action are prohibitive. In such a context, bargaining does not occur.

[4]A. Demsetz, "Toward A Theory of Property Rights," *American Economic Review Papers and Proceedings*, No. 57 (1967), p. 14.

[5]Lawrence Tribe, "Legal Frameworks for the Assessment and Control of Technology," *Minerva* (April, 1971), pp. 88-89.

[6]See the technical discussion of public goods externalities and water recreation in Paul Davidson, F. Gerard Adams and Joseph Seneca, "The Social Value of Water Recreational Facilities Resulting from an Improvement in Water Quality: The Delaware Estuary," in Kneese and Bower, *Water Research* (Baltimore: Johns Hopkins Press, 1966), pp. 182-187.

[7]The argument appears in "On Divergence Between Social Cost and Private Cost," *Economica*, Vol. 30 (1963), p. 309.

[8]A similar proposal made by the Treasury in 1970 to tax the lead content of gasoline was opposed by the oil industry, and didn't even clear the first congressional hurdle, the House Ways and Means Committee. In part because the oil industry is less likely to fight the sulphur tax, it is considered to have a much better outlook for success.

[9]E. S. Mills, *User Fees and the Quality of the Environment* (in preparation), cited in Robert M. Solow, "The Economist's Approach to Pollution and Its Control," *Science*, No. 173 (August 6, 1971), p. 502.

[10]Argued in Kenneth R. Reed, "Economic Incentives for Pollution Abatement: Applying Theory to Practice," *Arizona Law Review* No. 12 (1970), pp. 517-518.

[11]"Economic Incentives in Air-Pollution Control," in Harold Wolozin, ed., *The Economics of Air Pollution* (New York: W. W. Norton and Company, 1966), p. 77.

[12]These are discussed in Stanley S. Surrey, "Tax Incentives As A Device for Implementing Government Policy: A Comparison with Direct Government Expenditures," *Harvard Law Review* No. 83 (February, 1970), pp. 706-713.

[13]See *Hearings on the President's Proposal to Repeal Investment Tax Credit and to Extend Surcharge and Certain Excise Tax Rates* (Ways and Means Committee, House of Representatives, 91st Congress, 1st Session), pp. 145 ff.

[14]A February, 1970 report by the Conference Board in New York indicated that industry's 1969 capital appropriations for air and water pollution control dropped 56.9 percent below the 1968 appropriation, a drop in pollution control investments from less than four-tenths of one percent of 1968 gross revenues to less than two-tenths of one percent for 1969. Cited in Arnold W. Reitze and Glenn Reitze, "Tax Incentives Don't Stop Pollution," *American Bar Association Journal* No. 57 (February, 1971), p. 131. One estimate is that General Motor's budget for direct pollution control is about $40 million annually, about .17 of one percent of gross sales. This figure is about one-sixth of G.M.'s annual advertising budget. Cited in John C. Esposito. *The Vanishing Air* (New York: Grossman Publishers, 1970), p. 243.

[15]Paul R. McDaniel and Alan S. Kaplinsky, "The Use of the Federal Income Tax System to Combat Air and Water Pollution: A Case Study in Tax Expenditures," *Boston College Industrial and Commercial Law Review, Vol. XII* (February, 1971), p. 354.

[16]For much of the following material I am indebted to the discussion in Stanley S. Surrey, "Tax Incentives As A Device for Implementing Government Policy: A Comparison with Direct Government Expenditures," *op. cit.,* pp. 15-35.

[17]*Ibid.,* pp. 723-24.

[18]Paul R. McDaniel and Alan S. Kaplinsky, "The Use of the Federal Income Tax System to Combat Air and Water Pollution: A Case Study in Tax Expenditures," *op. cit.,* pp. 360-66.

[19]*Ibid.,* pp. 360-61.

[20]Marc J. Roberts has pointed out that marginal cost pricing presents a unique pricing problem. Since a river basin authority is operating a multi-part system and has the flexibility to treat first where the cost of treatment is least, the basin authority's marginal costs of removing additional waste will almost always be increasing and hence higher than its average cost. If all firms were charged the authority's marginal cost of abatement, a surplus would be generated. The river basin authority could avoid the surplus through a two-part tariff which incorporated a *negative* fee plus a variable fee based on the marginal cost of abatement. The negative fee would be a rebate given to each firm based on a non-pollution-related factor such as the number of employees or the dollar output of the firm.

A related problem is what happens when a new firm enters the system, which under marginal pricing will increase charges to each existing member since the expanded volume of effluent will have to be treated more intensively. One solution is to charge new firms a connection fee that reflects the costs of expanding the treatment system to accept their wastes. The fee could be fixed at some multiple of the annual negative basic charge and paid by making the new firm ineligible for the negative flat fee for an appropriate number of years. See Marc J. Roberts, "River Basin Authorities: A National Solution to Water Pollution," *Harvard Law Review* No. 83 (1970), pp. 1549-1553.

[21]The material in this section is summarized from the discussion in Kenneth R. Reed, "Economic Incentives for Pollution Abatement: Applying Theory to Practice," *op. cit.*, pp. 534-540.

[22]The net cost to a polluter who treats his own discharge is the difference between waste treatment expenditures and the value of recovered, salable by-products. The polluter will only recover these by-products if he treats his own waste; the existence of recoverable by-products will in part determine whether he will abate his own discharges, or will use the Emscher bulk treatment plants and pay the fee levied.

[23]See Allen Kneese, *Water Quality Management by Regional Authorities in the Ruhr Area*, in Hearings Before the Subcommittee on Air and Water Pollution, Senate Committee on Public Works, 89th Congress, 1st Session, part 3, pp. 942 ff. (1965), or the earlier article under the same title in *Papers and Proceedings of the Regional Science Association*, Vol. II (1963).

[24]Quoted in 115 *Congressional Record* S 14973 (November 25, 1969), cited in Kenneth R. Reed, "Economic Incentives for Pollution Abatement: Applying Theory to Practice," *op. cit.*, p. 539. To the extent that introduction of an effluent fee reduced the amount of liquid waste this figure would obviously be lower.

[25]The fact that an effluent fee approach will be the least expensive method of producing *any* desired level of pollution abatement has several interesting properties. Unlike many of the propositions about prices in welfare economics, this result does not require a world of perfect competition. It applies equally to monopolists or to oligopolists or to small firms producing heterogeneous products. The proposition holds even if the firms involved are not simple profit maximizers, but instead maximize their growth, their total revenues, their share of market, or any combination of these or a variety of other goals. Further, the proposition holds whatever the set of output levels or level of pollution abatement the society desires. It does not, for example, prejudge whether society should or should not reduce the number of private passenger cars in the process of decreasing air pollution. The only assumption inherent in this claim for an effluent fee approach is that a firm seeks to produce its chosen set of outputs at a minimum (private) cost. A formal

discussion of the effluent charge as a least cost solution is found in Allen V. Kneese, "Environmental Pollution: Economics and Policy," *American Economic Review* (May, 1971), p. 158.

[26]An effluent fee plan probably would not fall within the Air Quality Act's definition of an acceptable state control method, which is defined as one which directly limits the amount of pollution emitted. Since the effluent fee does not limit the amount of pollution but rather provides economic incentives to reduce emission levels, it apparently is outside the scope of the Act.

6

Legal Approaches

To Cost

Internalization

What do you do when a municipality decides that the highest and best use of a mighty river is an open sewer? What do you do when the Army Corps of Engineers or the Bureau of Reclamation decides to drown the Grand Canyon or most of Central Alaska, or insists upon destroying the delicate ecological balance of an entire state like Florida? Just what can you do?

SUE THE BASTARDS!

Industries and government can ignore your protests, ignore your picket signs . . . . But no one in industry or government ignores the scrap of legal cap that begins:

YOU ARE HEREBY SUMMONED TO ANSWER THE ALLEGATIONS OF THE COMPLAINT ANNEXED HERETO WITHIN TWENTY DAYS OR JUDGMENT WILL BE TAKEN AGAINST YOU FOR THE RELIEF DEMANDED.

Victor Yannacone[1]

600. Introduction[2]

In 1308, an unfortunate citizen of the city of London was executed by order of King Edward I for violation of a Royal Proclamation prohibiting the burning of high-sulphur coal instead of honest English oak in furnaces. Since 1308 there has been a decline in the severity of public and legal sanctions applied against those violating environmental laws, but public concern for the quality of the environment is being felt increasingly in the courtroom. Private citizens have brought suits against the federal government, the states, and private industry as well as against the

194

state and federal administrative agencies which are supposed to be protecting the environment. There are at least a hundred suits pending in federal and state courts at any given time which involve environmental or pollution issues. Conservation groups such as the Sierra Club and the Environmental Defense Fund have resorted to litigation as the most feasible means of halting potential environmental damage.[3]

The threat of being sued imposes on a polluter an expected "cost" of potential private damages, plus an expected "cost" of defending suits that will be induced by the fact of pollution. The expectation that such costs will be incurred acts as a spur to industry to apply its technology and management resources to reduce the social costs of pollution. Litigation offers another way in which the external costs of pollution can be internalized as a cost of production, either through damages paid—by the polluter buying off the plaintiff, or by the polluter ceasing his polluting operations. The polluter who anticipates litigation has a strong incentive to spend up to, but not more than, a dollar on pollution reduction for every dollar of expected claims plus expected legal costs likely to be levied against him. This is exactly the way we wish the polluter to behave, for it accomplishes the objective of internalizing pollution costs without forcing an administrative body to go through the difficult process of extracting from the polluter all he knows about alternative technologies by which his production process can be carried on.

If private suits proliferated, and if a large enough number of polluters were assessed damages, the pollution control industry would expand both its research and its capacity in response to demand for more efficient control devices. Eventually, the resulting internalization of pollution costs would tend to increase sales of nonpolluting industries as consumer demand, if at all elastic, shifted towards goods whose price did not include the surcharge of court-imposed damages.

In private suits against industrial polluters, plaintiffs usually seek injunctive relief—a court order prohibiting the activity which caused the pollution. Monetary damages may be requested along with the injunction. However, damages are not often requested alone in environmental cases because a damage award does not prevent continuation of the polluting practice, which in most cases is the prime target of the plaintiff.

Also, a legal action for damages alone may be difficult to sustain because of the problems of measuring actual damages, and of allocating the award fairly among the victims of the pollution. Except in rare cases such as poisoning by a single pollutant from a single source, it is often impossible to isolate the effects of one contaminating discharge from those of another. This is especially true for health claims because humans are subject to many kinds of contaminants for long periods of time, and as indicated earlier, contaminants in combination may have detrimental synergistic health effects not related to the individual pollutants involved.

Dollar damages may be hard to establish because much pollution injury is irreparable. Health damage, wildlife destruction, and generalized disruption of the ecosystem cannot be repaired by monetary damages. Further, even when a particular plaintiff is well-compensated for harm to himself and his property, damage awards ignore other individuals who are potential plaintiffs and who for various reasons have not been able to bring legal action.

Thus, when a damage action is brought, the court is faced with the problem of awarding damages in an amount that is subject to great dispute, and against a particular defendant who cannot equitably be singled out as the sole guilty party in causing the plaintiff's damages. The court is likely to be reluctant to make an award of damages under such circumstances. It will be less reluctant when the plaintiff requests injunctive relief, since it is easier to demonstrate that the polluter is causing some harm, and that the plaintiff has suffered some injury. Injunctive relief puts direct pressure on the polluter to change his industrial processes or to cease production. Injunctions oblige the polluter to find a suitable alternative technology, or to negotiate with the plaintiff for an agreement dissolving the injunction in exchange for a satisfactory payment, or to terminate the polluting part of the operation.

In practice, the extreme burden of proof that has been placed on the plaintiffs in environmental cases has prevented cases—through damages or injunctive relief—against all but the most blatant polluters. For example in the case of *Gerring* v. *Gerber* (1961), an injunction was denied because the odor from the defendant's cleaning establishment, while admittedly overpowering, was no more so than that which is expected from that type of business.[4] However, the growing amount of information about the harmful effects of various pollutants, and the growing public concern for a cleaner environment, suggest that a trend toward

greater success in actions for damages or injunctions against polluters will emerge.[5]

The cases filed to date present a great diversity of legal theories
ranging from constitutional claims to a pollution-free environment,
to more conventional legal theories of nuisance, trespass, and negligence. This chapter will briefly discuss the diverse theories for
environmental redress which have been put forward in various
cases, the limitations to effective legal cost-internalization, and the
real function of the legal approaches now in use. What follows is
not an exhaustive examination of all the judicial approaches potentially available to the victims of pollution, but it does indicate both
established and novel ways of looking at existing legal doctrines,
and hopefully suggests some wholly new approaches to pollution
abatement through the courts. The reader must appreciate, however, that many of the doctrines examined below are burdened by
either the weight of precedent, or by traditional judicial reluctance
to pioneer new and uncharted frontiers of the law.

CAUSES OF ACTION

601. Underlying Theory

Before a court can award damages or injunctive re-
lief, it must first have applied an appropriate legal theory. Historically, an individual whose person or property has been adversely
affected by the use to which his neighbor devoted his property
has been able to sue for damages or injunctive relief on the theories
of nuisance, negligence, or trespass. These traditional remedies,
considered below, were originally tightly structured legal concepts.
In this century they have merged to some extent, with the boundary areas between them becoming increasingly fuzzy.

The traditional remedies all require a balancing of conflicting
interests, and the value framework against which judges have performed this balancing historically has been weighted against environmental protection.[6] The courts have viewed both utility and
harm in economic terms, while economic externalities which extended over more than a small geographic area were generally
ignored. The objective of court decisions was always to encourage
industrial expansion and economic growth, even at the cost of

environmental damage; the common law doctrines now have the encrustations of a century of such attitudes.[7] This judicial attitude is well expressed in a 1954 Pennsylvania case in which the judge stated: "one's bread is more important than the landscape or clear skies. Without smoke Pittsburgh would have remained a very pretty village." [8]

Substantive law as it now exists is geared to the proprietary lawsuit and not to the suit to protect geographically diffused environmental values. The prospects for rapid change in judicial attitudes are promising, but uncertain. An examination of the available causes of action illustrates the variety of difficulties encountered in environmental litigation under present circumstances.

602. Nuisance

Nuisance law has traditionally been divided into areas known as "public nuisance" and "private nuisance." Public nuisance is the doing of, or failure to do something which injures the health, safety, or morals of the public, or creates a substantial annoyance or injury to the public. Private nuisance is a civil wrong for disturbance of rights in land, specifically for the unreasonable use of property so as to substantially interfere with the use and enjoyment by another of his property. While public nuisance has historically been associated with the removal of brothels, gambling dens, and similar institutions, its definition would seem to cover a situation where the air or water is being debased. However, the cases that have concerned smoke, dust, and water pollution have produced the finding that a private individual cannot sue to enjoin a public nuisance. The suit must be brought by the state or a federal attorney general in the name of the people of the state.[9] In 1972, there were only six states with statutes permitting individuals to sue to enjoin particular kinds of public nuisances.

The same act of pollution can create both a public and a private nuisance. Pollution of a waterway which destroyed its fishing would constitute a private nuisance where the river crossed private property and a public nuisance where public property (and public fishing) was involved.

Air pollution was recognized as a private nuisance as early as 1611, when an English court granted an injunction and damages to a plaintiff whose air had been corrupted by the defendant's hog sty. The defendant was found to be committing a nuisance even though he argued that a hog house was necessary to his sustenance, and that one ought not to have so delicate a nose as to be offended by the smell of hogs.[10] The following selection of cases suggests some more current examples of private nuisance applications, and some typical (and conflicting) judicial evaluations of the opposing equities involved.

In the frequently cited *Ducktown Sulphur* case,[11] the plaintiffs requested damages because pollutant discharges from the smokestacks of Ducktown's sulphur mills made it impossible for them to harvest their crops, largely destroyed the timber on their properties, and prevented them "from using and enjoying their farms and homes as they did prior to the inauguration of these enterprises." The court recognized the serious consequences of the pollution, but refused to grant injunctive relief. The court argued that since it was not possible for Ducktown to operate with less-polluting effect or to move to another more remote location, an injunction would compel it to stop operating its plants, making the property practically worthless and causing 10,000 people to lose their jobs. The court stated that:

> In order to protect by injunction several small tracts of land aggregating in value less than $1,000, we are asked to destroy other property worth nearly $2,000,000, and wreck two great mining and manufacturing enterprises. . . . The result would be practically a confiscation of the property of the defendants for the benefit of the complainants—an appropriation without compensation. . . . In a case of conflicting rights, where neither party can enjoy his own without in some measure restricting the liberty of the other in the use of property, the law must make the best arrangement it can between the contending parties, with a view to preserving to each one the largest measure of liberty possible under the circumstances.

The court did allow the plaintiffs to re-sue for monetary damages which were ultimately awarded.

In the 1911 *Hulbert* case,[12] the court took quite a different approach to an air pollution case which required a balancing of opposing equities. In *Hulbert*, the plaintiffs sought an injunction to require the defendant to stop discharging cement dust. The court found that the dust pollution was severe and not capable of being "dissipated by the strongest winds, nor washed off through the action of the most protracted rains"; that the value of the plaintiff's citrus fruit was decreased, that the presence of the dust on the leaves of the trees made harvesting of the crop very difficult and expensive, and that the presence of the dust in plaintiff's homes made life less pleasant.

The defendant argued that he was doing all he could to keep dust from escaping from his cement plant, that damages were sufficient to compensate plaintiffs for their injury, and that the court must consider the size of the cement plant payroll and its economic importance to the community in reaching a decision. The Supreme Court of California ruled that an injunction should be granted. The opinion admitted that the hardship inflicted upon the company by an injunction would be much greater than that suffered by the plaintiffs if the nuisance were permitted to continue, but argued that:

> It is by protecting the most humble in his small estate . . . that the poor man is ultimately enabled to become a capitalist himself. If the smaller interest must yield to the larger, all small property rights, and all small and less important enterprises, industries, and pursuits would sooner or later be absorbed by the large, more powerful few.

Both the doctrinal evolution in the law of nuisance and the economic analysis of one judge are illustrated in the 1963 *Renken* case.[13] Renken was a fruit grower in Wasco, Oregon who claimed that emissions from the Harvey Aluminum plant, consisting of particulates and gases, including fluorides, were harming his fruit trees. In examining Renken's request for an injunction, the court took careful note of the physical structure and chemical operation of the Harvey plant, with emphasis on the arrangements for exhaust and fume control. The court concluded that it was quite feasible to install cell hoods and electrostatic precipitators which would remove the particulates which were not removed by existing controls, and that such controls would reduce or eliminate the damage to the plaintiff's orchard. The court ruled that:

> While the cost of the installations of these additional controls will be a substantial sum . . . such expenditures would not be so great as to substantially deprive defendant of the use of its property . . . . If necessary, the cost of installing adequate controls must be passed on to the ultimate consumer. The heavy cost of corrective devices is no reason why plaintiffs should stand by and suffer substantial damage. . . . The defendant will be required to install proper hoods around the cells and electrostatic precipitators within

one year of the date of the decree. Otherwise, an injunction will [be issued as requested] by the plaintiffs.

In scrutinizing the evidence relating to the plant's equipment and processes, the court applied standards derived "from the best contemporary practice among qualified manufacturers." One commentator has suggested that the next appropriate step in a nuisance case might be to test the performance of the manufacturer not only by the criteria of technology actually available and in use, but also by the efforts he may or may not have made to develop new alternate technologies or engineering designs.[14]

The court's comment that "if necessary, the cost of installing adequate controls must be passed on to the ultimate consumer" is interesting both in that it ignores economic considerations of competitive market conditions and elasticity of demand in the aluminum industry, and in that it raises explicitly the evolving social view that the burden of compensating victims of pollution should be carried by the users of the product whose production caused the pollution. In requiring that the cost of corrective devices, however large, be borne by the manufacturer so long as it is not so great "as to substantially deprive defendant of the use of its property," the court indicates that its decision was limited only by the point at which confiscation might arise—which in most pollution cases would give the court a huge latitude to require corrective action by the polluter.

Two recent cases based upon a nuisance theory have shown that there is still strong judicial unwillingness to do more than award damages in the hope that this might indirectly induce abatement. In the 1970 *Jost* case,[15] plaintiff farmers sued a power cooperative for damages for injury to crops and diminution of the value of their farmlands. The court rejected defendant's arguments that the company's exercise of due care should defeat a nuisance charge, and that the social utility of the offending industry must be balanced against the harm done. However, the court refused a request for an injunction, and awarded only compensation through damages to the plaintiffs. If Dairyland Power increased its pollution in the future, provision was made for an increase in damages to the plaintiffs, but there was no requirement either for future injunctive relief, or for any provision to abate the pollution.

A New York court in the much-cited *Boomer* case was even more explicit in rejecting injunctive relief as too severe a remedy to impose on industry.[16] Boomer, the plaintiff and a landowner, brought suit against the Atlantic Cement Company, seeking an injunction to restrain Atlantic from emitting dust and raw materials in the operation of its plant. The court acknowledged that the cement plant was a source of air pollution and vibration nuisance, but denied an injunction stating that more research was needed to ameliorate pollution from cement plants. The court claimed that it was not the judiciary's place to spur such research. The court in its decision argued that:

> [Atlantic] expended more than $40,000,000 in the erection of one of the largest and most modern cement plants in the world. The company installed at great expense the most efficient devices available to prevent the discharge of dust and polluted air into the atmosphere.

The court chose to award permanent damages to Boomer; one effect of this remedy is that it terminated the lawsuit, for plaintiffs are precluded from future recovery because the defendant, by the payment of permanent damages, obtains what is known as a "servitude on the land." Several commentators have pointed out that, by paying the property owners permanent compensation for their land, a private company was able to seize private property and lay waste to the neighborhood.[17]

It is notable in *Boomer* that the court specifically chose not to use the long-established equitable remedy of an injunction that takes effect at a future date, thus allowing the defendant the opportunity to remedy existing nuisances. The remedy was rejected by concluding that technological breakthroughs in pollution control equipment were unlikely to take place in the near future, and that if at the end of a short period the entire industry had not found a technical solution to air pollution, the court would be hard put to close down one cement plant while leaving others in operation. The court did not consider that given the existing state of cement production technology, it was far less expensive for Atlantic to pay damage claims than to innovate research for pollution control devices, and the existence of continued damage claims would remove the incentive for either cement manufacturers or firms outside the industry to innovate new techniques or equipment. The effect of the *Boomer* decision on earlier case precedent is unclear; the precedent may be limited to those cases where the pollution cannot be abated by the most advanced pollution control devices, as opposed to situations where remedies are available although only at substantial cost to the polluter.

To the vagaries of the law must be added the fact that a private party seeking effective relief on a nuisance theory is also faced with a series of technical obstacles. The fact that a nuisance may be termed "public" has already been mentioned. In such a case the plaintiff must show special injury— which generally means that the plaintiff's damage must be different in kind rather than simply in degree from the harm suffered by the general public.

If a polluter has been active for some time, the legal doctrine of prescriptive rights may come into effect. Under a statute of limitations, his right to pollute would become absolute in regard to the particular plaintiff. However, many courts are refusing to recognize such a right because the defendant cannot meet various burdens of proof.

Another rule which may act against a potential plaintiff is that of "coming to the nuisance"—one example of which is the case where an individual may be found to have assumed an annoyance by moving nearer to a polluter. Coming to the nuisance would certainly weigh heavily in the balancing process of a court intent on comparing the relative equities of arguments.

In summary, a number of obstacles to an effective nuisance suit are frequently added to the currently ambiguous direction of current legal decisions. While it is frequently argued that the doctrine has potential for growth, nuisance at present must be said to be of only marginal effectiveness as a device for internalizing the costs of pollution.

603. Trespass

A number of pollution suits have attempted to use the theory of trespass, which is an unprivileged entry of a person or object on land occupied by another. The plaintiff's problems of proof are less under trespass than under nuisance. To establish trespass one need only show an intentional and unauthorized entry onto the land, while to show nuisance one must prove a substantial and unreasonable interference with the enjoyment of the land.

However, the theory of trespass requires a "direct" physical entry by a person or object, and courts have had conflicting opinions as to whether entry of smoke, fumes, or particulates onto a plaintiff's land qualifies as an "object."

For example, in the 1959 *Martin* case,[18] a group of Oregon cattle ranchers near a Reynolds Aluminum plant claimed that their cattle were poisoned by ingesting fluorides which escaped from the plant, and that forage and water on their land had been contaminated. Reynolds did not contest the facts, but argued that the mere settling of fluoride deposits upon land was not sufficient to constitute trespass. The court ruled:

> If we look to the character of [what] is used in making an intrusion upon another's land we prefer to emphasize the object's energy or force rather than its size. Viewed in this way we define trespass as any intrusion which invades the possessor's protected interest, whether that intrusion is by visible or invisible pieces of matter or by energy which can be measured only by the mathematical language of the physicist.

> We are of the opinion, therefore, that the intrusion of the fluoride particulates in the present case constituted a trespass.

There is still much conflict of opinion however, about whether air pollution (or water pollution) constitutes an "object," and cases since *Martin* have produced mixed results.[19] Also, some courts have held that if an intervening force such as wind or water carried the contaminants onto the plaintiff's land, that the entry is not "direct."

In summary, the fact that only plaintiffs in close proximity to the polluter have a cause of action, the difficulty of pinpointing which among many sources of pollution did the damage, the court's tendency to balance equities in trespass cases as in nuisance cases, and the cost of litigation against huge corporations, each discourages the filing of environmental trespass suits, and makes the trespass doctrine of only marginal value for effective pollution control on any large scale.

604. Negligence

The third conventional legal theory which is applicable to pollution cases is that of negligence. A direct causal relationship must be shown between the plaintiff's injury and the defendant's negligence, for negligence to be accepted by a court. In the 1958 *Blakely* case,[20] the plaintiff was allowed damages for negligence against Greyhound bus lines, for brain and nerve damage she allegedly suffered from inhaling carbon monoxide while a passenger on a bus with a defective exhaust system.

In the *Martin* case,[21] mentioned earlier, members of the Martin family brought a negligence suit against Reynolds Metals Company in which they claimed personal injuries arising from the fluoride compounds escaping from the Reynolds plant. The court ruled that:

> When [Martin] proved the emanation of fluoride compounds from the [Reynolds] plant, and the injury suffered by him as a result thereof, he made out a primafacie case of negligence on the part of the defendant.

In spite of the problems involved, a plaintiff may wish to pursue a negligence theory because of the greater likelihood of obtaining punitive damages than if the case were argued on nuisance or trespass theories. All but four states allow punitive damages, and about fifteen states award them with considerable frequency. Traditionally, punitive damages are awarded where there is malice, fraudulent or evil motive, or willful or wanton disregard of the interests of others. There is also justification for punitive damages when compensatory damages alone, although compensating the injured party, do not deter the polluter from committing similar acts in the future.

To date, the general "standard of care" problem in negligence cases allows the courts to balance the utility of allowing continued pollution in light of the general economic health of an area. What may prove to be the most productive approach in using negligence in pollution cases has yet to be tried—an application of the nuisance doctrine from the *Renken* case in a negligence case. If accepted by the court, a polluter would be negligent under the *Renken* doctrine unless he used the best available pollution control devices irrespective of their cost, so long as the expense does not bankrupt him. As in *Renken*, an unanswered question is what approach a court should take when a polluter uses available pollution control devices which are inadequate, but declines to conduct or share the cost of research to develop more efficient methods of pollution control for his industry.

605. Products Liability

The doctrine of products liability maintains that there is an implied warranty running from a manufacturer to the ultimate purchaser and to others who might be expected to use or utilize the product or service, that the goods are (among other things) not unreasonably dangerous. The logic of products liability is to insure that the cost of injuries resulting from defective products is borne by the manufacturer of the products, rather than by the injured persons who are powerless to protect themselves. Thus products liability shifts the costs of injuries from users of a defective product back to the manufacturer. To establish a manufacturer's liability it is sufficient to prove that the plaintiff was injured while using the product in the way it was intended to be used, and that the injury was a result of a defect in design or in manufacture of which the user was not aware.

An illustration of the possible use of products liability in environmental protection cases is given in the "Los Angeles Smog Case," filed in 1969.[22] Two citizens of Los Angeles, described as "C. Jon Handy, a land investment banker, and William R. Bernstein, a law student," suing for themselves, the People of The County of Los Angeles, the four minor children of C. Jon Handy, and all minor children similarly situated, sued the four major automobile makers and a number of oil companies for $15 billion because of their alleged critical role in the creation of Los Angeles smog. Named as defendants were General Motors, Ford Motor Company, Chrysler Motors, American Motors, the Automobile Manufacturers Association, Standard Oil Company of New Jersey, Gulf Oil, Mobil Oil, Texaco, Shell Oil, the American Petroleum Institute, Inc., the Secretary of Health, Education and Welfare, and the Attorney General of the United States. Three counts were listed in the suit, the first of which asked for an injunction that would require the automobile companies to alter, modify, or change their conventional internal combustion engines so that they did not cause smog, and to recall all existing automobiles in order to alter their engines so that they did not cause smog. The oil companies would be ordered to refine a "clean" motor fuel, and to refrain from adding tetraethyl lead or similar damaging substances to their fuels. The suit suggests that the doctrine of strict products liability can be used to internalize what are now costs external to the defendant companies, and in a way not possible through an action for nuisance.

Since the case has not yet been decided and there are no comparable cases known to the author, its implications can only be a subject of speculation. To continue their case, the plaintiffs will first have to satisfy some standard conditions appropriate to liability cases. They will have to demonstrate that automobile exhaust is the major factor in the causation of smog in Los Angeles, and that they have suffered serious injury and inconvenience because of this smog. Assuming that damages rather than an injunction are ultimately requested, they must also demonstrate that their damages can be reasonably evaluated in terms of dollars.

The defendants also must convince the court of their theory of "defective condition," which includes not just the specific defects of particular engines, but *all* engines of *all* motor vehicles currently in use in Los Angeles which are manufactured by the defendant motor car companies, and which emit exhaust which is a major component of Los Angeles' smog. The suit does not argue that the cars perform other than precisely as the manufacturers intended, and as their buyers expected. Most "defective condition" cases decided by the courts involve defective physical mechanisms, for example the failure of an altimeter to register the correct altitude, which leads to the crash of an airplane. The only cases analogous to the smog case have concerned food or drugs, which involved some risk or harm, and these have been ruled to be defective only when they are both "unreasonably dangerous," and when the manufacturer had reason to know of the danger but provided no warning.[23]

The case might turn on whether the plaintiffs can introduce evidence that contemporary motor vehicle technology is capable of eliminating major pollutants from automobile exhausts, or alternatively that different forms of carburetion exist that could utilize non-polluting forms of gasoline. The defendants would also have to indicate that automobiles embodying the improvements indicated could be priced and sold in numbers sufficient to maintain an economically viable automobile industry. At this point, the plaintiffs could argue that it was in the public interest to internalize the external costs of smog in the price of the automobile via the incremental costs of pollution control equipment.

If on the basis of such evidence the court were to support a finding of a smog-producing exhaust as being a "defective condition" and unreasonably dangerous, the court could consider remedies against the defendants, presumably with a balancing of equities, which would rule out either a $15 billion settlement, or a blanket injunction against internal combustion engines which emitted smog-producing exhaust. The key factor, from the standpoint of environmental law, would be the definition of defective condition, which would open the door to the use of a products liability theory as a much more effective weapon in pollution cases.

606. Abnormally Dangerous Activities

An abnormally dangerous (or extrahazardous, or ultrahazardous) activity is one which necessarily involves a risk of serious harm to persons or goods, and which cannot be eliminated simply by the exercise of extreme care. In *Luthringer* v. *Moore*,[24] an exterminator was held liable for damages resulting from hydrocyanic acid gas leaking from premises in which he used it to kill cockroaches. The precautions he had taken were considered appropriate, but the activity itself was ruled as being ultrahazardous by nature, and the defendant was thus liable for any damages which might occur, independent of the existence of any fault.

There are at least two major applications of the theory of abnormally dangerous activities to environmental law. A number of states have held the activity of drilling an oil well to be an ultrahazardous one which subjects the owners and drillers to liability if accidents occur. On February 20, 1969 the State of California, County of Santa Barbara, and Cities of Santa Barbara and Carpinteria filed suit against Union Oil, Mobil Oil, Gulf Oil, Texaco, and Peter Bawden Drilling, Inc. for injuries resulting from the blow-out of a well being drilled on part of the continental shelf in the Santa Barbara channel. The claim was for "no less than $500,000,000," and the damage was that petroleum "was deposited into and onto the waters, lands, fish, wildlife, and personal property of the State and all plaintiffs." As yet there is no ruling on whether liability without fault applies in this case.[25]

The second major application of the abnormally dangerous activities theory concerns environmental damage resulting from noise levels, sonic booms, and upper-atmospheric pollution resulting from flights by supersonic transport planes (SSTs). All editions and drafts of the *Restatement of Torts*, an outline of law usually followed by the courts, have regarded the operation of an SST as an abnormally dangerous activity which produces strict liability for ground injuries to persons or property caused by noise or sonic booms.[26] The issue of damage to the stratosphere from engine exhaust has not been treated either in legal cases or in the *Restatement*, but it is likely that the treatment would be the same.

Other than the applications of oil-well drilling and SSTs, a plaintiff in a pollution case would probably find it difficult to successfully argue abnormally dangerous activities unless he could also argue nuisance and/or trespass. To date the successful cases have been so few as to have had a negligible effect on internalizing the social cost of polluting activities.

607. Riparian Rights

The riparian doctrine concerns the right of each user of land on a waterway to a coequal use of water in the waterway. Persons whose waterway has been polluted may file a lawsuit against the alleged polluter.[27] Most states use the so-called "reasonable use" concept of riparian rights, which means that waste disposal may be reasonable in relation to the rights of other riparians (those who abut on the waterway). A definition of "reasonable" requires a balancing of equities similar to that carried out in nuisance or trespass law.

However, courts in determining "reasonableness," have tended to consider only economic aspects, and have rejected arguments as to the natural beauty or public health factors of the water. In the 1965 *Kennedy* case,[28] the court held that: "A riparian owner has no proprietary right in a beautiful scene presented by a river any more than any other owner of land could claim a right to a beautiful landscape." Such interpretations of riparian rights are probably of little value in environmental protection, except perhaps in highly specialized cases.

608. Public Trust Doctrine

A new and promising, but as yet untested approach to environmental protection law which relies on the so-called public trust doctrine has been proposed by Joseph Sax.[29] Public trust law considers that rivers, seashores, and public land are held in trust for the benefit of the public. Sax claims that "the function which the courts must perform . . . is to promote equality of political power for a disorganized and diffuse majority by remanding appropriate cases to the legislature after public opinion has been aroused." The function of the courts in the public trust area therefore will be one of insuring that the democratic process is followed. In a dispute between hunters and fishermen, and those who wished to drain a salt marsh to build luxury condominiums, the court would refer the case to a local, state, or federal political entity and then, having made sure that one interest is not underrepresented in the political process, the court would withdraw.

An example of a public trust case is *Gould* v. *Greylack Reservation Commission*,[30] a 1966 case in which a Massachusetts public parks commission had leased 4,000 acres of public land to a private organization for the development of a ski area. Five citizens of the county in which the land was located brought suit as beneficiaries of a public trust under which the land was held. The Supreme Judicial Court of Massachusetts held the lease invalid, questioning why the state would subordinate a public park to the use of private investors for a commercial development. Under the public trust doctrine as proposed by Sax, the plaintiffs might ask the court to invalidate the lease until the Massachusetts Legislature could vote on whether the interests of the citizens of the state were being served. Sax suggests several guidelines that a court might use in determining whether a particular resource decision has been improperly handled at the administrative or legislative level. Perhaps the most important of these guidelines are questions of whether the public property has been disposed of at less than market value where there is no obvious reason for the grant of a private subsidy, and whether the resource is being used for its natural purpose. The underlying assumption here is that a natural resource like a forest has its most beneficial public use when left in its natural condition.

609. Writ of Mandamus

A writ of mandamus is a court order directed to a public official which requires the performance of the public duties of his official office.[31] A number of studies of environmental protection problems have found that chronic nonenforcement of existing regulations, rather than the lack of effective regulations, has been the central characteristic of the failure of administrative agencies to protect the environment.[32] If an administrator's action involves an exercise of administrative discretion on a given question, then the courts will normally not interfere with the judgment because it is discretionary. However, where an interpretation is clear from the authorizing statute and the administrator or agency is acting erroneously, then the court can compel the agency to do its duty.

Mandamus achieved an important role in environmental protection with the passage of the National Environmental Policy Act in 1969, which requires all federal legislation and all actions of federal administrative agencies to include a statement on the impact of the proposal on man's environment, any adverse environmental effects which are unavoidable, alternatives to the proposed action, and the relationship between short-term uses of the environment and the maintenance and enhancement of long-term productivity. Thus, a full consideration of environmental factors by governmental agencies is now a congressional mandate, and a private citizen concerned about the effects of an agency's activity can seek a judicial review of the action by charging noncompliance with the National Environmental Policy Act. One suit brought under mandamus caused postponement of construction of the Trans-Alaska pipeline pending review of the environmental implications of the line, and consideration of alternative ways of moving oil from the Prudhoe Bay area to United States markets.

610. Stockholder Suits

At present, Security and Exchange Commission rules do not require management to submit to stockholders, proposals "primarily for the purpose of promoting general economic, political, racial, religious, social or similar causes," which probably includes environmental protection. However, if a stockholder can point to some specific economic detriment which might result from a corporation's continuing pollution, such as a possible damage judgment, then he could file a suit. The suit would ordinarily be based upon the theory of waste of corporate assets through management's failure to purchase and install pollution control equipment, so long as the expected cost of damage judgments in favor of victims of pollution exceeded the cost of the necessary control equipment.

Regardless of any waste of corporate assets, a stockholder might bring suit against pollution which exceeded government established emission levels on the basis that the corporate officers were guilty of a *per se* breach of fiduciary duty by being in violation of the law.

While there is some evidence that increased stockholder pressure is being brought to bear on polluters, it is problematic whether sufficient numbers of environmentally concerned stockholders exist to make the stockholder suit a more viable means of harassing reluctant managements.

A variant of the stockholder suit is exemplified by the General Motors proxy fight ("Campaign GM") in the spring of 1970. In late 1969, a group of Washington attorneys, working through the Project on Corporate Responsibility, drafted and submitted to General Motors management nine proposals dealing with minority employment, warranties, air pollution, the composition of the GM Board of Directors, and the formation of a shareholders' committee to advise management. GM management refused to place any of these proposals on the 1970 proxy ballot, and the Project lawyers appealed to the Securities and Exchange Commission. The SEC ordered, without any explanatory opinion, that two proposals be included on the proxy—one dealing with the formation of a share-holder committee to "prepare a report and make recommendations to the shareholders concerning the role of the corporation in society," the other to amend the by-laws to expand the Board to include three new "public interest" directors. At the May 22, 1970 stockholders meeting, the shareholder committee and expanded board proposals received the votes of 2.73 percent and 2.44 percent of the total shares and 7.19 percent and 6.22 percent of total shareholders respectively. The proxy proposals received support from eleven universities and colleges, eight religious organizations, and seven other organizations including the pension funds of New York City and San Francisco. The Project has indicated that it will fight future proxy battles with GM in the same manner, but that it will place major emphasis on the decision-making process and on possibilities for structural reform.

611. Constitutional Arguments

There may be a constitutional argument for the right to a pollution-free environment under the guarantees of the Fifth, Ninth, and Fourteenth Amendments to the Constitution. According to this argument, environmental degradation leads to a deprivation of "life, liberty, or property, without due process of law" [Amendments Five and Fourteen], and although the Constitution is not explicit about the right to be free from pollution, this is overcome by the Ninth Amendment, which reads: "The enumeration . . . of certain rights, shall not be construed to deny or disparage others retained by the people." [33]

In the *Hoerner Waldorf* case,[34] the Environmental Defense Fund sought an injunction on the constitutional argument that continued emission of sulphur oxides by Hoerner violated the rights of citizens guaranteed under the Ninth Amendment, and also violated the due process and equal protection clauses of the Fifth and Fourteenth Amendments. The argument used in the case is as summarized above, with the addition that it cites the Warren Court's decision in a right-to-birth-control-information case[35] that each of the specific rights listed in the Bill of Rights has "penumbras . . . that help give them life and substance." It is reasoned from this that there must surely be a right to an environment free from environmental poisons. A victory by the Environmental Defense Fund in the *Hoerner Waldorf* case would stand alongside *Brown v. Board of Education*[36] in its significance to the future of American constitutional law, and in its impact on society.

Several states have already introduced amendments to their own constitutions to formalize the right to a non-polluted environment. Article One of the Constitution of Pennsylvania was recently amended to read, in part:

> The people have a right to clean air, pure water, and to the preservation of the natural scenic, historic, and esthetic values of the environment. Pennsylvania's natural resources . . . are the common property of all the people, including generations yet to come. As trustee of these resources, the Commonwealth shall preserve and maintain them for the benefit of all the people.

612. Refuse Act of 1899

The Refuse Act of 1899 (more formally, the Rivers and Harbors Act of 1899), is a recently "rediscovered," and potentially very powerful tool in the hands of those concerned with water pollution control. Section 13 of the Act prohibits anyone, including individuals, corporations, municipalities, or other governments from discharging any "refuse" into navigable lakes, rivers, streams, or into the tributaries of such waters. The term "refuse" has been defined by the Supreme Court to include all foreign substances and pollutants, whether accidentally discharged or not, and whether valuable or of no value. The only exceptions to the Act are liquid sewage, and other materials if a permit is obtained from the Army Corps of Engineers. Although the Act enjoins United States attorneys "to vigorously prosecute all offenders," it has rarely been used until recently—largely because the Army Corps of Engineers has not insisted on permits, and has not bothered to bring offenders to the attention of the attorneys.

The Act provides criminal penalties of fines from $500 to $2,500 a day, or imprisonment from 30 days to a year. More importantly, it permits injunctions against continued dumping. Public service lawyers representing organizations such as the Environmental Defense Fund have seized upon this resurrected statute because it also provides that citizens bringing to United States attorneys information leading to conviction are entitled to half the fine. If the attorney does not act on the information supplied, the complaining citizen, in a *qui tam* action, can file suit himself.[37] The fine is important to environmental groups for the incentive it offers industrial employees and others to bring information to the attention of United States attorneys and to file suit if no action is taken.

The first person to be prosecuted under the criminal provisions of the Act was J. J. O'Donnell, President of the J. J. O'Donnell Woolens Company which had for decades poured dyes and soapy waste water into the Blackstone River in Grafton, Massachusetts. The conviction of Mr. O'Donnell in November of 1971 signalled a new approach of holding corporate executives criminally responsible for the water pollution caused by their plants. The theory behind this penalty is that recalcitrance will be overcome more quickly by this method than by the old practice of bringing criminal and civil charges against a company—which can hardly be thrown in jail.

The use of criminal law provisions against individuals such as Mr. O'Donnell raises a number of delicate moral, economic, and political questions. In a society in which corporations are run on the profit motive and pollution is a fact of industrial life, is it fair to penalize individuals or is it simply a hunt for a scapegoat? Is criminal action against a handful of individuals an effective mechanism for reducing pollution, or is it merely a political palliative?

Legally, there is no doubt about corporate responsibility. Executives have long been held responsible for the actions of their companies in antitrust and fraud cases. But pollution raises different kinds of issues. For one, criminal prosecutions tend to promote the "demonology myth" that pollution is caused by a few greedy and callous industrialists. The O'Donnell case bears witness to this argument. Mr. O'Donnell responded to his criminal conviction (and relatively low $2,500 fine) by terminating operations and by moving his plant out of Massachusetts. His textile mill, in what was once a thriving mill town, discharged its 160 employees.

Although the trend is to prosecute individuals, corporations are also beginning to be indicted under the Act, sometimes with remarkably large fines. The most dramatic example occurred in 1971 when Anaconda, which for years had dumped copper fragments from its wire-making plant at Hastings-on-Hudson in New York into the Hudson River, was fined $200,000 under the Act on a hundred-count indictment covering the first five months of 1971. The fine was by far the largest under the Act and is many times larger than the penalties so far levied under state antipollution legislation. Judge Thomas Croake commented that "pollution levies can no longer be shrugged off by corporations as a cost of doing business," and Anaconda would appear to agree—within five weeks it had completed installation of settling tanks to remove the copper from its discharges into the Hudson.

The likelihood that the Act will receive a broad interpretation is greatly increased by the recent flow of executive orders designed to minimize pollution, maximize recreation, and preserve natural resources. If the Refuse Act remains in force, and if the courts allow plaintiffs to file private *qui tam* actions and to collect penalty fees, the Refuse Act could become the most powerful single legal tool for preventing the pollution of navigable waters in the United States.

613. Other Legislation

It is obvious that there are situations in which immediate and decisive regulatory action is the only sensible approach to environmental pollution. Even if effluent fees or taxes are generally preferable to specific regulations, it is unlikely that we would ever regret simply having forbidden the disposal of heavy toxic metals like mercury where they can be consumed by animals or humans. We may also want to stop irreversible deterioration of certain natural resources at once. These are cases where the necessary user charges or taxes would be prohibitive.

This section will briefly review the provisions of federal pollution control statutes other than the Refuse Act. In general, little judicial history of these statutes is available to aid in assessing their value in bringing about pollution control or cost internalization. The most important statute, the National Environmental Policy Act of 1969, will be discussed in detail in Chapter Seven.

The Federal Water Pollution Control Act is the most important federal legislation on water pollution.[38] Under the Act, the pollution of interstate or navigable waters which endangers the health or welfare of any person is subject to abatement. Interstate waters are defined as all rivers, lakes, or other waters that flow across or form a part of state boundaries, including coastal waters such as the Great Lakes. Section Eleven of this Act provides for liability without fault for damages to any publicly-owned or privately-owned property resulting from the discharge of any oil, or from the removal of any such oil. Owners and operators of refineries and off-shore drilling rigs are liable to the government for the cost of removing spilled oil from the waters and shoreline up to a maximum liability of $14 million, and may also be fined up to $10,000. Curiously, the Act establishes strict liability to the federal government, which is capable of defraying cleanup costs from its own funds, but specifically denies strict liability to private actions in which the plaintiffs cannot afford to absorb their losses.

The Oil Pollution Act of 1961 makes it unlawful for a tanker or other ship to discharge oil within fifty miles from shore. Violation of the Act is a misdemeanor and carries a fine of from $500 to $2,500, or imprisonment not to exceed one year for each offense. There appear to have been no charges ever laid under this Act.

The Air Quality Act of 1967[39] was intended as a blueprint for an effort to deal with air pollution problems on a regional basis. The Act grants authority to the Secretary of Health, Education and Welfare to seek injunctions to abate the emission of contaminants anywhere in the country; to design "air quality control regions" for the purpose of implementing air quality standards; in the absence of effective state action, to establish and enforce ambient air quality standards for each region; and to establish federal interstate air quality planning commissions. While no provision is made for private suits or for monetary penalties, a writ of mandamus could certainly be directed at the Secretary of HEW, or at state officials to require performance under the Act.

The Federal Insecticide, Fungicide and Rodenticide Act[40] administered by the Department of Agriculture makes it unlawful to ship in interstate commerce any pesticide (dieldren, DDT, etc.) which is not registered under the Act. The principal purpose of the Act is to prevent misbranded articles from being sold in interstate commerce. However it may also be interpreted as preventing poisons which cannot be used safely from being registered. In the case of *Environmental Defense Fund* v. *Hardin*,[41] petitioners requested an order that the Secretary of Agriculture suspend and then cancel the registrations of pesticides containing DDT under the Insecticide Act. The court ordered the Department to begin cancellation proceedings within 30 days or to give detailed reasons for refusing to initiate proceedings.

There is no general state or federal law to protect the aesthetic quality of the environment, although the National Environmental Policy Act may afford some general protection through subsequent judicial interpretation. However, statutes are passed from time to time which are directed to the aesthetic or visual aspect of some project, area, or type of project. The Billboard laws are an example: The Federal Highway Act authorizes some control over billboards, junkyards, landscaping, and other aesthetic considerations.[42] The federal act does not prohibit a state statute which regulates (not "takes") without compensation or which is stricter than federal requirements.

At the federal level aesthetic considerations are proper under the welfare clause. In *Berman* v. *Parker*, Justice Douglas said:

> The concept of the public welfare . . . represents spiritual as well as physical, aesthetic, and monetary values. It is within the power of the legislature to determine that the community should be beautiful as well as healthy, spacious as well as clean, well-balanced as well as carefully patrolled . . . .[43]

Other such legislation includes a bill in California to ban gasoline-powered automobiles by 1975, and a New Jersey proposal to fine each commercial jet aircraft $2,500 for uncontrolled emissions on each take-off and landing. In the last two years alone, some 550 bills and amendments have been introduced in Congress dealing with the environment—almost certainly the highest concentration of Congressional attention on a single issue since World War Two.

CLASS SUITS

614. Class Actions

A class action is not a cause of action against polluters, but rather a procedure by which a group of persons involved in an issue such as pollution can sue as representatives of a class (or group) of persons even though the group which is suing does not include every member of the class. There are two principal requirements for the maintenance of a class action: the persons constituting the class must be so numerous that it is impractical to bring them all before the court, and the persons filing the class suit must be reasonably representative of all the members of the class. Class members must have aggregate individual claims of at least $10,000 in order to file suit in a federal court.[44] One practical problem with suits as small as $10,000, however, is that they do not offer sufficient contingent fee potential to induce lawyers to take the case on a contingent fee basis.

The economic value of a class action is that it reduces bargaining costs between the polluter and the victim, and among the victims. It enables individuals to combine their bargaining strength at minimal cost, and it presents courts with an aggregate claim which may shift the balance of equities away from the polluter. By presenting an aggregate damage claim, it may raise costs high enough so that the polluter finds it less expensive to abate his emissions than to run the risk of further class actions. Otherwise, faced with only a few plaintiffs claiming minimal damages, corporate polluters may react as did one executive of Reynolds Metals Company in a pollution suit where he testified: "It is cheaper to pay claims than to control fluorides." [45] A class suit allows a polluter to settle with the class representatives, before or after litigation, knowing that the entire class is represented and will be bound by the negotiated settlement.

The use of class actions in environmental litigation has not been common, although, for example, air pollution by a single firm, affecting a group of victims geographically clustered around the polluter where the harm caused to each individual is similar, would seem to present a classic situation for a class action suit.[46] The environmental class actions that have been filed have produced mixed results. One class action for $39 billion against virtually all industry and all municipal corporations in Los Angeles County was dismissed on the court's own motion.[47] In a more recent case, two Chicago aldermen sued the leading automobile, truck, and tractor manufacturers for $3 billion, alleging that they conspired to delay the research, development, and installation of air pollution control devices on their vehicles.[48]

In the *Storley* case,[49] 56 riparian plaintiffs representing 70 downstream farms brought a class action against the Armour & Company slaughterhouse for polluting a river. The suit was successful, and the court awarded damages. However, *Storley* is a class action only in the sense that one legal action was substituted for a number of separate ones. No firm rules for conditions under which a class action for pollution abatement might be brought, or for defining an acceptable representative of a class of pollution victims, were produced that are applicable to subsequent cases.

Federal agencies such as the National Air Pollution Control Administration have been openly encouraging private and class suits as a flexible means of solving local pollution problems, and of bringing to the forefront local environmental issues which should be solved through legislation; the NAPCA has offered their agency's assistance and technical competence in the conduct of such litigation. Class suits are particularly encouraged by these agencies in cases involving problems such as odors, which are difficult to control through the use of standards.

Given that a clearcut decision in the pollution class action field is still lacking, development of the class action concept into a truly effective cost-internalization tool will remain a challenge to environmental lawyers, and to the ability of the legal system to adapt its procedures and rules to changing technological requirements. Many environmental cases which might be litigated will remain unfeasible unless class plaintiffs can aggregate the total damage resulting from the pollution, and unless multiple polluters can be joined as class defendants, thus eliminating the barrier of proving causation where multiple polluters exist.

LIMITATIONS TO EFFECTIVE LEGAL COST-INTERNALIZATION

615. General Problems

Private suits as a device for implementing environmental protection encounter a number of inherent defects. As indicated earlier, establishing liability confronts sometimes intractable problems of proof, especially when the effects in question are intangible and thus difficult to measure, or where they are interacting and cumulative and thus difficult to attribute to one source. The most serious consequences of environmental pollution—damage to future generations, or the gradual erosion of the quality of human existence, cannot be readily associated with any single polluter or group of polluters, and could not in any event be translated into dollar damages.

Further obstacles to an effective legal role in internalizing industrial pollution costs may take several forms. The passive nature of the courts and their inability to initiate an investigation or injunctive suit, means that the questions reaching them typically involve only well-established problems and entrenched economic interests. Citizens have difficulty approaching the court until the injury is visible, or construction of potentially polluting facilities is well advanced. If the damage is only potential and not actual, the court may refuse to act. In a case against the Atomic Energy Commission, a court refused to consider whether thermal pollution of the Connecticut River ought to be enjoined or at least compensated, because the existing permit authorized only construction, not the operation of the nuclear power plant.[50] In another case, a court refused to issue an injunction against an environmentally-damaging highway project because substantial money had already been spent on land acquisition and preliminary planning.[51]

The considerable expense of private litigation against a corporate defendant severely restricts the number of suits possible. The extended court battle in the *Scenic Hudson* case[52] is estimated to have cost conservation groups more than half a million dollars and the Consolidated Edison Company of New York almost a million dollars. As a rule of thumb, to mount an effective environmental lawsuit where expert witnesses are required and the defendant is well financed will cost a minimum of $100,000. Costs of this magnitude force organizations such as the Environmental Defense Fund to make a careful selection of those suits with the greatest potential for publicity and precedent value.

The lack of predictability of litigation against any specific polluting industry has the effect of reducing the deterrent effect of the potential litigation, and also the incentive for abatement. Since episodic litigation is not foreseeable in the same way that government effluent charges are, and is not automatically triggered by a predeterminable action, industry reaction is frequently one of delaying cost internalization, and fighting suits as a deterrent while instituting only minimal antipollution measures.

616. Uneven Distribution of Costs

The unpredictable nature of private actions against polluters may lead to an uneven distribution of costs to particular enterprises, unduly burdening them to the advantage of those equally guilty of pollution, but who manage to avoid litigation. The social costs involved can be internalized with less strain if all the relevant competitors must internalize them, so that all pricing policies will be affected in similar fashion. It is unlikely that selective and random litigation will result in all forms of waste-producing enterprises being placed under the same cost-internalization requirements. Without a uniform distribution of costs, incentive for expenditures on improved pollution abatement is diminished, since each firm will calculate its probability of avoiding litigation, and will come up with an expected-cost-of-litigation-and-damages figure that is likely to be less than the cost of pollution control.

Those who advocate a broadening of common law actions to effectuate cost-internalization have recognized this problem, and have suggested that statutory arrangements to protect enterprises in selected industries from overwhelming liability is necessary. Such "insurance" arrangements would spread the cost burden of suits widely enough among firms to avoid penalizing any single enterprise that happened to be the target of a lawsuit for an accident that could have happened to any firm within an industry— for example, in offshore oil drilling. However, the risk must not be so widely diffused as to nullify the incentive for all firms to internalize the costs of their operations—this might be accomplished by having a high insurance "deductible," which varied inversely with the amount of pollution control equipment used by each operator.

FUNCTION OF LEGAL APPROACHES TO ENVIRONMENTAL PROTECTION

617. In General

The procedural and legal limitations of achieving effective internalization of pollution costs do not mean that the courts have no useful role to play in environmental protection. Private suits may be used in cases involving types or degrees of pollution that simply are not covered by existing statutes. For example, the 1967 Air Quality Act authorized the Secretary of Health, Education, and Welfare to establish air quality regions and ambient air standards, but specific regulations were not issued until mid-1971, with comprehensive standards still undetermined.

Private suits may also be used to fill gaps in existing enforcement of regulations. As pollution problems become more severe, overburdened agencies will have to become increasingly selective in prosecuting violations of pollution statutes. Private suits can be used to attack violations that agencies must ignore because of manpower and financial constraints. Where specific pollution is damaging to people located near its source but is minor relative to larger-scale pollution in the area, private enforcement through litigation may be the only way to force abatement.

Private suits may also provide a more sophisticated tool than regulatory response in dealing with the rapidly changing technology of pollution abatement. The ability of courts to hear new evidence and to shape novel remedies has led some writers to the conclusion that courts are more responsive than legislatures or administrative agencies to the impact of pollution, and the control techniques that might be applied.[53]

Private suits are certainly flexible from a time standpoint. The enactment of useful legislative change always takes time, a commodity which may become critical when particulate or other pollution suddenly reaches critical levels. An informed citizen can bring the problem to the attention of the court almost immediately; in the short run, the court is the arena in which industry lobbyists are least able to exercise their delaying tactics.

Lawsuits may also lead to the development of new public attitudes towards pollution by serving as a focal point for the gathering and dissemination of assumptions about the application and handling of technology. The very language used in the law may induce cultural and moral change. To require an industry to "internalize the social costs of its pollution" means little to the public at large, but to hold the same polluter liable for damages for the "nuisance" he has caused, or to hold him legally responsible for the "defect" in his products says a great deal, and is widely noted.

618. Publicity Function

An unrecognized benefit of the private suit against a polluter is its potential as a catalyst for inducing change elsewhere in the system. This is true particularly in our litigious society where the media pay front-page attention to the more dramatic court battles. Just as much of the most important civil rights legislation in the United States was induced by newsworthy, although ineffectual litigation, so much of the required legislation to protect the environment might be induced by successful (or even more by unsuccessful) private suits seeking to internalize the costs of pollution. A polluter-defendant in a suit, even if he "wins" the litigation, may be spurred to corrective abatement to avoid further unfavorable publicity.

619. Public Participation

Private suits enable the individual litigant to feel that he is capable of some involvement in the complex industrial activities that affect the quality of his life, that he is more than a passive inhabitant of an environment the future of which is beyond his control. To be accorded a court hearing to help determine whether an activity that harms him will be allowed to continue, and if so on what terms, has value in itself as an affirmation of the individual's right not to be reduced to a means towards someone else's technological or industrial end. The limited number of suits that can realistically be brought, given their expense, can provide direct benefits of participation to only a few. A less direct psychological satisfaction may accrue to the hundreds of thousands of citizens who are currently contributing to the Environmental Defense Fund and similar public organizations to assist their efforts in private litigation on behalf of the environment.

In fairness, something must also be said about the cost and nuisance that can be created for the legitimate corporation by crank suits instituted in spite of the expense involved. The small industrial corporation in particular is vulnerable to suits that are either unfair or vindictive, and which, even when won, can be extremely costly in terms of both money and executive time.

REFERENCES

[1]Victor Yannacone, *Sue the Bastards*, a speech delivered on "Earth Day," April 22, 1970, at Michigan State University, East Lansing, Michigan.

[2]The structure and part of the content of this chapter was inspired by a paper entitled *The Courts and Industrial Pollution Abatement*, by Barry R. Furrow, my research assistant at the Harvard Law School during 1970-71.

[3]For example *Environmental Defense Fund* v. *Hoerner Waldorf Corp.*, Civil No. 1694 (D. Mont., filed November 13, 1968); *Sierra Club* v. *Hickel*, Civil No. 51,464 (N.D. Calif., filed June 4, 1969); *Citizens Committee for Hudson Valley* v. *Volpe*, 302 F. Supp. 1083 (S.D. New York, filed June 28, 1969). An interesting case is *Diamond* v. *General Motors*, No. 947,429, where a multi-billion dollar suit was brought by a citizens group against thirteen major corporations, the Department of HEW, and the United States Attorney General for their alleged role in creating Los Angeles smog.

[4]*Gerring* v. *Gerber*, 219 NYS 2d 558 (1961).

[5]See "Developments in the Law—Injunctions," *Harvard Law Review*, No. 78 (1965), p. 994.

[6]See Coleman, "Possible Repercussions of the NEPA of 1969 on the Private Law Governing Pollution Abatement Suits," *Natural Resources Lawyer* (1970), p. 647.

[7]In an 1896 case, plaintiffs sued because defendant's coal mining operations had fouled the plaintiff's watercourse. The court concluded: "To encourage the development of the great natural resources of a country, trifling inconveniences to particular persons must sometimes give way to the necessities of a great community." Reference: *Penna. Coal Co.* v. *Sanderson*, 113 Pa. 126 (1896), p. 6 A. 459.

[8]*Waschack* v. *Moffat*, 109 A. 2d 310 (1954), p. 316.

[9]For a discussion, see W. Prosser, *Torts*, No. 89 (3rd edition, 1964), p. 488.

[10]*William Aldred's Case*, 77 Eng. Rep. 816 (K.B. 1611), cited in Julian Conrad Juergensmayer, "Control of Air Pollution Through The Assertion of Private Rights," *Duke Law Journal* (1967), p. 1125.

[11]*Madison* v. *Ducktown Sulphur, Copper & Iron Company*, 113 Tenn. 331 (1904).

[12]*Hulbert* v. *California Portland Cement Company*, 161 Cal. 239 (1911).

[13]*Renken* v. *Harvey Aluminum, Inc.*, 226 F. Supp. 169 (D.,Oregon 1963).

[14]Milton Katz, *The Function of Tort Liability in Technology Assessment* (Cambridge, Mass.: Harvard University Program on Technology and Society) Reprint Number 9 (1969), p. 615.

[15]*Jost* v. *Dairyland Power Company*, 172 N.W. 2d 647 (Wisc.,1970).

[16]*Boomer* v. *Atlantic Cement Company*, 309 NYS 2d 312 (1970).

[17]See Patrick E. Murphy, "Environmental Law: New Legal Concepts in the Antipollution Fight," *Missouri Law Review*, No. 36 (1971), pp. 81-82. For an expansion of the "Taking of Property" concept see R. Lester, "Nuisance As A 'Taking of Property'," *University of Miami Law Review,*No. 17 (1963) p. 537.

[18]*Martin* v. *Reynolds Metals Company*, 342 P. 2d 790 (1959), *cert. denied* 362 U.S. 918 (1960).

[19]Cases similar to *Martin* in that they also involved the Reynolds Aluminum plant at Troutdale, Oregon but which had quite different outcomes are *Arvidson* v. *Reynolds Metals Company*, 125 F. Supp. 481 (W. D.,Wash. 1954), *aff'd.* 236 F. 2d 224 (9th Cir. 1956), and *Fairview Farms* v. *Reynolds Metals Company*, 176 F. Supp. 178 (D. Ore. 1959), both of which are discussed in Juergensmeyer, "Control of Air Pollution Through the Assertion of Private Rights," *op. cit.*, pp. 1138-1142. The history of applying a trespass theory to water pollution cases is limited. Courts have allowed recovery under a trespass theory for damage to oyster beds resulting from dredging operations causing silt, or from sewage discharged into oyster beds. See *Mason* v. *United States*, 123 Ct. Cl. 647 (1952).

[20]*Greyhound Corporation* v. *Blakely*, 262 F. 2d 401 (9th Cir. 1958).

[21]*Martin* v. *Reynolds Metals Company*, 342 P. 2d 790 (1959).

[22]C. Jon Handy and William R. Bernstein, *For Themselves and On Behalf of The People of The United States That Are Similarly Situated* v. *General Motors, Inc.*, Civil Action No. 69-1548-R (C.D. Cal., August 7, 1969). The short title and the discussion of the *Handy* case come from Milton Katz, *op. cit.*, pp. 623-638.

[23]There are a vast number of drug products liability cases to choose from. A recent one is *Basko* v. *Sterling Drug, Inc.*, 416 F. 2d 417 (1st Cir. 1969).

[24]*Luthringer* v. *Moore*, 190 P. 2d 1 (1948).

[25]*State of California* v. *Union Oil Company*, No. 84594, Superior Court of Santa Barbara County, California (February 20, 1969). Since the Santa Barbara blow-out, federal law [section 250.42(a)] has been amended to make pollution of the high seas by drilling or production of

oil by definition an abnormally dangerous activity, thus imposing the rule of liability without fault on such activities. To not impose liability in such cases would be equivalent to imposing a tax on victims of blow-outs and turning the proceeds over to the oil industry as a subsidy.

[26]See *Restatement (Second) of Torts* 520A, and comments a through d (1964).

[27]The riparian doctrine is accepted in 31 eastern states. In most of the western states the rule of prior appropriation ("he who gets there first, controls") is followed.

[28]*Kennedy* v. *Moog Servocontrols, Inc.*, 264 N.Y.S. 2d 606 (Sup. Ct. 1965).

[29]Joseph Sax, "The Public Trust Doctrine in Natural Resources Law: Effective Judicial Intervention," *Michigan Law Review*, No. 68 (1970), at 473.

[30]*Gould* v. *Greylack Reservation Commission*, 215 N.E. 2d 114 (1966).

[31]Strictly speaking, Rule 81(b) of the Federal Rules of Civil Procedure abolished mandamus, but it preserved the "relief heretofore available by mandamus." The courts have generally held that the remedies available before adoption of the new Federal Rules of Civil Procedure are still available under the new rules, and under the same principles as formerly governed its enforcements.

[32]See E. F. Cox, R. Fellmeth, J. Schultz, *The 'Nader' Report on the Federal Trade Commission* (New York: Grossman Publishers, 1969).

[33]See John C. Esposito, "Air and Water Pollution: What To Do While Waiting For Washington", *Harvard Civil Rights—Civil Liberties Law Review*, No. 32 (1970), pp. 45-51.

[34]*Environmental Defense Fund* v. *Hoerner Waldorf Corp.*, Civil No. 1694 (filed D. Mont., November 13, 1968).

[35]*Griswold* v. *Connecticut*, 381 U.S. 479 (1965).

[36]*Brown* v. *Board of Education*, 347 U.S. 483 (1954).

[37]A *qui tam* action is "brought by an informer, under a statute which establishes a penalty for the commission or omission of a certain act, and provides that the same shall be recoverable in a civil action, part of the penalty to go to any person who will bring such action and the remainder to the state or some other institution. . . ." In effect, the plaintiff sues for the mutual benefit of the state and himself. There is some question as to whether Congress intended citizens the right to bring *qui tam* actions to enforce the Refuse Act. The Act does not explicitly state that citizens have a right to sue directly, nor that they

do not. The prevailing view seems to be that citizen suits are possible. For a contrary argument, see "Commentary: Oil and Oysters Don't Mix—Private Remedies for Pollution Damage to Shellfish," *Alabama Law Review*, No. 23 (1970), pp. 121-124.

[38]33 U.S.C. 466, *et seq*; amended April 3, 1970 by the Water Quality Improvement Act of 1970, Public Law 91-224.

[39]81 Stat. 485, 42 U.S.C. 1857 *et seq*.

[40]7 U.S.C. 135 *et seq*.

[41]*Environmental Defense Fund* v. *Hardin* (D.C. Cir. May 28, 1970).

[42]23 U.S.C. 131 and 136.

[43]*Berman* v. *Parker*, 348 U.S. 26 (1954), p. 33. For a similar statement see *State* v. *Wieland*, 69 N.W. 2d 217 (Wisconsin 1955).

[44]One problem arises from the recent *Snyder* case, which held that class members in a federal diversity case must each meet the jurisdictional requirements in order to aggregate their claims to the required level. *Snyder* v. *Harris*, 394 U.S. 332 (1969), interpreting 28 U.S.C. 1331(a) (1964).

[45]Cited in John C. Esposito, "Air and Water Pollution: What To Do While Waiting For Washington," *op. cit.*, p. 36.

[46]Actions under the relevant statute, Rule 23(b)(3) of the Federal Rules, have arisen almost exclusively in antitrust and securities law situations.

[47]*Diamond* v. *General Motors, et al.*, No. 947,429, California Superior Court.

[48]*Kean, Wigoda et al.* v. *General Motors, Ford Motor Company, Chrysler Corporation, et al.*, No. 69c-1900, U.S. District Court for the Northern District of Illinois.

[49]*Storley* v. *Armour & Company*, 107 F. 2d 499 (8th Cir., 1939).

[50]*New Hampshire* v. *Atomic Energy Commission*, 406 F. 2d 170 (1st Cir. 1969).

[51]*Town of Bedford* v. *Boyd*, 270 F. Supp. 650 (S.D. New York, 1967).

[52]*Scenic Hudson Preservation Conference* v. *Federal Power Commission*, 354 F. 2d 608 (2nd Cir. 1965).

[53]There is considerable difference of opinion in the literature on this point. For a discussion see R. Stepp and S. Macaulay, "The Pollution Problem," in *Legislation and Special Analyses of the American Enterprise Institute for Public Policy Research*, 90th Congress, 2nd Sess. (No. 16, 1968), p. 12.

7

The National

Environmental

Policy Act

"A nation's history is written in
the book of its words, the book of
its deeds, the book of its art. A
people's history is also written
in what they do with the natural
beauty Providence bestowed upon
them."

Richard M. Nixon[1]

700. Introduction

Although Congress has been concerned with environmental legislation since the 1950's, the most comprehensive
legislation enacted to date is the National Environmental Policy
Act of 1969 (NEPA), signed into law by President Nixon on January 1st, 1970.[2] The statute marks an important departure from
existing federal environmental legislation in that it recognizes in
Title I the direct interest of the federal government in working
toward a healthful environment, rather than placing primary responsibility for environmental legislation on the states.[3] Title II of
the Act sets up a Council on Environmental Quality (CEQ) in the
Executive Office of the President. The functions of the Council are
to review and appraise the various programs and activities of the
federal government in light of the policy set forth in NEPA. Thus,
the main thrust of the Act is to insure that federal departments
and agencies proceed in their activities with due concern for environmental quality.

Examples of the rising public concern over the way in which federal policies and activities have contributed to environmental decay may be seen in the Santa Barbara oil well blowout; the impact of a jet airport adjacent to the Everglades National Park in Florida; the indiscriminate siting of steam-fired power plants; the dangers of spillage or leakage inherent in the various methods suggested for moving crude oil from the North Slope discovery in Alaska; the loss of publicly owned seashores and open spaces to industry and commercial developers; and federally sponsored or funded construction activities such as highways, airports, and other public works projects which proceed without reference to the desires of local residents.[4] NEPA is designed to deal with the basic causes and long-range implications of these environmental problems.

Section 101 of NEPA declares that it is national environmental policy that the federal government use all practicable means, consistent with other essential considerations of national policy, to improve and coordinate federal plans, functions, programs, and resources so that the nation may:

(1) fulfill the responsibilities of each generation as trustee of the environment for succeeding generations;

(2) assure for all Americans safe, healthful, productive, and aesthetically and culturally pleasing surroundings;

(3) attain the widest range of beneficial use of the environment without degradation, risk to health or safety, or other undesirable and unintended consequences;

(4) preserve important historic, cultural, and natural aspects of our national heritage, and maintain, wherever possible, an environment which supports diversity and variety of individual choice;

(5) achieve a balance between population and resource use which will permit high standards of living and a wide sharing of life's amenities; and

(6) enhance the quality of renewable resources and approach the maximum attainable recycling of depletable resources.

Under the Act, federal officials and agencies must consider whether adverse environmental impact will result before making *any* decision which affects the environment. Such consideration must be included in a "detailed statement" when legislative proposals or other major federal action are involved.

Federal officials must thus analyze the environmental impact of their proposed actions. Failure to consider an important environmental issue or inadequate consideration of such an issue is grounds to find noncompliance with NEPA where, had the issue been adequately considered, the decision might have been different. In legal terms, if a federal administrator does not adequately consider the environmental impact of his proposed actions, his decision to undertake the actions is considered arbitrary and capricious and subject to reversal in the courts. Further, a federal agency cannot justify a nonconsideration of environmental effects on the basis of ignorance of such effects. If there is inadequate knowledge about a particular problem, NEPA provides authority for the agency to obtain the required information.

If adequate consideration of environmental impact indicates that an action will have beneficial or neutral environmental effects, then the action is permissible under NEPA. If adverse environmental effects are shown, then the official or agency has a duty to consider alternatives to the proposed action. The consideration of alternatives must be as thorough as the consideration of environmental effects; inadequate consideration of an alternative is sufficient grounds to find noncompliance with NEPA, again because, had the alternative been adequately considered, it might have been adopted rather than the original proposal.

If an alternative is found which does not entail the adverse environmental effects of the proposed action, then the duty of federal officials under the Act requires that the alternative rather than the original proposal be adopted. If a conflict can be eliminated by the adoption of an environmentally nondestructive course of action, then it would be a breach of duty to adopt the environmentally destructive course of action.

Some proposals which have adverse environmental effects will not have alternatives which eliminate the adverse effects. In these cases, the federal official or agency has a responsibility under NEPA to reassess the justification for the proposed action. Senator Henry M. Jackson of Washington has pointed out that Congress intended that environmentally destructive courses of action be only infrequently permitted:

The basic principle of the policy is that we must strive in all that we do, to achieve a standard of excellence in man's relationship to his physical surroundings. If there are to be departures from this standard of excellence they should be exceptions to the rule and the policy. And as exceptions, they will have to be justified in the light of public scrutiny as required [by the Act].[5]

Under NEPA, the only permissible actions which have adverse environmental consequences are those where the long-term resulting social benefits outweigh the long-term environmental costs. The rules established by NEPA to govern this balancing of social equities are as follows:

First, values other than economic values are to be included in the weighing. Such values as diversity, aesthetics, and health are to be considered when determining whether an environmentally destructive action is to be permitted. To the extent that these values cannot be quantified, other procedures must be developed to insure that they receive "appropriate consideration."

Second, a much more thorough look at "public benefits" must be taken than is true under the "balancing of equities" test applied in nuisance cases. The benefits which accrue to the public, rather than to individuals, must be balanced against the losses accruing to the public.

Even where an agency succeeds in proving that an environmentally destructive action is justified by offsetting social benefits, it must take all possible steps to minimize the adverse effects of its action. In particular, consideration of alternative techniques of implementing the decision is important.

Throughout the process outlined, the burden of proof falls on the person or group which wishes to disturb the environment. This is a critical point, because it restructures a decision-making process which has virtually always subordinated the public's interest in environmental protection to a multitude of private interests. Those who wish to disturb the environment must now prove either that the proposed action will not impair environmental quality, or that social benefits will clearly outweigh social costs. They must also prove that no alternatives exist which would eliminate or minimize such effects, and the proof must be offered as part of a reviewable record.[6]

701. Procedural Duties

NEPA requires the preparation of a written statement, to be reviewed by the President, the Council on Environmental Quality, and the public, on the environmental impact of proposals for legislation which "significantly affect the quality of the human environment." [7] In the case of proposals for legislation, the written statement is supposed to allow Congress to determine whether a proposal is consistent with the national environmental policy without the need to plow through the administrative record. If the statement were not required, possible adverse effects would often be buried in the administrative record and would go unnoticed. When the statement is submitted, it must be accompanied by the comments of "appropriate Federal, State, and local agencies, which are authorized to develop and enforce environmental standards." The statement is specifically required to be an analysis of environmental impact rather than an attempt to justify a particular decision. The analytical character of the statement is emphasized by the NEPA requirement that the statement must be prepared by a "responsible official."

Reproduced below is an abbreviated copy of the U.S. Department of the Interior's environmental statement for the proposed Narrows Unit of the Missouri River Basin Project in Colorado, which was submitted in June of 1970 to satisfy NEPA requirements. Prior to its submission to the Council on Environmental Quality, the report had been reviewed by the member states of the Missouri River Basin, the Secretary of the Army, and several unnamed "interested Federal agencies." No revision was made based on the recommendations and views received.

It is of some interest that the environmental statement was transmitted to the Council on June 9th, 1970. Hearings on the House version of the bill approving the project (H.R. 6715) had been held the previous April 16th and 17th by the Subcommittee on Irrigation and Reclamation of the Committee on Interior and Insular Affairs, and the measure had been recommended for passage by the House. Hearings on the Senate bill (S. 3547) were scheduled for the next day, June 10th, by the Water and Power Resources Subcommittee of the Senate Committee on Interior and Insular Affairs.

In reading the environmental statement, consider to what extent it covers the five required factors: the environmental impact of the proposed action; whether there are any adverse environmental effects that cannot be avoided; whether there are alternatives to the proposed action; the relationship between long-term and short-term uses of the environment, and long-term maintenance of productivity; and, whether there are irreversible and irretrievable commitments of resources which are involved in the proposed action. Was the report written by an engineer, an economist, or an environmental protection expert?

ENVIRONMENTAL STATEMENT ON PROPOSED NARROWS UNIT, MISSOURI RIVER BASIN PROJECT, COLORADO, SUBMITTED IN CONFORMANCE WITH SECTION 102 (2) (C) OF THE NATIONAL ENVIRONMENTAL POLICY ACT OF 1969*

Nature of Activity

The proposed Narrows Unit of the Missouri River Basin Project is a multiple-purpose water and related land resources development located in the lower South Platte River Basin in northeastern Colorado. The proposed Unit would serve the functions of irrigation, flood control, recreation, and fish and wildlife enhancement, as well as potential future municipal and industrial water supplies. . . .

Description and Purpose of Proposed Development

The principal feature of the Narrows Unit would be Narrows Dam and Reservoir, to be constructed on the South Platte River near Fort Morgan. The Narrows Dam would be an earthfill structure about 146 feet high with a crest length of 22,100 feet. Three dikes having a combined length of about 12,700 feet also would be necessary. . . .

Rights-of-way adequate for construction and operation and

---

* Statement *by the United States Department of the Interior concerning the proposed Narrows Unit of the Missouri River Basin Project (June, 1970).*

maintenance of the dam and reservoir, associated relocations, and for recreation and fish and wildlife developments would require the acquisition of approximately 36,250 acres of land. Relocation of the Union Pacific Railroad and State Highway 144 would be required.

The construction of a fish hatchery and rearing ponds and the acquisition and development of the existing Jackson Lake Reservoir, now privately owned, are proposed for outdoor recreation and fish and wildlife enhancement. A wildlife management area and four public-use recreation areas are also proposed for development.

Because of inadequate water supplies, the areas irrigated within the lower South Platte River Basin, including the Narrows Unit service area, have been limited, and the full irrigation potential has failed to materialize. The frequent lack of sufficient surface water supplies has caused many irrigators to construct wells for pumping ground water for supplemental irrigation. Water supply shortages have been further intensified by severe droughts, which cause serious depletions of the surface water supply and result in a greater demand on the wells.

In the Narrows Unit service area there are 33 irrigation systems; none of these reservoirs are large enough to store adequate supplies for their associated ditch system. . . .

The lack of storage facilities is a major factor contributing toward the annual shortages of water. Twenty-three of the ditches, which serve 98.4 percent of the irrigable lands in the Lower South Platte Water Conservancy District, experienced an average annual diversion shortage of 178,000 acre-feet over the 1947-1961 period.

The water supply for the Unit would average 140,700 acre-feet annually, of which 119,400 acre-feet would be obtained from regulation of surplus streamflow and from direct-flow water rights associated with irrigated lands to be acquired for the Narrows Dam and Reservoir and 21,300 acre-feet from divertible return flows. . . .

Storage water would be released as necessary from the Narrows Reservoir to supplement irrigation within the service area, totaling 166,370 acres of irrigated land in the conservancy district. Supplemental releases would be conveyed downstream in the river channel to the diversion works of existing irrigation systems.

The supplemental water supply for Unit lands, analyzed on the basis of a 100-year period and an interest rate of 3-¼ percent, would yield $1,410,000 direct benefits and $222,000 indirect and public benefits, for total irrigation benefits of $1,632,000 annually.

The South Platte River Basin is subjected to deluge-type rainstorms that are erratic and incredibly violent. During the period 1844 to 1965 nine such storms occurred, resulting in major floods. Numerous smaller, though severe, floods also have occurred. The impact on the area is substantial, causing major losses to property, transportation facilities, irrigation systems, crops, and livestock, with resultant devastating effects on the economy. Operation of Narrows Dam and Reservoir will afford downstream flood protection. The Corps of Engineers estimates flood control benefits will amount to $1,600,000 annually. . . .

Both the construction of Narrows Dam and Reservoir and the rehabilitation of Jackson Lake Reservoir would provide recreation and fish and wildlife benefits. In addition, specific lands and facilities would be required for recreation and fish and wildlife purposes. Recommended minimum downstream flows for fish requirements would be met most of the time by reservoir seepage and normal project operations. Outdoor recreation activities will include picnicking, sightseeing, boating, water skiing, swimming, hiking, and camping. The National Park Service estimates that use will increase from 930,000 visitor days initially to almost 1-¼ million about 25 years after initial development. The recreation benefits have been evaluated at $1,410,000 annually.

The proposed fish and wildlife measures will jointly serve the purposes of mitigation and local and national enhancement of those resources. Total evaluated fish and wildlife benefits associated with the fishery, hunting, waterfowl use, and wildlife-oriented recreation are estimated to be $552,000 annually.

Adjusted annual equivalent benefits anticipated from development of the Narrows Unit total $5.2 million, of which $5.0 million are direct benefits.

The estimated construction cost of the Unit, based on January 1969 prices, is $68 million. Annual operation, maintenance, and replacement costs are estimated to be $313,000. Annual equivalent Federal costs for a 100-year period of analysis at 3-¼ percent interest are computed to be $2.75 million.

The ratio of total annual benefits to annual equivalent costs is 1.9 to 1. The ratio of direct benefits to costs is 1.8 to 1.

The total construction costs ($68 million) have been allocated to the functions of the Unit as follows: irrigation, $21.1 million; flood control, $24.4 million; recreation, $15.8 million; fish and wildlife enhancement, $6.6 million; road relocation, $135,000.

Effect of Proposed Development on Quality of the Environment

This assessment of the probable effect of the Narrows Unit on the quality of the human environment reflects the views and recommendations of those Federal and State agencies which participated directly in formulating the recommended plan of development or indirectly through the review process.

(1) Impact on environment. The South Platte River watershed is a broad rolling plain through which the river has formed a wide valley of flood plains and bench lands on river terrains. The bench lands are situated from 20 to 200 feet higher than the flood plains. The river has a gradient of 8 to 10 feet per mile.

The Unit area . . . is normally semi-arid with widely varying annual precipitation. This climate provides abundant sunshine, with warm days and cool nights during the growing season, making the area especially favorable for agriculture and associated industries, although the natural precipitation is adequate to support only highly speculative dryland farming and livestock grazing. The project area does not constitute a unit of environment that is either scarce or unique.

The Narrows Unit will have a favorable impact on the natural environment and economy throughout the South Platte River system within and downstream from the project area. Beneficial impacts would include creation of a new reservoir having a water surface area of approximately 15,000 acres; establishment of a new reservoir fishery; conversion of 5-½ miles of low quality warm water stream fishery to a good cold water fishery; the development and operation of 15,765 acres of project lands as a wildlife management unit to mitigate loss and damages to the fish and wildlife resources and to enhance the project for upland game and waterfowl; stabilization of a 2,500-acre offstream reservoir environment specifically to maximize the benefits therefrom for fish and wildlife and recreation purposes. . . . The Unit would provide a much-needed water-oriented recreation outlet for this region of Colorado.

No downstream water quality effects are anticipated which would interfere with present or proposed beneficial uses of water from the South Platte River. Operation of the Narrows Unit will reduce the salinity and sediment content of the downstream flows.

At the present time, the economic environment of the project area is one of instability with wide fluctuations in income from year to year due primarily to variations in rainfall and water supply for irrigation. This has resulted in a deterioration of the well-being of the area residents. The additional water supply, flood protection, fish and wildlife, and recreational developments and opportunities provided by the Unit would contribute substantially to the improvement of the well-being of the residents of the area.

The difference in irrigated crop values produced in the project area has varied as much as $4 million from one year to the next. A study developed for Nebraska indicates that $6.68 of economic activity occurs within the State for one dollar of increased value attributable to irrigated crop production. On this basis, a reduction of $4 million in crop production translates into a total economic activity decrease of about $27 million. Such wide variations have occurred as recently as 1965. Conversely, with the project in place, economic stability occurs and indications are that total economic activity would increase by about $25 million annually.

(2) **Adverse environmental effects.** Certain adverse effects on the environment will occur with the project. These will include the inundation by the reservoir of 15.5 miles of natural stream environment and approximately 15,000 acres of land. The loss of approximately 1,100 fur bearers and 1,000 ducks annually associated with the habitat will be mitigated as a part of the proposed fish and wildlife development. There will be no loss of unique archaeological or geological features. The project will require the acquisition of a total of approximately 36,000 acres of predominantly agricultural lands and the dislocation of about 40 farm units associated therewith. Three small settlements, involving about 150 families and one cemetery, will require relocation.

(3) **Alternatives to the proposed action.** There is no alternative course of action to the proposed plan which would create equivalent benefits for meeting social, economic, and environmental objectives within the State of Colorado at comparable economic costs.

(4) Relationship of short-term uses versus long-term needs. The resources which would be committed to this proposed development are not subject to depletion in the same sense as are coal or oil deposits. Water is a renewal resource. Land productivity can be maintained and enhanced with proper care while being irrigated. Therefore, the water and land resources are not lost, nor is their future development for other purposes having higher values precluded.

Thus, a common relationship exists between local short-term use of these resources and the need to maintain and enhance the long-term productivity.

(5) Irreversible commitment of resources. The only resource commitments of an irretrievable nature involved in this proposed development are enumerated under item (2) discussed previously.

702. The Engineering Fallacy

The environmental statement on the proposed Narrows Unit of the Missouri River Basin Project is one of the more straightforward and accurate statements filed under the NEPA requirement in the first 24 months of its existence. It has its obvious problems—one can, and should, question the calculations of benefits which yield a cost-benefit ratio of 1 to 1.9, and a cost-to-direct-benefit ratio of 1 to 1.8, or the use of an agricultural multiplier of 6.68 when such a value is normally never assumed by economists to exceed 1.2 or 1.3. The real problem, though, is one common to virtually every statement filed in the first 24 months, and will be referred to as the engineering fallacy.[8]

A simple example will suffice to illustrate the fallacy. In the New York City area at the present time, there is great pressure and urgency to construct a fourth jetport. Every projection indicates that there will be 85 million passengers using New York airports by 1980, so there must be a fourth, and perhaps a fifth jetport to service them. If you accept the premise in the last sentence, you have already been conned by the engineering fallacy. If there are no additional airport facilities in New York in 1980, there will not be 85 million passengers. If some of the people who really require airport access cannot get it in New York, they will simply locate elsewhere. Some persons will simply not fly, others will use alternate airports at some distance from the city. Some persons will be prepared to accept long delays in "stacked" aircraft, but there are physical and economic limits to how far that "solution" can be extended.

Consider a second example. In 1960, the citizens of California authorized the largest single bond issue ever floated by a single state—billions of dollars for the California Water Plan. The Plan was concerned with transporting the fresh water from the north to the majority of the people, and thus the bond-issue voters, in the south. Every indication was that southern California would require water for an additional 9 million people by 1985. The problem was how to get the water to the people.

The engineering fallacy was apparent again in the California Plan. The problem could easily have been stated (but wasn't) as follows: "How do we get the people to the water?" a problem that would be physically easier, financially cheaper, and ecologically immensely wiser. Going one step further, however, one might ask: Why get the people and the water together at all? State a need, buttress it with growth projection statistics, and the engineering fallacy will focus your thinking on solutions. But who says it is a problem to begin with? If we don't build the dams and aqueducts of the Water Plan, southern California just might *not* grow by 9 million people. People and industries, learning of the forecast water shortage, might go elsewhere, or might stay home. We would not have to pay the cost of the California Water Plan altering virtually every remaining body of fresh water in the state, leaving none in its natural condition. And we would not have to speculate what this might do to the complex ecology of the Central Valley, the land, and the wildlife.

Getting back to the Department of the Interior's environmental statement: point out to an engineer that the South Platte River in northeastern Colorado sometimes floods its lowlands, and he proposes building a dam—or in this case, one dam and three dikes. Point out to him that the dam will eliminate the fish run on the river and he proposes a fish ladder and artificial gravel spawning pits. Point out that one railroad and one state highway will be suddenly under water and he proposes relocating them. Point out that 15,000 acres of natural stream environment and 36,000 acres of good agricultural land, as well as 40 farms and three villages will be inundated, and he proposes calling in a planner to build a model city for the displaced persons. What he will *never* do is reconsider whether the Narrows Unit dam of the Missouri River Basin Project should be built or not. Altogether NEPA may require him to consider the environmental implications of doing nothing, his whole background and training as an engineer distort his perspective.

Since the development of environmentally nondestructive alternatives is an important component of the substantive duty of federal agencies under NEPA, it is important that they do define "alternative courses of action." Nonaction is always one alternative, but consideration of alternatives should not be limited to this pair. However, when considering positive alternatives, the engineering fallacy may arise again in determining which alternatives are economically or technologically feasible, given that feasibility depends on an allocation of resources that NEPA is designed to change.

For example, in deciding whether to build another freeway through downtown Boston, one is tempted to argue that there is no alternative system of mass transportation that is technologically feasible. But it was the original federal decision to subsidize highway construction rather than rapid transit that now makes it technologically and economically unfeasible to build other forms of mass public transportation.

Economic impracticality is often cited as an obstacle to the adoption of environmentally nondestructive alternatives because of an incorrect analysis of short-term costs and benefits. When the Tennessee Valley Authority says it cannot afford to pay enough for coal to allow the damage done by strip mining to be repaired, it is attempting to pass the cost of its operation to the public in decreased environmental quality instead of increased power costs. Such a decision should be stated in the environmental statement in just this way, rather than viewing this type of economic impracticality as an obstacle to the adoption of alternative courses of action.

Technological impracticality must be viewed not only in relation to cost, which is well understood, but also in relation to time. Given enough time (and enough money), technological alternatives can probably be developed for most environmentally destructive actions. The question that must be asked is whether the need for a particular project is so immediate as to rule out the possibility of delay so that adverse environmental effects can be eliminated. For example, proponents of nuclear power plants raise the spectre of power shortages if such facilities are not constructed immediately. They tend to disregard the fact that the environmental consequences of such plants are very uncertain. The question becomes whether we Americans can change our power consumption habits enough to allow us to wait to eliminate harmful environmental effects before building nuclear plants. The answer depends on a whole series of economic, social, and political variables. Until we know whether these variables can be manipulated to allow time to develop alternatives, the claim of technological impracticality should be rejected.

703. Administrative and Judicial Interpretation

The performance of federal agencies in implementing the NEPA has been spotty, but seems to be becoming more consistent. The Department of Transportation did not issue a statement on the environmental effects of the SST until several months after the vote on the appropriations request in the House of Representatives, but later did delay the extension of runways at New York's Kennedy Airport pending review of the environmental impact by the National Academy of Sciences. Under pressure from Congressman Dingell, the International Boundary Commission delayed approval of the use of chemical defoliants along the United States-Canadian border while it solicited the comments of the affected states (but not, curiously, the comments of the affected Canadian provinces).

In several recent judicial proceedings the NEPA has been cited as authority to deny actions where adverse environmental effects might result. In *Zabel* v. *Tabb*,[9] the owners of land underlying Boca Ciega Bay in Florida required the issuance of a permit by the United States Army Corps of Engineers to fill in eleven acres of tidelands for use as a commercial mobile trailer park. Several state agencies and about seven hundred concerned citizens filed protests with the Corps. The United States Fish and Wildlife Service also opposed the application for a dredge and fill permit because such construction "would have a distinctly harmful effect on the fish and wildlife resources of Boca Ciega Bay."

The Secretary of the Army denied the application on the grounds that issuance of the permit would cause irreparable damage to the fish and wildlife resources. The landholders then brought suit in federal district court asking that the Secretary of the Army be required to issue a permit. The district court, relying on past interpretations of the Rivers and Harbors Act, held that the Secretary was without authority to deny a permit for reasons other than the obstruction of navigation. However, on appeal to the United States Court of Appeals for the Fifth Circuit, the court held that the Fish and Wildlife Coordination Act, when read together with NEPA, did give the Secretary of the Army power to prohibit an action where the ecology was endangered, and upheld the denial of the permit. Although NEPA was not in existence at the time Zabel was denied a permit by the Secretary, the court said that judicial review of an administrative decision must be made in terms of the applicable standards at the time of the court's decision.

In the *Wilderness Society* v. *Hickel* case,[10] the plaintiffs were the Wilderness Society, Friends of the Earth, and the Environmental Defense Fund, Inc., who argued that Walter J. Hickel, then Secretary of the Interior, should not be allowed to issue permits for the construction of the 789 mile long oil pipeline from Prudhoe Bay to Valdez, Alaska because the Trans-Alaska Pipeline System (TAPS) threatened the wilderness ecosystem of Alaska's North Slope. Specifically, it was claimed that the pipeline would cross high-risk earthquake terrain, and that there was a strong possibility that the pipeline would rupture and spill oil, causing irreparable damage to the environment. Second, the heated oil passing through the pipeline could irreparably melt and erode Alaska's delicate permafrost. Third, the pipeline road would use from 12 to 20 million cubic yards of gravel which would be taken from the rivers and streams of the public domain. Fourth, oil spills from tanker loading operations at Valdez would irreparably damage the Pacific Coast from Alaska to Seattle. An injunction was granted on the basis that Secretary Hickel had filed an environmental statement under NEPA which took into account road construction, but he did not consider the total environmental impact of the pipeline construction which would accompany the road. The injunction is important because it reverses the more common approach which is to issue licenses contingent on future compliance with vague standards. Projects of the size of TAPS gain great momentum and once initial construction is undertaken they are difficult to stop no matter what detrimental environmental effects may occur. For example, despite proven geological faults in the Santa Barbara Channel, and despite the occurrence of one disastrous oil spill, oil companies are still permitted to drill new wells in that area.

NEPA has also been used with some success in conjunction with other environmental protection statutes. The Environmental Defense Fund filed a petition with the Department of HEW in April of 1970 to force the Secretary to set emission standards for gasoline to implement the Clean Air Act and NEPA. The Clean Air Act itself does not require standards to be set for air pollution, but in combination with NEPA it can be argued to so require. Similarly, the Environmental Defense Fund filed a petition with the Federal Aviation Administration in May of 1970 to require the immediate setting of environmental standards to apply to the SST, citing NEPA and the Aircraft Noise Abatement Act as authorities. EDF requested standards for sideline noise, sonic booms, passenger radiation, and atmospheric pollution, claiming that a lack of standards would make it impossible to set later standards which would restore environmental quality as envisioned in the policy statement of NEPA.

In each of these proceedings, there is evidence that NEPA is beginning to affect the decisions of governmental agencies that have in the past been accused of being insensitive to environmental factors. For example the Atomic Energy Commission, which had always claimed that it had no power to consider environmental factors other than radiation damage resulting from its operations, has now instituted new procedures requiring license applicants to supply an environmental impact statement prior to public hearings for nuclear power reactor licenses. The Army Corps of Engineers have begun studying alternative ways to complete the controversial Cross-Florida Barge Canal with the objective of leaving more of the Oklawaha River free of dams. And, the Department of Transportation has rejected an application for a bridge permit where the proposed bridge would have led to the destruction of certain historic sites, thus having the sort of adverse environmental effect prohibited by NEPA. As federal agencies become more familiar with the substantive and procedural requirements of NEPA and their effect on statutory authority, it is to be hoped that they will increasingly incorporate this national policy into their decisions.

704. NEPA and Tort Law

Section 101(c) of NEPA provides that: "The Congress recognizes that each person should enjoy a healthful environment and that each person has a responsibility to contribute to the preservation and enhancement of the environment." This section and the responsibility of the federal judiciary to further the national policy suggest that the Act might have ramifications in the area of private tort law which currently offers the private citizen his only method of redress against polluters.

As indicated in the previous chapter, the present structure of tort law upon which NEPA is superimposed is one in which a plaintiff in a pollution abatement suit must base liability on one or more of the traditional doctrines of nuisance, trespass, negligence, or on a doctrine of strict liability such as products liability or liability for abnormally dangerous activities. Although only negligence among these requires a finding of fault on the part of the polluter, each calls for a process of weighing conflicting interests.

With few exceptions, the balancing of equities involved in the weighing process has treated primarily economic considerations, and has not taken into account the fact that a plaintiff's personal aesthetic interest in a clean environment is paralleled by the community's interest in abating pollution, and that this individual and group interest often outweighs the social utility of a polluter's contribution to the local economy. Now that Congress has articulated for the first time in the Act a recognition of each person's fundamental right to a healthful environment, it may be that the guarantee of the continued enjoyment of this right will weigh more heavily than before when it comes time for the court to balance conflicting interests.[11]

The narrowest impact which NEPA might have is to provide a basis for the abrogation of some common law defenses such as the polluter's acquiring over time the right to maintain a private nuisance or a trespass, and the victim's "coming to the nuisance" barring or at least making more difficult the recovery of damages. A broader impact would be the abrogation of some of the technicalities which make it difficult for a victim to make a case; such as the need for the victim in a public nuisance action to show special damages, or the rule that trespass occurs only where there are direct and not consequential damages. These implications arise directly from the recognition in section 101(c) of the Act that enjoyment of the right to a healthful environment is dependent on others respecting their duty to "contribute to the preservation and enhancement of the environment."[12]

705. NEPA and State Laws

A very broad effect on state law could be achieved under the theory that section 101(c) of NEPA sets up a federal right and duty which states must effectuate through their own systems of laws and provisions for private actions and remedies. If this argument were aimed only at overcoming the common law defenses and rules which hamper victims of pollution within the framework of the traditional common law remedies, then the resulting impact on state tort law and on the internalizing of costs of pollution would be substantial. If the argument were broadened to require the states to create new causes of action similar to NEPA the effect on state law and on effective cost internalization would be far greater, as the private victim would no longer be forced to sue under all the existing rubrics which private law has evolved.

A number of states have to date produced statutes which parallel or in some cases exceed NEPA in providing remedies. The Illinois General Assembly passed an Environmental Protection Act which established a Pollution Control Board, an Environmental Protection Agency, and an Institute for Environmental Quality. The Institute's function parallels that of the Council on Environmental Quality established under Title II of NEPA: it will carry out research and work with other state agencies in search of long-range solutions to environmental problems. The Pollution Control Board can promulgate standards for the control of air, water, and land pollution, refuse disposal, noise, and atomic radiation. The Agency may file complaints with the Board alleging violation of the Act or of a regulation, after which the polluter has the burden of showing that compliance with the law would create an "arbitrary or unreasonable hardship." The Board can issue cease and desist orders, impose money penalties, and grant individual variances.

In New York, an Environmental Conservation Law went into effect on June 1st, 1970 which declares a state environmental policy and creates a Department of Environmental Conservation to manage the environmental effort. The Department is the New York counterpart of the CEQ. The New York law goes beyond NEPA in that it empowers the Commissioner of Environmental Conservation to bring summary action against any person engaging in an activity which presents an imminent danger to the environment. Statutes similar to New York's have been passed in Connecticut, Illinois, and Kentucky.

Probably the toughest state environmental statute in the country and the one best suited to local conditions is the Vermont Environmental Protection Act passed in late 1970, which has been used as a basis for almost thirty individual actions against polluters in its first six months of existence. Vermont's environmental problem is acute because the state is used as a recreation area by city dwellers from Boston to Washington. This has produced both a Florida-type land boom in recreation land, and a general disregard for environmental protection on the part of these transient residents. Land developers have in many cases subdivided land into half- and quarter-acre lots with no provisions for central sewage. In some cases these developments are at altitudes of over 2500 feet where the ability of the land to absorb waste is low because of underlying bedrock. Where the soil cover is shallow, septic tanks overflow and wastes seep downhill into wells, streams, and lakes. Also large-scale building over 2500 feet, such as occurs with the development of ski areas, upsets fragile watersheds and other ecological balances, thus destroying fish and other wildlife.

The major provision of the Vermont statute is the establishment of a state environmental board and nine district commissions to establish comprehensive state capability, development, and land-use plans. A state-wide zoning law was established for all developments over 10 acres, with all construction for any purpose above 2500 feet altitude included. All included developments must be licensed and approved by one of the district commissions, which are empowered to hold public hearings and compel attendance of witnesses and production of evidence. An interesting feature is that there is no exemption for municipal development projects such as schools, waterworks, or industrial parks.

Another provision allows the state to buy land while still allowing farmers to work it. This allows the state to block a development without imposing economic hardships on existing farmers because of high taxes. This provision was needed because when a development comes into an area land values increase, and land becomes assessed at its market value rather than its value as farm land. Farmers are thus often forced to sell to the developers. In Windham County in Vermont, which includes many ski areas as well as a 23,000 acre International Paper development, an owner of a 55 acre wooded lot who paid $24 in taxes in 1967 would pay $690 in 1972. Each of these new laws, particularly those tailored to local problems as is Vermont's, helps assure compliance with NEPA while relieving conservationists of the costs and attendant perils of suing the federal government for compliance.

While state enactment of environmental protection laws is hopeful, the most promising approach to pollution abatement is on a worldwide basis, an approach which will be discussed briefly in Chapter Eight.

REFERENCES

[1] From President Nixon's environmental message to Congress, 1971

[2] Public law 91-190, 91st Congress, 1st Session (January 1, 1970), 42 U.S.C. 4331 *et seq.*

[3] For example, the Air Quality Act states as a Congressional finding "that the prevention of air pollution at its source is the primary responsibility of states and local governments."

[4] The structure and part of the content of the first two sections of this chapter were inspired by an excellent paper entitled *Title I of the National Environmental Policy Act of 1969*, by Ronald C. Peterson, a third year student at Yale Law School, which was written during 1970 while he was in residence at the Center for Law and Social Policy in Washington, D.C. under Yale's intensive semester program.

[5] *Congressional Record,* No. 115, Senate 17451 (December 20, 1969).

[6] In practice, the "action-forcing" requirement of a reviewable record has not worked out uniformly well. The language of NEPA seems to warrant the assumption that environmental statements must be circulated and made public before an agency decides to act. Yet the Act does not say positively when the statements are to be submitted or made public. Russell E. Train, Chairman of the White House Council on Environmental Quality, issued guidelines which indicated that a draft environmental statement should be prepared and circulated for comment to other agencies, but that only the final completed statement need be made public. However, some agencies have decided that "timely" publication is months after they have proposed an action, and even months after they have gone ahead with it. Thus, William M. Magruder, head of SST development, did not submit a draft impact statement to other agencies and the public until nine months after the Administration first asked for $290 million for the SST program, and did not make public the final impact statement and comments until after the House had first voted on the bill.

[7] The only major federal actions exempted from the requirement that a detailed statement be prepared are some which affect water quality. Under the Water Quality Improvement Act of 1970, a certification procedure was set up to secure advance compliance with water quality

standards. When compliance with water quality standards is secured from an appropriate state or interstate agency, NEPA statement filing requirements do not apply. However, exemption under this procedural requirement does not exempt water projects from other duties under NEPA where compliance with standards is required.

[8]A number of enlightening examples are given in a fascinating article to which I am indebted for a number of insights: Gene Marine, "The Engineering Mentality," *Project Survival* (Chicago: HMH Publishing Company, 1971), pp. 205-220.

[9]*Zabel* v. *Tabb*, 430 F. 2d 199 (5th Cir. 1970).

[10]*Wilderness Society* v. *Hickel*, Civ. No. 728-70 (D.D.C. April 23, 1970), *Environment Law Digest*, Vol. 70 (1970), p. 1.

[11]It should be noted that the Act in its final form states only that each person *should* enjoy a healthful environment; the legislative history is ambiguous as to whether this means that each individual has the "right" to a healthful environment, with the power to enforce it. In the original Senate bill the section contained somewhat stronger language referring to an inalienable right to a healthful environment, but this wording was stricken in the compromise with the House version of the Act. However, the Act does speak in positive terms of the "responsibility" of each person to contribute to the enhancement of the environment, and the section by section analysis retains strong language about the importance of a healthful environment even though at no point does it call it a right.

[12]These and other impacts on the technicalities of tort law are discussed in great detail in Virginia Coleman, "Possible Repercussions of the National Environmental Policy Act of 1969 on the Private Law Governing Pollution Abatement Suits," *Natural Resources Lawyer*, Vol. III, pp. 647-693.

8

The

Stockholm

Conference

Could there, one wonders, be any undertaking
better designed to meet the world's needs,
to relieve the great convulsions of anxiety
and ingrained hostility that now rack
international society, than a major international effort to restore the hope, the
beauty, and the salubriousness of the natural
environment in which man has his being?

George F. Kennan[1]

800. Introduction

Stockholm, Sweden was host to the first United
Nations Conference on the Human Environment, from June 5th
to 16th, 1972, which brought together almost a complete cross-
section of the world's 3.5 billion people with delegates from 114
nations. (The only major industrialized nation which boycotted the
conference was the Soviet Union.) The conference represented
what many saw as the beginning of a new era of international
collaboration to improve the earth's deteriorating quality of life.

The conference produced agreement, in principle, that nations,
despite their sovereignty, have mutual responsibilities for such
common property as the oceans and the atmosphere, and have
responsibilities to each other for constructive environmental
efforts. The nations were unanimous in their acknowledgement that
a worldwide environmental emergency existed, in sectors ranging
from urban blight to insecticide pollution, and that concerted international action was required. The meetings produced a 200-point

program of international action, designated a permanent organization within the United Nations to coordinate these actions, and adopted a code of principles to serve as guidelines for future national performance. The Conference's conclusions are pending ratification by the United Nations General Assembly.

Recognition of the need for internationally coordinated treatment of environmental pollution occurred precipitously. In 1967, when Sweden's U.N. delegates first urged an international meeting, the response was indifference. In 1969, when the issue was raised again, the General Assembly voted almost unanimously for the two-week debate in Stockholm. U Thant, then Secretary-General of the U.N., chose Maurice Strong, a Canadian industrialist as secretary-general of the conference. Strong turned out to be an ombudsman for the developing countries, who now numerically dominate the U.N. but who were at first reluctant to support the conference. They pointed out that the environmental problem facing the Third World nations was poverty; and that pollution was largely a disease of affluence.

In 1970, Strong requested that every country in the U.N. make a survey of national environmental conditions and problems, and submit a report prior to the conference. Two hundred international organizations, 20 U.N. agencies, and 100 internationally-known scientists were also asked for their ideas on the state of the environment. This pre-conference request forced countries of the world to set up a committee, involve their responsible people, and, in many cases, make their first surveys of the resources, needs, the state of pollution, the physical and social conditions in urban and rural settlements, plant and animal life, and their views on useful approaches to the environmental problem.

Strong then assembled experts from the U.N. and the Smithsonian Institution to evaluate the reports and to formulate six action plans on cities, natural resources, pollutants, information, economic aspects of environment, and the structure of an organization for continuing the work after the conference. Intergovernmental groups under a 27-nation Preparatory Committee were asked to draft concrete proposals on marine pollution, soil conservation, monitoring and resource conservation, and on a Declaration on the Human Environment. The document that emerged from this work, some 900 pages in length, was distributed to all participating nations.

"Mini-Stockholms" also were held in Rensselaerville, New York, on organization questions; in Founex, Switzerland, on problems of the developing countries; and in Canberra, Australia, on scientific monitoring problems.

The Founex conference, in June of 1971, was of special interest in that it focused the issues that would confront the industrialized countries in Stockholm. The report from Founex clearly stated that in the view of the majority of the participants, "dire poverty is the most important aspect of the problems which afflict the environment of the majority of mankind." The environmental problems listed by developing countries were: poor water supplies, inadequate sewerage, sickness, nutritional deficiency, and bad housing— all of which were aggravated by rapid population growth. Further, these countries stated their fear that if environmental measures increased the price of goods produced in the rich countries, the rich might try to impose protective taxes on imports from countries with less rigorous standards. The poor countries were also afraid that some exports, such as lead and high-sulfur fuel, would be displaced by nonpolluting technology; that recycling would reduce the demand for raw materials; and that fruits and vegetables containing DDT and similar substances would be banned. There was an expressed need that some early-warning system be worked out to inform developing countries of such pending advancements.

The pre-conference documentation in Founex urged all nations to limit the growth of their demand for energy, and ignored the fact that much of this growth is due to the replacement of human labor by electric power as part of the industrialization process. The effort to reduce industrial energy consumption thus ran headlong into the desire of the developing countries for higher levels of production. Since energy generation is never free of environmental impact (if only through heat emissions), the result was both an impasse, and the dropping of the demand for limited growth in energy production from the Stockholm sessions. Finally, there was apprehension in Founex that the cost to the developed nations of environmental protection would leave less money for already diminishing foreign aid.

Perhaps as a result of the meticulous pre-conference planning, the Stockholm sessions themselves were unexpectedly productive. The general accomplishments of the sessions were summarized by Maurice Strong in an interview with the Swedish press:

> . . . we set up machinery to work toward short and long range goals. To take issue with the technical questions, like who actually does the polluting in a given situation, there will be a monitoring

system, as part of a global assessment program. And there will be exchange of information and research programs on such questions as, for example, the encroachment of the deserts, substitutes for DDT, better methods of waste disposal, recycling, new clean technologies. And of course there will be measures proposed on problems like water and soil contamination—so crucial for developing countries, some of whom lose more capital each year through soil contamination than they receive in foreign aid. As for the depletion of plant life, where, for example, the practice of monoculture in relation to the green revolution is extinguishing many types of plant life which it took millions of years to evolve, we propose genetic banks to preserve them.[2]

Specific results of the conference included the approval of an "action program" involving 200 recommendations in fields that ranged from monitoring climate change or oceanic pollution to promoting birth control and the preservation of the world's vanishing diversity of plant and animal species. An Environmental Fund was approved to cover that part of the international effort not paid by specialized agencies and national governments. Those pledges which were made suggest that the fund will reach about $100 million, which is considered the minimum requirement for the first five years of operation.

An interesting series of conference recommendations were aimed at fears that the rapid adoption by farmers of standard crops is weakening the gene pool on which the long-term survival of such crops is dependent. Where a single strain or group of strains is used over a wide geographic area, the crops are vulnerable to blights against which they have no defenses. It is usually in wild or exotic strains that blight-resistant properties are found—strains which are fast vanishing. Thus, a recommendation of the conference was that governments initiate emergency programs to explore and collect species which are imperiled, and to store seeds and otherwise preserve and develop breeds for posterity.

One proposal that pitted the Third World nations against the industrialized nations was a proposal by India and Libya that an international fund or financial institution be set up to provide seed capital to help developing nations improve their housing. The Third World members easily passed this plan, but the 15 nations voting against it included virtually all of the more affluent countries who were expected to contribute to the plan.

801. The National Reports

The reports submitted by 78 nations on the state of the environment in their particular country produces both a sense of the immensity and diversity of the worldwide environmental problem as well as a feeling for the honesty and dedication with which solutions are being sought. The first report, by Afghanistan, concludes that:

The population explosion, depletion of natural resources, inadequate waste disposal systems, unavailability of adequate potable water, the widespread introduction of DDT into the ecosystems, the countryside destruction of natural pastures by overgrazing and conditions related to the underdeveloped status of the country are the most important ecological problems in Afghanistan.

India submitted the most comprehensive survey, contained in four lengthy volumes. While for India population and poverty are the most crucial environmental problems, much of the Indian report discussed the fate of the country's wildlife. The report cited the increase in human population, which has upset the delicate balance of nature, producing species that are injurious to man and his products which are increasing in numbers as a result of man's slaughter of their natural predators. According to the report, "In India it is a case of the giants being superseded by the pygmies. The wild elephant, the rhinoceros, and wild buffalo, the lion, the tiger, and the wild bear, the black buck, the musk deer, the nilgai and the wild ass, the mongoose, the fox and wild cat, the golden eagle, the pink headed duck, the peacock, the Great Indian bustard, the florican, the quail and the partridge either have become extinct or are fast disappearing. What have multipled are the mosquitoes and sand fleas, ticks and mites, the caterpillars, moths, locusts, ants, beetles, and insects of all sorts which attack crops, the sparrows and the saragas, the monkeys and the langurs, the mice and rats which do great damage to the crops and seem to be yearly increasing in numbers and in their ravages."

Holland's report indicates that it faces perhaps the most crucial environmental problem in Europe. Not only is Holland the most densely populated country in Europe, with 350 people per square kilometer, but the problems of effluents and waste disposal are bing, no fighting back. I was soon out of air so a couple of the other fellows took over and I busted for the surface. They had him on shore in a jif. Doyle was blue as a whetstone and as limp as your mother's dish rag. We draped him over the boulder that was serving as ballast for the diving plank, pushed on him a couple of times, and a lot of water came out of him from somewhere. His eyes began to roll and he coughed. One of the Benear Twins had read something about artificial respiration in school. Benear worked him over.

Somehow between us, or because of the fact that Someone was watching over us, Doyle came around. I never did know if he was close to drowning, if he had suffered a concussion by jumping in the water the way he did, or if it was shock from the low water temperature.

Regardless of the cause, it had a sobering effect on that particular crop of colts.

After putting our clothes on, we made a secret pact that had to do with Doyle staying under the water too long. Doyle put it to us in this way. "If my folks ever hear of you fellows having to haul me out they will never let me come here again and perhaps you will get the axe, too."

His idea made sense. He was a leader. We decided to never mention the incident. From then on we were prancing colts no more.

The secret was never told. In three score of years it has not been made public knowledge, as far as I know, until this writing.

Doyle's mother, Myrtle, and father, Homer, have both passed away as well as the former colt. He enlisted in the Marines (he really was a tough gutsy guy) and was in the Death March on Bataan when the Japs had us by the throat. Fate decreed that he was to give his life for his country as a hero and not to lose it as a colt in the depths of the old swimming hole.

The elementary school in Lennon, Michigan, is named the Doyle Knight School in his honor.

A HERO'S MONUMENT

Comment

This episode does not exactly coincide with the mood of this book but the author feels good about putting it here as a personal tribute to a hero, Doyle Knight, with whom I was privileged to share some boyhood days.

CHAPTER III

SUGAR SHANTY

THERE HAVE BEEN many yarns spun and written about sugar shanties. Here are a couple of happenings that took place in that setting. One was a putrid day and the other a sweet, sweet night.

Our neighbor Roy had a beautiful rolling wood lot of hard maple trees that he tapped each spring. The wood lot was like a park. The few boys of the neighborhood were allowed free rein of this property and cherished it as if it were their own.

In the middle of these woods, erected on a well drained south slope, was a sugar house. It contained all the necessary equipment for making maple syrup from the sap that was collected from the trees. There was a large hearth, custom-built from stone picked up from the adjoining fields with the top row being of Middlesworth firebrick, so as to provide an even surface to set the sap pan on. The hearth would accommodate wood up to ten feet long. An elevated raw sap supply was anchored outback on the rise behind the shanty. It would gravity-feed into the evaporating pan on the hearth. The flow of sap could be regulated by a wooden spigot inside the shanty. There was a chimney for the smoke and an opening all the way around the cozy building at the eaves to let the steam from the boiling sap escape. There was a bunk for resting (you seldom found time to sleep) on each side of the leather-strap hung door. It opened on the south side directly

A WORKING SUGAR SHANTY

in front of the business-end of the hearth. Sometimes Roy would ram a dead sapling into the hearth twenty feet long, leave the shanty door open, and keep shoving it into the fire as it was consumed. This saved a lot of chopping. There were a few nails to hang your hat and coat on. Lordy! It would get hot in there even though it was built of rough-sawn hardwood boards. It had to have been nailed up when the lumber was green because the boards had warped as they cured and they were so hard you could not even carve your initials in them. You did not have to hunt for a knothole to see what was going on out in the woods. You could look out the cracks anywhere.

Precocious Sanitation Engineers

Roy, who liked kids, gave us boys the responsibility for keeping the place in order during the off-season. That was eleven months out of a year. The red squirrels would chew a set of leather hinges off the door every year and the "be-cussed" woodchucks would go back to work undermining the place as soon as our backsides went over the hill. When they had the dirt floor altered to their liking they seemed to move on to the next project and a den of skunks took possession or maybe ran out the woodchucks. We never knew exactly how the franchise changed hands.

A couple of us kids went back during summer vacation, which was a third of the year, with a couple of our mother's garden spades, with the idea of cleaning the shanty and leveling off the floor where the woodchucks had piled up mounds of dirt. We were about ten years old. When we opened the door the place did not look bad; but it sure smelled bad. Something had done a job at the edge of the hearth that looked like a pile of ground up crickets. Ken was the older and he knew about such things.

"Skunks eat crickets. I bet there is a skunk back in there," Ken said, as he pointed his spade into the dark hole under the evaporating pan which was greased and upside down on the arbor. We both got down on our knees with spades pointed inward. There was a rustle. We were gritty kids. No matter what was under the pan, it was taking its life in its own hands; only it was they.

The battle was decisive and disastrous for our side. Ken's new dog, Curly, was right in the line of fire with us. He was only a pup and he didn't know any better either.

It was a hot, muggy, late afternoon. The stench seemed to smother us. We both began to cry, cough, and spit, in that order. After we had each gone through the routine about three times, plus rolling in the grass like Curly, I saw Kenny button up his bottom lip. He was a real tough kid.

"Let's go over where Dad is," suggested Ken. He was across the road and south about twenty rods, hoeing corn and whistling.

We had come by him about an hour ago and all he had said was, "Don't you fellows get into any trouble with those big shovels." He knew what we were up to because we had planned it for a week.

Curly arrived at Charlie's corn row much ahead of us. He got a potent whiff of Curly, stopped hoeing, and began throwing clods of dirt at the dog to keep him away. Poor Curly took off for the barn with his yet undocked tail between his legs.

After the hostile reception Ken's dad had given Curly, we were a bit cautious in our approach. We could see from a distance that he was muttering something to himself. Of course, he had to have been watching our progress across the corn field from out of the corner of his eye, after being forewarned by Curly.

Suddenly, he dropped the hoe and held up both hands.

"Whoa! Don't come any closer. I've got corn to hoe. Go see your mother. Where're the shovels?"

We just pointed toward the woods. Of course, he knew exactly where they were. He put his head down and kept chopping corn. As we passed him on the windward side, we saw him shake his head and blow his nose real hard one time. We did not get any help there.

As we rounded the corner of the granary, Ken's mother, Jennie, was out with the broom lambasting Curly off the kitchen stoop. Lucky that we had Curly along or we might have got it the same way. Now we knew what to watch out for.

Ken blurted out between half sobs, "Curly was between and behind us when disaster struck. How could he smell so bad?" I

MEPHITIS MEPHITIS

Skunks are equipped to dig their own burrows, but seldom do. They are usurpers and would rather take possession of a woodchuck hole because they are roomier.

Their number one defense is a putrid spray. This spray will travel 20 feet against a strong wind and 4 miles with that same wind. When this sticky, greenish fluid strikes an intruder it causes choking, coughing, temporary blindness and even a possibility of a blackout. This debilitating material will dissipate with time and become only a lingering disagreeable odor.

didn't think he smelled too bad now, because I didn't notice it like at first when we lost the battle. My lips didn't even taste like they did at first.

We started toward the house. Jennie and Grandma Stein were both out on the stoop now. Curly stood about halfway between the barn and the house. His ears were down, his back was humped up, and he looked as if he did not have a friend left in the whole world. We were worse off, but did not know it.

"Kenneth! Kenneth! Do you hear me? If you ever let that pup of yours come to the house smelling like that again, we will have to do away with him." Grandma Stein stood right behind Ken's mother nodding her approval.

She continued to yell out toward us. "We almost gagged. He must have had a hold of a skunk's tail. Tie him up out in the orchard and come on to the house. I want to get you cleaned up and ready for that church meeting tonight. Stanley should go home, his mother will be wondering about him. You both look filthy."

When in trouble a country kid goes up into the haymow to figure things out. It was a place of solitude. A place to meditate. Up the ladder we went dragging Curly up with us. Why not? Curly had already saved our skins twice. He was a great pup and on his way to becoming a great dog. Right now, he really was the only friend we both had—for sure.

The first thing we did was smell each other all over like dogs do. Then we both smelled Curly. We came to the conclusion that none of us smelled very bad. I noticed that Ken's face, where the tears had not run, was thick with dark bluish-green specks and his clothes looked kind of a faded yellow all across the blue overall bib. I did not say "nuthin" about it even to him. We were tired and felt kind of sick and overcome by the whole thing. Shortly, the three of us curled up and went to sleep together in the haymow.

Ken's father woke us up in the morning by yelling from the top of the ladder at the opposite end of that mow of loose hay.

"Come and get it, you skunk hunters." We rubbed our eyes and bounced on the loose hay over to where he had left a pile of pancakes that were shedding melted butter down over their sides and about a gallon of warm milk. We figured that we were in for bad trouble for having slept in the haymow all night without permission. I did not even go home. My folks did not know where I was! We had done a thousand forbidden things. We would both get the razor strop, and good!

Charlie put us at ease real quick, for there he was already back down on the barn floor alternately standing and bending over laughing as hard as we had ever seen this big man carry on. Tears of laughter were streaming down over his jowls, as they had over ours the afternoon before from fear and the vile secretion.

"You fellows stay right where you are and keep Curly with you. We don't need any of "youse" down here. Grandma Stein will be out here in a bit. She is going to give all three of you a bath from head to foot with her homemade soft soap and vinegar. After she finishes with you guys, you hold Curly for her. Hang your dirty clothes in the tool shed. She is going to bring you clean ones as soon as Stan's dad brings his down."

"We don't stink anymore," we said. Charlie just held his arms up to the heavens and walked out of view. At least my folks knew where I was. That was a relief.

We shared the milk and pancakes with Curly. By noon, we both had our feet under our own mother's dinner table, and life for the sugar shanty janitors was back to normal.

Ken and I were amazed by the lack of punishment and the few remarks that were made about the commotion we had caused. Finally, when we could stand the suspense no longer, we asked Steven Hatch, my dad's hired man, what he had heard about us, if anything.

We were playing it safe by going through a third party. Steve was a blunt, rough talking guy, who would do most anything for us boys.

"Nobody had to say anything," he said. "We could smell ya a mile agin the wind. Ya still stink! I had to bury your mother's spade out in the garden, don't know if she can even use it agin. We don't want the thing around the barn. What in the world did you do, walk in on a den of skunks while they were having a p------g contest?"

The Sweet Night Shift

The spring that followed our losing the battle with the skunks turned out to be a fine one for the making of maple syrup. A spell of abnormally warm weather had blown into this mitten of Michigan on a southwest wind. Did it make the sap run! The supply tank was full and the buckets on the trees were running over before neighbor Roy realized it.

Roy had tapped the trees only a couple of days before so that this would be all choice first-run syrup. To keep the pails from running over, it was necessary to gather sap from the trees three times a day and maintain the evaporator at a rolling boil around the clock.

Our neighbor had sap literally running over the top of his boots. In addition, he had livestock chores to do and a responsive young wife to look after, so he asked Ken and young Perk if we would spell him in the sugar shanty one night. We jumped for joy at the invitation. There was no money involved; pay never entered our minds. The maple syrup was only fetching two dollars for an eleven pound gallon and you could buy a new pair of mittens for fifteen cents. Money was of no account. This opportunity to help a friend was of more consideration and besides he would help us out should we ever get in a jam.

Roy suggested that we go over to the chicken coop and help ourselves to a dozen eggs.

"You fellows might get hungry before morning," he said. "Don't let the fire go out or the pan boil dry."

It was a big all-night responsibility for a couple of kids. Our folks never worried about us. This was our way of life, and we loved every minute of it.

Getting back to the food, we filled our pockets in the chicken coop so we might have had two dozen eggs instead of one. Who cared? They were only worth ten cents a dozen and you had to trade them for groceries to get that.

Upon arriving at the sugar shanty to relieve Roy, we put all those eggs into the pan of boiling, rolling, frothing maple sap. Every time we felt a little hungry, we would take the skimmer down from its hook and fish out two or three apiece. They were real good. The sap added a sweet taste as egg shells are porous.

All that we had to drink throughout the night was cold sap from a bucket that hung on the nearest maple tree. So there we were — a pair of country kids with a big all-night job to do and getting sweeter by the hour.

Roy knew best. We should have taken his advice. One dozen eggs would have been enough. We polished off those eggs washed down with a generous supply of raw cold sap, and nothing else. No salt, pepper, cheese, crackers, bread, cookies; no "nuthin."

We both came down sick with the heaves in the middle of the night — real sick. Ken would go outside the shanty and throw up while young Perk was stoking the fire. Then we would switch. It got to be routine. We both became so sick that the fire nearly went out one time, but we had to stay with it. We could not let Roy down, even though we thought at least one of us would die right there in the woods outside Roy's sugar shanty before the night was over.

I remember asking Ken one time, "Have I turned inside out yet?"

"Nope," he replied, "I think you are going to make it. You just look like a puckery green apple. Green apples come around, if you don't touch them until they get ripe. I think I am the one who is going to die. When I look away, everything looks cloudy. Sometimes I feel like I am floating on a big white cloud. Perk, do you think I am on my way to heaven?"

"Ken, how could you be on your way to heaven after all the deviltry we have been into lately? How about the time we threw the dead snake in the vent of the preachers privy?" Of course, we didn't know his wife was inside and there was no reason for her to head for the manse with her drawers down showing her fat pink bottom and screaming bloody murder. The snake was stone dead. He couldn't hurt her. "We were lucky nobody saw us with that dead spotted adder before we found a place to put it. The fiery preacher would have burnt us at the stake."

"How about the time last week when we switched those rotten hen's eggs we found in the straw stack for some fresh ones in your mother's basket and took them to Pat Cook's Store, and traded them for licorice? Remember Ken, how we smeared the handle of the hired man Ed's favorite dung fork with fresh cow manure? We cannot die here now. We are not ready. We have to live because neither one of us is going to heaven."

This series of recollections shook Ken up and he decided that we would fight it through the night and not give up. Once in awhile Ken would bring up something about Sunday School.

"Perk," he probed me, "did that whale puke up Jonah because he puked in the whale's belly? I know just how Jonah felt. I couldn't stand any whale blubber either right now. You know Perk, it must be terrible to die if we are only half dead now."

By this time there was a ray of light in the eastern sky. This was a sure sign that help was on the way. Dawn was making a good wide crack, when we heard Roy's team coming with the "pun."

"Whoa, Nel" was one of the finest sounds we had ever heard in all our young lives. Roy opened the shanty door and started to shove more wood into the hearth when he turned and got a look at us.

"Say, what has happened to you fellows?" he asked. "You are green. Come over here in the light so I can get a good look at you. My land!" Roy exclaimed. "Look at this pile of egg shells! That's what the matter is. Climb inside the sap tank on the pun and lay down. Let me build up the fire a bit then we will skid you fellows on home to your mothers."

We laid real quiet on the bottom of the sweet smelling sap tank. We did not say a thing. It wasn't necessary. It had all been said for us.

The ride home was fuzzy. I did not remember much about it. Roy had it all figured out when he mentioned the pile of egg shells and the sweet, sweet sap.

I was fifty years old before I could look at a boiled egg without gagging and maple sap fresh off the tree still spins me out.

CHAPTER IV

SOLD TO THE MAN WITH THE BIG CIGAR

T O GET RIGHT to the point, this chapter has to do with public auction sales. There is a timeworn statement that says, "A writer does his best work on familiar subject matter."

Having worked within the auction profession in various capacities for thirty years throughout the eastern half of the United States and Ontario, I find that making the decisions on what to include and what to leave out is more trying than the actual writing. The material will be extremely varied. I have merchandised everything by the auction sale method from the dispersal of a backwoodsman's estate, to a yearly production sale of thoroughbreds for and to sophisticates.

Beholding a Major Event

As a starter, let us go back and recant the joyful impression of an early country farm auction as experienced by a barefoot toeheaded boy. The thing that came to mind when an auction was mentioned to a kid was the big free sack lunch at noon. If the sale was on Saturday, we would go with our dads after chores in the morning and stay all day. If it was on a school day, the free time expendable at the auction was much less, and limited by decree of our teacher. The teacher was usually liberal in this respect being as how the school board members, who approved of her teaching and paid her monthly wages, were farmers.

If there was an auction within running distance of the country school, the teacher would let us boys have an extra long noon hour to hit off to the sale. Usually the shortest distance was cross lots over rail fences, creeks and stone piles. Our dads would all be there, we would crowd into the lunch line ahead of them and latch onto a free bag and a tin cup. In the bag would be two thick sandwiches each made from crusty slices of homemade bread and filled with anything from wild strawberry jam to salt pork. There would be a couple thick blackstrap molasses cookies and also some fruit, depending on the season of the year. For the tin cup, there was all the coffee or tea you could drink. The boys did not care for those drinks so we would dilute the stuff about half with fresh milk straight from a cow's teat. Off to the cow stable we would go for the milk. The cows' bags were full and hurting by this time because the man selling out never milked his cows clean the morning of the auction. He wanted them to look full in the udder when sold, which was usually about the middle of the afternoon. Cows that were not giving much milk would not be milked at all in the morning.

When a bunch of schoolboys did go to the cowshed to dilute their coffee with warm milk, they sometimes carried a good thing too far. By this I imply that a depredation called "squirt in the face" often took place.

It would begin in a prankish way by someone squeezing a large front teat and squirting milk at the kid working on the cow directly across the aisle. The compliment would be returned almost immediately. A milk war was on.

Often a man interested in buying a cow would just happen to be sauntering down the same aisle looking them over before they were sold and get caught in the cross-fire.

A soprano yip was the sign to vamoose. Before a hand could be laid on any of the young rascals, they evaporated into thin air. They could be found shortly, standing innocently with their respective fathers in the crowd where the selling was currently taking place.

A word here about the tin cups as long as it has surfaced. The auctioneer always brought these cups, perhaps three or four hundred of them. They were usually imprinted with his name or his mark. Today this is called a logo. When you finished with your cup you tossed it into the nearest burlap bag. These bags would be hanging all over the place. Sometimes boys would pitch in a few fresh road-apples to dilute the tin. The auctioneer would take the cups home and his wife would wash them up in preparation for the next auction. This custom of using tin cups has long since been condemned but I never knew of any contamination stemming from them.

Women were never present at a country auction except to prepare the free food. It was a man's world. We boys loved it. Girls did not mean a thing to us at that time in our lives. Oh boy!

The clerk was an important man at the auction. He was a professional who handled the money and the record. He was either hired by the farmer selling out, or by a local bank to protect its interest in the proceedings. The auctioneer was the best dressed man in the crowd, drove the fastest horse and rode up in the flashiest buggy. He would be a dominating portly gentleman that ran the show with as much authority as a captain did his ship on the Great Lakes. He would be a ready wit and tell a few risqué stories on the hired girl or the schoolmarm for the natives to carry back home. They would not fit in here.

The most important portion of the auction for us would take place when they sold the horses. Good driving and buggy horses were always in demand, but the big money was laid on the line for the matched work teams. In selling a team, the off horse would be placed up for bid first, then the near horse. After the auctioneer had secured the highest figures that the bidders were willing to pay for the team as individuals, the two amounts would be totaled by the clerk. This figure is where the bidding would resume if the horses were to be kept together as a team. The boys would cry if a team was split. This would happen when the bid as a team did not exceed the total of the two when sold separate. We

BILL AND BUSTER

A team named Bill and Buster weighing close to a ton each are hitched here to a set of "bobs" and hauling winter wood in deep snow on the farm of Calvin Hall near Pickford, Michigan.

These matched bay geldings are being kept in condition by their owner Dean Bawks who has his mind set on taking some of those cash prizes at the Chippewa County Fair horse pulling contests.

knew all the neighbors' horses by sight and their names. After the selling of a team, either single or double, the harnesses on their backs would be sold. Usually the collar and pad would stay with the horse because they were worn in to fit a particular shoulder and had little value for use elsewhere. You see how a boy's mind revolved around the free lunch, the auctioneer and the beautiful horses.

I do recall that farm implements were a minor portion of the auction which is in direct contrast to the emphasis of the present day. The tools might include walking and sulky plows, an A-tooth drag, a newfangled spring-tooth harrow, a cornfield marker, a log land roller, an eleven-hose grain drill, hand corn planters, cultivators, wagons, racks, a mower, a buck rake, tedder, grain and corn binders, a stump puller, a "pun" or two, a maple syrup making outfit, and there was once in awhile a new machine called a manure spreader.

The money was in livestock. Every farmer had about all the domestic animals on his premises that were available, including poultry. There would be turkeys, geese, ducks, chickens and even pea fowl. There would be sheep, hogs, cattle, and horses which were the power source. Within these various types of stock would be plenty of breakdowns (categories) for an auctioneer and he would have a quip or short story as he began each class.

Some of these quips and stories we would carry back home and retell to the hired men at the barn, but never in or anywhere near the house and the womenfolk. If we retold the auctioneer's off-colored jokes to the wrong people, we would get our hides tanned.

I remember one statement, of printable quality, that an auctioneer used to make when he put a nondescript filly up for bids. "Men, we do not know very much about the background of this young mare except that she was sired by Woebegone and damned by Everybody. How much am I bid to start her? Do I hear sixty-five dolla?" And so it went.

An itinerant auctioneer was a contact with the outside world. He was not always the same person but always cast in the same mold. The panoramic projection of the world outside our immediate community as depicted by the itinerant auctioneers was in conflict with the information provided by circuit riding preachers. Personally, the view of the exterior as presented by the auctioneers was much more appealing to a boy than the fire and brimstone of the theologians.

As seen from the eyes of the country youth, a neighborhood auction was a major event. It was something not to be missed unless you were in bed with the chicken pox. It was on a par with a chivaree, barn raising, box social or the Christmas program at the schoolhouse. Auctions made a lasting impression on us as a youth. To many, the transient auctioneer was a hero and some of the local youth aspired to be likewise. A few were persevering enough and followed through, including this one.

The Overall Traveler

Many years later, as an auctioneer, I was calling a sale near Flushing for a four-corners businessman by the name of Stevens. To be liquidated were the service station equipment, shelf inventory, tools, and contents of the second story living quarters. Frank Zelahi, a young up-and-coming auctioneer, was assisting. We had finished selling the business items and had moved the crowd upstairs to the household goods. The place was packed with humanity and oh, was it hot! There were some fine items to be sold. Frank handed me a beautiful old "Gone with the Wind" lamp that had been electrified. It would be worth a small fortune on today's market. It was an original with matching fount and globe. We were successful in selling this signed hand-painted heirloom at a most satisfactory price of forty dollars. Just as I was attempting to pass it over a couple of heads to the new owner, a barefoot boy in patched bib overalls dashed from behind me, hell-bent for the great outdoors. He caught the electrical plug at the end of that lamp cord between his toes. I juggled that beautiful lamp a couple of times trying desperately to save it. Frank lunged for the boy but to no avail. He was as slippery as an eel. The kid took a second foothold and as we all yelled for him to stop, he simply lowered his head and burrowed through that crowd like a weasel going through a stump pile. You know what happened. Perk ended up on his derriere amongst the brass lamp parts with the glass fount and globe all around him in small pieces. About then the recent buyer started to yell, because the clerk had already taken payment from her for the long-gone, by the way of a boy, antique. Also by that time, the auctioneer had unceremoniously picked himself up and started looking every which way for the barefoot traveler in the patched bib overalls. We could not find him, nor could we locate a mother, father, sister or even a grandmother. Evidently, the lad had automatically declared himself a ward of probate court because no one, and I emphasize *no one*, would admit even remote kinship. To make it more puzzling we could not even find where he went.

It figures that someone had a bit of liability. We gave the buyer her money back and carried on with the auction. I am retired now from my chosen profession. For many years I have been expecting that sometime, somewhere a penitent young man would come forward, maybe with a son of his own in tow, and say, "Remember me, I'm the barefoot kid who caught the lamp cord in my toe," and we would end up having a big laugh. He never has.

Little Red Dogs

Children and youth are always welcome at auctions. The atmosphere and environment are conducive both mentally and physically to healthy growth. In the modern auction they like the lunch wagon and especially the hot dogs. More than once a bawling confused child has been pacified with a free trip to the lunch wagon as guest of the auctioneer. It is a good investment, because there is nothing that will harm an auction more than to have a sniffling, whimpering, bawling kid under foot or hanging around the auction stand. What he is seeking is attention or sympathy. He usually gets it from the crowd. This puts him in competition with the show already in progress and it is distracting to say the least. Never underestimate the power of a child or of a woman over a crowd of men!

This next vignette is the opposite of hilarious. However, it was not tragic and it does have a happy ending.

I was making an auction in Livingston County, Michigan, for a family that was retiring from the contracting business. They were an affluent couple. Their steading included a fine man-made lake surrounded on three sides by heavy woods.

The auction was well along when a young couple came up to the edge of the stand and interrupted me between items, asking if I would put out a call for their four-year-old daughter. A few minutes later they returned with a description of how the child was dressed. Deep concern was written all over their faces. I repeated the call over the P.A. system the second time.

Some teenage lovers who had been strolling on the lakeshore

said they had seen some children playing at the edge of the water and that one was about the age of the missing child.

About half of our crowd took off on the run to the lake where the footprints of small children were found. Under these circumstances, the show did not have to go on. Hysteria was rapidly taking over the event, fueled by the apprehensions of the fearful young parents.

Just at the moment we had decided to shut down the sale and organize a search party, the little girl burst into being.

If you ever see a more tearful and thankful group of people, you will have to do a lot of traveling.

After the crowd had calmed down and emotions had subsided the parents asked the child, "Where have you been? Why did you run off?" They tried to explain to the child in a simple manner, that they had been worried and concerned for her safety.

"Daddy, I was over there in the woods watching the little dogs play," she answered. Upon critical observation by several curious adults, the "little dogs" turned out to be a family of noisy red squirrels. They are fascinating for adults to feed and watch, to say nothing of the interest they would hold for a small child.

This was an auction in which squirrels nearly stole the show.

Tearful Tyke

A tearful tike grabbed me around the knee one-time, looked up and said, "I lost my daddy."

I broke the chant and replied, "Aren't you the one who is lost?'

"No, I'm at Perk's Auction," was her answer. This was a cute incident but also one of my greatest compliments.

COUNTRY AUCTION

Cattle Dog Lost?

There was the occasion when I held a farm auction in a south of Durand neighborhood, where people were so clannish that if you had a serious misunderstanding with any one of the natives, you'd best pull up stakes and move on. During the middle of the afternoon before selling the large machinery, we sold a very well-trained registered Collie cattle dog. The successful bidder was a local farmer who knew the dog's ability well. The price arrived at was substantial. After the auction was concluded, the buyer said to me, "Well, I'm going to get my dog and go for home."

The dog was allowed the freedom of the steading, as usual, but did not seem to be in the immediate vicinity at the moment.

The dog buyer looked up the proprietor and said, "Walt, I guess I will take the dog now."

Well! That dog was not about to be taken. After a quick search of the buildings and the dog's old haunts, it was the naked truth that the expensive dog had vanished.

Shortly thereafter, everyone remaining on the premises was looking for the high-selling cattle dog. The railroad passed about twenty rods west of the buildings and someone mentioned they had seen a couple of boys playing with a dog down by the tracks a spell back. Of course we all went to the tracks to look around. South down the tracks about half a mile there appeared to be a couple of boys walking the rails with something in between them. Walter put two fingers in his mouth and whistled very loud and shrill through his teeth. Immediately you could see that there was a commotion down the tracks and it was not a train wreck.

The good cattle dog came back as fast as he could travel and the boys kept going away from us a hell of a lot faster than they had been. When the dog returned to the crossing where our group stood there were two pieces of baling twine tied to his collar, evidently tied on by the boys so that they could lead him away between them. We were amazed that the dog was able to break free and return.

Slave Auction

Humoristic situations were all over the place at a Slave Auction held as a benefit for their church, by a Youth Fellowship group. Each so-called slave was catalogued on a pass-out mimeographed sheet as to sex, age, weight, height, talent, and job experience. They were a choice group of young people not out passing the tin cup but willing to give eight hours of work to their church in the amount that their new master was willing to bid. It was the kind of town where an auction did not have to be advertised, everybody knew. As auctioneer, I was the recipient of several order bids from merchants in the small town. They could not attend but wished to patronize this sale. I was not successful in filling any of them. The slaves all sold above their bids.

Before the auction opened, there was a parade around the hall of the volunteer slaves. To the side of the auctioneer's podium they had arranged a series of three circular step platforms. The highest was for the display of the slave currently under the hammer. The boys would get on these stages, roll up their sleeves and flex their muscles. The girls, being Free Methodists, did not flex a thing but one could see that they were adequately endowed nevertheless. One mother bought her own daughter as a slave after some fast bidding.

We asked her publicly, "Why did you do that?"

Her reply was, "I never can get Cindy to do anything around the house. Now, for eight hours she is going to work cleaning and scrubbing in our home as a church slave. If she doesn't I am going to ask for a refund." She sounded like a mean old woman. Why didn't she buy the services of somebody else's daughter?

The last to settle their bill at this Slave Auction was a pair of attractive young women. They had purchased the sale topper, the most expensive slave that was sold. Their acquisition was a strapping six-footer capable of handling most any job in that community that needed to be done. They peeled off the cash and turned to leave.

"Wait a minute, if you don't mind," I said. "What kind of a job do you have for your slave?" I sensed by their reaction that I had hit a tender spot. They were reluctant to talk. Finally one blurted out that they did not have a job for him.

"Why did you bid?" I asked. "This slave cost you a lot of money."

"Well you see, it is kind of a fishhook deal," she answered.

"Fishhook deal? What is a fishhook deal?"

"That is when you hook into something big and hope you can land it," she replied. "Should we tell him?" she asked her taller partner.

"Sure, maybe he would have some suggestions, he seems to be a live wire," the partner replied.

"We hope the action is along these lines. Charlie is one of a kind with many talents. We are both seniors in high school and have been seriously looking at men. You go around and around and come right back to Charlie as the standard of quality that you compare all the rest of them to, as my dad is always saying about everything he buys. However, this dude has a problem. During the last semester he has allowed himself to be dominated completely by a little snot who is only a sophomore. So—we have bought Charlie for eight hours and asked him to work from two until ten p.m. next Saturday."

"What is your strategy?"

"Actually the only work he is going to be asked to do is mow the lawn out at our cottage on Silver Lake which will take about fifteen minutes. Some of his other labors will be swimming, water-skiing, enjoying a big cookout, dancing on the deck and perhaps even a moonlight skinny dip. He does not have to leave at ten. We hope he doesn't. I don't know how this will turn out but at least we are going to give him a change of scenery for eight hours. Now, do you have any suggestions?"

"No suggestions, but oh! For the life of a slave."

The Old Skinflint Game

An old circuit traveling auctioneer who was always trying to date his vocation historically by hitching it to other businesses would usually open his case by saying, "We all know what the oldest business in the world is. Payment for the use of money is second and auctioneering, called bartering in ancient times, is third. Now, if you will lend an ear I will tell you how they were all tied in together."

There would be some variations in his story from sale to sale depending on who was in the crowd. He would continue with a risque supposition. "Suppose you just happened to be a Neanderthal man instead of standing here before me on the front porch of this old house as you are today. One of your early ancestors is dying to partake of the charms of the damsel back up under a cliff of yon mountain. She meets you at the entrance to her cave backed up by her three big gorilla-like brothers, all of whom have skull splitters in their hands, demanding three pieces of flint each large enough to cover her palm. You have only one. You borrow two more. You spend them all on the damsel. Then there comes a time of reckoning. You must pay back the two flint you borrowed plus one for usury. This task is not as pleasant as the spending.

You bring together all the skins you have, snare some fur bearers and steal a few more. Finally, in desperation, in the act of paying off this debt, you secure the services of a professional barterer (auctioneer) who trades for you. He has the expertise of a super salesman especially in the trading of skins for flint stone. Now you understand how auctioneering, in the ancient times and still in some remote areas, is called the old skinflint game."

Double Dry Out

A coincidental string of events triggered the liquidation by auction of the Nostalgialand Museum. The inventory to be sold was large and valuable. It was located in Alba where the name of every business began with the name of the owner. It was a two-day event. Saturday, July 2nd, and Monday, July 4th, were the dates selected. Shorty Ash was my aide, plus the regular clerks. Shorty, always an opportunist and sometimes a conniver, made a deal with a businessman down state. In lieu of the commission for selling a brace of Kentucky long rifles in this museum auction, we were to have the use of his resort home over the weekend. It was located on beautiful Torch Lake, a resort community, about forty miles from the sale location.

We cashed out that first day's sale Saturday night, with eight hundred and fifty well sold items under our belt. Shorty and Perk took off for the resort home dead tired and hungry as a pair of she wolves. All the grub we could find in that gorgeous shack was a half a bowl of sugar and some dog food. That was a discouraging end to a beautiful day. By the time we had located an after-hours oasis and chuck wagon, it was getting into the wee hours of Sunday morning. Shorty was fond of his liquids. We slept straight through until early afternoon and awoke only to once again seek food. It turned out to be a late Sunday afternoon dinner. A strong wind was blowing offshore and a beautiful twilight was soon with us. Shorty was as restless as a young tom cat under a barrel. I was in a relaxed mood contemplating strategy for the last day of the auction.

A boom! Boom! And boom! Again! Fourth of July eve! A gentle knock at the door followed. There stood a holiday-dressed matron; short, thick, and in organdy. Over her shoulder we counted five children all under twelve years old. They were her grandchildren.

"Could we watch the fireworks from your dock?" she asked. "The view from there would be perfect. Our dock next door is short and the view is blocked by tree limbs."

"Certainly," was our reply, "and may we join your party?"

They were a fine looking bunch of grandchildren, well scrubbed and very alert.

Out we went to the dock for a view of the fireworks display. Under her arm, the matronly one carried a sheath of newspapers. Shorty and I fell in line and brought up the rear in this Third of July parade to the dock. She spread a section of newspaper over the edge of the dock as each grandchild was seated. Then she laid one out for herself. The draft of a breeze under the dock and over the water, caused her newspaper to blow straight out instead of folding down over the edge. Grandmother took more than the usual care and precaution to fold her beautiful but bulky summer dress about her ample posterior before sitting down. She seemed to have shed the grandmotherly image as she glanced back toward us to see if we were noticing. We were only paying gentlemanly attention.

Shorty nudged me, "Perk, you have been away from home too long."

She squatted to take her place on the section of newspaper she had laid out for herself and ker-splash! She had skidded off the edge. Down she went into the dredged boat channel. The children became panicky. They all jumped up yelling and crying. Almost in unison it was, "Save our Grandma."

When Shorty had a day to relax he imbibed a bit, so his reflexes were not the sharpest. It was up to Perk. All that was visible of the youngish plump grandmother was a few bubbles and a tent-like portion of white organdy dress inside out. It was no trouble to locate her — no trouble to bring her back to the surface coughing and spitting — but there was no way to lift her back onto that dock which was two feet above the lake level. Shorty was on the dock consoling the nervous children. He also was the hero of this dunking. He grasped my hand and towed us both to the safety of the shore.

Grandma, attired in her soggy translucent dress, sent the children back out to the dock to watch the fireworks, sworn to secrecy about her misfortune. The three of us retired to the cottage. Now, you know how some auctioneers have spent the evening before a large sale. Yes, drying out somebody's grandmother and drying out a faithful friend. Regardless of the most unusual events that took place on the evening before, there was one whale (big 'un) of an auction that last day on the Fourth of July in Alba. Everyone, including our client, had quite a bang, but no more dunkings.

Bonnie's Dilemma

Johnny Potter used liquid spirits if an occasion caused him stress in any way. He had been over into the hills south of Holly to an auction held for the account of a James Mott. Now James and he were first rate friends, and he had fetched a fair wagon and rack over to be sold as a consignment. Well, because of socializing he did not get his wagon lined up with the farm implements and it did not get sold as was the intent. The auction was over. The bids were all in. The auctioneer was all done. The crowd had dispersed. Johnny Potter still had the wagon and it was still his. He meant for it to be sold along with Mott's stuff but somewhere a gear slipped a cog. Too many free drinks. Guess he even forgot to tell the auctioneer that he wanted it sold.

After one more for the road, Potter decided to get that wagon and rack straight back home before dark, as straight as he would be able to drive with his tractor.

About twenty minutes later, the auctioneer took off down the same road, "hell bent for election," with that underslung one-hundred-twenty mile an hour Bonneville headed just as straight for his home. On that particular piece of gravel about half way to town there is a very steep hogback downhill curve called Pepper Hill. Johnny Potter with his tractor and wagon on behind had hit down that same twisting grade all of five minutes before, but they never reached the bottom of the hill. The unkeyed drawpin had bobbed up out of the tractor drawbar because of the agitating washboard ridges in the gravel road and had released the wagon from the tractor.

Potter said, "I seed the wagon gaining on us so I pulled the tractor off the gee and that darn fool wagon passed us up. It went right on by without even tooting. It got along fine by hitself, 'til it gained full speed near the bottom of the hogback where it forgot to take the curve. The tongue skidded along until it snagged in the high grass and low brush at the edge of the road. Then that fool of a wagon cartwheeled into those saplings where you see it now resting. Resting up on its side. I should bury hit right thar, except I need it."

Johnny Potter had a long chain about as long as the road was wide and he was fixing to get that wagon rolled up and over those saplings and back on the road. It was good thinking on his part to attempt to salvage the outfit as long as nothing interfered with his plans.

By the time that Bonneville carrying the heavy footed auctioneer broke over the crest of Pepper Hill at a mile a minute throwing stones every which way, Johnny had fumbled around and managed to hook up the chain. It was hooked from the tractor drawbar directly across the road to the high side of the wagon rack that was held up by the brush. The Bonneville did not have a lot of time to figure out the situation. A quick observation disclosed a variation on the height of that chain. At the tractor drawbar, it was about a foot off the road and on the end attached to the wagon, it was five feet high. There never has been a Bonneville so confused before or since. There was about four-hundred feet of downhill loose gravel, before Waterloo.

Pepper Hill is so steep that kids have to push their bicycles up it. You know that old Bonnie would aim for one end of that log chain stretched across the roadway, then change its mind and start for the other end. It kept it up, high side then the low side, for about five sashays. At a hundred feet away the auctioneer behind the wheel was getting a bit out of patience with its carrying on and he started to open the door to jump plumb clear of its crazy actions, when you know that Bonneville settled right down, stopped that old stuff of throwing rocks, grabbed the middle of the road by the belly and eased up to that taut log chain like a kitten to a dish of warm milk. It only nudged the chain enough to shake that wagon down off the brush it was trespassing upon.

All at once the attitude of the man behind the wheel changed. He was proud of that Bonnie again, whereas a few seconds before, he was about to abandon it forever.

One Daniel Ford's steading is back up over Pepper Hill a short spell. The man behind the wheel remarked later that he was pleased that Mr. Ford had not seen the fracas. Bonnie was nursed back off the chain having twisted only one bumper guard. The wagon was straightened around, a piece of fence wire was twisted around the drawpin so that it would not jump out again and Johnny Potter was aimed up Andersonville Road toward home. There is no verification that he ever made it.

Karl and Kaska

Once upon a time there was a jolly St. Nicholas type of farmer who was fortunate enough to snare for himself a beautiful devoted Polish wife, Kaska, from out of the city. However, within a short span as life goes, Karl began to age prematurely because of a couple of obvious self-admitted over-indulgences that he loved and enjoyed. So they sold the farm because Karl could not handle it any more even with Kaska's help. He had means to hire help but preferred not to have another man around. She was young and friendly. Only he knew that she was so receptive and responsive. That was the way he wanted to keep it.

They phoned up Perk, who got paid for chanting and claimed a date in the fall to sell for them at auction, eighteen good butcher steers, their oats, corn, hay, straw, a John Deere Model B tractor and all the matching implements that went with it, wheelbarrows, a churn, small buildings on skids, copper boilers, crocks, kegs, casks (Karl made real good stuff for himself), all their furniture, including his mother's spindle back rocker, a new washer and dryer he had bought for Kaska, five old fat hens for soup and plus and plus. They were not going to sell the pickup truck. It was of sentimental value, because it had been so good to and for them. Karl out-wheeled her brothers with it when they ran away to get married. They wanted to use it to move the few articles they were keeping and to peddle their own sale bills.

Before Karl ran off with his child bride (he was far past middle age), he had a lot of drinking friends. He was well-known in every tavern in the vicinity. He swore off public imbibing and had not seen any of them for five years. This new life with Kaska was much better, but he was craving to meet his old cronies on common ground one more time at the tavern in the town. He knew that the auction bills had to be spread around and that Perk always did this for his customers. For this personal reason not yet shared with Kaska, he wanted to do his own bill peddling. He would ask her to go and drive, but stay in the pickup.

Perk acquiesced to his desire. A route was laid out by the auctioneer who explained to him that it was important to post the auction bills in local banks, hardwares, feed mills, food markets, etc., which he wholeheartedly agreed to do. Taverns were not mentioned. There was no use running a good thing in the ground, but Perk was aware of his plans. As related from a party twice removed, it turned out to be a real chore for Kaska. Some of those country four corners had as many as three oases. Four towns a day were about all Karl could handle. After the first stop his tongue would loosen. After the second, he would be a bit unsteady and have trouble finding the pickup door handles. The third stop was attended by burdensome obstacles. The fourth was his swan song. Kaska would recruit his drinking buddies to help and they would drop the tailgate and roll soused Karl into the back of the pickup for the trip back home. Kaska would drive the pickup into the shed and forget the whole thing until morning.

About eight a.m. she would see Karl around the buildings doing his chores as always. She would holler out that breakfast was ready and to come and get cleaned up. Shortly thereafter the pair would set out once more to peddle auction bills. It took four days and yet the coverage was limited.

We had a large crowd at Karl's auction. There was lots of babbling and fun. It was a country holiday, but do you know those tavern hangers-on don't have much money or a credit rating with the local bank worth a hoot. Karl had to find this out for himself; the hard way. Everything was sold for whatever it brought. There was no second time around.

It was a subnormal auction when the prices received were taken into consideration. However, from Karl's point of view it was a howling success and his greatest party.

The Contenders

Humorous and sometimes rather strange happenings take place between competing bidders at an auction. Bidders are usually stressed by the activity and are likely to say or do things that are not in harmony with their usual behavior. Most of the friction or contrasting happy moments develop because of the contending bidders being friends, neighbors, or relatives. The same things could develop between contending bidders who hate each others guts. Because this is a happy book we will not mention those ramifications.

When the bidding on a given item slows down and its price escalates to value, the number of bidders narrows down usually to only two. Within a community these two could well be and usually are more than shouting acquaintances. In a small crowd at this point in the selling, the remaining bidders will sort each other out. Casual friends will continue to bid against each other until one quits.

The winner will then customarily rush over to the side of the losing bidder and make an apologetic remark something like this. "Harry, I didn't know you wanted that old wheelbarrow or I would have stopped bidding long ago."

"That's O.K.," Harry replies. "I only wanted the old thing to wheel chicken manure from the coop to the garden. Now I know where I can borrow a conveyance to do that job."

An exchange between neighbors out of necessity has to be subtle. Friends come and go. It is relatively easy to make a new one should you lose an old one. With neighbors it is a porcupine of yet another quill. Neighbors are nailed down. They stay put for years and are not easily shed, unless one moves out. Sometimes this is financially unrewarding; so with neighbors a little more discretion must be practiced than with friends. One cannot afford to lose the goodwill of a neighbor over a two-bit bid. Of course, a two-bit bid could be twenty-five cents or twenty-five dollars.

Julie the Jewel

Elmer was selling his dairy cows, young cattle and related milking equipment at public auction. He only had thirty-seven milkers, but within this number was one registered Holstein cow of outstanding conformation with an excellent Dairy Herd Improvement Association (DHIA) record for both milk and fat. She was right in every way, five years old and scaling out at over fourteen hundred pounds in her working clothes. She was a jewel and about as valuable. Elmer knew that and so did all of his neighbors. Two of them had approached him secretly before the sale with solid propositions to buy her privately. He thanked them and refused to be tempted into being a partner to any nefarious scheme. There was so much interest in this one outstanding cow that the clerk of the auction started a betting pot on her selling price with each person putting in a dollar and being entitled to make one guess. Many guessed the amount of money they personally would bid. They were losers from the beginning.

There were to be some hurt feelings, bent personalities, poor losers, but only one winner. An event like this could rupture the tranquillity of a whole country neighborhood. In no way did Elmer wish to be a contributor to this possible dissension. He talked to his auctioneer Lorn about it.

Lorn, being experienced in matters of this kind said, "Elmer, you just let me handle it and everything will end up A-OK. Run your jewel cow out just the same as you do all the rest. When I start the bidding at one thousand dollars you put a frown on your face and I will take it from there."

So it was. Auctioneer Lorn was no dummy. He secured a bid not to exceed two thousand dollars from the order buyer, Bill

Huff, for out of state shipment. Lorn calculated this should solve a touchy situation and make everyone happy.

The sale looked good for Elmer's neighbors, the cow (her pet name was Julie), and the price; until Lorn's phone rang late in the evening of the night before the auction. It was his client's married daughter.

"Lorn, my husband and I have had a go-around and have come to a decision that is going to affect the direction of the remainder of our lives. It is because of Dad's Julie cow. Imagine a cow doing this to us? We are going to buy Julie tomorrow at the auction."

"Do you realize how much she may cost?" a startled Lorn fired right back.

"It doesn't matter too much what she costs. We have been saving several years to build a new house. Now the house is out the cowshed door," replied the daughter-in-law. "The cow Julie is the result of a lifetime of constructive dairy herd improvement by this family, and we have decided that it be continued by Julie and the heifers that we can raise from her. There are two heifers among the young cattle that are her daughters. We may buy those also. We have decided to establish a new herd on the Julie cow and her get."

This determined talk shook up the auctioneer. Should he go back to the order buyer for outstate shipment and get him to raise his two thousand dollar bid? Would this bidding by a family member, even be it unknown to the owner, Elmer, really antagonize the community? There were a couple of changes that would have to be made. The Julie cow would have to be sold last in the mature cow sale order and the bidding for the daughter-in-law's account would have to be done by number with her name being revealed only after the conclusion of the auction.

This is a perfect example of why auctioneers age prematurely. Lorn remained in control. He said nothing to the order buyer. When he made out the selling order for cows in milk, he switched Julie from third to last because it was certain to depress prices if the crowd should find out that she was bought by a member of the family.

To further cloud the issue, Lorn took an order to buy without limit from the daughter-in-law. Only Lorn knew that the selling price would be more than two thousand. It was twenty-one hundred.

An auctioneer with Lorn's experience prepared for any eventuality. He had a verbal understanding with the daughter-in-law to stay low-key. So low-key in fact, that she was not to put in a visible appearance, but they agreed on a sign. It was this. If the big old barn tomcat came air-borne out of the open milk house window it was a signal to cease bidding for her account on the Julie cow. The tomcat never showed and the daughter-in-law won the dollar pot with a guess of $2150.00.

Strip Show Leaves Auctioneer Naked

Birds of a feather bidding on the same item at a public auction can cause reactions both pro and con. It depends on the attitude and tolerance of the relatives.

Estate auctions of household goods that contained antiques and treasured heirlooms that were sold for a family that included stepparents and many stepchildren usually became the equivalent of a one ring circus. Competition for specific items could get a little hairy.

One time a couple of women got into a hassle over an old steelyard that I was selling out of a granary, formerly in the possession of their great-grandfather. The deceased, it seems, had bivouacked with several women and his descendants were numerous. The fact that he had become well-heeled at some point in his life's journey attracted a host of legitimate, illegitimate and spurious claimants. Probate Court had weeded some of them out. Court action had progressed to the point of turning the great-grandfather's visible assets into cash. Thus the auction.

Bidding on the steelyard had escalated its price to a ridiculous level. One of the buxom bidders blew her cool, grabbed the balance weight hanging on the steelyard, and threw it at the other scoring a direct hit in the area of her bare midriff. It knocked the wind out of her. After gasping a couple of moments to get her breath back and becoming very red with anger, she made a lunge at her adversary. She succeeded in securing a hold somewhere in the area of the nape of the neck and with one tremendous jerk tore out the entire back panel of a form-fitting flowery summer dress. This caused much tittering by the men, and concern by the auctioneer who somehow had to remain in control and on top of the situation. The strip show staged by the rending of the cloth was followed by some fast face slapping by both of the "disputees."

"Hey, this fracas has gone far enough," yelled the auctioneer. "You women are going to do one of two things. Stop the fighting and behave yourselves so that we can continue this sale, or what is left of you two go on out there in the orchard and have it out."

The combatants took off for the orchard snarling obscenities at each other. Needless to say, most of the auction crowd took off too, following them at a safe distance. The auctioneer stood on his selling stand stripped naked. I mean by that, he had lost his crowd. A better show was in progress, for free, under the apple trees.

Those two women were scrappers from the word go. There was scratching, screaming, pulling hair, biting and tearing clothing until a siren was heard wailing perhaps a mile up the road. Someone had called the law.

Now, the fastest switch took place one would ever see. The crowd returned from the orchard to the auction platform, the auctioneer resumed chanting, the infuriated women melted away together (you would not believe your eyes) into an adjacent corn field. An officer parked his cruiser at the road and walked up to the shed.

The auctioneer stopped his chant as the officer inquired, "How are things? We had a report of a disturbance at this address."

"Everything is just fine," replied the auctioneer.

Spouse Competition

Closer relatives than those can also get themselves tangled up when bidding, namely married couples. It is not unusual for a couple to attend an auction together after having talked over at home what they would like to buy. At a large local auction a couple can become separated one from the other by visiting and circulating among friends. All at once the item they had previously decided to try to buy is placed up for bids. They each look around and not seeing their spouse proceed to bid on the item. Many times the article of their choice will be knocked down to one of them with the other serving as the flabbergasted contending bidder. This is a common expensive occurrence and is extremely humorous for the onlookers and lucrative for the owner.

If the occurrence is recognized by a bystander and brought to the attention of the auctioneer, or if the auctioneer himself recognizes the bidders as a married couple, the bids on that particular item will be declared off and it will be started over once again. Outside of that, it is a legal sale, not retractable once the item is declared sold, and the couple involved will always be the butt of the usual snide remarks about getting their act together.

CHAPTER V

ON THE FAIR CIRCUIT

A CTIVITIES FOR THE exhibitors at a fair can be divided into two segments; before the judging and after. The judges usually make their placings as soon as possible after the opening day. This lends color to the fair for the days that follow, as the prized ribbons, banners and trophies are put out on display for the passersby to see. Up to the time of the judging, it is pretty much a blood and guts situation, especially in the livestock departments. It is every exhibitor for himself. Remarks among competitors are brief and fraternizing is at a bare minimum.

All serious activity builds up to a climax on show day. This is the day referred to as "the wedding day." This is the day of the judging. It's the time when all exhibits are to look and act their best. The tension is not visible, but it is there; sometimes thick enough to cut with a knife or to cause a squabble.

The judges of the various classes and breeds, quietly and deliberately, make their placings. It is usually a long and tiring ordeal for all. There is some beating of the gums and gnashing of teeth by the herdsmen and owners. The judges, being well qualified, handle feedback with dispatch. The die has been cast. There is no reconsideration. There is no instant replay. Each exhibitor now knows exactly where he stands in this show and how many coveted ribbons and rosettes he has won. He now has time to go back to his show box, dig out the premium book and from it tabulate

MICHIGAN STATE FAIR 1912

Judging Scotch Shorthorn Cattle. This is the two year cow class. The judge's back is to the camera. He is wearing a derby hat.

MICHIGAN STATE FAIR, DETROIT 1912

Scene at edge of a midway showing clothing styles and price of a still popular refreshment.

his cash winnings; the most pleasant of chores, especially if the judge has looked kindly upon his exhibit this day. He also notices in the premium book the release time of 5 p.m. next Sunday. That is several days hence.

Hairy Spiders and Rodents

The stock will have to be fed, watered, groomed and the exhibit kept clean and attractive, but there will be plenty of time for other things. This is the pattern of all fairs throughout the Great Lakes Area. So, when the pressure was off and the work done the country boys were not unlikely to kick up their heels a bit. These country boys consisted of owners, herdsmen, hired hands and hangers-on who just came along for the ride. Their frolic was of many patterns.

Their pet aversion was to frighten, cajole or out-slick the city slickers who were always available in droves. Scare the pants off them by dropping a simulated hairy spider of mammoth proportions right down in front of a brace of teenage girls by means of an almost invisible thread, and then listen for their shrieks and screams as they went running out a far door.

A live mouse or a rat would scatter a whole alley full of middle aged women; yes and even some of the men and boys. This was great sport for the country ruffians.

Crowd Thinning

On a weekend the crowds traipsing through the livestock barns would become oppressive. There would be much dust and debris. The air would become foul and oxygen would seem to be deficient. The cattle would begin to pant and become restless. It would be impossible to tote feed pans and water buckets through and about this excessive stream of foot traffic. There was only one solution. Turn the largest, meanest, bellowing bull in the barn loose.

Then the herdsman would begin to yell from all corners of the show barn. "Bull loose, run for the exits." This would clear the barn before you could yell the third time.

Of course, there was actually no bull loose. He might be out of his stall and be bellowing at the end of an aisle somewhere, but he always had a neck strap attached to a strong rope that was anchored to a post or to three or four country cattlemen. This was definitely a crowd thinning operation — then you could do chores and breathe again.

Homemade Entertainment

A mock livestock auction was an instrument used by the ruffians to provide themselves with all the entertainment they needed. Sometimes more than was expected. The proceedings were well planned right down to the last detail, in the pattern of a modern purebred livestock sale. For those who are not familiar with this type of selling, we will set the stage for you.

The location of the sale ring was of prime importance. It had to be in or near an area of heavy foot traffic. There was need for some type of barrier between the livestock selling and the bidders. This was provided by using bales of straw and hay. This so-called ring was about twenty-five feet in diameter. It had to have an entrance and an exit for the stock as well as space for a couple of ringmen to work as they assisted the auctioneer in taking bids. There was an auctioneer's stand in a raised position overlooking the ring and the area where bidders (suckers) would stand. The auctioneer would be fortified with a sound system and homemade signs would be stuck up around the fairgrounds. They might read something like this:

```
BLUE RIBBON LIVESTOCK

A U C T I O N

Saturday night  9:00 P.M.

in front of

Cattle Show Barn
```

The time was deliberately selected to coincide with the conclusion of the first grandstand show. The people would pile down out of those stands with blood in their eye, looking for excitement before they had to go home. The promoters, at the opportune time, would slide into gear the "darn-dest" fictitious auction sale you could ever hope to attend.

The Cheapskate

The auctioneer would start warming up his tonsils by reeling off the terms of the sale, introducing the ringmen and the clerk, giving the reason for the sale and the outstanding prize winning livestock that was going to be sacrificed to the highest bidders. His speel might go something like this.

"Buyers, bidders, speculators, spectators, ladies and gentlemen, you are all to be congratulated for having the keen foresight to be here at this most propitious time. You have often heard people say, if only my foresight was as good as my hindsight. Hallelujah! You are 'he-ah.' In honor of the occasion please do this for me. Place both of your hands behind your back and shake hands with yourself. Congratulate yourself on your foresight. Wonderful. Thank you. Now you know yourself. That is a start.

"Without further delay and before we proceed with the greatest auction of prize winning livestock ever put on the auction block in this county, let me make known to you the sales force for 'thee' event. The sales manager of this history making event is standing on my right panting — whoops, excuse the remark — that is just his red necktie hanging out, Mr. C. U. Loiter of Wapakoneta, O-hi-o. On my left the clerk, and we are privileged to have the E-steamed Vice-chairman of the Last National Bank of Saginaw, Mr. Her-man Du-Chek. Mr. Du-Chek take a bow. Also, for this evening's auction our very capable ringmen, if you please. On the right and catching bids from the rafters, treetops and other inaccessible areas, Mr. Shorty Upper, representing "The Mistequay Cattleman," published in New Lothrop, Michigan. On the left side of the ring and also watching for bids down the alley and in behind this auctioneer, Mr. I. B. Higher, southern fieldman for that great Canadian Livestock Journal, "The Wawa Trader." It is great to have you down here working with us in the low country, Mr. Higher. Oh yes, we almost forgot — Miss Gloria Stack who we are crowding a bit here in the middle of the auction stand. Mr. Du-Chek could you pl-ea-se give her a little more room. Miss Stack is our pedigree reader and after the conclusion of this auction she will be available on a first-come, first-serve basis in the fifth cattle stall on the left — to read your palm, for a small fee. She is a reader from the word go.

"She just flew in from Tuscaloosa, Alabama, especially to assist us with this sale. In transit, her luggage was misdirected or lost, so she is stranded here temporarily with hardly a thing to wear. What a Stack-er— ah, I mean — we all feel for you Miss Stack. It couldn't have happened to a better figure and we are blessed with a beautiful warm evening. Oh well, you win some and you lose some. That completes the introductions except I am your auctioneer and my name is Colonel Socko Filtchem.

"The terms of this sale are not cash. Please contact Mr. Du-Chek before you leave as to shipping instructions for any purchases you make.

"The sale order will be sheep first, followed by hogs, cattle and with horses last. The auctioneer and his staff are acting as sales agents only, now and forever. Nothing is forever. Amen."

With that introduction blasting out over the intercom, about 500 people would be waiting aghast for the next shoe to drop, and it soon would. Immediately into the ring would come the Grand Champion Suffolk Ram completely garnished with ribbons. Gloria, in the low cut halter, would race through a fictitious pedigree. She could talk a man into most anything.

Auctioneer Filtchem would take off at 300 dolla a 50 and 4 hundred. Ringmen Higher secures 5 hundred and yells to the auctioneer who chants for a fifty. Higher yells back "Ye-aahh" for a fifty while ringman Shorty Upper continues to bore in a dry hole. Clerk Du-Chek picks up seven fifty behind the auction stand. After a brief period of additional chanting the auctioneer calls for quiet. This pause in the bid taking is what is called a "take down" by the professionals.

"The owner of this champion ram has a word. Mr. Walter Wooley, if you would please."

"This ram of mine that we are selling here tonight has two outstanding characteristics. One is this great fleece he is carrying. The other is the gleam in his eye. Now, you do not get these qualities in your flock by chance. It has to be bred into them. This ram, Sir Lancelot, is more than willing to do this for you."

That speech brought forth a hundred dollar bid. Ringman Upper quips that Wooley's speech was worth $100.00 and he could prove it. Who could argue with him because the crowd was there and saw it happen. Col. Filtchem cries for one thousand even money. It does not come.

"Eight-fifty do you want'im at nine hundred." No response.

The auctioneer says "sold" in a very dejected manner. Why not? Why shouldn't he be crestfallen? The ram was worth a thousand dollars and he had to sell him for only eight hundred and fifty. What a bargain. The crowd moans in responsive sympathy.

"The cheapskate," someone yells out from the multitude.

"Who is the cheapie that bought him?"

A well dressed portly gentleman steps up to clerk Du-Chek who shuffles about a pile of papers and announces over the intercom, "The buyer of this champion Suffolk Ram, Sir Lancelot, is Far Away Ranch, Havre, Montana, at eight hundred and fifty dollars."

The crowd gasps and in unison repeats in awe, "Havre, Montana," as they crowd in a bit closer. They are in the palm of our hand. It was great sport.

The sale order would be followed to a tee and the show acted out in all seriousness by the main characters. The crew was like a group of actors and on stage without a union card. A total of ten head from each class of livestock make up a forty-lot auction. No local bidders were ever allowed to buy anything. All sales were made to far away fictitious bidders with grandiose names and addresses.

This, in addition to causing the local populace to stand in awe of our abilities, also protected us from any legal complications except when an unusual or favorable circumstance presented itself.

Sow and Matching Lady

Such a circumstance was taken advantage of at one of the well-prepared mock auctions that was held in the beef cattle barn of the Michigan State Fair in De-troit City. Things were getting lively at the cattle auction and an exhibitor in the swine barn decided he would like to share in the fun. He drove over to the ring the largest aged sow in the barn. She weighed all of seven-hundred pounds and was so clean that her skin showed pink through her white hair. She acted like a pet as she rooted about the ring. Bidding was fast and furious.

The auctioneer noticed a thickset lady directly opposite him who was totally engrossed (sucked in) by the proceedings. What made the auctioneer notice this well dressed city lady was her resemblance to the sow being sold—white hair, pink skin and a rooter. The lady looked up at the auctioneer in admiration of his talent and blinked. The auctioneer, being an opportunist, sensed a golden moment and almost immediately said, "Sold to the lady in the pink dress!" The auctioneer called for the next lot to continue on with the auction, but this was not to be the order of business.

"Who me; did I buy that big hog?"

"Yes," replied a ringman," would you please give us your name and address, and that will be $1100.00 please."

"What can I do with that hog in my flat? What will the neighbors think? How did I buy this monster?" She yelled out so loud

HISTORICAL MARKER
Also the site of many hilarious auctions

loins, hams, shoulders, etc. and rendered into white shortening. No fatty tissue from anywhere within the carcass was overlooked.

The rendering of lard was a critical and sometimes dangerous job. The fat was cut into small cubes and placed in kettles over a steady fire. The grease would cook from the tissue and leave as residue the cracklings. Cracklings were edible and could be classified as an early American confection. If rendered too long or at too high a temperature, the lard would not turn out white as desired but be of a tan color. There was also the chance of the lard catching on fire or someone being burned with hot grease.

The small intestines were used for link sausage. They had to be segregated from other innards, flushed clean (what a job), turned inside out and hung up to dry until needed. The tripe was secured in almost the same manner but it was easier to work with because it was larger. This lining of the stomach was rubbery and not as easily damaged as the sausage casings.

Caleb, the New Craftsman

The making of sausage was one of the methods used to preserve meat. Germans turned out Braunschweiger and Frankfurters, the Italians brought in the secrets of making Salami and the Scandinavians introduced Goteborg. Demand exceeded supply. It was not long before a good sausage maker was classified as a craftsman. He was on the same level as a barn framer.

It was hand labor and began at the chopping block where large pieces of meat were cut by hand-forged two-handed cleavers and multiple-blade rocker knives. Woe be it for an animal live or dead, that got in the way. There was always a new joke circulating concerning what had provided the tangy flavor to Caleb's latest batch of sausage.

Salt and smoking were the prime preservers. Seasonings like sage, pepper, savory, oregano, rosemary and saltpeter were also used when available.

Metal meat grinders did not come around until after the Civil War. Previous to that time the grinding units were made of wood.

FORGED MEAT CHOPPERS
Used before grinders were invented.

PRIMITIVE MEAT CUTTER
Used in the early 1700's.

WOOD MEAT CUTTER
Improved design dated 1824.

The meat grinder was turned by hand from the business end of a crank. It would have a central rotating axle studded with a spiral set of square iron teeth. Projecting from the inside walls of this wood grinder would be a set of knives. The speed of production depended on the strength of the operator's arm.

The stuffing of the casings followed. A large canister was filled with well-seasoned ground meat. A wood plunger would be inserted that fit the hole in the canister, precisely. A casing would be fitted onto the nozzle at the opposite end. The sausage maker would place the top of the plunger firmly against his midsection and pull back on the canister with both hands. His production in this case depended upon the strength of his arms and belly muscles.

This was a bustin' a gut job. Not only was the sausage maker's gut in jeopardy, but the casing at the far end of the canister could blow, too. Barrel chested men with strong stomachs were in demand for this task.

At a country butchering bee one might find as many as twenty hogs hanging on the meat pole. It would be concluded by early

HAND SAUSAGE STUFFERS
It was a job where both brawn and belly were necessary qualifications.

afternoon with a potluck dinner. By the time dinner was over and the joshing and story telling had run its course, the hogs would be cooled out to the degree that they could be loaded into the respective owner's wagon boxes and returned to the place of origin. It was an important day with plenty of socializing.

From there on out the pork was consumed fresh, cured, smoked, pickled and made into highly seasoned sausage and headcheese according to the likes of the owner and his family. This new supply of meat would be consumed so as to dovetail in with their yield from the next butchering bee.

Oxen to Beef

Beef butchering was also a major event within the early communities, but it never was as prominent as hog butchering. The fact that it was not an event participated in by the entire family had much to do with it. This was a man's job.

A good young cow was the most essential animal on an early farm. When fresh she produced milk, from which cream, butter and cheese were made. Her bull calves were unsexed and called steers. If they were strong and sturdy, they were trained to "gee" and "haw" and placed under the yoke and called oxen. They became beasts of burden and were in some respects far superior to horses for use in early agriculture.

When any of these bovines faltered, they were promptly replaced and soon became beef, plus several other essentials.

The yield from a beef butchering was many fold. Leather was made by tanning the hide. It accommodated about every need that there was for a strong material which was flexible. It was used for everything from door hinges to harnesses.

The fat was the exclusive lubricant before the discovery of oil and was more valuable than the nourishing meat. Some cattle were bred especially for their superior ability to pile up gobs of fat about their rumps and briskets. When rendered it became tallow and was used to reduce friction on everything that turned, from a wagon axle to the drivers of a steam locomotive. Much of the tallow was also used for candle making.

Some of the other by-products were gelatin from the hooves; tools, handles, toys and utensils from the horns and bones; and a darn good fly swatter from the tail switch.

The important product was beef, which was easier to preserve than pork. It was used fresh, spiced, salted, corned, smoked and dried.

The Stockman's Cane

There were so-called practical and impractical jokers throughout the countryside in early days. Allow me to tell you of one of these hand-me-down episodes that took place in a log barn on a Sabbath evening at chore time. It had to do with cattle. Some of the cattle that are a part of this episode were in the process of being milked, while at least one had gone to his reward by the way of a beef butchering bee.

Jon was not a young man. He was aged beyond his years because of permanent injuries suffered in a fall from a barn. It was summertime and he was in the stable milking. There was some social event going on up at the big house.

Three young women dressed in the lacy dresses of the day had wandered away from the party and for the lack of anything more exciting to do were soon visiting pleasantly with Jon in the cow stable. He finished milking one cow and because they knew Jon was crippled, one of the girls, who was a milkmaid herself, offered to drive the cow from the stable for him.

"Take that stick from the peg up yonder and give her a little rap on the rump."

Jon stayed with his three-legged milking stool and slid over to the next cow. He noticed that the girls were handling and somewhat admiring the stick or homemade stockman's cane that one had used to drive the dry cow out the barn door.

"Jon, this is a neat stick you have here for driving cattle. I wish we had one like it for our barn. How did you find one with a loop on the top? I've never seen a stick like this before and it is so smooth, long and slender. It has what it takes. It has a nice feel."

Jon did not know exactly how to answer so he beat about the bush with the three knowledgeable country girls. He continued his milking. They persisted.

Finally Jon softened, "I'll tell you what you do. Come here and take my jackknife and cut a small piece from that stick and see if you can tell me what it might be."

After some difficulty, they whittled off a fair sample of the persuader for a more detailed examination. None of the three could identify it as a definite kind of wood for Jon. However, one came up with a possible answer.

"The stuff softens up and becomes slippery when I hold it in my hand. Is that slippery elm, Jon?"

"Nope," came back the answer.

Yet another of the girls offered her idea. "It looks and smells more like the beef jerky dad made one time, than anything else."

The third girl crowded into the act and pleaded. "Give me a small piece to chew on and I'll bet you a setting of duck eggs that I can tell you what it is."

Jon had finished the chores and could hold out on them no longer.

"Girls, if you really must know I will tell you. That is the tool from the big Durham Bull we butchered last year." They squealed like only country girls can, turned on their heels and took off on a run for the party at the big house. This narrative in essence, does little more than demonstrate how little was wasted, even from a beef.

Taking the Hide

There were definite differences in butchering a beef versus butchering a hog. Beef butchering was hard, particular work. One animal was slaughtered at a time. The yield would run between six and nine hundredweight and it would be shared within the immediate neighborhood. Beef was less inclined to spoil than pork. During the cold months it could be kept and consumed fresh without concern. Beef has the quality of aging gracefully. Dried beef has always been popular. Beef cured by jerking and drying was called jerky. Corned beef was a method of preserving by submerging it in a brine solution. Grinding of beef was unheard of and canning was strictly experimental. Many people were poisoned and a few died from eating beef that had been canned improperly.

Before the butchering of a beef, be it a cow, bull, steer or heifer, food and water would be withheld. The cattle would be led out to the skinning area where a block and tackle had been previously located with the upper block hooked into a barn beam, tree limb or whatever, as much as twenty feet above ground.

The equipment needed was trivial. A heavy white ash gambrel was a must. No toggled up equipment could be tolerated. The gambrel had to have provision for pins to be placed on either side of each beef shank to stop all sliding. Should a heavy beef carcass shift only fractionally, it would be likely that the whole thing would come tumbling down and maim some worker. Butcher, boning and skinning knives had to be sharp and kept sharp with a steel. Some salt was needed to sprinkle on the hide once it was removed and a good long stick should be handy to keep the dogs at a distance.

With the exception of a bad acting bull, shooting was not done at the time of the kill. Most cattle butchers carried along a small maul with a special long handle. If the business end of the maul was the size of a U.S. half dollar, that would be fine. The slammer, as the specialist was called, would draw a hypothetical cross on the forehead of the animal to be slaughtered. The ends of this cross would be anchored by the horns as they emerged from the hair on the pole and by the eyes. If an animal could be thumped precisely at this intersection of lines, he would go down and out like a light. Without delay, the head must be raised up or pulled back, depending which way the animal fell, and a large knife would be used to cut the throat from ear to ear close to the jawbone. The heart continued to beat and pumped the body dry of blood, or nearly so. At this time, the block and tackle was attached to one back leg with a short chain and the animal was raised so that his back was off the ground as far forward as the kidney area. This insured a well-bled carcass.

No skinning would be attempted until signs of life were no longer noticeable. Many country butchers have been cut seriously by an animal kicking a knife from their grasp, when they were a bit too anxious to get on with the job.

A carcass is opened by inserting a knife under the hide between the dewclaws of the swinging free back leg. Continue to open the hide to the hock plus eight inches toward the rump. Skin out this leg and remove it by passing the knife through the flat joint immediately below the knuckle. Insert one end of the gambrel between the leg cord and bone, and secure the pins. Transfer block and tackle to this leg and skin out the other in the same manner. When the gambrel is inserted in both rear hocks and made secure, begin to raise the carcass. There is usually an evil-smelling discharge of liquids from the first stomach, at this time, through the gullet.

Go at the hide opening again. With a short-bladed sharp knife, open the hide from hock to hock down through the crotch. From this opening, cut at right angles from tail to navel. Grasp the half-moon skinning knife and work down from all four corners of this intersection in the crotch. Do not cut the hide or slash the meat. As downward pressure is exerted by pulling with one hand on the hide, sever only the white connecting tissue.

Hides from cattle were so essential to the early settler's well-being that if a person helping with the skinning so much as scored a hide, he was asked to forget it. He was what was called "black-balled" from skinning.

An incompetent skinner was often demoted and delegated as the rope man. His job was to continue to hoist as the hide fell away. He operated the block and tackle on instructions from the head butcher.

As the hide continued to drop from the beef, a further opening from the middle of the stomach over the brisket and down the dewlap across the throat slit and to the point of the jaw was made. The meat was kept clean by not rolling off the hide until clear of ground contamination. It was all "up, up and away."

At about his time in the proceedings, the head butcher began the opening of the body cavity. The front legs were removed to the knees by the same method as was used on the back legs which were already high above and secured in the gambrel.

The head butcher would skin out the head (a messy job) and remove and scrape the tongue. The beef head would be disjointed and separated from the body. It would be taken to the butcher's table, washed, meat removed to the bone and the horns sawed off. There was always close examination of the skull at this time, to ascertain if the slammer had directed his maul to that precise predetermined point, before it was tossed out for the dogs to fight over.

The skinners continued to skin and the head butcher opened the neck up to the brisket. If the animal was young, he would remove the sweetbreads before cutting and sawing up through the breastbone to the heart and lung cavity. The upper end of the breastbone petered out into gristle. This was a most delicate area. Behind the gristle was the diaphragm, which by this time, was being pressured by the bloated stomachs. The last stroke of the bucksaw or heavy butcher knife would meet little resistance and squish! Even a top butcher could get into really bad trouble. There is no way he could tie up a beef stomach with string. After the initial breakthrough, he would have to plug the hole in the damn stomach with whatever was closest. That would be his hands. If working alone, the next thing he would do was yell for help.

"Abigail! Abigail run out to the corn sheller and fetch me some corncobs. Do you hear, woman? Hurry Abigail — Oh! good. Stand to one side so as not to soil your apron. When I move my hand to one side, crowd in a cob. It will take about three."

They did the best they could but the hole in the stomach continued to drip a brownish fluid called gastric juice down on the front quarters. The drip plus the first explosion was not in the least complimentary to the quality of the meat. There was no quick solution. Only, that the offal had to go as soon as possible.

Upstairs, goes the butcher. A short ladder was best unless the beef was small or the butcher extremely tall. Upstairs he went with a knife to the crotch betwixt the hindquarters. Careful cutting along the inside of the rounds, brought him up short at the aitchbone. This was sawed cautiously because when this bone parted there would be a shifting of weight on the gambrel. If the hocks were not secured properly to the gambrel, the entire carcass could slip off center and fall from the heights to the ground.

With a successful parting of the aitchbone, the bum gut and bladder may be knifed out with ease. The bladder was usually saved, inflated and used by the children as a plaything. The large intestine was pulled loose and placed outside the carcass. This left the bloated third stomach raising up into the butchers face. Now, it was time to open the belly of the beast by holding back the set of innards with one hand and cutting the tough belly liner with the other, bottom to top. The innards of a young animal might hang but usually a larger older animal would let go at the diaphragm windpipe junction. It is like old bones, they lose their genuflection. Old guts lose their elasticity. If they should take off, the butcher would just stand clear of the three stomachs and their entourage. So far so good.

The butcher might ask you, as an interested spectator, if you would like to take a look inside at this time. Not inside the house for a cup of coffee, but inside the beef for a look-see into his digestive cavity. You will find it an empty room with the furnishings gone except for a pair of sectionalized brownish-red glands about the size of a man's hand attached to the top of the loin. If the cattle is in good rig, by being given access to all the unhusked bundled corn he could eat, these glands may not be visible because of being completely encased in fat. These are the kidneys. While your head is inside the carcass look down. Your view is blocked off by the diaphragm. Extending both ways from the belly opening parallel with the ribs is a border of thin lean muscle which gradually subsides into a veil of taut white tissue.

The butcher makes two quick slashes through the diaphragm and exposes the heart and lungs. The heart is enclosed in yet another sac that holds a small amount of clear fluid.

You are curious. You ask, "What happened to the liver?"

That is a good question. The liver has already taken off. It is under that pile of stomachs and their associates. Here, take a look. There it is, at least twelve pounds or more. The butcher retrieves it from the pile and does some fancy cutting about the ducts until he comes across a fragile appearing sac loaded with what looks like a venomous fluid. It is. It is the gall bladder and contains enough bitterness to render the entire beef inedible if this bile is spread about in vulnerable areas, thus say the old-timers. Bile is thought to have some dubious medicinal value but no one has ever become ill enough to down any of it. However, in cattle, this so-called evil fluid is drained off into the duodenum and is said to aid their digestion.

The liver is trimmed. The heart is secured and trimmed. The lungs are thrown to the dogs. A little washing of capillary blood from the neck about completes the bee, except — the most precise and one of the hardest jobs at a beef butchering bee is yet to come. It takes the strength and skill of several people. One bad slash, and pounds of the best meat in the carcass will be mutilated. It is the halving of the beef. The oxtail is unjointed from the spinal column at the top of the carcass. A bucksaw is best for opening a cut to the first breakaway vertebra. After that it is broadaxed all the way. In the judgment of the head butcher, whosoever misses the mark is disqualified and the most accurate wielder of the broadaxe is awarded the oxtail. It is the source of choice small pieces of meat and has the best joints for soup stock in the entire carcass. Once divided the halves are raised to maximum height allowed by the block and tackle and out of reach of leaping dogs. After the meat sets up or hardens which is usually overnight, it is

EARLY MEAT MARKET
Stocked for the holiday trade.

quartered, trimmed of any foreign material and made ready for consumption.

Mutton and By-Products

There were sheep slaughtering bees in which the yield was lamb and mutton. I will delete the details because it followed closely the procedure of a beef butchering bee. The meat had greater dietary value than either pork or beef and was particularly used by country people with digestive troubles. Mutton fat or tallow was also considered superior to both lard and beef fat. Wool was clipped from the pelts and used the same as the fleeces shorn from the live sheep in springtime. The clipped pelts were salted, cured and used for everything from making a collar pad for a sore-shouldered workhorse to house slippers for the family.

Tar and Ticks

Sheep shearing was usually done at neighborhood bees. The young country boys had input here that was of more than a passing interest. They could not catch ewes and drag them to the shearing platform because the ewes were too large. Boys were not allowed to box and tie fleeces because this job was too particular. As might be surmised, boys were not allowed to stand idly by and watch. They were kept busy another way.

Even an expert manual sheep shearer would nick every animal several times, because of their wiggling and twisting. As soon as a sheep was shorn it was turned over to the boys. Their job was to dab pine tar on every one of those cuts. By the time all of the sheep had been run through this process the boys would be covered with blood, pine tar—and sheep ticks.

It was a common custom to go over to the chicken coop and leg up a half dozen cawing hens and throw them into the pen with the newly shorn flock. The hens would wise up fast. They would start walking the backs of the sheep and pick off the ticks like they would pick earthworms off the lawn after a spring shower.

A person could not handle sheep at shearing time without becoming infested with ticks, especially if he was wearing wool clothing. Sheep ticks do not like humans and they will get off as soon as possible, but they are slow and deliberate. It might take them a couple of days to exit, unless the host made an effort to hunt them down.

The posterior of a full grown sheep tick is by far the largest part of his body. By bringing a goodly amount of pressure to bear with the ends of one's fingers, the tick will pop loud enough to be heard all over a room. A young boy who loved to tantalize his mother and sisters would leave the sheep shed ladened with a healthy supply of ticks. When opportunity presented itself, he would reach into a pocket and sort out a plump tick. A move with his hand toward the neck of one of his sisters would follow. This was feinting that he had picked a tick off from her. Then, much to the amusement of the menfolk, he would pop it.

Connivers

A look-see into poultry butchering was directly the opposite. Country people did get together to kill poultry of all kinds for shipment in barrels by train to the city. The market for poultry and even eggs in the countryside and its villages was very limited because everyone kept poultry regardless of where they lived. The market was in the city. It took cooperative effort between neighbors to prepare a few barrels of iced fowl to roll on the 3:40 p.m. fast train bound for Detroit.

A poultry bee took specialists, too. They were the sticker, the scalder, pluckers, drawers and finishers. The interesting sidelight was not in the work but in the potluck held soon afterwards. The scalder and the pluckers would always get their heads together. The water would somehow become too hot. The feathers would seize and the pluckers would pay no heed. The skin on several chickens would be torn, particularly about the crop and breast. There was no way they would be accepted in the city in damaged condition. They had to be eaten. There was no time or need to do anything but cook them up for the potluck. So it was; the socializing was then done on a full stomach.

The same conniving would work when killing turkeys, ducks, geese or what have you.

Poultry Pluckers

Deviation from the subject of food here, is because of the value of a by-product from ducks and geese. This also ties into this text because there was a double demand for good pluckers. Duck feathers and goose down were country basics and city essentials. Cornhusk and straw mattresses were standard for "pore folk." When one made, acquired or fell heir to a feather tick, he was sleeping high on the "hawg," and never alone. It was an item to be shared.

The feather yield from a poultry butchering that included

ducks and geese was always saved for bedding, but the quality was not the best. They would be wet from the scalding and were difficult to dry without becoming mildewed and musty smelling.

"Good gracious," as Norrie Desmond used to say, "who wants to get up in the morning smelling like a duck?"

Also, pioneer women thought that feathers plucked from live birds gave off a pleasant aroma and that the feathers had more resiliency than those taken from poultry that had been butchered. It was argued that they wore better and lasted longer because the natural oils had not been washed from the feathers in scalding. So there you have it, pro and con. This is also an excellent example of a topic that was used for discussion at a monthly Grange meeting.

So — there were plucking bees. Not everyone could be a participant even though he wanted to. Later this inability to perform was identified by a new word; allergy. This could have been where the term "goose bumps" originated. Minute fuzz from the feathers and especially from the down would cause the plucker's body to break out. Particles of fuzz were also inhaled while working and this further fueled the fires for those who were allergic.

There was yet another element that decimated the pluckers. It was the ideology of reincarnation. During early days, throughout the countryside, many people seriously believed that after death they would return to earth in another physical form, such as a dog, cat, horse, goose or whatever. There was much discussion over religion and specifically reincarnation. There were many of these believers. The last thing in the world many of them would wish to be was a dry plucker. In their way of looking at it there was a humanitarian difference between a wet plucker and a dry plucker. If one pulled feathers wet, it was from a dead fowl that had already given up his life for humanity and his soul had already passed on to a new body. Dry pluckers yanked, pulled and stripped feathers and down from live poultry and it was painful to the "pullee." Reincarnates did not relish this possible torturing of their ancestors. To be a dry plucker one had to be callous. Most early settlers were not. They were meek and mild because of the uncertainty of life in those days. Their close association with nature fostered an attitude of humbleness. Good dry pluckers, consequently, were not in surplus. Sometimes it was difficult to get a bee organized. Once it was set up the details became fuzzy, so following is only a rough outline of the actual event.

A plucking bee was a fluffy affair run by the strong-willed women of the community. The women were always in poultry and the funds or other assets accrued were theirs to do with as they pleased. This is why the poultry in the barnyard was sometimes better cared for than the kids in the house.

The ducks and geese were caught after dark the night before they were to be plucked and placed in crates. Come morning, they were loaded on a light wagon with a spring seat and before the sun was too high, off went the wife and children with an ample potluck basket of food to some neighbor's steading for the annual plucking bee. The timing depended on the weather. The quality of late spring weather brought on the moulting season. When the ducks and geese began to lose their winter feathers about the farmyard, it was time to hold the bee. One of the men said that these plucking bees didn't make any sense and that the work could have just as well been done at home. The women disagreed. They would not admit it to the menfolk in so many words, but the real reason was so that the women could get together and talk — yes! Gossip! It was good for the soul after a long confining winter.

"Matilda's children have all come down with chicken pox and she won't be able to get away today. Poor thing. Do you know that this very plucking bee was the only day she had away from home last year, by herself, mind you."

"The schoolmarm is being courted by at least three hired men in the neighborhood and they all chew tobacco. You know she is boarding with us this month. Every night a different one walks her home. My husband Elmer says that as soon as the weather gets a bit warmer they won't be walking her straight to our place, but will be stopping under that big sycamore tree down by the spring. When that starts, he's going to begin hitching up Old Bess every night to go fetch her home by himself. He doesn't have time to stop right in the middle of spring work and go looking for another teacher for the district. He is the moderator of the school board. Well, do you know what I told that man of mine?"

"Elmer," I said, "that getting elected to the school board has plumb gone to your head. I've read most of the words in that school law book they gave you and I can't find a thing about the moderator being the guardian of young school teachers. If she should come sick every morning so that she couldn't teach that is no business of yours, except you would have to hire another teacher with the approval of the other two board members. You betcha I got him out of that idea in a hurry. I can read that law book better than he can. Don't tell anybody. He only went to the fourth grade."

This is a fair to middlin' sample of the gossip.

It was a field day for all the able-bodied neighborhood women that could stand the plucking, both mentally and physically. It was mean work but still recreation and a change of pace because of the socializing.

The last statement about sums up the reason for holding a bee of any type, except that there were many of these jobs that could not be accomplished within a family. Plain brawn and usually experienced assistance was needed. It also was a training ground for the young people within these families. By this method they became qualified to go out and establish homes of their own with that girl they met across the hair sorting table at the hog butchering bee.

Barn Building

A barn raising was looked forward to as a colossal event not only for the family involved but for the entire community. It was a social thing. In truth, it was all fun. The backbreaking labor was never taken into consideration. A series of local bees were usually held as a means of assisting the owner in preparing the materials to be used for the main event.

The actual raising of the barn was the culmination or climax rather than the beginning, as those who are not informed might be led to believe.

Any decisions made were family decisions. Families lived, worked and played as a unit. Once the die was cast, it was full

TIME OUT FOR THE PHOTOGRAPHER
This barn raising was not over. The ridge pole was yet to be raised plus the supporting rafters. Ninety people are in this picture.

steam ahead. The children would walk to school the next day and spread the word.

"We are going to have a barn raising. Will ya-all come?"

The news was carried home to other families by their children. Immediately it became the first statement in conversation wherever people met, often by stopping their rigs in the middle of the road. Within a week the good news had spread for twenty miles by word of mouth, which was the only means of communication.

"Philander McLain is going to build a new barn, come next fall."

"Gracious me," the wife would reply, "that's less than a year hence. They will have to hustle."

Thus, the word was out. In response to the word came felicitations, congratulations, offers of help, suggestions, expressions of sympathy and solicitations by craftsmen for possible use of their particular talents, etc. The project had to be squeezed into the crowded routine of daily and seasonal tasks. This was accomplished by stepping up the pace and stretching the hours of the day. The day began earlier and lasted longer into the evening.

It was a family undertaking and there were decisions to be made.

"Dad, say Dad! Where are we going to put the barn?"

Philander would answer after some heavy pondering, "I guess we better call Ma and your sisters and go out on the buzz pile and figure that one out. They should have more to say 'bout that than us, seeing as how they will be doing chores and slopping the "hawgs" all summer while we menfolk are in the field."

Family conferences settled the major points. They would have a south barnyard extending to the creek. There would be a rock foundation with the southwest corner anchored on that grey granite boulder. The horse stalls would be in the corner closest to the house and that was the way it went. There was a well-thought-out reason to back-up each determination, and that is the manner in which each steading was put together and in turn, the entire countryside.

The amount of folding money that would be transferred from one person to another in a barn building project, during this era, was minimal. Barter, trading work and community bees were the method of exchange. Hard cash was scarce. Everybody traded the same way. A nest egg was not needed. All that was needed was the desire and a strong body.

There were two kinds of barn raisings. One was where an all-out professional effort was made. A craftsman, called a framer, was hired and he made all preparations for a large one-day event. Every piece of material needed would be on the grounds down to the last roof board and shingle. The bents would be framed and supported on blocks awaiting the pike poles of a hundred or more strong-armed men. The mortised joints fit. The pins were driven by young daredevils standing on eight inch beams with forty-pound beetles clutched in their hands while thirty feet off the ground. It was "heave ho, men" and a new barn would come into being.

"Easy men, now all together. Good! Hold her right there.

Ebner, toss him a pin." They continued until all was in place, including the roof.

The other barn raising event would need help only in raising the bents. The owner with his sons and hired hands would later lay the sub-floor, put on the siding, use a froe to split the shingles, etc. The barn dance would be held when all was completed. At such time, all those who helped to raise the frame would be present with other guests for a high old time. It was usually held on a Saturday night or on a convenient holiday.

The first visible action, on the part of the landowner, would be in providing drainage for the site. The tools used would be a team, walking plow, and both a board and a slip scraper plus some lazy-back shovels. Once the building site was selected it was rearranged by landscaping so that water would get away from the foundation quickly. The barnyard had to be well drained so that livestock would stand high and dry during all kinds of weather.

The most important part of a new barn was the wall. There were two ways to go. This foundation could be provided by hauling large deadheads in from the fields and laying the sills directly on top of them. This was a floating foundation that would move, rise and fall, with the freezing and thawing. These large rocks had to be so aligned that the weight of the barn and its eventual contents were distributed evenly. This was a painstaking job. Usually neighbors were consulted.

The other type of foundation was a chinked stone wall built up to a desired height to support the building from forty-two inches below ground level. This was considered a safe depth and was below the frost line. Thus there was not supposed to be any movement because of the effects of the weather. It was permanent and thought to be the best of the two styles. However, the labor was many times over that required to build the barn on a floating foundation and the skill of a stonemason was necessary.

There were yet many other tasks to be performed before the barn raising bee took place.

Logs were selected on the stump during the previous fall or before sap began to rise in the trees early the same year in which the barn was to be built. Trees were girdled and allowed to air cure while standing. There was much contention, and lively discussion about this timber-seasoning method while chawing tobacco around the pot-bellied stove at the country store in the wintertime.

About this time the owner would call in a framer for consultation. A framer would review the dimensions and come up with a complete bill of materials needed right off the top of his head. Perhaps the two of them would even go out into the woods and size up the trees that had been selected for the new barn. If they were a little short — what did they do? They borrowed a few trees from a neighbor. Trees were one thing that most every early settler had in surplus.

"Sure, help yourself Philander. When I raise a barn you can pay me back. Reckon it will be ten years."

The trees were cut and either broadaxed or hauled to a mill. Out came sills, posts, purlin plates, braces, rafters, joists, flooring, siding, roof boards, etc. — "the whole ball of wax."

The sills were placed on the wall and mortised. The floor joists were set in the sill and temporarily pinned. Flooring was laid over the joists more as a worktable than anything else. Nothing was finalized at this stage because there was more curing and shrinking of the wood to take place.

The upright sections of framing which included both ends and several bents along the length of the barn were laid out. They were all assembled laying flat on the ground.

This was precision work. Everything had to fit, even to the rafters. The professional framer was usually called back to oversee the raising.

After careful consideration, a date would be set for the barn raising. Every last soul within convenient driving distance would be notified, invited and expected to show up.

This meant strong men with pike poles from 12 to 18 foot long, good strong country women who could cook all day and dance all night, every young person of "courtin' " age and the whole kit and caboodle of youngsters.

There was no event under the stars that communities attended en masse like they did barn raisings.

When a social event was held at a church only the parishioners of that particular sect attended. School doings were usually limited to those people who resided in that one country school district but a raising was for everybody—even the hired men and the hired girls—the schoolmarm, "Oh, ain't she pretty"—the minister (a pike pole never caressed his hands)—all the business people, "iffin it was nye to a village"—hucksters passing through—gandy dancers—tramps—musicians—and the saloon keeper with his fast team and buckboard loaded to the gills with kegs to supplement the homemade applejack.

More important than liquid refreshments was the food. It took a mountain of food to feed the multitude, so assembled. The feast began about high noon. The eating never stopped until "three o'clock in the morning," when the swinging on the corner, clogging and stomping ceased because of sheer exhaustion.

There was another demand for nourishment. It was for the horses. Fifty to seventy-five horses would be tied to trees, fence posts, hitching rails and fancy cast iron tie blocks. Some of the more affluent would fetch along their own hay and a nose bucket of oats, but most of them would depend upon their host's feed supply for their horses. That many hay burners would about clean out a small haymow in the fifteen hours they were on the premises, to say nothing about the hole they would make in the oat bin. Most of the drivers made it a practice to take off out of their own driveways with their horses hungry. They always figured that a hungry horse was a fast horse and he would have all day to eat at the expense of the host, once they arrived at the site of the barn raising.

A barn raising was an institution. Few barns were exactly the same. Their style was dictated by the needs and the character of the owners. Consequently, barns and other buildings throughout the countryside, that have outlived their owners, preserve for present viewers individualities of the past.

Corn Husking and the Mating Game

Barns were kept neat and clean because of plain country pride. Because they were presentable and large, they also were used for social activities. Common work-related bees were held within barns. Usually when the labor was completed the socializing began. There were some exceptions to this rule. One was the annual winter husking bee in which socializing stood on equal footing with the work. Let me explain to you why it was considered as being of equal importance.

Acreages of cleared land were small and every bit of fodder that could be gleaned from them was stored in the barn to feed the livestock during the off season. Hand planted fields of corn were cut with a corn knife, bound into bundles and shocked in the field as soon as the kernels on the ears dented. These stalks contained a lot of natural plant juices and were very nutritional. They were left in a shock in the field until they dried down. They called it passing through a "sweat." The shocks were hauled to the barn and put under cover as soon as possible after cider making time.

It was customary to place a keg of cider (containing the proper accouterments) in the mow first. Time and the insulating effects of the stalked corn piled on top and all about the keg imparted a flavor to the end product that was made available by no other process known to that day or since.

The resulting corned applejack served as the pot of gold at the base of the rainbow when the husking was finished.

Well-known Laurie Brunson said this about a husking bee, "They'd come in an shuck m'corn, sing and have the best time. You've never seen such a good time as they had! I wish you could go to a corn shuckin' sometime."

Most of the participants were young or at least single, except for the farmer and his wife who owned the corn. No money changed hands for shucking. In exchange, the young people expected plenty of food throughout the day with the privilege of having an unchaperoned party which lasted well into the night or even until the next morning—all in the barn.

During the day any young man who shucked out a red ear was entitled to run down, catch and kiss the girl of his choice. As the day matured, the girls were not so hard to catch. The more husking he did, the greater his chances were of finding red ears. Girls shucked too. Not as vigorously as the boys, but occasionally a girl would find a red ear. This she would hide within her clothing until such time as she could secretly reveal it to the young man of her choice. He would grab the ear and proceed to collect the premium amid a swirl of cornstalks, squeals and giggles. If the pair was sufficiently amorous, they might lose themselves in the fluffy pile of husks that were always separated from the stalks and ears.

Once the keg of corned applejack was located the socializing began in earnest. There would be music and dancing and plenty of pairing off.

No decent young woman was allowed to go to a husking bee unless her parents considered her to be of marriageable age, sufficiently skilled in the culinary arts and able to maintain a home of her own. When it appeared that the time had arrived for the young people, to strike out on their own as judged by the family elders, a husking bee was a perfect example of the vehicle used to grease the skids.

CHAPTER IX

COUNTRY CONTRAPTIONS AND COMPLICATIONS

S INCE THE TELEPHONE was first introduced to local subscribers in about 1903, the people of the Great Lakes area
have adopted it for their very own. Congenial people are apt
to socialize via the wire more than the average. People who are
more frugal, both with their time and money, use the telephone
more than others. This in turn leads into a variance of topics.
Because of these recreational and economic benefits, a Scottish
immigrant, Alexander Graham Bell, inventor of the telephone in
1876, and his disciples have always been regarded as extra special
by the inhabitants of this fresh water area.

Party Line Telephone

The country party line was a primitive apparatus when compared to modern day telecommunications. It was the source of

CENTRAL SWITCHBOARD
A three unit switchboard as used at the Davison, Michigan exchange. One of these consoles would be sufficient for a small country town and the surrounding community.

much humor, gossip and some business. Perhaps it would be enlightening to explain briefly what a country party line telephone was and how it operated. It has not been over the hill very long but long enough so that most of the people now using a telephone have never heard of it. A good descriptive beginning would be to say that nothing about it was automatic. The heart of the operation was the central switchboard that was manned around the clock. It was located in a private home rather than in an office. The control center was completely manual. It might contain as many as a hundred circuits or lines. Some of these country lines might have as many as twenty subscribers. There were only a few private lines. These would be doled out carefully to the most important people and to the essential businesses. There would be a few outside circuits for long distance calls, but by far it was a local enterprise.

Subscribers on a party line might be billed each quarter of a year at the rate of $1.25 per month plus the long distance calls that were made from his number. Each subscriber was assigned a signal ring. There were no numbers, per se. When his presence was wanted at the wall telephone installed in his home or business, the central operator would manually ring his signal. For example, it might be one long and three shorts. The eight or ten other subscribers on the same line also heard the ring of one long and three shorts on line seventeen. They all knew each other's ring by heart, and this ring was for the Widow Prosser's place. Not wanting to miss prime gossip in the making, everyone who was available and heard the one long and three shorts, made a mad dash for the receiver and cupped a hand tightly over the mouthpiece to shut out all possible incoming domestic noises.

Sometimes so many people would take down their receivers to listen that the interference would make it impossible for the talking parties to carry on their conversation.

When a receiver was taken off the hook, the release of weight of same put the contraption into gear, or in other words, caused a contact to be made. It plugged in the nefarious listener, but not without warning the people already on the line by sounding a pronounced click. This sound would draw uncomplimentary remarks from the people wishing to talk. These remarks were orbital in character and ranged from slander to humor. It was also an excellent time in which to unload on your neighbor who had been cutting cross-lots on your land. He was not supposed to be listening to your conversation but you knew that he was, so this was a golden opportunity to give him a piece of your mind, indirectly.

"Harry, you know that good-for-nothin' that borrowed my posthole digger and never brought it back, the fellow that lives across the road and down a spell? Well! His horses got out last night. They came up to our place and trampled our garden and ate all the sweet corn. Now, if he doesn't come up here, like a man that he isn't, and pay for the damages I am going to turn a bill over to an attorney for collection. Harry, they are a family of nincompoops. They have kids over there that are four years old and still in diapers. They can't raise what they have and now have another one on the way. It looks like a downright case of child neglect. All this neighborhood needs is a couple more backsliders

SUBSCRIBER'S WALL TELEPHONE

*The new method of communicating with the outside. It would bring help in
an emergency and trouble if you were looking for it.*

like him and we are on the way to hell on a handcar. Oh, his wife
is not to blame, but I think he has something missing from his
upper story."

And so the derogatory statements would be forthcoming as long
as the listener remained on the line. When the listener would get
so mad that he could not stand it any longer he had two choices.
To open up and reply to slanderous remarks would be to reveal
his identity and start a wholesale retort. The other option would
be to hang up, which is what the talkers were wanting him to do
in the first place.

Party lines were "tailor made" for country women. As they
matured and became grandmothers their techniques improved.
Their tactics depended on conditions and upon their personalities. Personalities that were warped by the hardships and impov-
erishment of their times. One of few channels available for them
to use to vent their pent-up feelings and to serve as a safety valve
was the telephone. Idle talk and malicious gossip were their bag

and they were properly identified as wags by the men. Suppose there were a couple of old country women on your party line passing back and forth choice bits of gossip and you wanted to get them off to make an important business call. You listened a bit until you could identify them and pleasantly asked them if you could have the line to call the blacksmith, Charlie Dunkle.

"My best mare Roxy has thrown a shoe. I can't work her on the sulky plow like she is. It looks like winter is coming on fast and I want to finish that fall plowing."

"A likely story," one wag retorts. "It must have taken you a long time to come up with that fancy excuse. We have heard them all. We were not born yesterday. We have only been on this line for two hours and pay our $1.25 monthly toll same as you do. Why don't you get off the line yourself and go back to your whittling because we want to talk about you next. What we have to say might burn your ears."

The central (operator) was a power in these small communities. If she liked you and you were tolerable when the phone was out of order she would do most anything for you at any hour of the day or night. On the contrary, if you did not pay your telephone bill on time, complained about poor service and were obnoxious, you might as well have your phone disconnected because she would not put out a fire call for you, if your barn was burning.

The apparatus at the central switchboard was wired up so that by throwing a master switch the operator could activate all thirty lines (or whatever) simultaneously. This was used to inform the community of various emergency situations as quickly as possible. Calling for help to fight a fire was the primary use. Twelve rings in rapid succession brought everyone to the telephone on the run for directions to the fire. The central operator would open all circuits and make an announcement as to the name of the unfortunate family whose property was on fire and the location. The fastest transportation was by horseback, but it was difficult to carry a bucket for fighting fire while astride a galloping horse. Most people would throw the harness on their fastest driver, hitch him to their fastest rig and pick up neighbors enroute. If it was a serious fire, the operator would repeat the all circuits alarm.

The same notification system was also used for lesser calamities, but never the twelve rings. They were reserved for a fire, exclusively. Ten rings might be used to inform the subscribers of the death of a prominent citizen. Eight was often used to advertise a church supper, box social or even a chivaree.

A subscriber (or a voting member, if it was a mutual company) on a party line could ring any other subscriber on that particular line without going through the overworked central switchboard. The signal of two long rings was usually reserved, by custom, for notification to all of an emergency within that immediate neighborhood. These emergencies would not concern the entire countryside, but were important to those living locally.

Two long strong rings, "This is Sadie Shaw, our bull has busted the barnyard board fence, the men are on the back forty mowing and they cannot hear me ringing the dinner bell for help. He has chased my Johnny up that Snow Apple tree and he is pawing and bellowing around the roots of that tree like a spring tornado. I need someone to help me let the heifer out of her pen to calm him down 'til the menfolk come up for supper."

In spite of serious limitations the party line telephone system was a definite improvement over the ringing of dinner bells, yelling across the valley, Indian smoke signals or beating upon a hollow log, as we reach back into primitivistic life.

The Drummer's Role

Because of the unending demands for strenuous physical labor to keep body and soul united, the early settlers were always on the alert for short cuts to arrive at an end, labor saving ideas and lastly, new inventions.

Drummers, entrepreneurs and con men out for the fast buck literally flooded the hinterlands with their products. The people were gullible. The traveler did not have to possess much sales ability to make a good return for his efforts.

Many items were merchandised that fell short of their promised goal. Much culling of new inventions took place. A hundred years later when I came along this was still going on and it continues even today. Allow me to share with you some fine points on a few items I happened to use and skin my knuckles on, among other things.

I have no intention of downgrading all the early labor saving implements that were invented for use in agriculture. Still, I think that it is of importance to share with posterity some of the unique moments of my association with a few of the more prominent machines.

The McCormick Binder

Cyrus McCormick invented the reaper in 1831 and by the time I ceased being the gleam in my father's eye, it was called the binder, with an optional newfangled swinging contraption called the bundle carrier. Other accessories were a set of trucks that mounted under the tongue to take the weight of the machine off from the horses' necks, and a combination tin toolbox, whip socket and oil-can holder mounted under the drivers seat.

Three good horses could swing a seven foot cut for half a day at a good clip, if it was cool. During a hot afternoon the driver could go to shocking up what he had cut in the morning, and let the horses swat flies under a tree, or put on a fresh team and keep that bull wheel a rolling. Yep, that bull wheel was the source of all power. It drove the pitman that was connected to the cutter bar, the rollers that drove the three canvasses and the almighty important unpredictable knotter that tied the twine about the bundle of grain.

One time my grandfather had a hired hand who was an excellent teamster but a poor machinist. The hand was chomping at the bit wanting to show everyone that he could cut ten acres of wheat a day without hanging the horses' hides on the fence. Every time he came around the field to where we were shocking bundles, "Gramps" would stop him to rest the horses and to look the binder over. This hand did not know what an oil can was intended for. He was all speed and hell on horses.

At one stop he had a complaint. "You know Willie, this cutter

THE GRAIN BINDER
This one lacks a bundle carrier. Note the fly nets on the horses.

bar just gets lower and lower on me. I have the lever up in the last notch and the knives sometimes run in the dirt." "Gramps" looked over the situation.

It was that "dad gum" bull wheel. The driver had hit too many rocks and ditches going too fast, trying to make the ten acres a day. That drive wheel which normally was forty inches in diameter had been reduced by slam-bang compaction to a ball of scrap iron about one half that height. It was still rotating, doing a job, but in a much smaller circle. The hired hand did not cut the ten acres that day or the next. It was a major repair job. Forge welding was not possible. It required a new wheel.

There were all sorts of controls on this binder. One was a foot trip pedal which controlled the bundle carrier. When the knotter tied a bundle it was expelled down the side of the shield that covered the bull wheel toward the ground. Earlier binders strung bundles along the ground helter-skelter. With the bundle carrier, they could be dumped in rows as you cut around and around the field in bunches of six to eight. However, there was no catch, lock, spring or other resistance of any kind to hold that heavy load of bundles from dumping, except for the pressure of the driver's foot encased in sort of a stirrup on that pedal. Your leg would get so tired that you thought you had lost it for sure before the job was done.

The real "wing ding" of that McCormick was the knotter. It was as tempermental as a Fordson Tractor. The variables that spawned its intemperance were numerous, such as the twine being twisted, too thick or too thin; the driver not keeping the butt lever in proper adjustment for the changing length of the straw; thistles or other coarse weeds winding about the needle; straw too tough or dry; the knotter slipping a cog and going out of time or even a rabbit or snake becoming impaled on the needle. I have heard modern farmers curse the knotter on a hay baler. They were born a century too late to get in on this main event. The main event they missed was the knotter on an early McCormick grain binder. The best tool the operator could have was a sharp jackknife. Twine, green weeds, damp straw all in turn would have to be cut away during a day's work with this labor saver. Many farmers were impaled upon the needles of those early McCormicks. There was a warning that said, "Place binder out of gear before working with knotter" — but they would never take time to do it — too busy — all hurry up. If the knotter was tripped and a horse took a step reaching for a bite of grain, so as to move the bull wheel, up came the needle, quick as you could say scat, and through the muscle of an arm or the palm of one's hand. It was geared high. One could not react fast enough to get out of its way.

The driver was perched on a slotted cast iron seat that was molded to fit the universal male buttocks, but it never did. He never seemed to conform. He was a misfit. This was a place where a sheep pelt came into heavy use. There were no springs, no rubber tires. The driver vibrated until he gave up and let his teeth chatter, especially if one was traveling crossways of the way the field was drilled.

In front of the driver was a pair of footrests, one of which was never used because one foot was always stuck in the bundle carrier stirrup. The lines that he drove the horses with were always in his hands, except when he was doing one of his juggling acts. The juggling was necessary when he was required to adjust one or more of several levers. The most trying one to move was the bundle butt adjustment lever which lay across the top of the binder to his right. It was a piece of strap iron with notches in it. The handle was made by turning the strap iron a quarter turn after heating it white hot in the forge. When the straw was short, the driver brought it toward him and when the straw was long, he went the opposite direction. This caused the twine to be tied in the middle of the sheath. When the straw was long and the grain was rolling up between the canvasses at a rapid clip, it was almost impossible to pull that lever back when there was short grain in the offing.

The only way the cutter bar could be adjusted for height was by raising or lowering the bull wheel and the outer table canvas wheel. Directly in front of the driver a bit above the foot rests were two stubby levers. One of these was to adjust the tilt of the table and cutter bar and the other was to control the height of the reels. These levers were so short they were counterfeits. They gave the driver no leverage. They were simply gut pullers and caused a bushel of trouble in the grain fields. It was not uncommon for a driver to be struggling with the pair of gut pullers (if you moved one to a different notch they both had to be adjusted) and to drop his lines. Before you could say "Whoa!" the lines, one or both, would be wound up in the canvas rollers and be pulling your horses severely right or left. Never would they be pulled back on their haunches because both lines were never pulled equally.

The usual result here was a runaway, which was a common occurrence especially if you were working green broke mustangs. One harvest our family had a good farmhand. His name was Ed S-shu-mor-ee. Never did know how to spell his last name because he had a severe speech impediment and that was the way it sounded. All the men in the family were shocking grain because that was considered of more importance than running the binder, especially if a rain was coming. The very thing I have mentioned happened to Ed. In his struggles with the two handfuls of levers, Ed dropped one line. It gave the horses a quick jerk, the line broke, and they were off to where they pleased. Ed was a good horseman. He stayed on the seat clutching the stubby levers for dear life. Where the horses pleased was over in a hollow under a piss elm tree. Somehow those four tough mustangs were short on communication. They did not have their directions synchronized. They hit the elm shade they were aiming for, but three of them went to the off side. This cartwheeled the binder around the tree and the impact tossed Sh-shu-mor-ee up into some low branches. He was unhurt but very excited, which is the worst thing that can happen to one with a speech impediment.

Nobody could understand a thing he said for a week. The binder was wrecked. A new one only cost $126.00 and grain was about as much per bushel as it is at this writing, only it took more manual labor to gather it in.

Regardless of my sometimes humorous and critical personal observations, farmers of the Great Lakes Watershed are forever grateful to Cyrus McCormick for placing his reaper in the crack of the door that finally opened wide and introduced the industrial revolution to agriculture.

Model 101 Corn Picker by Deere

If you were to place the position of number one on an agricultural crop it would have to be placed on corn. In the beginning, it was a hand job from the time seed was dropped into the soil until it was placed on the food table or used to feed livestock. Logically, much attention was given to eliminating this hard manual labor.

Improvements in methods and machinery soon brought us to the mechanical harvesting of corn. This was a far cry from the husking bee, but the transition consumed fewer years than most of us would like to admit.

THEY SOLD THE HORSES

A McCormick Binder of later design is teamed up with a Fordson that does not runaway — only balks. It took an extra man and gasoline but no oats.

John Deere, from the time he developed the first steel mold-board plow, was an innovator. He was quick to grasp new concepts. Sometimes too quick, or I might add, placed them on the market before proper field testing. So it was with his infamous 101 Corn Picker.

It was built to mount on most standard two or three-plow-size row-crop tractors. By row-crop I am referring to the narrow front-end type of iron horse power plant. Of course, they were especially manufactured to fit John Deere Model A and Model B Tractors. They were useable on other makes of tricycle type farm tractors by securing an adapter kit. It was said by company block men that any red-blooded farm boy could mount one of these contraptions onto his tractor in seven minutes. Actually it was

Complete View of No. 101 Corn Picker with Tractor (Manufactured 1941-1947)

101 NEVER STOOD FOR A THING
It was a machine that could not be aimed like a gun.

much closer to seven hours. It was one and a half tons of malleable and sheet iron mounted on one lonesome wheel. John Deere slipped a big cog right there. In all of God's creation I do not think there was ever a more difficult piece of machinery to maneuver about, either by itself or when attached to its host tractor.

The number 101 never stood for a thing because it picked one row at a pass, except it could have meant by way of warning, that it was only good for 101 rows. The length of the rows would have been irrelevant.

All the "heft" was on the left side of the tractor, once it was mounted. A corn wagon to receive the ears from the picker elevator was attached to a drawbar built into the picker. This was supposed to have some counterbalancing effect. It had none, except when the wagon was heavily loaded, which was seldom.

With dry footing, the side draft could be compensated for by keeping one's right foot on the wheel brake. This would bring the front end of the tractor about so it could be aimed down the corn row. If the corn rows were crooked there was not much of any place to aim. Shortly, one would smell something burning. It would be a hot brake; tomorrow you could count on being in the brake relining business. You had to have a good brake, at least on one side, to hold her straight.

So much for dry footing. Suppose there had been a rain, some snow or a bit of ice. Suppose that in the process, the ground had softened so that the outrigger wheel sunk in a couple inches. If any of these weather conditions prevailed (and they are not uncommon in the fall season), how do you think the front end of that tractor would have reacted? I will tell you. It would have made a half-moon turn in spite of all the operator could do to prevent it. Few rows of corn are planted in that pattern. It was enough to make you reach in your jacket pocket for that trusty husking peg and a pinch of snuff and go at the job by hand.

The only way to harvest a corn crop with a J.D. 101 was to plan on supplementary assistance. The field would require ten shoats per acre or perhaps it would have been best to start with the hogs and leave the 101 in the shed.

Fiery Fordson

The Fordson was an early farm tractor concocted to replace two teams of horses and take the drudgery out of making a living for the eighty acre farmer. It was a wonderful dream that did not quite materialize. It did not develop to the aspired heights because of mechanical inadequacies, but it accomplished a first. It was the first machine to introduce the element of stress to the peaceful countryside. As the years have rolled by these stressful situations that materialized matured into humorous memories. At this writing farming is still one of the top ten most stressful occupations.

This beast of burden was not a junker. It was not a disgrace to

FORDSON TRACTOR

A good view of the front wheels, the armstrong starter and scars in the radiator core from the buck sheep's goring.

its namesake. The tractor was just plain tempermental. It was as if it were programmed into a negative human disposition. It was composed of pig iron, a small percentage of steel, some copper and a bit of brass. Let's put it this way. It was vulnerable to misuse and had the ability to reciprocate. Taking the front end first, as you were walking around this battleship grey culprit, you barked your knee on the extended hand crank. Yes, the crank to turn the engine. Yes, to start this horse of iron. This was one of many very unreliable parts of this tractor.

This crank extended to the engine through an opening below the radiator shell. A spring was slipped over the inner end of this crank so that you had to exert considerable inward pressure at the same time as you tried to spin her. The inner end was drilled so a three-eighths pin was inserted at right angles to engage some notches that were recessed back inside of a small flat belt pulley, that drove the large radiator cooling fan. After a couple of hours of steady hand cranking, which was about par, it was difficult to get that pin to hang into those notches because of the lubrication furnished by the sweat that had run down your arm. So — the pin skittered out of its notch and you on the business end of the crank went into a heap on the terra firma much to the amusement of whomever was watching. About this time you had arrived at the point of impatience, where it was no joking matter.

That crank had another booby trap. It was the spark. You see, there was no battery, no alternator or generator, but to provide the fire, there was a super hot or more likely a cold, cold magneto apparatus bolted to the flywheel that was located deep in the bowels of this beast of stress. The control for its spark of life was mounted on the steering post under the steering wheel along with the throttle lever. The setting of this spark lever was not a mathematical or engineering decision. Why so much care in the set of the spark? Because, the setting of the spark was the sum total. If it happened to be in a notch coinciding with the disposition of the engine it would fire off. If not the cranker would fire off into the great blue beyond and land on his arse. Only one more comment on the advance or retarding of the spark. It never would fire properly two days in a row from the same notch. We would try to back it into a corner. We tried all the fundamentals like regulating it according to the humidity, barometric pressure or temperature. We toiled with those critters for ten years and never did come up with the why. Why? Two to one it would buck or kick versus firing up. So the odds were that you would lose your touch and your temper. Thus the stress.

As you stepped away from this armstrong engine starter you whacked your shin on the extended crank handle once again. Ouch! It drew your attention to the fragile unprotected copper radiator core. No fins, grill or guard.

A neighbor was raising a new span of horses by the way of a half-sister pair of fillies. They were cavorting about the inside barn lot. The Fordson was stalled there while hot and it absolutely refused to blast off again until all the components cooled off. Neighbor Nelson spun the crank until his wife rang the dinner bell. When he came back out after dinner for the second round with the battleship grey dum-dum, it had not moved. It was still

Moon Glow

Captain Jack Brown was lord and master of the S.S. Emperor for the Canadian Steamship Lines. He was a despot. He was a tyrant who was never in error and never spared his extensive vocabulary on an officer or seaman who dared suggest that he might be — "dammit, I am right whether right or wrong."

This sister ship of the Haggerty was inbound for Chicago with a load of rye for Seagrams. It was three bells. The wind was calm. The air was heavily laden with fog and the coal smoke from thousands of Chicago south side homes. Visibility was down to one hundred feet. Wheelsman Robinson rang for Captain Jack. Captain Jack routed out all hands for watch. Someone suggested that they throw out the hook. This statement brought out the pent up fury of Captain Jack on them all. "Take her in and we will snub her up at dawn."

But where, thought the wheelsman to himself as they continued to inch along through water below and soup above. He knew Chicago and Calumet C Grain Elevator was to port because he could smell it. The key was Calumet Light at the end of the break water. The wheelhouse was dark as pitch. Captain Jack was outside on the starboard wing that was three steps lower than the wheelhouse.

He brought everyone to an alert by shouting, "Thar she glows," meaning, of course, that he had sighted the Calumet Light. "Take her in Robinson. I am going to my bunk and don't ring me for any of your nonsense. That's an order."

One good squint from his dark raised wheelhouse and Robinson knew that the glow that the Captain had identified was not Calumet Light. It was the moon. Robinson also knew that the captain did not want to take the S.S. Emperor to the moon. He rang the mate. They consulted, discussed and cussed Captain Jack, each other and themselves at length.

The captain is right, right or wrong. Their real task was to circumvent his order. So — the mate ordered the engines cut to fast idle and spared the hook. The noise of the anchor chains running out would have awakened an enraged captain. The crew violated a few regulations that morning until an off-shore breeze came up and finally blew off the soup. They located the light three hours late and tied up at Calumet C in mid-morning. Shortly thereafter, Captain Jack Brown appeared on deck, signed the papers and took off for business downtown without a word of condemnation or praise.

The docking at Calumet C on their next trip was during daylight. The captain was up in the wheelhouse with Robinson as usual.

Everything was routine. There were no problems. The captain was in a tolerable mood. They were alone. Captain Brown curled his lip a bit, squinted more pronounced than usual and yielded one of his rare half smiles.

"It is a damn sight better today than the last time we put in here. If it hadn't been for the moon being out to steer by we would have run her hard aground."

Aye Sir," replied Robinson.

In their years of association that followed the incident was never mentioned again. Nuthin' sifted to the crew. Most everyone knew that the captain was always right, whether wrong or right. That was a standing order.

He Pulled a Knife on Me

There has always been ample material available to assist in the development of humor within the situations provided by the division of age groups, cultures and life styles of the geographical boundaries of the Great Lakes. Sometimes it is a combination of more than one of these divisions. This setting is in an area of high-density population, in a city where traditions of the past are now being challenged by modern liberalism.

I am referring to Detroit and of its beloved old Corktown. This was a section roughly bounded by Trumbull, Henry, Fourth Street and Michigan Avenue. It is now, except for a few stubborn pockets, crime ridden and in a state of decay. This deterioration is typical of the pattern which has encompassed the inner cities. Corktown formerly was beautiful and Irish to the hilt. It was

from one of these remaining pockets of a proud people that Paddy
(Patrick) had taken his leave to confront the Saints. A wake was in
progress. It was late, extremely late. In fact, it was so late that it
was early. The crowd that was so evident earlier in the evening
had dwindled. Dwindled to the extent that as the door closed
softly once more, there remained only two of Paddy's stalwarts to
man the wake until dawn.

Across the street was a saloon with lights glaring and music
blaring. Its patrons were typical of all that had destroyed the old
Corktown. The enticement was great. Thirst overwhelmed the
two vigilants of the wake, and there it was all put together for
them, just across the street. Neither was willing to stay alone with
Paddy while the other went for some liquid refreshment. After
much and sometimes heated discussion they decided to take
Paddy to the saloon with them. It was not the neighborhood place
he was used to, but Paddy might enjoy himself one more time
before interment, just sitting at the rail. It would be like old home
to him.

They carefully removed his body from the casket and had to
rustle up shoes and a hat. It appeared as though they were going
to plant him without footwear.

Much to their surprise he was easy to handle as they supported
him between them down the steps and across the street. His feet
did not function but that was natural for Paddy. The two of them
had brought him home like this several times on Saturday night.
He looked good and was well dressed, too. Perhaps, these were
the best clothes he had ever had on.

"And what's for your friend in the middle," the bartender
asked.

"He is on the wagon this morning," one replied, as he pulled the
felt hat farther down over Paddy's eyes. A couple of rounds later
they were feeling smug about their venture and thinking of
returning Paddy to his box when a fight erupted back in the
shadowy recesses of the joint. Before they could clear out, the
fight spread to include the three late patrons. A call for the police
riot squad went out. A bewhiskered giant took a roundhouse
swing at the three Irishmen standing at the bar. Two of them saw
it coming and ducked in an act of self-preservation, leaving
Paddy totally unprotected and unsupported. Wham! The round-

house punch caught him flush on the jaw. The riot squad came charging in both exits. All the patrons were lined up against the wall, except Paddy. There he lay all crumpled up on the floor near the bar along with the other debris. A couple officers rolled him face up.

"He's not out, he's dead! Stone cold! Who hit him?" shouted the Lieutenant.

Several patrons, too loaded to know better, immediately identified the whiskered giant as the guilty one. "He is the one that slugged him and right in the kisser!"

"He really laid it on him!"

"The fellow didn't have a chance!" These were some of the comments.

"Sir, it appears that you are in bad trouble. This man is dead," stated the Lieutenant. "What do you have to say for yourself?"

"It was like this officer, the man lying there pulled a knife on me and I was only acting in self defense. I am sorry, but what else could I do?"

CHAPTER XI

SOCIAL ACTIVITIES — PRO AND CON

Our forefathers lived an extremely drab existence by today's standards. Some of the more cognizant individuals realized that their lives left much to be desired. There were excesses of hard labor, inconvenience and suffering. On the opposite side of the existence equation, there was a surplus amount of emotional energy that went unused for long periods of time. When an opportunity presented itself to balance out this pioneer subsistence, they were likely to go into excess. These opportunities were few and far between. Travel was slow and tiring. Distances were great when the speed of travel was taken into consideration. The population was thin. Yet, the need of this emotional balance, in spite of these strong deterrents, spawned many interesting innovations that became a part of Americana. Camp meetings, box socials, quilting bees, barn raisings, husking bees and chivarees were some of the events that filled this void.

Sugaring Off

A sugaring-off party was a social event held to celebrate the successful conclusion of the maple syrup season. It was a sweet affair of springtime for the young and the young-at-heart when both the sap of the maple tree and the juices of the country youth flowed naturally.

Modern entrepreneurs have grasped the reins from those early settlers who held neighborhood sugar parties and turned them into great events named Maple Syrup Festivals. They are scheduled each spring by selected towns and small cities throughout the Great Lakes area and the Province of Ontario.

Sugaring-off was the main event which climaxed days of back-breaking labor, nights without sleep, and the end of the first spell of drudgery in the new year. One of the good things about it was that it did not require a lot of preparation.

The location would be in the massive kitchen of a country home with the wood-fired kitchen range serving as the center of activity. The ingredients were; maple syrup, tubs of snow or ice, homemade fried cakes, a few quarts of sour pickles, liquid refreshments to compliment the mood of the gathering and a house full of young people chaperoned by a sprinkling of straight laced parents to keep the boys from "kicking over the traces" and the girls from removing their tightly laced corsets.

Syrup, fresh up from the woodlot sugar shanty, was brought to a slow boil on the kitchen range as the young folk gathered about to watch, jostle, tell jokes and to sort out the opposite sex. The syrup in the kettles would be boiled on down until it hardened in the old-time cook's water test. Then it would be poured out into thin ribbons on the snow or ice. It hardened quickly because of the cooling and was then eaten from the fingers like sticks of candy.

When one became as sweet inside as he could stand, he would chaw down a dill pickle and go after more of the congealed maple syrup. It wouldn't be unusual for someone to get burned trying to grab a stick of maple sugar before it had cooled. Another casualty, or even several, might develop by taking too much aboard. This would require a trip to a location out behind the woodpile, there to gag and heave ho until relieved. The evening was seldom scratched for this reason even though the agonized might be green about the gills for an hour or so.

Courting games such as spin the bottle were played, group singing around the parlor organ was expected and peering at the wonders of the little known outside world with the aid of slides as magnified by a stereoscope were the entertainment at a sugaring-off social. It was rare that a hoe-down was called, because that was strenuous exercise. Vigorous physical activity was not compatible with this type of extra-sweet social evening.

Gluttonous participants (there were always some) would curl up and go to sleep most anywhere; the haymow, a horse stall or even in the hired girl's room. This type of hangover, it has been said, brought about these following rules.

Rules of the Bedde

No spurs or sticky maple candy allowed.
Bedde limited to six.
Make it quicke, others may be waiting.
Those on sides wille gete up firste.
No crawling over top allowed.
Laste one up makes bedde.
Strangers not welcome
Those breaking slats or setting fire to tick
   wille NOT be accommodated in future.

Author unknown

All Saints' Day

Halloween, the eve of All Saints' Day or Allhallowmas, was in its beginning a historic Celtic Festival recognizing the end of summer. October 31 was considered as the eve of a new year by the Celts and later by the Anglo-Saxons and the Scots. It was a traditional date for bringing the cattle and sheep in from the pastures, rekindling of fires for the winter, and for renewing land lease agreements.

November was the darkest and dreariest month of the year for these people and was quite naturally associated with ghosts, witches, goblins and their likes. This eve of Halloween changed slowly into their realm of folk observances. It evolved from a religious and pastoral holiday into a fun festival for youth.

Likewise the Irish came from this primitive Celtic culture. In turn, Irish immigrants brought the custom of Halloween with them to the shores of America. This folk custom was quickly accepted by the socially starved early inhabitants of the Great Lakes area, Irish or not.

It was first called mischief night but soon succumbed back to the quasi All Saints' holiday, sub-title of Halloween. Because of the large number of early settlers who came straight from Ireland to Michigan, the new holiday was latched on to with more enthusiasm here than by some adjoining states. Because of this generous Irish infusion Michigan has enjoyed more, or should it be said suffered more, as the result of Halloween pranks.

Now, don't take me wrong. I am not giving the credits or debits (as it hits you personally) to the Irish. They only introduced this folk holiday. It was readily adopted by the populace.

Young people lived only between certain holidays like Christmas, 4th of July and Halloween. Of these three main events, Halloween was the most treasured by the boys, and required the most thought and advanced planning.

Preparation time was 365 days. On All Saints' Day a rough draft was made for proposed activities to take place on the following October 31st. Later, details were fine-honed to combat all eventualities so that a successful foray would be assured — usually.

There was an early rural mail carrier who drove a fast horse hitched to an all-weather buggy. There had been a bit of friction between this carrier and the local youth — so there had to be some retribution on Halloween. The U.S. Post Office in the village was a low hip-roofed building with a substantial flagpole up close in front. Wouldn't you know it, during the darkest time of the night the boys quietly removed this mail carrier's prized buggy from its shed, wheeled it to the post office and hoisted its parts piece by piece to the roof of the most important building in town by using the flagpole's rope and pulley. Up there, it was carefully reassembled so that in the morning it was resting straddle the peak — less horse. It is a wonder that they did not tie the horse up on the roof, too.

Another batch of laborious mischief was expended upon a particular and sometimes contankerous old farmer who got himself "kitty wampus" to the boys in a one-room country school. He had cut and shocked five acres of heavy corn beside a nearby well-traveled gravel road. When dawn broke on All Saints' Day, a couple hundred large shocks were lined up on the crown of that narrow country road. Rigs had to use the ditch, including the mail carrier.

The tipping over of outhouses was the first bit of deviltry of the evening. Few families were spared this impropriety. It was a "heave-ho and over she goes." Sometimes even with a user inside screaming.

In one instance a dozen wiry boys all crowded in together on the door side of a well-built three-holer. They grasped for handholds. The outhouse came up faster than most. It had a fancy brass doorknob. This knob caught one of the younger boys right under his leather belt. Up, up and away he went, kicking and clawing in an attempt to shake himself loose. In this effort he was successful — while the privy was teetering on its axis at about a 45 degree angle.

This youngster had been tagging along with a group of larger boys attempting to make a good impression on them by serving his apprenticeship in an aggressive manner so as to insure his being included in the inner circle the next time around.

He slid back down that privy door expecting to land on solid ground. He didn't.

The Chivaree

The Chivaree was an event of short notice and sometimes even on the spur of the moment. There had to be an organizer. Every community had one. The wheels started turning as soon as the word was out that "thar was going to be a weddin."

A chivaree was a crude vehicle by which a newly married couple was welcomed into the community. It was their premiere social event. Not to have one was a disgrace and a sure signal that the participants were not welcome, or that the new couple would have a difficult time of being accepted socially. It would be an uphill struggle, to say the least.

Once in a great while, post wedding socializing would backfire or not develop as was expected. This would happen when the couple was not so-called regular folk.

Otterburn Widow

There was a widow who lived in a weather-beaten clapboard house down by old Otterburn way. She was not solicitous of her neighbors or her neighbor's children, which was uncommon in that day. The children used to tease this widow and their parents did little to deter them. One of their favorite pranks was to steal up to her door and knock and then run out of sight before she came to answer. All the same, they still did errands for her, got groceries, mailed letters, etc.

At that time a comic strip in the local paper featured "The Nebbs." Mr. Nebb had discovered a well or spring whose waters supposedly possessed healing and invigorating powers. He called it "Noxage."

The Otterburn widow lived in a fantasy world and expressed a desire for some of this water. The comic strip was the real thing to her. She was certain that it would cure her "rheumatiz." One of the neighbors, to lead her on, told her that he was going to visit a relative and could bring her a jug of "Noxage."

That evening, he filled the jug from the widow's own well. This information was liberally shared with those that comprised the settlement. The widow soon reported a gain in health. She gave all the credit to the "Noxage" and asked the same neighbor to buy her a couple additional jugs. He secured them at the same place and would take no pay either for the "Noxage" or for his trouble. Otterburn was in stitches. There was more to come.

The widow felt so chipper that she began mailing letters to Lonely Hearts Clubs. These letters had a way of becoming "unsealed" before reaching the post office as did the replies, before they reached her. Word spread. She became the local joke.

Mail went out to "Seers and Sawbuck" and "Monkey Wards." Packages soon returned. Small tears in the packages revealed brightly colored fabrics. She was making for herself some new dresses and such.

Several times, well dressed middle-aged men were seen to get off the morning passenger train and make a beeline for her modest house. They never asked directions. They knew exactly where to go. In spite of other inconsistencies she was a good cook and housekeeper. None of the men stayed. They all were observed boarding the returning afternoon train. It was said that they were all respectable and had purchased round-trip tickets.

It was later reported, via the grapevine, that a wedding was in the offing. A portly gentleman with a large suitcase got off the morning train. No one in town had observed him there before. He was a stranger. It looked like the winner takes all. Like the others, he asked no questions and knew exactly where to go.

In the middle of the afternoon a man of the cloth drove his horse and buggy right up to the widow's house. He was dressed in black with a black hat and with Bible in hand. One of the neighbors and his wife were asked to come over and be witnesses. This neighbor was a fun loving person and so he took it upon himself to, in turn, invite all the local young folks and youngsters to come over too. He arranged a sign with them to let them know when the ceremony was about to begin and he left the kitchen door ajar. A large hound dog had been befriended by one of the girls. He came in with the young people as they crowded quietly in the back door. This hound went immediately into the parlor and flopped himself down right in front of the bridal pair while the Parson was putting them through their vows.

The bride could hardly wait for the ceremony to end. She was embarrassed by the presence of the hound and knew the kids were in the kitchen. She heard their giggles. As soon as the pair had been proclaimed man and wife, instinct told her to chase the interlopers out of her home. After tripping over the hound, her skirts and a couple of rag rugs, she burst into the kitchen screaming and flailing her arms. The back door had been left open to provide for a quick get-away, just in case. The group made good use of it.

They decided to return in the evening and have some more fun at the expense of the newlyweds. They were encouraged by the Otterburn neighborhood men.

Old wash tubs and pans were rounded up. One older boy "borrowed" his father's shotgun. Another, who played in a band, brought his trumpet. Pockets were filled with stones to throw on the metal roof of the "Noxage" widow's house. By the time all this equipment was collected and the crowd assembled the house was dark and quiet.

By a prearranged signal, all hell cut loose. It was a bang! Bang! Crash! Boom! Everybody was on the front lawn yelling for treats and for the new bride and groom to come out.

Only one appeared and it was right now! It was the furious bride. She looked like a phantom clad only in a long white nightie. She stood on the front porch cracking a long black-snake bullwhip. They had seen this menacing weapon only once before when she had used it to frighten children from an apple tree which stood in her front yard. She screamed at the young people and threatened to get the sheriff. The chivaree good-time committee disbanded.

Next day the ticket agent at the Otterburn depot reported selling a one-way ticket to a portly gentleman for the early westbound train.

The groom was never seen again. He should have purchased a round-trip ticket like the rest of her suitors. They were cheaper.

The New Family

A chivaree with a "ya all come" attitude and everyone in the vicinity in attendance was a steed of a different speed. Two or three young bucks on horseback would take off in predetermined directions after supper. They would yell to everybody they saw. "Chivaree tonight, 10 o'clock at the old VanVleet place. The schoolmarm was married up with Ebenezer's boy, Daniel, this noon and they came home on the afternoon train. Pass it on." And of course, they did.

The word of this socializing was accepted by the community with a welcome, "It's 'bout time we all got together."

Precisely at 10 p.m. about a hundred natives moved stealthily to the now darkened VanVleet place from all directions after having tied their horses and rigs to trees back up the road a goodly piece.

The firing of a shotgun was a pre-arranged signal for the advance of the troops on the newlyweds' sleeping quarters. The younger men with buggy whips made it to the house first, with the womenfolk bringing up the rear with amply filled baskets of food. The object was to rout the newly-wedded couple out of their honeymoon nest and have them light the lamps, open the door wide, and welcome all their friends and neighbors.

Several shotgun blasts followed the initial signal so that the honeymooners must have surmised that something was afoot or on horseback. Next, the whips were brought to bear against the clapboard siding of the house on all sides. On the inside of the house this made a tremendous racket. The honeymooners had to be out of bed and alerted by now. Some pairs would play up to being mulish, then those on the chivaree would have to take more drastic action. Some of the things they would do could be kind of wild, but never destructive. It was all in fun. Like getting some livestock or poultry into the house by opening a window. Geese were good because they would do a lot of honking when inside among strange surroundings. If that wouldn't get the newlyweds out of bed they would go out to the pig pen and steal a few shoats out of their nest, shove them into the house and let them root and squeal about. As a last resort, if nothing else worked, the boys would heist one of their most nimble to the roof with a short board under his arm. He would place it over the fireplace chimney. This would smoke them out. However, at most chivarees, the shotgun blasts, ringing of dinner bells, and the yelling of the crowd would bring them to the door.

At one chivaree it was a long time before the principals came out.

When they finally showed, someone asked, "What took you so long?"

"We were busy," the bridegroom replied.

The season of the year and the size of the crowd would determine where the party was held. It could be in the yard, on the barn floor or inside the house. The newlyweds would have, hopefully, prepared themselves somewhat by having cigars for the men and candy for the women and youngsters.

Somebody would break out a fiddle and banjo. Soon they would be into the "Chicken Reel." Two or three might have a jug of hard cider for fortification against a long night of boot stomping. By 2 a.m. out would come the food baskets. It would be broad daylight before the last stragglers made their way home from the latest chivaree.

The new couple could sleep the ruckus off with the satisfaction that they had been accepted as a part of the community. This was imperative at a time when families were so dependent on one another.

And so we have concluded this writing by describing a celebration that heralded the establishment of a new family — and thus our nation was built.